MARKET SHARE REPORTER

The INVESTEXT database was employed in the compilation of *Market Share Reporter*, 3rd Edition. INVESTEXT is a database which offers the complete text of company and industry reports written by analysts at more than 100 of the world's leading investment banks and consulting and research firms. INVESTEXT currently includes 200,000+ reports which cover 11,000 companies and 53 industries. The INVESTEXT database may be accessed from any PC with a modem. Hard copies of all reports are also available directly from Thomson Financial Networks. Thomson Financial Networks also has available three additional databases: BONDTEXT, which offers data and analysis on corporate, government, and municipal debt; MARKINTEL MASTER, which contains major market studies; and MARKINTEL, a companion file to MARKINTEL MASTER, which contains extensive market research reports by Frost and Sullivan, Inc. Information on any of these databases may be obtained by contacting Thomson Financial Networks at the address or phone numbers listed below.

INVESTEXT
Thomson Financial Networks
11 Farnsworth Street
Boston, MA 02210
(617) 345-2000 U.S.
(800) 662-7878 U.S.
(800) 544-5651 Canada
(071) 836-8223 U.K.

(617) 330-1986 FAX

ISSN 1052-9578

MARKET SHARE REPORTER

AN ANNUAL COMPILATION

OF REPORTED MARKET SHARE

DATA ON COMPANIES,

PRODUCTS, AND SERVICES

1 9 9 3

ARSEN J. DARNAY

MARLITA A. REDDY

 **Gale Research Inc.** · DETROIT · WASHINGTON, D.C. · LONDON

Arsen J. Darnay and Marlita A. Reddy, *Editors*

Editorial Code & Data Inc. Staff

Helen S. Fisher and Larisa Volchegurskaya, *Associate Editors*
Mahmood Kalam, Annemarie Muth, Musadiq Shah, and Susan Turner, *Contributors*
Nancy Ratliff, *Data Entry Associate*

Gale Research Inc. Staff

Donna Wood, *Coordinating Editor*

Mary Beth Trimper, *Production Director*
Catherine Kemp, *Production Assistant*

Cynthia D. Baldwin, *Art Director*
Bernadette M. Gornie, *Graphic Designer*

∞™ The paper used in this publication meets the minimum requirements of American National Standard for Information Sciences — Permanence Paper for Printed Library Materials, ANSI Z39.48-1984.

This book is printed on recycled paper that meets Environmental Protection Agency Standards.

TABLE OF CONTENTS

TABLE OF TOPICS

The *Table of Topics* lists all topics used in *Market Share Reporter* in alphabetical order. One or more page references follow each topic; the page references identify the starting point where the topic is shown. The same topic name may be used under different SICs; therefore, in some cases, more than one page reference is provided.

INTRODUCTION

Market Share Reporter (MSR) is a compilation of market share reports from periodical literature and brokerage reports. The third edition covers the period 1990 through 1992; while dates overlap slightly with the second edition, *MSR*, 3rd Edition, has completely new or updated entries. As shown by reviews of previous editions plus correspondence and telephone contact with many users, this is a unique resource for competitive analysis, diversification planning, marketing research, and other forms of economic and policy analysis. Third edition features include—

- More than 2,000 entries, all new or updated.

- SIC classification, with entries arranged under 449 SIC codes.

- Corporate, brand, product, service and commodity market shares, with a significant increase (66%) in coverage of companies and brands.

- Coverage of private and public sector activities.

- National and international scope.

- Comprehensive indexes, including products, companies, brands, places, sources, and SICs.

- Table of Topics showing topical subdivisions of chapters with page references.

- Graphics.

MSR is, thus, a one-of-a-kind resource for ready reference, marketing research, economic analysis, planning, and a host of other disciplines.

Categories of Market Shares

Entries in *Market Share Reporter* fall into four broad categories. Items were included if they showed the relative strengths of participants in a market or provided subdivisions of economic activity in some manner that could assist the analyst.

- **Corporate market shares** show the names of companies that participate in an industry, produce a product, or provide a service. Each company's market share is shown as a percent of total industry or product sales for a defined period, usually a year. In some cases, the company's share represents the share of the sales of the companies shown (group total) — because shares of the total market were not cited in the source or were not relevant. In some corporate share tables, brand information appears behind company names in parentheses. In these cases, the tables can be located using either the company or the brand index.

- **Institutional shares** are like corporate shares but show the shares of other kinds of organizations. The most common institutional entries in *MSR* display the shares of countries, states, provinces, or regions in an activity. The shares of not-for-profit organizations in some economic or service functions fall under this heading.

- **Brand market shares** are similar to corporate shares with the difference that brand names are shown. Brand names include equivalent categories such as the names of television programs, magazines, publishers' imprints, etc. In some cases, the names of corporations appear in parentheses behind the brand name; in these cases, tables can be located using either the brand or the company index.

- **Product, commodity, service, and facility shares** feature a broad category (e.g. household appliances) and show how the category is subdivided into components (e.g. refrigerators, ranges, washing machines, dryers, and dishwashers). Entries under this category cover products (autos, lawnmowers, polyethylene, etc.), commodities (cattle, grains, crops), services (telephone, child care), and facilities (port berths, hotel suites, etc.). Subdivisions may be products, categories of services (long-distance telephone, residential phone service, 900-service), types of commodities (varieties of grain), size categories (e.g., horsepower ranges), modes (rail, air, barge), types of facilities (categories of hospitals, ports, and the like), or other subdivisions.

- **Other shares.** *MSR* includes a number of entries that show subdivisions, breakdowns, and shares that do not fit neatly into the above categorizations but properly belong in such a book because they shed light on public policy, foreign trade, and other subjects of general interest. These items include, for instance, subdivisions of governmental expenditures, environmental issues, and the like.

Coverage

The third edition of *Market Share Reporter* covers essentially the same range of industries as previous editions. However, all tables are *new* or represent *updated* information (more recent or revised data). Also, coverage in detail is different in certain industries, meaning that more or fewer SICs are covered or product details *within* an SICs may be different. For these reasons, it is recommended that previous editions of *MSR* be retained rather than replaced.

MSR reports on *published* market shares rather than attempting exhaustive coverage of the market shares, say, of all major corporations and of all products and services. Despite this limitation, *MSR* holds share information on more than 5,600 companies, more than 1,500 brands, and more than 2,900 product, commodity, service, and facility categories. Several entries are usually available for each industry group in the SIC classification; omitted groups are those that do not play a conventional role in the market, e.g., U.S. Postal Service (SIC 43) and Private Households (SIC 88).

Coverage by SIC is comparable with the second edition: 449 SIC categories versus 416. Variation in coverage from previous editions is due in part to publication cycles of sources and a different mix of brokerage house reports for the period covered (due to shifting interests within the investment community).

As pointed out in previous editions, *MSR* tends to reflect the current concerns of the business press. In addition to being a source of market share data, it mirrors journalistic preoccupations, issues in the business community, and events abroad. Important and controversial industries and activities get most of the ink. Heavy coverage is provided in those areas that are —

- large, important, basic (autos, chemicals)

- on the leading edge of technological change (computers, electronics, software)

- very competitive (toiletries, beer, soft drinks)

- in the news because of product recalls, new product introductions, mergers and acquisitions, lawsuits, and for other reasons

- relate to popular issues (environment, crime), or

- have excellent coverage in their respective trade press.

In many cases, several entries are provided on a subject each citing the same companies. No attempt was made to eliminate such seeming duplication if the publishing and/or original sources were different and the market shares were not identical. Those who work with such data know that market share reports are often little more than the "best guesses" of knowledgeable observers rather than precise measurements. To the planner or analyst, variant reports about an industry's market shares are useful for interpreting the data.

Publications appearing in the September 1991 to December 1992 period were used in preparing *MSR*. As a rule, material on market share data for 1991 was used by preference; in response to reader requests, we have included historical data when available. In some instances, information for earlier years was included if the category was unique or if the earlier year was necessary for context. In a few other cases, projections for 1993 and later years were also included.

"Strange" Market Shares

Some reviewers of the first edition questioned — sometimes tongue-in-cheek, sometimes seriously — the inclusion of tables on such topics as computer crime, endangered species of fish, children's allowances, governmental budgets, and weapons system stockpiles. Indeed, some of these categories do not fit the sober meaning of "market share". A few tables on such subjects are present in the third edition as well — because they provide market information, albeit indirectly, or because they are the "market share equivalents" in an industrial classification which is in the public sector or dominated by the public sector's purchasing power.

Organization of Chapters

Market Share Reporter is organized into chapters by 2-digit SIC categories (industry groups). The exception is the first chapter, entitled *General Interest and Broad Topics*; this chapter holds all entries that bridge two or more 2-digit SIC industry codes (e.g. retailing in general, beverage containers, advanced materials, etc.) and cannot, therefore, be classified using the SIC system without distortion. Please note, however, that a topic in this chapter will often have one or more additional entries later—where the table could be assigned to a detailed industry. Thus, in addition to two tables on food containers in the first chapter, numerous tables appear later on glass containers, metal cans, etc.

Within each chapter, entries are shown by 4-digit SIC (industry level). Within blocks of 4-digit SIC entries, entries are sorted alphabetically by topic, then alphabetical by title.

SIC and Topic Assignments

MSR's SIC classifications are based on the coding as defined in the *Standard Industrial Classification Manual* for 1987, issued by the Bureau of the Census, Department of Commerce. This 1987 classification system introduced significant revisions to the 1972 classification (as slightly modified in 1977); the 1972 system is still in widespread use (even by the Federal government); care should be used in comparing data classified in the new and in the old way.

The closest appropriate 4-digit SIC was assigned to each table. In many cases, a 3-digit SIC had to be used because the substance of the table was broader than the nearest 4-digit SIC category. Such SICs always end with a zero. In yet other cases, the closest classification possible was at the 2-digit level; these SICs terminate with double-zero. If the content of the table did not fit the 2-digit level, it was assigned to the first chapter of *MSR* and classified by topic only.

Topic assignments are based on terminology for commodities, products, industries, and services in the SIC Manual; however, in many cases phrasing has been simplified, shortened, or updated; in general, journalistically succinct rather than bureaucratically exhaustive phraseology was used throughout.

Organization of Entries

Entries are organized in a uniform manner. A sample entry is provided below. Explanations for each part of an entry, shown in boxes, are provided on the facing page.

1

★ 1229 ★
Autos (SIC 3711)   2   3

Top-Selling Cars   4

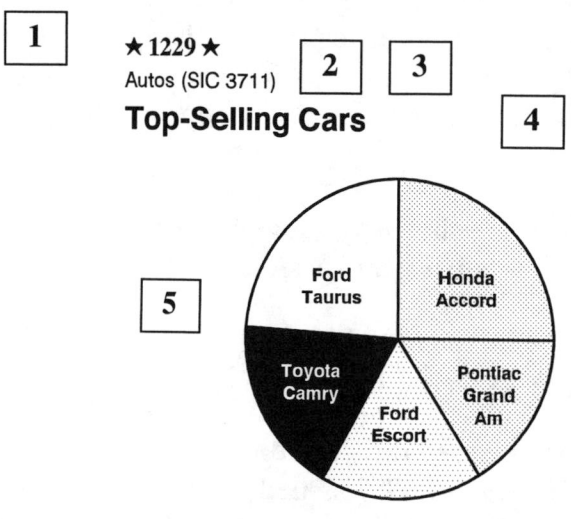

5

Top-selling car brands for the first half of 1992 are shown in number of units sold. Relative shares are shown in percent.   6

	Units sold	% of Group
Honda Accord	191,662	25.4%
Ford Taurus	181,189	24.0
Toyota Camry	137,906	18.3
Ford Escort	124,212	16.5
Pontiac Grand Am	120,059	15.9

7

8

Source: *USA TODAY*, July 14, 1992, p. 1B, from Autodata.   9

| 1 | *Entry Number.* A numeral between star symbols. Used for locating an entry from the index. |

| 2 | *Topic.* Second line, small type. Gives the broad or general product or service category of the entry. The topic for Top-Selling Cars is Autos. |

| 3 | *SIC Code.* Second line, small type, follows the topic. General entries in the first chapter do not have an SIC code. |

| 4 | *Title.* Third line, large type. Describes the entry with a headline. |

| 5 | *Graphic.* When a graphic is present, it follows the title. Some entries will be illustrated with a pie or bar chart. The information used to create the graphic is always shown below the pie or bar chart. |

| 6 | *Note Block.* When present, follows the title and is in italic type. The note provides contextual information about the entry to make the data more understandable. Special notes about the data, information about time periods covered, market totals, and other comments are provided. Self-explanatory entries do not have a note block. |

| 7 | *Column headers.* Follow the note block. Some entries have more than one column or the single column requires a header. In these cases, column headers are used to describe information covered in the column. In most cases, column headers are years (1990) or indicators of type and magnitude ($ mil.). Column headers are shown only when necessary for clarity of presentation. |

| 8 | *Body.* Follows the note block or the column header and shows the actual data in two or more columns. In most cases, individual rows of data in the body are arranged in descending order, with the largest market share holder heading the list. Collective shares, usually labelled "Others" are placed last. |

| 9 | *Source.* Follows the body. All entries cite the source of the table, the date of publication, and the page number (if given). In many cases, the publisher obtained the information from another source (original source); in all such cases, the original source is also shown. |

Continued entries. Entries that extend over two adjacent columns on the same page are not marked to indicate continuation but continue in the second column. Entries that extend over two pages are marked *Continued on the next page.* Entries carried over from the previous page repeat the entry number, topic (followed by the word *continued*), title, and column header (if any).

Use of Names

Company Names. The editors reproduced company names as they appeared in the source unless it was clearly evident from the name and the context that a name had been misspelled in the original. Large companies, of course, tend to appear in a large number of entries and in variant renditions. General Electric Corporation may appear as GE, General Electric, General Electric

Corp., GE Corp., and other variants. No attempt was made to enforce a uniform rendition of names in the entries. In the Company Index, variant renditions were reduced to a single version or cross-referenced.

Country Names. Names of countries are reproduced as they were given in the source. Countries known by name or abbreviation (e.g., U.S.A., C.I.S., U.K., and others) may appear abbreviated or fully spelled out. For instance, the United Kingdom sometimes appears under its name, as U.K., as Great Britain, and as GB. As in the second edition, there are numerous references to the one-time German Democratic Republic, i.e. East Germany. In the pertinent tables, the designation used by the source (East Germany, Eastern Germany, etc.) was left unchanged. In the *Place Names Index*, however, all such references are rendered as Germany, Eastern.

Use of Numbers

Throughout *MSR*, tables showing percentage breakdowns may add to less than 100 or fractionally more than 100 due to rounding. In those cases where only a few leading participants in a market are shown, the total of the shares may be substantially less than 100.

Numbers in the note block showing the total size of the market are provided with as many significant digits as possible in order to permit the user to calculate the sales of a particular company by multiplying the market total by the market share.

In a relatively small number of entries, actual unit or dollar information is provided rather than share information in percent. In such cases, the denomination of the unit (tons, gallons, $) and its magnitude (000 indicates multiply by 1,000; mil., multiply by 1,000,000) are mentioned in the note block or shown in the column header.

Data in some entries are based on different kinds of currencies and different weight and liquid measures. Where necessary, the unit is identified in the note block or in the column header. Examples are long tons, short tons, metric tons or Canadian or Hong Kong dollars, British pounds, yen, French Francs, etc.

Graphics

Pie and bar charts are used to illustrate some of the entries. The graphics show the names of companies, products, and services when they fit on the charts. When room is insufficient to accommodate the label, the first word of a full name is used followed by three periods (...) to indicate omission of the rest of the label.

In the case of bar charts, the largest share is always the width of the column, and smaller shares are drawn in proportion. Two bar charts, consequently, should not be compared to one another.

Sources

The majority of entries were extracted from newspapers and from general purpose, trade, and technical periodicals normally available in larger public, special, or university libraries. All told, 1,660 sources were used; of these, 440 were primary print sources. Many more were reviewed but lacked coverage of the subject. These primary sources, in turn, used 1,220 original sources. These totals reflect a 100% increase in the number of sources cited in the second edition.

A substantial number of entries were obtained under a special arrangement with Investext®, a service of Thomson Financial Networks, 11 Farnsworth Street, Boston, MA 02210. Investext is an on-line source for company and industry analysis. Data included in *Market Share Reporter* were extracted from the Investext database using search parameters developed by Gale's editorial staff and Investext staff. For comprehensive information on Investext services — and to obtain full copies of reports containing cited market shares (on paper or on-line) — please call Investext at (800) 662-7878 or (617) 345-2000; or FAX (617) 330-1986. Thomson Financial Networks also has available three additional databases: Bondtext®, which offers data and analysis on corporate, government, and municipal debt; MarkIntel Master®, which contains major market studies; and MarkIntel®, a companion file to MarkIntel Master®, which contains extensive market research reports by Frost & Sullivan, Inc. Information may be obtained by contacting Thomson Financial Networks at the address or phone numbers listed above.

In many cases, the primary source in which the entry was published cites another source for the data, the original source. Original sources include other publications, brokerage houses, consultancies and research organizations, associations, government agencies, special surveys, and the like. Most entries from Investext are extracted from brokerage reports which, in turn, may cite an original source.

Since many primary sources appear as original sources elsewhere, and vice-versa, primary and original sources are shown in a single Source Index under two headings. Primary sources included in *MSR* almost always used the market share data as illustrative material for narratives covering many aspects of the subject. We hope that this book will also serve as a guide to those articles.

Indexes

Market Share Reporter features five indexes and an appendix.

- **Source Index**. This index holds 1,660 references in two groupings. *Primary sources* (440) are publications where the data were found. Investext, Thomson Financial Networks, is included under primary sources. *Original sources* (1,220) are sources cited in the primary sources. Each item in the index is followed by one or more entry numbers arranged sequentially, beginning with the first mention of the source.

- **Place Names Index**. This index provides references to 289 global regions (Europe, Oceania), countries of the world, U.S. states, and Canadian provinces. The decrease in the number of geographic references is due to the editors' desire to focus more heavily on company and brand shares, which more than doubled since the second edition. References are to entry numbers.

- **Products, Services, and Issues Index**. This index holds more than 2,900 references to products and services in alphabetical order. The index also lists subject categories that do not fit the definition of a product or service but properly belong in the index. Examples include *budgets, conglomerates, crime, defense spending, economies, lotteries*, and the like. Some listings are abbreviations for chemical substances, computer software, etc. which may not be meaningful to those unfamiliar with the industries. Wherever possible, the full name is also provided for abbreviations commonly in use. Each listing is followed by one or more references to entry numbers.

- **Company Index**. This index shows references to nearly 5,700 company names by entry number. Companies are arranged in alphabetical order. The listing is international: major corporations (AT&T, IBM) will be found next to Korean conglomerates and Dutch banks. In some cases, the market share table from which the company name was derived showed the share for a combination of two or more companies; these combinations are reproduced in the index.

- **Brand Index**. The Brand Index shows references to 1,539 brands by entry number. The arrangement is alphabetical. Brands include names of publications, computer software, operating systems, etc., as well as the more conventional brand names (Coca Cola, Maxwell House, Budweiser, etc.)

- **Appendix - SIC Coverage**. The book's appendix shows SICs covered by *Market Share Reporter*. The listing shows major SIC groupings at the 2-digit level as bold-face headings followed by 4-digit SIC numbers, the names of the SIC, and a *page* reference (rather than a reference to an entry number, as in the indexes). The page shows the first occurrence of the SIC in the book. *MSR*'s SIC coverage is quite comprehensive, as shown in the appendix. However, many 4-digit SIC categories are further divided into major product groupings. Not all of these have corresponding entries in the book.

Acknowledgements

Market Share Reporter, 3rd Edition, owes much to the many helpful comments received from users of the book in writing and by telephone. Users pointed out errors and inconsistencies in previous editions, asked for specific topics to be covered, and gave us encouragement by words of praise. *MSR* could not have been produced without the help of many people in and outside of Gale Research. The editors would like to express their special appreciation to Investext, Thomson Financial Networks, which added a special dimension to the book; Ms. Donna Wood (Senior Editor, Gale Research), who served as editorial coordinator; Ms. Deborah Devine (Manager, Customer Support & Training at Investext); and to the staff of Editorial Code and Data, Inc.

Comments and Suggestions

Comments on *MSR* or suggestions for improvement of its usefulness, format, and coverage are always welcome. Although every effort is made to maintain accuracy, errors may occasionally occur; the editors will be grateful if these are called to their attention. Please contact:

Editors
Market Share Reporter
Gale Research Inc.
835 Penobscot Building
Detroit, Michigan 48226-4094
Phone: (313) 961-2242 or (800) 347-GALE
Fax: (313) 961-6815

MARKET
SHARE
REPORTER

General Interest and Broad Topics

★1★

Advanced Armor

Advanced Armor Use Worldwide

Percent distribution, by type, is shown as percent of value in 1990 for North America and Western Europe.

Land vehicles 42.0%
Personal protection 38.0
Shipboard 10.0
Architectural 5.0
Aircraft 4.0
Other 1.0

Source: *Ceramic Industry*, August 1991, p. 13, from Kline & Co.

★2★

Advanced Armor

Advanced Armor Worldwide

Percent distribution of materials used in North America and Western Europe is shown as percent of value in 1990.

Polymer composite 45.0%
Advanced metal 24.0
Fabric 23.0
Ceramic 8.0

Source: *Ceramic Industry*, August 1991, p. 13, from Kline & Co.

★3★

Advanced Materials

Ceramic-Matrix Composites Market

CMC (ceramic-matrix composites) market shares, by application, are shown in percent, based on totals of $130.75 million in 1990 and $249.2 million in 1995 (forecast).

	1990	1995
Wear parts	40.9%	47.9%
Cutting tools	24.5	23.1
Aerospace and military	26.4	18.9
Engines	3.1	5.6
Energy-related and industrial applications	5.1	4.5

Source: *JOM*, June 1992, p. 44.

★4★

Advanced Materials

Raw Material Fiber Worldwide Market

Shares by type of fiber are shown in percent, based on an estimated total market of $795 million in 1990. The "Other" category includes boron, ultra-high molecular weight polyethylene (UHMWPE), and other polymer fibers.

Carbon 67.7%
Aramid 23.1
HS-Glass 3.2
Ceramic 2.9
Other 3.2

Source: *U.S. Industrial Outlook 1992*, p. 17-9, from Kline & Company.

★ 5 ★

AIDS Cost

Global AIDS-Care Budget

Percent distribution is shown in percent, based on an estimated AIDS spending total of $56.5 billion.

Care
  Developed countries 50.0%
  Developing countries 3.0
Research
  Developed countries 23.0
  Developing countries 2.0
Prevention
  Developed countries 20.0
  Developing countries 2.0

Source: *The Economist*, August 1992, p. 89, from Global AIDS Policy Coalition, Harvard.

★ 6 ★

Beverage Containers

Soft Drink Container Market

Shares of soft-drink container shipments, by type of container, are shown in percent for 1991, and estimated for 1992 and 1993.

	'91	'92	'93
Cans	44.7%	45.2%	45.4%
Plastic bottles	25.3	25.4	25.3
Bulk	20.7	20.5	20.7
Non-returnable bottles	9.1	8.8	8.4
Returnable bottles	0.2	0.1	0.1

Source: Investext, Thomson Financial Networks, March 23, 1992, from Merrill Lynch Capital Markets.

★ 7 ★

Building Materials

Building Material Producers

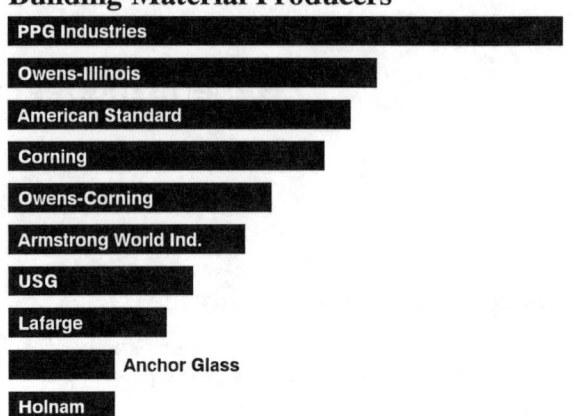

Companies are ranked by 1991 sales, shown in millons of dollars. Percent shares are based on a group total of $27,237 million.

	Sales ($ mil.)	% of Group
PPG Industries	$ 5,725	21.0%
Owens-Illinois	3,852	14.1
American Standard	3,595	13.2
Corning	3,287	12.1
Owens-Corning	2,783	10.2
Armstrong World Ind.	2,439	9.0
USG	1,840	6.8
Lafarge	1,569	5.8
Anchor Glass	1,167	4.3
Holnam	979	3.6

Source: *Fortune*, April 20, 1992, p. 260.

★ 8 ★

Building Materials

Building Materials Shipments

Segment distribution is shown as percent of total value of shipments in 1991 and 1992. Figures are estimates. "Lumber" includes softwood and hardwood lumber, softwood flooring and fence lath. "Millwork" includes wood millwork with metal and plastic overlays, doors, wooden windows, moldings, blinds and shutters, stairwork, porch columns and rails, and trellises. "Preserved wood" includes pressure-treated lumber, plywood, timbers, poles, and posts, and fire retardant treated (FRT) lumber and plywood. "Reconstituted wood" includes particle hardboard, fiberboard, insulation board, and oriented strand board/waferboard.

	1991	1992
Lumber	30.2%	30.4%
Ready-mix concrete	22.8	22.7
Millwork	16.8	16.6
Softwood veneer and plywood	8.3	8.4
Reconstituted wood	5.2	5.2
Gypsum products	4.6	4.6
Preserved wood	4.1	4.2
Concrete block and brick	4.0	4.0
Hardwood veneer and plywood	3.9	4.0

Source: *Hardware Age*, February 1992, p. 50, from *Industrial Outlook 1992.*

★ 9 ★

Building Materials

Construction Materials

Distribution of industry shipments in 1992 is shown in percent, based on a forecast total of $44.172 billion, expressed in 1987 dollars. N.e.c. stands for "not elsewhere classified."

Ready-mix concrete	28.2%
Fabricated structural metal	17.3
Concrete products, n.e.c.	13.7
Hydraulic cement	9.5
Prefab metal buildings	5.7
Gypsum products	5.6
Flat glass	5.4
Plumbing fixture fittings	5.3
Concrete block and brick	4.9

Metal sanitary ware	2.2%
Plastic plumbing fixtures	2.2
Vitreous plumbing fixtures	0.0
Ceramic wall/floor tile	0.0

Source: *U.S. Industrial Outlook 1992*, p. 7-1, from U.S. Dept. of Commerce and Bureau of the Census and International Trade Administration.

★ 10 ★

Business Travel

Business Travel Expenditures

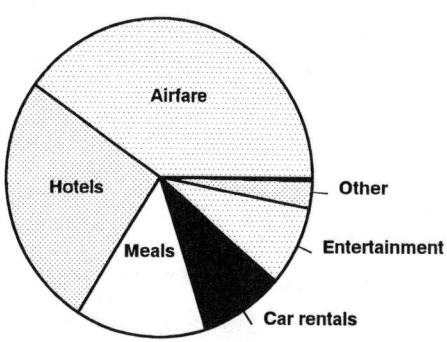

Shares, by end use, of total business travel dollars are shown in percent.

Airfare	40.8%
Hotels	25.6
Meals	14.2
Car rentals	8.5
Entertainment	7.5
Other	3.4

Source: *INC.*, April 1992, p. 40, from Doubletree Hotel study, in association with *Business Travel News.*

★ 11 ★

Carload Products

Major Products Hauled on Trains

Top 10 products hauled on trains are shown with millions of carloads. Percent shares are based on group total.

	Carloads (mil.)	% of Group
Coal	5.91	38.8%
Farm products	1.69	11.1
Chemicals	1.53	10.1
Food	1.31	8.6

Continued on next page.

★ 11 ★ *Continued*

Carload Products

Major Products Hauled on Trains

Top 10 products hauled on trains are shown with millions of carloads. Percent shares are based on group total.

	Carloads (mil.)	% of Group
Minerals	1.20	7.9%
Cars/trucks	1.09	7.2
Lumber	0.78	5.1
Pulp/paper	0.61	4.0
Petroleum	0.57	3.7
Stone/clay/glass	0.53	3.5

Source: *USA TODAY*, June 25, 1992, p. 3A, from *Railroad Facts*.

★ 12 ★

Computer Viruses

Computer Virus Experience - 1991/92

Average number of virus outbreaks per office in January 1992. Data are based on a survey of 300 companies with at least 300 personal computers per office. The names shown are the names of viruses. A computer virus is a destructive computer program that multiplies itself and transports itself on diskettes as part of "infected" programs or data.

Michelangelo	18.2
Stoned	4.3
Jerusalem	1.6
Joshi	1.0

Source: *The New York Times*, March 8, 1992, p. 8, from Dataquest.

★ 13 ★

Computer Viruses

Computer Viruses - 1992

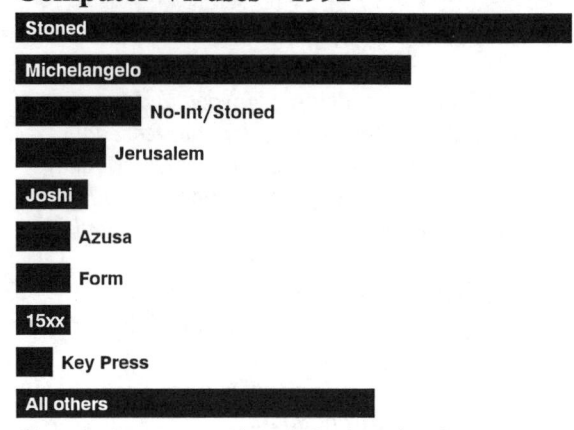

Shares of computer virus infection, by virus name, are shown as percent of total occurrences for the first half of 1992.

Stoned	31.1%
Michelangelo	21.8
No-Int/Stoned	7.2
Jerusalem	5.0
Joshi	4.2
Azusa	3.3
Form	2.8
15xx	2.5
Key Press	2.2
All others	20.0

Source: *Information Week*, July 6, 1992, p. 16, from McAfee Assoicates.

★ 14 ★

Conglomerates

Japan's Sogo Shosha

Gross sales of the nine largest "sogo shosha" (general traders) in 1990 are shown in billions of yen; relative market shares are shown in percent for the same period.

	Sales (Y bil.)	% of Group
C. Itoh	20,595.9	16.2%
Marubeni	19,448.2	15.3
Sumitomo	19,212.6	15.1
Mitsui	18,234.1	14.4
Mitsubishi	17,421.3	13.7
Nissho Iwai	13,343.2	10.5
Tomen	6,768.1	5.3

Continued on next page.

★ 14 ★ *Continued*

Conglomerates

Japan's Sogo Shosha

Gross sales of the nine largest "sogo shosha" (general traders) in 1990 are shown in billions of yen; relative market shares are shown in percent for the same period.

	Sales (Y bil.)	% of Group
Nichimen	6,184.8	4.9%
Kanematsu	5,850.4	4.6

Source: *TOKYO Business Today*, January 1992, p. 56, from company reports.

★ 15 ★

Conglomerates

Korea's Chaebol

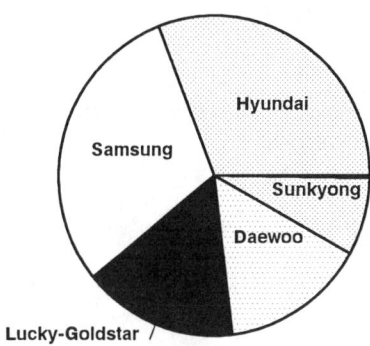

Korea's leading conglomerate or chaebol *sales are shown in billions of dollars for 1991. Company shares are shown as percent of group total sales.*

	Sales ($ bil.)	% of Group
Hyundai	$ 51	31.1%
Samsung	49	29.9
Lucky-Goldstar	26	15.9
Daewoo	25	15.2
Sunkyong	13	7.9

Source: *Fortune*, May 4, 1992, p. 109.

★ 16 ★

Construction

Construction in the U.S.

Value, by type of construction, is shown in billions of dollars for 1990, 1991, and 1992; market shares are shown in percent. The total value of new construction $402.8 billion in 1990; $380.4 billion in 1991; and $381.1 billion in 1992.

	'90	'91	'92
Residential	$ 40.9	$ 40.2	$ 42.5
Private nonresidential	34.6	33.4	31.2
Public works	24.5	26.3	26.2

Source: *U.S. Industrial Outlook 1992*, p. 5, from U.S. Department of Commerce, Bureau of the Census, and International Trade Administration.

★ 17 ★

Construction

Construction Industry Leaders in Europe

Company sales in 1990 are shown in billions of ECUs (European currency units). Percent shares are based on group total.

	ECU (bil.)	% of Group
Generale des Eaux	16.0	34.1%
Lyonnaise/Dumez	10.2	21.7
Bouygues	7.9	16.8
Schneider	7.2	15.4
SGE	5.6	11.9

Source: *International Management*, April 1992, p. 75.

★ 18 ★

Construction

Top 10 Construction Companies - Japan

Companies are ranked by 1991 declared income, shown in millions of Yen. Relative market shares are shown in percent.

	Income (Y mil.)	% of Group
Shimizu Corp.	127,877	15.0%
Kajima Corp.	114,087	13.4
Taisei Corp.	101,811	11.9
Sekisui House	94,025	11.0

Continued on next page.

★ 18 ★ *Continued*

Construction

Top 10 Construction Companies - Japan

Companies are ranked by 1991 declared income, shown in millions of Yen. Relative market shares are shown in percent.

	Income (Y mil.)	% of Group
Takenaka Corp.	91,418	10.7%
Daiwa House Industry	88,054	10.3
Ohbayashi Corp.	71,592	8.4
Kumagai Gumi	69,023	8.1
Toda Construction	49,547	5.8
Hazama Corp.	45,580	5.3

Source: *TOKYO Business Today*, July 1992, p. 37.

★ 19 ★

Consumer Debt

Consumer Debt - 1990

Distribution is shown in percent, based on a total of $3.4 trillion. "Other" includes home improvement loans.

Mortgages/home equity loans	76.0%
Auto	8.3
Revolving credit cards	6.8
Non-installment credit	2.0
Mobile homes	0.6
Other	6.3

Source: *Black Enterprise*, September 1991, p. 102, from Federal Reserve System and BE Research.

★ 20 ★

Convenience Store Products

Convenience Store Product Categories

Top 10 categories are ranked by percent of merchandise purchases.

Tobacco	24.9%
Beer	12.7
Fast food	12.1
Soft driks	9.1
Milk and milk products	5.6
Candy and gum	5.2
Salty snacks	4.6

Groceries	4.4%
Publications	4.3
Bread and cakes	3.7

Source: *National Petroleum News*, June 1992, p. 129.

★ 21 ★

Cotton

Cotton Industry Segments

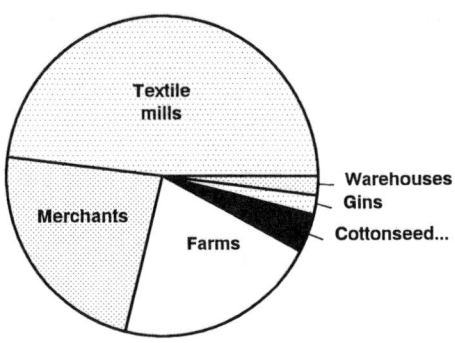

Segment distribution is shown in percent, based on a total of $28.396 billion.

Textile mills	48.0%
Merchants	22.6
Farms	21.1
Cottonseed oil mills	4.1
Gins	2.2
Warehouses	1.9

Source: *America's Textiles International*, February 1992, p. 30, from National Cotton Council of America.

★ 22 ★

Data Losses

Federal Government Data Losses

Distribution of personal computer data losses, by cause, is shown in percent.

Errors and omissions	65.0%
Employee tampering	19.0
Natural disasters and power outages	8.0
Water damage	5.0
Computer viruses	3.0

Source: *Government Executive Computing*, March 1992, p. 20, from Robert Courtney, Inc.

Education

Private Company Expenditures on Training

Private companies spend $30 billion a year on training. Shares, by type of job, are shown in percent.

Jobs for college graduates
Professionals 27.0%
Managers 22.0
Professional sales 9.0
Technicians and supervisors 8.0
Jobs for non-graduates
Technicians and supervisors 11.0
Skilled crafts 9.0
Laborers, drivers, and production workers . 5.0
Retail sales and service workers 5.0
Clerical and data 4.0

Source: *The Economist*, August 22, 1992, p. 21, from American Society of Training and Development.

★ 24 ★

Electronics

Electronics and Computer Company Sales

Company sales are shown in millions of dollars for fiscal 1991. Percent shares are based on group total.

	Sales ($ mil.)	% of Group
Digital Equipment	$ 13911.0	11.9%
Rockwell Intl. Corp.	11927.4	10.2
General Motors	11540.6	9.9
Raytheon Co.	9274.2	7.9
TRW Inc.	7913.0	6.8
Texas Instruments Inc. . . .	6784.0	5.8
Apple Computer Inc.	6308.8	5.4
Honeywell Inc.	6192.9	5.3
Litton Industries Inc.	5219.0	4.5
Intel Corp.	4778.6	4.1
Eaton Corp.	3381.0	2.9
Galileo Electro-Optics Corp. . .	3221.3	2.8
EAC Industries	3095.0	2.6
Anaren Microwave Inc. . . .	3040.1	2.6
Bowmar Instrument Corp. . . .	2688.5	2.3
Venturian Corp.	2126.8	1.8
Genisco Technology	1991.3	1.7
Perceptronics Inc.	1737.8	1.5
IRT Corp.	1702.5	1.5
Ramtek Corp.	1701.8	1.5

	Sales ($ mil.)	% of Group
Espey Mfg. & Electronics Corp.	.$ 1676.4	1.4%
Verdix Corp.	1524.9	1.3
Western Microwave Inc.	1377.9	1.2
EIP Microwave Inc.	1348.2	1.2
Tektronix Inc.	1330.9	1.1
Zenith Electronics Corp.	1321.6	1.1

Source: *Aviation Week & Space Technology*, May 25, 1992, p. 41.

★ 25 ★

Electronics

Electronics Leaders - Japan

Companies are ranked by electronics sales, shown in millions of dollars. Relative market shares are shown in percent.

	Sales ($ mil.)	% of Group
Matsushita	.$ 33,320	17.0%
NEC	26,179	13.3
Toshiba	25,179	12.8
Hitachi	22,853	11.6
Fujitsu	21,031	10.7
Sony	20,419	10.4
NTT	14,969	7.6
Mitsubishi	11,776	6.0
Canon	11,683	5.9
Sharp	9,000	4.6

Source: *Electronic Business*, February 10, 1992, p. 32.

★ 26 ★

Electronics

Electronics Leaders - U.S.

Companies are ranked by electronics sales, shown in millions of dollars. Relative market shares are shown in percent.

	Sales ($ mil.)	% of Group
IBM	$ 69,018	39.6%
AT&T	16,832	9.7
Xerox	13,583	7.8
Hewlett-Packard	13,233	7.6
Digital Equipment	12,943	7.4
GM Hughes	11,723	6.7
Motorola	10,885	6.2
Unisys	10,111	5.8
General Electric	9,430	5.4
Texas Instruments	6,567	3.8

Source: *Electronic Business*, February 10, 1992, p. 32.

★ 27 ★

Employment

Petroleum Industry Employment

Employment distribution by industry segment is shown in percent, based on total of 1,548,674 employees. Data are current as of January, 1991.

Gasoline stations, retail	41.8%
Oil and gas extraction, mining	25.4
Petroleum products, wholesale	12.9
Gas distribution	10.4
Petroleum refining	7.6
Pipelines, except gas	1.2
Oils and greases, refining	0.8

Source: *National Petroleum News*, June 1992, p. 54, from Independent Petroleum Association of America.

★ 28 ★

Energy

Energy Use in Japan

Distribution of power sources is shown in percent.

Oil	29.0%
Nuclear	27.0
Gas	21.0
Hydro	13.0
Coal	10.0

Source: *Business Week*, June 22, 1992, p. 76, from Ministry of International Trade and Industry.

★ 29 ★

Energy

Energy Use in the U.S.

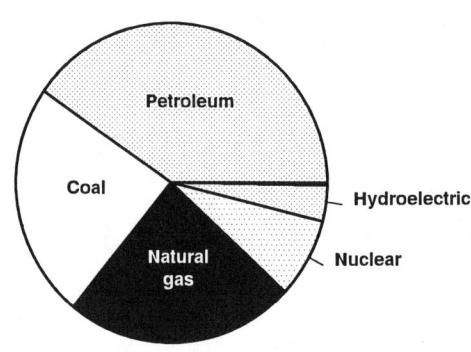

Distribution, by source, is shown in percent for 1973 and 1990.

	1973	1990
Petroleum	47.0%	41.0%
Coal	17.0	24.0
Natural gas	30.0	24.0
Nuclear	1.0	8.0
Hydroelectric	4.0	4.0

Source: *USA TODAY*, February 20, 1992, p. 9A, from Energy Information Administration.

★ 30 ★

Energy

Heating Fuels by Type - Canada

Percent distribution of heating fuels by type is based on a total of 9,873,000 households. Data are shown for 1991.

Piped gas	44.2%
Electricity	33.5
Oil	16.8
Wood	4.5
Bottled gas	0.7
Other	0.3

Source: *National Petroleum News*, June 1992, p. 82, from Statistics Canada.

★ 31 ★

Event Sponsorship

Corporate Sponsorship of Events

Distribution of estimated corporate financial sponsorship of events is shown in percent.

Sports	66.0%
Music/entertainment tours	10.0
Festivals/fairs	9.0
Cause marketing	8.0
Arts/cultural	7.0

Source: *Advertising Age*, March 23, 1992, from International Events Group.

★ 32 ★

Exercise

Exercise Preferences

Exercise preferences are ranked according to millions of exercise equipment units sold in 1990 and 1991.

	1990
Exercise cycles	2.6
Cross-country ski exercisers	0.8
Stair climbers	0.8

Source: *USA TODAY*, May 19, 1992, p. 1C, from National Sporting Goods Association.

★ 33 ★

Flooring Materials

Flooring Materials

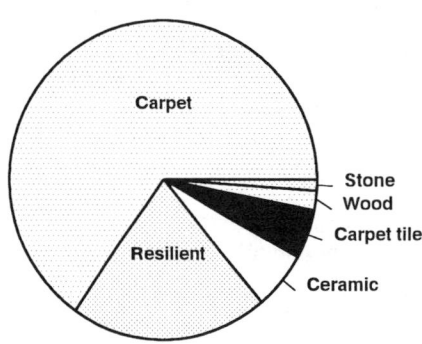

Percent distribution is shown, by material, based on total board feet sold in 1990.

Carpet	66.0%
Resilient	21.0
Ceramic	5.6
Carpet tile	4.7
Wood	1.7
Stone	0.7

Source: *Ceramic Industry*, April 1992, p. 12, from Keyser Ciprus Inc.

★ 34 ★

Flooring Materials

Flooring Materials - Canada

Percent distribution is shown, by material, based on total board feet sold in 1990.

Carpet	63.7%
Resilient	18.3
Ceramic	12.3
Carpet tile	3.3
Wood	1.4
Stone	1.0

Source: *Ceramic Industry*, April 1992, p. 12, from Keyser Ciprus Inc.

★ 35 ★

Food and Consumer Goods

European Biggest Food and Consumer Goods Producers

Company 1990 sales are shown in billions of ECUs (European currency units). Percent shares are based on group total.

	ECU (bil.)	% of Group
Unilever NV	20.2	34.7%
Grand Metropolitan	13.1	22.5
Unilever plc	11.0	18.9
BSN	7.7	13.2
Allied-Lyons	6.2	10.7

Source: *International Management*, April 1992, p. 75.

★ 36 ★

Food Containers

Food and Beverage Container Market

Shares, by type of container, are shown in percent, based on totals of $7.37 billion units for 1990 and $9.99 billion units for 1991.

	1990	1991
Metal cans	57.8%	58.0%
Plastic cups	35.1	35.6
Brick-style cartons	7.1	6.4

Source: *Packaging*, January 1992, p. 36, from Frost & Sullivan.

★ 37 ★

Food Containers

Food Container Demand for Materials

Percent shares by type of material are based on a total of 82.0 billion units in 1990.

Plastic containers	34.0%
Metal cans	30.0
Glass containers	15.0
Paperboard	15.0
Composite containers	3.0
Aluminum foil trays	2.0
Aseptic packaging	1.0

Source: *Packaging*, January 1992, p. 42, from The Freedonia Group.

★ 38 ★

Food Marketing

Food Marketing System Contribution

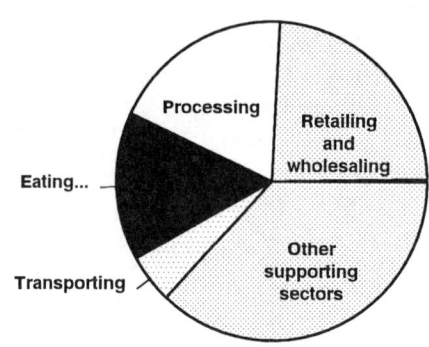

The food marketing system added $491.0 billion to the value of raw food products in 1989 through processing, storage, transportation, and services. Shares by food system segment are shown in percent.

Retailing and wholesaling	24.0%
Processing	19.0
Eating and drinking places	15.0
Transporting	5.0
Other supporting sectors	37.0

Source: *FoodReview*, July 1991, p. 42.

★ 39 ★

Foreign Aid

Foreign Aid from the U.S.

Segment distribution of foreign aid provided by the United States is shown in percent, based on totals of $16,746 million in 1991, $15,745 million in 1992 (estimate) and $15,685 million in 1993 (estimate).

	1991	1992	1993
Security	60.1%	49.9%	48.0%
Economic and humanitarian .	25.4	30.2	32.0
International organizations . .	7.1	10.0	10.5
Multilateral banks	7.5	10.0	9.5

Source: *The Wall Street Journal*, August 10, 1992, p. A12, from The Carnegie Endowment for International Peace.

	% of invest.	Capital ($ mil.)	% of Group

★ 40 ★

Foreign Aid

U.S. Food International Donations

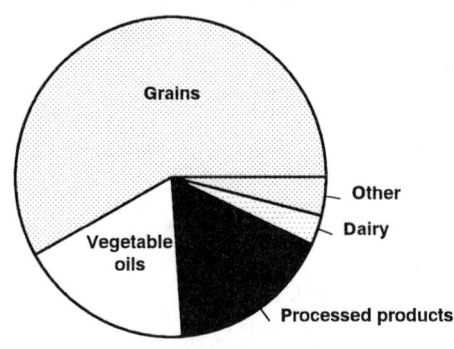

Shares of value of food aid shipped in fiscal years 1987-89 are shown in percent.

Grains	58.0%
Vegetable oils	18.0
Processed products	17.0
Dairy	3.0
Other	4.0

Source: *FoodReview*, July 1991, p. 47.

★ 41 ★

Foreign Investment

Foreign Investment in Romania

Chief foreign investments in Romania in 1991 are shown in terms of foreign company percent of each investment and foreign company capital in millions of U.S. dollars. Dollar shares are shown in percent. (Headquarters locations are in parentheses).

	% of invest.	Capital ($ mil.)	% of Group
Phoceene de Metallurgic (France)	54.0%	$ 14.50	23.7%
Bouygues (France)	51.0	8.00	13.1
Colgate-Palmolive (U.S.)	60.0	7.50	12.3
Siemens (Germany)	49.0	6.50	10.6
Soc. de Expl. Manantiales (Spain)	52.0	6.48	10.6
Coca-Cola (U.S.)	51.0	5.80	9.5
Ciments Francais (France)	90.0	4.00	6.5
Alcatel (France)	56.5	3.40	5.6

	% of invest.	Capital ($ mil.)	% of Group
Quadrant Amroq (U.S.)	75.0%	$ 2.10	3.4%
Sikor (France)	65.0	1.40	2.3
Tangarut (Holland)	75.0	1.00	1.6
Goldstar (Korea)	50.0	0.50	0.8

Source: *Industrial Investor* special section, March 1992, p. 12.

★ 42 ★

Foreign Investment

Foreign-Owned Firms in the U.S.

Foreign-owned firms in U.S. employ 4% of the workforce. Percentage of industry's workforce for foreign-owned firms is shown by category.

Cement	61.0%
Polyester and nylon	60.0
Lead and zinc (mining)	55.0
Liquor	43.0
Household audio and equipment	40.0

Source: *USA TODAY*, July 31, 1992, p. 1B, from Commerce and Labor departments.

★ 43 ★

Foreign Investment

Top Japanese Investors in the U.S.

Value of disclosed deals is shown in millions of dollars. Relative market shares are shown in percent.

	Value ($ mil.)	% of Group
Matsushita Electric Industrial	$ 6,208.7	24.6%
Sony	6,195.0	24.5
Bridgestone	2,600.0	10.3
Saison Group	2,150.0	8.5
Dai-Ichi Kangyo Bank	1,580.0	6.3
Aoki	1,530.0	6.1
Dainippon Ink & Chemicals	1,317.9	5.2
Mitsubishi Corp.	1,273.5	5.0
Mitsubishi Estate	1,262.0	5.0
Nippon Mining	1,142.3	4.5

Source: *Business Tokyo*, June 1992, p. 26.

★ 44 ★
Foreign Trade

Japanese Exporters

Japanese companies are ranked according to exports as percentage of revenue for fiscal years 1984 and 1991.

	1984	1991
Sharp	62.0%	45.0%
Nissan Motor	58.0	41.0
Sumitomo Metal	40.0	22.0
NKK Steel	41.0	20.0
NEC	34.0	18.0

Source: *USA TODAY*, November 9, 1992, p. B1, from Nihon Keizai Shimbun.

★ 45 ★
Foreign Trade

U.S. Agricultural Exports

Feed grains and products	
Animal products	
Oilseeds and products	
Fruits, nuts, and vegetables	
Wheat and products	
Rice	
Other	

1990 agricultural exports totaled 147,686 thousand metric tons with a value of $40,182 million. Distribution by product type is shown in percent.

	Vol. Share	Val. Share
Feed grains and products	47.1%	20.1%
Animal products	1.9	16.3
Oilseeds and products	16.1	15.2
Fruits, nuts, and vegetables	3.5	12.9
Wheat and products	19.6	11.0
Rice	1.7	2.1
Other	10.2	22.4

Source: *FoodReview*, July 1991, p. 50, from *Foreign Agricultural Trade of the United States*, USDA, and ERS.

★ 46 ★
Foreign Trade

U.S. Agricultural Imports

Shares of 1990 agricultural imports, by product, are based on a total of $22,514 million, shown in percent.

Fruit, nuts, and vegetables	21.4%
Meat	12.6
Coffee	8.9
Cocoa and products	4.6
Bananas	4.1
Sugar	3.3
Vegetable oils	3.2
Other	41.9

Source: *FoodReview*, July 1991, p. 50, from *Foreign Agricultural Trade of the United States*, USDA, and ERS.

★ 47 ★
Forest Products

Forest Product Manufacturers

Companies are ranked by dollar sales in 1991. Relative market shares are based on a total of $100,193 million.

	Sales ($ mil.)	% of Group
International Paper	$ 12,703	12.7%
Georgia-Pacific	11,524	11.5
Weyerhaeuser	8,702	8.7
Kimberly-Clark	6,830	6.8
Stone Container	5,399	5.4
Scott Paper	5,000	5.0
Champion International	4,786	4.8
Mead	4,579	4.6
James River (VA)	4,562	4.6
Boise Cascade	4,044	4.0
Union Camp	2,967	3.0
Jefferson Smurfit	2,942	2.9
Temple-Inland	2,507	2.5
Westvaco	2,322	2.3
Manville	2,100	2.1
Willamette Industries	2,005	2.0
Louisiana-Pacific	1,714	1.7
Sonoco Products	1,704	1.7
Federal Paper Board	1,435	1.4
Bowater	1,291	1.3
Potlatch	1,242	1.2
Bemis	1,142	1.1
Fort Howard	1,138	1.1

Continued on next page.

★ 47 ★ *Continued*
Forest Products

Forest Product Manufacturers

Companies are ranked by dollar sales in 1991. Relative market shares are based on a total of $100,193 million.

	Sales ($ mil.)	% of Group
First Brands	$ 1,073	1.1%
ITT Rayonier	979	1.0
Consolidated Papers	882	0.9
Chesapeake	841	0.8
Gaylord Container	724	0.7
Tambrands	666	0.7
Longview Fibre	645	0.6
St. Joe Paper	608	0.6
P.H. Glatfelter	577	0.6
Ply Gem	562	0.6

Source: *Fortune*, April 20, 1992, p. 272.

★ 48 ★

Gifts

Gift Market

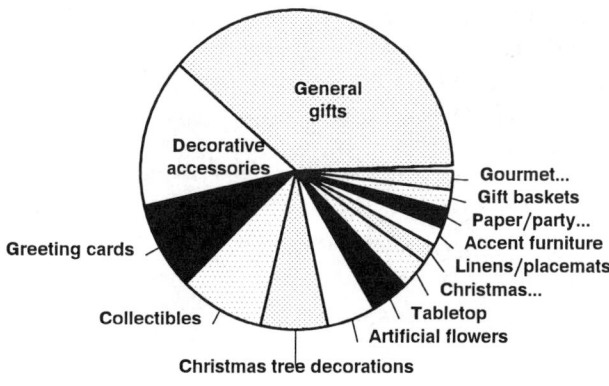

Segment distribution of products sold by gift retailers is shown in percent for 1990.

General gifts	38.0%
Decorative accessories	15.0
Greeting cards	9.0
Collectibles	9.0
Christmas tree decorations	7.0
Artificial flowers	5.0
Tabletop	4.0
Christmas decorations	3.0
Linens/placemats	2.0
Accent furniture	2.0

Paper/party goods	2.0%
Gift baskets	2.0
Gourmet specialty foods	2.0

Source: *Gifts & Decorative Accessories*, May 1992, p. S-14.

★ 49 ★

Health

Health Spending by Source of Funds

U.S. health spending in 1989 by source of funds is shown in billions of dollars, based a total of $604 billion.

Consumer	
Private insurance	33.1%
Out of pocket	20.7
Charities	4.3
Federal	
Medicare	16.9
Veterans military	6.1
Medicaid	5.8
Sate and local	
State medicaid	4.5
Other state and local	8.6

Source: *Fortune*, July 1, 1991, p. 46.

★ 50 ★

Information

Data Information Services

Data information sources are shown with revenue in millions of dollars for 1991. Shares by sources are shown in percent.

	Rev. ($ mil.)	Share
Paper yellow pages	$ 9,200	59.5%
Paper white pages	2,400	15.5
Direct marketing list services	2,000	12.9
Directory assistance	1,800	11.6
Electronic white pages	25	0.2
Electronic yellow pages	12	0.1
CD-ROM-based white pages	8	0.1
Magnetic tape	8	0.1

Source: *The Wall Street Journal*, April 6, 1992, p. B1.

★ 51 ★

Licensed Products

Licensed Product Sales in the U.S.

Percent shares, by product, are based on retail sales of $63.5 billion in 1991.

Apparel/accessories	32.1%
Toys/games	11.8
Gifts/novelties	10.7
Home furnishings/housewares	10.7
Publishing/stationery	10.2
Food/beverages	9.3
Health and beauty aids	6.1
Electronics	5.7
Sporting goods	3.3

Source: *Discount Merchandiser*, June 1992, p. 24, from *The Licensing Letter*.

★ 52 ★

Minority Business

Black-Owned Businesses

Sales of the leading black-owned firms in 1991 are shown in millions of dollars; relative market shares are shown in percent for the same period.

	Sales ($ mil.)	% of Group
TLC Beatrice International Holdings . . .	$ 1,542.0	57.5%
Johnson Publishing Co.	261.4	9.8
Philadelphia Coca-Cola Bottling Co.	256.0	9.5
H.J. Russell & Co.	143.6	5.4
Barden Communications . . .	91.2	3.4
Garden State Cable TV	88.0	3.3
Soft Sheen Products	87.9	3.3
RMS Technologies	79.9	3.0
Stop Shop and Save	66.0	2.5
The Bing Group	64.9	2.4

Source: *The New York Times*, May 7, 1992, p. C5, from *Black Enterprise*.

★ 53 ★

Minority Business

Leading Women-Owned Businesses

Revenues for 1991 are shown in millions of dollars; relative market shares are shown in percent for the same period.

	Rev. ($ mil.)	% of Group
Axel Johnson Group	$ 829	10.7%
Minyard Food Stores	700	9.0
Warnaco Group	548	7.1
Jockey Intl.	450	5.8
Esprit	450	5.8
Astronautics	415	5.4
Jenny Craig	412	5.3
Copley Newspapers	405	5.2
Chas. Levy	350	4.5
Lundy Packaging	350	4.5
Gear Holdings	280	3.6
Johnson Publishing	252	3.2
Owen Healthcare	250	3.2
Carole Little	205	2.6
Sunshine Jr. Stores	203	2.6
Tootsie Roll	200	2.6
Donna Karan Co.	200	2.6
Owen Steel	192	2.5
Resort Condominiums Intl. . . .	180	2.3
Adrienne Vitadinni	160	2.1
Lillian Vernon	160	2.1
Copeland Lumber Yards	152	2.0
Software Spectrum	146	1.9
Redken Laboratories	140	1.8
Rose Acre Farms	127	1.6

Source: *USA TODAY*, April 23, 1992, p. 2B, from *Working Woman*.

★ 54 ★

New Product Development

New Product Development

The number of products introduced between September of 1991 and September of 1992 is shown in thousands.

	'91	'92
Foods	6,463	5,947
Health and beauty aids	2,939	3,515
Beverages	1,397	1,243
Household goods	634	675
Pet products	320	336
Other	198	195

Source: *The Wall Street Journal*, October 28, 1992, p. B1, from Marketing Intelligence Service Ltd.

★ 55 ★

Packaging

Cigarette Packaging Global Market

Shares, by company, of the cigarette packaging market are shown in percent.

G.D.(Italy)	40.0%
Hauny(Germany)	30.0
Focke(Germany)	30.0

Source: Investext, Thomson Financial Networks, February 18, 1992, from Studio Albertini.

★ 56 ★

Packaging

Cigarette Packing Global Market

Shares, by company, of the global market in cigarette packing are shown in percent.

	Soft Pack	Rigid Pack
SASIB (Switzerland)	50.0%	-
G.D. (Italy)	45.0	65.0%
Hauny (Germany)	5.0	-
Mollins (U.K.)	-	-
Focke (Germany)	-	35.0

Source: Investext, Thomson Financial Networks, February 18, 1992, from Studio Albertini.

★ 57 ★

Packaging

Medical Packaging by Type - Europe

Market segmentation, by material, is shown in percent, based on a total usage of 28,700 tons in 1990.

Paper	46.7%
Plastic films	45.3
Aluminum foils	5.9
Tyvek	2.1

Source: Investext, Thomson Financial Networks, May 1, 1992, from Barclays de Zoete Wedd Securities.

★ 58 ★

Packaging

Medical Packaging Use - Europe

Market segmentation is shown in percent, based on a total usage of 28,700 tons in 1990.

Reels	79.1%
Bags	10.3
Pouches	8.1
Tubing	2.4

Source: Investext, Thomson Financial Networks, May 1, 1992, from Barclays de Zoete Wedd Securities.

★ 59 ★

Patents

Federal Patents by Department

Distribution of federal patents by department is shown in percent, based on total of 1,802 patents in 1990.

Navy	25.0%
Dept. of Energy	25.0
HHS	13.0
Army	11.9
NASA	9.7
Air Force	7.9
Dept. of Agriculture	4.1
Dept. of Commerce	1.7
Dept. of Interior	0.8
Dept. of Veterans Affairs	0.4
EPA	0.3
Dept. of Transportation	0.1

Source: *Government Executive*, November 1991, p. 39, from Commerce Department Technology Administration.

★ 60 ★

Patents

U.S. Patents in Electronics and Instrumentation

Companies are ranked by numbers of U.S. patents issued in electronics and instrumentation in 1991. Shares of the group are shown in percent.

	No. of Patents	% of Group
Toshiba	895	24.2%
Hitachi	869	23.5
Mitsubishi	793	21.5
Motorola	572	15.5
IBM	563	15.2

Source: *Electronic Business*, February 24, 1992, p. 26, from *MicroPatent*.

★ 61 ★

Pet Care Products

Pet Care Product Market

Pet care product sales are shown in billions of dollars. Shares, by type of product, are shown in percent, based on total sales in 1989.

	Sales ($ bil.)	Share
Dog food	$ 4.12	39.0%
Cat food	2.67	25.3
Dog/cat accessories	1.87	17.7
Dog snacks	0.805	7.6
Flea/tick products	0.567	5.4
Cat box filler	0.492	4.7
Cat treats	0.030	0.3

Source: *Grocery Marketing*, November 24, 1991, p. 30, from Frost & Sullivan Inc.

★ 62 ★

Plumbing Fixtures

Plumbing Fixture Production

Production of selected plumbing fixtures is shown in thousands of units for 1990. Shares of the group are shown in percent.

	Units (000)	% of Group
Water closet bowls	8,785	26.8%
Flush tanks	8,147	24.9
Lavatories	7,422	22.7
Kitchen sinks	4,514	13.8
Bathtubs	3,343	10.2
Whirlpool baths	285	0.9
Urinals	231	0.7

Source: *U.S. Industrial Outlook 1992*, p. 7-14, from U.S. Department of Commerce.

★ 63 ★

Plumbing Fixtures

Plumbing Parts Market

Value of shipments is shown in millions of dollars for 1991. Shares, by type, are based on a total shipment value of $5,926 million.

	($ mil.)	Share
Plumbing fittings	$ 2,980	50.3%
Plastics plumbing fixtures	1,089	18.4
Metal sanitary ware	1,006	17.0
Vitreous plumbing fixtures	851	14.4

Source: *U.S. Industrial Outlook 1992*, p. 7-15, from U.S. Department of Commerce.

★ 64 ★

Politics

Health Care Campaign Contributors

The top congressional campaign contributions from health and insurance sources are shown for the 18 months ended June 30, 1992. Totals include individual contributions. PAC stands for political action committee.

American Medical Assn. PAC	$ 1,108,039
American Dental Assn. PAC	655,564
Independent Insurance Agents of America PAC	433,567
American Family PAC	394,150

Continued on next page.

★ 64 ★ *Continued*

Politics

Health Care Campaign Contributors

The top congressional campaign contributions from health and insurance sources are shown for the 18 months ended June 30, 1992. Totals include individual contributions. PAC stands for political action committee.

American Academy of
  Ophthalmology PAC . . . . $ 356,413
Prudential Insurance   349,960
American Council of Life Insurance . .   301,716
American Hospital Assn. PAC   301,129
Podiatry PAC   289,250
American Chiropractic Assn. PAC . . .   257,049

Source: *The Wall Street Journal*, November 27, 1992, p. A8, from Citizen Action.

★ 65 ★

Politics

Political News Coverage

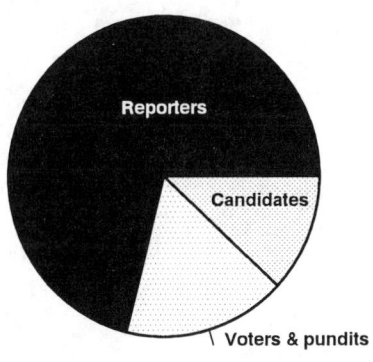

Percent distribution of speaking time on network nightly news is shown in percent for the period from September 7 to November 3, 1992.

Reporters 71.0%
Voters & pundits 17.0
Candidates 12.0

Source: *USA TODAY*, November 30, 1992, p. 1A, from Center for Media and Public Affairs.

★ 66 ★

Private Labels

Private-Label Product Sales

Data represent supermarket categories with private-label sales of more than $20 million in the 52-week period ended Sept. 16, 1992. Sales are shown in millions of dollars; private label as percent of the total category is shown in percent.

	Sales ($ mil.)	Share
Pies & cakes	$ 111.6	29.5%
Internal analgesics	138.1	13.6
Disposable diapers	318.4	13.0
Mouthwash	38.5	11.9
Cold/allergy/sinus remedies . .	72.1	10.4
Hot cereal	101.4	9.2
Frozen desserts	30.0	5.4
Cold cereal	333.5	4.7
Frozen chicken	30.0	3.6
Cigarettes	130.4	1.7

Source: *The Wall Street Journal*, October 20, 1992, p. B1, from Information Resources Inc.

★ 67 ★

Repair Services

Maintenance and Repair Spending

Spending on maintenance and repair by category is shown in billions of dollars for 1991. Percent shares are based on group total.

	($ bil.)	% of Group
Autos	$ 90.0	69.4%
Computers	16.6	12.8
Telecommunications hardware . .	15.6	12.0
Copiers	5.4	4.2
Medical electronics	2.1	1.6

Source: *The Wall Street Journal*, June 22, 1992, p. B1, from Automotive Service Industry Association.

★ 68 ★

Research

International Research Companies in the U.S.

Companies are shown with U.S. research revenues in millions of dollars in 1991. Relative shares are shown in percent. The total market was $2.06 billion in 1991.

	Rev. ($ mil.)	% of Group
A.C. Nielsen Co.	$ 492.0	29.6%
Arbitron Co	201.7	12.1
Information Resources Inc. . . .	183.9	11.1
IMS International	165.0	9.9
Westat	86.9	5.2
Marlitz Marketing Research . .	59.6	3.6
M/A/R/C Group	56.1	3.4
Abt Associates	55.3	3.3
NFO Research	45.6	2.7
Gallup Organization	43.5	2.6
Market Facts	40.7	2.4
MRB Group	37.3	2.2
Walker Group	30.9	1.9
Intersearch	28.2	1.7
Burke Marketing Research . . .	24.9	1.5
Marketeam/Doane Marketing Research	6.5	0.4
FRC Research	6.4	0.4
Shifrin Research	6.3	0.4
Strategy Research	6.0	0.4
Directions for Decisions	5.6	0.3
Louis Harris & Associates . . .	9.1	0.5
Wirthlin Group	9.0	0.5
Response Analysis	8.8	0.5
ICR Survey Research Group . .	8.6	0.5
McCollum Spielman Worldwide	8.4	0.5
Field Research	8.3	0.5
Newman-Stein	8.0	0.5
Market Measures	7.7	0.5
Marketing Analysts	7.0	0.4
Pretesting Co.	6.6	0.4

Source: *Advertising Age*, June 22, 1992, p. S4.

★ 69 ★

Research

Research Company International Shares

Companies are shown with international research revenues in thousands of dollars. Percent shares are based on total of $1.3 billion for the group in 1991.

	Rev. ($000)	% of Group
A.C. Nielsen Co.	$ 708,000	54.2%
IMS International	344,000	26.3
Research International	102,300	7.8
MRB Group	59,106	4.5
Millward Brown	40,300	3.1
Information Resources Inc. . . .	23,800	1.8
Louis Harris & Associates . . .	13,680	1.0
Gallup Organization	4,500	0.3
Harte-Hanks Marketing Services	2,000	0.2
Walker Group	1,591	0.1
Starch INRA Hooper	1,500	0.1
BASES Group	1,000	0.1
Decision Research	980	0.1
BRX/Global	900	0.1
Wirthlin Group	900	0.1
Burke Marketing Research . . .	600	0.0
Pretesting Co.	540	0.0
Rothstein-Tauber	315	0.0
National Analysts	200	0.0
Mediamark Research	115	0.0
Hamlin Harkins	100	0.0
Marketing Metrics	100	0.0
Marketing Analysts	94	0.0
Heller Research Group	65	0.0
American LIVES	35	0.0
Research & Forecasts	15	0.0

Source: *Advertising Age*, June 22, 1992, p. S4.

★ 70 ★

Retailing

Hard Lines Chains

Company revenues are shown in thousands of dollars. Percent shares are based on the group total.

	Rev. ($000)	% of Group
Toys "R" Us.	$ 6,124,209	40.0%
Tandy	2,519,149	16.5

Continued on next page.

Retailing

Hard Lines Chains

Company revenues are shown in thousands of dollars. Percent shares are based on the group total.

	Rev. ($000)	% of Group
Circuit City	$ 1,886,907	12.3%
Blockbuster Entertainment . .	868,003	5.7
Best Buy	589,763	3.9
Pier 1 Imports	552,480	3.6
House of Fabrics	493,062	3.2
Tiffany	491,906	3.2
Fabri-Centers of America . . .	468,904	3.1
Highland	420,759	2.7
Hancock Fabrics	388,001	2.5
Oshman's	202,102	1.3
Good Guys	155,013	1.0
Lionel	148,648	1.0

Source: *Chain Store Age Executive*, April 1992, p. 72, from company reports.

Retailing

Retail Leaders

Retail revenue is shown in billions of dollars for 1991; relative market shares are shown in percent for the same period. Figures for Sears Roebuck do not include All State Insurance, Coldwell Real Estate Group, or Dean Witter Financial Services.

	Rev. ($ bil.)	% of Group
Wal-Mart	$ 43.9	25.3%
Kmart	34.6	19.9
Sears Roebuck	31.4	18.1
J.C. Penney	16.2	9.3
Dayton Hudson	16.1	9.3
May Company	10.6	6.1
Federated	6.9	4.0
R.H. Macy	6.8	3.9
Dillards	4.0	2.3
Nordstrom	3.2	1.8

Source: *USA TODAY*, June 19, 1992, p. 1B, from Barnard's Retail Consulting Group.

Retailing

Retail Market by Outlet - Japan

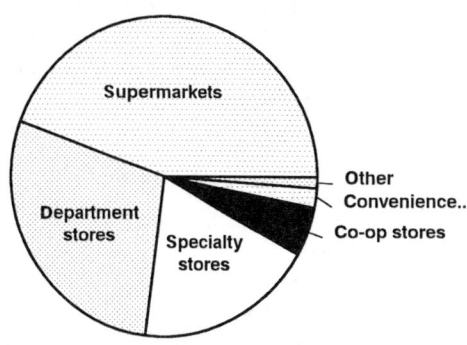

Shares of the total retail industry, by store type, are shown in percent for fiscal year 1990.

Supermarkets	44.86%
Department stores	29.44
Specialty stores	18.56
Co-op stores	4.51
Convenience stores	1.55
Other	1.08

Source: *Business TOKYO*, May 1992, p. 52, from Japan Company Handbook.

Retailing

Retailing by Channel

Shares are shown in percent, based on total sales of $982.907 billion by outlets with at least $1.0 billion in annual sales. The figure for home centers includes only consumer retail sales. The figure for mail order includes TV shopping.

Supermarkets	29.10%
Discount stores	9.66
Drug & proprietary stores	7.52
Department stores	7.25
Grocery stores	6.32
Auto and home supply stores	3.36
Women's ready-to-wear stores . . .	2.99
Furniture stores	2.93
TV, radio stores	2.91
Wholesale clubs	2.72
Home centers	2.25
Family clothing stores	2.08
Sporting goods and bicycle stores	1.56

Continued on next page.

★ 73 ★ *Continued*
Retailing

Retailing by Channel

Shares are shown in percent, based on total sales of $982.907 billion by outlets with at least $1.0 billion in annual sales. The figure for home centers includes only consumer retail sales. The figure for mail order includes TV shopping.

Shoe stores	1.45%
Jewelry stores	1.44
Hardware stores	1.43
Mail order	1.31
Off-price apparel stores	1.10
Floor covering stores	1.08
Household appliance stores	1.00
Men's, boys' clothing stores	0.88
Misc. general merchandise stores	0.87
Variety stores	0.84
Home furnishing stores	0.82
Bookstores	0.79
Hobby, toy, game shops	0.70
Music stores	0.67
Gift, novelty, and souvenir stores	0.64
Automatic merchandising machines	0.61
Paint, glass, and wallpaper stores	0.56
Catalog showrooms	0.54
Florists	0.53
Garden supply stores	0.45
Optical goods stores	0.40
Stationery stores	0.37
Sewing, piece goods stores	0.33
Camera, photo supply stores	0.27
Infants' and childrens' stores	0.27

Source: *Discount Merchandising*, June 1992, p. 78.

★ 74 ★
Retailing

Retailing Giants

Volume of the 25 largest retailers reached $332.235 million in 1991. Relative shares are shown in percent.

	Sales ($ 000)	% of Group
Wal-Mart	$ 43,886,902	13.2%
KMart	34,580,000	10.4
Sears Merch. Group	31,432,900	9.5
Kroger	21,350,530	6.4
American Stores	20,822,956	6.3

	Sales ($ 000)	% of Group
J.C. Penney	$ 16,201,000	4.9%
Dayton Hudson	16,115,000	4.9
Safeway Stores	15,119,200	4.6
A&P Supermarkets	11,590,991	3.5
May Dept. Stores	10,615,000	3.2
Winn-Dixie	10,074,331	3.0
WoolWorth	9,914,000	3.0
Melville	9,886,183	3.0
Albertson's	8,680,467	2.6
Southland	8,076,012	2.4
Federated Dept.	6,932,300	2.1
R.H. Macy	6,760,000	2.0
Walgreen	6,733,044	2.0
Price Club	6,598,053	2.0
Food Lion	6,438,507	1.9
Supermkts. General	6,425,000	1.9
The Limited	6,149,218	1.9
Toys "R" Us	6,124,209	1.8
Publix	6,100,000	1.8
Montgomery Ward	5,630,000	1.7

Source: *Stores*, July 1992, p. 38.

★ 75 ★
Retailing

Top European Retailers

Company 1990 sales are shown in billions of ECUs (European Currency Units). Percent shares are based on the group total.

	ECU (bil.)	% of Group
Tengelmann	20.6	30.5%
Leclerc	14.5	21.5
Carrefour	11.0	16.3
J Sainsbury	10.9	16.1
Aldi	10.5	15.6

Source: *International Management*, April 1992, p. 75.

★ 76 ★

Retailing - Food

Broiler Market by Outlet

Volume shares by outlet are shown in percent for 1985, 1987, and 1989.

	'85	'87	'89
Domestic food market	92.0%	87.9%	84.9%
Retail grocery stores	53.8	52.4	51.2
Food service	38.2	35.5	33.7
Eating places	31.0	30.5	29.6
Fast food outlets	17.9	22.1	18.2
Other eating places	13.1	8.4	11.4
Government and institutions	7.2	3.0	1.9
Brokers	0.0	2.0	2.2
Exports	2.8	5.4	3.5
Renderers and pet food producers	5.2	6.7	11.6

Source: *FoodReview*, July 1991, p. 5, from "Broiler Industry Marketing Practices", National Broiler Council, and "Market Trends Driving Broiler Consumption".

★ 77 ★

Roofing

Commercial Roofing Market by Material

1990 market shares, by material, are shown in percent for new construction roofing and reroofing. "Other" includes tiles, PUF (polyurethane film), liquid-applied, and asphalt shingles.

	New Constr.	Re-roof.
Single-plies	36.9%	34.1%
Built-up roofing	30.0	31.7
Modified bitumen	13.2	17.2
Metal	13.9	13.5
Other	6.0	3.5

Source: *Shopping Center World*, July 1991, p. S2, from NRCA Annual Market Survey.

★ 78 ★

R&D

10 Leading Computer R&D Companies Worldwide

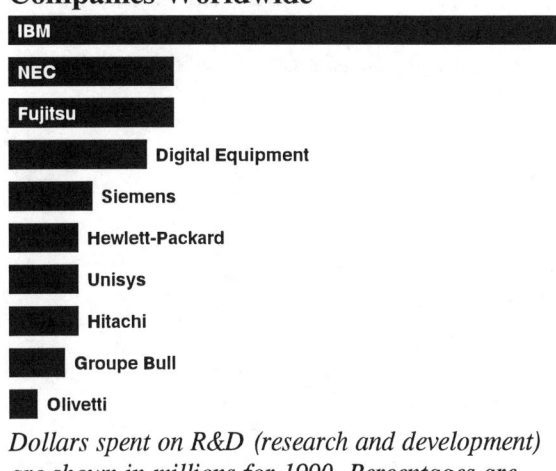

Dollars spent on R&D (research and development) are shown in millions for 1990. Percentages are based on a group total.

	($ mil.)	% of Group
IBM	$ 6,198	39.5%
NEC	1,901	12.1
Fujitsu	1,896	12.1
Digital Equipment	1,624	10.3
Siemens	873	5.6
Hewlett-Packard	853	5.4
Unisys	747	4.8
Hitachi	702	4.5
Groupe Bull	552	3.5
Olivetti	354	2.3

Source: *Financial World*, January 21, 1992, p. 53, from Gartner Group's Yardstick Top 100 Worldwide; Warner Computer and Services.

★ 79 ★

R&D

Cooperative R&D Agreements

Distribution of CRADAs (Cooperative Research and Development Agreements), by federal department, is shown in percent, based on a total of 607 agreements in 1990.

NASA	24.2%
Dept. of Agriculture	21.1
HHS	18.1
Dept. of Commerce	13.5
Army	13.2

Continued on next page.

★ 79 ★ *Continued*
R&D

Cooperative R&D Agreements

Distribution of CRADAs (Cooperative Research and Development Agreements), by federal department, is shown in percent, based on a total of 607 agreements in 1990.

Navy	3.3%
Air Force	2.1
Dept. of Interior	2.0
EPA	1.8
Dept. of Veterans Affairs	0.3
Dept. of Transportation	0.2
Dept. of Energy	0.2

Source: *Government Executive*, November 1991, p. 39, from Commerce Department Technology Administration.

★ 80 ★
R&D

Cooperative R&D Agreements

Percentages reflect numbers of active cooperative R&D agreements (CRADA), by department, based on a total of 460 CRADAs in 1990.

Agriculture	27.8%
Health and human services	23.9
Commerce	17.8
Army	17.4
Navy	4.3
Air force	2.8
Interior	2.6
Environment Protection Agency	2.4
Veterans' affairs	0.4
Transport	0.2
Energy	0.2

Source: *The Economist*, July 25, 1992, p. 23, from National Science Board, *Science & Engineering Indicators*.

★ 81 ★
R&D

Defense Research Grants

Institution shares are shown in percent, based on a total of $119.6 million in special grants for defense science projects.

Boston University	24.8%
Arctic Region Supercomputing Center	21.4
Louisiana State University	8.6
Marwood College, PA	8.6
U. Minnesota	8.6
Kansas State University	6.6
Northeastern University	5.1
U. Texas at Austin	5.1
Texas Regional Inst. for Environmental Studies	4.3
Monmouth College, NJ	2.0
Brandeis University	1.7
U. Wisconsin	1.4
George Mason University	0.6
U. South Carolina	0.4
U. St. Thomas at St. Paul, MN	0.4
New Mexico State University	0.3
Medical College of Ohio	0.2

Source: *Science*, December 6, 1992, p. 1449.

★ 82 ★
R&D

Federal Basic Research Budget

Shares of the federal basic research budget by department or agency are based on totals of $13,254 million in 1992 (enacted) and $14,322 million in 1993 (proposed).

	1992	1993
Health and Human Services	41.2%	40.5%
National Science Foundation	13.9	15.5
National Aeronautics and Space Administration	14.0	14.4
Department of Energy	13.5	13.0
Department of Defense	8.8	8.4
Department of Agriculture	4.6	4.5
Other agencies	4.0	3.7

Source: *Science*, Vol. 255, July 2, 1992, p. 672.

★ 83 ★
R&D

Federal Government Health Care R&D

1992 federal government spending on research and development, by type of illness, is shown in millions of dollars.

Cancer	$ 1984.0
HIV/AIDS	1164.0
Heart disease	729.0
Alzheimer's disease	282.0
Diabetes	279.0
Injuries	162.0
Stroke	94.0

Source: *The Wall Street Journal*, April 22, 1992, p. A6, from Public Health Service, Centers for Disease Control, and Alzheimer's Association.

★ 84 ★
R&D

Federal R&D Budget

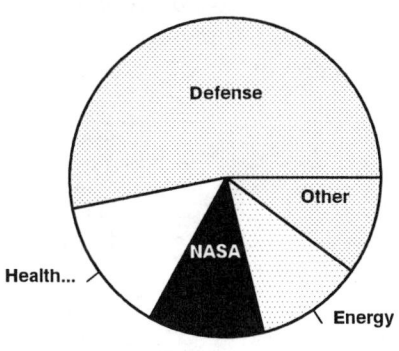

Shares of federal research and development budgets, by industry segment. Percentages are based on an R&D total of $67.7 billion.

Defense	53 %
Health & Human Services	14
NASA	12
Energy	11
Other	10

Source: *The Economist*, July 25, 1992, p. 22, from National Science Board, *Science & Engineering Indicators*.

★ 85 ★
R&D

Government Science Projects

Government spending on science projects is shown in millions of dollars for 1992 and 1993 (proposed).

Strategic Defense Initiative	$ 4,100
Space Station	2,029
Superconducting Super Collider	484
Human Genome Project	164

Source: *News & Comment*, February 1992, p. 673, from NASA, OMB, and DOD.

★ 86 ★
R&D

R&D Spending by U.S. Companies

Expenditures for 1990 are shown in millions of dollars; distribution of the group total is shown in percent.

	Expend. ($ mil.)	% of Group
General Motors	$ 5,341.5	21.7 %
IBM	4,914.0	20.0
Ford	3,558.0	14.5
AT&T	2,433.0	9.9
Digital Equipment	1,614.4	6.6
General Electric	1,479.0	6.0
Du Pont	1,428.0	5.8
Hewlett-Packard	1,367.0	5.6
Eastman Kodak	1,329.0	5.4
Dow	1,136.0	4.6

Source: *JOM*, January 1992, p. 40, from *Inside R&D*.

★ 87 ★
R&D

R&D Spending in Major Canadian Pharmaceutical Companies

Companies are ranked by research and development (R&D) spending, shown in millions of dollars. Percent shares are based on the group total.

	(mil.)	% of Group
Quadra Logic Technologies Inc.	$ 12.1	27.7 %
Allelix Biopharmaceuticals Inc.	7.5	17.1
Biomira Inc.	7.0	16.0

Continued on next page.

★ 87 ★ *Continued*
R&D

R&D Spending in Major Canadian Pharmaceutical Companies

Companies are ranked by research and development (R&D) spending, shown in millions of dollars. Percent shares are based on the group total.

	(mil.)	% of Group
Trimel Corp.	$ 7.0	16.0%
IAF BioChem International Inc.	6.3	14.4
Medicorp Inc.	1.5	3.4
Hyal Pharmaceutical Corp. . . .	1.3	3.0
IBEX Technologies Inc.	0.65	1.5
Deprenyl Research Ltd.	0.40	0.9

Source: *Report on Business Magazine*, October 1991, pp. 42-43.

★ 88 ★
R&D

Software Leaders in R&D

- SAS Institute
- Ashton-Tate
- BMC
- Softlab
- Legent
- Compuserve
- Software AG
- Lotus
- Ingres
- Boole

Software company expenditures on R&D are shown as percent of each company's revenues.

SAS Institute	45.0%
Ashton-Tate	26.0
BMC	24.0
Softlab	23.0
Legent	22.0
Compuserve	20.0
Software AG	20.0
Lotus	19.0
Ingres	19.0
Boole	18.0

Source: *Datamation*, February 15, 1992, p. 49.

★ 89 ★
R&D

Top Electronics R&D Spenders

Electronics R&D spending is shown as percent of sales for each company in 1990.

Cypress Semicond.	24.7%
Intergrated Device	19.9
Advanced Micro	19.2
Cadence Design	18.4
Ashton-Tate	17.2
Mentor Graphics	17.1
Applied Materials	17.1
Analog Devices	16.6
VLSI Technology	16.5
Cray Research	16.0

Source: *R&D Magazine*, December 1991, p. 14, from *Electronic Business*.

★ 90 ★
Supermarket Products

Supermarket Sales by Product

The top 25 products are ranked by supermarket sales for 52 weeks ended 9/29/91, shown in millions of dollars. Percent shares are based on the group total.

	Sales ($ mil.)	% of Group
Rice	$ 981,332	8.0%
Internal analgesics	964,881	7.8
Sauces	810,881	6.6
Drink mixes	794,275	6.4
Biscuits/dough	758,161	6.2
Frozen breakfast foods . . .	745,379	6.0
Mexican food	712,976	5.8
Cold/sinus tablets/cough . .	615,692	5.0
Gravy/sauce mixes	605,031	4.9
Other refrig. products	557,300	4.5
Frozen desserts/topping . . .	533,859	4.3
Mexican sauces	486,114	3.9
Creams	451,610	3.7
Sausage	410,295	3.3
Cat litter	376,446	3.1
Dry fruit snacks	369,724	3.0
Air fresheners	355,593	2.9
Pest control	303,426	2.5
Facial moisturizer/cleanser . .	282,222	2.3
Desserts-refrig.	236,415	1.9
Rug/upholstery cleaner . . .	228,148	1.9
Breadcrumbs/batters	199,517	1.6

Continued on next page.

★ 90 ★ *Continued*

Supermarket Products

Supermarket Sales by Product

The top 25 products are ranked by supermarket sales for 52 weeks ended 9/29/91, shown in millions of dollars. Percent shares are based on the group total.

	Sales ($ mil.)	% of Group
Feminine needs	$ 190,629	1.5%
Pizza-refrig.	179,437	1.5
Pasta-refrig.	176,121	1.4

Source: *Grocery Marketing*, January 24, 1992, p. 4.

★ 91 ★

Thermoses

Cooler & Jug Manufacturers

Estimated shares of the domestic market are shown in percent, based on a total of $300 million.

Coleman	28.0-35.0%
Igloo	31.0-34.0
Rubbermaid	17.0-33.0
Thermos	4.0

Source: Investext, Thomson Financial Networks, March 26, 1992, from The First Boston Corporation.

★ 92 ★

Trading

General Trading Leaders - Japan

Companies are ranked by 1991 declared income, shown in millions of Yen. Relative market shares are shown in percent.

	Income (Y mil.)	% of Group
Mitsubishi Corp.	91,576	24.2%
Sumitomo Corp.	83,754	22.1
Mitsui & Co.	51,789	13.7
C. Itoh & Co.	40,733	10.7
Marubeni Co.	39,845	10.5
Toyota Tsusho	18,362	4.8
Nissho Iwai	16,335	4.3
Nagase & Co.	12,526	3.3
Tomen Corp.	12,286	3.2
Nissei Sangyo	11,732	3.1

Source: *TOKYO Business Today*, July 1992, p. 40.

★ 93 ★

Transportation

Freight Transport by Modality

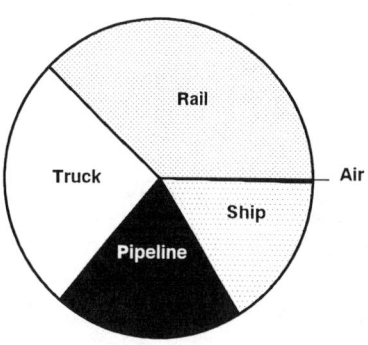

Shares are shown in percent, based on total ton miles in 1990.

Rail	37.6%
Truck	25.6
Pipeline	20.4
Ship	16.0
Air	0.3

Source: *Journal of Commerce*, June 25, 1992, p. 1A, from Association of American Railroads.

★ 94 ★

Transportation

Freight Transportation by Type

Shares by type of transportation are shown as percent of freight carried, based on tons carried per mile.

Railroads	37.6%
Trucks	25.6
Oil pipelines	20.4
Waterways	16.1
Air	0.3

Source: *USA TODAY*, June 25, 1992, p. 3A, from *Railroad Facts*.

★ 95 ★

Volunteerism

Volunteer Causes

Percentage of employee volunteer programs in each area is shown based on a poll of 454 human resources, community relations, and public affairs executives.

Education 74.0%
Health 47.0
Youths in crisis 47.0
Environment 41.0
Homelessness 41.0

Source: *USA TODAY*, August 7, 1992, p. 1D, from The Conference Board.

★ 96 ★

Voting Equipment

Voting Equipment

Voting methods used in the November 3, 1992 U.S. presidential election are shown in percent.

Computer card 60.0%
Lever pull 25.0
Paper ballot 10.0
Electronic machine 5.0

Source: *USA TODAY*, November 3, 1992, p. 1A, from Federal Election Commission.

SIC 01 - Agricultural Production - Crops

★ 97 ★
Crops (SIC 0100)

Crop Acreage

Planted acreage in the U.S. is shown in millions with relative percent distribution for 1991.

	Acres Planted	% of Group
Corn	75.9	32.9%
Wheat	70.0	30.3
Soybeans	59.8	25.9
Cotton	14.1	6.1
Sorghum	11.0	4.8

Source: *Farm Journal*, February 1992, p. 6.

★ 98 ★
Gardening (SIC 0100)

Gardening Market

Lawn and garden retail sales, by category, are shown in millions of dollars for 1989, 1990, and 1991. Relative market shares are shown in percent.

	1989	1990	1991
Flower gardening	$ 61.6	$ 59.5	$ 54.7
Vegetable gardening	34.0	36.2	39.3
Herb gardening	1.9	2.2	3.8
Berry growing	2.4	2.1	2.1

Source: *The Wall Street Journal*, March 11, 1992, p. B1, from National Gardening Association.

★ 99 ★
Cash Grain (SIC 0110)

Cash Grain Supply

Cash grain supply is shown in millions of bushels for 1990-91 and 1991-92, combined. Percentages are based on group totals.

	Bushels (mil.)	% of Group
Corn	9,282	62.9%
Wheat	3,309	22.4
Soybeans	2,167	14.7

Source: *Futures*, May 1992, p. 26.

★ 100 ★
Hops (SIC 0139)

Hops by Variety

U.S. hops yield, by variety, is shown in thousands of lbs. for 1990.

Variety	
Banner	2,046
Aquila	2,009
Cluster	1,899
Nugget	1,782
Galena	1,779
Chinook	1,775
Eroica	1,728
Olympic	1,700
Cascade	1,630
Fuggles	1,410
Willamette	1,364
Perle	1,083
Tettnanger	1,044
Mt. Hood	744
Other	1,262

Source: *Washington Agricultural Statistics*, October 1991, p. 71.

★ 101 ★

Berries (SIC 0171)

Biggest Berry Producers

Leading berry growers in the U.S. are listed with thousands of acres per grower. Relative shares are shown in percent.

	Acres (000)	% of Group
Cherryfield Foods, Inc.	7,376	26.3%
Jasper Wyman & Son	6,910	24.7
A.D. Makepeace Co.	1,475	5.3
Northland Cranberries, Inc.	1,433	5.1
Atlantic Blueberry Co.	1,320	4.7
Haines & Haines, Inc.	1,080	3.9
Beaton Cranberries, Inc.	807	2.9
Reiter Affiliated Cos.	770	2.8
Adkin Blue Ribbon Pkg. Co. Inc.	750	2.7
N.T. Gaurgiulo, Inc.	750	2.7
A.R. Demarco Enterprises Inc.	725	2.6
Sandy Farms, Inc.	682	2.4
Bob Jones Ranch	550	2.0
Variety Farms Inc.	550	2.0
Habelman Brothers Co.	525	1.9
Fujii Farms	515	1.8
All Natural Farms, Inc.	460	1.6
Reenders Blueberries Farms	460	1.6
E.W. Bowker Co. Inc.	435	1.6
Bertino Brothers	425	1.5

Source: *Fruit Grower*, August 1992, p. 8.

★ 102 ★

Grapes (SIC 0172)

Grape Crush Production

Shares by varietal are shown in percent, based on a 1991 total grape crush production of 2,564 thousand tons.

Colombard	23.7%
Thompson seedless and other raisin varieties	11.0
Chenin blanc	9.7
Zinfandel	8.7
Chardonnay	8.5
Tokay and other table varieties	6.1
Cabernet sauvignon	5.2%
Grenache	3.9
Sauvignon blanc	3.2
All others	20.1

Source: *Wines & Vines*, April 1992, p. 22, from "Preliminary Grape Crush Report 1991" and California Department of Food & Agriculture.

★ 103 ★

Grapes (SIC 0172)

Largest Grape Growers

The top 20 grape growers in the U.S. are listed with thousands of acres per grower. Relative shares are shown in percent.

	Acres (000)	% of Group
Simpson Farm Co.	12,000	10.5%
Giumarra Vineyards Corp.	10,000	8.8
Delicato Vineyards	8,365	7.3
Dole Food Co., Inc.	8,000	7.0
J&L Farms	7,827	6.9
Golden State Vintners	7,800	6.8
Sun World International	7,500	6.6
Wine World Estates	6,000	5.3
E&J Gallo Winery	5,400	4.7
Met West Agribusiness	5,400	4.7
Royal Madera Vineyards	4,300	3.8
Sutter Home Winery	4,052	3.6
Vino Farms Inc.	4,000	3.5
Frank A. Logoluso Farms Inc.	3,500	3.1
The McCarty Co.	3,550	3.1
Stimson Lane Wine & Spirits Ltd.	3,360	2.9
Lucich Farms	3,265	2.9
Valley Farm Management, Inc.	3,262	2.9
Scheid Vineyards & Management Co.	3,205	2.8
Pandol & Sons	3,200	2.8

Source: *Fruit Grower*, August 1992, p. 9.

★ 104 ★

Nuts (SIC 0173)

Nut Consumption in the U.S.

*Market segmentation is shown in percent, based on a
total of 2.217 billion lbs. (shelled basis) in
1991.*

Peanuts for food	80.5%
Almonds	8.2
Walnuts	5.7
Pecans	5.7

Source: Investext, Thomson Financial Networks, January
27, 1992, from Donaldson, Lufkin & Jenrette Securities.

★ 105 ★

Nuts (SIC 0173)

Tree Nut Growers

*Leading tree nut producers in the U.S. are listed with
thousands of acres per grower. Relative shares are
shown in percent.*

	Acres (000)	% of Group
Paramount Farming Co.	35,603	29.0%
S&J Ranch	10,600	8.6
Dole Food Co., Inc.	8,200	6.7
Farmers Investment Co.	6,643	5.4
Tejon Farming Co.	6,360	5.2
Mont Pelier Orchard Management/		
Vista Ranch Management . . .	5,388	4.4
Diamond AgraIndustries	5,300	4.3
Lassen Land Co.	5,165	4.2
Braden Farms, Inc.	4,675	3.8
Pacific Coast Farms	4,094	3.3
Big Valley	4,000	3.3
MacFarms of Hawaii, Inc. . . .	3,800	3.1
Stahmann Farms, Inc.	3,750	3.1
Blackwell Land Co.	3,324	2.7
Nuts Unlimited, Inc.	3,295	2.7
Mockingbird Hill Farms	3,200	2.6
Mauna Loa Macadamia		
Nut Corp.	2,470	2.0
Haley Farms	2,408	2.0
Hortsville Ranch	2,406	2.0
Belridge Farms	2,209	1.8

Source: *Fruit Grower*, August 1992, p. 8.

★ 106 ★

Citrus Fruits (SIC 0174)

Citrus Giants

*The 20 leading citrus growers in the U.S. are listed
with thousands of acres per grower. Relative shares
are shown in percent.*

	Acres (000)	% of Group
Ben Hill Griffin Inc.	30,000	11.8%
Turner Foods Corp.	28,061	11.1
Berry Citrus	20,000	7.9
Coca-Cola	17,000	6.7
U.S. Sugar Corp.	16,434	6.5
Orange-Co. of Florida	16,391	6.5
Becker Holding Corp.	15,500	6.1
A. Duda & Sons, Inc.	14,750	5.8
Crittenden Fruit Co. Inc.	14,000	5.5
Barron Collier Co./Silver		
Strand Div.	10,258	4.0
Paramount Farming Co.	10,000	3.9
S&J Ranch	9,800	3.9
Collier Enterprises Agribusiness .	7,900	3.1
Alico, Inc.	7,694	3.0
Bernard Egan & Co.	7,550	3.0
Dole Food Co., Inc.	7,300	2.9
Gracewood Inc.	6,002	2.4
Royal Palm Citrus		
Management, Inc.	5,018	2.0
Alcoma Packing Co., Inc. . . .	5,000	2.0
Graves Brothers Co.	4,850	1.9

Source: *Fruit Grower*, August 1992, p. 9.

★ 107 ★

Orchard Fruits (SIC 0175)

Apple and Pear Producers

*The top 20 apple and pear growers in the U.S. are
listed with thousands of acres per grower. Relative
shares are shown in percent.*

	Acres (000)	% of Group
Brewster Heights Packing	5,700	11.5%
Naumes, Inc.	5,330	10.8
Jack Frost/Marley Orchards . . .	3,423	6.9
Evans Fruit Farm	3,400	6.9
Northwestern Fruit &		
Produce Co.	2,942	6.0
E&J Gallo Winery	2,700	5.5
Broetje Orchards	2,670	5.4

Continued on next page.

★ 107 ★ *Continued*

Orchard Fruits (SIC 0175)

Apple and Pear Producers

The top 20 apple and pear growers in the U.S. are listed with thousands of acres per grower. Relative shares are shown in percent.

	Acres (000)	% of Group
Fruit Hill Orchard Inc.	2,500	5.1%
Borton & Sons Inc.	2,150	4.4
B&D Farms, Inc.	2,000	4.0
Fowler Brothers Inc.	1,950	3.9
National Fruit Product Co. Inc.	1,885	3.8
Dole Food Co., Inc.	1,800	3.6
Met West Agribusiness	1,800	3.6
Orchard Management Co./ Senseny South Corp.	1,635	3.3
Mount Levels Orchards	1,600	3.2
Associated Fruit Co.	1,521	3.1
Hudson Valley Farms, Inc.	1,490	3.0
Pacific Fruit Growers & Packers, Inc.	1,465	3.0
Niagara Orchards Inc.	1,422	2.9

Source: *Fruit Grower*, August 1992, p. 7.

★ 108 ★

Orchard Fruits (SIC 0175)

Stone Fruit Producers

The top 20 stone fruit growers in the U.S. are listed with thousands of acres per grower. Relative shares are shown in percent.

	Acres (000)	% of Group
Gerawan Farming	4,300	9.2%
Lane Packing Co.	4,010	8.6
Taylor Orchard	3,300	7.1
Valley View Packing Co.	3,250	7.0
California Prune Packing Co.	3,122	6.7
Fowler Packing Co., Inc.	2,660	5.7
Evans Farm	2,550	5.5
Cherry Ke Inc.	2,140	4.6
Ito Packing Co., Inc.	2,120	4.5
J.H. Satcher Jr. & Sons Farms	2,000	4.3
Big Six Farm	1,950	4.2
J.W. Yonce & Sons Farms Inc.	1,914	4.1
Miami Valley Fruit Farm, Inc.	1,810	3.9
D.W. DuBose & Sons, Inc.	1,800	3.9
Sun World International	1,800	3.9

	Acres (000)	% of Group
J.R. Wood Inc.	1,667	3.6%
Lewis F. Holmes & Son	1,600	3.4
Met West Agribusiness	1,600	3.4
Marchese Farms	1,550	3.3
Chappell Farms Inc.	1,500	3.2

Source: *Fruit Grower*, August 1992, p. 7.

★ 109 ★

Figs (SIC 0179)

Dried Fig Production

Shares of the dried fig market are shown in percent for the years 1988 to 1990.

	1988	1989	1990
Adriatic	31.0%	33.0%	41.0%
Calimyrna	40.0	38.0	31.0
Mission	23.0	24.0	24.0
Kadota	6.0	5.0	4.0

Source: *1991 Statistical Review of the California Fig Industry*, California Fig Institute/California Fig Advisory Board, 1990, from California Crop and Livestock Reporting Service (1990 estimates only).

SIC 02 - Agricultural Production - Livestock

★110★
Cattle (SIC 0210)

Fed Cattle Production

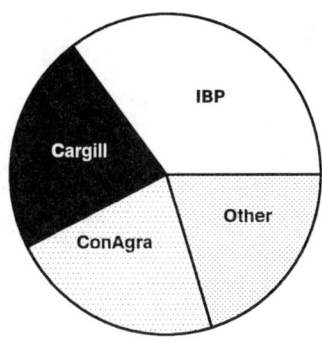

Estimated company shares of the 1992 market are shown in percent.

IBP	35.3%
Cargill	22.2
ConAgra	22.2
Other	20.2

Source: Investext, Thomson Financial Networks, February 7, 1992, from Donaldson, Lufkin & Jenrette Securities.

★111★
Livestock (SIC 0210)

Livestock Slaughter

Market distribution by species is shown in percent, based on a total of 126.209 head in 1990.

Hogs	67.7%
Cattle	26.3
Sheep and lambs	4.6
Calves	1.5

Source: *Meat Facts*, 1991, p. 17, from U.S. Department of Agriculture.

★112★
Meat (SIC 0210)

Meat Production

Estimated company shares of the 1992 market are shown in percent.

IBP	13.6%
ConAgra	13.5
Cargill	7.7
Tyson	6.8
Other	58.4

Source: Investext, Thomson Financial Networks, February 7, 1992, from Donaldson, Lufkin & Jenrette Securities.

★113★
Hogs (SIC 0213)

Hog Production by County

The leading hog-producing counties in the United States are ranked according to the number of hogs produced.

Sampson (NC)	896,710
Sioux (IA)	871,562
Lancaster (PA)	782,391
Delaware (IA)	745,649
Plymouth (IA)	623,187
Washington (IA)	572,879
Dubuque (IA)	515,476
Henry (IL)	512,809
Carroll (IA)	509,281
Cuming (NE)	475,728

Source: *USA TODAY*, April 7, 1992, p. 3A, from 1991 U.S. Department of Agriculture survey and 1987 Census of Agriculture.

★ 114 ★
Pork (SIC 0213)

Pork Production

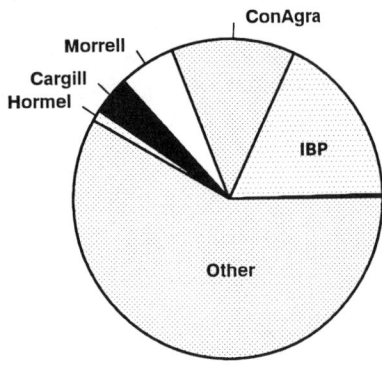

Estimated company shares of the 1992 market are shown in percent.

IBP	17.6%
ConAgra	13.3
Morrell	5.9
Cargill	3.6
Hormel	1.1
Other	58.5

Source: Investext, Thomson Financial Networks, February 7, 1992, from Donaldson, Lufkin & Jenrette Securities.

★ 115 ★
Poultry (SIC 0251)

Broiler Production

Estimated company shares of the 1992 market are shown in percent.

Tyson	20.7%
ConAgra	9.6
Gold Kist	8.6
Perdue	6.4
Pilgrim's Pride	5.7
Cont. Grain	3.9
Hudson Foods	3.8
Cargill	1.2
Other	40.0

Source: Investext, Thomson Financial Networks, February 7, 1992, from Donaldson, Lufkin & Jenrette Securities.

★ 116 ★
Poultry (SIC 0251)

Poultry Producers

Shares of the domestic market are shown in percent.

Tyson Foods	19.0%
ConAgra Inc.	9.0
Gold Kist, Inc.	8.0
Perdue Farms, Inc.	6.0
Pilgrim's Pride Corporations . . .	5.0
Wayne Poultry Division	3.0
Hudson Foods, Inc.	3.0
Seaboard Farms, Inc.	3.0
Townsends, Inc.	3.0
Foster Farms	3.0
Showell Farms, Inc.	2.0
Marshall Durbin Companies	2.0
Fieldale Farms Corporation	2.0
McCarty Farms, Inc.	2.0
Simmons Industries, Inc.	2.0
Allen Family Foods, Inc.	2.0
Wampler-Longacre Chicken, Inc. . .	2.0
Cagle's Inc.	1.0
Sanderson Farms, Inc.	1.0
Herider Farms, Inc.	1.0
George's, Inc.	1.0
B.C. Rogers Poultry, Inc.	1.0
Green Acre Farms	1.0
Cargill, Inc.	1.0
Choctaw Maid Farms, Inc.	1.0
Other	16.0

Source: Investext, Thomson Financial Networks, June 30, 1992, from Prudential Securities, Inc.

★ 117 ★
Poultry (SIC 0251)

Turkey Production

Estimated company shares of the 1992 market are shown in percent.

ConAgra	16.1%
Philip Morris	8.7
Carolina	8.7
Rocco	8.5
Hormel	7.3
Cargill	7.0
Other	43.8

Source: Investext, Thomson Financial Networks, February 7, 1992, from Donaldson, Lufkin & Jenrette Securities.

★118★

Pets (SIC 0270)

Domestic Pet Market

Number of pets owned by Americans in 1990 is shown in millions.

Dogs 54
Cats 54
Fishes 95
Birds 14
Small animals 9

Source: *Hardware Age*, June 1992, p. 89.

★119★

Landscape Architecture (SIC 0781)

Largest Landscape Architects

Top 10 firms are shown with gross 1990 billings for landscape architecture and planning fees (in millions of dollars) and with relative shares for the group.

	($ mil.)	% of Group
CRSS, Inc.	$ 27	19.4%
Sasaki Associates, Inc.	24	17.3
EDAW, Inc.	21	15.1
The SWA Group	15	10.8
Belt Collins & Associates . . .	10	7.2
Edward D. Stone, Jr. & Associates	10	7.2
Johnson Johnson & Roy, Inc. . .	9	6.5
Wallace Roberts & Todd . . .	9	6.5
Peridian, Inc.	8	5.8
Hellmuth, Obata & Kassabaum Inc.	6	4.3

Source: *Landscape Architecture*, September 1991, p. 60.

SIC 08 - Forestry

★ 120 ★
Trees (SIC 0800)

Lumber Exports from the U.S.

Shares of the U.S. lumber export market, by variety of tree, are shown in percent. Shares are based on a total of 1,918,565 cubic meters.

Red Oak 31.0%
White Oak 27.0
Ash 7.0
Yellow Poplar 6.0
Maple 5.0
Red Alder 5.0
Cherry 3.0
Beech 2.0
Other hardwood 14.0

Source: *AgExporter*, August 1991, p. 24.

★ 121 ★
Timber (SIC 0811)

Christmas Trees

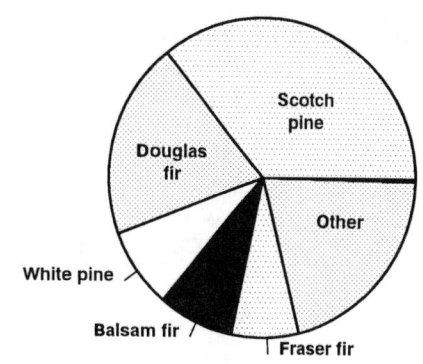

Shares, by type, are shown in percent.

Scotch pine 36.0%
Douglas fir 20.0
White pine 8.0
Balsam fir 8.0
Fraser fir 7.0
Other 21.0

Source: *USA TODAY*, December 9, 1992, p. 1A, from National Christmas Tree Assn.

★ 122 ★
Timber (SIC 0811)

Christmas Trees by Material

Shares are shown in percent, based on a total of 72.0 million trees sold in 1991.

Artificial 50.4%
Real 49.6

Source: *USA TODAY*, December 9, 1992, p. 2D, from National Christmas Tree Assn.

SIC 09 - Fishing, Hunting, and Trapping

★ 123 ★

Fish (SIC 0912)

Seafood Consumption

Domestic consumption of the five most popular seafoods is shown in pounds per capita.

Tuna	3.60
Shrimp	2.40
Cod	1.12
Alaska pollock	0.99
Salmon	0.97

Source: *USA TODAY*, November 20, 1992, p. 1D, from National Fisheries Institute.

SIC 10 - Metal Mining

★ 124 ★

Metal Mining (SIC 1000)

Metal Mining Leaders

Companies are ranked by 1991 sales, shown in millions of dollars. Percent shares are based on group total.

	Sales ($ mil.)	% of Group
Phelps Dodge	$ 2,434	27.1%
Asarco	1,910	21.3
Cyprus Minerals	1,679	18.7
Newmont Mining	623	6.9
Precision Castparts	588	6.5
Newmont Gold	573	6.4
Freeport-McMoran Copper & Gold	468	5.2
Homestake Mining	411	4.6
Battle Mountain Gold	170	1.9
Amax Gold	128	1.4

Source: *The 1992 Business Week 1000*, p. 190.

★ 125 ★

Metal Mining (SIC 1000)

Nonferrous Metal Mining Leaders - Japan

Companies are ranked by 1991 declared income, shown in millions of Yen. Relative market shares are shown in percent.

	Income (Y mil.)	% of Group
Nippon Light Metal	22,733	20.6%
Sumitomo Metal Mining . . .	19,138	17.4
Nippon Mining	18,837	17.1
Furukawa	11,870	10.8
Mitsubishi Materials	10,637	9.7
Shin-Etsu Handotai	7,485	6.8
Ryobi	5,580	5.1
Dowa Mining	4,795	4.4

	Income (Y mil.)	% of Group
Mitsubishi Nuclear Fuel	4,512	4.1%
Showa Aluminum	4,507	4.1

Source: *TOKYO Business Today*, July 1992, p. 38.

★ 126 ★

Metals (SIC 1000)

Nonferrous and Ferroalloy Metals

1991 sales of nonferrous and ferroalloy metals, by company, are shown in millions of dollars and percent share of market.

	Sales ($ mil.)	Share
Aluminum Co. of America . .	$ 9,884.1	25.7%
Alcan Aluminum	7,748.0	20.2
Reynolds Metals	5,730.1	14.9
Amax	3,771.6	9.8
Inco	2,999.2	7.8
Phelps Dodge	2,434.3	6.3
Asarco	1,909.9	5.0
Cominco	1,133.7	3.0
Newmont Mining	622.8	1.6
Kenmetal	617.8	1.6
Handy & Harman	462.5	1.2
Homestake Mining	411.0	1.1
Unc	360.6	0.9
Brush Wellman	267.5	0.7
Oregon Metallurgical	54.2	0.1

Source: *Chemicalweek*, May 6, 1992, p. 31, from Standard & Poor's Compustat Service.

★ 127 ★

Platinum (SIC 1099)

Platinum Market Use in the Western Hemisphere

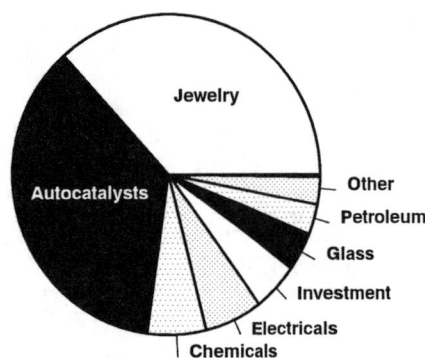

Shares by end use are shown in percent, based on total net demand of 3,660,000 ounces troy in 1990.

Jewelry	37.0%
Autocatalysts	36.0
Chemicals	6.0
Electricals	6.0
Investment	5.0
Glass	4.0
Petroleum	3.0
Other	3.0

Source: *International Management*, February 1992, p. 37.

SIC 12 - Coal Mining

★ 128 ★

Coal (SIC 1200)

Coal Consumption

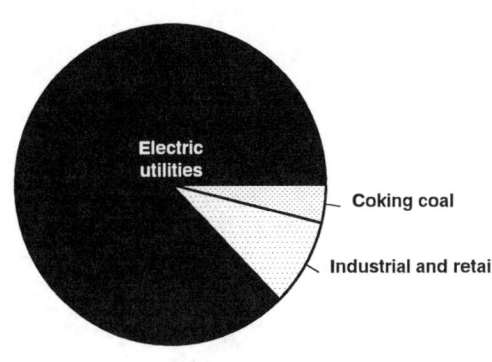

Distribution of domestic consumption is shown in percent, based on a forecast total of 912 million tons in 1992. Figures include anthracite.

Electric utilities	87.1%
Industrial and retail	9.0
Coking coal	3.9

Source: *Coal*, February 1992, p. 9, from National Coal Association.

★ 129 ★

Coal (SIC 1200)

Coal Consumption by End Use - U.S.

Consumption of coal in the U.S., by end use, is shown in millions of short tons for 1990, 1991, and 1992. Figures for 1991 are an estimate; those for 1992 include other industrial, transportation, residential, and commercial consumption.

	'90	'91	'92
Electric utilities	771.7	782.0	816.0
Coke plants	39.8	34.0	37.0
Residential and commercial	6.7	-	-
Other industrial and transportation	76.1	82.0	83.0

Source: *U.S. Industrial Outlook 1992*, p. 2, from U.S. Department of Energy, Energy Information Administration.

★ 130 ★

Coal (SIC 1200)

Coal Mining Production

Coal production, by company, is shown in thousands of tons mined per seam.

A&G Coal	1,000-4,000
Bruce Coal	800
Bullion Hollow	1,400-1,600
Dotson & Rife	1,800
Elk Run single section	3,000-6,000
Kinney Branch	2,000-3,500

Source: *Coal*, August 1991, p. 32.

★ 131 ★

Coal (SIC 1200)

Coal Producers

Company sales are shown in millions dollars for 1991. Percent shares are based on group total of $2,866 million.

	Sales ($ mil.)	% of Group
Pittston	$ 1,946	67.9%
Nerco	920	32.1

Source: *The 1992 Business Week 1000*, 1992, p. 176.

★ 132 ★

Coal (SIC 1200)

Coal Production - Australia

Raw production figures in 1990 are shown for the country's ten largest mines; share of the group is shown in percent.

	Tons (mil.)	% of Group
Goonyella/Riverside	13,407,020	17.6%
Peak Downs	10,005,380	13.1
Blair Athol	8,353,620	10.9
Saraji	7,898,440	10.3
Curragh	6,727,600	8.8
Hunter Valley No.	6,655,990	8.7
Meandu	6,620,240	8.7
Norwich Park	5,980,920	7.8
Newlands	5,537,840	7.3
Blackwater	5,149,650	6.7

Source: *Coal*, March 1992, p. 46, from *Australian Black Coal Statistics 1990*, and Joint Coal Board/Queensland Coal Board.

★ 133 ★

Coal Mining (SIC 1220)

Coal Mining Company Production

Company shares are shown in percent, based on 1991 total production of 24.3 million tons. Data for CSX Group do not include Aracoma, which is under development.

CSX Group
Elk Run	12.8%
Omar	5.0
Peerless Eagle	2.9
Purchased coal	28.9

Other	0.4%
NS Group	
Rawl Sales	22.7
Martin County	11.6
Sydney Coal	11.2
Vantage Mining	0.4
Other	0.4
Other and new operators	3.7

Source: *Coal*, March 1992, p. 36.

SIC 13 - Oil and Gas Extraction

★ 134 ★

Oil & Gas (SIC 1300)

Oil and Gas Company Sales

Company sales are shown in millions of dollars for 1991. Percent shares are based on a group total $395,404 million.

	Sales ($ mil.)	% of Group
Exxon	$ 104,217	26.4%
Mobil	56,432	14.3
Chevron	40,900	10.3
Texaco	38,322	9.7
Amoco	25,325	6.4
Atlantic Richfield	17,037	4.3
USX-Marathon Group	13,975	3.5
Phillips Petroleum	13,259	3.4
Sun	11,930	3.0
Occidental Petroleum	10,096	2.6
Unocal	9,845	2.5
Coastal	9,549	2.4
Ashland Oil	9,201	2.3
Amerada Hess	6,416	1.6
Fina	3,336	0.8
Kerr-McGee	3,274	0.8
Mapco	2,783	0.7
Pennzoil	2,685	0.7
Diamond Shamrock	2,576	0.7
Tosco	1,980	0.5
Burlington Resources	1,754	0.4
Murphy Oil	1,690	0.4
Oryx Energy	1,601	0.4
Union Texas Petroleum Holdings	1,080	0.3
Valero Energy	1,012	0.3
Unocal Exploration	878	0.2
Mitchell Energy & Development	864	0.2
Louisiana Land & Exploration	825	0.2
Maxus Energy	791	0.2
Enron Oil & Gas	388	0.1
Santa Fe Energy Resources	380	0.1

	Sales ($ mil.)	% of Group
Apache	$ 357	0.1%
Anadarko Petroleum	337	0.1
Triton Energy	219	0.1
BP Prudhoe Bay Royalty Trust	93	0.0

Source: *The 1992 Business Week 1000*, 1992, p. 176.

★ 135 ★

Oil & Gas (SIC 1300)

Petroleum Service Companies

Company sales are shown in millions of dollars for 1991. Percent shares are based on a group total of $22,585 million.

	Sales ($ mil.)	% of Group
Halliburton	$ 7,019	31.1%
Schlumberger	6,145	27.2
Dresser Industries	4,607	20.4
Baker Hughes	2,747	12.2
CBI Industries	1,615	7.2
Noble Affiliates	250	1.1
Helmerich & Payne	202	0.9

Source: *The 1992 Business Week 1000*, 1992, p. 180.

★ 136 ★

Natural Gas (SIC 1311)

Natural Gas Consumption - 1992

Percent shares of natural gas consumption are based on a 1992 total of 19.67 trillion cubic feet.

Industrial	36.8%
Residential	25.1
Commercial	15.0
Utilities	14.1
Plant fuel	6.2
Pipeline	2.9

Source: *National Petroleum News*, July 1992, p. 33, from Energy Information Administration.

★ 137 ★

Oil (SIC 1311)

Crude Oil and Product Importers

Company shares are based on a 1990 U.S. total volume of 7,954,000 barrels per day.

Chevron	9.11%
Star	7.81
Exxon	6.07
Amoco	5.97
Sun Shell	4.76
Mobil	4.69
BP America	4.22
Amerada Hess	3.83
Coastal	3.60
Other	46.22

Source: *National Petroleum News*, June 1992, p. 70, from Energy Information Administration, Petroleum Supply Monthly, and Special Report, March 1991.

★ 138 ★

Oil (SIC 1311)

Crude Oil Importers

Company shares are based on a 1990 U.S. total volume of 5,876,000 barrels per day.

Chevron	11.15%
Star	10.38
Amoco	7.73
Shell	5.99
Exxon	5.53
Sun	5.36
Mobil	5.26
BP America	4.59
U.S. Steel	3.81
Koch	3.76
Other	33.94

Source: *National Petroleum News*, June 1992, p. 70, from Energy Information Administration, Petroleum Supply Monthly, and Special Report, March 1991.

★ 139 ★

Oil (SIC 1311)

Crude Oil Production in Argentina

Company shares are shown in percent, based on a national total of 489,037 barrels per day in the third quarter of 1991. YPF (Yacimientos Petroliferos Fiscales) is a state-owned energy company.

Perez Companc	17.4%
Total Austral	9.0
Amoco Ankina Production Co	8.4
Astra	5.7
Occidental	5.0
Bridas	3.6
Tecpetrol	3.0
Cadispa	1.8
Pluspetrol	1.8
Capsa	1.5
10 other private operators	2.3
YPF and other provinces	40.5

Source: *Euromoney* supplement, February 1992, p. 6.

★ 140 ★
Oil (SIC 1311)

Oil Reserves Worldwide

Reserve volume is shown in millions of barrels;
relative market shares are shown in
percent.

	Reserves (mmbbl)	% of Group
Royal Dutch Shell	9,681	23.5%
Exxon	6,713	16.3
British Petroleum	4,437	10.8
Mobil	3,322	8.1
Chevron	3,156	7.7
Arco	2,831	6.9
Texaco	2,711	6.6
Amoco	2,446	5.9
Phillips	1,056	2.6
USX-Marathon	868	2.1
Unocal	799	1.9
Occidental	646	1.6
Amerada Hess	638	1.5
Oryx	541	1.3
Santa Fe Energy	229	0.6
Maxus	205	0.5
Kerr-McGee	160	0.4
Burlington Resources	141	0.3
Pennzoil	139	0.3
Murphy Oil Corp.	93	0.2
Louisiana Land	84	0.2
Mesa Inc.	83	0.2
Apache Corp.	80	0.2
Anadarko	46	0.1
Noble Affiliates	44	0.1
Enron Oil & Gas	20	0.0
Chieftan	7	0.0
Wainoco	6	0.0
Nuevo	3	0.0
Cabot Oil & Gas	1	0.0

Source: Investext, Thomson Financial Networks, June 23, 1992, from Rauscher Pierce Refsnes, Inc.

★ 141 ★
Oil (SIC 1311)

Petroleum Products Global Market

Sales of 12 leading petroleum product companies
worldwide, are shown in billions of dollars, totaling
$583.41 billion in 1990. Relative market shares are
shown in percent.

	Sales ($ bil.)	% of Group
Royal Dutch/Shell	$ 107.20	18.0%
Exxon	105.89	18.0
British Petroleum	59.54	10.0
Mobil	58.77	10.0
ENI	41.76	7.0
Texaco	41.24	7.0
Chevron	39.26	7.0
Elf Aquitaine	32.94	6.0
Amoco	29.28	5.0
Total-CFP	23.59	4.0
Petroleos de Venezuela	23.47	4.0
Petrobas	20.47	4.0

Source: *Business Horizons*, November 1991, p. 18.

★ 142 ★
Natural Gas (SIC 1321)

Gas Reserves Worldwide

Reserve volume is shown in billions of cubic ft.;
relative market shares are shown in
percent.

	Reserves (bcf)	% of Group
Royal Dutch Shell	53,064	25.6%
Exxon	42,799	20.6
Mobil	18,756	9.0
Amoco	18,700	9.0
British Petroleum	10,923	5.3
Chevron	9,399	4.5
Arco	8,203	4.0
Unocal Corp.	6,858	3.3
Texaco	6,277	3.0
Phillips	5,639	2.7
Burlington Resources	4,887	2.4
USX-Marathon	4,077	2.0
Amerada Hess	2,551	1.2
Occidental	2,378	1.1
Oryx	2,041	1.0
Anadarko	1,744	0.8
Enron Oil & Gas	1,585	0.8
Mesa Inc.	1,368	0.7

Continued on next page.

★ 142 ★ *Continued*

Natural Gas (SIC 1321)

Gas Reserves Worldwide

*Reserve volume is shown in billions of cubic ft.;
relative market shares are shown in
percent.*

	Reserves (bcf)	% of Group
Pennzoil	926	0.4%
Louisiana Land	843	0.4
Kerr-McGee	842	0.4
Cabot Oil & Gas	716	0.3
Maxus	672	0.3
Murphy Oil Corp.	659	0.3
Apache Corp.	602	0.3
Noble Affiliates	397	0.2
Wainco	214	0.1
Santa Fe Energy	171	0.1
Nuevo	136	0.1
Chieftan	78	0.0

Source: Investext, Thomson Financial Networks, June
23, 1992, from Rauscher Pierce Refsnes, Inc.

★ 143 ★

Natural Gas (SIC 1321)

Natural Gas Reserves - U.S.

*Reserve volume is shown in billions of cubic ft.;
relative market shares are shown in
percent.*

	Reserves (bcf)	% of Group
Amoco	11,649	14.0%
Exxon	10,155	12.2
Chevron	6,569	7.9
Mobil	6,237	7.5
Royal Dutch Shell	5,967	7.2
Arco	5,798	7.0
Burlington Resources	4,887	5.9
Texaco	4,697	5.6
Unocal Corp.	4,043	4.9
Phillips	3,817	4.6
British Petroleum	2,865	3.4
USX-Marathon	2,267	2.7
Occidental	2,249	2.7
Oryx	1,775	2.1
Anadarko	1,699	2.0
Enron Oil & Gas	1,456	1.7
Mesa Inc.	1,368	1.6
Amerada Hess	1,058	1.3
Pennzoil	892	1.1

	Reserves (bcf)	% of Group
Cabot Oil & Gas	716	0.9%
Maxus	635	0.8
Apache Corp.	602	0.7
Kerr-McGee	541	0.6
Louisiana Land	521	0.6
Murphy Oil Corp.	396	0.5
Santa Fe Energy	171	0.2
Nuevo	136	0.2
Noble Affiliates	84	0.1
Chieftan	64	0.1
Wainco	46	0.1

Source: Investext, Thomson Financial Networks, June
23, 1992, from Rauscher Pierce Refsnes, Inc.

★ 144 ★

Oil and Gas Field Services (SIC 1381)

Drilling in Eastern Europe

*Percent distribution of 1,061 wells drilled in 1990
(estimate) are shown by type of well, activity,
outcome, or status.*

Oil	41.0%
Gas	20.4
Dry	17.6
Suspended	17.1
Service	4.0

Source: *World Oil*, August 1992, p. 82, from
governmental agencies.

★ 145 ★

Oil and Gas Field Services (SIC 1381)

Drilling in Far East

*Percent distribution of 10,248 wells drilled in 1990
(estimate) are shown by type of well, activity,
outcome, or status.*

Oil	73.0%
Service	23.5
Gas	1.9
Dry	1.2
Suspended	0.3

Source: *World Oil*, August 1992, p. 24, from API.

★ 146 ★

Oil and Gas Field Services (SIC 1381)

Drilling in Middle East

Percent distribution of 959 wells drilled in 1990 (estimate) by type of well, activity, outcome, or status.

Oil	72.1%
Dry	13.4
Service	6.4
Suspended	5.2
Gas	3.0

Source: *World Oil*, August 1992, p. 24, from API.

★ 147 ★

Oil and Gas Field Services (SIC 1381)

Drilling in North America

Percent distribution of 33,223 wells drilled in 1990 (estimate) are shown by type of well, activity, outcome, or status.

Oil	37.5%
Gas	33.2
Dry	27.0
Service	2.3
Suspended	0.1

Source: *World Oil*, August 1992, p. 24, from API.

★ 148 ★

Oil and Gas Field Services (SIC 1381)

Drilling in South America

Percent distribution of 2,130 wells drilled in 1990 (estimate) are shown by type of well, activity, outcome, or status.

Oil	78.9%
Dry	14.1
Gas	3.7
Suspended	1.7
Service	1.6

Source: *World Oil*, August 1992, p. 24, from API.

★ 149 ★

Oil and Gas Field Services (SIC 1381)

Drilling in Western Europe

Percent distribution of 877 wells drilled in 1990 (estimate) are shown by type of well, activity, outcome, or status.

Oil	36.0%
Dry	26.2
Gas	21.0
Service	9.8
Suspended	7.0

Source: *World Oil*, August 1992, p. 24, from API.

★ 150 ★

Oil and Gas Field Services (SIC 1381)

Drilling Outside the U.S.

Shares are shown in percent, based on totals of 21,342 wells in 1991 (estimate) and 22,058 wells in 1992 (forecast).

Offshore	91.8%
Onshore	8.2

Source: *World Oil*, February 1992, p. 85.

★ 151 ★

Oil and Gas Field Services (SIC 1381)

U.S. Drilling Wells

Shares are shown in percent, based on 1990 total of 29,107 wells.

Oil	38.4%
Gas	32.0
Dry	26.9
Services and other	2.7

Source: *World Oil*, February 1992, p. 54, from API.

★ 152 ★

Oil and Gas Field Services (SIC 1381)

World Drilling - 1990

*Percent distribution of 48,287 wells drilled in 1990
(estimate) are shown by type of well, activity,
outcome, or status.*

Oil	46.4%
Gas	25.2
Dry	21.7
Service	6.3
Suspended	0.5

Source: *World Oil*, August 1992, p. 24.

SIC 14 - Nonmetallic Minerals, Except Fuels

★ 153 ★

Crushed and Broken Stone (SIC 1429)

Crushed Stone Companies - Leaders

The 10 leading producers of crushed and broken stone are ranked according to number of work sites in 1990.

Vulcan Materials Co.	153
Martin Marietta Aggregates	141
Beazer USA Inc.	99
Rogers Group Inc.	29
CSR America	21
Tarmac America	14
Dravo Basic Materials Co.	13
General Dynamics Material Service	9
Genstar Stone Products Co.	7
Michigan Limestone Operations	2

Source: *Rock Products*, February 1992, p. 25.

★ 154 ★

Sand and Gravel (SIC 1440)

Sand and Gravel Producers - U.S.

The leading producers of sand and gravel are ranked according to combined tonnage of all plants as of December 31, 1990. Relative market shares are shown in percent. The figure provided for Beazer USA covers the period from July 1989 to June 1990, and includes the combined production of Beazer East and Beazer West divisions for that fiscal year. NA indicates that information was not provided by the company.

	Tons	% of Group
Beazer USA	32,436,000	29.3%
CalMat	30,193,000	27.3
CSR America	20,900,000	18.9
Dravo Basic	NA	
Teichert & Son	NA	
Meyer Material	NA	

	Tons	% of Group
Texas Industries	6,600,000	6.0%
Owl Rock	6,546,497	5.9
Florida Rock	NA	
C.L. Pharris	5,420,548	4.9
Vulcan Materials	5,150,700	4.7
Material Service	NA	
Martin Marietta	3,454,507	3.1
Tarmac America	NA	
Tanner	NA	

Source: *Rock Products*, August 1991, p. 45.

★ 155 ★

Construction Sand and Gravel (SIC 1442)

Sand and Gravel Companies - Leading Producers

The 10 leading sand and gravel producers are ranked according to number of work sites in 1990.

Beazer USA Inc.	40
CSR America Inc.	29
CalMat Co.	27
Ashland Oil Inc.	26
Tarmac America	18
Dravo Basic Materials Co.	12
Lafarge Corp.	11
Meyer Material Co.	8
Teichert & Son Inc., A.	8
Lone Star Northwest	4

Source: *Rock Products*, February 1992, p. 25.

SIC 15 - General Building Contractors

★ 156 ★

Construction (SIC 1500)

Construction Market in Canada

Market shares, by type, are shown as percent of $10,201 million spent on construction starts in the first half of 1992.

Residential	47.0%
Engineering	20.4
Institutional	15.6
Commercial	14.9
Industrial	2.2

Source: *The Globe and Mail*, July 29, 1992, p. B5, from CanaData.

★ 157 ★

Roofing (SIC 1500)

Commercial Roofing Market

1990 commercial roofing market shares, by type of job, are shown in percent, based on an industry total of $11.58 billion.

Reroofing	71.5%
New construction	28.5

Source: *Shopping Center World*, July 1991, p. S1.

★ 158 ★

Nonresidential Construction (SIC 1540)

Nonresidential Construction

Shares of nonresidential construction spending, by type of construction, are shown in percent, based on totals of $67.5 billion in 1990 and $71.4 million in 1991 (forecast).

	1990	1991
Institutional	41.2%	54.3%
Retail	20.8	20.5
Industrial	14.5	18.1
Hotel	5.9	5.3
Office	17.5	1.8

Source: *Heating/Piping / Air Conditioning*, January 1992, p. 109.

★ 159 ★

Nonresidential Construction (SIC 1541)

Nonresidential Construction by Type

Nonresidential construction, by type, is ranked according to preliminary 1991 floor areas, measured in millions of square feet.

Stores and other commercial	360
Educational	160
Manufacturing buildings	105
Office buildings	100
Hospital and health	67
Other nonresidential buildings	146

Source: *Heating/Piping/Air Conditioning*, January 1992, p. 95, from F.W. Dodge.

★ 160 ★
Utility Construction (SIC 1541)

Utility Construction

Distribution of construction spending by investor-owned electric utilities is shown in percent for 1992, based on an estimated total of $27.029 billion.

Generating plants	
Coal 16.5%
Nuclear 9.5
Other 8.9
T&D facilities	
Distribution 36.3
Transmission 13.8
Other	
General/misc. plants 8.5
Nuclear fuel 6.5

Source: *Electrical World*, May 1992, p. 7, from Edison Electric Institute.

★ 161 ★
Retail Construction (SIC 1542)

Interior Space Retail Contractors

The 25 leading retail contractors of interior space are ranked according to square footage of construction from June 1986 to June 1991.

De Jager Construction Inc. 9,072,000
E M J Corp. 8,270,242
Porter McLeod Inc.	
Construction Services 6,370,000
The Whiting-Turner Contracting Co. . . 6,238,000
Weekes Construction Inc. 6,238,000
Herbert & Boghosian Inc. 5,938,000
Robert E. Bayley Construction Inc. . . 5,792,000
Tony Crawford Construction 5,695,080
Phillips Construction Co. Inc. 5,507,432
Hale-Mills Construction Inc. 5,396,201
S M I Construction Co. 5,114,520
Tribble & Stephens Co. 5,016,427
L.M. B. Construction Co. Inc.. 4,850,000
Dicon Inc. 4,687,278
McCrory Construction Co. Inc. 4,669,850
Gillam & Associates Inc. 4,247,922
State Construction Corp. 4,212,556
The Weitz Co. Inc. 4,184,726
C.D. Build Group Ltd. 4,120,000
R.A.S. Builders Inc. 3,974,400
Hoar Construction 3,896,559
Pepper Construction 3,887,300

Elder-Jones Inc. 3,774,000
Fisher Development Inc. 3,753,621
Miller Building Corp. 3,676,475

Source: *Shopping Center World*, September 1991, p. 30.

★ 162 ★
Retail Construction (SIC 1542)

Shell Space Retail Contractors

The leading retail contractors of shell space are ranked according to amount of square footage of construction from June 1986 to June 1991.

McDevitt & Street Co. 12,486,952
Tribble & Stephens Co. 11,728,291
E M J Corp. 10,296,388
Hoar Construction 8,431,759
Phillips Construction Co. Inc. 8,098,624
S A E Pinkerton and Laws 7,853,961
Hale-Mills Construction Inc. 6,232,497
I M C Inc. 6,215,120
The Whiting-Turner Contracting Co. . 5,765,000
Dicon Inc. 4,993,207
McCrory Construction Co. Inc. . . . 4,894,600
Robert E. Bayley Construction Inc. . . 4,504,000
Gillam & Associates Inc. 4,247,922
Paul H. Schwendener Inc. 4,088,340
The Lathrop Co. 4,077,272
Pepper Construction Co. 4,030,300
Tarlton Corp. 4,025,000
Keene Construction Co. of	
Central Florida Inc. 3,878,966
Rentenbach Constructors Inc. 3,873,731
Stewart & Perry Construction Inc. . . 3,631,900
Inland Construction Co. 3,600,000
Charles Pankow Builders Ltd. 3,154,000
L.M.B. Construction Co. Inc. 3,100,000
Brice Building Co. Inc. 3,000,000
The Law Co. Inc. 2,983,868

Source: *Shopping Center World*, September 1991, p. 31.

SIC 16 - Heavy Construction, Except Building

★ 163 ★

Heavy Construction (SIC 1600)

Heavy Construction Contractors - Canada

Volume is shown in thousands of Canadian dollars for 1991; relative market shares are shown in percent for the same period. Category includes both building and roads.

	Volume ($000 Cdn.)	% of Group
PCL Construction Group Inc.	$ 1,438,700	18.6%
Ellis-Don Ltd.	950,000	12.3
Banister Continental Ltd.	700,000	9.1
Delta Catalytic Corp.	600,000	7.8
Magil Construction Ltd.	421,000	5.4
Matthews Group Ltd.	375,000	4.9
Dominion Bridge	330,000	4.3
Eastern Construction Co. Ltd.	300,175	3.9
Group Herve Pomerleau	296,676	3.8
Commonwealth Construction Co.	270,500	3.5
Canron	270,000	3.5
Cana Ltd.	266,300	3.4
Comstock Canada	237,470	3.1
Stuart Olson Construction Inc.	236,000	3.1
Atlas-Gest	202,000	2.6
George Wimpey Canada Ltd.	193,719	2.5
Peter Kiewit Sons Co. Ltd.	171,158	2.2
Milne & Nicholls Ltd.	160,659	2.1
Majestic Contractors Ltd.	155,588	2.0
Dominion Co.	154,700	2.0

Source: *Heavy Construction News*, June 1991, p. 12.

★ 164 ★

Heavy Construction (SIC 1611)

Roadbuilders - Canada

Volume is shown in Canadian dollars for 1990; relative market shares are shown in percent for the same period.

	Volume ($ Cdn.)	% of Group
George Wimpey Canada Ltd.	$ 193,719,000	20.1%
Armbro Inc.	93,440,000	9.7
Bot Construction Ltd.	85,488,000	8.9
Dufferin Construction	75,000,000	7.8
North American Construction	75,000,000	7.8
Con-Strada Construction Inc.	45,000,000	4.7
Graham Bros. Construction Ltd. Group	44,250,000	4.6
Everall Construction Ltd.	40,000,000	4.1
Pennecon Ltd.	39,419,332	4.1
Bell Construction	35,000,000	3.6
Peters Bros. Paving Ltd.	34,500,000	3.6
Jack Cewe Ltd.	32,500,000	3.4
Meloche Inc.	30,000,000	3.1
Arthur A. Voice Construction Co. Ltd.	22,000,000	2.3
Cruickshank Construction Ltd.	21,914,776	2.3
Standard Paving Maritime Ltd.	21,010,000	2.2
South Rock Ltd.	20,000,000	2.1
Cantex Eng. & Const. Co. Ltd.	20,000,000	2.1
Argo Industries Ltd.	19,000,000	2.0
Allan G. Cook Ltd.	18,162,000	1.9

Source: *Heavy Construction News*, June 1991, p. 12.

★ 165 ★

Heavy Construction (SIC 1620)

Contracting Leaders - Canada

Volume is shown in Canadian dollars for 1990; relative market shares are shown in percent for the same period.

	Volume ($ Cdn.)	% of Group
PCL Construction Group Inc.	$ 1,438,700,000	22.2%
Ellis-Don Ltd.	950,000,000	14.6
Delta Catalytic Corp.	600,000,000	9.2
Magil Construction Ltd.	421,000,000	6.5
Dominion Bridge	330,000,000	5.1
Eastern Construction Co. Ltd.	300,175,000	4.6
Pomerleau Group	296,676,000	4.6
Canron	270,000,000	4.2
Cana Ltd.	266,300,000	4.1
Stuart Olson Construction Inc.	236,000,000	3.6
Atlas-Gest Inc.	202,000,000	3.1
Milne & Nicholls Ltd.	160,659,000	2.5
Dominion Co.	154,700,000	2.4
Bird Construction Co. Ltd.	152,941,850	2.4
V.K. Mason Construction Ltd.	137,000,000	2.1
Cooper Corp. Ltd.	132,000,000	2.0
A.V. Carlson Constructors Inc.	130,000,000	2.0
Eton Construction Ltd.	110,076,318	1.7
Jackson-Lewis Co. Ltd.	106,000,000	1.6
Bondfield Construction Co.	98,000,000	1.5

Source: *Heavy Construction News*, June 1991, p. 12.

★ 166 ★

Pipeline Construction (SIC 1623)

Pipeline Construction in 1991 - Worldwide

World pipeline construction, by segment, is shown in thousands of miles. Total construction for 1991 was 10,730 miles.

Natural gas pipelines	7,886
Products pipelines	1,037
Replacement/repair pipelines	1,204
Crude oil pipelines	603

Source: *Pipeline & Utilities Construction*, January 1992, p. 40.

★ 167 ★

Pipeline Construction (SIC 1623)

Pipeline Construction in 1992 - Canada

Anticipated pipeline construction in Canada, by type, is shown in thousands of miles for 1992. Total pipeline construction is expected to amount to 1,087 miles in 1992.

Gas transmission	817
Gas distribution	260

Source: *Pipeline & Utilities Construction*, January 1992, p. 41.

★ 168 ★

Pipeline Construction (SIC 1623)

Pipeline Construction in 1992 - U.S.

Anticipated pipeline construction, by type, is shown in thousands of miles for 1992. The total U.S. pipeline construction is expected to amount to 19,931 miles in 1992.

New construction pipelines	19,321
Gas mains/distribution pipelines	14,395
Gas transmission pipelines	4,098
Repair/rehabilitation/ replacement pipelines	610
Crude oil pipelines	492
Products pipelines	336

Source: *Pipeline & Utilities Construction*, January 1992, p. 41.

SIC 17 - Special Trade Contractors

Roofing (SIC 1761)

Roofing Market

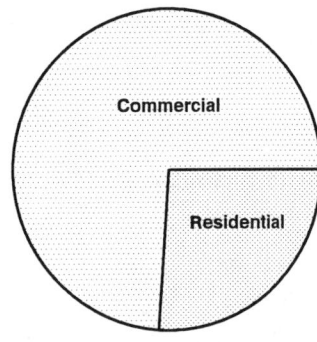

Roofing market segments are shown in percent, based on a total of $16.40 billion in 1992 (projected).

Commercial 74.0%
Residential 26.0

Source: *Buildings*, May 1992, p. 57.

Roofing (SIC 1761)

Roofing Market by Job-Type

Market shares by job-type are shown in percent, based on a total of $16.40 billion in 1992.

New construction 80.0%
Reroofing 20.0

Source: *Buildings*, May 1992, p. 57.

SIC 20 - Food and Kindred Products

★171★

Fast Food (SIC 2000)

Fast Food Sales in U.K.

Shares of U.K. fast food sales, by type of food, are shown in percent, based on a total market of 5.0 billion pounds.

Sandwiches	.22.0%
Hamburgers	.16.4
Fish and chips	.12.8
Pizzas	.12.0
Chinese-food takeaways	9.2
Chicken	6.0
Indian-food takeaways	4.2
Others	.17.5

Source: *Accountancy*, February 1992, p. 86.

★172★

Food (SIC 2000)

Food Companies in Mexico

Revenues of major food companies investing in Mexico are shown in billions of dollars.

Sara Lee	$ 11.600
Kraft General Foods	10.400
CPC International	5.100
Dean Foods	2.000
Pepsico Foods	0.672
Stokely	0.272

Source: *Food Engineering*, April 1992, p. 25, from A.T. Kearney.

★173★

Food (SIC 2000)

Food Expenditures - U.S.

Shares of U.S. food expenditures, by category, are shown in percent.

Labor	.35.0%
Farm value	.24.0
Packaging	8.0
Advertising	4.5
Depreciation	4.5
Transport	4.0
Fuels and electricity	4.0
Before-tax profits	3.0
Rent	3.0
Net interest	3.0
Repairs	1.5
Other	5.5

Source: *Hoard's Dairyman*, January 25, 1992, p. 62.

★ 174 ★

Food (SIC 2000)

Food Market by Manufacturer

Companies are ranked by dollar sales in 1991. Relative market shares are based on $195,494 million in sales.

	Sales ($ mil.)	% of Group
Philip Morris	.$ 48,109	24.6%
Conagra	19,505	10.0
Sara Lee	12,456	6.4
Archer-Daniels	8,586	4.4
Ralston Purina	7,394	3.8
Borden	7,235	3.7
General Mills	7,153	3.7
H.J. Heinz	6,682	3.4
Cambell Soup	6,230	3.2
CPC International	6,200	3.2
Quaker Oats	6,101	3.1
Kellogg	5,787	3.0
Chiquita Brands	4,627	2.4
Tyson Foods	3,922	2.0
Farmland Industries	3,652	1.9
Agway	3,490	1.8
Hershey Foods	2,902	1.5
Geo. A. Hormel	2,836	1.5
Land O'Lakes	2,458	1.3
Intl. Multifoods	2,192	1.1
Dean Foods	2,159	1.1
Central Soya	2,000	1.0
Mid-America Dairymen . . .	1,742	0.9
Del Monte	1,435	0.7
McCormick	1,428	0.7
Gold Kist	1,268	0.6
Gerber Products	1,203	0.6
Savannah Foods & Ind. . . .	1,203	0.6
Wm. Wrigley Jr.	1,160	0.6
Interstate Bakeries	1,107	0.6
Smithfield Foods	1,072	0.5
Domino Sugar	1,058	0.5
Ocean Spray	946	0.5
AG Processing	866	0.4
Universal Foods	834	0.4
Flowers Industries	831	0.4
Tri Valley Growers	825	0.4
Doskocil	820	0.4
Thorn Apple Valley	818	0.4
Pilgrim's Pride	788	0.4
Hudson Foods	765	0.4
Imperial Holly	718	0.4
Riceland Foods	641	0.3

	Sales ($ mil.)	% of Group
Prairie Farms Dairy	$ 638	0.3%
Sun-Diamond Growers . . .	603	0.3
Amer. Maize-Prod.	534	0.3
Wisconsin Dairies Coop.	533	0.3

Source: *Fortune*, April 20, 1992, p. 268.

★ 175 ★

Food (SIC 2000)

Food Processing Companies

Company sales are shown in millions of dollars for 1991. Percent shares are based on a group total of $137,460 million.

	Sales ($ mil.)	% of Group
Conagra	.$ 20,485	14.9%
Sara Lee	12,651	9.2
IBP	10,388	7.6
Archer Daniels Midland	8,801	6.4
General Mills	7,486	5.4
Ralston Purina	7,448	5.4
Borden	7,235	5.3
H.J. Heinz	6,553	4.8
CPC Internatioal	6,189	4.5
Campbell Soup	6,133	4.5
Kellogg	5,787	4.2
Quaker Oats	5,570	4.1
Chiquita Brands International . .	4,627	3.4
Tyson Foods	3,978	2.9
Dole Food	3,216	2.3
Hershey Foods	2,899	2.1
Geo.A. Hormel	2,764	2.0
International Multifoods	2,271	1.7
Dean Foods	2,168	1.6
Pet	1,878	1.4
McCormick	1,428	1.0
Gerber Products	1,209	0.9
Savannah Foods & Industries . .	1,200	0.9
Wm. Wrigley Jr.	1,149	0.8
Pioneer Hi-Bred International .	1,131	0.8
Universal Foods	843	0.6
Flowers Industries	838	0.6
J.M. Smucker	480	0.3
Lance	450	0.3
Tootsie Roll Industries	208	0.2

Source: *The 1992 Business Week 1000*, 1992, p. 174.

★ 176 ★

Food (SIC 2000)

Leading Food and Beverage Manufacturers

Sales of 12 leading food and beverage manufacturers worldwide, are shown in billions of dollars. Relative market shares are shown in percent based on a total of $230.13 billion in 1990.

	Sales ($ bil.)	% of Group
Philip Morris	$ 44.32	19.0%
Unilever	39.97	17.0
Nestle	33.36	14.0
Pepsico	17.80	8.0
Conagra	15.52	7.0
Grand Metropolitan	14.77	6.0
Ferruzi	13.97	6.0
Sara Lee	11.65	5.0
Anheuser Busch	10.75	5.0
Coca-Cola	10.41	5.0
BSN	9.72	4.0
Archer-Daniels-Midland	7.89	3.0

Source: *Business Horizon*, November 1991, p. 17.

★ 177 ★

Food (SIC 2000)

Meat Market

Shares of the meat market in the U.S., by category, are shown in percent for the years 1985 and 1990.

	1985	1990
Red meat	61.2%	53.2%
Poultry	32.2	40.0
Fish	6.6	6.8

Source: *Food Engineering*, December 1991, p. 12, from American Meat Institute.

★ 178 ★

Food (SIC 2000)

Nationality Food Market

Market segmentation, by product ethnicity, is based on a volume total of 696 million lbs. and a value total of $1,750 million. Data are shown in percent for 1990.

	Vol. Share	Val. Share
Italian	38.4%	39.1%
Mexican	42.9	37.3
Oriental	8.7	15.5
Jewish	6.6	5.7
Other	3.4	2.3

Source: *Quick Frozen Foods International*, October 1991, p. A6, from Arbitron SAMI.

★ 179 ★

Food (SIC 2000)

Private-Label Grocery Products

Segment distribution is shown in percent, based on a total of $14.13 billion in sales for the year ending June 30, 1991.

Milk	39.3%
Fresh bread and rolls	10.9
Cheese	9.6
Ice cream	6.4
Frozen vegetables	5.9
Sugar	4.4
Shelved vegetables	4.4
Frozen juice	4.3
Carbonated beverages	4.2
Shelved juice	3.8

Continued on next page.

★ 179 ★ *Continued*
Food (SIC 2000)

Private-Label Grocery Products

Segment distribution is shown in percent, based on a total of $14.13 billion in sales for the year ending June 30, 1991.

Refrigerated juice 3.6%
Shelved fruit 3.2

Source: *The New York Times*, January 14, 1992, p. C5, from Information Resources Inc.

★ 180 ★
Food (SIC 2000)

Red Meat, Poultry, Seafood Consumption

Consumption of red meat, poultry and seafood is shown in lbs. per capita in 1990.

Red meat 112.3
Poultry 63.6
Fish and shellfish 15.4

Source: *Restaurant Business*, March 1992, p. 2, from USDA.

★ 181 ★
Frozen Food (SIC 2000)

Frozen Food by Category

Market segmentation is based on totals of 28,458 million lbs. and $53,692 million, shown in percent for 1990.

	Vol. Share	Val. Share
Fish and seafood	8.4%	31.0%
Prepared foods	24.2	29.1
Vegetables	33.4	15.1
Poultry	15.5	9.5
Juices and drinks	9.8	7.5
Meat	4.8	5.4
Fruits	3.9	2.4

Source: *Quick Frozen Foods International*, October 1991, p. A5, from Arbitron SAMI.

★ 182 ★
Frozen Food (SIC 2000)

Frozen Food Consumption in Italy

Market segmentation is shown in percent, based on a total consumption of 380,300 tons of quick frozen food in 1990.

Vegetables 50.9%
Potatoes 15.1
Fish 12.1
Snacks 7.7
Pasta dishes 3.4
Poultry 3.1
Meat 3.0
Milk products 2.2
Seafood molluscs 2.1
Fruit and juices 0.3

Source: *Quick Frozen Foods International*, October 1991, p. A24.

★ 183 ★
Frozen Food (SIC 2000)

Frozen Food Consumption - Germany

Market segmentation is shown in percent, based on total value of 1,615,919 Deutschmarks in 1990.

Poultry 26.9%
Potato products 20.6
Vegetables 17.4
Ready meals 14.3
Fish/shellfish 7.9
Bakery products 5.8
Meat and game 5.2
Fruit, fruit juices 1.4
Pasta and pasta dishes 0.5
Dairy products and desserts 0.1

Source: *Quick Frozen Foods International*, October 1991, p. A21, from German Frozen Food Institute and ZMP and German Association of Poultry Processors.

★ 184 ★
Frozen Food (SIC 2000)

Frozen Food Retail Sales - 1991

Percent distribution of retail sales, by food category, is based on a total of $17,924,034,852 for the 52-week period ending December 1, 1991.

Ice cream and novelties 24.6%
Dinners and entrees 23.2
Continued on next page.

★184★ *Continued*

Frozen Food (SIC 2000)

Frozen Food Retail Sales - 1991

Percent distribution of retail sales, by food category, is based on a total of $17,924,034,852 for the 52-week period ending December 1, 1991.

Meat and fish	9.8%
Juices and drinks	9.5
Plain vegetables	9.0
Pizza	6.6
Desserts	4.7
Breakfast foods	3.9
Potatoes and onion rings	3.8
Baked goods	1.8
Prepared vegetables	0.9
Fruit	0.8
Other frozen foods	1.4

Source: *Quick Frozen Foods International*, April 1992, p. 135, from Information Resources, Inc.

★185★

Frozen Food (SIC 2000)

Prepared Frozen Food Market

Segment distribution is shown in percent, based on a volume total of 6,879 million lbs. and a value total of $15,262 million. Data are shown for 1990.

	Vol. Share	Val. Share
Poultry (breaded, precooked) . . .	18.3%	17.2%
Entrees (including pouches) . . .	11.6	13.6
Nationality foods	10.1	11.5
Dinners (platters) and lunches . .	7.6	9.2
Pizza	6.6	7.7
Seafood specialties	4.9	7.4
Bakery products	7.8	6.1
Breakfast items	5.4	6.0
Prepared vegetables	5.2	4.3
Vegetable creams	7.7	4.1
Dessert pies	5.2	3.8
Snacks	2.3	3.2
Meat pies	3.1	2.3
Pie and pastry shells	1.1	0.9
Miscellaneous	3.1	2.7

Source: *Quick Frozen Foods International*, October 1991, p. A7, from Arbitron SAMI.

★186★

Frozen Foods (SIC 2000)

Supermarket Pizzas

Tombstone
Tony's
Red Baron
Totino's
Stouffer's
Private labels
Celeste
Jack's
McCain Ellio's
Jeno's
Other

Sales of the top 10 supermarket frozen pizza brands accounted for 81.4% of the $1.2921 billion market for the 52 weeks ending May 16, 1992. Shares are shown in percent.

	Sales	Share
Tombstone	$ 221.7	17.2%
Tony's	158.4	12.3
Red Baron	137.3	10.6
Totino's	132.0	10.2
Stouffer's	112.3	8.7
Private labels	82.2	6.4
Celeste	59.8	4.6
Jack's	54.4	4.2
McCain Ellio's	52.4	4.1
Jeno's	40.0	3.1
Other	241.6	18.6

Source: *Advertising Age*, July 20, 1992, p. 20, from A.C. Nielsen ScanTrack.

★ 187 ★
Vegetables (SIC 2000)

Vegetable Consumption in 1990

Consumption of fresh vegetables in the U.S. in 1990 is shown in pounds, based on a total consumption per person of 111 pounds.

Iceberg lettuce	27.8
Onions	18.6
Tomatoes	15.4
Cabbage	8.7
Carrots	8.0
Broccoli	3.4

Source: *USA TODAY*, November 3, 1992, p. 7A, from *1992 Statistical Abstract of the United States*.

★ 188 ★
Meat (SIC 2010)

Top Meat Companies

Sales of top 20 meat companies totaled $54.510 billion in 1990. Relative shares are shown in percent.

	($ mil.)	% of Group
Con Agra, Inc.	$ 12,500	22.9%
IBP, Inc.	10,185	18.7
Excel Corporation	5,500	10.1
Tyson Foods, Inc.	3,825	7.0
Sara Lee Corporation	3,000	5.5
Geo. A. Hormel & Co.	2,681	4.9
Oscar Mayer Foods Corp.	2,500	4.6
John Morrell & Co.	2,100	3.9
BeefAmerica, Operating Co., Inc.	1,800	3.3
International Multifoods U.S. Food Service Group	1,500	2.8
Perdue Farms, Inc.	1,250	2.3
Idle Wild Foods, Inc.	1,233	2.3
Gold Kist, Inc.	1,040	1.9
Doskocil Cos., Inc.	919	1.7
Smithfield Foods, Inc.	853	1.6
Hyplains Beef Co., Inc.	734	1.3
American Foods Group	729	1.3
FDL Foods, Inc.	725	1.3
Pilgrim's Pride Corp.	721	1.3
Farmland Foods, Inc.	715	1.3

Source: *Meat Facts*, 1991, p. 30, from *Meat & Poultry*.

★ 189 ★
Meat (SIC 2011)

Meat Production

Segment distribution is shown in percent, based on a production total of 38.785 billion lbs. of meat in 1990.

Beef	58.6%
Pork	39.6
Lamb and mutton	0.9
Veal	0.8

Source: *Meat Facts*, 1991, p. 17, from U.S. Department of Agriculture.

★ 190 ★
Luncheon Meat (SIC 2013)

Lunch-Kit Sales

The lunch-kit market is shown, by brand, with sales in millions of dollars based on supermarket sales for the 52 weeks ended on October 4, 1992.

Oscar Mayer Lunchables	$ 130.2
Bryan Lunch 'n Munch	13.0
Hillshire Farm Lunch 'n Munch	11.7
Charlie's Lunch Kit	4.5
Hillshire Farm Lite	1.7
Lunch to Go	0.5
Eckrich Lunch Makers	0.4
Bryan Lite	0.2

Source: *The Wall Street Journal*, November 3, 1992, p. B1, from Information Resources, Inc.

★ 191 ★
Poultry (SIC 2015)

Broiler Companies - U.K.

Market shares are shown in percent, based on an annualized total output of 675 million birds.

Hillsdown	13.0%
Unigate	9.0
Marshall	7.0
Facenda	6.0
Sun Valley	6.0
Grampian	5.0
Padley	4.0
Favor Parker	4.0
Moy Park	4.0
Webb	3.0
Lloyd Maunder	2.0

Continued on next page.

★ 191 ★ *Continued*

Poultry (SIC 2015)

Broiler Companies - U.K.

Market shares are shown in percent, based on an annualized total output of 675 million birds.

Imports 18.0%
Other 19.0

Source: *Financial Times*, February 11, 1992, p. 22.

★ 192 ★

Poultry (SIC 2015)

Frozen Poultry Market

Market segmentation is shown in percent, based on a volume total of 4,406 million lbs. and a value total of $5,134 million. Data are shown for 1990.

	Vol. Share	Val. Share
Turkey	47.0%	50.6%
Chickens	33.9	24.2
Raw turkey roasts	3.1	6.4
Table eggs	9.2	5.8
Cooked turkey products	2.4	5.3
Pan turkey roasts	2.2	4.4
Ducks	1.5	2.0
Rock cornish roasts	0.6	1.2
Other poultry	0.1	0.1

Source: *Quick Frozen Foods International*, October 1991, p. A9, from U.S. Department of Agriculture and National Agricultural Statistics Service.

★ 193 ★

Poultry Products (SIC 2015)

Egg Substitute Producers

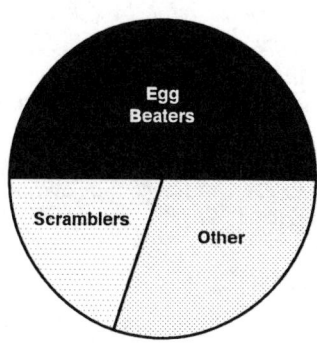

Brand shares of frozen egg substitute sales are shown in percent for 1991. Manufacturers are shown in parentheses.

Egg Beaters (Fleischmann) 55.0%
Scramblers (Worthington) 22.0
Other 33.0

Source: Investext, Thomson Financial Networks, May 21, 1992, from The Ohio Company.

★ 194 ★

Dairy Products (SIC 2020)

Margarine Producers

Shares, by company, are shown in percent.

Unilever 32.0%
Nabisco 22.0
Other 46.0

Source: Investext, Thomson Financial Networks, February 14, 1992, from Nomura Research Institute Europe Ltd.

★ 195 ★
Cheese (SIC 2022)

Cheese Consumption

Per capita cheese consumption by type is shown in lbs. Percentages are based on a total of 34 lbs. in 1991. "Other American" includes Colby, Monterey Jack, curd. "Italian" includes Romano, Provolone, Parmesan.

	Lbs.	Share
American Cheddar	9	26.5%
Mozzarella	8	23.5
Processed cheese	4	11.8
Processed spread	3	8.8
Cream	2	5.9
Other American	2	5.9
Blue	2	5.9
Ricotta	1	2.9
Swiss	1	2.9
Italian	1	2.9
All other	1	2.9

Source: *Detroit Free Press*, July 8, 1992, p. C1, from International Trade Administration; Agriculture Department.

★ 196 ★
Baby Food (SIC 2023)

Baby Food by Brand

Shares, by brand, of the baby food market are shown in percent for 1989, 1990, and 1991.

	1989	1990	1991
Gerber	69.9%	70.3%	71.0%
Heinz	12.7	14.2	14.4
Beech-Nut	17.3	14.7	13.6

Source: Investext, Thomson Financial Networks, March 19, 1992, from Paine Webber Inc.

★ 197 ★
Baby Food (SIC 2023)

Baby Food Market Shares

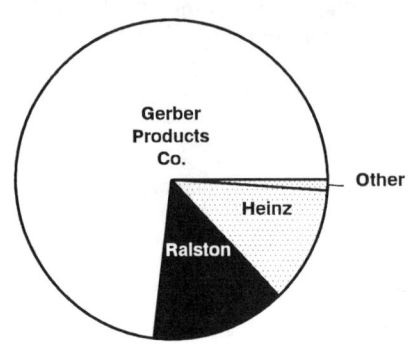

Company shares are shown in percent for the year-to-date.

Gerber Products Co.	73.0%
Ralston	14.0
Heinz	12.0
Other	1.0

Source: Investext, Thomson Financial Networks, May 28, 1992, from Donaldson, Lufkin & Jenrette Securities.

★ 198 ★
Baby Food (SIC 2023)

Baby Food Supermarket Sales

Shares of the baby food market, shown in percent, are based on a total of $878 million in sales in 1991.

Gerber	71.0%
Beech-Nut	15.0
Heinz	11.0
Other	3.0

Source: *The New York Times*, June 11, 1992, p. C6, from Information Resources, Inc.

★ 199 ★

Infant Formula (SIC 2023)

Supermarket Formula Brands

Sales of top 10 supermarket infant formula brands accounted for 98.5% of the $1.6082 billion market for the 52 weeks ending May 16, 1992. Shares are shown in percent.

	Sales	Share
Similac	$ 566.0	35.2%
Enfamil	350.2	21.8
Isomil	222.8	13.9
SMA	121.4	7.5
Prosobee	113.1	7.0
Gerber	59.2	3.7
Nursoy	55.2	3.4
Carnation Follow-Up	38.4	2.4
Good Start	30.5	1.9
Nutramigen	27.6	1.7
Other	23.8	1.5

Source: *Advertising Age*, July 20, 1992, p. 20, from A.C. Nielsen ScanTracks.

★ 200 ★

Frozen Desserts (SIC 2024)

Frozen Dessert Shares

Manufacturers and their brand shares of the ice cream, frozen novelty, and sherbet market are shown in percent, based on an industry total of $61.0 million in advertising expenditures in 1991.

Philip Morris	13.0%
Jell-O Frozen Pudding Pops	4.8
Breyers Ice Cream	3.1
Kool-Aid Frozen Kool Pops	2.1
Other	3.0
Nestle SA	11.6
Carnation Bon Bons	4.4
Flintstones Pushups	1.3
Other	5.9
Dreyers Grand Ice Cream, Inc.	6.6
Edys Ice Cream	2.5
Dreyers Grand Frozen Yogurt	2.0
Edys Frozen Yogurt	1.1
Dreyers Ice Cream	0.2
Other	0.8
Borden, Inc.	3.6
Borden Ice Cream	1.5
Lady Borden Ice Cream	0.8
Meadow Gold Ice Cream	0.5

Borden Frozen Yogurt	0.3%
Other	0.5
Grand Metropolitan	3.4
Haagen Dazs Ice Cream	3.4
Blue Bell Creameries	2.1
Blue Bell Ice Cream	2.1
Empire of Carolina, Inc.	2.2
Klondike Ice Cream Bars	1.5
Klondike Lite Ice Cream	0.7
Eskimo Pie	1.7
Eskimo Pie Sugar Free Ice Cream Bars . .	1.5
Other	0.2
Agway, Inc.	0.2
Hood Free Ice Cream	0.2
All Other	55.7

Source: Investext, Thomson Financial Networks, April 27, 1992, from Wheat First Butcher & Singer, Inc.

★ 201 ★

Frozen Desserts (SIC 2024)

Frozen Novelties

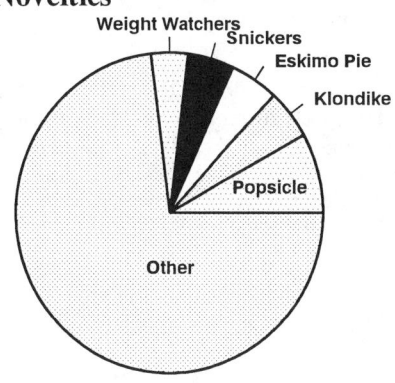

Unit brand shares for the 12 weeks ending December 1991 are shown in percent, based on sales by U.S. grocery stores with at least $2.0 million annual volume (all commodities). The figure for Eskimo Pie does not include Welch's or Heath brands.

Popsicle	7.6%
Klondike	5.4
Eskimo Pie	5.3
Snickers	4.8
Weight Watchers	4.3
Other	72.6

Source: Investext, Thomson Financial Networks, April 27, 1992, from Wheat First Butcher & Singer, Inc.

★ 202 ★

Milk (SIC 2026)

Milk Consumption

Per capita milk consumption, by type, is shown in gallons in 1971 and 1991.

	1971	1991
Low-fat milk	4.0	11.6
Whole milk	23.0	9.6
Skim milk	1.4	2.8

Source: *USA TODAY*, October 21, 1992, p. 1D, from U.S. Department of Agriculture.

★ 203 ★

Yogurt (SIC 2026)

Yogurt Producers - Belgium

Shares are shown in percent. 74,000 tons of yogurt were consumed in 1990.

BSN	30.0%
Stassano	14.0
Jacky/Chambourcy (Nestle)	8.0
Other	48.0

Source: Investext, Thomson Financial Networks, February 20, 1992, from UBS Phillips & Drew Global Research Group.

★ 204 ★

Yogurt (SIC 2026)

Yogurt Producers - France

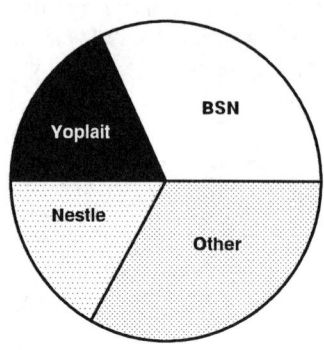

Shares are shown in percent. 913,000 tons of yogurt were consumed in 1990.

BSN	32.0%
Yoplait (Sodiaal)	18.0
Nestle	17.0
Other	33.0

Source: Investext, Thomson Financial Networks, February 20, 1992, from UBS Phillips & Drew Global Research Group.

★ 205 ★

Yogurt (SIC 2026)

Yogurt Producers - Germany

Shares are shown in percent. 649,000 tons of yogurt were consumed in 1990.

Muller	16.0%
BSN	13.0
Herrmann	10.0
Sudmilch	8.0
Bauer	7.0
Nestle	6.0
Other	40.0

Source: Investext, Thomson Financial Networks, February 20, 1992, from UBS Phillips & Drew Global Research Group.

★ 206 ★
Yogurt (SIC 2026)

Yogurt Producers - Italy

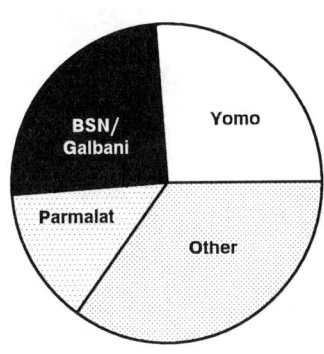

Shares are shown in percent. An estimated 200,000 tons of yogurt were consumed in 1990.

Yomo	26.0%
BSN/Galbani	25.0
Parmalat	14.0
Other	35.0

Source: Investext, Thomson Financial Networks, February 20, 1992, from UBS Phillips & Drew Global Research Group.

★ 207 ★
Yogurt (SIC 2026)

Yogurt Producers - Spain

Danone
Yoplait
Nestle
Other

Shares are shown in percent. 316,000 tons of yogurt were consumed in 1990.

Danone (BSN)	60.0%
Yoplait	15.0
Nestle	12.0
Other	13.0

Source: Investext, Thomson Financial Networks, February 20, 1992, from UBS Phillips & Drew Global Research Group.

★ 208 ★
Yogurt (SIC 2026)

Yogurt Producers - U.K.

Shares are shown in percent. 247,000 tons of yogurt were consumed in 1990. The figure for Northern Foods includes Eden Vale.

Northern Foods	33.0%
Unigate	26.0
Other	41.0

Source: Investext, Thomson Financial Networks, February 20, 1992, from UBS Phillips & Drew Global Research Group.

★ 209 ★
Soup (SIC 2030)

Ready-to-Serve Soup Market

Company shares are based on total sales of $137.2 million for the January-February, 1992 period, shown in percent.

Chunky	36.3%
Home Cookin'	16.9
ConAgra	9.0
Campbell	6.0
Other	31.8

Source: *Advertising Age*, April 6, 1992, p. 12, from Nielsen Marketing Research.

★ 210 ★
Soup (SIC 2030)

Soup/Sauce Producers

Shares, by company, are shown in percent.

Lipton	50.0%
CPC	7.0
Other	43.0

Source: Investext, Thomson Financial Networks, June 15, 1992, from Kidder, Peabody & Company, Inc.

★ 211 ★

Soups (SIC 2030)

Supermarket Soups

Shares of supermarket soup sales are shown by brand for the 52 weeks ending May 16, 1992. Percentages are based on a total market of $2.1006 billion.

	Sales	Share
Campbell's	$ 1,580.7	75.3%
Progresso	170.9	8.1
Private lables	120.9	5.8
Swanson	63.0	3.0
College Inn	39.9	1.9
Healthy Choice	38.6	1.8
Snow's	10.9	0.5
Health Valley	7.4	0.4
Pritikin	7.2	0.3
Sweet Sue	6.5	0.3
Other	54.6	2.6

Source: *Advertising Age*, July 20, 1992, p. 20, from A.C. Nielsen ScanTrack.

★ 212 ★

Canned Vegetables (SIC 2033)

Canned Vegetables Industry Leaders

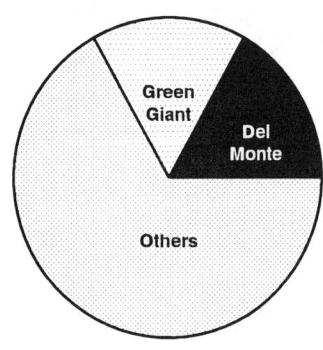

Company shares are shown in percent.

Del Monte	17.0%
Green Giant	16.0
Others	67.0

Source: Investext, Thomson Financial Networks, March 2, 1992, p. 13, from Merrill Lynch Capital Markets.

★ 213 ★

Sauces (SIC 2033)

Spaghetti Sauces

Brand shares are shown in percent, based on a total of $1.2 billion in sales.

Ragu	42.0%
Prego	26.0
Hunt's	12.0
Other	20.0

Source: *Advertising Age*, February 17, 1992, p. 59.

★ 214 ★

Salad Dressings (SIC 2035)

Salad Dressing Producers

Shares are shown in percent.

Kraft	24.0%
Hidden Valley Ranch	23.0
Other	53.0

Source: Investext, Thomson Financial Networks, January 30, 1992, from Prudential Securities, Inc.

★ 215 ★

Sauces (SIC 2035)

Mayonnaise Market

Shares, by company, are shown in percent.

CPC	50.0%
Kraft	23.0
Other	27.0

Source: Investext, Thomson Financial Networks, June 15, 1992, from Kidder, Peabody & Company, Inc.

★ 216 ★
Sauces (SIC 2035)

Pasta Sauces - Restaurant Market Penetration

Percentages reflect consumer preference in choice of pasta sauces served in restaurants. Data are shown for 1988 and 1991.

	1988	1991
Marinara/tomato	78.0%	92.0%
Alfredo	39.0	59.0
Garlic & oil	30.0	45.0
White clam	32.0	39.0
Pesto	21.0	33.0
Red clam	18.0	24.0

Source: *Restaurant Business*, January 1992, p. 2.

★ 217 ★
Frozen Fruits (SIC 2037)

Frozen Fruit Market

Market segmentation is shown in percent, based on a volume total of 1,117,688 thousand lbs. and a value total of $1,308,971 thousand.

	Vol. Share	Val. Share
Strawberries	35.3%	35.9%
Blueberries	10.5	16.4
Peaches	9.9	9.2
Cherries	10.7	8.5
Apples	11.2	7.8
Red raspberries	2.4	4.1
Purees, non-citrus	3.8	2.8
Blackberries	1.2	1.4
Apricots	1.5	1.3
Cherries, sweet	1.2	1.0
Boysenberries	0.7	0.6
Black raspberries	0.2	0.4
Plums and prunes	0.1	0.1
Loganberries	0.1	0.1
Miscellaneous	11.2	10.5

Source: *Quick Frozen Foods International*, October 1991, p. A10, from American Frozen Food Institute, U.S. Department of Commerce, U.S. Department of Agriculture, and American Institute of Food Distribution.

★ 218 ★
Frozen Juices (SIC 2037)

Frozen Juice and Beverage Market

Market segmentation is shown in percent, based on a total value of $4,077,688 thousand. Data are shown for the 1989-90 season.

Frozen concentrated orange juice	41.8%
Orange concentrate for chilled juice and remanufacture	24.2
Fruit drinks and synthetics	8.6
Non-citrus concentrates	5.5
Grape juice	5.1
Ades (lemon, lime, etc.)	5.0
Apple juice and cider	4.2
Grapefruit juice	0.9
Tangerine juice	0.2
Single strength and citrus purees	0.1
Miscellaneous	4.3

Source: *Quick Frozen Foods International*, October 1991, p. A11, from Florida Citrus Processors Association, American Food Institute, and U.S. Department of Commerce.

★ 219 ★
Frozen Vegetables (SIC 2037)

Frozen Vegetables - Australia

Market shares, by company, are shown in percent, based on a 1989 total of $247 million.

Nestle	48.0%
McCain	26.0
Griffs	13.0
Kraft	5.0
Other	8.0

Source: *Quick Frozen Foods International*, January 1992, p. 126.

★ 220 ★
Fruit Juices (SIC 2037)

Orange Juice Market

Company shares are shown as percent of the 1991 total orange juice market.

Coca-Cola Foods' Minute Maid	22.6%
Tropicana Products	21.5
Citrus Hill	7.8
Others	48.1

Source: *Advertising Age*, July 6, 1992, p. 2.

★ 221 ★
Frozen Hamburgers (SIC 2038)

Frozen Beefburgers/Hamburgers - Australia

Market shares, by company, are based on 1989 total of $18.1 million, shown in percent.

Birdseye	24.3%
I&J	24.0
Barons Table	14.7
Other	37.0

Source: *Quick Frozen Foods International*, January 1992, p. 126.

★ 222 ★
Frozen Meals (SIC 2038)

Frozen Dinner Producers

Company shares are shown in percent, based on an estimated market of $1.2 billion.

ConAgra	43.0%
Campbell Soup Co.	34.0
Kraft General Foods	8.2
Tyson	6.9
Other	7.9

Source: *Advertising Age*, February 17, 1992, p. 59, from Nielsen Marketing Research.

★ 223 ★
Frozen Meals (SIC 2038)

Frozen Ready Meal Producers - Australia

Company shares are based on a 1989 market total of $69 million, shown in percent.

Herbert Adams	22.4%
Wedgewood	22.0
Big Ben	13.6
Woolworths	7.5
Buttercup	7.4
Farmland (Coles)	5.7
Franklins	3.7
Black & Gold	3.0
Sargent's	2.1
Other	12.6

Source: *Quick Frozen Foods International*, January 1992, p. 126.

★ 224 ★
Frozen Pastry (SIC 2038)

Frozen Fruit Pies - Australia

Company shares are shown in percent, based on 1989 market total of $22.2 million.

Nanna's	47.8%
Sara Lee	16.1
House brands/generic	22.1
Others	14.0

Source: *Quick Frozen Foods International*, January 1992, p. 126.

★ 225 ★
Frozen Pastry (SIC 2038)

Frozen Savory Pastry Producers - Australia

Company shares are based on 1989 total of $84 million in sales, shown in percent.

Petersville	33.0%
McCain	17.0
House brands	40.0
Other	10.0

Source: *Quick Frozen Foods International*, January 1992, p. 126.

★ 226 ★
Frozen Pastry (SIC 2038)

Frozen Unbaked Pastry - Australia

Company shares are shown in percent, based on a 1989 total of $22.4 million in sales.

Pampas	75.9%
Sara Lee	3.0
I&J	2.8
Other	18.3

Source: *Quick Frozen Foods International*, January 1992, p. 126.

★ 227 ★
Frozen Snacks (SIC 2038)

Frozen Chinese Snacks - Australia

Company shares are shown in percent, based on a 1989 total of $15.5 million.

Ho Mai/Golden Wok	.60.0%
Marathon	.30.0
Other	.10.0

Source: *Quick Frozen Foods International*, January 1992, p. 126.

★ 228 ★
Flour and Cereal Products (SIC 2040)

Flour and Cereal Product Consumption

Shares by type of product are based on per capita consumption of flour and cereal products in 1970 and 1990, shown in percent.

	1970	1990
Wheat flour	82.5%	74.3%
Corn products	7.6	11.9
Rice	5.3	9.0
Oat products	3.1	4.0
Barley products	0.6	0.5
Rye flour	0.9	0.3

Source: *FoodReview*, July 1991, p. 12.

★ 229 ★
Flour Products (SIC 2041)

Refrigerated Dough Manufacturers

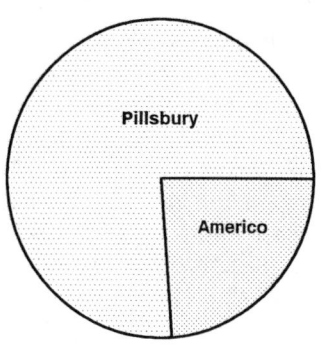

Company shares are shown in percent.

Pillsbury	.76.0%
Americo	.24.0

Source: Investext, Thomson Financial Networks, March 2, 1992, from Merrill Lynch Capital Markets.

★ 230 ★
Milling (SIC 2041)

Milling Capacities - U.S.

Capacities of U.S. flour mills are shown in thousands of hundredweights (cwt) for 1990. Data for the following large milling firms include capacities of smaller milling firms which they have acquired, shown in parentheses: ConAgra, Inc. (International Multifoods Corp., Peavey Co., Colorado Milling and Elevator Co., Standard Milling, Sunshine Biscuits); ADM (Dixie-Portland Flour Mills, Centennial Mills, Acme-Evans); Cargill (Seaboard Allied Milling Corp., Ross Industries); and Pillsbury, Inc. (Tennant and Hoyt Co.). Market shares are shown in percent.

	(000 cwt)	Share
ConAgra	276.5	25.2%
ADM Milling Co./ADM Holding Co.	224.7	20.5
Cargill, Inc.	149.2	13.6
Pillsbury, Inc..	119.7	10.9
General Mills, Inc.	66.7	6.1
Cereal Food, Proc., Inc.	68.3	6.2
Bay State Milling Co.	50.7	4.6
Nabisco Brands, Inc.	28.0	2.6
Mennel Milling Co.	22.7	2.1

Continued on next page.

★ 230 ★ *Continued*

Milling (SIC 2041)

Milling Capacities - U.S.

Capacities of U.S. flour mills are shown in thousands of hundredweights (cwt) for 1990. Data for the following large milling firms include capacities of smaller milling firms which they have acquired, shown in parentheses: ConAgra, Inc. (International Multifoods Corp., Peavey Co., Colorado Milling and Elevator Co., Standard Milling, Sunshine Biscuits); ADM (Dixie-Portland Flour Mills, Centennial Mills, Acme-Evans); Cargill (Seaboard Allied Milling Corp., Ross Industries); and Pillsbury, Inc. (Tennant and Hoyt Co.). Market shares are shown in percent.

	(000 cwt)	Share
North Dakota Mill	18.0	1.6%
Italgrani USA, Inc.	15.6	1.4
Amber Milling Co.	15.0	1.4
Fisher Mills, Inc.	15.0	1.4
Midwest Grain Products	14.0	1.3
Bartlett Milling Co.	13.0	1.2

Source: *Food Review*, April 1991, p. 36, from *Milling Directory/Buyers' Guide*.

★ 231 ★

Milling (SIC 2041)

Milling Companies

Capacities of the 18 largest wheat and rye milling companies totaled 1,195,940 CWT (hundredweights). Relative shares are shown in percent.

	CWTs	% of Group
ConAgra Inc.	284,600	23.8%
Cargill, Inc.	225,400	18.8
ADM Milling Co.	221,700	18.5
General Mills, Inc.	73,000	6.1
Cereal Food Processors, Inc.	69,800	5.8
Pillsbury Inc.	69,400	5.8
Bay State Milling Co.	55,000	4.6
Italgrani U.S.A., Inc.	29,240	2.4
Nabisco Brands, Inc.	28,000	2.3
Amber Milling Co.	23,000	1.9
The Mennel Milling Co.	22,700	1.9
North Dakota Mill & Elevator	20,000	1.7
Bartlett Milling Co.	16,500	1.4
Fisher Mills Inc.	15,000	1.3

	CWTs	% of Group
Midwest Grain Products, Inc.	14,000	1.2%
Star of the West Milling Co.	9,900	0.8
Shawnee Milling co.	9,500	0.8
Siemer Milling Co.	9,200	0.8

Source: *Milling & Baking News*, p. 10.

★ 232 ★

Cereal (SIC 2043)

Breakfast Cereal Producers

Shares of the $7.5 billion ready-to-eat cereal market are shown in percent.

Kellogg	38.0%
General Mills	28.0
Post	11.0
Quaker	7.0
Ralston	6.0
Nabisco	4.0
Private label	5.0
Other	1.0

Source: *The Wall Street Journal*, December 16, 1991, p. B1.

★ 233 ★

Cereal (SIC 2043)

Cereal Makers

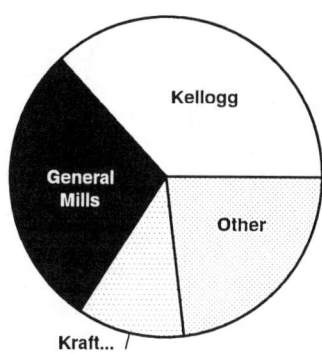

Leading manufacturer shares of the $7 billion ready-to-eat cereal market are shown for the 52 weeks ended April 18, 1992. Shares are shown in percent.

Kellogg	36.5%
General Mills	29.4
Kraft General Foods' Post Division	11.3
Other	22.8

Source: *Advertising Age*, July 20, 1992, p. 3, from Nielsen Marketing Research.

★ 234 ★

Cereal (SIC 2043)

Cereal Outside North America

Manufacturer shares of the ready-to-eat cereal market are shown in percent.

Kellogg	52.0%
Weetabix	6.6
Quaker Oats	4.2
CPWI	4.0
Sanitarium	3.5
Uncle Toby's	2.9
Private label	10.0
Other	0.5

Source: Investext, Thomson Financial Networks, May 28, 1992, from The First Boston Corporation.

★ 235 ★

Cereal (SIC 2043)

Ready-to-Eat Cereal Market

Market shares, by company, are shown in percent for 1989, 1990, and 1991.

	1989	1990	1991
Kellogg	39.7%	37.5%	37.5%
General Mills	23.4	24.3	25.4
Post/GF	10.9	11.3	11.5
Quaker Oats	7.9	7.8	7.6
Private Label	5.2	6.5	7.4
Ralston Purina	5.6	6.1	4.7
Nabisco	4.8	4.4	3.3
Other	2.5	2.1	2.6

Source: Investext, Thomson Financial Networks, May 11, 1992, from The First Boston Corporation.

★ 236 ★

Cereal (SIC 2043)

RTE Cereal Manufacturers

Company shares of the RTE (ready-to-eat) cereal market are shown in percent for 52 weeks of each year ending in October.

	1989	1990	1991
Kellogg Co.	39.8%	37.2%	37.2%
General Mills	26.2	28.0	28.8
General Foods	10.1	10.5	11.1
Quaker Oats	7.8	7.3	7.0
Ralston Purina	6.2	6.9	5.7
Nabisco	4.6	4.3	4.3
Private label	5.3	5.8	6.8

Source: Investext, Thomson Financial Networks, January 21, 1992, from Prudential Securities Inc.

★ 237 ★

Cereal (SIC 2043)

RTE Cereal Market

Company shares are shown as percent of the U.S. RTE (ready-to-eat) cereal market in 1989, 1990 and 1991.

	'89	'90	'91
Kellogg	39.7%	37.5%	38.8%
General Mills	23.4	24.3	23.8
Post/General Foods	10.9	11.3	11.2
Quaker Oats	7.9	7.4	7.4
Ralston-Purina	5.6	6.1	4.7

Continued on next page.

★ 237 ★ *Continued*

Cereal (SIC 2043)

RTE Cereal Market

Company shares are shown as percent of the U.S. RTE (ready-to-eat) cereal market in 1989, 1990 and 1991.

	'89	'90	'91
Nabisco	4.8%	4.4%	3.4%
Private-label brands	5.2	6.5	7.4
Other	2.5	2.5	3.3

Source: *FW*, June 11, 1991, p. 45, from Nielson Marketing Research.

★ 238 ★

Cereal (SIC 2043)

Supermarket Cereal

Sales of the top 10 supermarket ready-to-eat cereal brands accounted for 33.4% of the $7.041 billion market for 52 weeks ending May 16, 1992. Shares are shown in percent.

General Mills' Cheerios	$ 331.7	4.7%
Kellogg's Frosted Flakes	306.2	4.3
Kellogg's Corn Flakes	231.9	3.3
General Mills' Honey Nut Cheerios	229.7	3.3
Kellogg's Rice Krispies	227.8	3.2
Kellogg's Raisin Bran	203.8	2.9
Kellogg's Frosted Mini-Wheats	183.0	2.6
Kellogg's Froot Loops	165.4	2.3
General Mills' Lucky Charms	142.6	2.0
Private labels	340.2	4.8
Other	4,678.7	66.6

Source: *Advertising Age*, July 20, 1992, p. 20, from A.C. Nielsen ScanTrack.

★ 239 ★

Flour Products (SIC 2045)

Cake Mix Manufacturers

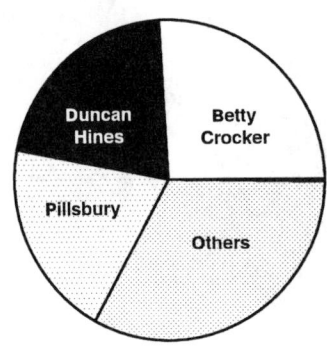

Shares are shown in percent.

Betty Crocker	26.0%
Duncan Hines	21.0
Pillsbury	20.0
Others	33.0

Source: Investext, Thomson Financial Networks, March 2, 1992, from Merrill Lynch Capital Markets.

★ 240 ★

Corn Syrup (SIC 2046)

High Fructose Corn Syrup - North America

Company shares are shown in percent for 1992.

ADM	30.7%
Staley	24.0
Cargill	18.4
CPC	11.0
American Maize	9.0
Roquette	5.4
Coors	1.5

Source: Investext, Thomson Financial Networks, February 7, 1992, from Donaldson, Lufkin & Jenrette Securities.

★ 241 ★

Pet Food (SIC 2047)

Cat and Dog Food Sales

Cat and dog food sales totaled $6,401.0 million in 1991. Market shares are shown in percent.

Dog food

Dry dog food	.31.0%
Canned dog food	.17.6
Dog treats	. 7.7
Moist dog food	. 2.0
Soft-dry dog food	. 2.9

Cat food

Canned cat food	.22.0
Dry cat food	.13.9
Moist cat food	. 2.4
Cat treats	. 0.5

Source: Investext, Thomson Financial Networks, April 10, 1992, from Wheat First Butcher & Singer, Inc.

★ 242 ★

Pet Food (SIC 2047)

Cat Treat Brands

Brand shares are shown in percent, based on sales of $34.5 million in 1990 and $35 million in 1991 (estimate).

	1990	1991
Pounce (Quaker Oats)	8.5%	6.0%
Bonkers (Beatrice)	7.0	6.0
9-Lives Finicky Bits (Heinz)	4.0	4.4
Whisker Lickins (Ralston Purina) . .	3.0	2.9
Others	12.0	15.7

Source: Investext, Thomson Financial Networks, April 10, 1992, from Wheat First Butcher & Singer, Inc.

★ 243 ★

Pet Food (SIC 2047)

Moist Cat Food

Brand shares are shown in percent, based on sales of $170.0 million in 1990 and $154.0 million in 1991 (estimate).

	1990	1991
Tender Vittles (Ralston Purina) . . .	57.9%	60.1%
9-Lives/Tender Meal (Heinz) . . .	13.8	13.4
Happy Cat (Ralston Purina)	15.9	12.0
Moist Meals (Quaker Oats)	0.9	0.0
All others	11.5	14.4

Source: Investext, Thomson Financial Networks, April 10, 1992, from Wheat First Butcher & Singer, Inc.

★ 244 ★

Pet Food (SIC 2047)

Pet Food Manufacturers

Company shares are shown in percent, based on 1991 total market.

Ralston Purina	.26.0%
Nestle	.15.0
Mars	.13.0
Heinz	.11.0
Quaker Oats	.11.0
Alpo	. 8.0
Others	.16.0

Source: Investext, Thomson Financial Networks, March 2, 1992, from Merrill Lynch Capital Markets.

★ 245 ★

Pet Food (SIC 2047)

Pet Food Market Shares

Company shares are shown in percent, based on a total of $6,401.0 million in 1991.

Ralston Purina	.24.2%
Friskies PetCare (Nestle)	.14.9
Kal Kan (Mars)	.12.5
Heinz	.11.4
Quaker Oats	. 9.0
Alpo (Grand Met USA)	. 8.6
All others	.19.4

Source: Investext, Thomson Financial Networks, April 10, 1992, from Wheat First Butcher & Singer, Inc.

★ 246 ★

Pet Food (SIC 2047)

Pet Food Market Shares

Market shares, by company, are shown in percent.

Ralston Purina	26.0%
Carnation	15.0
Kal Kan	13.0
Heinz	11.0
Quaker Oats	11.0
Alpo	9.0
Other	15.0

Source: Investext, Thomson Financial Networks, May 11, 1992, from The First Boston Corporation.

★ 247 ★

Pet Food (SIC 2047)

Pet Food Producers

Manufacturer shares are shown in percent based on $4.74 billion in supermarket sales in the year ended February 22, 1992.

Ralston Purina Co.	25.9%
Nestle USA/Friskies Petcare	15.0
Mars/Kal Kan Foods	12.9
Heinz Pet Products	11.3
Quaker Oats Co.	10.9
Grand Met/Alpo Petfoods	9.2
Other	14.8

Source: *Advertising Age*, April 20, 1992, p. 45, from Nielsen Marketing Research.

★ 248 ★

Baked Goods (SIC 2050)

Baked Goods by Outlet

Shares, by segment, are shown as percent of retail sales.

Five leading wholesalers	55.0%
Other wholesale	16.0
In-store	17.0
Freestanding	12.0

Source: *Restaurant Business*, March 20, 1992, p. 2, from FIND/SVP.

★ 249 ★

Baked Goods (SIC 2051)

Bread and Cake Bakers

Leading bread and cake bakers are ranked by 1989 sales, shown in millions of dollars; relative market shares are shown in percent.

	Sales ($ mil.)	% of Group
Continental Baking Co.	$ 1,836	25.6%
Campbell Taggart, Inc.	1,400	19.5
Interstate Bakeries, Corp.	1,079	15.0
Flowers Industries, Inc.	782	10.9
Pepperidge Farm, Inc.	548	7.6
Best Foods Baking Group	530	7.4
Entenmann's, Inc.	502	7.0
Sara Lee Bakery	502	7.0

Source: *Food Review*, April 1991, p. 40, from *Bakery Production and Marketing*.

★ 250 ★

Baked Goods (SIC 2051)

Bread Products

Market segmentation is shown in percent.

White bread	35.6%
Soft variety	27.7
Specialty	18.8
Buns	13.9
Rolls	4.0

Source: Investext, Thomson Financial Networks, February 4, 1992, from Prudential Securities, Inc.

★ 251 ★

Baked Goods (SIC 2051)

Cakes, Pies, and Pastries

Shares are shown in percent, based on an industry total of $74.0 million in advertising expenditures in 1991.

Kellogg Co.	
Kelloggs Pop Tarts	33.3%
Mrs. Smiths Frozen Desserts	7.7
Mrs. Smiths Ready/Serve Desserts	2.6
Ralston Purina	
Hostess Light Snack Cakes	5.1
Hostess Snack Cakes	0.9
Other	0.1
Phillip Morris Cos.	

Continued on next page.

★ 251 ★ *Continued*
Baked Goods (SIC 2051)

Cakes, Pies, and Pastries

Shares are shown in percent, based on an industry total of $74.0 million in advertising expenditures in 1991.

Entenmann's Baked Goods	7.7%
Other	0.4
McKee Baking Co.	
Little Debbie Cakes	11.0
H.J. Heinz Co.	
Weight Watchers Frozen Desserts	3.5
Sara Lee	
Sara Lee Frozen Cakes	4.6
Other	7.1
Campbell Soup Co.	
Pepperidge Farm Frozen Desserts	0.4
Other	1.2
Anheuser-Busch Cos. Inc.	
Break Cakes	0.5
Interstate Bakeries Corp.	
Dolly Madison Cakes	2.2
All other	11.7

Source: Investext, Thomson Financial Networks, April 28, 1992, from Wheat First Butcher & Singer, Inc. and leading national advertisers.

★ 252 ★
Baked Goods (SIC 2051)

Sweet Biscuit Market - European Community

Company shares are based on industry sales of $9.4 billion, shown in percent.

UB	7.8%
BSN	7.0
Bahlsen	3.6
PFI/GMI	1.1
Other/local	80.5

Source: Investext, Thomson Financial Networks, May 18, 1992, from Dean Witter Reynolds.

★ 253 ★
Cookies and Crackers (SIC 2052)

Cookie and Cracker Manufacturers

Leading cookie and cracker bakers are ranked by 1989 sales, shown in millions of dollars. Percent shares are shown as a percent of group total.

	Sales (000)	% of Group
Nabisco Biscuit Co.	$ 2,163	44.1%
Keebler Co.	1,379	28.1
Sunshine Biscuits, Inc.	540	11.0
Lance, Inc.	432	8.8
McKee Baking Co.	395	8.0

Source: *Food Review*, April 1991, p. 40, from *Bakery Production and Marketing*.

★ 254 ★
Cookies and Crackers (SIC 2052)

Cookie Market Shares

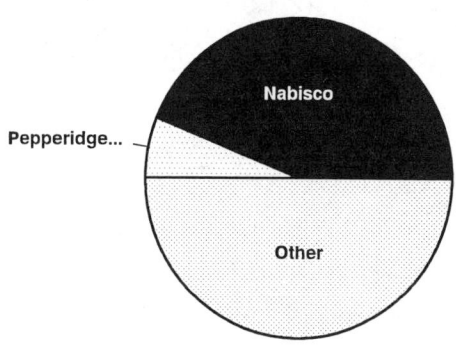

Company shares are shown as percent of the $3.2 billion cookie market.

Nabisco	44.0%
Pepperidge Farm	6.0
Other	50.0

Source: *Advertising Age*, July 13, 1992, p. 4.

★ 255 ★

Cookies and Crackers (SIC 2052)

Major Cookie Brands

Supermarket unit sales and market shares for major cookie brands are shown for the 52 weeks ended June 13, 1992.

	Units	Share
Nabisco	410.2	28.2%
Keebler	180.2	12.4
Sunshine	96.0	6.6
Pepperidge Farm	36.2	2.5
Total private label	199.1	13.7
Other	532.4	36.6

Source: *The Wall Street Journal*, July 13, 1992, p. B1, from Nielsen Marketing Research.

★ 256 ★

Confectionery (SIC 2060)

Candy Retail Sales - Australia

Candy retail sales were $U.S.1.235 billion in 1990 and $U.S.1.238 billion in 1991 (estimated). Segment distribution is shown in percent.

	1990	1991
Chocolate bars	16.8%	16.5%
Molded chocolate blocks	9.4	9.7
Boxed chocolates	6.5	5.2
Other chocolate	8.2	8.9
Total chocolate	40.9	40.3
Non-chocolate candies	18.3	19.5

Source: *Candy Industry*, July 1992, p. H 17, from *Australian Supermarket News*.

★ 257 ★

Confectionery (SIC 2060)

Candy Snack Manufacturers

Confectionery companies are ranked according to sales from candy and tobacco distributors to retail outlets in 1990. Market shares are shown in percent. Total cumulative share for top 25 companies is 90.07%.

Hershey Chocolate Co.	17.56%
Mars Inc.	16.72
American Chicle Div. Warner-Lambert	11.62
Wm. Wrigley	10.03
RJR Nabisco	8.90
Nestle U.S.A.	7.78
Leaf Inc.	3.93%
Topps	1.97
Tootsie Roll Ind.	1.51
E.J. Brach	1.49
Ferrero U.S.A.	1.14
Procter & Gamble	0.90
Fleer Corp.	0.79
Impel Marketing	0.78
GoodMark Foods	0.62
Ferrara Pan Candy	0.54
Phoenix Confections	0.51
Upper Deck Card Co.	0.45
Van Melle	0.43
Just Born	0.43
Keebler	0.42
Cornnuts, Inc.	0.42
Sathers Inc.	0.41
Ragold Inc.	0.40
Storck U.S.A.	0.32
Other	9.93

Source: *Candy Industry*, 1991, p. H6, from ICC/ACCUTRACKS.

★ 258 ★

Confectionery (SIC 2060)

Candy Snack Market

Market shares, by type, are shown in percent, based on 1990 sales from candy and tobacco distributors to retail outlets.

Chocolate bars	34.0%
Chewing/bubble gum	23.2
Chocolate other	11.2
Non-chocolate bars	9.6
Mints/rolls	9.0
Non-chocolate other	8.7
Pops and others	4.2

Source: *Candy Industry*, 1991, p. H6, from ICC/ACCUTRACKS.

★ 259 ★
Confectionery (SIC 2060)

Confectionery Products

Segment distribution is shown in percent.

Bar chocolate candy 28.79%
Bagged chocolate candy 20.65
Non-chocolate bagged candy 18.31
Gum 16.18
Roll candy 6.37
Boxed chocolates 5.88
Miscellaneous 3.82

Source: *Discount Merchandiser*, June 1992, p. 61, from survey.

★ 260 ★
Confectionery (SIC 2060)

Specialty Food Companies

Top specialty food companies are shown with percent market shares, based on sales for year ended March 1991.

Lindt & Sprungli 15.8%
Pez 12.6
Commerce Foods (La Vosgienne) 6.5
Callard & Bowser 5.6
Jacobs Suchard (Tobler) 4.1
Nestle (Sarotti, Perugina) 4.0
Farley Candy 3.5
Foreign Candy (Black Forest) 3.3
Droste 3.2
Abuelita (Mexican candies) 2.3
Ghirardelli 2.3
I.A.C. (Elite) 1.7
Ricola 1.5
Koala (gummy products) 1.5
E.J. Brach 1.3
Other 30.8

Source: *Candy Industry*, July 1991, p. H7, from SFTI.

★ 261 ★
Sweeteners (SIC 2060)

Caloric Sweetener Consumption

Percent distribution of the sweetener market by segment is based on per capita consumption in 1990.

Refined (cane and beet) sugar 46.7%
Corn sweeteners
  High fructose corn syrup 35.7
  Glucose 13.8
  Dextrose 2.8
Honey 0.7
Edible syrups 0.3

Source: *FoodReview*, July 1991, p. 12.

★ 262 ★
Chocolate (SIC 2064)

Chocolate Bar Makers - Australia

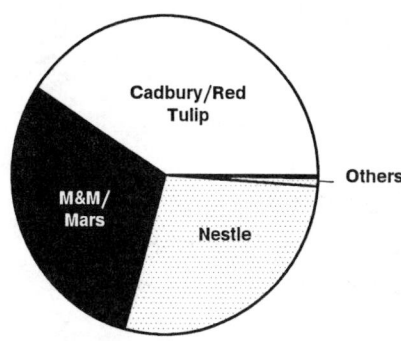

1991 manufacturer shares of Australian chocolate bar market are shown, by type, in percent.

Cadbury/Red Tulip 41.0%
M&M/Mars 30.0
Nestle 28.0
Others 1.0

Source: *Candy Industry*, July 1992, p. H17, from *Australian Supermarket News*.

★ 263 ★

Chocolate (SIC 2064)

Chocolate Brand Shares

Chocolate brand shares are shown in percent, based on sales for year ended 9/91. Manufacturers are shown in parentheses.

Snickers (M&M/Mars)	10.8%
Reese's Peanut Butter Cups (Hershey) . . .	8.8
M&M's Peanut Chocolate Candies (M&M/ Mars)	7.4
M&M's Plain Chocolate Candies (M&M/ Mars)	6.0
Kit Kat (Hershey)	4.6
Milky Way (M&M/Mars)	4.5
Butterfinger (Nestle)	3.7
Hershey's Milk Chocolate with Almonds (Hershey)	3.3
Other	50.9

Source: *Candy Industry*, January 1992, p. H7.

★ 264 ★

Chocolate (SIC 2064)

Chocolate Brands

The 10 leading chocolate brands in 1991 represented 53.5% of the chocolate brands market. Manufacturers' names are in parentheses. Market shares are shown in percent.

Snickers (M&M/Mars)	9.5%
Reese's Peanut Butter Cups (Hershey) . . .	8.7
M&Ms Peanut Chocolate Candies (M&M/ Mars)	7.3
M&Ms Plain Chocolate Candies (M&M/ Mars)	6.0
Kit Kat (Hershey)	4.7

Milky Way (M&M/Mars)	4.6%
Butterfinger (Nestle)	3.9
Hershey's Milk Chocolate with Almonds (Hershey)	3.3
Crunch (Nestle)	3.0
Hershey's Milk Chocolate (Hershey)	2.7
Other	46.5

Source: *Candy Industry*, July 1992, p. H7, from *ICC/ Accutracks Candy/Snacks Report.*

★ 265 ★

Confectionery (SIC 2064)

Best Selling Lollipop Brands

The 10 leading lollipop brands dominated the 1991 market with an 83.0% share. Manufacturers' names are in parentheses. Brand shares are shown in percent.

Blow Pops (Tootsie Roll)	21.5%
Tootsie Pops (Tootsie Roll)	17.3
Charms Pops (Tootsie Roll)	14.7
Ring Pops (Topps)	8.3
Dum Dum Pops (Spangler)	5.6
Push Pops (Topps)	5.6
Saf-T-Pops (Spangler)	3.4
Disney Pops (American Candy)	2.6
Tootsie Bunch Pops (Tootsie Roll)	2.1
Life Saver Pops (LifeSavers)	1.9
Other	17.0

Source: *Candy Industry*, July 1992, p. H 9, from ICC/ Accutracks Candy/Snacks Report.

★ 266 ★

Confectionery (SIC 2064)

Breathmint Candy Brands

Breathmint candy brands are shown with percent shares, based on sales for year ended 9/91. Manufacturers are shown in parentheses.

LifeSavers (LifeSavers)	26.9%
Certs (American Chicle)	19.6
Breath Savers (LifeSavers)	12.8
Tic Tac (Ferrero)	10.6
Certs Sugarfree (American Chicle)	6.1
LifeSavers Holes (LifeSavers)	4.7
Certs Mini Mints (American Chicle)	4.1
Mentos (Van Melle)	4.0
Fruit Juicers (LifeSavers)	2.8

Continued on next page.

★ 266 ★ *Continued*

Confectionery (SIC 2064)

Breathmint Candy Brands

Breathmint candy brands are shown with percent shares, based on sales for year ended 9/91. Manufacturers are shown in parentheses.

Clorets (American Chicle) 2.7%
Other 5.7

Source: *Candy Industry*, January 1992, p. H7.

★ 267 ★

Confectionery (SIC 2064)

Candy and Snack Suppliers

The 15 largest candy and snack suppliers for the 12 months ended January 1992 dominated the market with an 85.47% share. Shares are shown in percent.

M & M/Mars 17.93%
Hershey Chocolate USA 17.01
American Chicle Group 11.06
Wm. Wrigley Jr. Co. 9.83
RJR Nabisco 8.71
Nestle Foods Corp. 7.99
Leaf Inc. 3.75
Sathers, Inc. 1.95
The Topps Company, Inc. 1.84
Tootsie Roll Industries Inc. 1.27
E.J. Brach Corp. 1.07
The Upper Deck Co., Inc. 0.98
SkyBox International 0.72
Ferrero USA 0.70
Beatrice 0.65
Other 14.53

Source: *Candy Marketer*, May 1992, p. 45, from ICC/ Accutracks.

★ 268 ★

Confectionery (SIC 2064)

Candy - Supermarket Sales

Segment distribution of 1991 sales is based on a total volume of 3.575 million units and total sales of $2.603 billion.

	Unit Share	$ Share
Chocolate candies	56.2%	41.1%
Non-chocolate candies	16.6	20.2
Chocolate miniatures	5.4	17.4

	Unit Share	$ Share
Chocolate special	3.2%	6.8%
Breathmints	6.9	4.2
Marshmallows	3.4	3.6
Hard roll candies	6.1	3.2
Lollipops	1.1	1.4
Non-chocolate miniatures	0.6	1.2
Candy kits	0.1	0.3
Dietetic non-chocolate	0.2	0.3
Dietetic chocolate	0.1	0.3

Source: *Candy Industry*, July 1992, p. H5, from Nielsen Marketing Research.

★ 269 ★

Confectionery (SIC 2064)

Confectionery Products

Segment distribution of sales by candy and tobacco distributors is shown in percent. Figures are based on totals of $2.488 billion in 1990 and $2.697 billion in 1991. N.S.K. stands for not specified by kind.

	1990	1991
Chocolate bars	45.5%	46.0%
Non-chocolate bars	10.8	11.5
Chocolate, other packs	11.5	11.3
Non-chocolate, other packs . . .	10.7	11.2
Mints and hard rolls	11.7	10.9
Cough suppressants/throat drops .	3.2	3.0
Lollipops	2.0	2.0
Chocolate changemakers	2.3	2.0
Non-chocolate N.S.K.	1.4	1.0
Chocolate N.S.K.	0.4	0.5
Granola bars	0.5	0.5

Source: *Candy Industry*, July 1992, p. H6, from ICC/ ACCUTRACKS.

★ 270 ★

Confectionery (SIC 2064)

Confectionery Vending Sales

Segment distribution of confectionery vending sales, based on totals of $449.5 million in 1990 and $477.3 million in 1991 is shown in percent.

	'90	'91
Chocolate bars	79.5%	78.8%
Non-chocolate bars	14.7	15.1
Mints/hard roll candies	3.8	3.9
Granola bars	2.0	2.2

Source: *Candy Industry*, July 1992, p. H10, from DEBS Vending Report.

★ 271 ★

Confectionery (SIC 2064)

Hard Roll/Breath Mint Leaders

The top 10 breath mint brand shares represented 97.8% of the breath mint market in 1991. Manufacturers' names are in parentheses. Market shares are shown in percent.

Certs (American Chicle)	29.3%
Life Savers (LifeSavers)	27.1
Breath Savers (LifeSavers)	12.9
Tic Tac (Ferrero)	10.4
Life Saver Holes (LifeSavers)	4.9
Mentos (Van Melle)	4.3
Clorets (American Chicle)	3.1
Velamints (Ragold)	2.1
Fruit Juicers (Lifesavers)	2.0
Reeds Rolls (Amurol Products)	1.6
Other	2.2

Source: *Candy Industry*, July 1992, p. H 8, from ICC/ Accutracks Candy/Snacks Report.

★ 272 ★

Confectionery (SIC 2064)

Lollipop Brands

Lollipop brand shares, shown in percent, are based on sales for year ended 9/91.

Bio Pops (Tootsie Roll)	22.0%
Tootsie Pops (Tootsie Roll)	17.5
Charms Pops (Tootsie Roll)	13.9
Ring Pops (Topps)	8.1
Dum Dum Pops (Spangler)	5.9
Push Pops (Topps)	5.7
Saf-T-Pops (Spangler)	3.7
Disney Pops (American Candy)	2.2
Tootsie Bunch Pops (Tootsie Roll)	1.9
Thumb Fun (Topps)	1.8
Other	17.3

Source: *Candy Industry*, January 1992, p. H7.

★ 273 ★

Confectionery (SIC 2064)

Non-Chocolate Candies

The top 10 brand shares of non-chocolate candy sales constituted 41.8% of the non-chocolate candy brands market in 1991. Manufacturers' names are in parentheses. Market shares are shown in percent.

Sathers non-chocolate items (Sathers) . . .	7.2%
Skittles Bite Size Candies (M&M/Mars) . .	6.4
Starburst Fruit Chews (M&M/Mars) . . .	5.8
E.J. Brach non-chocolate items/E.J. Brach .	4.3
Y&S Candies (Hershey)	4.2
Jolly Ranchers (Leaf)	3.2
Pay Day (Leaf)	3.1
Now & Later (Phoenix)	3.0
Tootsie Roll (Tootsie Roll)	2.4
Sweetarts (Sunline/Nestle)	2.3
Other	58.2

Source: *Candy Industry*, July 1992, p. H 8, from ICC/ Accutracks Candy/Snacks Report.

★ 274 ★

Confectionery (SIC 2064)

Non-Chocolate Candy Brand Shares

Brand shares are shown in percent, based on sales for year ended 9/91.

Skittles Bite Size Candies (M&M/Mars) . .	6.4%
Starburst Fruit Chews (M&M/Mars)	5.9

Continued on next page.

★ 274 ★ *Continued*

Confectionery (SIC 2064)

Non-Chocolate Candy Brand Shares

Brand shares are shown in percent, based on sales for year ended 9/91.

Sathers non-chocolate items (Sathers)	5.6%
E.J. Brach non-chocolate items (Brach)	4.2
Y&S Candies (Hershey)	4.2
Jolly Rancher (Leaf)	3.4
Pay Day (Leaf)	3.2
Now & Later (Phoenix)	3.1
Tootsie Roll (Tootsie Roll)	2.5
Sweetarts (Sunline/Nestle)	2.2
Other	59.3

Source: *Candy Industry*, January 1992, p. H7.

★ 275 ★

Confectionery (SIC 2064)

Sugar Confection Market - European Community

Company shares are based on industry sales (excluding chocolate) of $8.6 billion, shown in percent.

Cadbury	5.8%
Warner Lambert	4.7
PFI/GMI	0.2
Other/Local	89.3

Source: Investext, Thomson Financial Networks, May 18, 1992, from Dean Witter Reynolds.

★ 276 ★

Chocolate (SIC 2066)

Chocolate Bar Producers

Shares of the domestic market are based on a total of $5.0 billion in 1991.

Hershey	34.6%
Mars	31.6
Nestle	9.9
Brach	9.4
Nabisco	2.5
Other	12.0

Source: *USA TODAY*, February 29, 1992, p. 4B, from Merrill Lynch.

★ 277 ★

Chewing Gum (SIC 2067)

Chewing Gum Leaders

Manufacturer shares are shown in percent based on a total market of $1.3 billion in 1991.

Wm. Wrigley Jr. Co.	42.6%
Warner-Lambert Co.'s American Chicle Group	23.9
Planter LifeSavers Co.	17.5
Other	16.0

Source: *Advertising Age*, April 27, 1992, p. 50, from Nielsen Marketing Research.

★ 278 ★

Chewing Gum (SIC 2067)

Chewing Gum Manufacturers

Shares are shown in percent for 1991.

Wrigley	47.0%
American Chicle	23.7
Lifesavers	16.9
Other	12.5

Source: Investext, Thomson Financial Networks, January 23, 1992, from Shearson Lehman Brothers, Inc.

★ 279 ★

Chewing Gum (SIC 2067)

Chewing Gum Market Shares by Brand

Chewing and bubble gum brand shares are shown in percent, based on sales for year ended 9/91.

Extra (Wrigley)	15.5%
Trident (American)	11.6
Care Free (LifeSavers)	8.6
Doublemint (Wrigley)	8.2
Big Red (Wrigley)	6.0
Dentyne (American Chicle)	5.9
Juicy Fruit (Wigley)	5.0
Spearmint (Wrigliy)	4.7
Bubble Yum (LifeSavers)	4.7
Bubblicious (American Chicle)	4.5
Other	25.3

Source: *Candy Industry*, January 1992, p. H7.

★ 280 ★

Chewing Gum (SIC 2067)

Chewing Gum Vending Sales

Segment distribution of chewing gum vending sales, based on totals of $27.3 million in 1990 and $27.9 million in 1991, is shown is percent.

	'90	'91
Sugared gum	59.0%	58.8%
Sugar-free gum	41.0	41.2

Source: *Candy Industry*, July 1992, p. H 10, from DEBS Vending Report.

★ 281 ★

Chewing Gum (SIC 2067)

Chewing Gums

1991 shares of 10 best-selling chewing gum brands accounted for 75.1% of the market. Manufacturer names are in parentheses. Brand shares are shown in percent.

Extra (Wrigley)	16.2%
Trident (American Chicle)	11.8
Care Free (LifeSavers)	8.7
Doublemint (Wrigley)	8.1
Big Red (Wrigley)	6.2
Dentyne (American Chicle)	5.5
Juicy Fruit (Wrigley)	4.9
Spearmint (Wrigley)	4.8
Bubble Yum (LifeSavers)	4.7
Bubblicious (American Chicle)	4.4
Other	24.9

Source: *Candy Industry*, July 1992, p. H 10, from ICC/ Accutracks Candy/Snacks Report.

★ 282 ★

Chewing Gum (SIC 2067)

Gum Market

Segment distribution of sales by candy and tobacco distributors is shown in percent. Figures are based on totals of $752 million in 1990 and $806 million in 1991. N.S.K. stands for not specified by kind.

	1990	1991
Sugar-free gum	37.0%	39.8%
Sugared stick gum	34.6	34.1
Chunk bubble gum	14.1	13.9
All other gum	13.7	12.0
Gum N.S.K.	0.5	0.2

Source: *Candy Industry*, July 1992, p. H6, from ICC/ ACCUTRACKS.

★ 283 ★

Chewing Gum (SIC 2067)

Gum - Supermarket Sales

Segment distribution of 1991 sales is based on totals of 113 million units (1,000 stick equivalents) and $506 million.

	Unit Share	$ Share
Sugar-free chewing gum	36.6%	37.2%
Sugared chewing gum	41.1	36.4
Sugared bubble gum	11.6	14.1
Sugar-free bubble gum	10.7	12.3

Source: *Candy Industry*, July 1992, p. H5, from Nielsen Marketing Research.

★ 284 ★

Nuts (SIC 2068)

Snack Nut Market

Company shares are shown in percent, based on 1990 sales $1,200 million.

Planters	42.0%
Fisher	6.0
Johh B. Sanfilippo	5.0
Azar	4.0
Flavor House	4.0
Other	38.0

Source: Investext, Thomson Financial Networks, April 6, 1992, from William Blair & Company.

★ 285 ★
Fats and Oils (SIC 2070)

Fat and Oil Consumption

Fat and oil consumption per capita is shown in lbs. for 1989.

Fats and oils, fat-content basis	60.9
Vegetable	50.4
Animal	10.5
Fats and oils, product-weight basis	63.9
Salad cooking oils	23.9
Shortening	21.5
Margarine	10.2
Butter	4.3
Lard (direct use)	1.8
Edible tallow (direct use)	0.9
Other edible fats and oils	1.3

Source: *FoodReview*, July 1991, p. 10.

★ 286 ★
Fats and Oils (SIC 2070)

Oil Milling Market in the U.S.

Shares, by company, are shown in percent.

ADM	30.0%
Cargill	25.0
Beghin-Say	10.0
Other	35.0

Source: Investext, Thomson Financial Networks, June 4, 1992, from Credit Lyonnais Laing.

★ 287 ★
Cooking Oil (SIC 2079)

Cooking/Salad Oil Market

Shares, by company, are shown in percent.

Wesson	26.0%
Procter & Gamble	24.0
CPC	16.0
Other	44.0

Source: Investext, Thomson Financial Networks, June 15, 1992, from Kidder, Peabody & Company, Inc.

★ 288 ★
Alcoholic Beverages (SIC 2080)

Beverage Per Capita Consumption

U.S. adult per capita consumption of specified beverages is shown in gallons for 1991.

Beer	33.3
All wine	2.65
All wine under 14 percent alcohol	2.43
Table wine	2.00
All wine over 14 percent alcohol	1.80
Distilled spirits	0.22

Source: *Wines & Vines*, June 1992, p. 20.

★ 289 ★
Beverages (SIC 2080)

Beverage Company Sales per Employee

Company sales per employee are in dollars.

A & W Brands	$ 677,846
Glenmore Distill.	643,176
Coca-Cola	426,515
Seagram Co. Ltd.	348,125
Philip Morris	304,577
American Brands	281,243
Canandaigua Wine	276,685
Labatt (John)	245,426
Brown-Forman	239,363
Anheuser-Busch	236,476
Coca-Cola Enterprises	212,318
Coca-Cola Beverages	193,665
Coors (Adolph)	174,145
Cadbury Schweppes	171,499
Coca-Cola Bott. Cons.	150,712
Genesee Brewing	140,977
Molson Cos.	131,885
Whitman Corp.	94,494
Pepsico Inc.	57,801

Source: *Beverage World*, July 1991, p. 34, from Nordby International.

★ 290 ★

Beverages (SIC 2080)

Beverage Consumption in 1991

Beverage market penetration in 1991 is shown in percent.

Soft drinks	64.0%
Coffee	51.0
Juices	47.0
Milk	47.0
Tea	31.0
Cappuccino	0.4
Espresso	0.6

Source: *Detroit Free Press*, May 6, 1992, p. 1C, from 1991 Coffee Drinking Study, National Coffee Association of USA.

★ 291 ★

Beverages (SIC 2080)

Beverage Consumption - U.S.

Shares of stomach are shown in percent. Figures for 1991 are estimated. Coffee and tea data are based on a three-year moving average to counterbalance inventory swings. The wine category includes wine coolers.

	1990	1991
Soft drinks	26.1%	26.0%
Coffee	14.5	14.5
Beer	13.2	12.6
Milk	10.6	10.4
Bottled water	5.0	5.2
Tea	3.8	3.7
Juice	3.4	3.5
Powdered drinks	3.1	3.1
Wine	1.1	1.0
Distilled spirits	0.9	0.8
Other	18.2	19.2

Source: Investext, Thomson Financial Networks, February 26, 1992, from Wheat First Butcher & Singer, Inc.

★ 292 ★

Beverages (SIC 2080)

Beverage Industry Leaders

Companies are ranked by 1991 sales, shown in millions of dollars. Percent shares are based on group total of $56,581 million.

	Sales ($ mil.)	% of Group
Pepsico	$ 19,771	34.9%
Coca-Cola	11,572	20.5
Anheuser-Busch	10,996	19.4
Coca-Cola Enterprises	4,051	7.2
J.E. Seagram	3,680	6.5
Whitman	2,866	5.1
Adolph Coors	1,918	3.4
Brown-Forman	1,126	2.0
Dr. Pepper/Seven-Up	601	1.1

Source: *Fortune*, April 20, 1992, p. 260.

★ 293 ★

Beverages (SIC 2080)

Beverage Market

Shares of beverage consumption at table-service restaurants are shown in percent. Data are based on a study of beverage consumption patterns in 10,920 households.

Coffee	29.0%
Soft drinks	27.0
Tea	23.0
Beer	8.0
Wine	3.0
Milk	3.0
Fruit juice	2.0
Liquor	2.0
Other nonalcoholic	3.0

Source: *Restaurants & Institutions*, September 4, 1991, p. 22.

★ 294 ★

Beverages (SIC 2080)

Beverages by Type

Segment distribution of the 1991 market is shown in percent.

Carbonated soft drinks	25.0%
Tap water	19.0
Milk	15.0
Beer	12.0
Coffee	11.0
Juice	6.0
Other	12.0

Source: *The New York Times*, May 2, 1992, p. 19Y, from Information Resources and Coca-Cola Company.

★ 295 ★

Beverages (SIC 2080)

Supermarket Drink Brands

Sales of 10 leading supermarket shelf stable drink brands accounted for 82.5% of the $1.7537 billion market for 52 weeks ending May 16, 1992. Market shares are shown in percent.

Ocean Spray	$ 393.1	22.4%
Gatorade	314.8	17.9
Hi-C	172.1	9.8
Tropicana	137.6	7.8
Hawaiian Punch	85.7	6.6
Kool-Aid	77.8	4.9
Capri Sun	77.5	4.4

Squeezit	$ 47.3	4.4%
Welch's	28.0	2.7
Private labels	115.7	1.6
Other	304.1	17.5

Source: *Advertising Age*, July 20, 1992, p. 20, from A.C. Nielsen ScanTrack.

★ 296 ★

Beverages (SIC 2080)

Top Beverage Manufacturers

Companies are ranked by 1991 sales, shown in millions of dollars. Percent shares are based on group total of $49,347 million.

	Sales ($ mil.)	% of Group
Pepsico	$ 19,608	39.7%
Coca-Cola	11,572	23.5
Anheuser-Busch	10,996	22.3
Coca-Cola Enterprises	4,051	8.2
Adolph Coors	1,917	3.9
Brown-Forman	1,203	2.4

Source: *The 1992 Business Week 1000*, p. 170.

★ 297 ★

Liquor (SIC 2080)

Best-Selling Liquor Brands

Market shares, by brand, are shown in percent for 1990 and 1991, based on sales in millions of 9-liter cases. Table includes brands with sales more than one million 9-liter cases. Manufacturers' names are in parentheses.

	'90	'91
Bacardi (Bacardi Imports)	4.8%	4.6%
Smirnoff (Heublein Inc.)	3.8	3.7
Seagram's Gin (Seagram Co.)	2.4	2.6
7 Crown (Seagram Co.)	2.5	2.5
Bacardi Breezer (Bacardi Imports) . .	2.4	2.5
Jim Beam (James Beam)	2.3	2.3
Popov (Heublein Inc.)	2.2	2.3
Jack Daniel's (Brown-Forman Corp.) .	2.1	2.1
Canadian Mist (Brown-Forman Corp.)	2.1	2.0
Absolut (Carillon Importers)	1.7	1.8
Canadian Club (Hiram Walker) . . .	1.4	1.5
V.O. (Seagram Co.)	1.4	1.5
Gordon's Gin (Schenley)	1.4	1.4
Gallo Brandy (E&J Gallo)	1.4	1.4

Continued on next page.

★ 297 ★ *Continued*

Liquor (SIC 2080)

Best-Selling Liquor Brands

Market shares, by brand, are shown in percent for 1990 and 1991, based on sales in millions of 9-liter cases. Table includes brands with sales more than one million 9-liter cases. Manufacturers' names are in parentheses.

	'90	'91
Gordon's Vodka (Schenley)	1.4%	1.4%
Dewar's (Schenley)	1.4	1.4
Jose Cuervo (Heublein Inc.)	1.2	1.3
Windsor Supreme (James Beam)	1.3	1.3
Balck Velvet (Heublein Inc.)	1.2	1.2
Kahlua (Hiram Walker)	1.1	1.2
J&B Rare (Paddington)	1.1	1.1
Crown Royal (Seagram Co.)	0.9	1.1
Ancient Age (Ancient Age)	0.8	1.0
Kamchatka (James Beam/Heublein)	0.9	0.9
Gilbey's Vodka (James Beam)	0.8	0.9
Early Times (Brown-Forman Corp.)	0.8	0.8
Tanqueray (Schieflin & Somerset)	0.9	0.8
Southern Comfort (Brown-Forman Corp.)	0.8	0.8
Christian Bros Brandy (Heublein)	0.7	0.8
Skol (Glenmore Distillers)	0.7	0.8
Kessler (James Beam)	0.9	0.8
Gilbey's Gin (James Beam)	0.7	0.8
Stolichnaya (Monsieur Henri)	0.7	0.7
Lord Calvert (James Beam)	0.7	0.7
Johnnie Waller Red (Schiefflin & Sommerset)	0.7	0.6
Wolfschmict (James Beam)	0.6	0.6
Balley's Irish Cream	0.6	0.6

Source: *Beverage Industry*, June 1992, p. 34, from Wheat First Securities.

★ 298 ★

Liquor (SIC 2080)

Leading Liquor Brands

Sales, in thousands of cases, and market shares, in percent, are shown by brand with company names in parentheses. Data refer to 1991.

	Cases (000)	Market Share
Bacardi rum (Bacardi Imports)	7,055	4.8%
Smirnoff vodka (Heublein)	6,090	4.1
Seagram's gin (House of Seagram)	4,100	2.8%
Seagram 7 Crown (House of Seagram)	3,930	2.7
Popov vodka (Heublein)	3,755	2.6
Jim Beam (Jim Beam Brands)	3,515	2.4
Canadian Mist (Brown-Forman)	3,350	2.3
Jack Daniel's (Brown-Forman)	3,250	2.2
E&J brandy (E&J Gallo Winery)	2,490	1.7
Absolut vodka (Carillon)	2,455	1.7

Source: *Advertising Age*, February 10, 1992, p. 44, from *IMPACT Databook*.

★ 299 ★

Liquor (SIC 2080)

Liquor Manufacturers

Company shares are shown in percent based on a total market of 163.614 million cases in 1990 and 156.337 million cases (estimated) in 1991.

	1990	1991
James Beam	9.4%	12.1%
Heublein Inc.	12.8	10.4
Seagram Co. Ltd.	14.3	9.4
Bacardi Corporation	8.1	7.5
Brown Forman Corporation	6.9	6.3
Hiram Walker Inc.	7.4	6.0
Schenley	6.8	5.3
Glenmore Distillers	4.8	4.5
Paddington	2.9	2.7
Schieffelin & Somerset	2.5	2.3
Carillon Importers	2.2	2.1
Other	31.3	40.9

Source: Investext, Thomson Financial Networks, January 21, 1992, from Wheat First Butcher & Singer, Inc.

★300★
Beer (SIC 2082)

Beer Market - U.K.

Shares of the United Kingdom beer market, by brewer, are shown in percent.

Bass	23.0%
Courage	20.0
Carlsberg-Tetley	19.0
Whitbread	14.0
S&N	12.0
Other	12.0

Source: Investext, Thomson Financial Networks, June 8, 1992, from Nikko Securities Co., (Europe) Ltd.

★301★
Beer (SIC 2082)

Beer Production by Brand

Shares are shown in percent based on totals of 188.1 million barrels in 1989; 193.2 million barrels in 1990; and 189.2 million barrels in 1991.

	1989	1990	1991
Budweiser	26.3%	25.5%	24.7%
Miller Lite	10.7	10.6	10.3
Coors Light	5.5	6.0	6.3
Bud Light	5.6	5.9	6.3
Busch	4.7	4.9	5.2
Milwaukee's Best	3.5	3.6	3.8
Miller Genuine Draft	2.5	3.1	3.4
Old Milwaukee	3.7	3.3	3.1
Miller High Life	4.0	3.4	3.0
Natural Light	1.4	1.7	2.3
All others	32.1	32.1	31.6

Source: *Beverage World*, March 1992, p. 82, from Beverage Marketing Corporation.

★302★
Beer (SIC 2082)

Breweries in the U.S.

Shares of domestic production are shown in percent. G. Heileman does not include Pittsburgh Brewing Products; S & P includes Falstaff, General, Pearl, Pabst, and Olympia breweries; Pittsburgh Brewing does not include G. Heileman contract packing volume. Shares are based on totals of 184.2 million barrels in 1989; 190.2 million barrels in 1990; and 188.2 million barrels in 1991.

	1989	1990	1991
Anheuser-Busch	43.8%	45.5%	45.7%
Miller	22.7	22.9	23.2
Coors	9.6	10.1	10.4
Stroh	10.0	8.6	8.0
G. Heileman	6.8	6.0	5.5
S & P Industries	4.1	4.0	4.0
Genesee	1.2	1.2	1.2
Latrobe	0.4	0.4	0.4
Pittsburgh Brewing	0.4	0.3	0.3
Hudepohl-Schoenling	0.3	0.2	0.2
All other domestic	0.7	0.9	1.3

Source: *Beverage World*, March 1992, p. 82.

★303★
Beer (SIC 2082)

Brewers - Global Leaders in 1990

Brewers are ranked by beer sales in millions of hectoliters; market shares are shown in percent.

	Vol.	Share
Anheuser-Busch	101.5	18.3%
Heineken	53.50	9.6
Miller Brewing	51.90	9.4
Fosters Brewing	36.00	6.5
Kirin	32.40	5.8
Brahma	26.00	4.7
BSN	23.80	4.3
Antarctica	23.00	4.1
Adolph Coors	22.60	4.1
SAB	22.00	4.0
Carlsberg	21.40	3.9
Guinness	20.00	3.6
Modelo	19.60	3.5
Stroh	19.00	3.4
Asahi	16.00	2.9
Heileman	14.40	2.6
Bass	14.00	2.5

Continued on next page.

★ 303 ★ *Continued*
Beer (SIC 2082)

Brewers - Global Leaders in 1990

Brewers are ranked by beer sales in millions of hectoliters; market shares are shown in percent.

	Vol.	Share
Interbrew	13.90	2.5%
San Miguel	13.50	2.4
Lion	10.50	1.9

Source: Investext, Thomson Financial Networks, February 14, 1992, from Barclays De Zoete Wedd Securities.

★ 304 ★
Beer (SIC 2082)

Brewery Shares Worldwide

Sales of the world's leading breweries in 1990 are shown in millions of hectoliters; relative market shares are shown in percent for the same period. Volumes for Fosters, Guinness, and Lion/National are for 1991, following acquisitions.

Anheuser-Busch	101.5	18.3%
Heineken	53.5	9.6
Miller Brewing	51.9	9.4
Fosters Brewing	36.0	6.5
Kirin	32.4	5.8
Brahma	26.0	4.7
BSN	23.8	4.3
Antarctica	22.6	4.1
Adolph Coors	22.6	4.1
SAB	22.0	4.0
Carlsberg	21.4	3.9
Guiness	20.0	3.6
Modelo	19.6	3.5
Stroh	19.0	3.4
Asahi	16.0	2.9
Heileman	14.4	2.6
Bass	14.0	2.5
Inerbrew	13.9	2.5
San Miguel	13.5	2.4
Lion/National	10.5	1.9

Source: Investext, Thomson Financial Networks, January 29, 1992, from Nomura Research Institute Europe Ltd.

★ 305 ★
Beer (SIC 2082)

Near Beer by Brand

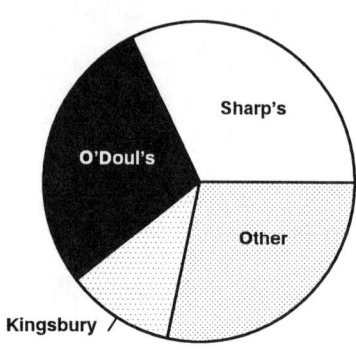

Brand shares are shown in percent, based on a total of 24.1 million cases of near beer sold in 1991.

Sharp's	32.4%
O'Doul's	28.2
Kingsbury	11.2
Other	28.2

Source: *The Wall Street Journal*, March 30, 1992, p. B1, from *Impact*.

★ 306 ★
Beer (SIC 2082)

Standard Lager Market

Brands are ranked according to thousands of barrels sold.

Hofmeister	171
Heineken	125
Carling	112
Kestrel	90
John Smith's	73
Norseman	69
Miller Pilsner	66
Tennent's Pilsner	57
Whitbred Best	56
Stones	53
Skol	49
Harp	48
Tartan	40
McEwan's Export	39
Mansfield Bitter	38
Castlemaine	34
Newcastle Brown	27
Websters	27

Continued on next page.

★306★ *Continued*

Beer (SIC 2082)

Standard Lager Market

Brands are ranked according to thousands of barrels sold.

Carlsberg Special Brew	27
Budweiser	24
Stella Artois	24
Tennent's Super	21
Boddington's	21
Holsten Pilsner	20
Beck's	16
Foster's	14
Kronenbourg	14
Grolsch	11

Source: Investext, Thomson Financial Networks, June 8, 1992, from Nikko Securities Co., (Europe) Ltd.

★307★

Beer (SIC 2082)

Top Supermarket Beers

Supermarket beer sales are shown by brand for 52 weeks ending May 16, 1992 in millions of dollars. Percentages are based on a total market of $5.0088 billion.

	Sales	Share
Budweiser	$ 848.4	16.9%
Miller Lite	436.6	8.7
Coors Light	363.4	7.3
Bud Light	338.4	6.8
Miller Genuine Draft	222.5	4.4
Busch	198.4	4.0
Milwaukee's Best	152.5	3.0
Natural Light	151.2	3.0

	Sales	Share
Bud Dry	$ 110.7	2.2%
Miller High Life	108.5	2.2
Other	3078.2	41.5

Source: *Advertising Age*, July 20, 1992, p. 20, from A.C. Nielsen ScanTrack.

★308★

Champagne (SIC 2084)

Leading Champagne Brands

Wholesale shipments in 1991 are shown in thousands of nine-liter cases; relative market shares are shown in percent.

	Cases (000)	% of Group
Andre	4,200	44.8%
Cook's	1,545	16.5
Korbel	1,105	11.8
Freixenet	1,050	11.2
J. Roget	880	9.4
Martini & Rossi	600	6.4

Source: *The Wall Street Journal*, December 12, 1992, p. B1, from M. Shanken Communications Inc.

★309★

Wine (SIC 2084)

Australian Wine Market

Estimated product shares are shown in percent, based on total liters sold.

Casks	53.0%
Table wine	26.0
Sparkling wine	11.0
Sherry port	10.0

Source: Investext, Thomson Financial Networks, June 5, 1992, from McIntosh & Company.

★310★

Wine (SIC 2084)

Domestic Wine Market

Market shares, by company, are shown in percent for 1991.

E & J Gallo	30.4%
Heublein	9.0
Canandaigua	4.9

Continued on next page.

★ 310 ★ *Continued*
Wine (SIC 2084)

Domestic Wine Market

Market shares, by company, are shown in percent for 1991.

Franzia (Wine Group)	4.6%
Vintners International	3.3
Almaden	2.9
Sebastiani	2.2
Sutter Home	2.0
Bronco	1.7
Gibson	1.6
Guild	1.6
Robert Mondavi	1.6
Beringer (Wine World)	1.5
Glen Ellen	1.5
Mogen David	1.2
Lamont	1.0
Delicato	0.9
F. Korbel	0.5
Christian Brothers	0.4
Sonoma	0.3
C. Mondavi	0.3
Giumarra	0.3
California Growers	0.3
East-Side	0.2
Weibel	0.1
M&H	0.1
Mirrasou	0.1
Wente	0.1
Louis Martini	0.1
Other domestic	13.4

Source: Investext, Thomson Financial Networks, June 8, 1992, from Wheat First Butcher & Singer, Inc.

★ 311 ★
Wine (SIC 2084)

Premium Wine Industry

Market shares, by company, are shown in percent for 1991.

Gallo	19.0%
Sebastiani	7.3
Sutter Home	7.0
Glen Ellen	4.4
Robert Mondavi	3.4
Blossom Hill	2.2
Other	56.7

Source: Investext, Thomson Financial Networks, June 8, 1992, from Wheat First Butcher & Singer, Inc.

★ 312 ★
Wine (SIC 2084)

Wine Cooler Industry

Market shares, by company, are shown in percent for 1989, 1990, and 1991. Figures for 1991 are estimates.

	1989	1990	1991
E & J Gallo	35.2%	43.6%	44.6%
Seagram	36.5	39.6	39.5
Stroh	5.6	4.4	5.1
Brown-Forman	6.1	4.0	4.6
Canandaigua	3.8	3.2	3.4
Universal Brands	3.0	1.3	1.4
Other	9.8	4.0	1.4

Source: Investext, Thomson Financial Networks, June 8, 1992, from Wheat First Butcher & Singer, Inc.

★ 313 ★
Wines (SIC 2084)

Largest Wine Producers

Total storage capacity by company is shown in thousands of gallons. Percentages are based on the group total.

	Gal. (000)	% of Group
E & J Gallo	330,000	30.6%
Grand Metropolitan plc	135,166	12.5
Canandaigua Wine Co.	94,800	8.8
Vintners International	84,500	7.8
Vie-Del Company	50,000	4.6
JFJ Bronco Winery	43,800	4.1
ERLY Foods	43,000	4.0

Continued on next page.

★ 313 ★ *Continued*

Wines (SIC 2084)

Largest Wine Producers

Total storage capacity by company is shown in thousands of gallons. Percentages are based on the group total.

	Gal. (000)	% of Group
The Wine Group	42,800	4.0%
Delicato Vineyards	39,500	3.7
F. Korbel & Bros./Hick Clrs.	34,000	3.2
Golden State Vintners	28,500	2.6
Robert Mondavi Winery	21,500	2.0
Giumarra Vineyards	16,000	1.5
Wine World	13,894	1.3
Sebastiani Winery	13,000	1.2
Gibson Wine Co.	10,940	1.0
Delano Growers Grape Products	8,250	0.8
ASV Wines/Arroyo Seco Vyds.	7,583	0.7
Fetzer Vineyards	7,200	0.7
Stimson Lane Wine & Spirits	7,090	0.7
Oak Ridge Vyds./Royal Host Brandy	7,000	0.6
Charles Krug Winery	6,000	0.6
Seagram Classics Wine Co.	5,750	0.5
Sutter Home Winery	5,300	0.5
Frutec	5,200	0.5
Wente Bros.	4,000	0.4
The Wine Alliance	3,698	0.3
Paramount Distillers	3,575	0.3
Klein Family Vintners	3,300	0.3
Warner Vineyards	3,000	0.3

Source: *Wines & Vines*, July 1992, p. 43.

★ 314 ★

Wines (SIC 2084)

Wine Market by Class

Shares of U.S wine market (including imported wines) by class are shown in percent, based on totals of 467 million gallons in 1991 (estimate) and 446 million gallons in 1992 (forecast).

	1991	1992
Table wine	67.7%	69.3%
Coolers	13.5	12.1
Sparkling wine	7.3	7.2
All other	11.6	11.4

Source: *Wines & Vines*, January 1992, p. 19, from Wine Institute.

★ 315 ★

Applejack (SIC 2085)

Draught Cider - U.K.

Shares of on-licensed trade for 12 months ended December/January 1992 are shown in percent.

Strongbow	30.2%
Dry Blackthorn	24.5
Woodpecker	10.2
Olde English	9.3
Autumn Gold	4.3
Other	21.5

Source: Investext, Thomson Financial Networks, May 1, 1992, from Rowan, Dartington & Co. Securities Ltd.

★ 316 ★

Applejack (SIC 2085)

Packaged Cider - U.K.

Shares of on-licensed trade of packaged half-pints are shown in percent for 12 months ended December/January 1992. Manufacturers are shown in parentheses.

Diamond White (Taunton)	26.4%
Woodpecker (Bulmer)	13.7
Strongbow (Bulmer)	9.7
Autumn Gold (Taunton)	9.4
Merrydown (Merrydown)	4.4
Dry Blackthorn (Taunton)	4.3
Olde English (Gaymer)	2.7
Other	29.4

Source: Investext, Thomson Financial Networks, May 1, 1992, from Rowan, Dartington & Co. Securities Ltd.

★ 317 ★

Applejack (SIC 2085)

Take-Home Cider Sales - U.K.

Brand shares are shown in percent for 12 months ended December/January 1992. Manufacturers are shown in parentheses.

Strongbow (Bulmer)	15.3%
Olde English (Gaymer)	10.8
Woodpecker (Bulmer)	8.0
Merrydown (Merrydown)	5.1
Dry Blackthorn (Taunton)	3.8
Private label	30.4
Other	26.6

Source: Investext, Thomson Financial Networks, May 1, 1992, from Rowan, Dartington & Co. Securities Ltd.

★ 318 ★

Tequila (SIC 2085)

Best-Selling Tequila Brands in the U.S.

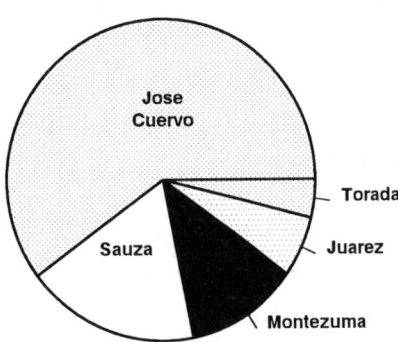

Tequila sales by brand are shown with number of cases for 1991. Percent shares are based on group total.

	No. of Cases	% of Group
Jose Cuervo (Heublein) . . .	2,080,000	60.4%
Sauza (Domecq Importers) . .	610,000	17.7
Montezuma (Barton Brands) .	400,000	11.6
Juarez (David Sherman) . . .	210,000	6.1
Torada (Sazerac)	145,000	4.2

Source: *Adweek's Marketing Week*, June 15, 1992, p. 5, from Impact Data Bank.

★ 319 ★

Whiskey (SIC 2085)

Scotch Whiskey Producers Worldwide

Shares are shown in percent, based on a total volume of 71.5 million nine-liter cases in 1990. Glenmore Distilleries Company is owned by Guinness.

United Distillers	34.1%
HWAV (Allied Lyons)	13.1
Seagram	10.7
IDV (Grand Met)	8.3
Wm Grant	5.8
White & Mackay (American Brands) . . .	3.7
Highland Distillers	3.1
Berry Bros. & Rudd	2.9
Glenmore Distilleries	1.8
La Martiniquase	1.6
Other	15.0

Source: Investext, Thomson Financial Networks, January 29, 1992, from Nomura Research Institute Europe Ltd.

★ 320 ★

Beverages (SIC 2086)

Soft Drink Market by Manufacturer

Company shares are shown as percent of the total U.S. market in 1990 and 1991.

	1990	1991
Coca-Cola	41.0%	41.3%
Pepsi-Cola	33.1	32.9
Dr Pepper/Seven-Up	9.5	10.2
Cadbury Beverages	3.2	3.3
The Royal Crown Cola Co.	2.6	2.4
A & W Brands, Inc.	1.7	1.7
Others	8.9	8.2

Source: *Beverage World*, March 1992, p. 70, from Beverage Marketing Corporation.

★ 321 ★

Bottled Water (SIC 2086)

Bottled Water Sales Worldwide

Companies are ranked according to annual output, in millions of liters, for 1990.

Contrexeville	884
Volvic	639

Continued on next page.

★ 321 ★ *Continued*
Bottled Water (SIC 2086)

Bottled Water Sales Worldwide

Companies are ranked according to annual output, in millions of liters, for 1990.

Arrowhead	586
Perrier	363
Poland Spring	318
Vicky St. Yorre	188
Oasis/Ozarka	183
Great Bear	145
Zephyr Hills	113
Vichy Celestin	65
Buxton	33
Other French springs	92
Other U.S. springs	89
Various Brazilian springs	37
Various Spanish springs	88

Source: Investext, Thomson Financial Networks, June 17, 1992, from Merrill Lynch Capital Markets.

★ 322 ★
Bottled Water (SIC 2086)

Water by the Bottle

Perrier

McKesson

Anjou International

Suntory

Evian

Other

Company shares of the $2.7 billion wholesale market for bottled water in the United States are shown in percent.

Perrier	22.5%
McKesson	8.3
Anjou International	4.5
Suntory	4.4
Evian	3.3
Other	56.9

Source: *The New York Times*, March 20, 1992, p. C4, from *Beverage Marketing*.

★ 323 ★
Soft Drinks (SIC 2086)

Carbonated Soft Drink Global Market

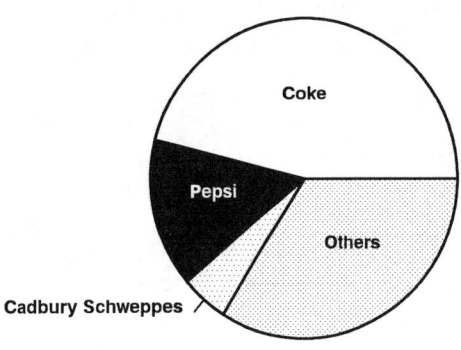

Global market shares are shown in percent.

Coke	46.0%
Pepsi	15.0
Cadbury Schweppes	5.0
Others	34.0

Source: *Financial Times*, January 16, 1992, p. 10, from *Jesse Meyers' Beverage Digest*.

★ 324 ★
Soft Drinks (SIC 2086)

Carbonated Soft Drinks by Type

Segment distribution of the 1991 soft drink market is shown in percent based on a total of approximately $48.0 billion.

Caffeinated cola	48.0%
Caffeine-free cola	10.4
Lemon-lime	9.8
Dr. Pepper	3.9
Orange	3.7
Root beer	3.7
Ginger ale	3.5
Citrus	3.4
Unsweetened seltzer	2.2
Cream	1.4
Grape	1.2
Grapefruit	1.0
Mineral water	1.0

Continued on next page.

★ 324 ★ *Continued*

Soft Drinks (SIC 2086)

Carbonated Soft Drinks by Type

Segment distribution of the 1991 soft drink market is shown in percent based on a total of approximately $48.0 billion.

Tonic water	0.7%
Sweetened seltzer	0.4
Club soda	0.4
Other	5.3

Source: *The New York Times*, May 2, 1992, p. 19Y, from Information Resources and Coca-Cola Company.

★ 325 ★

Soft Drinks (SIC 2086)

Cola-Flavored Soft Drink Brands

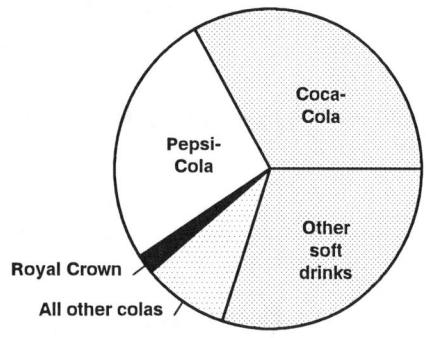

Shares of the total soft drink market for 1989 and 1990 in the U.S., are shown in percent. (Cola-flavored soft drinks made up 69.5% of the total soft drink market in 1989 and 69.9% in 1990).

	1989	1990
Coca-Cola	33.0%	33.3%
Pepsi-Cola	25.6	25.7
Royal Crown	2.1	2.0
All other colas	8.8	8.9
Other soft drinks	30.5	30.1

Source: *U.S. Industrial Outlook 1992*, p. 32-38, from Wheat First Securities.

★ 326 ★

Soft Drinks (SIC 2086)

Diet Soft Drink Market

Shares of total soft drink market for 1989 and 1990 in the U.S., shown in percent. (Diet soft drinks made up 27.9% of the total soft drink market in 1989 and 29.4% in 1990. This segment includes decaffeinated diet soft drinks).

	1989	1990
Coca-Cola	12.6%	13.0%
Pepsi-Cola	8.0	8.5
Seven-Up	0.9	1.3
Dr. Pepper	0.5	0.4
Other diet brands	5.9	6.2
Other soft drinks	72.1	70.6

Source: *U.S. Industrial Outlook 1992*, p. 32-38, from Wheat First Securities.

★ 327 ★

Soft Drinks (SIC 2086)

Iced Tea Producers

Shares of the ready-to-drink iced tea market are shown in percent.

Pepsi/Lipton Tea Partnership	38.2%
Snapple Beverage Corp.	15.6
Nestea	7.7
Tetley	2.1
Other	36.4

Source: *Advertising Age*, May 4, 1992, p. 4, from Nielsen Marketing Research.

★ 328 ★

Soft Drinks (SIC 2086)

Lemon-Lime Soft Drink Market

- ■ Coca-Cola
- ■ Seven-Up Co.
- ▮ Pepsi Co. Inc.
- ▮ A&W Brands
- ▮ All other lemon-lime
- ■ Other soft drinks

Shares of lemon-lime soft drink market for 1989 and 1990 in the U.S., are shown in percent. (Lemon-lime soft drinks made up 12.0% of the total soft drink market in 1989 and 11.7% in 1990).

	1989	1990
Coca-Cola	4.9%	4.9%
Seven-Up Co.	3.9	3.8
Pepsi Co. Inc.	1.6	1.3
A&W Brands	0.4	0.5
All other lemon-lime	1.2	1.2
Other soft drinks	88.0	88.3

Source: *U.S. Industrial Outlook 1992*, p. 32-38, from Wheat First Securities.

★ 329 ★

Soft Drinks (SIC 2086)

Soft Drink Brand Shares - Hispanic Market

Brand shares of soft drinks purchased by Hispanics are shown in percent for 1991.

Coca-Cola Classic	27.1%
Pepsi-Cola	15.5
Diet Coke	9.6
Seven-Up	7.1
Diet Pepsi	4.7
Dr Pepper	4.7
Sprite	4.4
Caffeine Free Diet Coke	2.5
Royal Crown	1.7
Mountain Dew	1.2
Other	21.5

Source: *Beverage World*, December 1991, p. 135, from Data Bank USA.

★ 330 ★

Soft Drinks (SIC 2086)

Soft Drink Brands - C-Store Sales

Brand shares of the C-store (convenience store) market are shown in percent for the first 10 months of each year.

	1989	1990	1991
Pepsi-Cola	27.7%	22.9%	25.4%
Coke Classic	20.2	21.8	17.2
Mountain Dew (all)	6.3	7.7	9.9
Diet Coke	7.1	7.9	7.4
Diet Pepsi	7.6	6.4	6.6
Sprite	3.8	4.1	3.4
Other	27.1	29.2	30.1

Source: *Beverage World*, November 1991, p. 83, from Data Bank USA.

★ 331 ★

Soft Drinks (SIC 2086)

Soft Drink Brands - Foodstore Sales

Brand shares of the domestic foodstore universe are shown in percent for 1981, 1986, 1991.

	1981	1986	1991
Regular Pepsi	22.4%	18.2%	16.1%
Coca-Cola Classic	21.6	15.1	15.9
Diet Coke	0.0	6.0	7.4
Diet Pepsi	3.7	4.3	5.7
Regular Dr Pepper	3.4	2.8	3.3
Mountain Dew	3.0	2.6	3.2
Regular 7Up	5.2	4.1	2.9
Regular Sprite	2.1	2.3	2.6
Slice	0.0	3.0	1.6
A&W Root Beer	1.3	1.0	1.2
Diet 7Up	1.9	1.9	1.2
Diet Dr. Pepper	1.3	0.6	0.9
New Coke	0.0	2.3	0.8
Other	31.4	35.8	37.2

Source: *Beverage World*, March 31, 1992, p. 2, from Nielsen Marketing Research.

★ 332 ★

Soft Drinks (SIC 2086)

Soft Drink Companies - C-Store Sales

Company shares of the C-store (convenience store) soft drink market are shown in percent for the first 10 months of the year.

	1989	1990	1991
Pepsi-Cola	45.3 %	40.6 %	45.7 %
Coca-Cola	35.8	40.1	33.5
Dr Pepper	5.5	5.8	6.8
Seven Up	4.2	3.6	3.6
Royal Crown	2.0	1.8	1.9
All other	7.3	8.2	8.6

Source: *Beverage World*, November 1991, p. 83, from Data Bank USA.

★ 333 ★

Soft Drinks (SIC 2086)

Soft Drink Franchisors - Hispanic Market

Coca-Cola

Pepsi-Cola

Seven-Up

Dr Pepper

Royal Crown

All other

The leading franchisors in 1991 are shown with shares of sales of soft drinks to Hispanics. Shares shown in percent.

Coca-Cola	49.8 %
Pepsi-Cola	26.5
Seven-Up	7.1
Dr Pepper	4.7
Royal Crown	2.7
All other	9.3

Source: *Beverage World*, December 1991, p. 135, from Data Bank USA.

★ 334 ★

Soft Drinks (SIC 2086)

Soft Drink Leaders

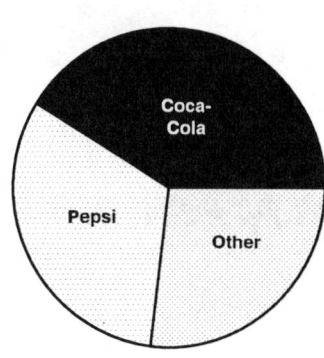

Company shares are shown as percent of 1991 total market.

Coca-Cola	41.0 %
Pepsi	32.0
Other	27.0

Source: *Advertising Age*, June 1, 1992, p. 49, from *Beverage Digest*.

★ 335 ★

Soft Drinks (SIC 2086)

Soft Drink Market

Segment distribution of supermarket sales in 1991 is based on a total of 2.6 billion cases. Citrus drinks include orange and lemon-lime.

Cola (caffeinated and caffeine-free)	58.3 %
Citrus	17.9
Water	4.7
Dr. Pepper	3.9
Root beer	3.7
Other	8.0

Source: *The New York Times*, May 3, 1992, p. 10F, from Information Resources.

★336★

Soft Drinks (SIC 2086)

Soft Drink Market by Manufacturer

Company shares are shown as a percent of the total U.S. market in 1990 and 1991.

	1990	1991
Coca-Cola	41.0%	41.3%
Pepsi-Cola	33.1	32.9
Dr Pepper/Seven-Up	9.5	10.2
Cadbury Beverages	3.2	3.3
The Royal Crown Cola Co.	2.6	2.4
A & W Brands, Inc.	1.7	1.7
Others	8.9	8.2

Source: *Beverage World*, March 1992, p. 70, from Beverage Marketing Corporation.

★337★

Soft Drinks (SIC 2086)

Soft Drink Producers

Percent shares are based on total volume sales of 11,692.1 million gallons in 1989; 11,996.1 million gallons in 1990; and 12,200.4 million gallons in 1991. National Beverage includes Shasta and Faygo brands.

	1989	1990	1991
Coca-Cola	40.0%	41.0%	41.3%
Pepsi-Cola	33.0	33.1	32.9
Dr Pepper/Seven-Up	9.5	9.5	10.2
Cadbury Beverages	3.2	3.2	3.3
Royal Crown	2.6	2.6	2.4
A&W Brands	1.7	1.7	1.7
National Beverages	1.7	1.7	1.7
Monarch	1.6	1.6	1.6
Barq's	0.4	0.5	0.6
Double-Cola	0.5	0.5	0.5
All others	5.4	4.7	3.9

Source: *Beverage World*, March 1992, p. 69, from Beverage Marketing Corporation.

★338★

Soft Drinks (SIC 2086)

Sucrose - Fructose Soft Drink Market

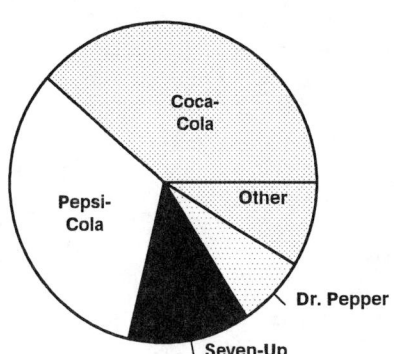

Shares of sucrose-fructose soft drink market for 1989 and 1990 in the U.S., are shown in percent. (Sucrose-fructose soft drinks made up 72.1% of the total soft drink market in 1989 and 70.6% in 1990).

	1989	1990
Coca-Cola	27.4%	27.4%
Pepsi-Cola	23.7	23.3
Seven-Up	8.9	8.5
Dr. Pepper	5.1	5.4
Other	7.0	6.0

Source: *U.S. Industrial Outlook 1992*, p. 32-38.

★339★

Flavoring Extracts (SIC 2087)

Flavor Producers

Company shares of the domestic flavors market are shown in percent, based on a total of $610.0 million in 1989.

Int'l Flavors & Fragrances	16.0%
Universal Foods	13.0
Quest	12.0
Compton & Knowles	11.0
Fries & Fries	7.0
FDO	6.0
Florasynth-Lautier	5.0
Hercules	5.0
Other	25.0

Source: Investext, Thomson Financial Networks, January 8, 1992, from J.C. Bradford & Co.

★ 340 ★

Fruit Beverages (SIC 2087)

Fruit Beverage Market

Estimated company wholesale figures are shown in millions of dollars for 1991. Percent shares are based on a total market of $9,052.5 million in 1991.

	Sales ($ mil.)	Share
Coca-Cola Foods	$ 1,688.0	18.6%
Tropicana	1,095.0	12.1
Ocean Spray	820.0	9.1
Procter & Gamble	813.0	9.0
Welch's Juices & Drinks	343.8	3.8
Dole Juices	224.7	2.5
Veryfine Juices & Drinks	210.0	2.3
Del Monte Juices	180.0	2.0
Tree Top Juices	151.3	1.7
Mott's USA Juices	148.8	1.6
All Others	3,378.7	37.3

Source: *Beverage World*, May 1992, p. 49, from *Beverage Marketing Annual Industry Survey*.

★ 341 ★

Seafood (SIC 2090)

The Fish Market

Segment distribution of the fish and seafood market is shown as percent of supermarket sales.

Fish	42.0%
Shrimp	30.0
Lobster	7.0
Prepared entrees (uncooked)	6.0
Prepared entrees (cooked)	5.0
Clams and other shellfish	4.0
Scallops	4.0
Soups	2.0

Source: *Supermarket Business*, November 1991.

★ 342 ★

Seafood (SIC 2092)

Frozen Seafood Market

Segment distribution is based on a volume total of 2,396,196 thousand lbs. and a value total of $16,801,266 thousand. Data are shown in percent for 1990.

	Vol. Share	Val. Share
Shrimp	28.1%	47.0%
Fillets	29.6	26.5
Crab meat	2.8	4.6
Breaded shrimp	4.8	3.8
Steaks	6.6	3.2
Portions	12.3	3.1
Lobster tails	1.3	3.1
Scallops	3.4	3.0
Catfish	5.3	2.3
Oysters	1.8	1.3
Sticks	2.7	0.8
Trout	0.5	0.2
Miscellaneous	1.0	1.0

Source: *Quick Frozen Foods International*, October 1991, p. A8, from U.S. Department of Commerce and American Institute of Food Distribution.

★ 343 ★

Coffee (SIC 2095)

Coffee Consumption by Flavoring Treatments

The popularity of different methods of enhancing the taste of coffee is shown in percent for 1962 and 1991.

	'62	'91
Black	28.0%	38.0%
Sweetener and creamer	42.0	31.0
Creamer only	20.0	22.0
Sweetener only	10.0	09.0

Source: *Detroit Free Press*, May 6, 1992, p. 1C, from 1991 Coffee Drinking Study, National Coffee Association of USA.

★ 344 ★
Coffee (SIC 2095)

Coffee Consumption per Capita

The number of cups of regular or decaffeinated coffee consumed per person per day is shown for the years 1962 and 1991.

	'62	'91
Regular	4.2%	3.4%
Decaf	2.6	2.4

Source: *Detroit Free Press*, May 6, 1992, p. 1C, from 1991 Coffee Drinking Study, National Coffee Association of USA.

★ 345 ★
Coffee (SIC 2095)

Coffee Market Shares by Brand

Estimated market shares for 1991 are shown in percent.

General Foods
Maxwell House Regular	16.5%
Maxwell House Decaffeinated	2.0
Maxwell House Private Collection . . .	0.6
Master Blend	8.8
Sanka	1.6
Yuban Regular	2.2
Yuban Decaffeinated	0.3
Brim (Includes Max-Pax)	1.3

Procter & Gamble
Folgers Regular	22.5
Folgers Decaffeinated	3.9
Flakes	4.8
Maryland Club	0.3
Butternut	0.6

Nestle
Hills Brothers	9.6
MJB	3.8
Chase & Sanborn	4.0
Tasters Choice	0.3
Chock Full O'Nuts	3.2
All Others	13.7

Source: Investext, Thomson Financial Networks, March 16, 1992, from Wheat First Butcher & Singer Inc.

★ 346 ★
Coffee (SIC 2095)

Coffee Producers

Shares are shown in percent. Figures are estimated for 1991. Procter & Gamble acquired Maryland Club and Butternut in October 1989.

	1989	1990	1991
General Foods	32.1%	33.0%	33.3%
Procter & Gamble	32.2	32.7	32.1
Nestle	13.5	16.0	17.7
Chock Full O'Nuts	3.4	3.4	3.2
Winterpark Investment Group	1.3	-	-
Other	17.5	14.9	13.7

Source: *Advertising Age*, May 4, 1992, p. 46, from John C. Maxwell, Jr.

★ 347 ★
Coffee (SIC 2095)

Coffee Shares by Brand

Shares are shown in percent. Figures are estimated for 1991.

	1990	1991
General Foods		
Maxwell House Regular	16.3%	16.5%
Maxwell House Decaf	2.0	2.0
Maxwell House Private Collection .	0.5	0.6
Master Blend	8.6	8.8
Sanka	1.8	1.6
Yuban Regular	2.2	2.2
Yuban Decaf	0.3	0.3
Brim (incl. Max-Pax)	1.3	1.3
Procter & Gamble		
Folgers Regular	22.7	22.5
Folgers Decaf	4.0	3.9
Folgers Flakes	4.9	4.8
Maryland Club	0.4	0.3
Butternut	0.7	0.6
Nestle		
Hills Brothers	8.9	9.6
MJB	3.65	3.8
Chase & Sanborn	3.2	4.0
Taster's Choice	0.3	0.3
Chock Full O'Nuts	3.4	3.2
Other	14.9	13.7

Source: *Advertising Age*, May 4, 1992, p. 46, from John C. Maxwell, Jr.

★ 348 ★

Coffee (SIC 2095)

Instant Coffee Producers

Shares are shown in percent. Figures are estimated for 1991. "Other" includes Borden in 1991.

	1990	1991
General Foods	36.3%	35.8%
Nestle	33.3	32.6
Procter & Gamble	24.7	25.3
Borden	0.3	-
Other	5.4	6.3

Source: *Advertising Age*, May 4, 1992, p. 46, from John C. Maxwell, Jr.

★ 349 ★

Coffee (SIC 2095)

Instant Coffee Shares by Brand

Shares are shown in percent. Figures are estimated for 1991. "Other" in 1991 includes Kava.

	1990	1991
General Foods		
Maxwell House Regular	19.8%	19.7%
Maxwell House Decaf	1.7	1.6
Maxim	1.2	1.1
Sanka	8.3	8.2
Freeze Dried Sanka	0.6	0.6
Yuban	0.8	0.8
Brim	0.8	0.7
International Coffees	3.1	3.1
Nestle		
Nescafe Regular	7.1	6.8
Nescafe Decaf	2.6	2.5
Taster's Choice Regular	11.4	11.2
Taster's Choice Decaf	5.6	2.6
Sunrise	0.8	1.6
Hils Brothers	2.6	2.6
MJB	1.6	1.6
Chase & Sanborn	1.6	1.7
Procter & Gamble		
Folgers Regular	17.8	18.0
Folgers Deacaf	5.9	6.2
Highpoint	1.0	1.1
Borden		
Kava	0.3	-
Other	5.4	6.3

Source: *Advertising Age*, May 4, 1992, p. 46, from John C. Maxwell, Jr.

★ 350 ★

Coffee (SIC 2095)

Regular and Instant Coffee Consumption

Consumption of regular and instant coffee is shown in percent for the years 1985 and 1991.

	'85	'91
Regular	77.0%	83.0%
Instant	23.0	17.0

Source: *Detroit Free Press*, May 6, 1992, p. 1C, from 1991 Coffee Drinking Study, National Coffee Association of USA.

★ 351 ★

Snacks (SIC 2096)

Salty Snack Producers

Company shares of the $5.1 billion market in 1991 are shown in percent.

Frito-Lay	49.0%
Borden	8.7
Other	42.3

Source: *Advertising Age*, March 23, 1992, p. 20, from Nielsen Marketing Research.

★ 352 ★

Snacks (SIC 2096)

Savory "Salty" Snack Market - European Community

Company shares are based on industry sales of $7.3 billion, shown in percent.

PFI/GMI	22.5%
UB	14.2
BSN	5.0
Bahlsen	4.6
San Carlo	3.2
Convent	3.1
Borden	0.3
Other/local	47.1

Source: Investext, Thomson Financial Networks, May 18, 1992, from Dean Witter Reynolds.

★353★

Snacks (SIC 2096)

Snack Market - Belgium

Company shares are based on industry sales (excluding chocolate) of $0.5 billion, shown in percent.

PFI/GMI	11.0%
UB	6.0
BSN	2.0
Bahlsen	1.0
Warner Lambert	1.0
Other/local	79.0

Source: Investext, Thomson Financial Networks, May 18, 1992, from Dean Witter Reynolds.

★354★

Snacks (SIC 2096)

Snack Market - France

Company shares are based on industry sales (excluding chocolate) of $4.1 billion, shown in percent.

BSN	20.0%
Bahlsen	5.0
PFI/GMI	3.0
UB	2.0
San Carlo	2.0
Other/local	67.0

Source: Investext, Thomson Financial Networks, May 18, 1992, from Dean Witter Reynolds.

★355★

Snacks (SIC 2096)

Snack Market - Greece

Company shares are based on industry sales (excluding chocolate) of $0.3 billion, shown in percent.

PFI/GMI	19.0%
Warner Lambert	7.0
Other/local	74.0

Source: Investext, Thomson Financial Networks, May 18, 1992, from Dean Witter Reynolds.

★356★

Snacks (SIC 2096)

Snack Market - Netherlands

Company shares are based on industry sales (excluding chocolate) of $1.3 billion, shown in percent.

PFI/GMI	9.0%
UB	4.0
BSN	1.0
Warner Lambert	1.0
Other/local	86.0

Source: Investext, Thomson Financial Networks, May 18, 1992, from Dean Witter Reynolds.

★357★

Snacks (SIC 2096)

Snack Market - Portugal

Company shares are based on industry sales (excluding chocolate) of $0.3 billion, shown in percent.

PFI/GMI	14.0%
UB	4.0
Warner Lambert	3.0
Other/local	79.0

Source: Investext, Thomson Financial Networks, May 18, 1992, from Dean Witter Reynolds.

★358★

Snacks (SIC 2096)

Snack Market - Spain

Company shares are based on industry sales (excluding chocolate) of $1.6 billion, shown in percent.

PFI/GMI	14.0%
Warner Lambert	7.0
Borden	1.0
UB	1.0
Other/local	77.0

Source: Investext, Thomson Financial Networks, May 18, 1992, from Dean Witter Reynolds.

★ 359 ★

Deli Items (SIC 2099)

Deli Service Items

Shares, by type, are based on total supermarket deli sales.

Sliced meats	33.4%
Cheese	13.8
Salads	11.1
Fried/barbeque chicken	10.5
Pizza	8.0
Sandwiches	7.7
Hot entrees	6.2
Refrigerated entrees	5.6
Barbeque ribs	2.4
Other	1.3

Source: *Supermarket Business*, February 1992, p. 53.

★ 360 ★

Deli Items (SIC 2099)

Prepackaged Deli Items

Market penetration in supermarket self-serve cases is shown in percent.

Sandwiches	95.0%
Salads	88.0
Refrigerated entrees	83.0
Desserts	81.0

Source: *Supermarket Business*, February 1992.

★ 361 ★

Deli Items (SIC 2099)

Supermarket Deli Market Penetration

Figures shown are percent of supermarkets that offer each type of deli service.

Salad bar	50.0%
Soup bar	50.0
Hot pizza section	48.0
Fresh pasta section	39.0
Tortilleria	22.0
Ice cream stand	18.0
Yogurt machines	18.0
Sushi bar	4.0

Source: *Supermarket Business*, February 1992, p. 53.

★ 362 ★

Dressings (SIC 2099)

Salad Dressings

Brand shares are shown in percent, with manufacturers' names in parentheses. Percentages are based on a total market of $650 million.

	Fall 1990	Fall 1991
Wishbone (Unilever)	18.0%	20.5%
Hidden Valley Ranch (Clorox)	13.0	16.5
Other	69.0	63.0

Source: Investext, Thomson Financial Networks, January 24, 1992, from Kidder, Peabody & Company, Incorporated.

★ 363 ★

Pasta (SIC 2099)

Pasta Producers

Shares, by company, are shown in percent.

Borden	30.0%
Hershey	23.0
CPC	12.0
Other	35.0

Source: Investext, Thomson Financial Networks, June 15, 1992, from Kidder, Peabody & Company, Inc.

★ 364 ★

Pasta (SIC 2099)

Pasta Shares - France

Company shares of the 1989 market are shown in percent.

Panzani	33.0%
Rivoire et Carret	14.0
Lustucru	13.0
Barilla	8.0
Other and private label	32.0

Source: Investext, Thomson Financial Networks, February 27, 1992, from Barclays de Zoete Wedd Securities.

★ 365 ★

Pasta (SIC 2099)

Pasta Shares - Italy

Company shares of production are shown in percent for 1989.

Barilla	33.0%
Panzani Agnesi	9.0
Buitoni	6.0
Other	52.0

Source: Investext, Thomson Financial Networks, February 27, 1992, from Barclays de Zoete Wedd Securities.

★ 366 ★

Pasta (SIC 2099)

Pasta Shares - U.K.

Company shares of the 1989 market are shown in percent. Category includes dried pasta only.

Pasta Foods	30.0%
Buitoni	13.0
Sitoni	5.0
Napolina	4.0
Barilla	2.0
Private label	35.0
Other	11.0

Source: Investext, Thomson Financial Networks, February 27, 1992, from Barclays de Zoete Wedd Securities.

★ 367 ★

Pasta (SIC 2099)

Pasta Shares - West Germany

Company shares of the 1990 market are shown in percent. Category includes dry pasta only.

Sonnen Bassermann/Birkel	29.0%
3-Glocken	26.0
Bernbacher	7.0
Buck	5.0
Other and private label	33.0

Source: Investext, Thomson Financial Networks, February 27, 1992, from Barclays de Zoete Wedd Securities.

★ 368 ★

Peanut Butter (SIC 2099)

Leading Peanut Butter Brands

Brand shares for 1991 are shown as percent of the $1.0 billion domestic market.

Jif	34.0%
Skippy	20.0
Peter Pan	15.2
Other	30.8

Source: *Advertising Age*, February 17, 1992, p. 56, from Nielsen Marketing Research.

★ 369 ★

Peanut Butter (SIC 2099)

Peanut Butter Market

Shares, by company, are shown in percent.

Procter & Gamble	34.0%
CPC	21.0
ConAgra	15.0
Other	30.0

Source: Investext, Thomson Financial Networks, June 15, 1992, from Kidder, Peabody & Company, Inc.

★ 370 ★

Peanut Butter (SIC 2099)

Supermarket Peanut Butter

Sales of the 10 leading supermarket peanut butter brands accounted for 96.4% of the $974.4 million market for 52 weeks ending May 23, 1992. Shares are shown in percent.

	Sales	Share
Jif	$ 304.9	31.3%
Skippy	195.8	20.1
Peter Pan	143.8	18.1
Simply Jif	31.7	14.8
Smucker's	27.0	3.9
Reese's	18.8	2.8
Adams	13.4	1.9
Laura Scudder's	13.2	1.4
Private label	176.4	1.4
Generic	7.1	0.7
Other	36.3	3.6

Source: *Advertising Age*, July 20, 1992, p. 20, from A.C. Nielsen ScanTrack.

★ 371 ★
Prepared Foods (SIC 2099)

Sandwich Ingredients Sales

The five most popular sandwich ingredients are shown with sales in millions of dollars. Peanut butter sales figures are based on the 52 weeks ended September 23, 1992.

Packaged cold cuts	$ 2,425.0
Packaged sliced cheese	1,415.0
Canned tuna	1,124.0
Peanut butter	908.7
Jelly/jam	365.1

Source: *The Wall Street Journal*, November 3, 1992, p. B4, from Information Resources, Inc.

★ 372 ★
Tortillas (SIC 2099)

Tortilla Producers

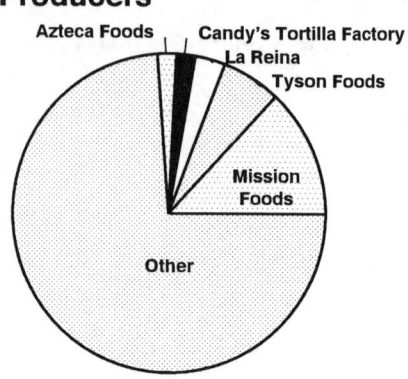

Shares of an estimated $1.725 billion market in 1991 are shown in percent.

Mission Foods	13.3%
Tyson Foods	5.8
La Reina	2.9
Candy's Tortilla Factory	1.9
Azteca Foods	1.7
Other	74.4

Source: *The New York Times*, September 23, 1992, p. C1, from company reports.

SIC 21 - Tobacco Products

★373★

Tobacco Products (SIC 2100)

Tobacco Product Manufacturers

Companies are ranked by 1991 sales, shown in millions of dollars. Percent shares are based on a group total of $81,989 million.

	Sales ($ mil.)	% of Group
Philip Morris	$ 48,064	58.6%
RJR Nabisco Holdings	14,989	18.3
Amercan Brands	14,064	17.2
Universal	2,907	3.5
Dibrell Brothers	1,059	1.3
UST	907	1.1

Source: *The 1992 Business Week 1000*, p. 171.

★374★

Tobacco Products (SIC 2100)

Tobacco Products

Segment distribution is shown in percent.

Cigarettes	70.27%
Lighters/accessories	10.82
Cigars	9.29
Tobacco products	7.66
Miscellaneous	1.96

Source: *Discount Merchandiser*, June 1992, p. 60, from survey.

★375★

Cigarettes (SIC 2111)

9th-Grader Cigarette Brand Preference

Data reflect self-reported brand preference in a survey of 9th-graders in 10 U.S. communities in 1990. According to U.S. surgeon general, approximately 90% of smokers become regular smokers before age 21.

Marlboro	43.0%
Camel	30.0
Newport	20.0
Winston	3.3
Other	2.8

Source: *USA TODAY*, March 25, 1992, p. 11A, from Centers for Disease Control.

★376★

Cigarettes (SIC 2111)

Cigarette Brand Shares

Shares of the domestic market are shown in percent for 1991.

Marlboro	25.8%
Winston	7.5
Salem	5.4
Newport	4.7
Doral	4.6
Kool	4.6
Camel	4.0
Benson & Hedges	3.2
Merit	3.1
Virginia Slims	2.8
Cambridge	2.8
Vantage	2.0
Pall Mall	1.9
Bristol	1.6
Kent	1.6
Carlton	1.5

Continued on next page.

Cigarettes (SIC 2111)

Cigarette Brand Shares

Shares of the domestic market are shown in percent for 1991.

Viceroy	1.4%
Montclair	1.3
Generic	1.3
Pyramid	1.2
Raleigh Extra	1.2
Now	0.9
More	0.8
Parliament	0.8
True	0.7
Alpine	0.6
Tarreyton	0.5
Capri	0.5
Misty	0.5
Sterling	0.5
Magna	0.5
Eve	0.4
Bucks	0.4
Richland-20	0.4
Lucky Strike (non-filter)	0.4
Century	0.3
Raleigh	0.3
Malibu	0.3
American	0.3
L&M	0.2
Bull Durham	0.2
BelAir Regular	0.2
Barclay	0.2
Lucky Strike (filter)	0.1
Lark	0.1
BelAir Low	0.1
Chesterfield	0.1
Richland-25	0.1

Source: Investext, Thomson Financial Networks, May 28, 1992, from Prudential Securities, Inc.

★ 377 ★

Cigarettes (SIC 2111)

Cigarette Brand Shares - Argentina

Shares, by brand, are shown in percent for 1991. KS stands for king size.

Nobleza Piccardo (BAT)

Derby KS	12.8%
Jockey Club ES K.S.	6.8

Jockey Club K.S.	5.5%
Derby Suaves	5.2
43/70 King Size Regulars	4.2
Derby 10	3.4
Parisiennes Filtre	2.7
Derby Suaves 100	1.6
43/70 100s	1.5
Conway KS	1.3
Derby Suaves 10	1.1
Jockey Club 100s	1.0
Jockey Club ES 100s	1.0
Jockey Club ES 10s	0.8
Jockey Club 10	0.6
Pall Mall 100s	0.5
Camel KS	0.5
43/70 10s	0.4
Colt	0.3
Derby	0.2
Jockey Club 120s	0.1
Others	1.0

Massalin Particulares (PM)

Marlboro King	12.1
LeMans Suave	5.4
Marlboro Box	4.3
Philip Morris KS	2.7
LeMans Suave 100	2.5
L & M KS	2.3
Imparciale 100s	2.3
Chesterfield KS	1.9
Parliament KS	1.8
Particulares Long Size	1.7
Colorado KS	1.1
LeMans Suaves 10	1.1
LeMans KS	1.0
Marlboro Box 10	0.9
Wilton KS	0.9

Source: Investext, Thomson Financial Networks, March 25, 1992, from Wheat First Butcher & Singer, Inc.

★ 378 ★

Cigarettes (SIC 2111)

Cigarette Brand Shares - Finland

Market shares, by brand, are shown in percent for 1991.

Marlboro	25.0%
Belmont Extra Mild	7.8
Belmont 2002	7.8
Marlboro Box	6.2
Marlboro Lights	1.9

Continued on next page.

★ 378 ★ *Continued*
Cigarettes (SIC 2111)

Cigarette Brand Shares - Finland

Market shares, by brand, are shown in percent for 1991.

Marlboro Menthol	3.5%
Marlboro Lights Menthol	2.3
Marlboro Lights Box	2.2
Belmont Filter	1.9
Belmont 2002 Menthol	1.1
Form Special	0.5
Partner	0.2
Boston	0.2

Source: Investext, Thomson Financial Networks, March 25, 1992, from Wheat First Butcher & Singer, Inc.

★ 379 ★
Cigarettes (SIC 2111)

Cigarette Brand Shares - France

Market shares, by brand, are shown in percent for 1991.

Seita	
Group of Gauloises	29.7%
Group of Gitanes and Brunes Superiors	10.5
Group of Royales	4.7
Gailia	0.2
Group of Francaises	0.1
Other	2.2
Philip Morris	
Marlboro	19.6
Philip Morris	5.0
Other	1.2
Rothmans International	
Peter Stuyvesant Group	8.7
Rothman Group	2.5
Dunhill Group	1.7
Other	0.8
Reynolds	
Camel Filter	7.8
Other	0.9

Source: Investext, Thomson Financial Networks, March 25, 1992, from Wheat First Butcher & Singer, Inc.

★ 380 ★
Cigarettes (SIC 2111)

Cigarette Brand Shares - Japan

Market shares, by brand, are shown in percent for 1991.

Mild Seven	21.8%
Mild Seven Lights	12.9
Seven Stars	10.0
Caster Mild	8.2
Mild Seven Super Lights	6.3
Cabin 85 Mild Box	5.0
Mild Seven FK	3.5
Hi Lite	3.2
Hope	3.1
Caster	2.8
Peace	1.9
Echo	1.8
Seven Stars Custom Lights Box	1.8
Hi Lite Mild	1.6
Cabin 85 Super Mild Box	1.3
Mi-Ne	0.3
Mini Star	0.3
Sometime	0.3
Mild Seven Menthol	0.2
Shinsei	0.2
Partner	0.2
Marlboro	0.2
Caster Special Box	0.2
Cabin 100s Mild Box	0.2
Mr. Slims	0.2
Marlboro Lights	0.1
Cabin 85 Super Mild	0.1
Beside	0.1
With Class	0.1
Other	0.9

Source: Investext, Thomson Financial Networks, March 25, 1992, from Wheat First Butcher & Singer, Inc.

★ 381 ★
Cigarettes (SIC 2111)

Cigarette Brands

Unit sales figures are shown by brand in billions. Percent shares are based on total industry sales of 390.4 billion cigarettes.

	Units (bil.)	Share
Marlboro	130.2	33.4%
Winston	68.0	17.4

Continued on next page.

★ 381 ★ *Continued*
Cigarettes (SIC 2111)

Cigarette Brands

Unit sales figures are shown by brand in billions. Percent shares are based on total industry sales of 390.4 billion cigarettes.

	Units (bil.)	Share
Salem	28.0	7.2%
Newport	24.1	6.2
Kool	24.0	6.1
Doral	23.3	6.0
Camel	20.4	5.2
Merit	16.5	4.2
Benson & Hedges	16.4	4.2
Virginia Slims	14.5	3.7
Others	25.0	6.4

Source: *USA TODAY*, June 25, 1992, p. 2B, from *The Maxwell Report*.

★ 382 ★
Cigarettes (SIC 2111)

Cigarette Company Shares - Australia

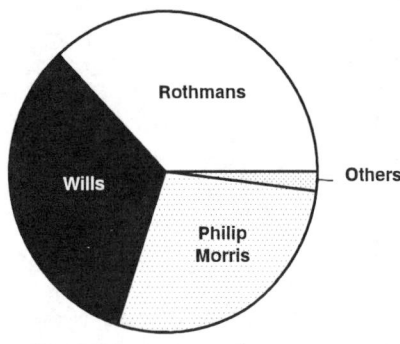

Market shares, by company, are shown in percent for 1981.

Rothmans	37.2%
Wills	33.1
Philip Morris	28.1
Others	1.6

Source: Investext, Thomson Financial Networks, March 25, 1992, from Wheat First Butcher & Singer, Inc.

★ 383 ★
Cigarettes (SIC 2111)

Cigarette Company Shares - Eastern Germany

Company shares of an estimated market of 30.4 billion cigarettes are shown in percent.

Philip Morris	44.0%
Rothmans	16.0
BAT	11.0
RJ Reynolds	7.0
Other	22.0

Source: *Financial Times*, January 31, 1992, p. 17.

★ 384 ★
Cigarettes (SIC 2111)

Cigarette Company Shares - France

Market shares, by company, are shown in percent for 1991.

Seita	47.4%
Philip Morris	25.8
Rothmans International	13.7
Reynolds	8.7
American Tobacco	1.8
BAT	1.5
Others	1.1

Source: Investext, Thomson Financial Networks, March 25, 1992, from Wheat First Butcher & Singer, Inc.

★ 385 ★
Cigarettes (SIC 2111)

Cigarette Company Shares - Japan

Market shares, by company, are shown in percent for 1991.

Japan Tobacco Inc.	82.3%
Philip Morris	11.3
Brown & Williamson/BAT	3.7
R. J. Reynolds	2.0
Rothmans	1.4
American Tobacco	1.2
BAT	-
Others	0.10

Source: Investext, Thomson Financial Networks, March 25, 1992, from Wheat First Butcher & Singer, Inc.

★ 386 ★
Cigarettes (SIC 2111)

Cigarette Company Shares - Japan

Japan Tobacco	
Philip Morris	
Brown & Williamson	
R.J. Reynolds	
Others	

Company shares of Japan's cigarette market shown in percent.

Japan Tobacco	83.5%
Philip Morris	10.1
Brown & Williamson	3.7
R.J. Reynolds	2.0
Others	0.7

Source: *Business TOKYO*, June 1992, p. 41, from Tobacco Institute of Japan and U.S. Department of Agriculture.

★ 387 ★
Cigarettes (SIC 2111)

Cigarette Company Shares - U.K.

Shares of the Big Three (U.K. cigarette companies) are shown for 1986 and 1990.

	1986	1990
Gallaher	36.0%	43%
Imperial Tobacco	39.0	34
Rothmans	10.0	14
Other	15.0	9

Source: *Tobacco*, May 1992, p. 3, from *Euromonitor*.

★ 388 ★
Cigarettes (SIC 2111)

Cigarette Consumption - Eastern Europe

Per capita annual consumption is shown for each country.

Poland	2,493
Hungary	2,485
Yugoslavia	2,355
Bulgaria	2,109
East Germany	1,875
Czechoslovakia	1,724

Russia	1,548
Romania	1,412
Albania	860

Source: *Financial Times*, January 31, 1992, p. 17, from Nomura Research Institute Europe.

★ 389 ★
Cigarettes (SIC 2111)

Cigarette Contraband - Canada

The contraband cigarette market in Canada is shown, by agent, in percent.

Large- /small-scale prof. smugglers	70.0%
Cross-border shoppers	30.0

Source: *The Globe and Mail*, May 22, 1992, p. A6, from RCMP estimates.

★ 390 ★
Cigarettes (SIC 2111)

Cigarette Discount Brands

Shares of the five leading discount brands are shown in percent.

Marlboro	23.2%
Winston	7.2
Salem	5.3
Doral	4.8
Camel	4.4

Source: *USA TODAY*, October 30, 1992, p. 2B, from Nielsen Marketing Research.

★ 391 ★
Cigarettes (SIC 2111)

Cigarette Exports from Canada

Recipients of Canada's 1.5 billion exported cigarettes are shown with their percentage of the market. "Other" includes airlines, ships, diplomats, and European sales.

United States	80.0%
St.-Pierre-Miquelon	10.0
Other	10.0

Source: *The Globe and Mail*, May 22, 1992, p. A6, from Revenue Canada, RCMP.

★ 392 ★

Cigarettes (SIC 2111)

Cigarette Global Manufacturers

Shares of cigarette manufacturing are shown in percent.

Hauny(Germany)	65%
Mollins(U.K.)	25
SASIB(Switzerland)	10

Source: Investext, Thomson Financial Networks, February 18, 1992, from Studio Albertini.

★ 393 ★

Cigarettes (SIC 2111)

Cigarette Industry - U.S.

Market shares, by company, are shown in percent. The figures for the first quarter of 1992 are an estimate, provided by Philip Morris.

	'90	'91	1Q '92
Philip Morris U.S.A.	42.3%	43.4%	41.6%
RJR Nabisco	29.6	27.8	30.6
Brown & Williamson	10.3	11.1	9.3
Lorillard	7.6	7.3	7.7
American Brands	6.8	7.0	7.3
Liggett Group, Inc.	3.4	3.4	3.5

Source: Investext, Thomson Financial Networks, June 15, 1992, from The Robinson-Humphrey Co., Inc.

★ 394 ★

Cigarettes (SIC 2111)

Cigarette Market

Value brand segment represented 19% of the total cigarette market in 1990. Shares of cigarette market are shown in percent by type of value brand.

Branded generic (low-price brand)	10.4%
Black and white/private label	3.6
Subgeneric (lower price than branded generics)	3.5
Price-offs (cigarettes with on-pack coupons)	0.8
Value 25s (25 cigarettes at price of 20-pack)	0.7
Other	81.0

Source: *DM*, September 1992, p. 56.

★ 395 ★

Cigarettes (SIC 2111)

Cigarette Market - U.K.

Segmentation of consumer sales is shown in percent for 1989 and 1990.

	1989	1990
King size	66.4%	66.7%
Longer length	25.3	26.0
Other tipped	6.4	5.5
Plain	2.0	1.8

Source: *Tobacco*, May 1992, p. 3, from *Euromonitor*.

★ 396 ★

Cigarettes (SIC 2111)

Cigarette Production in Canada

End use of the 12 billion cigarettes produced in Canada is shown in percent.

Sold, smoked in Canada	87.5%
Exported	12.5

Source: *The Globe and Mail*, May 22, 1992, p. A6, from Revenue Canada Excise Duty Directorate.

★ 397 ★

Cigarettes (SIC 2111)

Cigarette Vending Brands - U.K.

1992 forecasted shares of cigarette vending market, by brand, are shown in percent.

Benson & Hedges Special Filter	37.3%
Silk Cut King Size	14.1
Regal Kingsize	9.8
Embassy No 1 Kingsize	7.1
John Player Superkings	5.0
John Player Special Kingsize	4.7
Marlboro Kingsize	3.4
Berkeley Superkings	3.3
Embassy Tipped	3.0
Rothmans Kingsize	2.5
Other	9.8

Source: *Tobacco*, May 1992, p. 3, from *Euromonitor*.

★ 398 ★

Cigarettes (SIC 2111)

Supermarket Cigarette Sales

| Marlboro |
| Winston |
| Salem |
| Doral Light & Full Flavor |
| Camel |
| Merit |
| Benson & Hedges |
| Virginia Slims |
| Kool |
| Cambridge |
| Other |

Sales of the 10 leading supermarket cigarette brands accounted for 63.1% of the $9.8717 billion market for the year ending January/February 1992. Shares are shown in percent.

	Sales	Shares
Marlboro	$ 2,060.1	20.9%
Winston	806.1	8.2
Salem	599.2	6.1
Doral Light & Full Flavor	529.0	5.4
Camel	398.8	4.0
Merit	390.0	4.0
Benson & Hedges	375.4	3.8
Virginia Slims	370.1	3.7
Kool	365.5	3.7
Cambridge	329.5	3.3
Other	3,648.0	36.9

Source: *Advertising Age*, July 20, 1992, p. 20, from A.C. Nielsen ScanTrack.

★ 399 ★

Cigars (SIC 2121)

Large Cigar Sales

Cigar manufacturers are shown with brand shares in percent, based on a total of 1.822 billion units in 1991. Brands listed under Consolidated Cigar include those of American Cigar, which it acquired in 1986. Phillies acquired Erik in 1988.

Swisher International
King Edward	24.1%
Optimo	2.5
Corral Wodiska y Co.	0.9

Other	7.1%

Consolidated Cigar
Muriel	8.1
Dutch Masters	6.0
Antonio y Cleopatra	4.6
El Producto	3.5
Backwoods	1.6
La Corona	0.7
Roi-Tan	0.6
Other	2.0

Havatampa
| Cuesta-Rey | 0.9 |
| Phillies | 1.0 |

Phillies
| Erik Filter Menthol | 3.0 |

General Cigar
White Owl	5.1
Garcia y Vega	4.9
Robert Burns	2.6
William Penn	2.2
Tijuana Smalls	1.7
Other	0.9

House of Windsor
| House of Windsor | 2.7 |

M&N Standard Cogar
| Rigoletto | 1.0 |

Source: Investext, Thomson Financial Networks, March 23, 1992, from Wheat First Butcher & Singer, Inc.

★ 400 ★

Smokeless Tobacco (SIC 2131)

Dry Snuff Producers

Volume shares of the domestic market in 1991 are shown in percent, based on a total of 6.382 million lbs.

Conwood	40.0%
Helme	34.0
U.S. Tobacco	18.0
B&W	8.0

Source: Investext, Thomson Financial Networks, April 28, 1992, from Wheat First Butcher & Singer, Inc.

★ 401 ★
Smokeless Tobacco (SIC 2131)

Loose Leaf Smokeless Tobacco

Shares of the domestic market in 1991 are shown in percent, based on a total of 63.664 million lbs. Figures may not add due to rounding.

Pinkerton
Red Man	28.0%
Golden Blend	9.0
Granger	4.0
Workhorse	1.0
Other	1.0

Conwood
Levi Garrett	23.0
H.B. Scott	2.0
Taylors Pride	2.0
Rough Country	1.0
Scotten, Dillon	1.0
Red Fox and others	3.0
National	1.0
Beech-Nut Regular	13.0
Beech-Nut Wintergreen	3.0
Beech-Nut Spearmint	1.0

Helme Tobacco
Chatanooga Chew	3.0
Other	6.0

Source: Investext, Thomson Financial Networks, April 28, 1992, from Wheat First Butcher & Singer, Inc.

★ 402 ★
Smokeless Tobacco (SIC 2131)

Moist Plug

Volume shares of the domestic market in 1991 are shown in percent, based on a total of 1.952 million lbs.

Pinkerton
Red Man	25.0%
Totems	10.0
R.J. Gold	3.0

Conwood
Levi Garrett	36.0
Taylors Pride	26.0

Source: Investext, Thomson Financial Networks, April 28, 1992, from Wheat First Butcher & Singer, Inc.

★ 403 ★
Smokeless Tobacco (SIC 2131)

Moist Snuff and Fine Cut Brands

Volume shares of the domestic market in 1991 are based on a total of 47.056 million lbs. Figures may not add due to rounding.

U.S. Tobacco
Copenhagen	47.0%
Skoal	37.0
Skoal Bandits	1.0
Happy Days	<1.0
Other	1.0

Conwood
Kodiak	8.0
Hawken	2.0

Helme Tobacco
Redwood	1.0
Silver Creek	1.0
Gold River	<1.0
Other	<1.0

Pinkerton
Red Man	<1.0
Other	<1.0

Source: Investext, Thomson Financial Networks, April 28, 1982, from Wheat First Butcher & Singer, Inc.

★ 404 ★

Smokeless Tobacco (SIC 2131)

Plug Producers

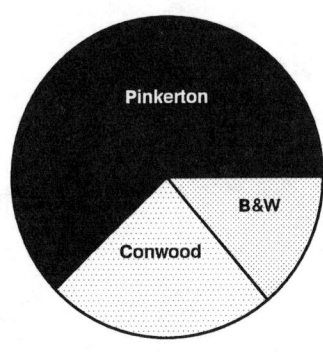

Volume shares of the domestic market in 1991 are shown in percent, based on a total of 4.494 million lbs.

Pinkerton 62.0%
Conwood 24.0
B&W 14.0

Source: Investext, Thomson Financial Networks, April 28, 1992, from Wheat First Butcher & Singer, Inc.

★ 405 ★

Smokeless Tobacco (SIC 2131)

Smokeless Tobacco Producers

Volume shares of the 1991 U.S. market are shown in percent, based on a total of 124.738 million lbs.

U.S. Tobacco 33.8%
Pinkerton 25.2
Conwood 23.7
National 9.7
Helme Tobacco 6.8
B&W 0.9
RC Owen 0.5
Other 1.2

Source: Investext, Thomson Financial Networks, April 28, 1992, from Wheat First Butcher & Singer, Inc.

★ 406 ★

Smokeless Tobacco (SIC 2131)

Twist/Roll Tobacco Producers

Volume shares of the domestic market in 1991 are shown in percent, based on a total of 1.190 million lbs.

Conwood 53.0%
R.C. Owen 47.0
RJR . . . . <1.0

Source: Investext, Thomson Financial Networks, April 28, 1992, from Wheat First Butcher & Singer, Inc.

SIC 22 - Textile Mill Products

★ 407 ★

Fabric Mills (SIC 2200)

Textile Manufacturers

Sales of 12 leading textile manufacturers worldwide, in billions of dollars, totaled $49.97 billion in 1990. Relative market shares are shown in percent.

	Sales ($ bil.)	% of Group
Toray Industries	$ 6.05	12.0%
Hyosung	5.26	11.0
Haci Omer Sabanci	5.13	10.0
Kanebo	4.63	9.0
Courtaulds	4.33	9.0
Levi Strauss	4.25	8.0
Teijin	4.11	8.0
Toyobo	3.69	7.0
Wickes	3.65	7.0
Coats Viyella	3.29	7.0
Unitika	2.96	6.0
VF	2.62	5.0

Source: *Business Horizons*, November 1991, p. 18.

★ 408 ★

Textile (SIC 2200)

Textile Manufacturer Global Shares

Market shares of the 12 largest textile companies in 1980 and 1990 are based on their world sales.

	1980	1990
Toray Industries	-	0.12%
Hyosung	0.08%	0.11
Haci Omer Sabanci	0.08	0.10
Kanebo	0.08	0.09
Courtaulds	0.16	0.09
Levi Strauss	0.11	0.08
Teijin	-	0.08
Toyobo	0.07	0.07
Wickes	-	0.07
Coats Viyella	-	0.07

	1980	1990
Unitika	0.06%	0.06%
VF	-	0.05
Burlington	0.12	-
JP Stevens	0.08	-
Coats Patons	0.06	-
Armstrong World	0.05	-
West Point Pepperell	0.05	-

Source: *America's Textile International*, May 1992, p. 37, from University Research Center.

★ 409 ★

Textile Fiber (SIC 2200)

Nylon Fiber Market - Asia/Pacific

Segment distribution is shown as percent of the total Asian/Pacific market.

Textile	61.0%
Carpet	10.0
Others	29.0

Source: Investext, Thomson Financial Networks, April 24, 1992, from Nomura Research Institute.

★ 410 ★

Textile Fiber (SIC 2200)

Nylon Fiber Market - Eastern Europe

Segment distribution is shown as percent of the total Eastern European market.

Textile	68.0%
Carpet	15.0
Others	17.0

Source: Investext, Thomson Financial Networks, April 24, 1992, from Nomura Research Institute.

★ 411 ★
Textile Fiber (SIC 2200)

Nylon Fiber Market - North America

Segment distribution is shown as percent of the total North American market.

Carpet	. 70.0%
Textile	. 19.0
Other	. 11.0

Source: Investext, Thomson Financial Networks, April 24, 1992, from Nomura Research Institute.

★ 412 ★
Textile Fiber (SIC 2200)

Nylon Fiber Market - West Europe

Segment distribution is shown as percent of the total West European market.

Textile	. 46.0%
Carpet	. 39.0
Other	. 15.0

Source: Investext, Thomson Financial Networks, April 24, 1992, from Nomura Research Institute.

★ 413 ★
Upholstery (SIC 2200)

Upholstery Fabrics

Distribution of sales is shown in percent.

Textures	. 28.0%
Jacquards	. 23.0
Velvets	. 19.0
Prints	. 18.0
Leathers	. 10.0
Vinyls	. 2.0

Source: *Furniture TODAY Annual Retail Marketing Guide*, 1992, p. 53.

★ 414 ★
Dyeing (SIC 2261)

Cotton Dyeing Processes - North America

Production of cotton, by dyeing process, is shown in percent.

Discontinuous jet dyeing	. 49.0%
Thermosol pad roll/pad steam	. 30.0
Package dyeing	. 21.0

Source: *ATI*, January 1992, p. 68, from BASF.

★ 415 ★
Textiles (SIC 2269)

Home Textile Sales

Shares by category are shown in percent, based on group totals for 1990 and 1991.

	1990	1991
Sheets and pillowcases	28.0%	28.6%
Bath towels	23.2	23.7
Mini blinds	20.0	19.9
Comforters	15.8	15.1
Vertical blinds	13.0	12.7

Source: *HFD*, February 24, 1992, p. 2A.

★ 416 ★
Carpets (SIC 2273)

Carpet Manufacturers

Shares are shown in percent, based on a market total of $7.10 billion in 1990. The figures for Shaw are based on fiscal year 1991.

Shaw	. 22.6%
Burlington	. 6.6
Salem	. 6.1
Queen	. 4.6
Karastan	. 4.5
Horizon	. 4.2
Other	. 48.6

Source: Investext, Thomson Financial Networks, January 7, 1992, from Wertheim Schroder & Co.

★ 417 ★

Carpets (SIC 2273)

Carpet Production by Type

Percent distribution of carpet shipments is shown, by type, based on a total of 1.250 million square yards in 1991 (estimate) and 1.325 million square yards in 1992 (forecast).

	1991	1992
Tufted broadloom	83.7%	83.0%
Automotive & industrial	4.8	5.3
Rugs & others	5.2	5.3
Needlepunch	3.6	3.4
Artificial grass	1.6	1.9
Woven	0.8	0.8
Knitted	0.4	0.4

Source: *Textile World*, May 1992, p. 70, from U.S. Department of Commerce.

★ 418 ★

Carpets (SIC 2273)

Carpet Shipments by Type

Shares of the U.S. tufted carpet market are shown in percent, based on shipment value totals of $6.2247 billion in 1985 and $7.9995 billion in 1990.

	1985	1990
Rugs (larger than 6x9)	87.5%	88.9%
Automotive & aircraft	6.6	5.6
Rugs (smaller than 6x9)	5.0	4.8
Artificial grass (non-athletic)	0.9	0.7

Source: Investext, Thomson Financial Networks, January 7, 1992, from Wertheim Schroder & Co.

★ 419 ★

Carpets (SIC 2273)

Commercial Carpet Use

Segment distribution is shown in percent.

Office buildings	43.0%
Hospitality facilities	17.0
Retail store facilities	17.0
Educational facilities	15.0
Health care facilities	8.0

Source: Investext, Thomson Financial Networks, June 26, 1992, from The First Boston Corporation.

★ 420 ★

Carpets (SIC 2273)

Tufted Carpet Use

Estimated shares of the 1992 market are shown in percent, based on a total of 1.140 billion square yards.

Residential remodeling	55.0%
Commercial remodeling	21.0
Residential construction	20.0
Commercial construction	4.0

Source: Investext, Thomson Financial Networks, January 7, 1992, from Wertheim Schroder & Co.

★ 421 ★

Textiles (SIC 2281)

Fabric Production in Pakistan

Fabric production is shown in thousands of square yards for 1990-91. Shares, by type, are shown percent.

	Sq. yds. (000)	Share
Cotton	257,411	80.4%
Blends	62,920	19.6

Source: *Textile World*, June 1992, p. 62.

★ 422 ★

Textiles (SIC 2281)

Yarn Production in Pakistan

Yarn production is shown in thousands of lbs. for 1990-91 period. Shares, by type, are shown in percent.

	Lbs (000)	Share
All-cotton	409,280	85.5%
Blends	69,499	14.5

Source: *Textile World*, June 1992, p. 62.

SIC 23 - Apparel and Other Textile Products

★ 423 ★

Apparel (SIC 2300)

Apparel Industry Leaders

Companies are ranked by 1991 sales, shown in millions of dollars. Percent shares are based on a group total of $18,205 million.

	Sales ($ mil.)	% of Group
Levi Strauss Assoc.	$ 4,903	26.9%
VF	2,989	16.4
Liz Claiborne	2,029	11.1
Fruit of the Loom	1,628	8.9
Hartmarx	1,215	6.7
Leslie Fay	837	4.6
Crystal Brands	827	4.5
Kellwood	811	4.5
Phillips-Van Heusen	808	4.4
Russell	805	4.4
Gitano Group	780	4.3
Warnaco Group	573	3.1

Source: *Fortune*, April 20, 1992, p. 260.

★ 424 ★

Apparel (SIC 2300)

Apparel Manufacturers

Companies are ranked by 1991 sales, shown in millions of dollars. Percent shares are based on a group total of $14,133 million.

	Sales ($ mil.)	% of Group
Nike	$ 3,212	22.7%
VF	2,952	20.9
Reebok International	2,734	19.3
Liz Claiborne	2,007	14.2

	Sales ($ mil.)	% of Group
Fruit of the Loom	$ 1,514	10.7%
Russel	805	5.7
Stride Rite	574	4.1
Jones Apparel Group	334	2.4

Source: *The 1992 Business Week 1000*, p. 170.

★ 425 ★

Apparel (SIC 2300)

Apparel Sales in Western Europe

Wholesale sales by category are shown in billions of dollars. Shares are shown as percent of group total.

	Sales ($ bil.)	% of Group
Activewear	$ 3.4	30.6%
Women's panties/foundations	3.3	29.7
Hosiery	2.9	26.1
Men's underwear	1.5	13.5

Source: Investext, Thomson Financial Networks, March 2, 1992, from Prudential Securities Inc.

★ 426 ★

Apparel (SIC 2300)

Jeans Market

Company shares are shown in percent, based on total sales of 386 million pairs of jeans sold in the 12 months ended February 1992.

Levi Strauss & Co.	20.2%
Wrangler	15.4
Other	64.4

Source: *Advertising Age*, May 25, 1992, p. 38, from MRCA Information Services.

★ 427 ★

Apparel (SIC 2300)

Leading Cap Makers

Percentages, based on total number of responses, reflect the Sporting Goods Business survey of screenprinting, heat lettering, and embroidery dealers, who indicated the single most used cap company name.

New Era 16.6%
Young An 6.7
Otto 6.3
Sportcap 5.8
Nissin 5.4

Source: *Sporting Goods Business*, March 1992, p. 14A.

★ 428 ★

Apparel (SIC 2300)

Soccer Shirts by Price

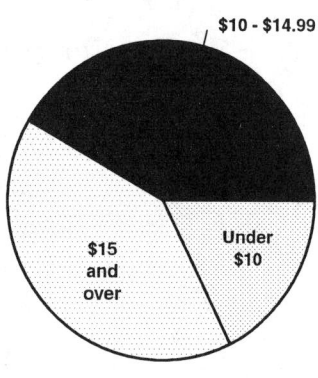

Figures represent percent shares of the soccer shirt market by price.

$10 - $14.99. . . . . 41.6%
$15 and over 40.9
Under $10 . . . . 17.5

Source: *Sporting Goods Business*, April 1992, p. 48.

★ 429 ★

Apparel (SIC 2300)

Soccer Shorts by Price

Figures represent percent shares of the soccer shorts market by price.

$15 or over 54.2%
$10 - $14.99. . . . . 28.2
Under $10 . . . . 17.6

Source: *Sporting Goods Business*, April 1992, p. 48.

★ 430 ★

Apparel (SIC 2300)

Sports Clothing Sales

1991 sports clothing sales, by type of sport, are shown in millions of dollars. Segment distribution is shown in percent.

	Sales	Shares
Swimming	$ 1,904.4	16.0%
Golf	1,525.4	12.8
Camping	1,495.5	12.6
Skiing	1,068.2	9.0
Aerobics	1,019.9	8.6
Hunting	938.1	7.9
Running/jogging	917.0	7.7
Bicycling	912.2	7.7
Fishing	854.7	7.2
Bowling	644.1	5.4
Tennis	613.9	5.2

Source: *Sporting Goods Business*, May 1992, p. 26, from NSGA.

★ 431 ★

Apparel (SIC 2300)

Top Athletic Shorts Makers

Percentages, based on total number of responses, reflect the Sporting Goods Business survey of screenprinting, heat lettering, and embroidery dealers, who indicated the single most used athletic shorts company name.

Augusta 21.4%
MJ Soffee 17.3
Russell 10.5
Don Alleson 9.5
Dodger 8.2

Source: *Sporting Goods Business*, March 1992, p. 14A.

★ 432 ★

Apparel (SIC 2300)

Top Fleece Product Manufacturers

Percentages, based on total number of responses, reflect the Sporting Good Business survey of screenprinting, heat lettering, and embroidery dealers who indicated the single most used fleece company name.

Russell	27.2%
Jerzees	22.2
Fruit of the Loom	18.0
Hanes	13.6
Discus	2.9
Lee	2.9

Source: *Sporting Goods Business*, March 1992, p. 14A.

★ 433 ★

Apparel (SIC 2300)

Top Golf/Placket Shirt Makers

Percentages, based on total number of responses, reflect the Sporting Goods Business survey of screenprinting, heat lettering, and embroidery dealers, who indicated the single most used golf/placket shirt company name.

Hanes	16.8%
Hartwell	10.9
Stedman	10.0
Outer Banks	9.1
Print-Ons	8.6

Source: *Sporting Goods Business*, March 1992, p. 14A.

★ 434 ★

Apparel (SIC 2300)

Top Jacket Makers

Percentages, based on total number of responses, reflect the Sporting Goods Business survey of screenprinting, heat lettering, and embroidery dealers, who indicated the single most used jacket company name.

Hartwell	15.1%
Holloway	14.8
Dunbrooke	11.8
Auburn	11.0
Westark	6.3

Source: *Sporting Goods Business*, March 1992, p. 14A.

★ 435 ★

Apparel (SIC 2300)

Top T-Shirt Makers

Percentages, based on total number of responses, reflect the Sporting Goods Business survey of screenprinting, heat lettering, and embroidery dealers, who indicated the single most used T-shirt company name.

Screen Strs Bst	27.3%
Russell	21.8
Hanes	18.2
Jerzees	13.8
Fruit of the Loom	6.7

Source: *Sporting Goods Business*, March 1992, p. 14A.

★ 436 ★

Apparel (SIC 2300)

Women's Apparel

Segment distribution is shown in percent.

Tops	33.61%
Dresses, skirts, suits	20.23
Bottoms	18.22
Intimate apparel	15.46
Activewear	6.16
Outerwear	2.70
Miscellaneous	3.62

Source: *Discount Merchandiser*, June 1992, p. 60, from survey.

★ 437 ★

Apparel (SIC 2321)

Men's Dress Shirt Makers

Company shares are shown in percent, based on the $2.4 billion men's dress shirt market in 1991.

Phillips-Van Heusen	9.9%
Arrow	9.2
Other	80.9

Source: *The Wall Street Journal*, May 22, 1992, p. B1, from MRCA Information Services.

★ 438 ★

Sweatshirts (SIC 2321)

Sweatshirt Manufacturers

Shares are shown in percent, based on an estimated total of $3.3 billion. Hanes includes Pannill and Champion.

Hanes 17.0%
Tultex 9.0
Russell 8.0
Bassett Walker 8.0
Fruit of the Loom 5.0
Other 5.0

Source: Investext, Thomson Financial Networks, June 25, 1992, from Oppenheimer & Co., Inc.

★ 439 ★

T-Shirts (SIC 2321)

T-Shirt Manufacturers

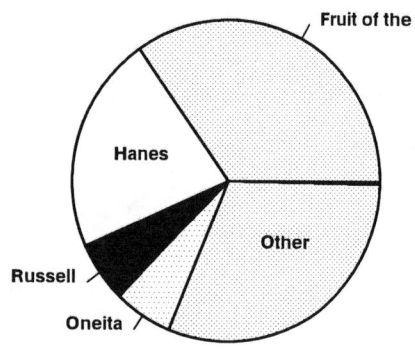

Shares are shown in percent, based on an estimated total market of $1.68 billion in 1991.

Fruit of the Loom 35.0%
Hanes 22.0
Russell 6.0
Oneita 6.0
Other 31.0

Source: Investext, Thomson Financial Networks, June 25, 1992, from Oppenheimer & Co., Inc. and industry surveys.

★ 440 ★

Millinery (SIC 2353)

Millinery Manufacturers - Leaders

Millinery sales for 1990 are shown in millions of dollars; relative market shares are shown in percent.

	Sales ($ mil.)	% of Group
Vatex Headwear Inc.	$ 130.0	24.2%
K-Products Inc.	80.0	14.9
Resistol Hats	50.0	9.3
Bollman Hat Co.	35.0	6.5
Paramount Cap Manufacturing Co.	35.0	6.5
George W. Bollman Co. Inc. . .	32.4	6.0
Universal Industries Inc.	30.0	5.6
Interco Inc. (International Hat Co.) . . .	25.0	4.7
New Era Cap Co. Inc.	25.0	4.7
Louisville Manufacturing Co. . .	19.0	3.5
Davis Clothing Co.	16.0	3.0
Four Seasons Garment Co. . . .	16.0	3.0
M. Grossman and Sons Inc. . .	15.0	2.8
Twin City Knitting Co.	15.0	2.8
AJD Cap Corp.	13.3	2.5

Source: *Infotrak*, 1991, p. 20, from Fairchild Fashion & Merchandising Group 1991.

★ 441 ★

Apparel (SIC 2360)

Boys' Apparel

Segment distribution is shown in percent.

Tops 36.63%
Bottoms 22.36
Furnishings 15.70
Activewear 13.61
Outerwear 7.52
Suits/sportcoats 1.11
Miscellaneous 3.07

Source: *Discount Merchandiser*, June 1992, p. 60, from survey.

★ 442 ★
Apparel (SIC 2360)

Girls' Apparel

Segment distribution is shown in percent.

Tops	23.82%
Bottoms	19.02
Intimate apparel	15.38
Dresses/skirts	14.23
Activewear	11.61
Outerwear	7.45
Miscellaneous	8.49

Source: *Discount Merchandiser*, June 1992, p. 60, from survey.

★ 443 ★
Apparel (SIC 2360)

Men's Apparel

Segment distribution is shown in percent.

Tops	32.43%
Bottoms	25.35
Furnishings	17.16
Activewear	8.60
Suits/sportcoats	6.74
Outerwear	6.52
Miscellaneous	3.20

Source: *Discount Merchandiser*, June 1992, p. 60, from survey.

★ 444 ★
Curtains and Draperies (SIC 2391)

Curtain and Drapery Market

Segment distribution is shown in percent for 1991.

Draperies	42.2%
Curtains	40.6
Roller shades	10.9
Top treatments	6.4

Source: *HFD*, February 24, 1992, p. 14A.

★ 445 ★
Comforters (SIC 2392)

Comforter Manufacturers

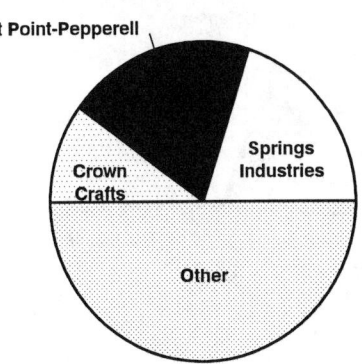

Estimated shares of sales of comforters and accessories are shown in percent.

Springs Industries	20.0%
West Point-Pepperell	20.0
Crown Crafts	10.0
Other	50.0

Source: Investext, Thomson Financial Networks, June 19, 1992, from William Blair & Company.

★ 446 ★
Home Furnishings (SIC 2392)

Bed Coverings Market

Segment distribution is shown in percent for 1990.

Bed ensembles	36.0%
Comforters	33.4
Bedspreads	16.1
Quilts	7.0
Down comforters	5.8
Duvet covers	1.2
Bedding accessories	0.5

Source: *HFD*, February 24, 1992, p. 10A.

★ 447 ★

Tents (SIC 2394)

Tent Manufacturers

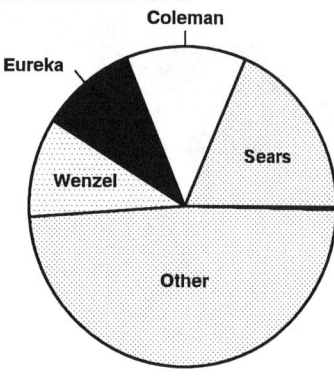

Estimated shares of the domestic market are shown in percent, based on a total of $240 million.

Sears	15.0%
Coleman	10.0
Eureka	8.0
Wenzel	8.0
Other	39.0

Source: Investext, Thomson Financial Networks, March 26, 1992, from The First Boston Corporation.

★ 448 ★

Sleeping Bags (SIC 2399)

Sleeping Bag Manufacturers

Estimated shares of the domestic market are shown in percent, based on a total of $225 million.

Coleman	31.0%
Wenzel	21.0
Sears	8.0
Ero	4.0
Other	36.0

Source: Investext, Thomson Financial Networks, March 26, 1992, from The First Boston Corporation.

SIC 24 - Lumber and Wood Products

★ 449 ★

Sawmills (SIC 2421)

Lumber Producers - U.S. and Canada

1990 distribution of lumber production among the 20 North American leaders, expressed in million board feet per company. Relative market share is shown in percent.

	Vol. (mil. bd. ft.)	% of Group
Weyerhaeuser Co.	2,921	13.5%
Georgia-Pacific Corp.	2,664	12.3
Louisiana-Pacific Corp.	2,189	10.1
Canfor Corp.	1,431	6.6
Weldwood of Canada Ltd.	1,011	4.7
WTD Industries Inc.	996	4.6
West Fraser Timber Co. Ltd.	993	4.6
Sierra Pacific Industries	967	4.5
International Paper Co.	880	4.1
Fletcher Challenge Canada Ltd.	863	4.0
Champion International Corp.	819	3.8
MacMillan Bloedel Ltd.	795	3.7
Boise Cascade Corp.	783	3.6
Slocan Forrest Products Ltd.	680	3.1
Westar Timber Ltd.	626	2.9
Doman Industries	619	2.9
RSG Forest Productions Inc.	604	2.8
Northwood Pulp & Timber Ltd.	596	2.8
Donohue Inc.	595	2.8
Pope & Talbot Inc.	586	2.7

Source: *Forest Industries*, January/February 1992, p. 5.

★ 450 ★

Wood Panel (SIC 2430)

Wood Panel by Type

Distribution of domestic shipments in 1991 is shown in percent, based on a total of 33.7 million square feet. Structural panels include softwood plywood, oriented strand board, waferboard, and oriented waferboard.

Structural panels	72.1%
Hardboard	14.5
Particleboard	10.6
Medium-density fiberboard	2.8

Source: *Forest Industries*, March 1992, p. 21, from American Plywood Association, National Particleboard Association, and American Hardboard Association.

★ 451 ★

Wood Panel (SIC 2430)

Wood Panel Production - Canada

Distribution, by type, is shown in percent, based on an estimated total of 4.36 million cubic feet. OSB stands for oriented strand board.

Construction plywood	39.5%
Waferboard and OSB	36.5
Particleboard	24.0

Source: *Forest Industries*, March 1992, p. 22, from Statistics Canada.

★ 452 ★

Cabinets (SIC 2434)

Cabinet Makers

| Masco |
| WCI |
| Triangle Pacific |
| Bassett |
| American Woodmark |
| Other |

Estimated shares are shown in percent.

Masco	17.0%
WCI	6.0
Triangle Pacific	6.0
Bassett	3.0
American Woodmark	3.0
Other	65.0

Source: Investext, Thomson Financial Networks, May 26, 1992, from Kidder, Peabody & Company, Incorporated.

★ 453 ★

Softwood (SIC 2436)

Lumber Producers - North America

The 20 leading lumber producers in the U.S. and Canada are ranked by millions of board feet produced in 1990; relative share is shown in percent.

	Mil. Bd. Ft.	% of Group
Weyerhaeuser Co.	2,921	13.5%
Georgia-Pacific Corp.	2,664	12.3
Louisiana-Pacific Corp.	2,189	10.1
Canfor Corp.	1,431	6.6
Weldwood of Canada Ltd. . . .	1,011	4.7
WTD Industries Inc.	996	4.6
West Fraser Timber Co. Ltd. . .	993	4.6
Sierra Pacific Industries	967	4.5
International Paper Co.	880	4.1
Fletcher Challenge Canada Ltd. .	863	4.0
Champion International Corp. . .	819	3.8
MacMillan Bloedel Ltd.	795	3.7
Boise Cascade Corp.	783	3.6
Slocan Forest Products Ltd. . . .	680	3.1
Westar Timber Ltd.	626	2.9
Doman Industries	619	2.9
RSG Forest Products Inc. . . .	604	2.8
Northwood Pulp & Timber Ltd. .	596	2.8

	Mil. Bd. Ft.	% of Group
Donohue Inc.	595	2.8%
Pope & Talbot Inc.	586	2.7

Source: *Forest Industries*, January 1992, p. 5.

★ 454 ★

Mobile Homes (SIC 2451)

Mobile Home Manufacturers

The leading mobile home manufacturers are ranked according to 1991 sales in millions of dollars; relative shares are shown in percent.

	Sales ($ mil.)	% of Group
Fleetwood Enterprises	$ 1,410	51.5%
Clayton Homes	334	12.2
Skyline Corp.	313	11.4
Champion Enterprises	274	10.0
Schult Homes	161	5.9
Oakwood Homes	126	4.6
Cavalier Homes	66	2.4
Liberty Homes	53	1.9

Source: *Forbes*, December 23, 1991, p. 133, from Media General and Lotus One Source.

★ 455 ★

Firelogs (SIC 2499)

Firelogs by Brand

Shares are shown in percent for the year ending December 8, 1991. Shares did not add to 100% in original source.

Duraflame	54.0%
Other	45.0

Source: *Dealerscope Merchandising*, February 1992, p. 71, from IRI.

SIC 25 - Furniture and Fixtures

★456★

Furniture (SIC 2500)

Furniture Makers

Estimated shares are shown in percent.

Masco	9.0%
Interco	5.0
La-Z-Boy	4.0
Bassett	3.0
Ladd	3.0
Armstrong	3.0
Other	73.0

Source: Investext, Thomson Financial Networks, May 26, 1992, from Kidder, Peabody & Company, Incorporated.

★457★

Furniture (SIC 2500)

Furniture Makers - Canada

Manufacturer shares of Canada's furniture market are shown in percent based on total revenues of C$2,046.0 million in 1990 and C$1,802.0 million in 1991. Category includes businesses whose primary purpose is manufacture or marketing of household furniture. Revenue includes, however, sales from other furniture products. Figures for Strathearn House include Conant Ball, Nadeau, HPL, and Grange. Figures for Dorel include non-furniture baby products.

	1990	1991
Dorel Inds.	7.7%	9.6%
Palliser Furniture	7.5	9.3
Sklar-Peppler	3.7	3.9
Strathearn House	3.6	3.7
Carol Ann	2.4	2.8
Dutalier	2.0	2.5
El ran Furniture	2.0	2.4
Liberty Furniture	1.9%	2.1%
Shermag	1.9	2.0
La-Z-Boy Canada	1.8	1.8
Other	65.7	59.9

Source: *Furniture/Today*, June 8, 1992, p. 16, from Atkins Research Institute and *Furniture/Today* market research.

★458★

Furniture (SIC 2500)

Furniture Makers - Top 10

Companies are ranked by dollar sales in 1991. Relative market shares are based on a total of $14,170 million.

	Sales ($ mil.)	% of Group
Johnson Controls	$ 4,566	32.2%
Avery Dennison	2,545	18.0
Interco	1,597	11.3
LSS Holdings	1,085	7.7
Leggett & Platt	1,082	7.6
Herman Miller	884	6.2
Sealy Holdings	624	4.4
Hon Industries	612	4.3
La-Z-Boy Chair	609	4.3
Kimball International	565	4.0

Source: *Fortune*, April 20, 1992, p. 274.

★ 459 ★

Furniture (SIC 2500)

Furniture Makers - U.S.

Masco Furniture

Broyhill Lane

La-Z-Boy

LADD

Thomasville

Bassett

Mohasco

Klaussner

Ethan Allen

Sauder Woodworking

Other

Market shares are shown in percent, based on an industry revenue total of $16.020 billion in FY1990.

Masco Furniture	7.4%
Broyhill Lane	4.9
La-Z-Boy	3.5
LADD	3.2
Thomasville	2.7
Bassett	2.7
Mohasco	2.5
Klaussner	2.1
Ethan Allen	2.0
Sauder Woodworking	1.8
Other	66.1

Source: Investext, Thomson Financial Networks, April 10, 1992, from Oppenheimer & Co., Inc.

★ 460 ★

Furniture (SIC 2500)

Furniture Manufacturing Leaders

Top 25 U.S. manufacturers' shares are based on a 1990 industry total of $19,576 million, shown in percent.

Masco Furniture	6.05%
Broyhill/Lane	4.01
La-Z-Boy	2.88
Ladd	2.61
Thomasville	2.23
Bassett	2.23
Mohasco	2.02
Klaussner	1.74
Ethan Allen	1.66

Sauder Woodworking	1.48%
Leggett & Platt	1.25
Townhouse/Penthouse	1.23
Ashley	0.91
O'Sullivan	0.82
Stanley	0.81
Pulaski	0.67
Bernhardt	0.65
Douglas	0.62
Century	0.59
Berkline	0.58
Singer	0.57
Washington/Caraway	0.57
Bush	0.56
Flexsteel	0.56
Jackson	0.54

Source: Investext, Thomson Financial Networks, April 9, 1992, p. 92, from Raymond James & Associates, Inc.

★ 461 ★

Furniture (SIC 2500)

Furniture Market Shares by Product Type

Shares by product are shown as percent of 1991 total market.

Home theater/entertainment furniture	35.0%
Home office/computer furniture	25.0
Storage furniture	14.0
Bedroom furniture	12.0
Kitchen furniture	10.0
Other	4.0

Source: *HFD*, April 1992, p. 6.

★ 462 ★

Furniture (SIC 2500)

Furniture Sales by Type

Furniture sales by type are shown in billions of dollars for 1991. Percent shares are based on group total. RTA stands for ready-to-assemble.

	Sales ($ bil.)	% of Group
RTA furniture	$ 1.10	13.0%
Flat case goods	7.33	87.0

Source: *HFD*, April 1992, p. 12.

★ 463 ★
Furniture (SIC 2500)

Household Furniture Shipments

Household furniture shipment value was estimated to be $18,750 million in 1991. Shares, by type of furniture, are shown in percent.

Wood	42.1%
Upholstered	29.7
Mattresses and bedsprings	17.5
Metal	10.7

Source: *Furniture/Today*, 1992, p. 114, from Bureau of the Census and the International Trade Commission.

★ 464 ★
Furniture (SIC 2500)

Motion Upholstery Market

Shares are based on total 1990 shipments of inclining or reclining sofas, loveseats, sectionals, and modulars. Sales of free-standing reclining chairs are not included.

	Shpmt. ($ mil.)	Share
Mohasco	$ 92	12.0%
Berkline	78	10.0
Bench Craft	70	9.0
Townhouse/Penthouse	62	8.0
La-Z-Boy	45	6.0
Action	43	6.0
Klaussner	38	5.0
Peoploungers	37	5.0
Cleveland Chair	24	5.0
England/Corsair	15	3.0
Gentry Gallery	15	2.0
Silver Oaks	14	2.0
Easy Rest	12	2.0
Sheffield	11	1.0
Bradington Young	10	1.0

Source: "Annual Retail Marketing Guide," *Furniture/Today*, 1992, p. 33, from market research.

★ 465 ★
Furniture (SIC 2510)

Furniture Makers - North America

1991 distribution of revenues among the 25 leaders of the household furniture industry include contract shipments and bedding shipments, except in the case of Stanley and Leggett & Platt which include household furniture revenues only. Dorel revenues include unspecified sales of portable car seats and other infant products.

	Amt. ($ mil.)	% of Group
Masco Home Furnishings . .	$ 1,430.0	18.9%
Broyhill/Lane	819.3	10.8
La-Z-Boy	610.0	8.1
LADD	429.1	5.7
Thomasville	417.5	5.5
Bassett	401.6	5.3
Klaussner	357.5	4.7
Ethan Allen	335.0	4.4
Mohasco	334.3	4.4
Sauder Woodworking	300.0	4.0
Townhouse Penthouse	225.0	3.0
O'Sullivan	200.0	2.6
Ashley	180.0	2.4
Dorel	149.5	2.0
Palliser	144.4	1.9
Stanley	140.8	1.9
Sunbeam Outdoor Products . .	130.0	1.7
Berkline	126.5	1.7
Bush	126.2	1.7
Bernhardt	125.0	1.7
Leggett & Platt	121.0	1.6
Pulaski	120.6	1.6
Douglas	118.6	1.6
Singer	116.4	1.5
Century	111.5	1.5

Source: *Furniture/Today*, May 11, 1992, p. 8, from market research.

★ 466 ★

Furniture (SIC 2512)

Recliner Makers - 1991

Percent shares are based on estimated total shipments worth $1.03 billion. Shipments are for reclining chairs and for reclining chairs sold with motion upholstery groups only.

La-Z-Boy 36.1%
Action 18.4
Stratolounger 8.2
Franklin 5.3
Catnapper 5.2
Berkline 5.0
Barcalounger 3.7
Bench Craft 3.5
Shannon 2.9
Bassett Motion 2.5
Other producers 9.2

Source: *Furniture/Today*, "Annual Retail Marketing Guide", 1992, p. 35, from market research.

★ 467 ★

Furniture (SIC 2512)

Upholstered Furniture Sales

Shares of upholstery sales, by frame style, are shown in percent.

Contemporary 37.0%
Other traditional 25.0
Country 11.0
18th century 9.0
Early American 6.0
Tropical 4.0
Southwestern 2.0
French formal 1.0
Victorian 1.0
Other 2.0

Source: *Furniture/Today*, 1992, p. 51.

★ 468 ★

Beds (SIC 2515)

Bed Purchasing by Size

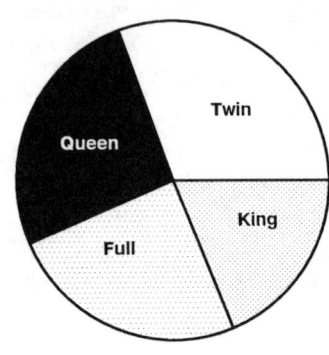

Bed purchasing, by bed size, is shown in percent for 1991.

Twin 30.5%
Queen 25.9
Full 25.1
King 18.5

Source: *HFD*, March 1992, p. 6, from IMR.

★ 469 ★

Beds (SIC 2515)

Bedding Sales by Type

The percentage of sleep sets, by type, is shown in percent.

Innerspring 75.0%
Flotation 13.0
Foam core 10.0
Futon 3.0

Source: *HFD*, March 1992, p. 6, from ISPA.

★470★

Aircraft Cabin Products (SIC 2531)

Aircraft Seat Manufacturers

Estimated shares of the non-16g aircraft seat manufacturing market are shown in percent.

BEAV	25.0%
Weber	19.0
Burns	16.0
Sicma	12.0
Recaro	8.0
Other	20.0

Source: Investext, Thomson Financial Networks, June 4, 1992, from Morgan Stanley & Co., Inc.

★471★

Aircraft Cabin Products (SIC 2531)

Commercial Aircraft Interior Products

Market shares, by company, are shown in percent.

BE Aerospace	11.0%
JAMCO	11.0
Weber Aircraft	8.0
SELL GmbH	7.0
Burns Aerospace	6.0
Grimes Aerospace	5.0
Sony Transcom	5.0
Matsushita	4.0
Rumbold	3.0
SICMA	3.0
MAG	2.0
Hughes Avionics	2.0
Koito	2.0
Inventum	2.0
Nordskog	2.0
Recaro	2.0
Other	25.0

Source: Investext, Thomson Financial Networks, June 4, 1992, from Morgan Stanley & Co., Inc.

★472★

Window Treatments (SIC 2591)

Window Accessories Market

Market shares, by type, are shown in percent for 1991.

Mini-blinds	38.0%
Vertical blinds	24.7
Drapery hardware	17.7
Pleated shades	17.7
Wood blinds	1.9

Source: *HFD*, February 24, 1992, p. 12A.

SIC 26 - Paper and Allied Products

★ 473 ★

Paper (SIC 2600)

Paper and Forest Product Leaders

Sales of 12 leading paper and forest products manufacturers worldwide, in billions of dollars, totaling $95.38 billion in 1990. Shares of the group are shown in percent.

	Sales ($ bil.)	% of Group
International Paper	$ 12.96	14.0%
Georgia-Pacific	12.67	13.0
Stora Kopperbergs Berg.	11.07	12.0
Weyerhaeuser	9.02	9.0
Noranda	8.12	9.0
Fletcher Challenge	7.13	7.0
Kimberly-Clark	6.45	7.0
Repola	6.04	6.0
Stone	5.77	6.0
James River	5.42	6.0
Scott	5.39	6.0
Svenska Cellulosa	5.33	6.0

Source: *Business Horizons*, November 1991, p. 18.

★ 474 ★

Pulp (SIC 2611)

Market Pulp Leaders

U.S. producers are ranked according to estimated 1992 capacity in millions of metric tons; relative market shares are shown in percent.

	Mil. m.t.	% of Group
Georgia-Pacific	1683	23.7%
Weyerhaeuser	1642	23.2
Stone Container	924	13.0
Champion International	617	8.7
Louisiana-Pacific	499	7.0
Federal Paper Board	354	5.0
International Paper	347	4.9

	Mil. m.t.	% of Group
Bowater	327	4.6%
Boise Cascade	227	3.2
Mead	150	2.1
Union Camp	113	1.6
Willamette	104	1.5
Temple-Inland	100	1.4

Source: Investext, Thomson Financial Networks, March 17, 1992, from Kidder, Peabody & Company, Incorporated.

★ 475 ★

Pulp (SIC 2611)

Pulp Market by Grade Worldwide

Percent shares of 1991 world pulp market, by grade, are based on total output of 43.456 million metric tons.

BSK	39.8%
BNK	29.9
Dissolving	8.0
Sulfite	7.1
UBK	6.1
CTMP	4.0
Nonwood	1.5
SGW	1.2
RMP/CMP/TMP	1.0
Semichemical	0.7
Recycled	0.6

Source: *Pulp & Paper*, August 1992, p. 48.

★ 476 ★

Pulp (SIC 2611)

Pulp Market by Grade - North America

Percent distribution by grade of the 1991 pulp market are based on total North American output of 16.288 million metric tons.

BSK	55.3%
BNK	19.4
Dissolving	10.0
CTMP	5.3
UBK	3.5
Sulfite	3.3
RMP/CMP/TMP	1.2
Nonwood	1.0
Recycled	0.7
SGW	0.3

Source: *Pulp & Paper*, August 1992, p. 48.

★ 477 ★

Paper (SIC 2620)

Paper by Type

Distribution of U.S. shipments is shown in percent for 1991, based on a total of 28.682 million tons.

Uncoated freesheet	42.2%
Newsprint	24.5
Coated groundwood	14.9
Coated freesheet	11.8
Uncoated groundwood	6.5

Source: *Graphic Arts Monthly*, January 1992, p. 38, from American Paper Institute.

★ 478 ★

Paper (SIC 2620)

Paper Product Manufacturers

Companies are ranked by 1991 sales, shown in millions of dollars. Percent shares are based on a group total of $13,829 million.

	Sales ($ mil.)	% of Group
Stone Container	$ 5,384	38.9%
Temple-Inland	2,507	18.1
Sonoco Products	1,697	12.3
Federal Paper Board	1,435	10.4
Bemis	1,142	8.3
Longview Fibre	644	4.7
St. Joe Paper	582	4.2
Greif Brothers	437	3.2

Source: *The 1992 Business Week 1000*, 1992, p. 171.

★ 479 ★

Newsprint (SIC 2621)

Newsprint Producers - Canada

Company shares are based on 1991 total Canadian capacity of 10,430,000 metric tons, shown in percent. Capacity for Abitibi-Price does not include that of its Thunder Bay, Ontario, mill which was closed for two years.

	Capacity (m.t.)	% of Group
Abitibi-Price Inc.	1,465,000	15.5%
Fletcher Challenge Canada Ltd.	1,072,000	11.4
Stone-Consolidated Inc.	834,000	8.8
Kruger Inc.	833,000	8.8
Quebec and Ontario Paper Co.	771,000	8.2
Canadian Pacific Forest Products Ltd.	643,000	6.8
MacMillan Bloedel Ltd.	590,000	6.3
Donohue Inc.	502,000	5.3
Daishowa Forest Products Ltd.	429,000	4.5
Irving Paper Ltd.	334,000	3.5
Spruce Falls Power and Paper Co. Ltd.	314,000	3.3
Boise Cascade Canada Ltd.	268,000	2.8
Domtar Inc.	258,000	2.7
Bowater Mersey Paper Ltd.	218,000	2.3
Alberta Newsprint	194,000	2.1

Continued on next page.

★ 479 ★ *Continued*

Newsprint (SIC 2621)

Newsprint Producers - Canada

Company shares are based on 1991 total Canadian capacity of 10,430,000 metric tons, shown in percent. Capacity for Abitibi-Price does not include that of its Thunder Bay, Ontario, mill which was closed for two years.

	Capacity (m.t.)	% of Group
James Maclaren Industries Inc.	191,000	2.0%
Stora Forest Industries	174,000	1.8
F. F. Soucy Inc.	160,000	1.7
Howe Sound Pulp and Paper Co.	95,000	1.0
Atlantic Newsprint Co.	85,000	0.9

Source: Newspaper and Newsprint Facts at a Glance 1991-92, from Canadian Pulp & Paper Association.

★ 480 ★

Newsprint (SIC 2621)

Newsprint Producers - North America

Capacity shares, by company, are shown in percent, based on a total of 18.490 million tons.

Abitibi-Price	13.3%
Canadian Pacific Forest Products	9.2
Bowater	8.6
Stone Container	6.7
Fletcher Challenge	6.2
MacMillan Bloedel	6.1

Kruger	5.9%
Boise Cascade	5.1
Champion International	4.9
Weyerhaeuser	4.8
Quebec and Ontario	4.6
Jefferson Smurfit	4.4
Other	20.3

Source: Investext, Thomson Financial Networks, February 21, 1992, from The First Boston Corporation.

★ 481 ★

Newsprint (SIC 2621)

Newsprint Producers - U.S.

Company shares are based on total U.S. capacity in 1991 of 6,477,000 metric tons and are shown in percent.

	Capacity (m.t.)	% of Group
Bowater Inc.	939,000	14.5%
Champion International	805,000	12.4
Smurfit Newsprint Corp.	709,000	10.9
Boise Cascade Corp.	539,000	8.3
North Pacific Paper Co.	524,000	8.1
Southeast Paper Manufacturing Co.	406,000	6.3
Augusta Newsprint Co.	352,000	5.4
Kimberly-Clark Corp.	310,000	4.8
Georgia-Pacific Corp.	295,000	4.6
Stone Container Corp.	279,000	4.3
Alabama River Newsprint Co.	220,000	3.4
Garden State Paper Co. Inc.	209,000	3.2
Newsprint South Inc.	209,000	3.2
Ponderay Newsprint Co.	205,000	3.2
Bear Island Paper Co.	203,000	3.1
FSC Paper Co. L.P.	132,000	2.0
Inland Empire Paper Co.	72,000	1.1
Manistique Papers Inc.	53,000	0.8
James River Corp.	16,000	0.2

Source: Newspaper and Newsprint Facts at a Glance 1991-92, from American Newspaper Publishers Association and and American Paper Institute.

★ 482 ★

Paper (SIC 2621)

Uncoated Free Sheet Producers in Canada

Canadian producer's shares are shown in percent based on total capacity of 1.153 million tons in 1988 and 1.702 million tons in 1993.

	1988	1993
Domtar Inc.	39.4%	40.7%
E.B. Eddy	11.2	8.5
Fraser Paper Ltd.	9.5	7.3
Canadian Pacific Forest Products Ltd.	10.4	20.9
Inland Paper	10.2	7.8
Rolland	11.2	8.5
Weyerhaeuser	8.1	6.2

Source: *Folio*, January 1991, p. 94, from Jaakko Poyry Consulting.

★ 483 ★

Paper (SIC 2621)

Uncoated Free Sheet Producers - U.S.

Company shares are shown in percent, based on total U.S. capacity of 11.897 million tons in 1988 and 13.675 million tons in 1993.

	1988	1993
International Paper/Hammermill	15.5%	14.3%
Champion	9.9	10.6
Boise Cascade	7.4	8.9
James River (CZ)	6.8	6.1
Georgia-Pacific	6.5	8.4
Nekoosa Papers	6.2	5.6
Union Camp	5.0	6.7
Westvaco	4.1	2.2
Mead	4.0	3.6
P.H. Glatfelter/Escusta	3.5	3.1
Simpson Paper (Plainwell)	3.5	3.2
Weyerhauser	3.4	3.1
Stora/Newton/Mohawk	1.8	1.6
Finch Pruyn & Co., Inc.	1.4	1.3
Potlatch	1.4	1.2
Allied Paper Inc.	1.3	1.2
Appleton Papers, Inc.	1.3	1.2
Fraser	1.3	1.1
Pentair Paper Co.	1.2	1.1
Temple Inland Inc.	1.2	1.1

	1988	1993
Willamette Industries	1.2%	3.1%
E.B. Eddy Group	1.2	1.1
Wausau	1.1	1.0
Warren	0.9	0.8
Grays Harbor Paper Co.	0.9	0.8
Kimberly-Clark Group	0.9	0.8
Sorg	0.8	0.8
Howard	0.6	0.6
Penntech	0.6	0.6
Scott Paper Co.	0.6	0.5
Lyons Falls Pulp & Paper	0.5	0.5
Lincoln Pulp & Paper	0.4	0.4
Badger	0.4	0.4
Valentine Pulp & Paper	0.4	0.3
Fitchburg Paper Corp.	0.3	0.3
Kerwin Paper Co.	0.3	0.3
Fletcher Paper Co.	0.3	0.2
Fox River Paper Co.	0.3	0.2
Shawano Paper Mills	0.3	0.2
Ward Paper Co.	0.2	0.2
Monadnock Paper Mills	0.2	0.2
Byron Weston Co.	0.2	0.2
Linweave Paper Co.	0.2	0.2
French Paper Co.	0.2	0.1
Rising Paper Co.	0.1	0.1
Crane & Co.	0.1	0.1
Potsdam Paper Mills	0.1	0.1
George A. Whiting Paper Co.	0.1	0.1
NVF Company	0.1	0.1
Minnesota Mining & Manufacturing	0.0	0.0
Southworth Co.	0.0	0.0
Esleek Manufacturing Co.	0.0	0.0

Source: *Folio*, January 1991, p. 94, from Jaakko Poyry Consulting.

★ 484 ★

Paper (SIC 2621)

Uncoated Groundwood Producers - Canada

Company shares are shown in percent, based on total capacity of 1.648 million tons in 1988 and 2.225 million tons in 1993. Shares are based on percent of the group's total.

	1988	1993
Abitibi-Price	17.8%	17.7%
Boise Cascade Canada Ltd.	10.7	11.3
Bowater Mercy	0.4	0.4

Continued on next page.

★ 484 ★ *Continued*

Paper (SIC 2621)

Uncoated Groundwood Producers - Canada

Company shares are shown in percent, based on total capacity of 1.648 million tons in 1988 and 2.225 million tons in 1993. Shares are based on percent of the group's total.

	1988	1993
Canadian Pacific	16.6%	14.9%
Consolidated-Bathurst Inc.	16.6	14.9
Domtar, Inc.	7.5	6.7
F.F. Soucy	2.2	1.9
K.C. of Canada	0.8	0.7
Kruger Pulp and Paper	0.6	3.3
Macmillan-Bloedel	17.4	15.6
Ontario Paper Co.	0.8	0.7
St. Mary's Paper Inc.	6.3	5.7
St. Raymond Paper Ltd.	2.4	1.0
Stone Consolidated	0.0	5.4

Source: *Folio*, January 1991, p. 96.

★ 485 ★

Paper (SIC 2621)

Uncoated Groundwood Producers - U.S.

Company shares are shown in percent, based on total U.S. capacity of 1.696 million tons in 1988 and 1.975 million tons in 1993. Shares shown are percent of the group's total.

	1988	1993
Appleton	2.2%	2.2%
Boise Cascade	2.5	2.6
Bowater	2.5	2.6
Champion	15.0	15.4
James River	5.0	5.1
Daishowa America	4.7	4.8
Fraser Paper Ltd.	9.1	9.3
Georgia-Pacific	2.5	2.6
Great Northern	16.9	14.5
Hennepin Paper Co.	1.3	1.3
Kimberly-Clark	5.6	5.8
Imperial Paper Co.	0.6	0.6
Lake Superior Paper Ind.	11.3	11.6
Lyons Falls Pulp & Paper	1.3	1.3
Madison Paper Co.	10.9	11.2
Manistique Paper	2.2	2.2
Mead Paper	2.5	2.6

	1988	1993
Pejepscot Paper	3.4%	3.5%
Seaman Paper	0.6	0.6

Source: *Folio*, January 1991, p. 96.

★ 486 ★

Paper (SIC 2631)

Unbleached Paperboard

Company shares are based on a 1992 total capacity of 22,353 thousand tons, shown in percent.

Stone Container Corp.	13.3%
Georgia-Pacific	9.9
International Paper	7.9
Jefferson Smurfit Corp.	7.2
Union Camp Corp.	6.8
Temple0Inland Inc.	6.7
Weyerhaeuser Co.	5.5
Gaylord Container Corp.	5.2
Potash Company of America, Inc. . . .	4.0
Wilamette Industries, Inc.	3.4
Westvaco Corp.	2.0
Longview Fibre Co.	1.9
Boise Cascade Corp.	1.5
Champion International Corp.	1.5
Chesapeake Corp.	0.7
Consolidated Papers, Inc.	0.7
Other	15.4

Source: Investext, Thomson Financial Networks, April 2, 1992, from Donaldson, Lufkin & Jenrette Securities.

★ 487 ★

Paper (SIC 2650)

Paperboard Products by Type

Value of shipments is shown in millions of dollars for 1991. Shares by type are shown in percent based on the group's total of $12,575 million in value of shipments.

	($ mil.)	% of Group
Sanitary food containers	$ 2,730	21.7%
Die-cut paper and board	2,156	17.1
Fiber cabs, drums, etc.	1,934	15.4
Stationery products	1,240	9.9
Setup paperboard boxes	562	4.5
Other paper products	3,952	31.4

Source: *U.S. Industrial Outlook*, 1992, p. 10-23.

★ 488 ★

Paper (SIC 2670)

Paper Flexible Packaging Materials

Value of shipments is shown in millions of dollars for 1991. Shares by type are shown in percent based on total shipments of $11,477 million.

	($ mil.)	% of Group
Bags: plastics/coated	$ 5,952	51.9%
Paper packaging, coated/ laminated	2,870	25.0
Bags: uncoated	2,655	23.1

Source: *U.S. Industrial Outlook*, 1992, p. 10-17, from U.S. Department of Commerce.

★ 489 ★

Paper Products (SIC 2670)

Consumer Paper Product Producers

Company shares are shown in percent, based on a total market of $10.348 billion in 1991. The category includes disposable diapers, facial tissue, toilet tissue, paper towels, and sanitary napkins.

Procter & Gamble	36.1%
Kimberly-Clark	24.8
Scott Paper	10.9
James River	5.4
Georgia Pacific	3.4
Johnson & Johnson	2.3
Private label	9.2
Generic	0.3
Other	7.6

Source: Investext, Thomson Financial Networks, January 24, 1992, from Kidder, Peabody & Company, Incorporated.

★ 490 ★

Recycled Materials (SIC 2670)

Recycled Materials

The rates at which various materials are recycled in the U.S. are shown in percent.

Paper	29.0%
Metals	23.0
Glass	20.0
Plastics	2.0

Source: *USA TODAY*, September 22, 1992, p. 1B, from U.S. Environmental Protection Agency.

★ 491 ★

Recycled Papers (SIC 2670)

Recycled Stock Paper Consumption

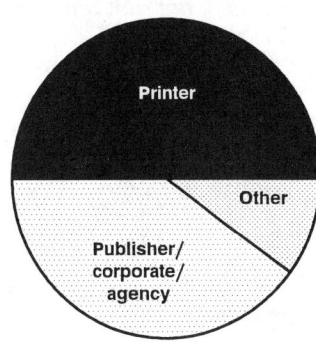

Recycled stock paper consumption, by user, is shown in percent.

Printer	50.0%
Publisher/corporate/agency	40.0
Other	10.0

Source: *High Volume Printing*, February 1991, p. 4.

★ 492 ★

Plastic Packaging (SIC 2671)

Interlocking Bag Market by Brand

Market shares, by brand, are shown in percent.

Zip Lock	56.1%
Glad	24.3
Reynolds	6.6
Private Label	13.0

Source: Investext, Thomson Financial Networks, June 2, 1992, from Shearson Lehman Brothers, Inc.

★ 493 ★
Plastic Packaging (SIC 2671)

Interlocking Bags - Selected Markets

Market shares, by brand, are shown in percent for selected markets.

	Food Store	Mass Merch.	Wrhse. Clubs
Zip Lock	54.9%	62.2%	60.9%
Glad	23.3	31.9	19.3
Reynolds	6.4	2.9	11.8
Private label	15.4	5.0	0.0

Source: Investext, Thomson Financial Networks, June 2, 1992, from Shearson Lehman Brothers, Inc.

★ 494 ★
Coated Paper (SIC 2672)

Coated Free Sheet Producers - North America

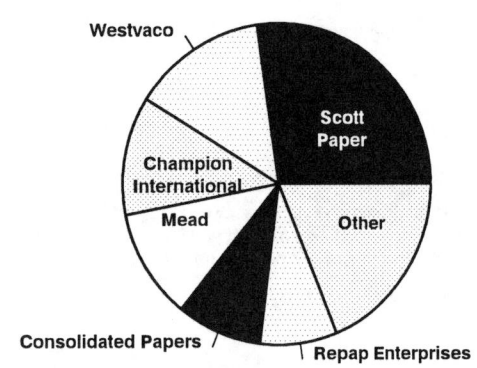

Shares are shown in percent, based on an industry annual capacity of 4.151 million tons.

Scott Paper	26.5%
Westvaco	14.2
Champion International	12.3
Mead	10.8
Consolidated Papers	9.2
Repap Enterprises	8.0
Other	19.0

Source: Investext, Thomson Financial Networks, January 6, 1992, from The First Boston Corporation.

★ 495 ★
Coated Paper (SIC 2672)

Coated Groundwood Producers - North America

Shares are shown in percent, based on an industry annual capacity of 5.198 million tons.

Champion International	13.9%
International Paper	11.9
Consolidated Papers	11.2
Repap Enterprises	10.1
Blandin Paper	6.4
Bowater	6.3
Mead	5.2
Other	35.0

Source: Investext, Thomson Financial Networks, January 6, 1992, from The First Boston Corporation.

★ 496 ★
Coated Paper (SIC 2672)

Coated Groundwood Producers - U.S.

Companies are ranked according to 1992 estimated capacity measured in millions of short tons; relative market shares are shown in percent.

	Mil. m.t.	Share
Champion International	725	16.2%
Consolidated Paper	620	13.9
International Paper	600	13.4
Bowater	485	10.9
Boise Cascade	310	6.9
James River	280	6.3
Mead	270	6.0
Weyerhaeuser	210	4.7
Others	963	21.6

Source: Investext, Thomson Financial Networks, March 17, 1992, from Kidder, Peabody & Company, Incorporated.

★ 497 ★

Disposable Diapers (SIC 2676)

Disposable Diaper Brand Shares

Brand shares are shown as percent of the total market for the 52 weeks ended May 18, 1991.

Kimberly-Clark (Huggies)	30.1%
Procter & Gamble (Pampers)	29.2
Luvs	20.4
Others	12.3

Source: *Advertising Age*, June 29, 1992, p. 3, from Nielsen Co.

★ 498 ★

Disposable Diapers (SIC 2676)

Disposable Diaper Market

Shares by company and brand are shown in percent. Estimated category size was $4.0 billion in 1991.

	Fall 1990	Fall 1991
Kimberly-Clark		
Huggies	30.5%	29.0%
Huggies Pull-Ups	4.0	8.5
Snuggems Ultra	0.5	0.6
Procter & Gamble		
Pampers (incl. Ultra Pampers) . . .	24.5	23.5
Luvs Deluxe	24.0	21.0

Source: Investext, Thomson Financial Networks, January 24, 1992, from Kidder, Peabody & Company, Incorporated.

★ 499 ★

Disposable Diapers (SIC 2676)

Disposable Diaper Market

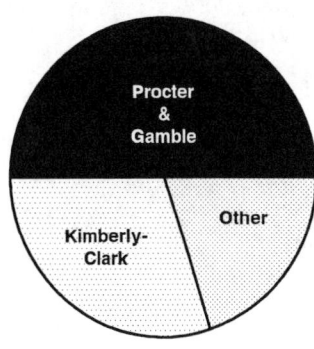

The $4 billion disposable diaper industry is dominated by two manufacturers whose market shares are shown in percent.

Procter & Gamble	50.0%
Kimberly-Clark	30.0
Other	20.0

Source: *The Wall Street Journal*, June 18, 1992, p. B10.

★ 500 ★

Disposable Diapers (SIC 2676)

Top Supermarket Diaper Brands

Sales of 10 leading supermarket disposable diaper brands account for 98.6% of the $2.1353 billion market for the 52 weeks ending May 16, 1992. Shares are shown as percent.

	Sales	Share
Huggies	$ 643.4	30.1%
Pampers	624.0	29.2
Luvs	436.3	20.4
Private labels	269.8	12.6
Fitti	31.7	1.5
Cozies	30.0	1.4
Drypers	28.8	1.3
Baby's Choice	22.9	1.1
Cuddles	11.7	0.5
Snuggems	11.5	0.5
Other	25.2	1.4

Source: *Advertising Age*, July 20, 1992, p. 20, from A.C. Nielsen ScanTrack.

★ 501 ★

Feminine Hygiene (SIC 2676)

Sanitary Napkin Market

Company and brand shares are shown in percent for 4th quater of 1991.

Kimberly Clark
Kotex	26.0%
New Freedom	9.0

Procter & Gamble
Always	30.0

Johnson & Johnson
Carefree	4.0
Stayfree	14.0
Sure & Natural	6.0

Tambrands
Maxi Thins	1.0
All others	10.0

Source: Investext, Thomson Financial Networks, April 10, 1992, p. 43, from Smith Barney, Harris Upham & Co.

★ 502 ★

Feminine Hygiene (SIC 2676)

Tampon Market

Company and brand shares are shown in percent for 4th quarter of 1991.

Tambrands
Tampax	56.0%

Playtex
Playtex	28.0

Johnson & Johnson
O.B.	10.0

Kimberly Clark
Kotex	6.0

Source: Investext, Thomson Financial Networks, April 10, 1992, p. 43, from Smith Barney, Harris Upham & Co.

★ 503 ★

Sanitary Paper (SIC 2676)

Sanitary Tissue Producers

Company shares are shown in percent, based on 1992 total capacity.

Scott Paper	18.0%
James River	18.0
Fort Howard	16.0
Procter & Gamble	13.0
Georgia-Pacific	9.0

Kimberly-Clark	8.0%
Chesapeake	3.0
Pope & Talbot	2.0
Potlatch	2.0
Other	11.0

Source: Investext, Thomson Financial Networks, April 3, 1992, p. 43, from S.G. Warburg & Co. Inc.

★ 504 ★

Sanitary Paper Products (SIC 2676)

Adult-Diaper Manufacturers

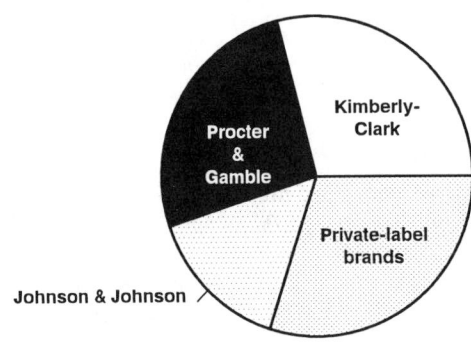

Shares of the $745.0 million incontinence product market are shown in percent for 1991.

Kimberly-Clark	29.0%
Procter & Gamble	26.0
Johnson & Johnson	15.0
Private-label brands	30.0

Source: *The Wall Street Journal*, March 20, 1992, p. B1, from Nonwoven Markets Publications.

★ 505 ★

Sanitary Paper Products (SIC 2676)

Bathroom Tissue Market

Shares by company and brand are shown in percent. Estimated category size was $2.6 billion in 1991.

	Fall 1990	Fall 1991
Georgia-Pacific		
Coronet	3.0%	2.5%
Softply	0.1	0.1
James River		
Northern	13.0	14.0
Aurora	1.0	0.3
Kimberly-Clark		

Continued on next page.

★ 505 ★ *Continued*

Sanitary Paper Products (SIC 2676)

Bathroom Tissue Market

Shares by company and brand are shown in percent. Estimated category size was $2.6 billion in 1991.

	Fall 1990	Fall 1991
Kleenex	-	3.5%
Procter & Gamble		
Charmin	23.0%	22.0
White Cloud	8.0	7.5
Banner	0.5	0.5
Scott Paper		
Scott	16.0	16.5
Cottonelle	8.0	8.0
Waldorf	0.3	0.2
Soft N Pretty	0.3	0.0

Source: Investext, Thomson Financial Networks, January 24, 1992, from Kidder, Peabody & Company, Incorporated.

★ 506 ★

Sanitary Paper Products (SIC 2676)

Sanitary Napkin Market

Shares by company and brand are shown in percent. Estimated category size was $1.050 billion in 1991.

	Fall 1990	Fall 1991
Johnson & Johnson		
Stayfree	14.0%	13.0%
Sure & Natural	6.0	6.0
Carefree	4.0	4.0
Modess	0.5	0.3
Kimberly-Clark		
Kotex	22.5	27.5
New Freedom	10.0	7.5
Procter & Gamble		
Always	28.5	32.0
Tambrands		
Maxithin	3.0	1.0

Source: Investext, Thomson Financial Networks, January 24, 1992, from Kidder, Peabody & Company, Incorporated.

★ 507 ★

Sanitary Paper Products (SIC 2676)

Tampon Manufacturers

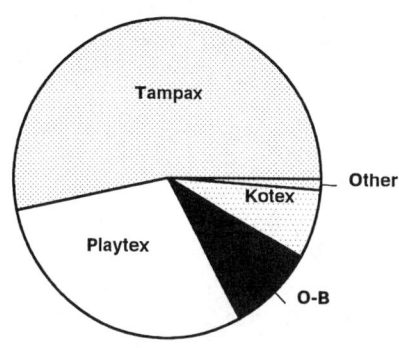

Dollar shares for September/October of 1991 are shown in percent.

Tampax	54.1%
Playtex	29.6
O-B	9.0
Kotex	6.8
Other	0.5

Source: Investext, Thomson Financial Networks, February 10, 1992, from Prudential Securities, Inc.

★ 508 ★

Sanitary Paper Products (SIC 2676)

Tampon Market

Shares by company and brand are shown in percent. Estimated category size was $660 million in 1991.

	Fall 1990	Fall 1991
Tambrands		
Tampax	45.5%	47.0%
Tampax Petal Soft	6.0	4.5
Tampax Kompak	2.0	4.0
Kimberly-Clark		
Kotex Security	7.5	8.0
Playtex		
Playtex Deodorant	16.0	18.0
Playtex	10.5	9.5
Playtex Portables	4.0	4.5
Johnson & Johnson		
O.B.	8.7	9.0

Source: Investext, Thomson Financial Networks, January 24, 1992, from Kidder, Peabody & Company, Incorporated.

★ 509 ★

Fluff (SIC 2679)

Fluff Use - Europe

Shares, by end use, are shown in percent, based on a potential market size of 81.0 billion SKr (Swedish Krona).

Operational/clinical	40.0%
Feminine hygiene	23.0-28.0
Baby diapers	15.0-17.0
Industrial tissue	13.0
Incontinence/other	8.0-10.0

Source: Investext, Thomson Financial Networks, February 21, 1992, from UBS Phillips & Drew Global Research Group.

SIC 27 - Printing and Publishing

★ 510 ★

Printing (SIC 2700)

Printing Consumption is the U.S.

Distribution, by industry, is shown in percent, based on a total market of $20.007 billion.

Social service and nonprofit	32.0%
Publishing (incl. software)	23.0
Banking and financial	14.1
Manufacturing and wholesale	12.9
Health care	4.9
Legal services	3.7
Food, lodging, and entertainment	2.8
Miscellaneous business services	2.2
Retail	2.1
Insurance	1.2
Education	1.0

Source: *Graphic Arts Monthly*, April 1992.

★ 511 ★

Printing (SIC 2700)

Printing Market in 1990

Estimated market segmentation is shown in percent for 1990, based on an industry total value of shipments of $117,371,000.

Commercial printing	44.1%
Packaging printing	30.8
General commercial	15.1
Forms and label printing	9.8
Specialty printing	7.6
Advertising	6.0
Publications	5.8
Trade services	5.7
Catalogs	3.5
Books	3.4
Direct mail	3.1
Financial and legal	3.0
Free-standing inserts	2.8
Greeting cards printing	2.1
Directories and scheduling	1.5

Source: Investext, Thomson Financial Networks, June 19, 1992, from William Blair & Company.

★ 512 ★

Printing and Publishing (SIC 2700)

Daily Newspaper Circulation - Global Leaders

The best selling daily newspapers are ranked by 1990 circulation, shown in millions; relative market shares for the same period are shown in percent.

	Circ. (mil.)	% of Group
Izvestia (Commonwealth of Independent States (CIS))	10.4	17.4%
Yomiuri Shimbun (Japan)	9.7	16.2
Pravda (Commonwealth of Independent States (CIS))	9.6	16.0

Continued on next page.

★ 512 ★ *Continued*

Printing and Publishing (SIC 2700)

Daily Newspaper Circulation - Global Leaders

The best selling daily newspapers are ranked by 1990 circulation, shown in millions; relative market shares for the same period are shown in percent.

	Circ. (mil.)	% of Group
Asahi Shimbun (Japan)	8.1	13.5%
Bild (Germany)	4.3	7.2
Mainichi Shimbun (Japan)	4.1	6.8
Renmin Ribao (People's Republic of China)	4.0	6.7
The Sun (England)	3.8	6.3
Daily Mirror (England)	3.1	5.2
Nihon Keizai Shimbun (Japan) . .	2.8	4.7

Source: *Newspaper and Newsprint Facts at a Glance 1991-92*, 1991, p. 22, from ABC London, *Editor & Publisher*, and independent verification.

★ 513 ★

Printing and Publishing (SIC 2700)

ELHI Textbook Sales by Publisher

Shares of the ELHI (elementary and high school) textbook market, by company, are shown in percent, based on sales in 1988, 1989, and 1990.

	1988	1989	1990
Macmillan/McGraw Hill . . .	13.6%	16.8%	16.1%
Simon & Schuster	10.5	12.1	13.4
HBJ	13.8	11.0	10.7
Scholastic	7.8	9.6	10.6
Houghton Mifflin	7.2	7.3	7.3
Scott Foresman	5.6	5.7	6.4
Others	41.5	37.5	35.5

Source: Investext, Thomson Financial Networks, May 13, 1992, from Raymond James & Associates, Inc.

★ 514 ★

Printing and Publishing (SIC 2700)

In-Plant Printing Budgets

25 biggest in-house printing budgets of wholesalers and retailers in millions of dollars for 1991. Relative budget shares are converted to percent.

	Budget ($ mil.)	% of Group
Albertson's	$ 11.00	10.9%
Spartan Stores	10.00	9.9
Publix Super Markets	9.00	8.9
Whirlpool	7.20	7.2
Rich's Department Stores . . .	6.20	6.2
Servistar	4.28	4.3
Target Stores	4.00	4.0
McCormick Press	4.00	4.0
Lawson Products	4.00	4.0
Supermarkets General	3.20	3.2
Super Valu Stores	3.20	3.2
Pep Boys	3.00	3.0
CVS	3.00	3.0
American Greeting	3.00	3.0
Bartell Drug	3.00	3.0
Fred Meyer	2.63	2.6
Brookshire Grocery	2.50	2.5
Anheuser-Busch	2.50	2.5
Agway	2.50	2.5
Canadian Tire	2.20	2.2
Philips Consumer Electronics . .	2.20	2.2
McCrory Stores	2.00	2.0
Affiliated Foods	2.00	2.0
Eckerd Drug	2.00	2.0
Amoco	2.00	2.0

Source: *In-Plant Reproductions*, August 1991, p. 18, from *In-Plant Reproductions* survey.

★ 515 ★

Printing and Publishing (SIC 2700)

Printing Giants

Sales of the 20 largest printers in the U.S. and Canada reached $21.260 billion in 1991. Relative shares are shown in percent.

	($ bil.)	% of Group
R.R. Donnelley & Sons Co. . . .	$ 3,900	18.3%
Hallmark Cards, Inc.	2,800	13.2
American Greetings Corp. . . .	1,573	7.4

Continued on next page.

★515★ *Continued*

Printing and Publishing (SIC 2700)

Printing Giants

Sales of the 20 largest printers in the U.S. and Canada reached $21.260 billion in 1991. Relative shares are shown in percent.

	($ bil.)	% of Group
Moore Business Forms, Inc.	$ 1,550	7.3%
Delux Corp.	1,474	6.9
Quebecor Printing, Inc.	1,386	6.5
Lawson Mardon Group	1,003	4.7
World Color Press, Inc.	800	3.8
Uanco, Inc.	700	3.3
Standard Register Co.	694	3.3
Valassis Communications, Inc.	636	3.0
Ringier America, Inc.	600	2.8
Banta Corp.	566	2.7
Arcata Graphics Co.	565	2.7
Sullivan Graphics	537	2.5
Treasure Chest Advertising Co., Inc.	530	2.5
Gibson Greetings, Inc.	522	2.5
Quad/Graphics, Inc.	500	2.4
Western Publishing Co., Inc.	466	2.2
Wallace Computer Services, Inc.	459	2.2

Source: *American Printer*, July 1992, p. 57.

★516★

Newspapers (SIC 2711)

Largest Newspaper Circulations

25 leading U.S. newspaper titles ranked by circulation as of Septermber 30, 1990. Parent companies are in parentheses. Relative shares of circulation are converted to percent.

	Circ. (000)	% of Group
Wall Street Journal (Dow Jones)	1,857	11.2%
USA Today (Gannett)	1,347	8.1
Los Angeles Times (Times Mirror)	1,196	7.2
New York Times (New York Times)	1,108	6.7
New York Daily News (Tribune)	1,098	6.6
Washington Post (Washington Post)	781	4.7
Chicago Tribune (Media General)	721	4.3

	Circ. (000)	% of Group
Newsday (Times Mirror)	714	4.3%
Detroit Free Press (Knight-Ridder)	636	3.8
SF Chronicle (Chronicle)	563	3.4
Chicago Sun-Times (Chicago Sun Times)	527	3.2
Boston Globe (Affiliated Publications)	521	3.1
Philadelphia Inquirer (Knight-Ridder)	520	3.1
New York Post (Peter Kalikow)	510	3.1
Detroit News (Gannett)	501	3.0
Star-Ledger (Advance Publications)	476	2.9
Houston Chronicle (Hearst)	442	2.7
Miami Herald (Knight-Ridder)	429	2.6
Plain Dealer (Advance Publications)	428	2.6
Minneapolis Star Tribune (Cowles Media)	407	2.4
Dallas Morning News (A.H. BeloCorp)	385	2.3
St. Louis Post-Dispatch (Pulitzer)	382	2.3
Boston Herald (News Corp.)	359	2.2
Orange County Register (Freedom)	354	2.1
St. Petersburg Times (Times Publishing)	353	2.1

Source: *Editor and Publisher International Yearbook 1991*, 1992, p. 64.

★517★

Newspapers (SIC 2711)

Largest Newspapers in the U.S.

Companies are ranked by average daily circulation for Monday through Friday for six months ended March 31, 1992. Relative market shares are shown for the same period.

	Circ.	% of Group
The Wall Street Journal	1,852,863	18.5%
USA TODAY	1,540,698	15.4
The New York Times	1,201,970	12.0
Los Angeles Times	1,164,388	11.6
The Washington Post	846,635	8.4
(New York) Daily News	781,796	7.8
Newsday	765,703	7.6

Continued on next page.

★ 517 ★ *Continued*
Newspapers (SIC 2711)

Largest Newspapers in the U.S.

Companies are ranked by average daily circulation for Monday through Friday for six months ended March 31, 1992. Relative market shares are shown for the same period.

	Circ.	% of Group
Chicago Tribune	733,775	7.3%
Detroit Free Press	587,952	5.9
San Francisco Chronicle	557,644	5.6

Source: *USA TODAY*, May 26, 1992, p. 7B, from Audit Bureau of Circulations.

★ 518 ★
Newspapers (SIC 2711)

Leading Newspapers

Figures are average daily circulation for Monday-Friday editions. Circulation includes bulk sales.

USA TODAY	1,839,851
Wall Street Journal	1,795,206
The New York Times	1,156,870
Los Angeles Times	1,154,762
The Washington Post	804,039
New York Daily News	777,496
Newsday	759,005
Chicago Tribune	727,750
Detroit Free Press	583,758
San Francisco Chronicle	561,803

Source: *USA TODAY*, November 25, 1992, p. 2B, from USA TODAY research.

★ 519 ★
Newspapers (SIC 2711)

Newspaper Companies - U.S. Leaders

Leading newspaper companies in the U.S. are ranked by average daily circulation at end of six months on March 31, 1991; relative shares for the same period are shown in percent.

	Circ.	% of Group
Gannett Co.	6,038,923	22.2%
Knight-Ridder Newspapers	3,901,818	14.3

	Circ.	% of Group
Newhouse Newspapers	3,069,635	11.3%
Times Mirror	2,988,022	11.0
Dow Jones	2,485,130	9.1
Thomson Newspapers	2,157,012	7.9
New York Times Co.	2,141,041	7.9
Scripps-Howard Newspapers	1,614,739	5.9
Tribune Co.	1,485,995	5.5
Cox Enterprises	1,358,475	5.0

Source: *Newspaper and Newsprint Facts at a Glance 1991-92*, from Morton Research, Lynch, Jones & Ryan.

★ 520 ★
Newspapers (SIC 2711)

Newspaper Giants

Top 20 newspaper revenues in 1991 totaled $18.3585 billion. Relative shares are shown in percent.

	($ mil.)	% of Group
Gannett Co.	$ 2,629.8	14.3%
Times Mirror Co.	1,973.8	10.8
Knight-Ridder	1,953.8	10.6
Advance Publications	1,714.0	9.3
New York Times Co.	1,274.4	6.9
Tribune Co.	1,141.6	6.2
Dow Jones & Co.	963.1	5.2
Cox Enterprises	709.0	3.9
E.W. Scripps	691.0	3.8
Hearst Corp.	680.0	3.7
Thomson Corp.	645.2	3.5
Washington Post Co.	642.7	3.5
Capital Cities/ABC	521.3	2.8
Media News Group	500.0	2.7
Central Newspapers	420.4	2.3
McClatchy Newspapers	412.1	2.2
Affiliated Publications	392.8	2.1
Copley Newspapers	386.5	2.1
Freedom Newspapers	382.0	2.1
Journal Register Co.	325.0	1.8

Source: *Advertising Age*, August 10, 1992, p. S-6, from *Advertising Age* estimates.

Newspapers (SIC 2711)

Newspaper Leaders in Lineage

Newspapers are ranked by column inches in 1991.

Dallas Morning News	6,221,759
Orange County Register	5,529,948
San Jose Mercury News	5,381,957
Los Angeles Times	5,092,315
Los Angeles Daily News	4,336,287
San Diego Union	4,156,344
Newark Star Ledger	4,024,765
Boston Globe	3,477,870
Cincinnati Enquirer	3,342,328
Contra Costa Times	3,298,482
Dallas Times Herald	3,263,251
New York Times	3,224,289
Baltimore Sun	2,919,513
Allentown Call	2,759,371
Bergen County Record	2,665,392
L.A./Torrance Breeze	2,585,843
San Francisco Chronicle & Examiner	2,487,195
San Diego Tribune	2,475,795
Riverside Press Enterprise	2,392,661
Asbury Park Press	2,382,131
L.A./Long Beach Press-Telegram	2,298,636
Fremont Argus	2,263,898
West Palm Beach Post	2,241,042
Hayward Review	2,105,701
San Bernardino Sun	2,030,792

Source: *Adweek*, May 4, 1992, p. 22, from leading national advertisers.

★ 522 ★
Newspapers (SIC 2711)

Newspapers in the U.S. - Leading Circulation

The best selling daily newspapers in the U.S. are ranked by 1990 circulation, shown in millions; relative market shares are shown in percent for the same period. Circulation totals are current as of March 31, 1991. The figure for USA TODAY *represents circulation of the national edition.*

	Circ. (mil.)	% of Group
The Wall Street Journal	1,919,355	19.0%
USA TODAY	1,503,496	14.9
Los Angeles Times	1,242,864	12.3
The New York Times	1,209,225	12.0

	Circ. (mil.)	% of Group
The Washington Post	838,902	8.3%
Newsday	825,902	8.2
Chicago Tribune	741,345	7.3
New York Post	644,738	6.4
Detroit Free Press	622,349	6.2
San Francisco Chronicle	570,364	5.6

Source: *Newspaper and Newsprint Facts at a Glance 1991-92*, from Audit Bureau of Circulations.

★ 523 ★
Newspapers (SIC 2711)

Newspapers with Joint Operating Agreements

Figures represent daily circulations in 1992.

Detroit Free Press	587,952
San Francisco Chronicle	557,644
Detroit News	421,006
Seattle Times	237,814
Pittsburgh Press	208,554
Seattle Post-Intelligencer	204,656
Cincinnati Enquirer	199,196
Pittsburgh Post-Gazette	153,832
Nashville Tennessean	140,430
San Francisco Examiner	130,146
Las Vegas Review-Journal	129,422
Salt Lake Tribune	116,289
Albuquerque Journal	115,565
Honolulu Advertiser	105,670
Cincinnati Post	100,925
Arizona Star	100,331
Honolulu Star-Bulletin	88,460
El Paso Times	65,626
Salt Lake City Desert News	62,335
Nashville Banner	61,257
Tucson Citizen	52,165
Las Vegas Sun	36,559
Albuquerque Tribune	36,016
El Paso Herald-Post	29,119

Source: *Adweek*, May 4, 1992, p. 23, from American Newspaper Publishers Association.

★524★

Newspapers (SIC 2711)

Newspapers with Separate Ownership and Operations

Figures represent daily circulations in 1992.

New York Times	1,201,970
Los Angeles Times	1,164,388
Washington Post	846,635
New York Daily News	781,796
Chicago Tribune	733,775
Chicago Sun-Times	530,856
Boston Globe	505,744
New York Post	470,987
Houston Chronicle	425,775
Rocky Mountain News	365,480
Boston Herald	335,666
Houston Post	296,878
New York Newsday	267,989
Sacramento Bee	263,084
Denver Post	262,041
Los Angeles Daily News	212,001
San Antonio Express-News	188,797
San Antonio Light	148,591
Trenton Times	83,266
Trentonian	75,518
Anchorage News	60,873
Anchorage Times	44,057
Sacramento Union	NA
Washington Times	NA

Source: *Adweek*, May 4, 1992, p. 23, from American Newspaper Publishers Association.

★525★

Newspapers (SIC 2711)

Sunday Newspapers - U.K.

Shares of circulation are shown in percent for 1991, based on a total of 2.677 million copies.

Sunday Times	43.4%
Sunday Telegraph	21.4
Observer	21.1
Independent on Sunday	14.2

Source: Investext, Thomson Financial Networks, May 1, 1992, from Panmure Gordon & Co., Ltd.

★526★

Publishing (SIC 2713)

Library Book Market in 1991

Libraries' share of the total book market, by category, is shown in percent for 1991.

University press	26.9%
Professional	21.8
Juvenile	13.8
Adult trade	8.8
Subscription reference	6.1
All books	8.8

Source: *Library Journal*, January 1992, p. 39, from BISG.

★527★

Magazines (SIC 2721)

Bridal Magazines

Paid circulation of major bridal magazines is shown for 1991. Relative market shares are shown for the same period.

	Paid Circ.	% of Group
Modern Bride	344,033	35.4%
Bride's & Your New Home	322,755	33.2
Bridal Guide	181,674	18.7
Elegant Bride	123,721	12.7

Source: *The Wall Street Journal*, April 2, 1992, p. B1, from company estimates.

★528★

Magazines (SIC 2721)

Consumer Magazines

The leading 40 paid circulation magazines are shown with circulation for the last half of 1991. "Paid" magazines are those that have at least 70% paid circulation.

Modern Maturity	22,450,003
Reader's Digest	16,269,637

Continued on next page.

★ 528 ★ *Continued*

Magazines (SIC 2721)

Consumer Magazines

The leading 40 paid circulation magazines are shown with circulation for the last half of 1991. "Paid" magazines are those that have at least 70% paid circulation.

TV Guide	15,053,018
National Geographic	9,763,406
Better Homes & Gardens	8,002,794
Good Housekeeping	5,188,919
McCall's	5,066,849
Ladies' Home Journal	5,065,135
Family Circle	5,065,131
Woman's Day	4,619,505
Time	4,073,530
Redbook	3,860,294
National Enquirer	3,758,964
Playboy	3,547,165
People	3,380,832
Sports Illustrated	3,297,493
Newsweek	3,224,770
Prevention	3,204,583
Star	3,102,026
American Legion Magazine	2,935,379
AAA World	2,800,733
Cosmopolitan	2,741,802
Southern Living	2,361,076
Scholastic Teen Network	2,333,967
U.S. News & World Report	2,237,009
Smithsonian	2,140,349
Glamour	2,081,212
V.F.W. Magazine	2,063,354
NEA Today	2,034,846
Motorland	2,022,412
Field & Stream	2,002,732
Money	1,933,864
Home & Away	1,881,346
Seventeen	1,851,665
Ebony	1,844,973
Country Living	1,839,065
Popular Science	1,837,026
Life	1,815,916
First for Women	1,764,430
Parents Magazine	1,752,474

Source: *Advertising Age*, February 17, 1992, p. 42, from Audit Bureau of Circulations.

★ 529 ★

Magazines (SIC 2721)

Leading Consumer Magazines

Top 40 consumer magazines are ranked by circulation figures for the first six months of 1990.

Modern Maturity	22,443,464
NRTA/AARP News Bulletin	22,105,308
Reader's Digest	16,396,919
TV Guide	15,837,064
National Geographic	10,182,911
Better Homes & Gardens	8,002,895
Family Circle	5,159,147
Good Housekeeping	5,105,094
McCall's	5,011,473
Woman's Day	4,612,833
Time	4,256,604
Guideposts	4,131,548
National Enquirer	4,019,187
Redbook	3,947,106
Star	3,615,692
Sports Illustrated	3,507,627
Playboy	3,436,471
Newsweek	3,227,522
People Weekly	3,176,166
Prevention	3,025,746
The American Legion Magazine	2,858,405
First for Women	2,764,667
Cosmopolitan	2,714,639
U.S. News & World Report	2,319,591
Smithsonian	2,295,985
Southern Living	2,295,241
Glamour	2,210,938
Field & Stream	2,006,253
Money	1,959,228
NEA Today	1,915,891
Motorland	1,902,234
Ebony	1,887,595
Home & Away	1,882,064
V.F.W. Magazine	1,861,182
Popular Science	1,820,471
Seventeen	1,754,194
Parents Magazine	1,751,839
Country Living	1,750,187
Life	1,734,105
Penthouse	1,700,964

Source: *Folio*, March 1991, p. 137, from Audit Bureau of Circulations.

★ 530 ★

Magazines (SIC 2721)

Leading Magazines

Circulation of the leading 40 magazines, both paid and unpaid, is shown for the second half of 1991.

The Cable Guide	6,951,677
Friendly Exchange	5,322,497
The Disney Channel Magazine	5,306,570
Episodes	1,945,484
Healthy Kids (Birth-3)	1,504,192
U (college paper)	1,358,914
Video Event	1,330,533
Expecting	1,262,838
Baby Talk	1,168,633
American Baby	1,168,269
Chevy Outdoors	1,065,006
Fantastic Flyer	1,059,926
Sports Illustrated for Kids	887,954
Avis Traveller	864,178
Guide for Expectant Parents	858,075
Price Club Journal	810,141
Heartland USA	800,000
Realtor News	743,131
Real Estate Today	732,131
Asia Magazine	655,308
Mas	629,863
PC World	613,197
Appleseeds	582,528
Where	565,489
Family	558,934
CompuServe	520,018
Careers	505,050
Child	502,863
Snowmobile	485,997
Vis a Vis	458,381
Continental Profiles	431,842
MacWorld	430,211
Coming Attractions	429,542
Sky	416,487
Satellite TV Week	389,626
MacUser	382,016
On Sat	376,215
Lotus	363,224
Video Preview Now Playing	339,967
Twentyone	320,160

Source: *Advertising Age*, February 17, 1992, p. 42, from Business Publications Audit of Circulation.

★ 531 ★

Magazines (SIC 2721)

Magazine Leaders

1991 shares of top 20 magazine revenues totaled $11.339 billion. Relative dollar shares are shown in percent.

	($ mil.)	% of Group
Time Warner	$ 1,928.0	17.0 %
Hearst Corp.	1,002.0	8.8
Advance Publications	859.0	7.6
Thomson Corp.	774.4	6.8
Reed International	760.0	6.7
Reader's Digest Association	729.2	6.4
International Data Group	627.0	5.5
New Corp.	575.0	5.1
McGraw-Hill	448.0	4.0
Meredith Corp.	441.7	3.9
Ziff Communications	436.0	3.8
Hachette Publications	389.0	3.4
New York Times Co.	352.7	3.1
Washington Post Co.	326.5	2.9
Capital Cities/ABC	321.0	2.8
K-III Holdings	302.8	2.7
Times Mirror Co.	291.5	2.6
National Geographic Society	279.7	2.5
Enquirer/Star Group	275.2	2.4
Petersen Publishing Co.	220.3	1.9

Source: *Advertising Age*, August 10, 1992, p. S-6, from *Advertising Age* estimates.

★ 532 ★

Magazines (SIC 2721)

Magazines by Gross Revenue

Estimated revenues for 1991 are shown in millions of dollars; relative market shares are shown in percent.

	Revenues ($ mil.)	% of Group
TV Guide	$ 884,123	14.9 %
People	663,423	11.2
Time	578,450	9.7
Sports Illustrated	563,323	9.5
Reader's Digest	440,146	7.4
Parade	388,690	6.5
Newsweek	377,835	6.4
Better Homes & Gardens	291,921	4.9
PC Magazine	271,543	4.6

Continued on next page.

★532★ *Continued*

Magazines (SIC 2721)

Magazines by Gross Revenue

Estimated revenues for 1991 are shown in millions of dollars; relative market shares are shown in percent.

	Revenues ($ mil.)	% of Group
U.S. News & World Report . .	$ 267,406	4.5%
Business Week	263,589	4.4
Good Housekeeping . . .	262,524	4.4
National Geographic . . .	246,402	4.1
Family Circle	225,765	3.8
National Enquirer	216,831	3.6

Source: *Advertising Age*, June 15, 1992, p. S-2, from Audit Bureau of Circulations.

★533★

Magazines (SIC 2721)

Magazines by Newsstand Revenue

Estimated revenues for 1991 are shown in millions of dollars; relative market shares are shown in percent.

	Revenue ($ mil.)	% of Group
TV Guide	$ 265.3	19.7%
People	189.5	14.1
National Enquirer	167.5	12.5
Star Magazine	138.0	10.3
Woman's World	74.6	5.5
Penthouse	64.7	4.8
Cosmopolitan	63.1	4.7
Family Circle	59.7	4.4
Globe	58.8	4.4
Soap Opera Digest	55.8	4.2
Playboy	50.4	3.7
Woman's Day	50.1	3.7
First for Women	37.1	2.8
National Examiner	36.3	2.7
Glamour	33.4	2.5

Source: *Advertising Age*, June 15, 1992, p. S-11, from Audit Bureau of Circulations.

★534★

Magazines (SIC 2721)

Magazines by Subscriber Revenue

Estimated revenues for 1991 are shown in millions of dollars; relative shares are shown in percent.

	Revenue ($ mil.)	% of Group
TV Guide	$ 339.7	15.1%
Reader's Digest	319.2	14.2
Time	225.4	10.0
Sports Illustrated	221.2	9.8
National Geographic	208.6	9.3
People	128.9	5.7
Newsweek	124.9	5.6
Better Homes & Gardens . . .	119.6	5.3
McCall's	89.3	4.0
U.S. News & World Report . .	86.2	3.8
Ladies' Home Journal	84.2	3.7
Cable Guide	83.4	3.7
Playboy	80.9	3.6
Consumer Reports	73.8	3.3
Good Housekeeping	64.3	2.9

Source: *Advertising Age*, June 15, 1992, pp. S-11, from Audit Bureau of Circulations.

★ 535 ★

Magazines (SIC 2721)

Non-Paid Circulation Magazines

Readership of top 12 non-paid circulation magazines for the first half of 1992 was 24.791 million subscribers. Relative shares are shown in percent.

	No. of Readers	% of Group
The Disney Channel Magazine	5,482,669	22.1%
Friendly Exchange	5,465,316	22.0
Healthy Kids (4-10)	2,003,716	8.1
Bounty InfantCare Guide	1,927,964	7.8
Healthy Kids (Birth-3)	1,504,695	6.1
Episodes	1,503,535	6.1
U.- National College Paper	1,325,713	5.3
Expecting Magazine	1,312,900	5.3
Baby Talk Magazine	1,152,467	4.6
Pocket Guide	1,116,708	4.5
Fantastic Flyer Magazine	1,059,926	4.3
American Baby	935,424	3.8

Source: *Advertising Age*, August 17, 1992, p. 39, from BPA.

★ 536 ★

Magazines (SIC 2721)

Paid-Circulation Magazines

Readership of top 20 paid-circulation consumer magazines for the first half of 1992 was 132.996 million subscribers. Relative shares are shown in percent.

	No. of Readers	% of Group
Modern Maturity	22,545,206	17.0%
Reader's Digest	16,257,903	12.2
TV Guide	14,919,872	11.2
National Geographic	9,787,145	7.4
Better Homes & Gardens	8,002,477	6.0
The Cable Guide	6,182,567	4.6
Good Housekeeping	5,101,237	3.8
Family Circle	5,038,434	3.8
Ladies' Home Journal	5,003,008	3.8
McCall's	4,650,901	3.5
Woman's Day	4,521,050	3.4
Time	4,159,533	3.1
Sports Illustrated	3,573,915	2.7
National Enquirer	3,469,529	2.6
People	3,444,104	2.6

	No. of Readers	% of Group
Playboy	3,402,180	2.6%
Redbook	3,356,086	2.5
Prevention	3,273,286	2.5
Newsweek	3,232,117	2.4
Star	3,075,526	2.3

Source: *Advertising Age*, August 17, 1992, p. 39, from ABC and BPA.

★ 537 ★

Magazines (SIC 2721)

Soap Opera Magazines

Magazines are shown with circulation in December 1991 and percent shares for the group.

	Circ.	% of Group
Episodes	1,500,000	36.6%
Soap Opera Digest	1,469,974	35.9
Soap Opera Weekly	550,000	13.4
Soap Opera Magazine	375,000	9.2
Soap Opera Update	200,000	4.9

Source: *Folio*, January 1992, p. 20.

★ 538 ★

Magazines (SIC 2721)

Top Bridal Magazines

1990 single copy sales of four leading bridal magazines are shown in number of issues sold and percent share of relative market.

	Circ.	% of Group
Bride's	270,021	32.2%
Modern Bride	251,547	30.0
Bridal Guide	197,554	23.5
Elegant Bride	120,483	14.3

Source: *Folio*, June 1991, p. 31.

★ 539 ★
Book Publishing (SIC 2731)

Bible Translations

Versions read by most people worldwide are shown in percent.

New International Bible	34.0%
King James Bible	25.0
New King James Bible	10.0
Living Bible	7.0
New American Bible	5.0
Other	19.0

Source: *USA TODAY*, September 28, 1992, p. 1D, from Spring Arbor Dist.

★ 540 ★
Book Publishing (SIC 2731)

Classic Book Market Penetration

Percentage of public high schools that assign each book is shown, based on a nationwide survey of 222 schools in 1963 and 322 schools in 1988. Authors' names appear in parentheses. A dash (-) stands for not in top ten for given year.

	1963	1988
Romeo and Juliet (Shakespeare)	-	90.0%
Macbeth (Shakespeare)	10.0%	81.0
Huckleberry Finn (Twain)	27.0	78.0
To Kill a Mockingbird (Lee)	-	74.0
Julius Caesar (Shakespeare)	77.0	71.0
The Pearl (Steinbeck)	-	64.0
The Scarlett Letter (Hawthorne)	33.0	62.0
Of Mice and Men (Steinbeck)	-	60.0
Lord of the Flies (Golding)	-	56.0
The Diary of a Young Girl (Frank)	-	56.0
Silas Marner (Eliot)	76.0	-
Our Town (Wilder)	46.0	-
Great Expectations (Dickens)	39.0	-
Hamlet (Shakespeare)	33.0	-
The Red Badge of Courage (Crane)	33.0	-
A Tale of Two Cities (Dickens)	33.0	-

Source: *The New York Times*, May 20, 1992, p. B8, from Clearinghouse on Reading and Communication Skills.

★ 541 ★
Book Publishing (SIC 2731)

Hardcover Book Sales by Category

Sales of hardcover books, by category, are shown as percent of unit volume.

Popular fiction	31.0%
Cooking/crafts	17.0
General nonfiction	15.0
Religious	7.0
Psychology/recovery	5.0
Technology/science/education	5.0
Reference	4.0
Art/literature/poetry	3.0
Travel/regional	1.0
Other	13.0

Source: *Publishers Weekly*, January 6, 1992, p. 14.

★ 542 ★
Book Publishing (SIC 2731)

Higher Education Publishing

Shares of textbook market by type are shown in percent, based on sales of $40.0 million in 1990.

Life sciences	40.0%
Computer information systems	16.5
Nursing	16.2
Computer science	14.2
Chemistry	7.3
Health	5.8

Source: Investext, Thomson Financial Networks, April 13, 1992, p. 13, from S.G. Warburg Securities.

★ 543 ★
Book Publishing (SIC 2731)

Higher Education Publishing Companies

Top ten college publishers are ranked by 1990 sales, shown in millions of dollars. Relative market shares are shown in percent.

	Sales ($ mil.)	% of Group
Simon & Schuster	$ 256	17.0%
McGraw-Holt	227	15.1
The Thomson Corp.	202	13.4
Harcourt Brace	185	12.3
Addison-Wesley	135	9.0

Continued on next page.

★ 543 ★ *Continued*
Book Publishing (SIC 2731)

Higher Education Publishing Companies

Top ten college publishers are ranked by 1990 sales, shown in millions of dollars. Relative market shares are shown in percent.

	Sales ($ mil.)	% of Group
Macmillan	$ 123	8.2%
HarperCollins	116	7.7
Times Mirror	105	7.0
John Wiley & Sons	77	5.1
Houghton Mifflin	76	5.1

Source: Investext, Thomson Financial Networks, April 13, 1992, p. 13, from S.G.Warburg Securities.

★ 544 ★

Book Publishing (SIC 2731)

Small Press Distributors

Leading shares of the small press book wholesaling market are shown in percent. (Figures add to more than 100% because bookstores buy from more than one wholesaler).

Ingram	60.6%
Baker & Taylor	39.1
Bookpeople	24.2
Inland	14.9
Gordon's	13.0
Pacific Pipeline	10.2
NASCORP	5.9
Koen	5.6
PGW	5.3
Spring Arbor	4.3
Bookslinger	4.0
New Leaf	4.0
Golden-Lee	3.7
The Distributors	3.1
Bookman	2.8
Consortium	2.8
L-S Distributors	2.2
Partners	1.9
Southern Books	1.9
Bookazine	1.6

Source: *Publishers Weekly*, November 15, 1991, p. 34, from Cahners Research.

★ 545 ★

Book Publishing (SIC 2731)

Trade Paper Book Sales by Category

Trade paper book sales, by category, are shown as percent of unit volume.

Cooking/crafts	17.0%
General nonfiction	16.0
Popular fiction	15.0
Psychology/recovery	9.0
Religious	8.0
Art/literature/poetry	7.0
Reference	7.0
Technology/science/education	7.0
Travel/regional	4.0
Other	10.0

Source: *Publishers Weekly*, January 6, 1992, p. 14.

★ 546 ★

Book Printing (SIC 2732)

Leading Book Printers

1990 sales by the 10 leading U.S. book printers were $1.9033 billion. Shares by company are shown in millions of dollars and percent of the group's share.

	Sales ($ mil.)	% of Group
R.R. Donnelley & Sons Co. . . .	$ 507.0	26.6%
Arcata Graphics Company . . .	331.3	17.4
Banta Corporation	182.0	9.6
Rand McNally	170.0	8.9
Ringier America Inc.	150.0	7.9
Jostens, Inc.	149.0	7.8
Bertelsmann Printing & Mfg. . .	96.0	5.0
Courier Corporation	88.0	4.6
Herff Jones, Inc.	80.0	4.2
Maple-Vail Book Mfg. Corp. . .	75.0	3.9
Taylor Publishing Co.	75.0	3.9

Source: *Graphic Arts Monthly*, October 1991, p. 51, from *Print Markets*.

★ 547 ★

Sports Cards (SIC 2759)

Sports Card Producers

Shares of the domestic market are shown in percent.

Fleer	30.0-35.0%
Topps	30.0-35.0
Other	30.0-40.0

Source: Investext, Thomson Financial Networks, April 7, 1992, from Merrill Lynch Capital Markets.

★ 548 ★

Trading Cards (SIC 2759)

Trading Cards by Type

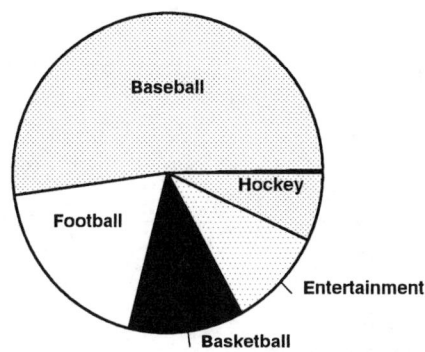

Shares, by category, are shown as percent of total sales.

Baseball	52.0%
Football	19.0
Basketball	12.0
Entertainment	10.0
Hockey	7.0

Source: *USA TODAY*, February 26, 1992, p. 1C, from Impel Marketing Inc.

★ 549 ★

Greeting Cards (SIC 2771)

Holiday Greeting Cards

Shares, by occasion, are shown as percent of 3.865 billion cards sold.

Christmas	59.5%
Valentine's Day	25.9
Easter	4.3
Mother's Day	3.9
Father's Day	2.6

Graduation	2.1%
Thanksgiving	1.0
Halloween	0.7

Source: *Business Week*, June 22, 1992, p. 44, from Greeting Card Assn.

★ 550 ★

Check Printing (SIC 2782)

Check Printing - U.K.

Shares of the personalized check market are shown in percent, based on a total of 520 billion units in 1990.

Bowater	18.3%
Bemrose	17.7
De La Rue	16.5
MB Clarke	13.9
BPCC (Forman)	9.7
Rochford Thompson	6.5
Kendrick and Jefferson	4.0
In House	9.4
Other	4.0

Source: Investext, Thomson Financial Networks, March 11, 1992, from Barclays de Zoete Wedd Securities.

★ 551 ★

Check Printing (SIC 2782)

Non-Personalized Check Printing - U.K.

Shares of the personalized check market are shown in percent, based on a total of 3.550 billion units in 1990. "Other" includes Kalamazoo.

Bowater	32.2%
MB Clarke	14.4
Bemrose	1.3
Waddington	1.3
Other	50.8

Source: Investext, Thomson Financial Networks, March 11, 1992, from Barclays de Zoete Wedd Securities.

SIC 28 - Chemicals and Allied Products

★ 552 ★

Chemicals (SIC 2800)

Biggest Chemical Producers

Sales of 12 leading chemical producers worldwide. Total sales were $212.56 billion in 1990. (Du Pont data exclude Conaco sales). Relative market shares are shown in percent.

	Sales ($ bil.)	% of Group
BASF	$ 29.18	14.0%
Hoescht	27.75	13.0
Bayer	26.06	12.0
Imperial Chemical Industries . .	23.35	11.0
Du Pont	22.06	10.0
Dow Chemical	20.01	9.0
Rhone-Poulenc	14.47	7.0
Montedison	13.03	6.0
Norsk Hydro	9.87	5.0
AKZO Group	9.51	4.0
Monsanto	9.05	4.0
Mitsubishi Kasei	8.22	4.0

Source: *Business Horizons*, November 1991, p. 16.

★ 553 ★

Chemicals (SIC 2800)

Chemical and Diversified Market

First quarter revenues of chemical and diversified companies (ended March 31, 1992 except as follows: figures for Cabot Corp. are from second fiscal quarter; figures for First Mississippi and Vigoro Corp. are from third fiscal quarter; figures for Univan Corp. are from fourth fiscal quarter). Revenues are shown in millions of U.S. dollars and market shares are shown in percent.

	($ mil.)	Share
Du Pont	$ 9,185	29.8%
Eastman Kodak	4,479	14.5
Tenneco	3,272	10.6

	($ mil.)	Share
Allied-Signal	$ 2,979	9.7%
W.R. Grace	1,326	4.3
Lyondell Petrochemical	1,028	3.3
Occidental Chemical	966	3.1
Kerr McGee	783	2.5
Arco Chemical	762	2.5
Chevron Chemicals	756	2.5
Hercules	744	2.4
Avery Dennison	670	2.2
Engelhard Corp.	630	2.0
Cabot Corp.	418	1.4
Lubrizol	415	1.3
Univar Corp.	410	1.3
Nalco Chemical	326	1.1
Ferro Corp.	273	0.9
NL Industries	226	0.7
Vulcan Materials	211	0.7
Inspiration Resources	200	0.6
Betz Laboratories	176	0.6
Loctite Corp.	147	0.5
Int'l Specialty Products	142	0.5
First Mississippi	123	0.4
Vigoro Corp.	118	0.4
Potash Corp. of Saskatchewan . .	74	0.2

Source: *Chemicalweek*, May 6, 1992, p. 12, from company reports and *Chemicalweek* calculations.

★ 554 ★

Chemicals (SIC 2800)

Chemical and Pharmaceutical Producers

Figures represent sales per employee in dollars and relative market shares in percent.

	Sales	% of Group
Shell	$ 598,737	8.2%
Neste	509,374	7.0

Continued on next page.

★ 554 ★ *Continued*
Chemicals (SIC 2800)

Chemical and Pharmaceutical Producers

Figures represent sales per employee in dollars and relative market shares in percent.

	Sales	% of Group
Norsk Hydro	$ 387,806	5.3%
Atochem	305,545	4.2
BP	293,656	4.0
Enichem	272,709	3.7
Elf Aquitaine	257,033	3.5
DSM	242,586	3.3
EMC	232,440	3.2
BASF	231,683	3.2
Laporte	225,063	3.1
Monsanto	218,958	3.0
Montecatini	216,815	3.0
Kemira	202,180	2.8
ICI	188,559	2.6
Sandoz	184,330	2.5
Degussa	183,031	2.5
Solvay	180,962	2.5
Nobel Industries	180,806	2.5
UCB	177,561	2.4
Huls	176,042	2.4
Hoechst	173,620	2.4
Rhone-Poulenc	169,082	2.3
Dyno Industrier	165,844	2.3
Ciba-Geigy	164,211	2.2
Bayer	162,943	2.2
Perstorp	157,287	2.1
AGA	151,446	2.1
Schering	148,458	2.0
Wacker Chemie	146,838	2.0
Akzo	146,542	2.0
Roche	144,008	2.0
BOC	123,670	1.7

Source: *ECN European Review Supplement*, December 1991, p. 10.

★ 555 ★
Chemicals (SIC 2800)

Chemical Company Revenues

Fourth-quarter 1991 revenues of diversified chemical companies are shown in millions of dollars. Shares are shown as percent of group total.

	($ mil.)	% of Group
Exxon Chemical	$ 5,436	18.8%
DuPont	3,780	13.1
Dow Chemical	2,678	9.2
Monsanto	1,660	5.7
Shell Oil	1,620	5.6
Occidental Petroleum	1,090	3.8
Amoco	943	3.3
W.R. Grace	941	3.2
Eastman Kodak	912	3.1
Chevron Corp.	907	3.1
Mobil Corp.	907	3.1
PPG Industries	840	2.9
Air Products and Chemicals	677	2.3
Rohm and Haas	660	2.3
Union Carbide	617	2.1
Texaco	592	2.0
Allied Signal	584	2.0
Ashland Oil	557	1.9
Quantum Chemical Corp.	443	1.5
BF Goodrich	419	1.4
FMC Corp.	396	1.4
Tenneco	290	1.0
Morton Int'l.	288	1.0
Imcera Group	273	0.9
Cabot	272	0.9
Freeport McMoRan	210	0.7
Olin Corp.	210	0.7
NL Industries	196	0.7
CBI Industries	182	0.6
Kerr-McGee	111	0.4
Inspiration Resources	104	0.4
Vulcan Materials	89	0.3
First Mississippi	77	0.3

Source: *Chemicalweek*, March 4, 1992, p. 25.

★ 556 ★
Chemicals (SIC 2800)

Chemical Industry Leaders in Europe

Company 1990 sales are shown in billions of European Currency Units (ECUs). Percent shares are based on group total.

	ECU (bil.)	% of Group
BASF	22.1	23.6%
Hoechst	21.9	23.4
Bayer	20.3	21.7
ICI	18.0	19.2
Rhone-Poulenc	11.4	12.2

Source: *International Management*, April 1992, p. 75.

★ 557 ★
Chemicals (SIC 2800)

Chemical Industry Leaders - Japan

Companies are ranked by 1991 declared income, shown in millions of Yen. Relative market shares are shown in percent.

	Income (Y mil.)	% of Group
Mitsubishi Petrochemical	40,187	22.3%
Shin-Etsu Chemical	25,832	14.3
Mitsubishi Kasei	25,393	14.1
Mitsui Petrochemical Industries	17,311	9.6
Ube Industries	16,889	9.4
Mitsui Toatsu Chemicals	14,017	7.8
Nippon Shokubai	13,629	7.6
Tokuyama Soda	9,905	5.5
Sumitomo Chemical	8,591	4.8
Nippon Sanso	8,450	4.7

Source: *TOKYO Business Today*, July 1992, p. 37.

★ 558 ★
Chemicals (SIC 2800)

Chemical Industry Sales - Australia

Segements of the Australian chemical industry are shown as percent of $7.68 billion in sales in 1990.

Synthetic resins and rubber	17.0%
Pharmaceutical and veterinary products	14.0
Soaps and detergents	11.0
Chemical fertilizers	10.0
Gases and organic industrial chemicals	10.0%
Inorganic industrial chemicals	9.0
Paints	9.0
Cosmetics and toiletries	5.0
Pesticides	5.0
Ammunition and explosives	4.0
Inks	4.0
Other	4.0

Source: *C&EN*, November 4, 1991, p. 16, from Australian Bureau of Statistics.

★ 559 ★
Chemicals (SIC 2800)

Chemical Market Leaders

Top 10 chemical company sales reached $45.6995 million in the first nine months of 1991. Relative shares are shown in percent.

	($ mil.)	% of Group
Dow Chemical	$ 14,244.0	31.2%
Monsanto	6,738.0	14.7
Union Carbide	5,359.0	11.7
W.R. Grace	4,971.9	10.9
American Cyanamid	3,851.3	8.4
Hercules	2,219.0	4.9
Air Products	2,206.5	4.8
Rohm & Haas	2,104.7	4.6
Arco Chemical	2,090.0	4.6
Ethyl	1,915.1	4.2

Source: *C&EN*, November 11, 1991, p. 10.

★ 560 ★

Chemicals (SIC 2800)

Chemical Plants in Serbia

Company percent shares are based on group total output in tons per year.

Pancevo 'HIP' Works	53.2%
Kikinda 'MSK' Works	20.0
Pancevo Petchem Complex	13.9
Zrenjanin 'FSK' Works	8.2
Sabac 'Zorka Hemijska' Works	2.7
Odzaci 'Hipol' Works	2.0

Source: *European Chemical News*, June 8, 1992, p. 10, from PlanEcon Inc.

★ 561 ★

Chemicals (SIC 2800)

Chemical Producers - 1991

Sales are shown in billions of dollars; relative market shares are shown in percent.

	Sales ($ bil.)	% of Group
Du Pont	$ 36.69	26.0%
Dow Chemical	18.81	13.3
Exxon Chemical	10.65	7.5
Monsanto	8.86	6.3
Hoechst Celanese	6.79	4.8
W.R. Grace	6.05	4.3
Lyondell	5.73	4.1
American Cyanamid	4.99	3.5
Union Carbide	4.88	3.5
Occidental Chemical	4.58	3.2
FMC Corp.	3.90	2.8
Amoco Chemical	3.80	2.7
Chevron Chemical	3.77	2.7
Mobil Chemical	3.76	2.7
Eastman Chemical	3.74	2.6
Shell Chemical	3.30	2.3
Air Products and Chemicals . . .	2.93	2.1
Arco Chemical	2.84	2.0
Rohm and Haas	2.76	2.0
Union Carbide Industrial Gases .	2.47	1.7

Source: *Chemicalweek*, March 4, 1992, p. 2, from company financial statements and *Chemicalweek* calculations.

★ 562 ★

Chemicals (SIC 2800)

Chemical - Leaders in Europe

Sales of the top 15 European chemical manufacturers are shown in billions of dollars for 1991; relative market shares are shown in percent.

	Sales ($ bil.)	% of Group
Hoechst	$ 28.8	14.1%
BASF	28.4	13.9
Bayer	25.8	12.7
ICI	21.9	10.8
Rhone-Poulenc	15.0	7.4
Ciba-Geigy	14.2	7.0
Royal Dutch/Shell	10.5	5.2
Akzo	9.2	4.5
Elf Atochem	9.0	4.4
Sandoz	9.0	4.4
Roche	7.7	3.8
Solvay	7.4	3.6
Huls	6.3	3.1
BP Chemicals	5.4	2.7
DSM	5.1	2.5

Source: *Chemicalweek*, April 1, 1992, p. 2, from company reports.

★ 563 ★

Chemicals (SIC 2800)

Chemicals Sales by Company

Companies are ranked by dollar sales in 1991. Percent shares are based on group total of $162,140 million.

	Sales ($ mil.)	% of Group
E.I. Du Pont De Nemours . . .	$ 38,031	23.5%
Dow Chemical	19,305	11.9
Monsanto	8,929	5.5
Union Carbide	7,346	4.5
W.R. Grace	6,949	4.3
Hoechst Celanese	6,856	4.2
Miles	6,197	3.8
Lyondell Petrochem.	5,757	3.6
American Cyanamid	5,040	3.1
BASF	4,962	3.1
FMC	3,932	2.4
Air Prods. & Chem.	2,950	1.8
Hercules	2,929	1.8
Rohm & Haas	2,775	1.7

Continued on next page.

★ 563 ★ *Continued*
Chemicals (SIC 2800)

Chemicals Sales by Company

Companies are ranked by dollar sales in 1991.
Percent shares are based on group total of $162,140
million.

	Sales ($ mil.)	% of Group
Ethyl	$ 2,575	1.6%
Sherwin-Williams	2,552	1.6
Quantum Chemical	2,486	1.5
B.F. Goodrich	2,472	1.5
EngelHard	2,436	1.5
Olin	2,290	1.4
Morton International	1,921	1.2
Dow Corning	1,877	1.2
Cabot	1,580	1.0
Lubrizol	1,485	0.9
Nalco Chemical	1,356	0.8
Great Lakes Chemical	1,348	0.8
IMC Fertilizer Group	1,133	0.7
Ferro	1,066	0.7
Inspiration Resources	1,062	0.7
Dexter	944	0.6
GAF	926	0.6
H.B. Fuller	855	0.5
NL Industries	842	0.5
Georgia Gulf	838	0.5
UCC Investors Holding	832	0.5
Wellman	806	0.5
CF Industries	803	0.5
Valhi	766	0.5
Baroid	708	0.4
Vista Chemical	705	0.4
Betz Laboratories	671	0.4
Valspar	633	0.4
Loctite	575	0.4
Arcadian	558	0.3
Sterling Chemicals	543	0.3
First Mississippi	539	0.3

Source: *Fortune*, April 20, 1992, p. 260.

★ 564 ★

Chemicals (SIC 2800)

Energy Companies - Chemical Earnings

Energy companies' chemical division third-quarter
profits for 1991, shown in millions of dollars. Market
shares are shown in percent.

	($ mil.)	Share
Du Pont	$ 286	42.8%
Exxon Chemical	85	12.7
Occidental Chemical	76	11.4
Atlantic Richfield Chemicals	53	7.9
Mobil Chemical	38	5.7
Ashland Chemical	26	3.9
Freeport-McMoRan	20	3.0
Chevron Chemical	17	2.5
Kerr-McGee Chemical	17	2.5
Amoco Chemical	13	1.9
Tenneco Chemicals and Minerals	12	1.8
Norsk Hydro	10	1.5
Tosco Corp.	8	1.2
Unocal Chemicals	4	0.6
Texaco Petrochemical	3	0.4

Source: *Chemicalweek*, November 6, 1991, p. 10, from
company reports and *Chemicalweek* calculations.

★ 565 ★

Chemicals (SIC 2800)

Flame Retardants in Plastics

Shares are shown in percent, based on a total
consumption of 272,500 tons in 1989.

Alumina trihydrate	65.0%
Organobromine	10.6
Phosphate esters	7.3
Antimony oxides	6.8
Organochlorine compounds	5.5
Chlorophosphates	4.8

Source: *Tin & Its Uses*, 1991, p. 1.

★ **566** ★

Chemicals (SIC 2800)

Paints and Coatings Sales

1991 sales of paints, coatings, inks, and pigments by company, shown in millions of dollars and as percent of the group's total.

	Sales ($ mil.)	Share
Sherwin-Williams	$ 2,541.4	43.4 %
Valspar	632.6	10.8
RPM	500.3	8.5
Benjamin Moore	463.0	7.9
Grow Group	412.1	7.0
UNC	360.6	6.2
Standard Brands Paint	293.6	5.0
Pratt & Lambert	239.0	4.1
Lilly Industrial Coatings	213.3	3.6
Guardsman Products	140.9	2.4
De Soto	58.9	1.0

Source: *Chemicalweek*, May 6, 1992, p. 32, from Standard and Poor's Compustat Services.

★ **567** ★

Chemicals (SIC 2800)

Speciality Chemical Companies in the U.K.

Sales figures are shown in millions of British pounds for 1991. Percent shares are based on group total.

	(L mil.)	% of Group
Croda International	$ 352.5	73.4 %
W Canning	74.3	15.5
Brent Chemicals	53.2	11.1

Source: *European Chemical News*, April 13, 1992, p. 12.

★ **568** ★

Chemicals (SIC 2800)

Specialty Chemicals

Specialty chemical company third-quarter 1991 revenues are shown in millions of dollars. Market shares are shown in percent.

	($ mil.)	Share
W.R. Grace	$ 1,622	31.2 %
Avery Dennison	609	11.7

	($ mil.)	Share
Engelhard	$ 572	11.0 %
Guardsman Products	367	7.0
Ecolab	361	6.9
Lubrizol	359	6.9
Nalco Chemical	346	6.6
Ferro	259	5.0
Betz Laboratories	170	3.3
International Specialty Products	129	2.5
Church & Dwight	123	2.4
Stepan	106	2.0
Calgon Carbon	73	1.4
Cambrex	40	0.8
MacDermid	35	0.7
Aceto	26	0.5
Chemdesign	9	0.2

Source: *Chemicalweek*, November 6, 1991, p. 10, from company reports and *Chemicalweek* calculations.

★ **569** ★

Chemicals (SIC 2800)

Top Chemical Firms - Japan

Japan's top 30 chemical firm are ranked by chemical sales for 1991 (year ended March 31), shown in billions of yen ($1 = Y130). (Data for Sumitomo Chemical, Showa Denko, Asalie Glass, and Kyowa Hakko Kogyo are for year ended December 31, 1990; data for Konica are for year ended April 30, 1991.) Relative market shares are shown in percent.

	(Y bil.)	% of Group
Mitsubishi Kasei	770.5	8.5 %
Sumitiomo Chemical	689.8	7.6
Asahi Chemical Industries	562.7	6.2
Toray Industries	523.3	5.8
Takeda Chemicals Ind.	490.7	5.4
Mitsubishi Petrochemical	434.4	4.8
Dainippon Ink & Chemical	388.0	4.3
Showa Denko	370.3	4.1
Idemitsu Petrochemical	361.1	4.0
Asahi Glass	351.0	3.9
Mitsui Petrochemical Ind.	330.8	3.6
Sanyo	325.1	3.6
Mitsui Toatsu Chemicals	324.2	3.6
Teijin	308.1	3.4
Kuraray	277.0	3.1
Mitsubishi Rayon	275.4	3.0
Tosoh	262.7	2.9

Continued on next page.

★ 569 ★ *Continued*
Chemicals (SIC 2800)

Top Chemical Firms - Japan

Japan's top 30 chemical firm are ranked by chemical sales for 1991 (year ended March 31), shown in billions of yen ($1 = Y130). (Data for Sumitomo Chemical, Showa Denko, Asalie Glass, and Kyowa Hakko Kogyo are for year ended December 31, 1990; data for Konica are for year ended April 30, 1991.) Relative market shares are shown in percent.

	(Y bil.)	% of Group
Kyowa Hakko Kogyo	223.7	2.5%
Toyobo	204.9	2.3
Kaneka	204.5	2.3
Ube Industries	188.2	2.1
Unitika	186.8	2.1
Ajinomoto	171.4	1.9
Konica	166.9	1.8
Shin-Etsu Chemical	156.9	1.7
Nippon Steel Chemical	149.5	1.6
Kanebo	141.0	1.6
Hitachi Chemical	111.0	1.2
Kao Corp.	77.1	0.8
Daikin Industries	47.8	0.5

Source: *Chemicalweek*, November 27, 1991, p. 38, from Comline International.

★ 570 ★

Chemicals (SIC 2800)

Top Chemical Producers - Brazil

Brazil's leading chemical companies are shown with 1990 sales in millions of dollars. (White Martins is a Union Carbide subsidiary; Glasurit is a BASF paints subsidiary). Relative shares are shown in percent.

	Sales	% of Group
Petrobras	$ 11,430	60.3%
Rhodia	674	3.6
Copene	665	3.5
Copesul	615	3.2
Hoechst	536	2.8
White Martins	523	2.8
Ciba-Geigy	469	2.5
Petroquimica Uniao	445	2.3
Bayer	419	2.2
Glasurit	365	1.9
BASF	357	1.9

	Sales	% of Group
Kodak	$ 338	1.8%
3M	301	1.6
Dow Quimica	285	1.5
Solvay	274	1.4
Petroflex	269	1.4
Du Pont	267	1.4
Poliolefinas	248	1.3
Tintas Coral	238	1.3
Salgema	229	1.2

Source: *Chemicalweek*, December 4, 1991, p. 42, from *Exame*.

★ 571 ★

Chemicals (SIC 2800)

World Top Chemical Companies

Company sales are shown in millions of dollars. Percent shares are based on the group's total.

	Sales ($ mil.)	% of Group
Hoechst	$ 28,528	11.5%
Bayer	25,635	10.3
BASF	24,121	9.7
Du Pont	22,844	9.2
ICI	22,104	8.9
Dow Chemical	18,807	7.6
Rhone-Poulenc	14,895	6.0
Ciba-Geigy	14,740	5.9
Shell Chemical	11,239	4.5
EniChem	10,861	4.4
Elf Atochem	9,578	3.8
Sandoz	9,401	3.8
Mitsubishi Kasei	9,180	3.7
Exxon Chemical	9,171	3.7
Akzo	9,060	3.6
Monsanto	8,864	3.6

Source: *European Chemical News*, June 8, 1992, p. 13.

★572★

Soda Ash (SIC 2812)

Soda Ash Producers Worldwide

Solvay
FMC
General Chemical
Rhone-Poulenc
Penrice
TG Soda Ash
North American

Percent shares of production capacity are based on an annual output of 16.8 million tons.

Solvay	37.5%
FMC	15.5
General Chemical	12.5
Rhone-Poulenc	11.9
Penrice	10.1
TG Soda Ash	7.1
North American	5.4

Source: *Chemicalweek*, April 29, 1992, p. 26, from Harriman Chemsult.

★573★

Industrial Gases (SIC 2813)

Argon Demand by End Use

Market distribution is shown as percent of a total demand of 13 billion cubic ft. in 1991.

Metal fabrication	45.0%
Steel	25.0
Lighting	7.0
Electronics	5.0
Other	18.0

Source: *C&EN*, December 2, 1991, p. 14.

★574★

Industrial Gases (SIC 2813)

Industrial Gas Market in Europe

Companies shares of the European market for industrial gases are shown in percent.

Air Liquide	26.0%
Air Products	15.0
AGA	13.0
BOC	12.0

Messer-Griesheim	11.0%
Linde	11.0
Union Carbide	3.0
Other	9.0

Source: Investext, Thomson Financial Networks, June 16, 1992, from UBS Phillips & Drew Global Research Group.

★575★

Industrial Gases (SIC 2813)

Industrial Gas Market Shares Worldwide

Global market shares, by company, are shown in percent.

Air Liquide	21.0%
BOC	17.0
Union Carbide	12.0
Air Products	10.0
AGA	6.0
Messer-Griesheim	6.0
Linde	5.0
Nippon Sanso	5.0
Other	18.0

Source: Investext, Thomson Financial Networks, June 16, 1992, from UBS Phillips & Drew Global Research Group.

★576★

Industrial Gases (SIC 2813)

Industrial Gas Producers

The world industrial gas market was $19 billion in 1991. Manufacturer's shares are shown in percent.

L'Air Liquide	21.0%
BOC	17.0
Union Carbide	13.0
Air Products	9.0
AGA	8.0
Messer Gresheim	5.0
Linde AG	4.0
Nippon Sanso	3.0
Others	20.0

Source: *Chemicalweek*, November 20, 1991, p. 53, from analyst reports.

★ 577 ★

Industrial Gases (SIC 2813)

Industrial Gas Sales Leaders

1990 world leading company sales are shown in millions of dollars, based on current exchange rates. Relative market shares are shown in percent. Data for BOC and Air Products and Chemicals are based on total sales for the year ended September 30. Data for Nippon Sanso are based on total sales for the year ended March 31.

	Sales ($ mil.)	% of Group
BOC (U.K.)	$ 3,494	22.3%
L'Air Liquide (France)	3,424	21.9
Union Carbide Industrial Gases (U.S.)	2,383	15.2
Air Products & Chemicals (U.S.)	1,640	10.5
AGA (Sweden)	1,423	9.1
Messer Griesheim (Germany) . .	1,198	7.7
Linde AG (Germany)	726	4.6
Nippon Sanso (Japan)	695	4.4
Liquid Carbonic (U.S.)	662	4.2

Source: *Chemicalweek*, November 20, 1991, p. 52, from company reports.

★ 578 ★

Industrial Gases (SIC 2813)

Nitrogen Demand by End Use

| Chemicals |
| Electronics |
| Petroleum refining |
| Metal fabrication |
| Food processing |
| Other |

Market distribution is shown as percent of a total demand of 770 cubic ft. in 1991.

Chemicals	35.0%
Electronics	20.0
Petroleum refining	15.0
Metal fabrication	10.0
Food processing	8.0
Other	12.0

Source: *C&EN*, December 2, 1991, p. 14.

★ 579 ★

Industrial Gases (SIC 2813)

Oxygen Demand by End Use

Market distribution is shown as percent of a total oxygen demand of 465 billion cubic ft. in 1991.

Steel	30.0%
Chemicals	15.0
Water treatment	12.0
Health	8.0
Petroleum refining	5.0
Other	30.0

Source: *C&EN*, December 2, 1991, p. 14.

★ 580 ★

Inorganic Pigments (SIC 2816)

Newest TiO2 Plants Worldwide

Titanium dioxide overcapacity will cause older, less efficient plants to be replaced by newer ones. All are chloride process plants except Tioxide in Malaysia. Production capacities are shown in thousands of metric tons per year and relative shares are shown in percent.

	(000) m.t./yr	% of Group
SCM (Australia/U.S.)	122	22.2%
Kerr-McGee (Australia/ Saudi Arabia)	110	20.0
Du Pont (U.S.)	90	16.4
Kronos (U.S.)	80	14.6
Kemira	52	9.5
Tioxide (Malaysia)	50	9.1
Ishihara (Singapore)	45	8.2

Source: *Chemicalweek*, April 22, 1992, p. 12, from International Business Management Associates.

★581★

Chemicals (SIC 2819)

Non-Agricultural Potash Sales - Canada

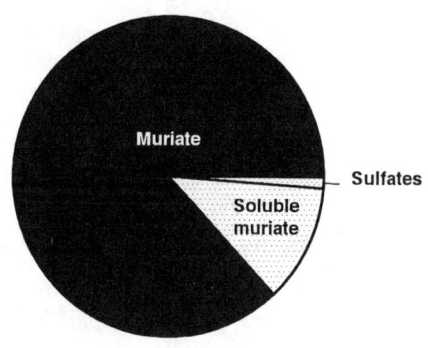

Segment distribution is shown in percent, based on total sales of 3,148 tons for the July-September period of 1991.

Muriate 87.0%
Soluble muriate 12.3
Sulfates 0.7

Source: *Potash & Phosphate Institute Press Release*, November 1991.

★582★

Inorganic Chemicals (SIC 2819)

Activated Carbon Production Worldwide

Market segmentation of activated carbon production capacity, by form, is shown in percent, based on a production capacity of nearly one billion lbs in 1991.

Granular and pellet 59.0%
Powder 41.0

Source: Investext, Thomson Financial Networks, June 18, 1992, from Kemper Securities Group, Inc.

★583★

Inorganic Chemicals (SIC 2819)

Catalysts by Type - North America

Segment distribution is shown in percent, based on totals of $3.354 billion in 1991 and $4.217 (projected) in 1996.

	1991	1996
Chemical	30.6%	32.3%
Environmental	25.0	28.4
Petroleum	16.0	15.1
Biocatalyst	20.5	13.8
Spent catalyst	7.9	10.4

Source: *Chemical Week*, July 1, 1992, p. 32, from Catalyst Consultants (Spring House, PA).

★584★

Inorganic Chemicals (SIC 2819)

Inorganic Chemical Production

Major chemical production is forecast for 1992 and shown in thousands of tons. Relative market shares are shown in percent.

	Tons (000)	% of Group
Sulfuric acid	44,803	40.8%
Ammonia	17,558	16.0
Phosphoric acid	12,700	11.6
Sodium hydroxide	12,776	11.6
Chlorine gas	11,689	10.6
Nitric acid	7,480	6.8
Hydrochloric acid	2,847	2.6

Source: *C&EN*, December 9, 1991, p. 39, from Bureau of the Census, International Trade Commission, Society of the Plastics Industry's Committee on Resin Statistics, and Fiber Economics Bureau.

★ 585 ★

Inorganic Chemicals (SIC 2819)

Non-Agricultural Potash Sales

Segment distribution is shown in percent, based on total sales of 126,540 tons for the July-September period of 1991.

Muriate	85.3%
Soluble muriate	13.7
Sulfates	1.1

Source: *Potash & Phosphate Institute Press Release*, November 1991.

★ 586 ★

Inorganic Chemicals (SIC 2819)

Phosphate Producers

```
FMC
Monsanto
A&W
Rhone-Poulenc
      Imports
```

Shares of phosphate production for the North American market in 1990 and 1992 are shown by company and percent.

	1990	1992
FMC	28.0%	35.0%
Monsanto	27.0	28.0
A&W	5.0	17.0
Rhone-Poulenc	15.0	16.0
Ocidental Chemical	11.0	-
Olin	10.0	-
Imports	4.0	4.0

Source: *Chemicalweek*, January 29, 1992, p. 28, from Albright & Wilson.

★ 587 ★

Inorganic Chemicals (SIC 2819)

Sodium Chlorate Producers

Percent shares of capacity are based on a total capacity of 597,000 metric tons per year.

Eka Nobel	31.7%
Kerr-McGee	20.8
Occidental Chemical	19.1

Huron Tech	12.1%
Elf Atochem	7.4
Georgia Gulf	4.0
Georgia Pacific	4.0
American Pacific	1.0

Source: *Chemicalweek*, April 1, 1992, p. 5, from SRI International, and *The Chemical Economics Handbook*.

★ 588 ★

Inorganic Chemicals (SIC 2819)

Sodium Chlorate Producers - Canada

Percent shares of capacity are based on a total capacity of 1,004,000 metric tons per year.

Sterling Chemical (Tenneco/A & W)	31.8%
Eka Nobel	23.4
Canadian Oxy	21.0
B.C. Chemicals	6.6
Albchem Industries	5.0
Weyerhaueser Canada (Saskatoon Chemicals)	4.7
PPG Canada	4.4
ICI Canada	2.2
Saint Anne Chemicals	1.0

Source: *Chemicalweek*, April 1, 1992, p. 5, from SRI International, and *The Chemical Economics Handbook*.

★ 589 ★

Plastics (SIC 2820)

Synthetic Materials Sales

1991 sales of fabricated rubber, plastic, and fiber products by company are shown in millions of dollars and percent share of market.

	Sales ($ mil.)	Share
Goodyear Tire & Rubber	$ 10,906.8	50.8%
Premark International	2,815.7	13.1
Gencorp	1,993.0	9.3
Rubbermaid	1,667.3	7.8
Cooper Tire & Rubber	1,001.1	4.7
Bandag	582.9	2.7
Carlisle Companies	500.8	2.3
Tredegar Industries	474.0	2.2
Sealed Air Corp.	435.1	2.0
Carlisle Plastics	343.6	1.6
Bamberger Polymers	203.5	0.9
American Biltrite	153.5	0.7

Continued on next page.

★ 589 ★ *Continued*
Plastics (SIC 2820)

Synthetic Materials Sales

1991 sales of fabricated rubber, plastic, and fiber products by company are shown in millions of dollars and percent share of market.

	Sales ($ mil.)	Share
American Filtrona	$ 144.0	0.7%
Raytech	103.3	0.5
Cimco	64.5	0.3
Versa Technologies	51.9	0.2
Selfix	37.0	0.2

Source: *Chemicalweek*, May 6, 1992, p. 30, from Standard & Poor's Compustat Services.

★ 590 ★
Plastics (SIC 2821)

Engineered Plastics

U.S. demand for engineered plastics, 1990, and projected demand for 1995 and 2000, are shown as percent. Percent shares are based on group totals of 746,200 tons for 1990, 982,800 tons for 1995, and 1,269,500 tons for the year 2000.

	1990 %	1995 %	2000 %
Polycarbonates	29.6%	29.8%	30.1%
Nylon	32.2	30.5	28.8
Thermoplastic polyester . . .	12.1	13.0	13.9
Polyphenylene oxide	10.5	10.3	10.1
Polyacetal	9.0	8.6	8.2
Other resins	6.5	7.9	8.9

Source: *JOM*, January 1992, p. 40, from The Freedonia Group.

★ 591 ★
Plastics (SIC 2821)

Major Plastics Production

Plastics production is forecast for 1992 and shown in thousands of tons. Relative market shares are shown in percent.

	Tons (000)	% of Group
Polyethylene, low density	11,856	27.3%
Polyvinyl chloride	9,170	21.1
Polyethylene, high density	9,013	20.8
Polypropylene	8,480	19.5
Polystyrene	4,860	11.2

Source: *C&EN*, December 9, 1991, from Bureau of the Census, International Trade Commission, Society of the Plastics Industry's Committee on Resin Statistics, and Fiber Economics Bureau.

★ 592 ★
Plastics (SIC 2821)

Plastics Market in USSR

Main plastics in USSR are shown with capacity, production and demand volume in 1991. Data are shown in thousands of tons.

	Capac.	Prod.	Demand
LDPE and HDPE . .	1410	1248	2857
PVC	731	665	1240
PS	607	540	1280
PP	141	130	453

Source: *European Chemical News*, July 22, 1991, p. 14, from Neste Chemicals International.

★ 593 ★
Plastics and Resins (SIC 2821)

ABS Resin Producers - Japan

Shares are shown in percent, based on a total ABS (acrylonitrile-butadiene-styrene) capacity of 617.8 thousand tons per year.

Japan Synthetic Rubber Co.	15.5%
Ube Cycon Co.	15.5
Monsanto Kasei Co.	13.1
Asahi Chemical Co.	11.6
Toray Industries Inc.	10.4
Sumitomo Naugatuck Co.	10.2
Denki Kagaku Kogyo Co.	8.8
Mitsubishi Rayon Co.	8.1

Continued on next page.

★ 593 ★ *Continued*
Plastics and Resins (SIC 2821)

ABS Resin Producers - Japan

Shares are shown in percent, based on a total ABS (acrylonitrile-butadiene-styrene) capacity of 617.8 thousand tons per year.

Daicel Chemical Co.	3.6%
Kanegafuchi Chemical Co.	3.1

Source: *Plastics Industry News*, January 1992, p. 3.

★ 594 ★

Plastics and Resins (SIC 2821)

HDPE Producers

Capacity shares of HDPE (high-density polyethylene) production are shown in percent for 1991. Percentages are based on a total U.S. capacity of 11.125 billion lbs.

Quantum Chemical	16.1%
Union Carbide	9.0
Dow Chemical	5.1
Other	69.8

Source: Investext, Thomson Financial Networks, April 1, 1992, from Prudential Securities Inc.

★ 595 ★

Plastics and Resins (SIC 2821)

LDPE Producers

Capacity shares of LDPE (low-density polyethylene) production are shown in percent for year-end 1991. Percentages are based on a total U.S. capacity of 8.0 billion lbs.

Quantum Chemical	20.6%
Dow Chemical	13.4
Union Carbide	6.2
Other	59.8

Source: Investext, Thomson Financial Networks, April 1, 1992, from Prudential Securities Inc.

★ 596 ★

Plastics and Resins (SIC 2821)

LLDPE Producers

Capacity shares of LLDPE (linear low-density polyethylene) production are shown in percent for year-end 1991. Percentages are based on a total U.S. capacity of 6.185 billion lbs.

Union Carbide	24.2%
Dow Chemical	20.9
Quantum Chemical	15.1
Other	52.1

Source: Investext, Thomson Financial Networks, April 1, 1992, from Prudential Securities Inc.

★ 597 ★

Plastics and Resins (SIC 2821)

PET Producers

Percent shares of U.S. capacity are based on annual total of 2,120 million lbs. of PET (polyethylene terephthalate).

Eastman Chemical	61.2%
Goodyear	20.9
Hoechst Celanese	15.1
ICI Americas	2.8

Source: *Chemicalweek*, April 1, 1992, p. 7, from company reports.

★ 598 ★

Plastics and Resins (SIC 2821)

Plastic Resins Market - Worldwide

The total market of 55.9 billion lbs. of plastic resins, by industry segment, is shown in percent for 1990.

Packaging	29.6%
Building/construction	21.1
Consumer, Institutional products	10.5
Electronic/electrical	5.7
Transportation	4.5
Furniture/furnishings	3.9
Adhesives/inks/coatings	2.5
Industrial/machinery	1.2
Other	21.0

Source: *The Wall Street Journal*, January 15, 1992, p. B2, from Society of the Plastics Industry.

★ 599 ★

Plastics and Resins (SIC 2821)

Plastics Production - Japan

Segment distribution is shown in percent, based on a total of 12.6 million metric tons produced in 1990.

Polyethylene	22.8%
Thermosets	16.4
Polyvinyl chloride	16.2
Polystyrene	15.3
Polypropylene	11.2
Acrylonitrile butadiene styrene	4.3
Polethylene terephthalate	3.6
Other	10.4

Source: *Chemicalweek*, November 27, 1992, p. 34, from Japan Plastics Industry Federation.

★ 600 ★

Plastics and Resins (SIC 2821)

Polycarbonate Makers - Europe

European chemical company shares are based on a total capacity of 266,000 thousand metric tons of polycarbonate in 1991, shown in percent.

Bayer (Belgium, Germany)	56.4%
GE Plastics (Netherlands)	22.6
Dow Europe (Germany)	13.5
EniChem (Italy)	7.5

Source: *Chemicalweek*, November 13, 1991, p. 10, from company reports.

★ 601 ★

Plastics and Resins (SIC 2821)

Polymer Producers in Eastern Europe

Company capacity is shown in thousands of tons; percent shares are based on the group's total.

	Tons (000)	% of Group
Czechoslovakia		
Litvinov	240	9.8%
Slovnaft	220	9.0
Neratowice	150	6.1
Novaky	91	3.7
Hungary		
TVK	435	17.7
BVK	200	8.1
Poland		
MZRIP	205	8.3
Wloclawek	200	8.1
Oswiecim	25	1.0
Tarnow	120	4.9
Yugoslavia		
Ina-oki	82	3.3
Ina-dina	70	2.8
Hip Pancevo	135	5.5
Hipol Odzaci	30	1.2
Sabac	40	1.6
Jugovinil	105	4.3
Ohis	48	2.0
Polichim	62	2.5

Source: *European Chemical*, April 6, 1992, p. 20, from CMAI.

★ 602 ★

Plastics and Resins (SIC 2821)

Polypropylene Producers - Latin America

Capacity of Latin America's top producers is shown in thousands of metric tons per year. Total capacity for the region is approximately 963,973 thousand metric tons per year.

Polibrasil	170
PPH	160
Indelpro (Himont/Grupo Alfa)	150
Propilco	120
Pemex	100
Petroken (IPAKO/Shell)	100
Propilven	70

Continued on next page.

★ 602 ★ *Continued*
Plastics and Resins (SIC 2821)

Polypropylene Producers - Latin America

Capacity of Latin America's top producers is shown in thousands of metric tons per year. Total capacity for the region is approximately 963,973 thousand metric tons per year.

Petroquima	55-65
Petroquima Cuyo	38

Source: *Chemicalweek*, February 19, 1992, p. 16, from Philip Townsend Associates.

★ 603 ★

Plastics and Resins (SIC 2821)

Recycled Plastics

Distribution of U.S. demand is shown in percent for 1990, based on an estimated total of 537.7 million lbs. Polyvinyl chloride does not include commercial scrap.

Polyethylene terephthalate	42.2%
High-density polyethylene	29.8
Low-density polyethylene	22.9
Polystyrene	3.7
Polypropylene	1.0
Polyvinyl chloride	0.4

Source: *Chemicalweek*, December 18, 1991, p. 30, from Council for Solid Waste Solutions.

★ 604 ★

Plastics and Resins (SIC 2821)

Recycled Plastics

Distribution of U.S. demand is shown in percent for 1990, based on an estimated total of 365 million lbs. Polyvinyl chloride does not include commercial scrap.

Polyethylene terephthalate	44.4%
High-density polyethylene	37.8
Low-density polyethylene	8.2
Polypropylene	5.2
Polystyrene	4.1
Polyvinyl chloride	0.3

Source: *Chemicalweek*, December 18, 1991, p. 30, from Chem Systems.

★ 605 ★

Plastics and Resins (SIC 2821)

Resin Demand in High-Visibility Packaging

Percent shares by type of resin are based on a 1990 total market of 120 million lbs.

Polyvinyl chloride (PVC)	26.0%
Polyethylenes	21.0
Polystyrene	20.0
Polycarbonate	13.0
Thermoplastic polyester	12.0
Other resins	9.0

Source: *Packaging*, January 1992, p. 42, from The Freedonia Group.

★ 606 ★

Plastics and Resins (SIC 2821)

Resin Industry by Major Market

Product breakdowns of the are shown in percent for 1989 and 1990.

	1989	1990
Packaging	28.0%	29.6%
Building and construction	21.1	21.1
Consumer and institutional	11.8	10.5
Electrical and electronic	6.0	5.7
Transportation	4.8	4.5
Furniture and furnishings	4.3	3.9
Adhesives, inks, coatings	2.3	2.5
Industrial/machinery	0.9	1.2
Other	20.8	21.0

Source: *Facts & Figures of the U.S. Plastics Industry*, August 1991, p. 24.

★ 607 ★

Plastics and Resins (SIC 2821)

Synthetic Resins

Distribution of domestic output is shown in percent for calendar year 1991, based on a total of 28.6893 billion kilograms.

Low-density polyethylene	40.2%
High-density polyethylene	32.1
Polyvinyl chloride	14.2
Polypropylene	11.8
ABS resins	1.5

Source: *Chemicalweek*, April 15, 1992, p. 25, from DRI/McGraw-Hill.

★ 608 ★

Plastics and Resins (SIC 2821)

Thermoset Market

Thermoset market categories, by material type, are shown in percent for 1990.

Phenolic	46.6%
Urea	23.7
Polyester	19.2
Epoxy	7.7
Melamine	2.8

Source: *Facts & Figures of the U.S. Plastics Industry*, August 1991, from SPI Major Market Report, SPI Committee on Resin Statistics, as compiled and by Ernst & Young.

★ 609 ★

Plastics and Resins (SIC 2821)

Thermosets by End Use

Thermoset markets, by end use, are shown in percent.

Building and construction	70.5%
Transportation	6.6
Electrical/electronic	3.5
Other adhesives, inks and coatings	19.4

Source: *Facts & Figures of the U.S. Plastics Industry*, August 1991, p. 41, from SPI Major Market Report, SPI Committee on Resin Statistics, as compiled and by Ernst & Young.

★ 610 ★

Plastics and Resins (SIC 2821)

Worldwide Silicone Market

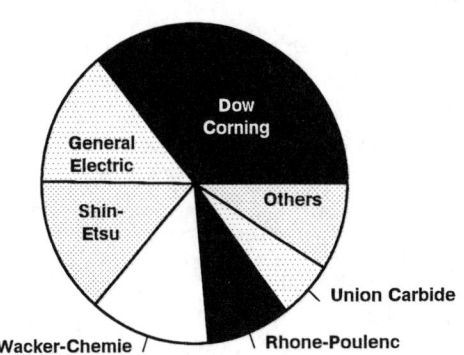

In 1991, the global silicone market was $5.2 billion. Manufacturers' shares are shown in percent.

Dow Corning	35.6%
General Electric	14.4
Shin-Etsu	13.5
Wacker-Chemie	13.0
Rhone-Poulenc	8.8
Union Carbide	5.8
Others	8.9

Source: *Chemicalweek*, February 19, 1992, p. 24, from SRI International.

★ 611 ★

Synthetic Rubber (SIC 2822)

Butyl Rubber Capacity - Global Shares

1991 butyl rubber capacity by company is shown in tons; shares of global market are shown in percent.

	Tons	Share
Exxon Chemical	388,000	52.6%
Bayer/Polysar	215,000	29.1
Japan Synthetic	50,000	6.8
Russia	85,000	11.5

Source: *European Rubber Journal*, April 1992, p. 19, from International Institute of Synthetic Rubber Producers.

★ 612 ★

Synthetic Rubber (SIC 2822)

Elastomer Consumption - North America

Shares, by type, are shown in percent based on actual consumption of 2.765 million metric tons in 1990 and estimated consumption of 2.671 million metric tons in 1991. SBR solid includes high styrene.

	1990	1991
SBR solid	28.4%	27.4%
Caboxylated SBR latex	18.1	18.3
Polybutadiene	14.3	14.8
TPE	9.4	10.2
EPDM	7.7	7.1
CR	2.8	2.7
NBR solid	2.5	2.7
SBR latex	1.8	1.8
NBR latex	1.3	1.4
Other synthetics	13.7	13.6

Source: *Rubber World*, May 1992, p. 20, from International Institute of Synthetic Rubber Producers.

★ 613 ★

Synthetic Rubber (SIC 2822)

Rubber Consumption - North America

Segment distribution is shown as percent of a total consumption of 2.399 million tons.

SBR solid	30.6%
X-SBR latex	20.4
Polybutadiene	16.5
Ethylene-propylene	7.9
Polychloroprene	3.0
NBR solid	3.0
SBR latex	2.0
NBR latex	1.5
Other synthetics	15.1

Source: *European Rubber Journal*, March 1992, p. 8, from Internationl Institute of Synthetic Rubber Producers.

★ 614 ★

Synthetic Rubber (SIC 2822)

Rubber Processing Market - U.S.

Shares of the U.S. rubber processing industry are shown in percent for 1991.

Farrel	80.0%
Other	20.0

Source: Investext, Thomson Financial Networks, March 17, 1992, from Paine Webber, Inc.

★ 615 ★

Synthetic Rubber (SIC 2822)

Rubber Processing Market - Worldwide

Shares of the worldwide rubber processing market are shown in percent for 1991.

Farrel	50.0%
Other	50.0

Source: Investext, Thomson Financial Networks, March 17, 1992, from Paine Webber, Inc.

★ 616 ★

Synthetic Rubber (SIC 2822)

Rubber Production - Worldwide

Worldwide rubber production by company is shown in thousands of tons. Percentages are based on a 1991 total production of 425,000 tons.

	Tons (000)	Share
E.I. du Pont (U.S.)	136	32.0%
Bayer (Germany)	60	14.1
Denki Kagaku (Japan)	45	10.6
Distugil (France)	40	9.4
Du Pont (U.K.)	33	7.8
Bayer/Polysar (U.S.)	27	6.4
Tosoh (Japan)	24	5.6
Du Pont-Showa Denko (Japan)	20	4.7
Russia, Omsk	20	4.7
China	20	4.7

Source: *European Rubber Journal*, December 1991, p. 24, from International Institute of Synthetic Rubber Producers.

★ 617 ★
Synthetic Rubber (SIC 2822)

U.K. Rubber Manufacturer Sales

Major U.K. rubber companies are ranked by 1989 sales, shown in millions of pounds. Percent shares are based on group total.

	(L mil.)	% of Group
Michelin Tyres Plc.		
Michelin (Fr.)	723.4	24.8%
Goodyear (GB) Ltd.	376.4	12.9
London Intl Group Plc.	351.3	12.0
Dunlop Ltd.	276.6	9.5
Pirelli Ltd.	235.6	8.1
Avon Rubber Plc.	228.6	7.8
SP Tyres (UK) Ltd.		
Industries (Japan)	186.4	6.4
BTR Industries Ltd.	143.2	4.9
Uniroyal Engelbert Tyres Ltd.	124.2	4.3
Gates Rubber Co. Ltd.	68.4	2.3
Arco Ltd.	57.9	2.0
James Walker Group Ltd.	52.9	1.8
Schleagel UK Ltd.	39.8	1.4
Dowty Woodville	27.6	0.9
Dowty Seals Ltd.	23.7	0.8

Source: *European Rubber Journal*, May 1992, p. 24, from ICC Business Ratios.

★ 618 ★
Synthetic Fibers (SIC 2823)

Synthetic Fiber Production

Synthetic fiber production is forecast for 1992 and shown in thousands of tons. Relative market shares are shown in percent.

	Tons (000)	% of Group
Polyester	3,456	41.9%
Nylon	2,495	30.3
Olefin and vinyon	1,821	22.1
Acrylic and modacrylic	473	5.7

Source: *C&EN*, December 9, 1991, from Bureau of the Census, International Trade Commission, Society of the Plastics Industry's Committee on Resin Statistics, and Fiber Economics Bureau.

★ 619 ★
Fibers (SIC 2824)

BCF Producers - Western Europe

Market shares are shown in percent based on a total of 168,000 metric tons. BCF stands for bulk continuous filament.

Du Pont	21.0%
Snia/Rhone Poulenc	18.0
Beaulieu	12.0
Aquafil	11.0
ICI	10.0
Allied-Signal (import)	9.0
Radicci	9.0
Akzo	8.0
ITC	2.0

Source: *Chemicalweek*, April 8, 1992, p. 24, from Snia.

★ 620 ★
Fibers (SIC 2824)

Polyamide Staple Fiber Makers - Western Europe

Market shares are shown in percent based on a total of 90,000 metric tons.

ICI	35.0%
Snia/Rhone Poulenc	28.0
Du Pont	20.0
Others	17.0

Source: *Chemicalweek*, April 8, 1992, p. 24, from Snia.

★ 621 ★
Organic Fibers (SIC 2824)

Nylon Carpet Fiber Producers

Capacity shares are shown in percent, based on an industry total of 2,440 billion lbs. as of January 1, 1992.

Du Pont	36.0%
Monsanto	25.0
BASF	18.0
Allied Signal	17.0
Wellman	2.0
Other	2.0

Source: Investext, Thomson Financial Networks, May 6, 1992, from Prudential Securities, Inc.

★ 622 ★
Organic Fibers (SIC 2824)

Poly Staple Fiber Producers

Capacity shares of the domestic market are shown in percent, based on an industry total of 2.605 billion lbs. in 1991.

Hoechst Celanese	31.0%
Du Pont	29.0
Wellman	26.0
Other	14.0

Source: Investext, Thomson Financial Networks, May 6, 1992, from Prudential Securities, Inc.

★ 623 ★
Synthetic Fibers (SIC 2824)

Synthetic Fibers Worldwide

| Polyester |
| Nylon and aramid |
| Acrylic/modacrylic |
| Other |

Segment distribution is shown in percent, based on a production total of 14.869 million metric tons in 1990.

Polyester	57.9%
Nylon and aramid	25.5
Acrylic/modacrylic	15.6
Other	1.1

Source: *Chemicalweek*, January 22, 1992, p. 20, from Fiber Organon.

★ 624 ★
Veterinary Pharmaceuticals (SIC 2830)

Animal Health Company - Worldwide

World leading animal health companies are shown with 1990 sales in millions of dollars and relative market shares in percent.

	($ mil.)	% of Group
Hoffmann-La Roche	$ 905	11.9%
Rhone-Poulenc	625	8.2
Pitman-Moore	615	8.1
SmithKline Beecham	574	7.5
MSD	570	7.5
Bayer	558	7.3

	($ mil.)	% of Group
Pfizer	$ 557	7.3%
BASF	494	6.5
Hoechst	377	5.0
Eli Lily	350	4.6
Solvay	292	3.8
Degussa	250	3.3
Upjohn	246	3.2
Ciba-Geigy	223	2.9
American Cyanamid	220	2.9
Sanofi	187	2.5
American Home Products	160	2.1
Monsanto	148	1.9
Akzo	140	1.8
Schering-Plough	120	1.6

Source: *European Chemical News*, July 1, 1991, p. 17, from Country NatWest WoodMac.

★ 625 ★
Dishwashing Compounds (SIC 2831)

Dishwashing Compound Market

Shares by company and brand are shown in percent. Estimated category size was $500 million in 1991.

	Fall 1990	Fall 1991
Benckiser		
Electrosol	8.0%	7.5%
Colgate-Palmolive		
Palmolive Liquid	9.0	10.5
Lever Brothers		
Sunlight	18.0	14.0
All	5.0	4.5
Procter & Gamble		
Cascade	53.0	56.0

Source: Investext, Thomson Financial Networks, January 24, 1992, from Kidder, Peabody & Company, Incorporated.

★626★

Antihistamines (SIC 2834)

Antihistamine Products

Brands are ranked according to their anticipated shares of the antihistamine market in 1992.

Seldane	49.0%
Hismanal	19.0
Seldane D	18.0
Claritin	9.0
Reactine	5.0

Source: Investext, Thomson Financial Networks, June 16, 1992, from Shearson Lehman Brothers, Inc.

★627★

Drugs (SIC 2834)

ACE Inhibitor Producers

Estimated shares of the 1991 domestic market are shown in percent. ACE stands for angiotensin converting enzyme.

Merck	55.0%
Vasotec	46.0
Prinivil	9.0
Bristol-Myers Squibb	38.0
Capoten	37.0
Monopril	1.0
ICI	6.0
Zestril	6.0
Warner Lambert	1.0
Accupril	1.0

Source: Investext, Thomson Financial Networks, January 3, 1992, from Morgan Stanley & Co. Inc.

★628★

Drugs (SIC 2834)

ACE Inhibitors

Manufacturer retail sales of ACE inhibitor drugs totaled $877 million in 1990 and $1.003 billion in 1991. Brand shares are shown in percent. ACE stands for angiotensin converting enzyme.

	1990	1991
Vasotec	41.0%	40.0%
Capoten	36.0	32.0
Zestril	8.0	10.0
Prinivil	7.0	8.0
Vaseretic	4.0	4.0
Capozide	3.0	3.0

	1990	1991
Prinzide	1.0%	1.0%
Zestoretic	1.0	1.0
Lotensin (new)	-	0.6
Altace (new)	-	0.2
Monopril (new)	-	0.2

Source: *Drug Topics*, March 23, 1992, p. 84, from PDS.

★629★

Drugs (SIC 2834)

Acetaminophen W/Codeine Manufacturers

1991 manufacturer shares are shown as percent of total sales through drugstore chains.

Lemmon	30.7%
Purepac	30.7
Barr	7.2
Rugby	5.4
Other	26.0

Source: *American Druggist*, July 1991, p. 54.

★630★

Drugs (SIC 2834)

Acne Remedies - U.K.

Estimated brand shares are shown in percent, based on a total OTC (over-the-counter) market of $26.0 million in 1991. Manufacturers' names are shown in parentheses.

Clearasil (P&G)	35.0%
Biactol (P&G)	20.0
Other	45.0

Source: Investext, Thomson Financial Networks, April 23, 1992, from Prudential Securities Inc.

★ 631 ★
Drugs (SIC 2834)

Acne Remedy Producers

Shares of the benzoyl peroxide acne product market are shown in percent.

SmithKline	44.0%
Procter & Gamble	35.0
Other	21.0

Source: Investext, Thomson Financial Networks, February 21, 1992, from Prudential Securities, Inc.

★ 632 ★
Drugs (SIC 2834)

Amoxicillin Manufacturers

1991 manufacturer shares are shown as percent of total sales through drugstore chains.

Apothecon	50.0%
SmithKline Beecham	18.9
Biocraft	17.7
Other	13.4

Source: *American Druggist*, July 1991, p. 54.

★ 633 ★
Drugs (SIC 2834)

Ampicillin Manufacturers

1991 manufacturer shares are shown as percent of total sales through drugstore chains.

Apothecon	46.7%
Biocraft	11.8
Wyeth-Ayerst	11.3
Warner Chilcott	8.7
Mylan	8.0
Rugby	5.3
Other	8.2

Source: *American Druggist*, July 1991, p. 54.

★ 634 ★
Drugs (SIC 2834)

Analgesic Brand Shares

Shares are shown in percent, based on a domestic market of $1.98 billion in revenues in 1991. Category includes narcotic and non-narcotic products.

Anaprox	12.8%
Darvocet	10.6
Dolobid	8.2
Fiorinal/Fioricet	4.6
Tylenol with Codeine	4.2
Anaprox	3.6
Generic	10.7
Other	45.4

Source: Investext, Thomson Financial Networks, February 3, 1992, from Morgan Stanley & Co. Inc.

★ 635 ★
Drugs (SIC 2834)

Analgesics

Brand shares are shown in percent for fiscal year 1992.

Excedrin	7.1%
Bayer	6.6
Others	86.3

Source: *Advertising Age*, July 13, 1992, p. 12.

★ 636 ★
Drugs (SIC 2834)

Antiarthritics Sales

Manufacturer retail sales of systemic antiarthritic drugs were $1.3 billion in 1990 and $61.2 million in 1991. Brand shares are shown in percent.

	1990	1991
Naprosyn	24.0%	19.0%
Voltaren	16.0	11.0
Feldene	16.0	9.0
Ansaid	8.0	5.0
Orudis	6.0	4.0
Lodine	3.0	3.0

Continued on next page.

★ 636 ★ *Continued*

Drugs (SIC 2834)

Antiarthritics Sales

Manufacturer retail sales of systemic antiarthritic drugs were $1.3 billion in 1990 and $61.2 million in 1991. Brand shares are shown in percent.

	1990	1991
Clinoril	4.0%	2.0%
Indocin	2.0	2.0
Tolectin	3.0	2.0
Others	18.0	43.0

Source: *Drug Topics*, March 23, 1992, p. 86, from PDS.

★ 637 ★

Drugs (SIC 2834)

Anticonvulsant Drugs

Shares of sales through drugstores and hospitals are shown in percent, based on a total market of $421.0 million in 1991. Manufacturers' names are shown in parentheses.

Dilantin and Dilantin 125 (Warner-Lambert)	33.0%
Tegretol (Ciba-Geigy)	24.0
Depakote (Abbott)	23.0
Depakene (Abbott)	5.0
Mysoline (American Home Products) . . .	3.0
Zarontin (Warner-Lambert)	2.0
Epitol (Lemanon)	1.0
Other	9.0

Source: Investext, Thomson Financial Networks, April 21, 1992, from Paine Webber Inc.

★ 638 ★

Drugs (SIC 2834)

Antidepressants Market

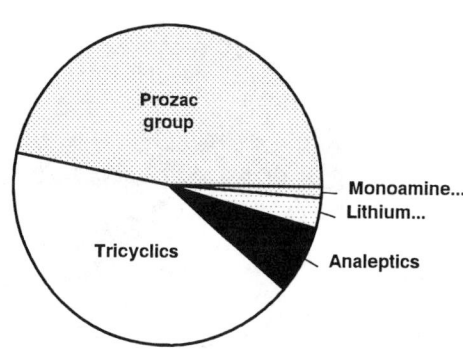

Manufacturer retail sales of antidepressant drugs were $800 million in 1990 and $903 million in 1991. Product shares are shown in percent.

	1990	1991
Prozac group	50.0%	47.0%
Tricyclics	39.0	42.0
Analeptics	6.0	7.0
Lithium products	4.0	3.0
Monoamine oxidase inhibitors . . .	1.0	1.0

Source: *Drug Topics*, March 23, 1992, p. 86, from PDS.

★ 639 ★

Drugs (SIC 2834)

Antilipemics Sales

Manufacturer retail sales of antilipemic drugs were $649 million in 1990 and $822 million in 1991. Brand shares are shown in percent.

	1990	1991
Mevacor	57.0%	61.0%
Lopid	25.0	25.0
Questran/Questran Light	11.0	5.0
Lorelco	4.0	3.0
Colestid	1.0	1.0
Pravachol	-	1.0
Others	2.0	4.0

Source: *Drug Topics*, March 23, 1992, p. 86, from PDS.

★ 640 ★

Drugs (SIC 2834)

Antiulcer Medications

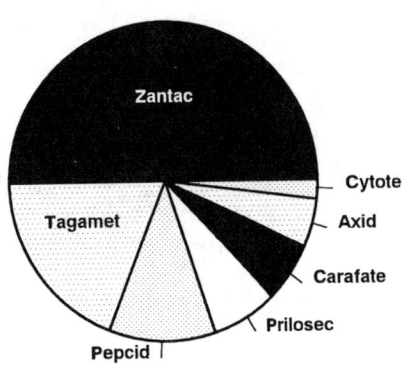

Manufacturer retail sales of antiulcer drugs were $1.6 billion in 1990 and $1.8 billion in 1991. Brand shares are shown in percent.

	1990	1991
Zantac	51.0%	50.0%
Tagamet	22.0	19.0
Pepcid	11.0	11.0
Prilosec	4.0	7.0
Carafate	7.0	6.0
Axid	4.0	5.0
Cytotec	1.0	2.0

Source: *Drug Topics*, March 23, 1992, p. 86, from PDS.

★ 641 ★

Drugs (SIC 2834)

Antiulcer Prescriptions

Oral, solid antiulcer prescription brand market shares are shown for the year-to-date 1992. Manufacturers' names are in parentheses.

Zantac (Glaxo)	44.43%
Tagamet (SKB)	20.02
Pepcid (MSD)	11.38
Carafate (Marion)	7.12
Axid (Lilly)	6.79
Prilosec (MSD)	6.43
Cytotec (G.D. Searle)	3.20
All others	0.63

Source: *Drug Topics*, June 22, 1992, p. 92.

★ 642 ★

Drugs (SIC 2834)

Anti-Cholesterol Drug Producers

Estimated shares of the domestic market are shown in percent, based on reported sales of $1.440 billion in 1991.

Merck	61.0%
Warner Lambert	25.0
Bristol-Myers Squibb	10.0
Other	4.0

Source: Investext, Thomson Financial Networks, January 3, 1992, from Morgan Stanley & Co. Inc.

★ 643 ★

Drugs (SIC 2834)

Anti-Cholesterol Drugs

Estimated brand shares of the domestic market are shown in percent, based on reported sales of $1.440 billion in 1991.

Mevacor	61.0%
Lopid	25.0
Questran	10.0
Other	4.0

Source: Investext, Thomson Financial Networks, January 3, 1992, from Morgan Stanley & Co. Inc.

★ 644 ★

Drugs (SIC 2834)

Best-Selling Drugs - 1990

Drug sales by brand are shown in millions of dollars for 1990. Brand shares are shown as a percent of group total.

	($ mil.)	% of Group
Zantac (Glaxo)	$ 1,305	19.5%
Cardizem (Marion Merrell Dow)	743	11.1
Procardia (Pfizer)	727	10.8
Prozac (Eli Lilly)	660	9.8
Mevacor (Merck)	600	8.9
Capoten (Bristol-Myers Squibb)	585	8.7

Continued on next page.

★ 644 ★ *Continued*
Drugs (SIC 2834)

Best-Selling Drugs - 1990

Drug sales by brand are shown in millions of dollars for 1990. Brand shares are shown as a percent of group total.

	($ mil.)	% of Group
Vasotec (Merck)	$ 570	8.5%
Tagamet (SmithKline Beecham)	560	8.4
Ceclor (Eli Lilly)	500	7.5
Naprosyn (Syntex)	455	6.8

Source: *Fortune*, July 29, 1991, p. 50, from *Medical Advertising News*.

★ 645 ★

Drugs (SIC 2834)

Beta Agonists for Asthma

Brand shares of the 1991 beta agonist market are shown in percent. Manufacturers' names are shown in parentheses.

Proventil (Schering-Plough)	42.5%
Ventolin (Glaxo)	36.5
Alupent (Boehringer Ingelheim)	7.1
Brethine (Ciba-Geigy)	3.7
Other	10.3

Source: Investext, Thomson Financial Networks, February 11, 1992, from Kidder, Peabody & Company, Incorporated.

★ 646 ★

Drugs (SIC 2834)

Beta Blockers

Manufacturer retail sales of beta-blocking drugs were $914 million in 1990 and $926.1 million in 1991. Brand shares are shown in percent.

	1990	1991
Tenormin	32.0%	33.0%
Lopressor	17.0	18.0
Inderal	16.0	13.0
Corgard	9.0	9.0
Tenoretic	5.0	5.0
Visken	3.0	3.0
Sectral	2.0	2.0
Trandate	2.0	2.0
Corzide	1.0	1.0

	1990	1991
Inderide	2.0%	1.0%
Propranolol Hcl	1.0	1.0
Other	10.0	12.0

Source: *Drug Topics*, March 23, 1992, p. 84, from PDS.

★ 647 ★

Drugs (SIC 2834)

Biotech Drug Sales

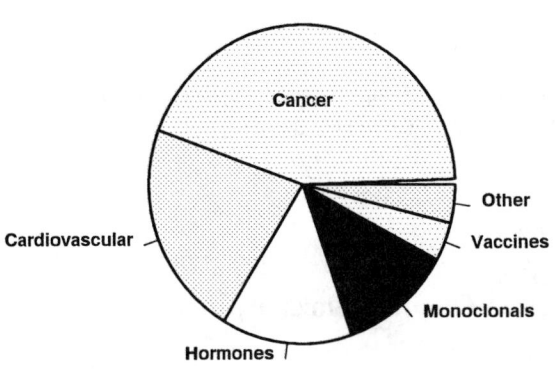

U.S. sales of biotech drugs, by category, totaling an estimated $1.67 billion in 1991 and $5.44 billion in 1996. Product shares are shown in percent.

	1991	1996
Cancer	24.0%	44.0%
Cardiovascular	38.0	22.0
Hormones	30.0	14.0
Monoclonals	1.0	12.0
Vaccines	7.0	4.0
Other	-	4.0

Source: *Fortune*, August 12, 1991, p. 80, from Ernst & Young.

★ 648 ★

Drugs (SIC 2834)

Biotechnology Drug Producers

Shares are shown in percent based on a revenue total of $2.607 billion for the 12 months ending April 1992.

Amgen	26.2%
Genentech	17.9
Life Technologies	6.6
Alza	5.4
Chiron	4.5

Continued on next page.

★ 648 ★ *Continued*

Drugs (SIC 2834)

Biotechnology Drug Producers

Shares are shown in percent based on a revenue total of $2.607 billion for the 12 months ending April 1992.

Genzyme	4.2%
Diagnostic Products Corp.	3.5
Genetics Institute	3.2
Biogen	2.4
Centocor	2.0
Immunex	2.0
Other	22.2

Source: Investext, Thomson Financial Networks, April 23, 1992, from Paine Webber Inc.

★ 649 ★

Drugs (SIC 2834)

Calcium Channel Blocker Market - U.S.

Brand shares are shown in percent.

Procardia XL	30.0%
Cardizem	20.0
Calan	19.0
Cardizem SR	14.0
Procardia	4.0
Isoptin	4.0
Cardizem CD	1.0
Other	8.0

Source: Investext, Thomson Financial Networks, June 16, 1992, from Shearson Lehman Brothers, Inc.

★ 650 ★

Drugs (SIC 2834)

Calcium Channel Blockers

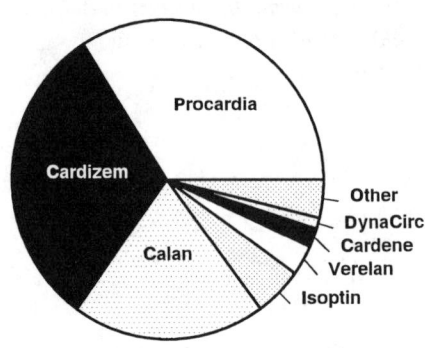

1991 sales of oral calcium channel blocking prescription drugs by brand, shown in percent of units (49.9 million) and percent of dollars ($1.513 billion).

	Rxs	Sales
Procardia	31.0%	34.0%
Cardizem	29.0	31.0
Calan	21.0	20.0
Isoptin	5.0	5.0
Verelan (new)	3.0	3.0
Cardene	3.0	2.0
DynaCirc (new)	1.0	1.0
Other	7.0	4.0

Source: *Drug Topics*, March 23, 1992, p. 82, from PDS.

★ 651 ★

Drugs (SIC 2834)

Cardiovascular Drugs

Sales of cardiovascular prescription drugs by type in 1990 ($4.2 billion) and in 1991 ($4.6 billion). Shares are shown in percent.

	1990	1991
Calcium channel blocker	30.0%	33.0%
ACE inhibitors	21.0	22.0
Beta-blockers	21.0	21.0
Vasodialators	12.0	10.0
Antihypertensives	9.0	8.0
Antiarrhythmics	5.0	5.0
Other	2.0	1.0

Source: *Drug Topics*, March 23, 1992, p. 82, from PDS.

★ 652 ★

Drugs (SIC 2834)

Cephalexin Manufacturers

1991 manufacturer shares are shown as percent of total sales through drugstore chains.

Biocraft	19.9%
Lemmon	19.2
Apothecon	15.2
Barr	9.9
Zenith	8.6
Warner Chilcott	7.3
Other	19.9

Source: *American Druggist*, July 1991, p. 54.

★ 653 ★

Drugs (SIC 2834)

Chest Rubs/Inhalants - Italy

Brand shares are shown in percent, based on a total market of $11.6 million for both categories combined in 1991.

Vicks VapoRub (P&G)	56.9%
Colyptol (RPR)	17.0
Vicks Inalante (P&G)	15.5
Other	10.6

Source: Investext, Thomson Financial Networks, April 23, 1992, from Prudential Securities Inc.

★ 654 ★

Drugs (SIC 2834)

Clonidine HCL Manufacturers

1991 manufacturer shares are shown as percent of total sales through drugstore chains.

Mylan	26.9%
Danbury	15.6
Lederle Standard	13.8
Purepac	10.6
Rugby	9.3
Geneva	6.3
Other	17.5

Source: *American Druggist*, July 1991, p. 54.

★ 655 ★

Drugs (SIC 2834)

Clorazepate Dipotassium Manufacturers

1991 manufacturer shares are shown as percent of total sales through drugstore chains.

Mylan	53.6%
Abbott	9.3
Goldline	6.6
Rugby	6.0
Warner Chilcott	6.0
Other	18.5

Source: *American Druggist*, July 1991, p. 54.

★ 656 ★

Drugs (SIC 2834)

Cough/Cold Remedies

Shares by category are shown in percent, based on sales of $1,947 million in 1990 and $2,168 million in 1991.

	'90	'91
Adult cold remedies	14.1%	64.6%
Cough syrups	48.3	20.3
Nasal decongestants	21.1	8.3
Sore throat remedies	12.4	5.1
Chest rubs	4.2	1.7

Source: Investext, Thomson Financial Networks, April 23, 1992, from Prudential Securities Inc.

★ 657 ★

Drugs (SIC 2834)

Diazepam Manufacturers

1991 manufacturer shares are shown as percent of total sales through drugstore chains.

Purepac	16.2%
Rugby	15.6
Danbury	14.3
Mylan	10.4
Warner Chilcott	7.1
Geneva	6.5
Goldline	5.8

Continued on next page.

★ 657 ★ *Continued*

Drugs (SIC 2834)

Diazepam Manufacturers

1991 manufacturer shares are shown as percent of total sales through drugstore chains.

Lederle	5.8%
Roche	5.2
Schein	5.2
Other	7.9

Source: *American Druggist*, July 1991, p. 56.

★ 658 ★

Drugs (SIC 2834)

Digestives Market - 1991

Shares, by type, are shown in percent, based on 1991 sales of $1,275 million.

Antacids	56.1%
Laxatives	43.9

Source: Investext, Thomson Financial Networks, April 23, 1992, p. 15, from Prudential Securities Inc.

★ 659 ★

Drugs (SIC 2834)

Dipyridamole Manufacturers

1991 manufacturer shares are shown as percent of total sales through drugstore chains.

Barr	32.0%
Danbury	12.4
Rugby	12.4
Boehringer Ingelheim	7.2
Geneva	6.5
Schein	5.9
Goldline	5.2
Other	18.4

Source: *American Druggist*, July 1991, p. 56.

★ 660 ★

Drugs (SIC 2834)

Doxycycline Hyclate Manufacturers

1991 manufacturer shares are shown as percent of total sales through drugstore chains.

Mylan	16.0%
Danbury	16.0

Mutual	13.6%
Barr	8.0
Purepac	7.4
Zenith	6.8
Rugby	5.6
Other	41.6

Source: *American Druggist*, July 1991, p. 56.

★ 661 ★

Drugs (SIC 2834)

Drug Manufacturer Sales

Company sales are shown in millions of dollars for 1991. Percent shares are based on group total of $65,159 millions.

	Sales (mil.)	% of Group
Bristol-Myers Squibb	$ 11,159	17.6%
Merck	8,603	13.6
American Home Products	7,079	11.2
Pfizer	6,950	11.0
Eli Lilly	5,756	9.1
Warner-Lambert	5,059	8.0
Rhone-Poulenc Rorer	3,824	6.0
Schering-Plough	3,616	5.7
UpJohn	3,426	5.4
Marion Merrell Dow	2,851	4.5
Syntex	1,958	3.1
Amgen	682	1.1
Sigma-Aldrich	589	0.9
Genentech	460	0.7
Perrigo	322	0.5
SPI Pharmaceuticals	226	0.4
Alza	140	0.2
Mylan Laboratories	117	0.2
Genzyme	109	0.2
Genetics Institute	83	0.1
Chiron	65	0.1
Biogen	61	0.1
Immunex	53	0.1
Centocor	53	0.1
Xoma	17	0.0
Synergen	14	0.0
Medimmune	14	0.0
Gensia Pharmaceuticals	5	0.0
U.S. Bioscience	3	0.0
Alliance Pharmaceutical	1	0.0

Source: *The 1992 Business Week 1000*, p. 180.

★ 662 ★
Drugs (SIC 2834)

Drug Manufacturers

First-quarter (ended March 31, 1992) revenues of drug companies (ended March 31, 1992). Revenues are shown in millions of U.S. dollars, and relative market shares are shown in percent.

	Rev. ($ mil.)	% of Group
Johnson & Johnson	$ 3,357	17.5%
Bristol-Meyers Squibb	2,783	14.5
Sandoz	2,707	14.1
SmithKline Beecham	2,086	10.9
Pfizer	1,761	9.2
Eli Lilly	1,557	8.1
Warner-Lambert	1,312	6.9
Schering-Plough	1,022	5.3
Rhone-Poulenc Rorer	898	4.7
Upjohn	872	4.6
Marion Merrell Dow	779	4.1

Source: *Chemicalweek*, May 6, 1992, p. 12, from company reports and *Chemicalweek* calculations.

★ 663 ★
Drugs (SIC 2834)

Drug Market - 1991

Drug market segments are shown in percent based on a total of $38.9 billion.

Tablets, capsules	76.0%
Injectables	10.0
Liquids	6.0
Topicals	6.0
Aerosols	2.0

Source: Investext, Thomson Financial Networks, March 23, 1992, from C.J. Lawrence, Morgan Grenfell Inc.

★ 664 ★
Drugs (SIC 2834)

Erythromycin Manufacturers

1991 manufacturer shares are shown as percent of total sales through drugstore chains.

Abbott	67.5%
Mylan	8.6
Barr	6.0
Upjohn	6.0
Other	11.9

Source: *American Druggist*, July 1991, p. 56.

★ 665 ★
Drugs (SIC 2834)

Ethical Pharmaceutical Global Producers

Shares are shown in percent for 1990.

Merck	3.6%
Bristol-Myers Squibb	2.8
Glaxo	2.8
SmithKline Beecham	2.4
Ciba-Geigy	2.4
Hoechst	2.3
Rhone-Poulenc Rorer	2.1
Takeda	1.9
Sandoz	1.9
Hoffman-La Roche	1.9
American Home Products	1.9
Eli Lilly	1.8
Pfizer	1.8
Bayer	1.8
Johnson & Johnson	1.7
Upjohn	1.4
Marian Merrell Dow	1.4
ICI	1.4
Boehringer Ingelheim	1.4
Sankyo	1.4
Wellcome	1.2
Schering-Plough	1.2
Schering AG	1.1
Fujisawa	1.0
Shionogi	1.0
Yamanouchi	1.0
American Cyanamid	0.9

Continued on next page.

★ 665 ★ *Continued*

Drugs (SIC 2834)

Ethical Pharmaceutical Global Producers

Shares are shown in percent for 1990.

Warner-Lambert	0.9%
Syntex	0.8
Eisai	0.8
Other	50.0

Source: Investext, Thomson Financial Networks, April 16, 1992, from Barclays de Zoete Wedd Securites.

★ 666 ★

Drugs (SIC 2834)

Furosemide Manufacturers

1991 manufacturer shares are shown as percent of total sales through drugstore chains.

Lederle	22.9%
Danbury	19.3
Mylan	16.3
Geneva	13.9
Rugby	6.6
Other	21.0

Source: *American Druggist*, July 1991, p. 56.

★ 667 ★

Drugs (SIC 2834)

Generic Drug Market by Segment - 1991

Percent shares by segment are based on total generic drug market of $7.45 billion.

Tablets, capsules	79.0%
Injectables	12.0
Liquids	4.0
Topicals	3.0
Aerosols	2.0

Source: Investext, Thomson Financial Networks, March 23, 1992, from C.J. Lawrence, Morgan Grenfell Inc.

★ 668 ★

Drugs (SIC 2834)

Generic Drug Market - U.S.

Shares of the U.S. generic drug market, by company, are shown in percent for 1989, 1990, and 1991.

	'89	'90	'91
Rugby-Darby	20.1%	19.6%	19.6%
IVAX Corporation	10.9	11.4	10.6
Ciba-Geigy	9.5	10.2	9.6
Mylan Laboratories	5.8	6.60	7.3
Schein-Henry, Inc.	4.6	4.90	5.8
Barr Laboratories	5.8	5.20	5.6
Moleculon	3.9	4.40	4.8
United Research Laboratories	5.2	5.20	4.3
American Cyanamid	5.3	4.80	4.1
Biocraft Laboratories	3.5	3.40	4.0
Warner Lambert	4.0	3.80	4.0
Major Pharmaceutical	4.5	4.40	4.0
A. L. Laboratories	2.8	3.30	3.9
Teva Pharmaceutical	2.3	2.80	3.1
Qualitest Products	4.9	3.30	2.8
Bioline Labs	1.8	1.8	1.5
Zenith Laboratories	1.3	1.3	1.3
Boehringer Ingelheim	1.0	1.2	1.3
Halsey Drug	0.7	0.9	0.9
Duramed	0.9	1.1	0.7
Pharmaceutical Resources	1.1	0.7	0.6

Source: Investext, Thomson Financial Networks, March 23, 1992, from C. J. Lawrence, Morgan Grenfell, Inc.

★ 669 ★

Drugs (SIC 2834)

Generic Drug Producers

Shares are shown as percent of total prescriptions.

	March 1991	March 1992
Rugby	24.8%	23.5%
Geneva	12.0	12.3
Goldline	12.9	12.1
Mylan	8.7	9.4
Barr	6.8	7.3
Warner	5.2	6.1
Biocraft	5.4	5.8
Purepac	5.7	5.8
Unit Res	5.5	5.2
Major	4.5	5.1
Lederle	4.8	5.0

Continued on next page.

★ 669 ★ *Continued*

Drugs (SIC 2834)

Generic Drug Producers

Shares are shown as percent of total prescriptions.

	March 1991	March 1992
Qualitest	3.6%	2.3%
Other	0.1	0.2

Source: Investext, Thomson Financial Networks, May 6, 1992, from Kidder, Peabody & Company, Incorporated.

★ 670 ★

Drugs (SIC 2834)

Gynecological Prescribed Remedies

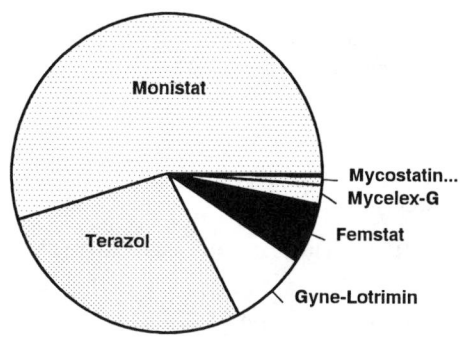

1990 market shares, by brand, are shown in percent.

Monistat (Johnson & Johnson)	55.0%
Terazol (Johnson & Johnson)	28.0
Gyne-Lotrimin (Schering-Plough)	8.0
Femstat (Syntex)	6.0
Mycelex-G (Miles)	2.0
Mycostatin Vaginal (Bristol-Myers Squibb)	1.0

Source: *American Druggist*, July 1991, p. 71, from HKS & Co. and Dow Jones.

★ 671 ★

Drugs (SIC 2834)

Hydrochlorothiazide Manufacturers

1991 manufacturer shares are shown as percent of total sales through drugstore chains.

Geneva	19.9%
Danbury	17.5
Purepac	17.5
Other	45.1

Source: *American Druggist*, July 1991, p. 56.

★ 672 ★

Drugs (SIC 2834)

Hydroxyzine HCL Manufacturers

1991 manufacturer shares are shown as percent of total sales through drugstore chains.

Rugby	30.1%
Geneva	23.3
Danbury	12.9
Mutual	11.0
Other	22.7

Source: *American Druggist*, July 1991, p. 57.

★ 673 ★

Drugs (SIC 2834)

Ibuprofen Manufacturers

1991 manufacturer shares are shown as percent of total sales through drugstore chains.

Boots	44.1%
Danbury	12.5
Mutual	8.6
Barr	7.2
Upjohn	5.9
Other	21.9

Source: *American Druggist*, July 1991, p. 57.

★ 674 ★
Drugs (SIC 2834)

Ibuprofen-based Product Market Shares

Brand shares are in percent for fiscal 1992.

Advil 50.0%
Motrin 15.0
Others 35.0

Source: *Advertising Age*, July 13, 1992, p. 12.

★ 675 ★
Drugs (SIC 2834)

Indomethacin Manufacturers

1991 manufacturer shares are shown as percent of total sales through drugstore chains.

Mylan 36.4%
Mutual 11.3
Lederle 9.9
Rugby 7.9
Merck 6.6
Goldline 5.3
Other 22.6

Source: *American Druggist*, July 1991, p. 57.

★ 676 ★
Drugs (SIC 2834)

Laxatives Market - 1991

Fiber-based bulking agents
Irritants and stimulants
Stool softeners
Mineral oils and salines

Shares, by category, are shown in percent, based on a 1991 sales total of $560 million.

Fiber-based bulking agents 40.0%
Irritants and stimulants 32.0
Stool softeners 18.0
Mineral oils and salines 10.0

Source: Investext, Thomson Financial Networks, April 23, 1992, from Prudential Securities Inc.

★ 677 ★
Drugs (SIC 2834)

Leading Antihistamines

1992 year-to-date brand shares of leading oral and solid antihistamines are shown in percent. Manufacturers' names are shown in parentheses.

Seldane (Merrell Dow) 54.1%
Hismanal (Janssen) 18.0
Tavist-1 (Sandoz) 4.1
Phenergan (Wyeth-Ayerst) 2.9
Promethazine HCI (Geneva Gen.) 2.2
Diphenhydramine HCI (Rugby) 2.1
Benadryl (Parke-Davis) 1.6
Diphenhydramine HCI (Geneva Gen.) . . . 1.5
Promethazine HCI (Rugby) 1.4
Diphenhydramine HCI (URL) 1.3
All other 10.8

Source: *Drug Topics*, April 20, 1992, p. 92, from Pharmaceutical Data Services Inc.

★ 678 ★
Drugs (SIC 2834)

Leading Pharmaceutical Companies

Sales by 12 leading pharmaceutical companies worldwide were $100.83 billion in 1990. Relative market shares are shown in percent.

	Sales ($ bil.)	% of Group
Ciba-Geigy	$ 14.48	14.0%
Johnson & Johnson	11.23	11.0
Bristol-Meyers Squibb	10.51	10.0
Sandoz	8.90	9.0
SmithKline Beecham	8.64	9.0
Merck	7.82	8.0
Hoffmann-LaRoche	9.96	7.0
American Home Products . . .	6.92	7.0
Pfizer	6.60	7.0
Procordia	6.34	6.0
Hoescht	6.22	6.0
Abbott	6.21	6.0

Source: *Business Horizons*, November 1991, p. 18.

★ 679 ★
Drugs (SIC 2834)
Liquid Diet Brands

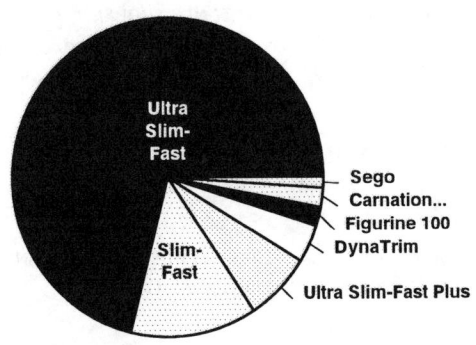

Brand shares are shown in percent for 13 weeks ended Sept. 20, 1992. Percentages are based on a total of $73.3 million in sales.

Ultra Slim-Fast 70.5%
Slim-Fast 13.2
Ultra Slim-Fast Plus 7.4
DynaTrim 3.8
Figurine 100 . . . . 1.9
Carnation Slender 1.6
Sego 0.9

Source: *The Wall Street Journal*, October 13, 1992, p. B1, from Information Resources, Inc.

★ 680 ★
Drugs (SIC 2834)
Lorazepam Manufacturers

1991 manufacturer shares are shown as percent of total sales through drugstore chains.

Mylan 26.5%
Danbury 16.8
Purepac 10.3
Rugby 7.7
Geneva 6.5
Wyeth-Ayerst 6.5
Goldline 5.8
Warner Chilcott 5.2
Barr 5.2
Other 9.5

Source: *American Druggist*, July 1991, p. 57.

★ 681 ★
Drugs (SIC 2834)
L-Thyroxine Sodium Manufacturers

1991 manufacturer shares are shown as percent of total sales through drugstore chains.

Geneva 19.7%
Marion 19.1
Daniels 12.5
Rugby 11.2
Boots 9.2
Rorer 7.9
Pharmaceutical Basics 7.2
Other 13.2

Source: *American Druggist*, July 1991, p. 60.

★ 682 ★
Drugs (SIC 2834)
Major Pharmaceutical Companies

Sales figures are shown in billions of dollars. Company shares are based on 1991 total sales, shown in percent.

	Sales ($ bil.)	Shares
Merck	$ 7.20	11.4%
Bristol-Myers	5.90	9.4
Lilly	4.03	6.4
American Home Products . . .	4.00	6.3
Pfizer	3.80	6.0
Others	38.20	60.5

Source: *Wall Street Journal*, April 9, 1992, p. B4, from U.S. Bureau of Labor Statistics.

★ 683 ★
Drugs (SIC 2834)
Methotrexate Manufacturers

1991 manufacturer shares of the oral methotrexate market are shown as percent of total sales through drugstore chains.

Lederle 77.5%
Barr 18.1
Other 4.4

Source: *American Druggist*, July 1991, p. 62.

★ 684 ★
Drugs (SIC 2834)

Methyldopa Manufacturers

1991 manufacturer shares are shown as percent of total sales through drugstore chains.

Geneva	30.4%
Danbury	14.9
Lederle	11.2
Rugby	9.9
Barr	7.5
Mylan	6.8
Other	19.3

Source: *American Druggist*, July 1991, p. 60.

★ 685 ★
Drugs (SIC 2834)

Nasal Decongestants - Germany

Brand shares of the OTC (over-the-counter) nasal decongestant market are shown in percent, based on a total market of $57.8 million in 1991. Manufacturer names are shown in parentheses.

Otriven (Zyma)	16.0%
Nasavin (Merck)	12.0
Olynth (Goedecke/W-L)	10.0
Wick Sinex (Blendax/P&G)	9.0
Sinuspret (Bionoric)	7.0
Rhinospry (Thomae/BI)	7.0
Endrine (Asche)	3.0
Ratiopharm	3.0
Other	33.0

Source: Investext, Thomson Financial Networks, April 23, 1992, from Prudential Securities Inc.

★ 686 ★
Drugs (SIC 2834)

Nasal Decongestants - Italy

Brand shares of the OTC (over-the-counter) nasal decongestant market are shown in percent, based on a total market of $33.1 million in 1991. Manufacturer names are shown in parentheses.

Sinex (Vicks)	39.0%
Rinazina (Maggioni Winthrop/Sterling)	17.0
Other	44.0

Source: Investext, Thomson Financial Networks, April 23, 1992, from Prudential Securities Inc.

★ 687 ★
Drugs (SIC 2834)

Nasal Decongestants - U.K.

Estimated brand shares are shown in percent, based on a total OTC (over-the-counter) market of $10.3 million in 1991. Manufacturers are shown in parentheses.

Sinex (P&G)	30.1%
Ofrivine (Zyma)	27.0
Other	42.9

Source: Investext, Thomson Financial Networks, April 23, 1992, from Prudential Securities Inc.

★ 688 ★
Drugs (SIC 2834)

Nicotine Patches

Brand shares of the domestic market, estimated at $700 million in 1992, are shown in percent. Manufacturers' names are shown in parentheses.

Habitrol (Ciba-Geigy)	42.9%
Nicoderm (Marion Merrell Dow)	39.3
Prostep (American Cyanamid)	10.7
Nicotrol (Warner-Lambert)	7.1

Source: *The New York Times*, August 19, 1992, p. C3, from Capital Institutional Services.

★ 689 ★
Drugs (SIC 2834)

Nicotine Patches by Brand

Shares by brand are shown in percent based on dollar sales for the weeks ended 04/24/92 and 02/28/92.

	Week 04/24	Week 02/28
Ciba-Geigy (Habitrol)	60.0%	57.0%
Marion Merrell Dow (Nicoderm)	27.0	42.0
American Cyanamid (ProStep)	13.0	1.0

Source: *The Wall Street Journal*, May 22, 1992, p. B1.

★ 690 ★
Drugs (SIC 2834)

Nifedipine Manufacturers

1991 manufacturer shares are shown as percent of total sales through drugstore chains.

Purepac	19.9%
United Research	17.2
Pfizer	13.2
Chase	11.9
Rugby	11.9
Lemmon	9.9
Other	16.0

Source: *American Druggist*, July 1991, p. 62.

★ 691 ★
Drugs (SIC 2834)

Nitroglycerin Manufacturers

1991 manufacturer shares are shown as percent of total sales through drugstore chains.

Parke-Davis	52.0%
Geneva	15.5
Purepac	12.2
Other	20.3

Source: *American Druggist*, July 1991, p. 60.

★ 692 ★
Drugs (SIC 2834)

NSAID Products

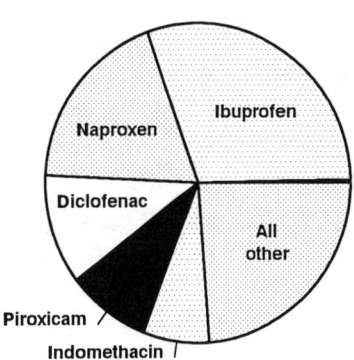

NSAID (Nonsteroidal anti-inflammatory drug) brand shares are shown in percent for 1991.

Ibuprofen	29.7%
Naproxen	19.1
Diclofenac	11.0
Piroxicam	8.5
Indomethacin	7.4
All other	24.2

Source: *Statistical Bulletin*, July 1992, p. 31.

★ 693 ★
Drugs (SIC 2834)

Oral Contraceptive Producers

Shares of the global market are shown in percent.

American Home Products	30.0%
Johnson & Johnson	25.0
Other	45.0

Source: Investext, Thomson Financial Networks, May 26, 1992, from Barclays de Zoete Wedd Securities.

★ 694 ★
Drugs (SIC 2834)

OTC Analgesics

Estimated shares of the OTC (over-the-counter) analgesics market are shown in percent, based on a total of $2.6 billion in 1990.

Acetaminophen	49.0%
Aspirin	30.5
Ibuprofen	20.5

Source: Investext, Thomson Financial Networks, February 3, 1992, from Morgan Stanley & Co. Inc.

★ 695 ★
Drugs (SIC 2834)

OTC Cough/Cold/Allergy Remedy Producers

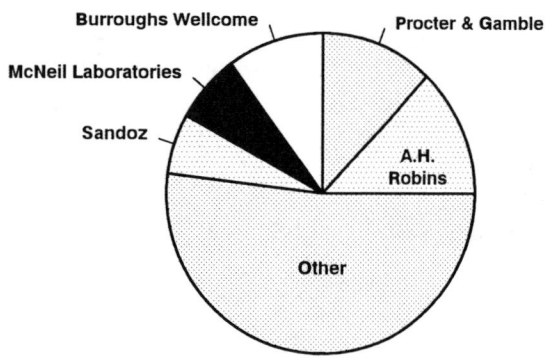

1991 company shares of the OTC (over-the-counter) cough/cold/allergy remedy market are shown in percent.

A.H. Robins	12.8%
Procter & Gamble	12.0
Burroughs Wellcome	9.6
McNeil Laboratories	7.1
Sandoz	6.1
Other	52.4

Source: *Advertising Age*, August 17, 1992, p. 43, from Nielsen Marketing Research.

★ 696 ★
Drugs (SIC 2834)

OTC Drug Producers - Europe

Company shares of the $12.0 billion OTC (over-the-counter) market are shown in percent for 1990.

Bristol-Meyers Squibb Co.	3.5%
Merck & Co.	3.1
American Home Products Corp.	3.0
Glaxo Holdings	2.6
Other	87.8

Source: *Advertising Age*, April 27, 1992, pp. I-32, from Euromonitor.

★ 697 ★
Drugs (SIC 2834)

Penicillin VK Manufacturers

1991 manufacturer shares are shown as percent of total sales through drugstore chains.

Apothecon	38.0%
Wyeth-Ayerst	15.3
Mylan	14.0
Biocraft	12.0
Other	20.7

Source: *American Druggist*, July 1991, p. 60.

★ 698 ★
Drugs (SIC 2834)

Phenobarbital Manufacturers

1991 manufacturer shares are shown as percent of total sales through drugstore chains.

Warner Chilcott	35.0%
Danbury	22.7
Lilly	11.0
Purepac	11.0
Other	20.3

Source: *American Druggist*, July 1991, p. 60.

★ 699 ★

Drugs (SIC 2834)

Potassium Chloride Manufacturers

1991 manufacturer shares are shown as percent of total sales through drugstore chains.

Warner Chilcott	14.1%
Robins	13.3
Copley	12.6
Rugby	9.6
Abbott	8.1
Ethex	8.1
Upsher-Smith	8.1
Adria	5.2
Other	20.9

Source: *American Druggist*, July 1991, p. 60.

★ 700 ★

Drugs (SIC 2834)

Sex Hormone Manufacturers

Shares of world production are shown in percent.

Schering	78.0%
Other	22.0

Source: Investext, Thomson Financial Networks, May 26, 1992, from Barclays de Zoete Wedd Securities.

★ 701 ★

Drugs (SIC 2834)

Sore Throat Remedies - Germany

Shares are shown by brand with manufacturers' names in parentheses.

Neo-Angin (Klosterfrau)	12.0%
Frubienzyms (Biotherax/BI)	9.0
Chlorhexamed (Blendax/P&G)	8.0
Dorithriein (Rentschler)	7.0
Lemocin (Sandoz)	7.0
Salviathymol (Galenika)	7.0
Hexoral (Goedecke/W-L)	6.0
Other	52.0

Source: Investext, Thomson Financial Networks, April 23, 1992, from Prudential Securities Inc.

★ 702 ★

Drugs (SIC 2834)

Steroids for Asthma

Brand shares of the 1991 beta agonist market are shown in percent. Manufacturers' names are shown in parentheses.

Azmacort (Rhone Poulenc Rorer)	39.2%
Vanceril (Schering-Plough)	34.4
Aerobid (Forest)	14.1
Beclovent (Glaxo)	12.3

Source: Investext, Thomson Financial Networks, February 11, 1992, from Kidder, Peabody & Company, Incorporated.

★ 703 ★

Drugs (SIC 2834)

Tetracycline Manufacturers

1991 manufacturer shares are shown as percent of total sales through drugstore chains.

Mylan	34.0%
Danbury	20.7
Rugby	9.3
Sandoz	8.7
Geneva	8.0
Goldline	5.3
Other	14.0

Source: *American Druggist*, July 1991, p. 62.

★ 704 ★

Drugs (SIC 2834)

Thioridazine HCL Manufacturers

1991 manufacturer shares are shown as percent of total sales through drugstore chains.

Mylan	34.0%
Danbury	20.7
Rugby	9.3
Sandoz	8.7
Geneva	8.0
Goldline	5.3
Other	14.0

Source: *American Druggist*, July 1991, p. 62.

★ 705 ★

Drugs (SIC 2834)

Thyroid Medication Manufacturers

1991 manufacturer shares are shown as percent of total sales through drugstore chains.

Armour	61.4%
Rorer	8.3
Luchem	6.9
Rugby	6.2
Other	17.2

Source: *American Druggist*, July 1991, p. 62.

★ 706 ★

Drugs (SIC 2834)

Timolol Maleate Manufacturers

1991 manufacturer shares are shown as percent of total sales through drugstore chains.

Merck	71.7%
Mylan	10.2
Other	18.1

Source: *American Druggist*, July 1991.

★ 707 ★

Drugs (SIC 2834)

Top 12 Pharmaceutical Firms in the World

Companies are ranked by 1991 sales of prescription drugs, shown in billions of dollars. Shares for the group are shown in percent.

	Sales ($ bil.)	% of Group
Merck and Co. (U.S.)	$ 6.60	12.7%
Glaxo (U.K.)	5.68	10.9
Bristol-Myers Squibb (U.S.)	5.36	10.3
Ciba-Geigy (Switzerland)	4.49	8.7
SmithKline Beecham (U.K./ U.S.)	4.21	8.1
Hoechst (Germany)	4.18	8.1
American Home (U.S.)	3.67	7.1
Lilly (U.S.)	3.66	7.1

	Sales ($ bil.)	% of Group
Hoffmann-La Roche (Switzerland)	$ 3.63	7.0%
Johnson & Johnson (U.S.)	3.60	6.9
Pfizer (U.S.)	3.47	6.7
Sandoz (Switzerland)	3.33	6.4

Source: *Science*, Vol 256, May 1, 1992, p. 608.

★ 708 ★

Drugs (SIC 2834)

Top Rxs by Dollar Volume

Top 10 retail prescription drugs are ranked by 1991 sales, shown in millions of dollars. Brand shares are shown as percent of group total.

	Sales ($ mil.)	% of Group
Zantac (Allen & Hanburys)	$ 916.1	19.6%
Procardia (Pfizer)	509.9	10.9
Mevacor (MSD)	504.7	10.8
Cardizem (Marion Labs)	474.7	10.2
Ceclor (Lilly)	428.8	9.2
Prozac (Lilly)	425.6	9.1
Vasotec (MSD)	404.4	8.6
Tagamet (SKB)	350.8	7.5
Xanax (Upjohn)	337.9	7.2
Naprosyn (Syntex)	323.1	6.9

Source: *Drug Topics*, March 23, 1992, p. 74, from Pharmaceutical Data Services Inc.

★ 709 ★

Drugs (SIC 2834)

Top Rxs by Unit Volume

Top 10 retail prescription drugs are ranked by 1991 sales, shown in millions of units. Brand shares are shown as percent of group total.

	Sales ($ mil.)	% of Group
Amoxil (Beecham)	23.4	13.1%
Premarin (Wyeth-Ayerst) . . .	22.0	12.3
Zantac (Allen & Hansburys) . .	19.3	10.8
Lanoxin (Burroughs Wellcome)	18.9	10.6
Xanax (Upjohn)	17.2	9.6
Synthroid (Flint)	16.3	9.1
Ceclor (Lilly)	16.0	9.0
Seldane (Merrell Dow)	15.4	8.6
Procardia (Pfizer)	15.3	8.6
Vasotec (MSD)	14.9	8.3

Source: *Drug Topics*, March 23, 1992, p. 74, from Pharmaceutical Data Services Inc.

★ 710 ★

Drugs (SIC 2834)

Verapamil Manufacturers

1991 manufacturer shares are shown as percent of total sales through drugstore chains.

Danbury	23.2%
Purepac	15.2
Searle	12.6
Warner Chilcott	10.6
Mylan	9.9
Rugby	9.3
Other	19.2

Source: *American Druggist*, July 1991, p. 62.

★ 711 ★

Diagnostic Substances (SIC 2835)

Hematology Diagnostic Producers

Shares are shown in percent. "Other" includes Genetic Systems and Organon Teknika.

Abbott	60.0%
Ortho	20.0
Other	20.0

Source: Investext, Thomson Financial Networks, February 7, 1992, from Surto & Co., Inc.

★ 712 ★

Test Kits (SIC 2835)

Blood-Glucose Strips by Brand

Shares are shown in percent, based on a total of $192 million for the year ending September 30, 1992.

LifeScan	28.7%
Chemstrip	26.4
Glucofilm	13.6
ExacTech	10.9
Glucostix	10.2
Tracer	8.8
Other	1.4

Source: *The Wall Street Journal*, November 12, 1992, p. B8, from Information Resources Inc.

★ 713 ★

Test Kits (SIC 2835)

Pregnancy Tests by Brand

Shares are shown in percent, based on a total of $155.9 million for the year ending September 30, 1992.

ept	24.8%
Fact	19.4
Clear Blue	17.9
First Response	15.0
Answer	9.8
Advance	7.3
Q-Test	4.9
Other	0.9

Source: *The Wall Street Journal*, November 12, 1992, p. B8, from Information Resources Inc.

★ 714 ★

Test Kits (SIC 2835)

Test Kits by Type

Shares are shown in percent, based on a total of $462.9 in sales for the year ending September 30, 1992.

Blood-glucose strips	42.0%
Pregnancy kits	34.1
Blood-glucose meters	12.9
Blood-pressure meters	5.2
Ovulation kits	3.7
Urinary test strips	2.1

Source: *The Wall Street Journal*, November 12, 1992, p. B1, from Information Resources Inc.

★ 715 ★

Detergent Chemicals (SIC 2840)

Detergent Chemicals Forecast

Domestic demand distribution is shown, by type, based on a projected total of 5.410 billion lbs. in 1994.

Builders	56.8%
Surfactants	36.4
Bleaches	1.1
Fabric softeners	0.9
Enzymes	0.8
Fragrances	0.5
Optical brighteners	0.5
Other	3.0

Source: *Chemicalweek*, January 29, 1992, p. 24, from Freedonia Group.

★ 716 ★

Detergents (SIC 2840)

Soap and Polish Sales

Procter & Gamble

Colgate-Palmolive

Clorox

Stanhome

NCH Corp.

Church & Dwight

1991 sales of soaps, synthetic detergents, and polishing products by company, are shown in millions of dollars and as percent of the total market.

	Sales ($ mil.)	Shares
Procter & Gamble	$ 27,026.0	73.8%
Colgate-Palmolive	6,060.3	16.6
Clorox	1,646.5	4.5
Stanhome	710.2	1.9
NCH Corp.	677.7	1.9
Church & Dwight	485.5	1.3

Source: *Chemicalweek*, May 6, 1992, p. 34, from Standard & Poor's Compustat Services.

★ 717 ★

Health & Beauty Aids (SIC 2840)

HBA Market

Segment distribution of the health and beauty aid market is shown as percent of supermarket sales.

Over-the-counter remedies	23.4%
Hair care	13.5
Oral hygiene	13.2
Feminine hygiene	10.4
Cosmetics & nail care	7.8
Personal deodorants	6.2
Shaving needs	5.0
Skin care/sun tan	4.0
Vitamins & supplements	3.4
Diet aids	3.2
First aid/wound care	2.5
Eye care/contact-lens care	2.4
Baby needs	1.8
Family planning	1.1
Other	2.1

Source: *Supermarket Business*, May 1992, p. 150.

★ 718 ★

Household Products (SIC 2840)

Household and Personal Care Companies

Shares of the household and personal care product core market are shown in percent for 1991. The category comprises laundry detergents, fabric softeners, dishwashing compounds, toilet soaps, shampoos, and toothpaste.

Procter & Gamble	47.3%
Lever Brothers	19.0
Colgate-Palmolive	10.1
Other	23.6

Source: Investext, Thomson Financial Networks, January 24, 1992, from Kidder, Peabody & Company, Incorporated.

★ 719 ★

Household Products (SIC 2840)

Household and Personal Care Market

Market segmentation is shown in percent for 1991, based on an industry total of $23.678 billion.

Disposable diapers	17.0%
Toilet tissue	11.0
Packaged detergents	8.7
Paper towels	7.1
Heavy-duty liquids	6.4
Cleansers	5.4
Shampoos	4.8
Toilet soap	4.8
Toothpaste	4.7
Deodorants	4.6
Sanitary napkins	4.4
Facial tissue	4.3
Fabric softener	3.5
Light-duty liquids	3.1
Conditioners	2.2
Dishwasher compounds	2.2
Liquid bleach	2.0
Mouthwash	2.0
Air freshener	2.0

Source: Investext, Thomson Financial Networks, January 24, 1992, from Kidder, Peabody & Company, Incorporated.

★ 720 ★

Detergents (SIC 2841)

Detergent Manufacturers - Japan

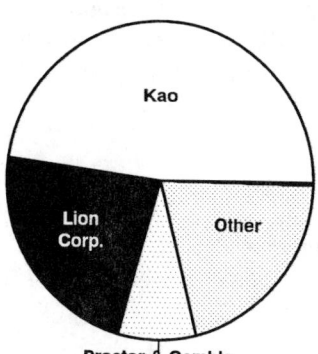

Shares of the 1991 market are shown in percent. "Other" includes Nippon Chemicals and Unilever.

Kao	48.0%
Lion Corp.	23.0
Procter & Gamble	8.0
Other	21.0

Source: *Chemicalweek*, January 29, 1992, p. 42, from Hewin International.

★ 721 ★

Detergents (SIC 2841)

Detergent Products - Japan

Segment distribution is shown in percent for 1991, based on a total of 639 thousand metric lbs.

Superconcentrates	74.8%
Conventional powders	
Phosphate-free	7.8
Phosphate-based	5.5
Conventional liquids	7.5
Multifunctional powders	3.9
Structured liquids	0.5

Source: *Chemicalweek*, January 29, 1992, p. 42, from Hewin International.

★ 722 ★

Detergents (SIC 2841)

Laundry Detergents

Market shares are shown in percent for fall of 1990 and fall of 1991. Estimated category size for 1991 was $3.6 billion. Total for Fab includes 1-Shot; total for Tide includes Tide with Bleach.

	Fall 1990	Fall 1991
Church & Dwight		
Arm & Hammer powder	3.0%	3.0%
Arm & Hammer liquid	1.5	1.5
Colgate-Palmolive		
Ajax	0.8	1.0
Ajax Liquid	1.4	2.0
Cold Power	0.1	0.1
Dynamo	1.2	0.8
Fab	2.0	1.5
Fab Liquid	0.7	0.5
Fresh Start	1.3	0.8
Lever Brothers		
All	2.5	1.5
All Liquid	4.0	4.5
Surf	5.0	4.0
Surf Liquid	3.0	2.5
Wisk Powerscoop	0.1	3.0
Wisk Liquid	8.0	8.0
Dow/Texize		
Yes Liquid	1.5	1.5
Clorox		
Clorox Detergent	2.0	0.5
Procter & Gamble		
Bold 3	2.0	2.0
Bold 3 Liquid	0.5	0.5
Cheer	5.0	5.5
Cheer Liquid	3.5	3.0
Lemon Dash	1.0	1.5
Liquid Lemon Dash	1.0	1.5
Era Liquid	3.0	3.0
Gain	1.0	2.5
Oxydol	1.8	2.5
Solo Liquid	1.5	2.0
Tide Powder	23.0	22.0
Tide Liquid	9.0	8.5
Dial		
Purex	1.5	1.5

	Fall 1990	Fall 1991
Purex Liquid	1.2%	1.5%
Dutch	0.2	0.2
Trend	0.5	0.6

Source: Investext, Thomson Financial Networks, January 24, 1992, from Kidder, Peabody & Company, Incorporated.

★ 723 ★

Detergents (SIC 2841)

Leading Dishwasher Detergent Manufacturers

Company and brand shares are shown as of June 1992.

Procter & Gamble (Cascade)	50.3%
Lever Bros. (Sunlight)	19.8
Colgate-Palmolive (Palmolive Automatic)	9.6
Benckiser (Electrasol)	9.2
Others	11.1

Source: *Advertising Age*, August 10, 1992, p. 3.

★ 724 ★

Detergents (SIC 2841)

Light-Duty Detergent Market

Shares by company and brand are shown in percent. Estimated category size was $735 million in 1991.

	Fall 1990	Fall 1991
Colgate-Palmolive		
Palmolive	17.0%	17.5%
Ajax	5.0	4.5
Lever Brothers		
Sunlight	9.0	10.0
Dove	5.5	6.0
Procter & Gamble		
Dawn	26.5	28.5
Ivory	14.5	12.0
Joy	11.5	11.0
Other	11.0	10.5

Source: Investext, Thomson Financial Networks, January 24, 1992, from Kidder, Peabody & Company, Incorporated.

★ 725 ★

Detergents (SIC 2841)

Top Supermarket Detergents

Sales of top 10 supermarket powder detergent brands accounted for 79.1% of the $2.0107 billion market for 52 weeks ending May 23, 1992. Shares are shown in percent.

	Sales ($ mil.)	% of Group
Tide	$ 466.6	23.2%
Tide with Bleach	286.5	14.2
Cheer	171.0	8.5
Surf	142.4	7.1
Arm & Hammer	111.4	5.5
Wisk Power Scoop	101.2	5.0
Gain	91.6	4.6
Bold	82.9	4.1
Fab	71.8	3.6
Oxydol with Bleach	66.3	3.3
Other	419.0	20.9

Source: *Advertising Age*, July 20, 1992, p. 20, from A.C. Nielsen ScanTrack.

★ 726 ★

Soap (SIC 2841)

Soap Manufacturers

Shares are shown in percent for 1983 and for 1991. The total market for toilet-soap in 1991 was $1.6 billion.

	1983	1991
Lever Bros.	24.0%	31.5%
Procter & Gamble	37.1	30.5
Dial	15.0	19.0
Colgate-Palmolive	6.5	8.0
Jergens	4.7	5.5
Other	12.7	5.5

Source: *The Wall Street Journal*, March 19, 1992, p. B1, from Packaged Facts Inc.

★ 727 ★

Soap (SIC 2841)

Toilet Soap Market

Shares by company and brand are shown in percent. Estimated category size was $1.145 billion in 1991, including both liquid and bar soap.

	Fall 1990	Fall 1991
Colgate-Palmolive		
Soft Soap Liquid	3.5%	4.5%
Irish Spring	4.5	4.0
Palmolive	1.0	0.7
Dial		
Dial	11.0	10.0
Dial Liquid	4.0	4.5
Tone	3.0	2.5
Pure & Natural	1.2	1.5
Kao/Jergens		
Jergens	4.0	3.5
Jergens Liquid	2.0	2.0
Gentle Touch	0.5	0.5
Lever Brothers		
Dove	15.0	13.5
Lever 2000	3.0	6.5
Caress	5.5	5.0
Shield	2.0	2.0
Lifebuoy	0.8	0.9
Lux	0.7	0.7
Procter & Gamble		
Ivory	8.0	7.0
Zest	8.0	6.5
Coast	5.5	4.5

Continued on next page.

★ 727 ★ *Continued*

Soap (SIC 2841)

Toilet Soap Market

Shares by company and brand are shown in percent. Estimated category size was $1.145 billion in 1991, including both liquid and bar soap.

	Fall 1990	Fall 1991
Camay	2.0%	4.0%
Safeguard	5.5	4.0
Ivory Liquid	3.5	2.5
Lava	0.5	0.5
Other	3.5	3.5

Source: Investext, Thomson Financial Networks, January 24, 1992, from Kidder, Peabody & Company, Incorporated.

★ 728 ★

Air Fresheners (SIC 2842)

Air Freshener Market

Shares by company and brand are shown in percent. Estimated category size was $225 million in 1991.

	Fall 1990	Fall 1991
Church & Dwight		
Arm & Hammer Spray	6.5%	8.5%
Drackett		
Renuzit	20.0	19.0
Renuzit Spray	7.5	6.5
Reckitt & Coleman		
Airwick StickUps	13.0	14.5
Wizard Spray	7.5	9.5
S.C. Johnson		
Glade Spray	31.0	32.0
Glade II	0.1	0.0
Other	14.4	10.0

Source: Investext, Thomson Financial Networks, January 24, 1992, from Kidder, Peabody & Company, Incorporated.

★ 729 ★

Bleach (SIC 2842)

Bleach Market

Shares by company and brand are shown in percent. Estimated category size was $625 million in 1991.

	Fall 1990	Fall 1991
Church & Dwight		
Arm & Hammer	1.0%	1.0%
Clorox		
Clorox Liquid (incl. Fresh		
Scent brands)	37.5	39.0
Clorox 2 Powder	14.5	13.0
Liquid Clorox 2	11.5	12.0
Airwick/Reckitt & Coleman		
Snowy Bleach Powder	1.0	0.7
Snowy Bleach Liquid	0.5	0.5
Dow/Texize		
Vivid	6.0	4.0
Dial		
Purex Liquid	1.8	2.0
Purex Powder	0.5	0.5
Procter & Gamble		
Biz	6.5	6.0
L&F		
Lysol Laundry Sanitizer	0.5	0.5
Private Label	17.0	20.0

Source: Investext, Thomson Financial Networks, January 24, 1992, from Kidder, Peabody & Company, Incorporated.

★ 730 ★

Cleaning Preparations (SIC 2842)

Specialty Cleaner Market

The specialty cleaner market, by segment, is shown with revenues in millions of dollars; relative market shares are shown in percent.

	Sales ($ mil.)	% of Group
Toilet-bowl cleaners	$ 209.0	37.0%
Abrasive cleaners	181.0	32.0
Nonabrasive cleaners	175.0	31.0

Source: *Advertising Age*, August 10, 1992, p. 34.

★ 731 ★

Cleaning Solutions (SIC 2842)

Cleaning Solution Market

Shares by company and brand are shown in percent. Estimated category size was $1.275 billion in 1991.

	Fall 1990	Fall 1991
Benckiser		
Lime-A-Way	1.8%	1.5%
Scrub Free Bathroom	2.0	1.5
Clorox		
Pine Sol	5.5	6.0
Soft Scrub	6.0	5.5
Formula 409	3.5	3.5
Clorox Clean-Up	-	3.0
Tackle	0.8	0.6
Colgate		
Ajax Powder	2.0	2.0
Ajax Liquid	0.5	0.5
Dow/Texize		
Dow Bathroom	3.5	3.5
Fantastik	3.0	3.0
Top Job	2.0	2.0
Spic & Span	2.0	1.5
Cinch	-	1.0
Mr. Clean Cleanser	0.2	0.2
Comet Cleanser	0.1	0.1
Vanish	5.5	4.0
L&F		
Lysol	4.5	5.5
Lysol Bathroom	4.5	3.5
Lysol Toilet	3.5	3.5
Lysol Direct	1.5	1.0
Procter & Gamble		
Comet Powder	5.5	5.0
Mr. Clean	3.5	3.5
Spic & Span Disinfectant	2.0	2.0
Other	36.6	36.6

Source: Investext, Thomson Financial Networks, January 24, 1992, from Kidder, Peabody & Company, Incorporated.

★ 732 ★

Fabric Softener (SIC 2842)

Fabric Softener Market

Shares by company and brand are shown in percent. Estimated category size was $815 million in 1991.

	Fall 1990	Fall 1991
Benckiser		
Cling Free	2.0%	2.5%
Free & Soft	0.1	0.1
Church & Dwight		
Arm & Hammer	1.0	1.5
Dial		
Toss N Soft	1.5	2.0
Sta-Puff	0.7	1.0
Lever Brothers		
Snuggle Liquid	13.0	13.0
Snuggle Sheets	6.5	6.5
Final Touch	10.7	9.4
Procter & Gamble		
Downy Liquid	34.5	35.5
Bounce	18.0	17.0
Downy Sheets	6.5	6.5

Source: Investext, Thomson Financial Networks, January 24, 1992, from Kidder, Peabody & Company, Incorporated.

★ 733 ★

Surfactants (SIC 2843)

Anionic Surfactants

Segment distribution of the U.S. market is shown in percent, based on a total of 2.178 million tons.

Soap	26.4%
Linear alkylbenzene sulfonate	23.0
Alkyl ethoxy sulfates	12.0
Alkyl sulfates	10.0
Other anionics	8.5
Quasi anionics	20.1

Source: *European Chemical News*, May 25, 1992, p. 26, from Hewin International.

★ 734 ★
Cosmetics (SIC 2844)

Eye Makeup Market

Company and brand shares are shown in percent for the 4th quarter of 1991.

Wasserstein-Perella
  Maybelline 43.0%
Procter & Gamble
  Cover Girl 32.0
  Clarion 2.0
Revlon
  Almay 3.0
  Max Factor 4.0
  Revlon 4.0
Unilever
  Aziza 5.0
All others 7.0

Source: Investext, Thomson Financial Networks, April 10, 1992, from Smith Barney, Harris Upham & Co.

★ 735 ★
Cosmetics (SIC 2844)

Face Makeup Market

Company and brand shares are shown in percent for the 4th quarter of 1991.

Procter & Gamble
  Cover Girl 55.0%
  Clarion 3.0
Wasserstein-Perella
  Maybelline 17.0
Revlon
  Almay 3.0
  Max Factor 5.0
  Revlon 6.0
All other 11.0

Source: Investext, Thomson Financial Networks, April 10, 1992, from Smith Barney, Harris Upham & Co.

★ 736 ★
Cosmetics (SIC 2844)

Lipstick Market

Company and brand shares are shown in percent for the 4th quarter of 1991.

Procter & Gamble
  Cover Girl 31.0%
  Clarion 3.0

Wasserstein-Perella
  Maybelline 23.0%
Revlon
  Max Factor 4.0
  Revlon 15.0
L'Oreal
  L'Oreal 6.0
Del Labs
  Flame Glo 1.0
  Lip Quencher 1.0
All others 16.0

Source: Investext, Thomson Financial Networks, April 10, 1992, from Smith Barney, Harris Upham & Co.

★ 737 ★
Cosmetics (SIC 2844)

Lipstick Market - Europe

Distribution of the wholesale market is shown by country, as percent of 107 million pounds in 1990.

France 30.9%
Germany 18.7
Italy 18.7
U.K. 11.2
Spain 7.5
Switzerland 5.1
Netherlands 2.8
Austria 2.8
Belgium 2.2

Source: *Financial Times*, February 14, 1992, p. 8, from European Forecasts.

★ 738 ★
Cosmetics (SIC 2844)

Makeup Leaders

Company shares are shown as percent of second-quarter 1992 sales at all outlets.

Cover Girl 21.5%
Maybelline 15.0
Revlon 15.0
L'Oreal 9.3
Other 39.3

Source: *The New York Times*, August 23, 1992, p. F12, from Merrill Lynch and Company and Nielsen Marketing Research.

★ 739 ★

Cosmetics (SIC 2844)

Makeup Leaders

Companies are shown with cosmetics sales (including lipstick, mascara, blush and nail polish) in millions of dollars at drug, mass merchandise and food stores. Percent shares are based on a 1991 total market of $ 2.12 billion.

	($ mil.)	Shares
Procter & Gamble	$ 721.9	34.0%
Revlon	477.7	22.5
Maybeline	350.2	16.5
L'Oreal	184.7	8.7
Other	385.5	18.3

Source: *The Wall Street Journal*, July 10, 1992, p. B2, from *Nielsen Marketing Research.*

★ 740 ★

Cosmetics (SIC 2844)

Nail Polish Market

Company and brand shares are shown in percent for the 4th quarter of 1991.

Procter & Gamble
  Cover Girl 27.0%
  Clarion 2.0
Wasserstein-Perella
  Maybelline 17.0
Revlon
  Max Factor 2.0
  Revlon 8.0
Unilever
  Cutex 10.0
L'Oreal
  L'Oreal 8.0
Del Labs
  Sally Hansen 8.0
All others 18.0

Source: Investext, Thomson Financial Networks, April 10, 1992, from Smith Barney, Harris Upham & Co.

★ 741 ★

Creams and Lotions (SIC 2844)

Facial Cleanser Brand Shares

Brand shares are shown as percent of total dollar sales.

Pond's 20.3%
Noxzema 17.9
Olay 6.3
Plenitude 2.8
Other 52.7

Source: *Discount Store News*, May 18, 1992, p. 64, from Syndicated Data.

★ 742 ★

Creams and Lotions (SIC 2844)

Hand and Body Lotion Makers

Company shares of hand and body lotion market are shown as percent of units sold.

Vaseline Intensive Care 23.6%
Jergens 8.7
Lubriderm 5.8
Nivea 5.3
Suave 5.0
Keri 4.3
Others 47.3

Source: *Discount Store News*, May 18, 1992, p. 64, from Syndicated Data.

★ 743 ★

Dental Care (SIC 2844)

Toothpaste

Shares are shown in percent for fall of 1990 and 1991. Estimated category size was $1.1 billion in 1991. Shares for Procter & Gamble are estimated.

	Fall 1990	Fall 1990
Beecham		
Aqua-Fresh	12.0%	10.5%
Carter-Wallace		
Pearl Drops	1.5	1.0
Church & Dwight		
Dental Care	5.0	8.0
Colgate-Palmolive		
Colgate (inc. Tartar Control)	26.0	24.0
Ultrabrite	2.3	2.5
Viadent	1.0	1.0

Continued on next page.

★ 743 ★ *Continued*
Dental Care (SIC 2844)

Toothpaste

Shares are shown in percent for fall of 1990 and 1991. Estimated category size was $1.1 billion in 1991. Shares for Procter & Gamble are estimated.

	Fall 1990	Fall 1990
Dentagard	0.1%	0.1%
Dep		
Topol	1.0	1.0
Lever Brothers		
Close-Up	7.0	6.0
Aim	4.0	2.0
Pepsodent	0.7	0.9
Procter & Gamble		
Crest (inc. Tartar Control)	33.5	36.0
Gleem	1.0	1.0

Source: Investext, Thomson Financial Networks, January 24, 1992, from Kidder, Peabody & Company, Incorporated.

★ 744 ★

Dental Care (SIC 2844)

Toothpaste Producers

Shares of dollar sales are shown in percent. "Other" includes Tom's of Maine, Dep Corp., Carter-Wallace, and Block Drug.

Procter & Gamble	37.5%
Colgate-Palmolive	29.5
SmithKline Beecham	10.5
Unilever	9.3
Church & Dwight	8.0
Other	5.2

Source: Investext, Thomson Financial Networks, March 10, 1992, from Bear, Stearns & Co., Inc.

★ 745 ★

Dental Care (SIC 2844)

Toothpaste Rivals

The $1.3 billion U.S. toothpaste market is dominated by two manufacturers whose shares are shown in percent.

Procter & Gamble Co.	36.0%
Colgate-Palmolive Co.	26.0
Other	38.0

Source: *The Wall Street Journal*, June 18, 1992, p. B5.

★ 746 ★

Deodorants (SIC 2844)

Deodorant Market

1991 shares of the $1.4 billion antiperspirant/ deodorant market, by manufacturer, are shown in percent.

Procter & Gamble	27.8%
Gillette	16.1
Mennen	15.9
Carter-Wallace	10.3
Bristol-Myers	8.4
Helene Curtis	8.1
Chesebrough	4.5
Other	8.9

Source: *Advertising Age*, March 30, 1992, p. 48, from Nielsen Marketing Research.

★ 747 ★

Deodorants (SIC 2844)

Deodorant Market

Shares by company and brand are shown in percent. Estimated category size was $1.085 billion in 1991.

	Fall 1990	Fall 1991
Procter & Gamble		
Secret	13.5%	13.5%
Sure	11.0	10.5
Old Spice	4.5	4.3
Mennen		
Speed Stick	13.5	13.5
Real	0.5	0.3

Continued on next page.

★ 747 ★ *Continued*

Deodorants (SIC 2844)

Deodorant Market

Shares by company and brand are shown in percent. Estimated category size was $1.085 billion in 1991.

	Fall 1990	Fall 1991
Helene Curtis		
Degree	5.5%	4.5%
Suave	3.0	4.0
Gillette		
Right Guard (inc. Sport Stick)	7.0	8.0
Dry Idea	5.0	4.0
Soft & Dri	3.7	4.0
Lever		
Power Stick	2.5	3.5
Brut 33	2.5	3.0
Carter-Wallace		
Arrid	10.5	10.0
Lady's Choice	1.2	0.8
Revlon		
Mitchum	3.5	3.5
No Sweat	1.5	1.0
Bristol-Myers		
Ban	8.5	7.5
Other	2.6	8.6

Source: Investext, Thomson Financial Networks, January 24, 1992, from Kidder, Peabody & Company, Incorporated.

★ 748 ★

Deodorants (SIC 2844)

Deodorant Producers

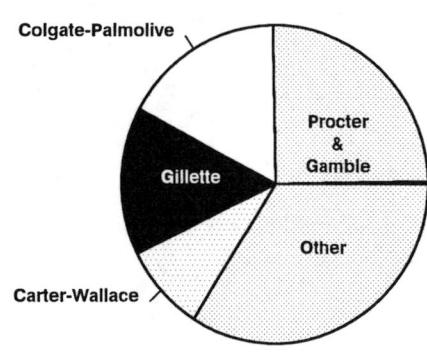

Shares of the domestic market are shown in percent. The figure for Colgate-Palmolive includes Mennen.

Procter & Gamble	25.1%
Colgate-Palmolive	16.6
Gillette	15.4
Carter-Wallace	9.2
Other	33.7

Source: *The Wall Street Journal*, September 18, 1992, p. B1, from Towne Oller & Associates.

★ 749 ★

Fragrances (SIC 2844)

Fragrance Producers

Estimated shares of the domestic fragrances market are shown in percent, based on a total of $495.0 million in 1989.

Int'l Flavors & Fragrances	25.0%
Givaudan	10.0
Florasynth-Lautier	10.0
Quest	4.0
Haarman & Reimer	4.0
Other	47.0

Source: Investext, Thomson Financial Networks, January 8, 1992, from J.C. Bradford & Co.

★ 750 ★

Hair Care (SIC 2844)

Men's Hair Coloring by Brand

Company shares are shown in percent.

Just for Men	44.0%
Grecian Formula	26.0
Option	23.0
Great Day	2.0
Other	5.0

Source: *Advertising Age*, June 12, 1992, p. 51, from Nielsen Marketing Research.

★ 751 ★

Hair Care (SIC 2844)

Men's Hair Coloring Producers

Company shares are shown in percent.

Clairol	52.1%
L'Oreal	28.3
Other	19.6

Source: *Advertising Age*, June 12, 1992, p. 3, from Nielsen Marketing Research.

★ 752 ★

Hair Care (SIC 2844)

Shampoo Market

Shares by company and brand are shown in percent. Estimated category size was $1.150 billion in 1991.

	Fall 1990	Fall 1991
Gillette		
White Rain	3.3%	4.0%
Silkience	0.7	0.5
Helene Curtis		
Suave	9.0	11.0
Finesse	4.5	4.0
Salon Selectives	4.0	4.0
Johnson & Johnson		
Johnson & Johnson	3.5	3.0
Agree	2.0	2.0
Lever		
Rave	1.5	2.0
Faberge Organics	1.0	0.5
Aqua Net	0.3	0.0
Timotei	0.2	0.0
Procter & Gamble		
Pert Plus	13.5	14.0

	Fall 1990	Fall 1991
Head & Shoulders (incl. Dry Scalp)	11.5%	10.0%
Sassoon	3.5	5.5
Prell	3.5	3.0
Ivory	3.0	2.0
Pantene	1.5	1.5
Revlon		
Flex	2.0	3.5
Other	31.5	43.5

Source: Investext, Thomson Financial Networks, January 24, 1992, from Kidder, Peabody & Company, Incorporated.

★ 753 ★

Personal Care Products (SIC 2844)

Personal Care Product Manufacturers

Companies are ranked by 1991 sales, shown in millions of dollars. Percent shares are based on group total of $50,421 million.

	Sales ($ mil.)	% of Group
Procter & Gamble	$ 28,229	56.0%
Colgate-Palmolive	6,060	12.0
Gillette	4,684	9.3
Avon Products	3,593	7.1
Clorox	1,679	3.3
International Flavors & Fragrances	1,017	2.0
Alberto-Culver	930	1.8
Ecolab	918	1.8
Stanhome	710	1.4
NCH	666	1.3
Tambrands	661	1.3
Block Drug	549	1.1
Church & Dwight	485	1.0
Neutrogena	239	0.5

Source: *The 1992 Business Week 1000*, p. 170.

★ 754 ★

Shaving Preparations (SIC 2844)

After-Shave Manufacturers

Shares of the domestic market are shown in percent. The figure for Colgate-Palmolive includes Mennen.

Colgate-Palmolive	21.3%
Procter & Gamble	21.2
Chesebrough-Pond's USA	10.2
Quintessence	7.0
Other	40.3

Source: *The Wall Street Journal*, September 18, 1992, p. B1, from Towne Oller & Associates.

★ 755 ★

Shaving Preparations (SIC 2844)

Shaving Cream Market

Shares by company and brand are shown in percent. Estimated category size was $175 million in 1991.

	Fall 1990	Fall 1991
Colgate-Palmolive		
Colgate	15.5%	19.0%
Gillette		
Foamy	15.5	17.0
Brush Plus	0.5	0.0
Hot One	0.1	0.0
S.C. Johnson		
Edge	32.0	32.0
Pfizer		
Barbasol	19.5	17.0
Procter & Gamble		
Noxema	10.5	9.0
Old Spice	3.5	3.0
Lever Brothers		
Brut	1.5	1.5
Other	1.4	1.5

Source: Investext, Thomson Financial Networks, January 24, 1992, from Kidder, Peabody & Company, Incorporated.

★ 756 ★

Shaving Preparations (SIC 2844)

Shaving Preparation Producers

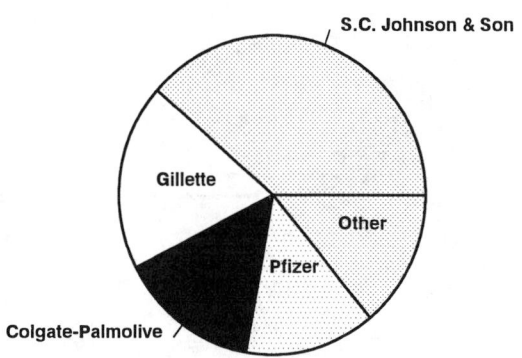

Shares of the domestic market are shown in percent.

S.C. Johnson & Son	39.1%
Gillette	18.7
Colgate-Palmolive	14.5
Pfizer	14.0
Other	13.7

Source: *The Wall Street Journal*, September 18, 1992, p. B1, from Towne Oller & Associates.

★ 757 ★

Sun Care (SIC 2844)

Sunless-Tanning Market

The sunless-tanning products market shares, by brand, are shown in percent. Figures are based on supermarket and drugstore sales during the 52 weeks ended September 30, 1992.

Coppertone	22.6%
Bain de Soleil	20.8
Hawaiian Tropic	18.6
Vaseline Intensive Care	12.5
Tropic Blend	6.9
Coppertone QT Lotion	4.7
Bonne Bell	1.4
Almay	1.1
Private label	9.4
Other	2.0

Source: *The Wall Street Journal*, October 29, 1992, p. B6, from Information Resources, Inc.

★ 758 ★

Sun Care (SIC 2844)

Suntan Products

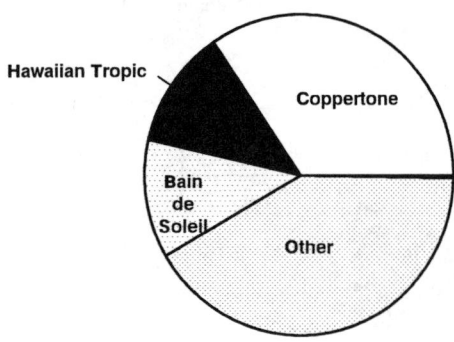

Brand shares of the food, drug, and mass merchandiser market for suntan products are shown in percent.

Coppertone	34.6%
Hawaiian Tropic	11.7
Bain de Soleil	11.6
Other	42.1

Source: *Advertising Age*, March 16, 1992, p. 16, from Nielsen Marketing Research.

★ 759 ★

Toilet Preparations (SIC 2844)

Antiperspirant/Deodorant Market

Company and brand shares are shown in percent for the 4th quarter of 1991.

Procter & Gamble
Old Spice	4.0%
Secret	13.0
Sure	10.0

Gillette
Dry Idea	4.0
Right Guard	8.0
Soft & Dri	5.0

Colgate-Palmolive
Mennen	17.0

Carter-Wallace
Arrid	9.0
Lady's Choice	1.0

Helene Curtis
Suave	4.0
Degree	4.0

Bristol-Myers Squibb
Ban	7.0

Unilever
Brut	3.0%
Powerstick	3.0

Revlon
Mitchum	3.0
All others	5.0

Source: Investext, Thomson Financial Network, April 10, 1992, p. 35, from Smith Barney, Harris Upham & Co.

★ 760 ★

Toilet Preparations (SIC 2844)

Dentifrice Market

Company and brand shares are shown in percent for the 4th quarter of 1991.

Procter & Gamble
Crest	35.0%
Gleem	1.0

Colgate-Palmolive
Colgate	22.0
Ultrabrite	3.0
Viadent	1.0

SmithKline Beecham
Aquafresh	10.0

Unilever
Aim	10.0
Close-Up	6.0
Pepsodent	1.0

Church & Dwight
Arm & Hammer	9.0

Source: Investext, Thomson Financial Networks, April 10, 1992, from Smith Barney, Harris Upham & Co.

★ 761 ★

Toilet Preparations (SIC 2844)

Face Cream and Lotion Market

Company and brand shares are shown in percent for the 4th quarter of 1991.

Procter & Gamble
Oil of Olay	35.0%
Noxzema	12.0

Unilver
Pond's	13.0

Revlon
Almay	2.0
Revlon	4.0

Continued on next page.

★ **761** ★ *Continued*

Toilet Preparations (SIC 2844)

Face Cream and Lotion Market

Company and brand shares are shown in percent for the 4th quarter of 1991.

L'Oreal	
Plenitude	5.0%
St Ives	
St Ives	4.0
Neutrogena	
Neutrogena	1.0
KAO	
Jergens	1.0
All others	23.0

Source: Investext, Thomson Financial Networks, April 10, 1992, from Smith Barney, Harris Upham & Co.

★ **762** ★

Toilet Preparations (SIC 2844)

Hair Conditioner Market

Company and brand shares are shown in percent for the 4th quarter of 1991.

Helene Curtis	
Suave	11.0%
Finesse	8.0
Salon Selectives	9.0
Procter & Gamble	
Ivory	3.0
Pantene	4.0
Prell	2.0
Vidal Sassoon	5.0
Alberto Culver	
VO5	6.0
Gillette	
Silkience	1.0
White Rain	4.0
S.C. Johnson	
Agree	3.0
Halsa	2.0
Dow Chemical	
Perma Soft	3.0
Style	1.0
Revlon	
Flex/Aqumrn/Intl	4.0
Playtex	
Jhirmack	3.0
Unilever	
Rave	2.0

Neutrogena	
Neutrogena	1.0%
All others	28.0

Source: Investext, Thomson Financial Networks, April 10, 1992, from Smith Barney, Harris Upham & Co.

★ **763** ★

Toilet Preparations (SIC 2844)

Hand and Body Lotion Market

Company and brand shares are shown in percent of the 4th quarter of 1991.

Unilever	
Vaseline Intensive	25.0%
Pond's	1.0
KAO	
Jergens	19.0
S.C. Johnson	
Soft Sense	4.0
Curel	5.0
Warner Lambert	
Lubriderm	9.0
Biersdorf AG	
Nivea	8.0
Helene Curtis	
Suave	5.0
Briston Myers	
Keri	5.0
Neurogena	
Neutrogena	3.0
All others	16.0

Source: Investext, Thomson Financial Networks, April 10, 1992, from Smith Barney, Harris Upham & Co.

★ **764** ★

Toilet Preparations (SIC 2844)

Mouthwash Market

Company and brand shares are shown in percent for the 4th quarter of 1991.

Warner Lambert	
Listerine	31.0%
Listermint	5.0
Procter & Gamble	
Scope	27.0
Pfizer	
Plax	12.0

Continued on next page.

★ 764 ★ *Continued*

Toilet Preparations (SIC 2844)

Mouthwash Market

Company and brand shares are shown in percent for the 4th quarter of 1991.

Johnson & Johnson
Act 4.0%
Dow Chemical
Cepacol 3.0
Colgate
Viadent 2.0
Unilever
Signal 2.0
Dep
Lavoris 1.0
All others 13.0

Source: Investext, Thomson Financial Networks, April 10, 1992, p. 3, from Smith Barney, Harris Upham & Co.

★ 765 ★

Toilet Preparations (SIC 2844)

Shampoo Market

Company and brand shares are shown in percent for the 4th quarter of 1991.

Procter & Gamble
Head & Shoulders 12.0%
Ivory 2.0
Pantene 2.0
Pert 13.0
Prell 2.0
Vidal Sassoon 6.0
Helene Curtis
Suave 8.0
Finesse 4.0
Salon Selectives 4.0
Revlon
Flex/Aquamarine/Intl 4.0
Johnson & Johnson
JNJ Baby Shampoo 4.0
Silkience . . . . --
White Rain 3.0
S.C. Johnson
Agree 2.0
Halsa 1.0
Dow Chemical
Perma Soft 1.0
Style 1.0
Playtex
Jhirmack 2.0

Unilever
Rave 2.0%
Neutrogena
Neutrogena T-Gel 2.0
All Others 25.0

Source: Investext, Thomson Financial Networks, April 10, 1992, from Smith Barney, Harris Upham & Co.

★ 766 ★

Toilet Preparations (SIC 2844)

Teeth-Whitener Brand Shares

Shares, by brand, of the $33.7 million market in drugstores and food stores are shown in percent and based on 12-month period ended May 1992.

Plus White 37.8%
Rembrandt 24.0
Stay-White 9.1
Natural White 8.8
White Step 7.4
Doctor's Teeth Whitener 6.4
Topol Mega White 3.3
Oxy white 1.2
All others 2.0

Source: *The Wall Street Journal*, July 6, 1992, p. 11, from Towne-Oller & Associates.

★ 767 ★

Toilet Preparations (SIC 2844)

Wet Shaving Market

Company and brand shares are shown in percent for the 4th quarter of 1991.

Gillette 69.0%
Warner Lambert
Schick 14.0
BIC 10.0
American Safety Razor
Persona 2.0
All others 5.0

Source: Investext, Thomson Financial Networks, April 10, 1992, from Smith Barney, Harris Upham & Co.

★ 768 ★
Toothpaste (SIC 2844)

Toothpaste Manufacturers

Company shares are shown in percent, based on a total domestic market of $1.3 billion.

Procter & Gamble	35.1%
Colgate-Palmolive	26.5
SmithKline Beecham	10.4
Unilever	9.2
Church & Dwight (Arm & Hammer)	7.0
Other	11.8

Source: *The Wall Street Journal*, March 2, 1992, p. B1, from Nielsen Marketing Research.

★ 769 ★
Paint (SIC 2851)

Architectural Paint Producers

Shares of the domestic market are shown in percent for 1991.

Sherwin-Williams	21.0%
Glidden	14.0
Benjamin Moore	8.0
PPG Industries	7.0
Kelly-Moore Paint Company	4.0
Valspar	4.0
Grow Group	3.0
Pratt & Lambert	3.0
Other	36.0

Source: Investext, Thomson Financial Networks, April 20, 1992, from Kidder, Peabody & Company, Incorporated.

★ 770 ★
Paint (SIC 2851)

Exterior Paint Color Preferences

Homeowners' color preferences are shown in percent.

White/off-white	34.0%
Beige/tan/brown	28.0
Gray	15.0
Blue	7.0
Green	6.0
Yellow	6.0
Red/pink	4.0

Source: *USA TODAY*, October 12, 1992, from Rohm & Haas Paint Quality Institute.

★ 771 ★
Paint (SIC 2851)

Paint Industry Leaders

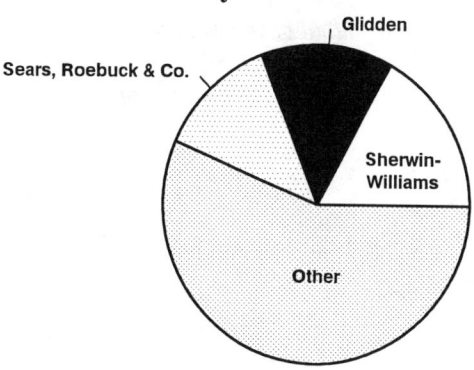

Largest manufacturer shares of the $8.6 billion paint industry are shown in percent.

Sherwin-Williams	17.0%
Glidden	13.5
Sears, Roebuck & Co.	13.0
Other	56.5

Source: *Advertising Age*, March 30, 1992, p. 50.

★ 772 ★
Organic Chemicals (SIC 2860)

Organic Chemicals

Distribution of domestic output is shown in percent for calendar year 1991, based on a total of 60.884 billion kilograms (or billion liters, in the case of benzene and toluene).

Ethylene	29.2%
Propylene	16.0
Benzene	9.9
Styrene monomer	6.7
Methanol	6.4
Toluene	5.8
Formaldehyde	4.7
p-xylene	4.1
Ethylene oxide	3.9
Cumene	3.2
Acetic acid	2.7
Acrylonitrile	2.0
Vinyl acetate	2.0
Isopropyl alcohol	1.0
Caprolactam	1.0
o-xylene	0.7

Continued on next page.

★ 772 ★ Continued

Organic Chemicals (SIC 2860)

Organic Chemicals

Distribution of domestic output is shown in percent for calendar year 1991, based on a total of 60.884 billion kilograms (or billion liters, in the case of benzene and toluene).

Toluene diisocyanate	0.6%
Perchloroethylene	0.2

Source: *Chemicalweek*, April 15, 1992, p. 25, from DRI/McGraw-Hill.

★ 773 ★

Intermediate Chemicals (SIC 2865)

Pesticide Intermediates

Percent distribution is based on a total 1990 market of $986 million.

Nitriles	18.8%
Amines	14.1
Carboxylic acids	10.5
Anilines	9.8
Organophosphorous compounds	9.7
Mercaptans	6.6
Phenols	6.4
Benzenes	5.5
Alkanes/alkenes	4.7
Bulk commodities	2.7
Pyridines	1.8
Alcohols	0.8
Aldehydes	0.8
Miscellaneous	7.7

Source: *Chemicalweek*, April 8, 1992, p. 46, from Frost & Sullivan International.

★ 774 ★

Organic Chemicals (SIC 2865)

Styrene Capacity - Japan

Idemitsu Kosan
Asahi Chemical
Mitsubishi Yuka
Nihon Oxirane
Nippon Styrene Monomer
Denki Kagaku
Nippon Steel
Tosoh Corp.

Distribution of Japanese styrene capacity, by producer, is shown in thousands of metric tons per year. (Nihon Oxirane is a joint venture of Arco Chemical/Sumitomo/Showa Denko; Nippon Styrene Monomer is a joint venture of Nippon Steel/Tosoh Corp.) Relative market shares are shown in percent.

	Tons (000)	% of Group
Idemitsu Kosan	491	20.2%
Asahi Chemical	480	19.7
Mitsubishi Yuka	460	18.9
Nihon Oxirane	335	13.8
Nippon Styrene Monomer	200	8.2
Denki Kagaku	180	7.4
Nippon Steel	180	7.4
Tosoh Corp.	110	4.5

Source: *Chemicalweek*, May 27, 1992, p. 23, from PCI Plastics.

★ 775 ★

Fire Retardants (SIC 2869)

Fire Retardant Use

Segment distribution is based on a domestic total of 746 million lbs. in 1991.

Plastic additives

Construction	32.0%
Electronics	30.1
Vehicles	17.4
Aerospace	11.7
Textile treatments	8.7

Source: *Chemicalweek*, April 15, 1992, p. 27, from The Freedonia Group.

★776★

Industrial Organic Chemicals (SIC 2869)

Chlorofluorocarbon Use

CFC (chlorofluorocarbon) market shares by application are shown in percent.

Solvents	53.0%
Refrigeraton	22.0
Rigid and flexible foam	8.0
Automobiles	8.0
Transport insulation	3.0
Fire extinguishers and propellants	2.0
Transport refrigeration	1.0
Other	3.0

Source: *Food Review*, April 1991, p. 27, from International Institute of Refrigeration and *Status of CFC's-Refrigeration Systems and Refrigerant Properties.*

★777★

Organic Chemicals (SIC 2869)

PA Producers - Western Europe

Production of PA (phthalic anhydride) and phthalates in Western European plants is shown in thousands of metric tons capacity per year. The 1991 total capacity was 887,000 metric tons. Market shares are shown in percent.

	Capacity (000 m.t./yr)	% Share
Alusuisse Italia (Italy)	105	11.8%
UCB (Belgium)	100	11.3
Huls (Germany)	95	10.7
BASF (Germany)	90	10.1
BP Chemicals (U.K.)	78	8.8
Pantochim (Sisas) (Belgium)	65	7.3
Exxon (Holland)	50	5.6
Bayer (Germany)	45	5.1
Sisas (Italy)	45	5.1
Cepsa (Spain)	36	4.1
Chemie Linz (Austria)	35	3.9
Atochem (France)	30	3.4
Reposa (Spain)	30	3.4
Neste (Sweden)	25	2.8

	Capacity (000 m.t./yr)	% Share
Gas de Portugal (Portugal)	18	2.0%
BASF Espanola (Spain)	17	1.9
Sopar (Belgium)	12	1.4
Bitmac (U.K.)	11	1.2

Source: *Chemicalweek*, February 5, 1992, p. 20, from Tecnon U.K.

★778★

Organic Chemicals (SIC 2869)

Petrochemicals - Japan

Mitsubishi Kasei
Mitsui Toatsu
Mitsubishi Petrochemical
Tosoh Corp.
Mitsui Petrochemical

1991 projected sales of the five leading Japanese petrochemical producers are shown in billions of yen ($1 = Y130). Relative market shares are shown in percent.

	Yen (bil.)	% of Group
Mitsubishi Kasei	760.0	32.6%
Mitsui Toatsu	440.0	18.9
Mitsubishi Petrochemical	435.0	18.7
Tosoh Corp.	360.0	15.5
Mitsui Petrochemical	334.0	14.3

Source: *Chemicalweek*, November 27, 1991, p. 16, from Comline International.

★779★

Sweeteners (SIC 2869)

Soft Drink Sweetener Producers

Shares, by company, are shown in percent.

Archer Daniels Midland	30.0%
Staley	21.0
Other	49.0

Source: Investext, Thomson Financial Networks, March 26, 1992, from Barclays De Zoete Wedd Securities.

★ 780 ★

Agrichemicals (SIC 2870)

Fertilizer Sales

1991 fertilizer sales by company are shown in millions of dollars and as percent share of market.

	Sales ($ mil.)	Shares
IMC Fertilizer Group	$ 1,131.2	29.7%
Freeport McMoran Resources .	903.7	23.7
Vigoro Corp.	557.6	14.6
First Mississippi	536.7	14.1
Mississippi Chemical	321.1	8.4
Potash Corp. of Saskatchewan .	269.8	7.1
Nu West Industries	92.2	2.4

Source: *Chemicalweek*, May 6, 1992, p. 30, from Standard & Poor's Compustat Services.

★ 781 ★

Agricultural Chemicals (SIC 2870)

Agricultural Potash Sales

Segment distribution is shown in percent, based on total sales of 1,087,979 tons for the July-September period of 1991.

Coarse muriate	53.2%
Granular muriate	32.7
Soluble muriate	7.0
Standard muriate	4.6
Sulfates	2.5

Source: *Potash & Phosphate Institute Press Release*, November 1991.

★ 782 ★

Agricultural Chemicals (SIC 2870)

Agricultural Potash Sales - Canada

Segment distribution is shown in percent, based on total sales of 51,377 tons for the July-September period of 1991.

Granular muriate	59.1%
Coarse muriate	37.1
Sulfates	2.0
Standard muriate	1.0
Soluble muriate	0.9

Source: *Potash & Phosphate Institute Press Release*, November 1991.

★ 783 ★

Agrichemicals (SIC 2879)

Agrichemicals by Application - Europe

Market shares for agrichemical products, by application, are shown in percent.

Cereals	38.2%
Vine crops	11.0
Beets	7.7
Maize	6.8
Fruits and vegetables	6.6
Other	29.7

Source: *European Chemical News*, July 1, 1991, p. 15.

★ 784 ★

Agrichemicals (SIC 2879)

Agrichemicals Market by Type

Shares of global agrichemicals market, by type, are shown in percent.

Herbicides	47.0%
Insecticides	25.0
Fungicides	20.0
Other	8.0

Source: *European Chemical News*, July 1, 1991, p. 15.

★ 785 ★

Pesticides (SIC 2879)

Pesticide Use

Residential	60.0%
Commercial	30.0
Institutional	4.0
Other	6.0

Source: *The New York Times*, November 1, 1992, p. F12, from Kline and Company.

★ 786 ★
Pesticides (SIC 2879)

Pesticides by Type

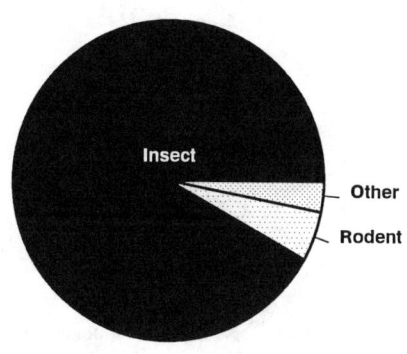

Distribution of dollars spent on pesticides is shown in percent.

Insect	92.0%
Rodent	5.0
Other	3.0

Source: *The New York Times*, November 1, 1992, p. F12, from Kline and Company.

★ 787 ★
Adhesives and Sealants (SIC 2891)

Adhesives and Sealants by Polymer Type

Shares, by polymer type, are shown in percent, based on a total market of 2,550 thousand tons.

Elastomer	29.0%
Vinyl	21.0
Tackifier	18.0
Acrylic	7.0
Olefin	6.0
Other	19.0

Source: *Chemicalweek*, March 11, 1992, p. 32.

★ 788 ★
Adhesives and Sealants (SIC 2891)

Adhesives and Sealants Use Worldwide

Shares, by end use, are shown as a percent of global total.

Paper, packaging, and related users	35.0%
Building and construction	24.0
Woodworking	21.0
Automotive	10.0
Others	10.0

Source: *Chemicalweek*, March 11, 1992, p. 28, from Henkel.

★ 789 ★
Adhesives and Sealants (SIC 2891)

Adhesives and Sealants Worldwide

Shares, by product type, are shown in percent.

Waterborn	45.0%
Hot melt	20.0
Solventborne	15.0
Reactive	10.0
Other	10.0

Source: *Chemicalweek*, March 11, 1992, p. 28, from Henkel.

★ 790 ★
Adhesives and Sealants (SIC 2891)

Adhesives Use

Shares of domestic consumption are shown, by market segment, based on an estimated total of $2.135 billion in 1992.

Building/construction	23.0%
Packaging	21.8
Automotive	21.8
Electronics	11.0
Aerospace	10.3
Dental	3.3
Transportation	2.9
Electrical	2.4
Medical	1.9
Appliances	1.7

Source: *Chemicalweek*, March 11, 1992, p. 26, from Strategic Analysis Inc.

★ 791 ★

Adhesives and Sealants (SIC 2891)

Adhesives, Sealants, and Coatings

Demand for adhesives, sealants and coatings by the U.S. electrical and electronics market amounted to $1.82 billion in 1990. Shares by product type are shown in percent, based on that total.

Wire coating	41.6%
Potting/encapsulating	19.7
PCB coating	11.6
Assembly adhesive	10.4
Coil impregnation	5.6
IC/hybrid coating	4.4
Die-attach adhesive	3.2
Other	3.5

Source: *Electronic Packaging & Production*, September 1991, p. 14, from Frost & Sullivan Inc.

★ 792 ★

Adhesives and Sealants (SIC 2891)

Environmentally Acceptable Coatings

The consumption of environmentally acceptable coatings, by type, is shown in percent for 1990. Distribution is based on an industry total of 1.044 billion gallons.

Waterborne	45.0%
Environmentally unacceptable	43.8
High-solids	6.0
Powder	4.8
Radiation-cure	0.4

Source: *Industrial Finishing*, March 1992, p. 23, from Business Communications Company.

★ 793 ★

Adhesives and Sealants (SIC 2891)

Sealants

Segment distribution of the domestic market is shown in percent for 1991.

Transportation	39.8%
Construction	34.1
Do-it-yourself	17.8
Other	8.3

Source: *Chemicalweek*, March 11, 1992, p. 27, from ChemQuest Group.

★ 794 ★

Coatings (SIC 2891)

Coatings and Linings

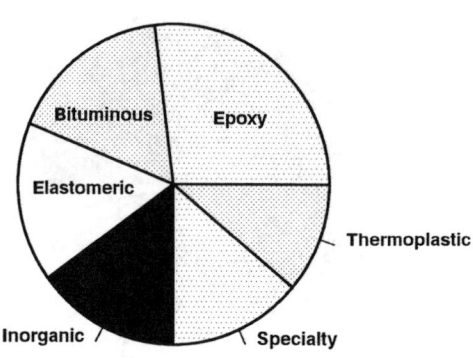

Segment distribution is shown for 1990 and forecast for 1995 in percent, based on respective totals of $700 million and $800 million.

	1990	1995
Epoxy	22.1%	26.9%
Bituminous	20.7	16.9
Elastomeric	14.3	15.6
Inorganic	13.6	15.0
Specialty	14.3	14.4
Thermoplastic	15.0	11.3

Source: *Industrial Finishing*, February 1992, p. 8, from Business Communications Co., Inc.

★ 795 ★

Coatings (SIC 2891)

Coatings by Type

Distribution of coatings used in 1991 is shown in percent, based on a survey of 4,000 finisher plants and 2,000 formulator plants.

Conventional	41.6%
High-solids	16.4
Powder	12.8
Waterborne	11.8
Two-component	11.6
Radiation-cure	2.0
Vapor-cure	1.4
Other	2.5

Source: *Industrial Finishing*, January 1992, p. 26.

★796★

Glue (SIC 2891)

Who Buys Industrial Glue

End-user shares of industrial specialty glues and all formulated glues are shown in percent, based on an estimated total of $2.060 billion in 1992.

Construction	23.0%
Automotive	21.8
Packaging	21.8
Electronics	11.0
Aerospace	10.3
Dental	3.3
Transportation	2.9
Electrical	2.4
Medical	1.9
Appliance	1.7

Source: *The New York Times*, May 31, 1992, p. F10, from Chemquest and Strategic Analysis, Inc.

★797★

Carbon Black (SIC 2895)

Carbon Black Manufacturing - Non-Socialist World

Manufacturers' shares are shown in percent, based on non-socialist world total of 11,747 million pounds for the end of 1990.

Cabot	33.0%
Degussa	13.5
Columbian	12.3
J.M. Huger	5.1
Sid Richardson	4.6
Witco Chemical	3.2
Non-major products	28.3

Source: Investext, Thomson Financial Networks, April 2, 1992, from C. J. Lawrence, Morgan Grenfell Inc.

★798★

Carbon Black (SIC 2895)

Carbon Black Market - Latin America

Manufacturer's shares are shown in percent, based on Latin American total of 1,136 million pounds for the end of 1990.

Cabot	66.7%
Non-major products	33.3

Source: Investext, Thomson Financial Networks, April 2, 1992, from C. J. Lawrence, Morgan Grenfell Inc.

★799★

Carbon Black (SIC 2895)

Carbon Black Market - North America

Manufacturer's shares are shown in percent, based on North American total of 3,945 million pounds for the end of 1990.

Cabot	26.9%
Columbian	22.4
J.M. Huger	15.1
Sid Richardson	13.6
Degussa	12.2
Witco Chemical	8.2
Non-major products	1.6

Source: Investext, Thomson Financial Networks, April 2, 1992, from C. J. Lawrence, Morgan Grenfell Inc.

★800★

Carbon Black (SIC 2895)

Carbon Black Market - Pacific Region

Manufacturer's shares are shown in percent, based on Pacific Region total of 3,436 million pounds for the end of 1990.

Cabot	24.9%
Witco Chemical	1.6
Columbian	1.0
Non-major products	72.5

Source: Investext, Thomson Financial Networks, April 2, 1992, from C. J. Lawrence, Morgan Grenfell Inc.

★ 801 ★

Carbon Black (SIC 2895)

Carbon Black Market - Western Europe

Manufacturer's shares are shown in percent, based on a Western Europe total of 2,945 million pounds for the end of 1990.

Cabot	40.8%
Degussa	33.5
Columbian	17.9
Non-major products	7.8

Source: Investext, Thomson Financial Networks, April 2, 1992, from C. J. Lawrence, Morgan Grenfell Inc.

★ 802 ★

Chemicals (SIC 2899)

EA Solder, Flux and Cleaners Worldwide

Segment distribution of EA (environmentally acceptable) solder, flux, and cleaners, is shown in percent, based on a 1990 total of $85.4 million.

EA flux	52.7%
EA cleaners/solvents	30.9
EA solder paste	14.1
EA no-clean process equipment	2.3

Source: *Electronic Packaging & Production*, September 1991, p. 11, from Business Communications Co. Inc.

★ 803 ★

Electronic Chemicals (SIC 2899)

Semiconductor Materials Market Worldwide

Shares of worldwide consumption of semiconductor materials are shown in percent for 1992 and 1993, based on industry totals of $9,686 million and $10,582 million respectively.

	1992	1993
Water fab materials		
Silicon wafers	22.9%	23.7%
Other substrates	2.9	3.1
Photomasks	12.4	12.3
Photoresists	2.7	2.8
Wet chemicals	4.8	5.0
Gases	6.6	6.9

	1992	1993
Deposition materials	2.8%	3.0%
Packaging materials		
Leadframes	13.6	14.0
Ceramic packages	10.7	12.8
Encapsulation resins	5.2	5.3
Bonding wire	3.7	3.8
Thick film pastes	2.0	2.2
Cerdip	1.7	0.9
Seal lids	2.3	2.1
Headers and cans	1.0	0.9
Other	4.5	4.2

Source: *Electronic Business*, May 18, 1992, p. 14, from Electronic Materials Report.

★ 804 ★

Gelatin (SIC 2899)

Softgel Capsule Producers Worldwide

Shares are shown in percent, based on an estimated global market of $445.0 million in fiscal 1992.

Scherer	67.0%
Other	33.0

Source: Investext, Thomson Financial Networks, January 20, 1992, from Paine Webber Inc.

★ 805 ★

Water Management Compounds (SIC 2899)

Water Management Compound Use

Distribution of domestic applications is shown in percent, based on a total market of $2.125 billion.

Cooling water	35.3%
Boiler water	24.0
Process water	19.1
Wastewater	15.8
Supply water	5.9

Source: *Chemicalweek*, May 13, 1992, p. 32, from Kline & Co.

★ 806 ★

Water Management Compounds (SIC 2899)

Water Management Compounds

Distribution of domestic demand is shown in percent, based on a total market of $1.740 billion in 1992.

Specialty chemicals
  Polyacrylamides 10.3%
  Ion exchange resins 6.6
  Activated carbon 4.4
  Quaternary ammonium compounds 3.7
  Polyamines 2.8
Formulated products
  Corrosion inhibitors 35.7
  Scale inhibitors 26.0
  Biocides 6.5
  Combustion additives 4.0

Source: *Chemicalweek*, May 13, 1992, p. 38, from SRI International and Health Performance Chemical Center.

★ 807 ★

Water Management Compounds (SIC 2899)

Water Management Compounds Worldwide

Distribution of global demand is shown in percent, based on a total market of $3.197 billion in 1992.

Specialty chemicals
  Polyacrylamides 14.9%
  Ion exchange resins 9.4
  Activated carbon 6.9
  Polyamines 3.3
  Quaternary ammonium compounds 2.0
Formulated products
  Corrosion inhibitors 30.6
  Scale inhibitors 22.4
  Biocides 6.2
  Combustion additives 4.3

Source: *Chemicalweek*, May 13, 1992, p. 37, from SRI International and Health Performance Chemical Center.

SIC 29 - Petroleum and Coal Products

★ 808 ★
Petroleum Products (SIC 2900)

Petroleum Products

Distribution of petroleum products supplied to the U.S. in 1992 is shown in percent, based on a forecast total of 16.92 billion barrels per day. This total includes both domestic production and imports.

Motor gasoline	42.3%
Distallate fuel oil	18.5
Jet fuel	8.8
Residual fuel oil	6.5
Other	23.9

Source: *U.S. Industrial Outlook 1992*, p. 4-2, from U.S. Department of Energy, Energy Information Administration.

★ 809 ★
Fuel (SIC 2911)

Fuel Generating Capacity in the U.S.

The U.S. share of generating capacity, by fuel, is shown in percent for the period from 1991 to 2000. Numbers may not add due to rounding.

Coal	43.0%
Oil/gas	27.0
Nuclear	14.5
Hydro	9.7
NUGS (Non-Utility Generating Source)	3.0
Other	2.8

Source: *Electrical World*, October 1991, p. 14, from NERC.

★ 810 ★
Gasoline (SIC 2911)

Gasoline Refiners - 1990

Company shares of the domestic market are shown in percent.

Shell	8.8%
Chevron	8.3
Texaco	7.8
Exxon	7.8
Amoco	7.5
Mobil	6.8
BP America	5.9
Citgo	5.4
Marathon	5.2
Sun	4.2
Phillips	3.5
Unocal	3.5
Arco	3.1
Conoco	2.6
Other	19.6

Source: *The Wall Street Journal*, January 2, 1992, p. B2, from *National Petroleum News*.

★ 811 ★
Petroleum Refining (SIC 2911)

Automotive Oil Sales by Type

Percent shares by type of automotive oil are based on 1990 sales (in terms of thousands of gallons).

SAE J-183a, engine oils	79.7%
Transmission/hydraulic fuels	15.1
Gear oils	3.6
Non-SAE J-183a, engine oils	1.7

Source: *National Petroleum News*, June 1992, p. 90, from National Petroleum Refiners Assn.

★ 812 ★

Petroleum Refining (SIC 2911)

Distillate Fuel Oil Sales by End Use

Percent shares are based on U.S. total sales of 46.31 trillion gallons in 1990.

On-highway	46.9%
Residential	13.2
Commercial	7.7
Farm	7.2
Railroad	7.0
Industrial	5.4
Vessel bunkering	4.8
Off-highway	3.9
Oil company	2.1
Military	1.7
All other	0.0

Source: *National Petroleum News*, June 1992, p. 56, from *Distillate, Kerosine, and Residual Fuel Oil Sales data,* Energy Information Administration, and *Fuel Oil and Kerosine Sales 1990, October 1991.*

★ 813 ★

Petroleum Refining (SIC 2911)

Industrial Lubricant Sales - 1990

Percent shares by type of lubricant are based on 1990 sales (in terms of thousand gallons).

General industrial oils	
Hydraulic oils	20.8%
Fire-resistant fluids	2.2
Gear oils	3.5
Other	11.3
Industrial engine oils	
Railroad diesel	3.6
Marine	5.9
Natural gas	4.4
Metalworking oils	10.8
Process oils	37.5

Source: *National Petroleum News*, June 1992, p. 90, from National Petroleum Refiners Assn.

★ 814 ★

Petroleum Refining (SIC 2911)

Kerosene Sales by End Use

Percent shares by end use are based on U.S. total kerosine sales of 728,313,000 gallons in 1990.

Residential	70.9%
Commercial	13.1
Industrial	10.5
Farm	3.0
All other	2.4

Source: *National Petroleum News*, June 1992, p. 60, from *Distillate, Kerosine, and Residual Fuel Oil Sales data,* Energy Information Administration, and *Fuel Oil and Kerosine Sales 1990, October 1991.*

★ 815 ★

Petroleum Refining (SIC 2911)

Oil Refiners - South Korea

Company shares, shown in percent, are based on a total refining capacity of 975,000 barrels per day in 1989 and 1.570 million barrels per day in 1991.

	1989	1991
Yukong	33.3%	34.7%
Honam	39.0	25.5
Ssangyong	9.2	19.1
Kyung In	9.2	14.3
Kukdong	9.2	6.4

Source: *Far Eastern Economic Review*, January 23, 1992, p. 50, from company data and industry estimates.

★ 816 ★

Petroleum Refining (SIC 2911)

Petroleum Refining Industry Leaders - Japan

Companies are ranked by 1991 declared income, shown in millions of Yen. Relative market shares are shown in percent.

	Yen (mil.)	% of Group
Showa Shell Sekiyu	46,396	26.1%
Tonen	32,698	18.4
Nippon Petroleum Refining Company	27,889	15.7
Mitsubishi Oil	22,378	12.6

Continued on next page.

★ 816 ★ *Continued*
Petroleum Refining (SIC 2911)

Petroleum Refining Industry Leaders - Japan

Companies are ranked by 1991 declared income, shown in millions of Yen. Relative market shares are shown in percent.

	Yen (mil.)	% of Group
Kashima Oil	14,636	8.2%
Juji Oil	8,997	5.1
Koa Oil	7,526	4.2
Nihonkai Oil	6,335	3.6
Nippon Steel Chemical	5,508	3.1
Seibu Oil	5,230	2.9

Source: *TOKYO Business Today*, July 1992, p. 37.

★ 817 ★
Petroleum Refining (SIC 2911)

Petroleum Refining Product Sales - Canada

Shares by product type are based on 1991 total sales (in terms of cubic meters), shown in percent.

Motor gas	47.8%
Diesel	23.2
Heavy fuel	11.7
Light fuel	8.4
Aviation turbine	6.5
Lubes and greases	1.3
Kerosine	1.0
Aviation gas	0.2

Source: *National Petroleum News*, June 1992, p. 76, from Statistics Canada.

★ 818 ★
Petroleum Refining (SIC 2911)

Petroleum Refining Products

Product shares are shown in percent, based on a total supply of 17.1 million barrels per day in December 1991.

Finished motor gasoline	42.1%
Distillate fuel oil	18.1
Jet fuel	8.8
Residual fuel oil	7.6
Other	23.4

Source: *National Petroleum News*, June 1992, p. 150, from Energy Information Administration, Petroleum Supply Monthly.

★ 819 ★
Petroleum Refining (SIC 2911)

Residual Fuel Oil Sales by End Use

Percent shares are based on U.S. total sales of 18.84 trillion gallons in 1990.

Electric utility	44.8%
Vessel bunkering	33.2
Industrial	11.8
Commercial	8.0
Oil company	1.7
Military	0.4
All other	0.2

Source: *National Petroleum News*, June 1992, p. 62, from *Distillate, Kerosine, and Residual Fuel Oil Sales data*, Energy Information Administration, and *Fuel Oil and Kerosine Sales 1990, October 1991*.

★ 820 ★
Petroleum Refining (SIC 2911)

Top Distillate Fuel Oil Importers

Company shares are based on a 1990 U.S. total volume of 277,000 barrels per day.

Amerada Hess	23.10%
Cargill	11.55
Global Petro	9.39
Coastal	7.58
Axel Johnson	4.69
Northville	4.69
G.E. Warren	4.69
Citgo	3.25
Aron J & Co.	2.53

Continued on next page.

★820★ *Continued*

Petroleum Refining (SIC 2911)

Top Distillate Fuel Oil Importers

Company shares are based on a 1990 U.S. total volume of 277,000 barrels per day.

Astroline	2.53%
Other	25.79

Source: *National Petroleum News*, June 1992, p. 70, from Energy Information Administration, Petroleum Supply Monthly, and Special Report, March 1991.

★821★

Petroleum Refining (SIC 2911)

Top Finished Motor Gasoline Importers

Company shares, shown in percent, are based on a 1990 U.S. total volume of 330,000 barrels per day.

Amerada Hess	13.94%
Getty	9.39
Bear Stearns	6.36
Mobil	6.36
Citgo	6.06
Cumberland Farms	5.76
C Itoh (Amer)	4.85
Coastal	4.55
Texport	4.55
Global Petro	4.24
Other	33.94

Source: *National Petroleum News*, June 1992, p. 70, from Energy Information Administration, Petroleum Supply Monthly, and Special Report, March 1991.

★822★

Petroleum Refining (SIC 2911)

Top Jet Fuel Importers

Company shares are based on a 1990 U.S. total volume of 103,000 barrels per day.

Amerada Hess	20.39%
Citgo	13.59
BP America	10.68
United Airlines	8.74
Defense Fuel Supp. Ctr.	7.77
Texport Cumberland Farms	6.80
PanAm World Airways	6.80
Texaco	6.80

Mobil	4.85%
Other	5.83

Source: *National Petroleum News*, June 1992, p. 70, from Energy Information Administration, Petroleum Supply Monthly, and Special Report, March 1991.

★823★

Petroleum Refining (SIC 2911)

Top Residual Fuel Oil Importers

Company shares are based on a 1990 U.S. total volume of 504,000 barrels per day.

Amerada Hess	18.4%
Coastal	9.72
Vitol S.A.	8.33
Chevron	7.94
Clarendon Marketing	7.14
Global Petro	6.75
Clark Trading	4.76
BP America	4.17
Solomon Inc.	3.57
Sun	3.37
Other	25.79

Source: *National Petroleum News*, June 1992, p. 70, from Energy Information Administration, Petroleum Supply Monthly, and Special Report, March 1991.

★824★

Petroleum Refining (SIC 2911)

WOCA Petroleum Coke Production by Type

Shares of WOCA petroleum coke production, by type, are shown in percent, based on a total of 35.7 million short tons. WOCA stands for World Outside Communist and formerly Communist Areas.

Fuel	73.0%
Calcined	27.0

Source: *Light Metal Age*, February 1992, p. 36.

★ 825 ★

Bottled Fuel (SIC 2992)

Camping Fuel Vendors

Estimated shares of the domestic market are shown in percent, based on a total of $65-70 million.

Coleman	59.0%
Western Industries	21.0
Other	20.0

Source: Investext, Thomson Financial Networks, March 26, 1992, from The First Boston Corporation.

SIC 30 - Rubber and Misc. Plastics Products

★ 826 ★

Tires (SIC 3011)

Car and Truck Global Market

Company shares of the global car and truck tire market are shown in percent for 1992.

Michelin	18.0%
Goodyear	16.5
Bridgestone	15.0
Others	50.5

Source: Investext, Thomson Financial Networks, April 6, 1992, from Paine Webber Inc.

★ 827 ★

Tires (SIC 3011)

Car and Truck Tire Market in Asia and Africa

Company shares of the Asian and African tire market are shown in percent for 1992.

Michelin	22.0%
Goodyear	4.0
Bridgestone	2.0
Others	72.0

Source: Investext, Thomson Financial Networks, April 6, 1992, from Paine Webber Inc.

★ 828 ★

Tires (SIC 3011)

Car and Truck Tire Market in Latin America

Company shares of the Latin American tire market are shown in percent for 1992.

Goodyear	33.0%
Bridgestone	23.0
Michelin	12.0
Others	32.0

Source: Investext, Thomson Financial Networks, April 6, 1992, from Paine Webber Inc.

★ 829 ★

Tires (SIC 3011)

Car and Truck Tire Market in North America

Company shares of the North American tire market are shown in percent for 1992.

Goodyear	29.0%
Michelin	24.0
Bridgestone	12.5
Others	34.5

Source: Investext, Thomson Financial Networks, April 6, 1992, from Paine Webber Inc.

★ 830 ★

Tires (SIC 3011)

Car and Truck Tire Market in Western Europe

Company shares of the Western European tire market are shown in percent for 1992.

Michelin 32.5%
Goodyear 13.0
Bridgestone 6.5
Others 48.0

Source: Investext, Thomson Financial Networks, April 6, 1992, from Paine Webber Inc.

★ 831 ★

Tires (SIC 3011)

OE Tire Manufacturers

Estimated brand shares of the OE (original equipment) tire market are shown in percent.

	1980	1985	1990
Goodyear	28.0%	32.0%	36.5%
Firestone	21.5	21.5	17.0
Uniroyal	24.4	22.0	17.0
Michelin	5.0	11.0	15.7
General	10.8	13.0	12.0
BF Goodrich	10.3	-	-
Other	-	0.5	1.8

Source: Investext, Thomson Financial Networks, January 16, 1992, from Smith Barney, Harris Upham & Co. and *Modern Tire Dealer.*

★ 832 ★

Tires (SIC 3011)

Replacement Tire Market - North America

North American company and brand shares are shown in percent for year-to-date.

Goodyear 15.0%
Michelin
  Michelin 8.5
  BF Goodrich 3.5
  Uniroyal 2.5
Bridgestone
  Firestone 7.5
  Bridgestone 3.5

Continental
  General 4.5%
  Continental 1.0
Pirelli
  Pirelli 2.0
  Armstrong 1.5
TBC Corp.
  Toyo 1.0
  Sumitomo/Dunlop 3.0
  Hankook 0.3
  Kumho 0.3
Jetzon-Laramie
Other private brands 15.0
Manufacturer's brands 13.0
  Kelly (Goodyear) 3.0
  Cooper/Falls (Cooper) 5.0
  Mohawk (Yokohama) 1.0
  Lee/Star (Goodyear) 2.0
  Centennial/Remington (Dunlop) . . . 2.0
Retailers 7.0
Importers 6.0
  Yokohama 1.5

Source: Investext, Thomson Financial Networks, May 28, 1992, from The First Boston Corporation.

★ 833 ★

Tires (SIC 3011)

Tire Market Leaders Worldwide

Manufacturer shares are shown in percent for 1990, based on the total world market.

Michelin (including Uniroyal Goodrich) . . . 20.5%
Goodyear 17.5
Bridgestone/Firestone 17.0
Continental (including General Tire) 7.0
Pirelli (including Armstrong Tire) 6.0
Sumitomo/Dunlop 6.0
Others 26.0

Source: Investext, Thomson Financial Networks, March 2, 1992, from Daiwa Institute of Research Europe Ltd.

★ 834 ★
Tires (SIC 3011)

Tire Market Worldwide

Sales of eight leading tire manufacturers worldwide, in billions of dollars, totaling $59.77 billion in 1990. Relative market shares are shown in percent.

	Sales ($ bil.)	% of Group
Bridgestone	$ 12.40	21.0%
Michelin	11.52	19.0
Goodyear	11.45	19.0
Pirelli	8.46	14.0
Continental	5.30	9.0
Pacific Dunlop	3.88	6.0
Sumitomo Rubber	3.79	6.0
Yokahama Rubber	2.96	5.0

Source: *Business Horizons*, November 1991, p. 18.

★ 835 ★
Tires (SIC 3011)

Tire Producers Worldwide

Shares of the global market, by company, are shown in percent for 1990.

Michelin	20.0%
Goodyear	16.0
Continental	7.0
Pirelli	6.5
Sumitomo	6.0
Yokohama	4.0
Toyo	2.0
Cooper	1.5
Hankook	1.5
Others	19.0

Source: *European Rubber Journal*, September 1991, p. 26.

★ 836 ★
Tires (SIC 3011)

Tire Producers Worldwide

Market shares of major tire producers are shown in percent.

Michelin	20.0%
Bridgestone	18.5
Goodyear	16.0
Continental	7.0
Pirelli	6.5
Others	32.0

Source: *FW*, June 9, 1992, p. 54, from *Nikkei Weekly*.

★ 837 ★
Athletic Shoes (SIC 3021)

Athletic Footwear Manufacturers

The top 20 athletic shoe makers are shown with 1991 sales in millions of dollars. Percent shares are based on the group total.

	Sales ($ mil.)	% of Group
Nike	$ 1,369	26.8%
Reebok	1,172	22.9
L.A. Gear	657	12.8
Keds	275	5.4
Rockport	232	4.5
Converse	200	3.9
Adidas	169	3.3
Avia	154	3.0
British Knights	145	2.8
Etonic	115	2.2
Asics Tiger	112	2.2
New Balance	90	1.8
K Swiss	81	1.6
Foot-Joy	71	1.4
Sperry	64	1.3
Saucony	45	0.9
Fila	43	0.8
Vans	42	0.8

Continued on next page.

★ 837 ★ *Continued*

Athletic Shoes (SIC 3021)

Athletic Footwear Manufacturers

The top 20 athletic shoe makers are shown with 1991 sales in millions of dollars. Percent shares are based on the group total.

	Sales ($ mil.)	% of Group
Pony	$ 42	0.8%
Tretorn	35	0.7

Source: *Fairchild Fact File/Fairchild Fashion & Merchandising Group - Footwear*, June 10, 1991, p. 17, from *Sportstyle*.

★ 838 ★

Athletic Shoes (SIC 3021)

Athletic Footwear Market Worldwide

Company shares are shown as percent of world market in 1991.

Nike	20.72%
Reebok	16.18
Adidas	9.89
LA Gear	5.23
ASICS	4.95
Aritmos	3.51
Keds	3.14
Converse	3.09
Others	33.29

Source: *The Wall Street Journal*, July 14, 1992, p. A15, from *Sporting Goods Intelligence*.

★ 839 ★

Athletic Shoes (SIC 3021)

Athletic Footwear - U.S. Market

Shares, by company, are shown in percent.

Nike	31.0%
Reebok	25.0
Other	44.0

Source: Investext, Thomson Financial Networks, March 19, 1992, from Shearson Lehman Brothers, Inc.

★ 840 ★

Athletic Shoes (SIC 3021)

Athletic Shoe Companies Worldwide

Percent shares are based on $11.3 billion in wholesale sales worldwide in 1991.

Nike	21.0%
Reebok	16.0
Adidas	10.0
LA Gear	5.0
Other	48.0

Source: *The Economist*, July 25, 1992, p. 7, from *Sporting Goods Intelligence*.

★ 841 ★

Athletic Shoes (SIC 3021)

Athletic Shoe Makers

Manufacturers' domestic shares are shown in percent based on sales of brand-name shoes in 1991.

Nike	29.79%
Reebok	22.83
LA Gear	7.98
Keds	5.92
Adidas	3.52
Converse	3.43
ASICS	2.83
Avia	2.32
British Knights	1.89
Etonic	1.75
New Balance	1.63
K-Swiss	1.61
Foot-Joy	1.37
Fila	1.32
Ellesse	1.00
Vans	0.79
Puma	0.77
Diadora	0.62
Saucony	0.62
Pony	0.60
Hi-Tec	0.60
Others	6.81

Source: *The Wall Street Journal*, June 9, 1992, p. B4, from Sporting Goods Intelligence.

★ 842 ★
Athletic Shoes (SIC 3021)

Athletic Shoes by Type

Segment distribution of the athletic shoe market is shown in percent, based on wholesale sales of $7.6 billion in 1990.

Basketball	22.0%
Children's	18.0
Cross-training	14.0
Tennis and other court	11.0
Running	10.0
Walking	8.0
Aerobics	7.0
Golf	4.0
Cleated	3.0
Other (cycling, bowling, etc.)	3.0

Source: *The New York Times*, January 5, 1992, p. 10F, from Sporting Goods Manufacturers Association.

★ 843 ★
Athletic Shoes (SIC 3021)

Outdoor Footwear Manufacturers

Major outdoor footwear companies are ranked by 1990 sales, shown in millions of dollars. Company shares are based on group total.

	Sales ($ mil.)	% of Group
Timberland	$ 101.8	29.2%
LaCrosse	45.8	13.2
Wolverine	43.5	12.5
Rocky Boots	40.0	11.5
Hermann's	34.1	9.8
Dunham	33.0	9.5
Hi-Tec	29.0	8.3
Lake-of-the-Woods	21.0	6.0

Source: *Fairchild Fact File/Fairchild Fashion & Merchandising Group - Footwear*, June 10, 1991, p. 18, from *Sportstyle*.

★ 844 ★
Athletic Shoes (SIC 3021)

Sneaker Manufacturers

Company shares are shown in percent, based on an estimated $5.5 billion in domestic sales in 1990.

Nike	30.0%
Reebok	24.0
L.A. Gear	10.0
Keds	5.0
Converse	4.0
Adidas	3.5
Other	23.5

Source: *The Wall Street Journal*, October 31, 1991, p. B1, from Adams Harkness & Hill Inc.

★ 845 ★
Films (SIC 3069)

Cinema Film Manufacturers

Company shares are shown in percent, based on total markets of $57.7 million in 1991, $64.6 million in 1992 and $72.6 million in 1993.

	'91	'92	'93
Kodak	40.7%	40.6%	40.2%
Vari-X	35.0	35.0	35.3
AGFA	17.3	17.2	17.9
Others	7.0	7.2	7.6

Source: Investext, Thomson Financial Networks, April 10, 1992, from Prudential Securities Inc.

★ 846 ★
Vinyl Sheet (SIC 3081)

Vinyl Sheet Producers

Shares are shown in percent.

Armstrong	45.0%
Congoleum	20.0
Mannington	20.0
Tarkett	10.0
Other	5.0

Source: Investext, Thomson Financial Networks, May 18, 1992, from Kidder, Peabody & Company, Incorporated.

★ 847 ★
Plastic Pipes (SIC 3084)

Plastic Drainage Market

Company shares of below-ground plastic drainage market are shown in percent. Data refer to December 1991.

Osma	28.0%
Polypipe	22.0
Hepworth	18.0
Marley	15.0
Uponor	10.0
Hunter	3.0
Brett	3.0
Terrain	1.0

Source: Investext, Thomson Financial Networks, April 7, 1992, from Nomura Research Institute Europe Ltd.

★ 848 ★
Plastic Containers (SIC 3085)

Plastic Container Producers

Shares are shown in percent, based on a total of $3.325 billion in sales.

Constar International	19.0%
Johnson Controls	15.0
Owens-Illinois	14.0
Graham Packaging	9.0
Plastic Container, Inc.	6.0
Silgan	6.0
U.S. Container	2.0
Other independents	5.0
Self manufacturers	24.0

Source: Investext, Thomson Financial Networks, June 29, 1992, from Merrill Lynch Capital Markets.

★ 849 ★
Plastic Containers (SIC 3085)

Plastic Pop Container Producers

Shares are shown in percent, based on a total of $1.140 billion in sales.

Constar International	36.0%
Johnson Controls	35.0
U.S. Container	7.0
Other independents	4.0
Self manufacturers	18.0

Source: Investext, Thomson Financial Networks, June 29, 1992, from Merrill Lynch Capital Markets.

★ 850 ★
Containers (SIC 3089)

Kitchen Container Producers

Company shares are shown in percent.

	1980	1992
Tupperware	75.0%	65.0%
Rubbermaid	25.0	35.0

Source: *USA TODAY*, March 3, 1992, p. 5B, from industry estimates.

★ 851 ★
Plastic Products (SIC 3089)

Plastic Static Control Product Market

Shares by product type are shown in percent, based on total sales of $257.0 million in 1991 and forecasted sales of $377.3 million in 1996.

	1991	1996
Film and film bags	26.5%	26.5%
Materials handling equipment	18.1	16.6
Flooring	14.4	15.9
Foam	11.7	11.7
Footwear, gloves, wrist straps, cords	6.0	4.9
Work surfaces	3.9	3.3
Others	19.5	21.2

Source: *Electronic Packaging & Production*, 1991, p. 14, from Business Communications Company.

★ 852 ★
Vinyl Tile (SIC 3089)

Vinyl Tile Manufacturers

Shares are shown in percent.

Armstrong	55.0%
Amtico	10.0
Kentile	8.0
Azrock	8.0
Tarkett	8.0
Other	11.0

Source: Investext, Thomson Financial Networks, May 18, 1992, from Kidder, Peabody & Company, Incorporated.

★ 853 ★
Prophylactics (SIC 3089)

Condom Brands

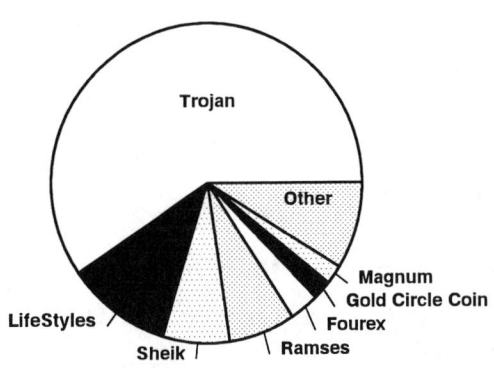

Shares are shown in percent, based on a total of 36.3 million packages sold through supermarkets and drugstores in the year ending October 31, 1992.

Trojan	59.7%
LifeStyles	11.1
Sheik	7.3
Ramses	6.5
Fourex	2.5
Gold Circle Coin	2.3
Magnum	1.5
Other	9.1

Source: *The Wall Street Journal*, November 24, 1992, p. B12, from Information Resources Inc.

★ 854 ★
Prophylactics (SIC 3089)

Condom Manufacturers

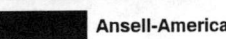

Shares are shown in percent, based on a total of $36.3 million packages sold through supermarkets and drugstores in the year ending October 31, 1992.

Carter-Wallace	61.6%
Schmid Laboratories	21.8
Ansell-Americas	11.1
Safetax	4.0
Other	56.5

Source: *The Wall Street Journal*, November 24, 1992, p. B12, from Information Resources Inc.

★ 855 ★
Prophylactics (SIC 3089)

OTC Contraceptives Market

Shares of OTC (over-the-counter) contraceptives market are shown in percent, based on projected sales of $457 million in 1992, $484 million in 1994 and $514 million in 1996.

	'92	'94	'96
Condoms	65.6%	66.9%	68.1%
Spermicides	34.4	33.1	31.9

Source: *Drug Topics*, February 17, 1992, p. 30, from Packaged Facts, Inc.

SIC 32 - Stone, Clay, and Glass Products

★856★

Glass (SIC 3200)

Glass Sales Worldwide

Segment distribution of the glass product market is shown in percent, based on 1991 sales of $44.2 billion.

Flat glass	30.0%
Lighting	18.0
Containers	18.0
Fiber glass	11.0
TV tubes and CRTs	10.0
Consumerware	6.0
Other	7.0

Source: *Ceramic Industry*, August 1992, p. 33.

★857★

Porcelain (SIC 3200)

Porcelain Enamel Sales Worldwide

Percent distribution by segment is based on a 1991 total of $7.7 billion.

Appliances	85.0%
Sanitaryware	12.0
Other	3.0

Source: *Ceramic Industry*, August 1992, p. 51.

★858★

Whiteware (SIC 3200)

Whiteware Sales Worldwide

Percent distribution by segment is based on 1991 sales of $8.2 billion.

Floor/wall tile	37.0%
Sanitaryware	29.0
Dinnerware/fine china	21.0
Foodserviceware	7.0
Artware	4.0
Other	2.0

Source: *Ceramic Industry*, August 1992, p. 39.

★859★

Flat Glass (SIC 3211)

Flat Glass

1990 shipment distribution is shown in percent, based on a total of 4.390 billion square feet. Raw flat glass includes insulating glass.

Raw flat glass	35.3%
Tempered glass	21.4
Laminated glass	16.9
Mirrors	8.2
Tinted and colored glass	6.3
Low-emissivity glass	6.0
Other	5.9

Source: *Glass Industry*, January 1992, p. 9, from The Freedonia Group, Inc.

★ 860 ★

Glass Containers (SIC 3221)

Glass Container Manufacturers

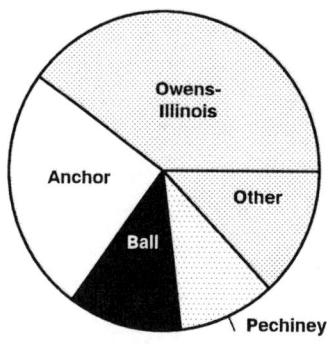

Approximate shares of the U.S. market are shown in percent.

Owens-Illinois	. 40.0%
Anchor	. 25.0
Ball	. 12.0
Pechiney	. 10.0
Other	. 13.0

Source: Investext, Thomson Financial Networks, January 16, 1992, from Bear, Stearns & Co., Inc.

★ 861 ★

Glass Containers (SIC 3221)

Glass Container Market

Domestic glass container market shares are shown in percent, based on dollar sales for the year-to-date.

Owens Illinois	. 40.0%
Anchor/Vitro	. 26.0
Ball-InCon	. 12.0
Foster Forbes	. 9.0
Kerr Glass	. 3.0
Other	. 10.0

Source: Investext, Thomson Financial Networks, March 5, 1992, from Paine Webber Inc.

★ 862 ★

Cement (SIC 3241)

Cement Consumption - North America

Estimated market shares, by category, are shown in percent for 1992.

	U.S.	Canada
Portland cement	96.5%	97.4%
Masonry cement	3.5	2.6

Source: Investext, Thomson Financial Networks, June 25, 1992, from Mabon Securities, Inc.

★ 863 ★

Cement (SIC 3241)

Cement Producers - Italy

Shares of the Italian cement market are shown in percent. "Other" includes 18 private companies.

Italcementi	. 36.4%
Unichem	. 14.4
Cementir	. 9.5
Cementeria Merone	. 5.2
Colacem	. 4.8
Buzzi	. 4.2
Sacci	. 3.4
Adriasebina	. 2.9
Cementizillo	. 2.5
Other	. 16.7

Source: Investext, Thomson Financial Networks, January 20, 1992, from Merrill Lynch Capital Markets.

★ 864 ★

Ceramic Refractories (SIC 3250)

Ceramic Refractories

Shares, by type, are based on 1990 sales of $4.8956 billion, shown in percent.

Brick and shapes	. 63.0%
Bulk refractories	. 30.0
Insulating ceramic fiber	. 3.0
Other	. 4.0

Source: *Ceramic Industry*, August 1991, p. 47.

★ 865 ★
Ceramics (SIC 3250)

Advanced Ceramic Component Market

Segment distribution is shown in percent, based on a total of $3.583 billion in 1990.

Electronic ceramics 79.9%
Ceramic coatings 10.4
Structural ceramics 9.8

Source: *JOM*, January 1992, p. 7, from Business Communications Company.

★ 866 ★
Ceramics (SIC 3250)

Advanced Ceramics Applications by Category

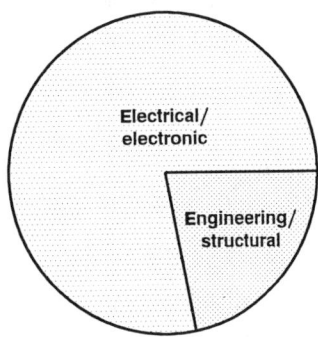

Shares of the worldwide advanced ceramics applications market, by category, are shown in percent, based on an industry total of $12.5 billion in 1991.

Electrical/electronic 77.6%
Engineering/structural 22.4

Source: *IDR*, January 1992, p. 24, from Survey estimate.

★ 867 ★
Ceramics (SIC 3250)

Advanced Ceramics Market

Segment distribution is shown in percent, based on a total of $4.175 billion in 1990.

Electronic ceramics 68.6%
Ceramic powders 11.0
Ceramic coatings 8.9
Structural ceramics 8.4
Ceramic-matrix composites 3.1

Source: *JOM*, January 1992, p. 7, from Business Communications Company.

★ 868 ★
Ceramics (SIC 3250)

Advanced Ceramics Sales Worldwide

Segment distribution is shown in percent, based on global sales of $13.594 billion in 1990.

Capacitors/substrates/packages 48.0%
Electrical porcelain 12.0
Engineering ceramics 10.0
Optical fibers 9.0
Other electrical/electronic 17.0
Other 4.0

Source: *Ceramic Industry*, August 1991, p. 25.

★ 869 ★
Ceramics (SIC 3250)

Advanced Ceramics Sales Worldwide

Percent distribution by segment is based on 1991 sales of $15.3 billion.

Capacitors/substrate packages 38.0%
Other electrical/electronic ceramics 25.0
Optical fibers 13.0
Engineering ceramics 11.0
Electrical porcelain 10.0
Other 4.0

Source: *Ceramic Industry*, August 1992, p. 27.

★870★
Ceramics (SIC 3250)

Whiteware Sales Worldwide

Shares, by type of whiteware, are shown in percent, based on a 1990 total of $6.1398 billion in sales.

Floor/wall tile	39.0%
Sanitaryware	33.0
Dinnerware/fine china	17.0
Artware	5.0
Foodserviceware	3.0
Other	3.0

Source: *Ceramic Industry*, August 1991, p. 33.

★871★
Ceramic Flooring (SIC 3253)

Ceramic Flooring Manufacturers

Shares are shown in percent.

American Olean	23.0%
Dal-Tile	17.0
Sikes Tile	15.0
Other	45.0

Source: Investext, Thomson Financial Networks, May 18, 1992, from Kidder, Peabody & Company, Incorporated.

★872★
Refractories (SIC 3255)

Refractory Sales Worldwide

Percent distribution by segment is based on 1991 sales of $5.8569 billion.

Bricks and shapes	56.0%
Bulk refractories	19.0
Insulating ceramic fiber	13.0
Other	12.0

Source: *Ceramic Industry*, August 1992, p. 45.

★873★
Ceramics (SIC 3264)

Ceramic Capacitor Global Market

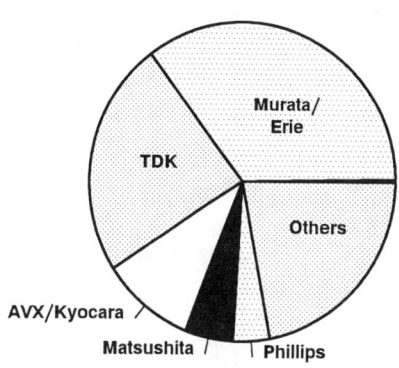

Company shares of the global market are based on total 1990 revenue of $2.98 billion.

Murata/Erie	34.7%
TDK	23.7
AVX/Kyocara	10.4
Matsushita	4.7
Phillips	4.3
Others	22.2

Source: *Electronic News*, May 11, 1992, p. 24, from Market Intelligence Research Corp.

★874★
Lime (SIC 3274)

Lime Demand by End Use

Market shares, by end use, are shown in percent, based on a total lime demand of 17.481 million tons in 1990.

Steel processing	29.3%
Chemical/industrial	14.9
Flue gas desulfurization	9.6
Construction	7.7
Pulp and paper	7.2
Water purification	6.1
Environmental, other	5.4
Ore, metal processing, other	4.9
Sugar processing	3.8
Magnesia extraction	3.7

Continued on next page.

★874★ *Continued*

Lime (SIC 3274)

Lime Demand by End Use

Market shares, by end use, are shown in percent, based on a total lime demand of 17.481 million tons in 1990.

Sewage treatment	2.7%
Miscellaneous uses	2.7
Precipitated calcium carbonate	1.5
Alkali production	0.6

Source: *Chemicalweek*, December 18, 1991, p. 15, from U.S. Bureau of Mines.

★875★

Plasterboard (SIC 3275)

Plasterboard Producers - France

Shares are shown in percent.

	1988	1991
BPB	55.0%	50.0%
Lafarge	40.0	40.0
Knauf	-	10.0
Other	5.0	-

Source: Investext, Thomson Financial Networks, May 20, 1992, from Barclays de Zoete Wedd Securities.

★876★

Plasterboard (SIC 3275)

Plasterboard Producers - Germany

Shares are shown in percent.

	1988	1991
Knauf	50.0%	46.0%
BPB	35.0	44.0
Lafarge	-	10.0
Other	15.0	-

Source: Investext, Thomson Financial Networks, May 20, 1992, from Barclays de Zoete Wedd Securities.

★877★

Plasterboard (SIC 3275)

Plasterboard Producers - U.K.

Shares are shown in percent.

	1988	1991
BPB	95.0%	65.0%
Lafarge	4.0	18.0
Knauf	-	17.0
Other	1.0	-

Source: Investext, Thomson Financial Networks, May 20, 1992, from Barclays de Zoete Wedd Securities.

★878★

Abrasive Products (SIC 3291)

Industrial Diamond Industry

Shares of the U.S. industrial diamond/cubic boron nitride market are shown in percent for 1991 and 1996, based on industry totals of $985.5 million and $1,400.5 million, respectively.

	1991	1996
Diamond, PCD	87.5%	80.2%
CBN, PCBN products	11.3	14.5
Diamond, diamond-like, CBN films, products	1.2	5.3

Source: *Ceramic Industry*, January 1992, p. 14, from Business Communications Co., Inc.

★879★

Paper Coatings (SIC 3295)

Paper Coatings - North America

Shares, by type, are shown in percent.

Kaolin	87.0%
Calcium carbonate	10.0
Other	3.0

Source: *Ceramic Industry*, September 1991, p. 17, from Industrial Minerals and Roskill Information Services Ltd.

★ 880 ★

Paper Coatings (SIC 3295)

Paper Coatings - Western Europe

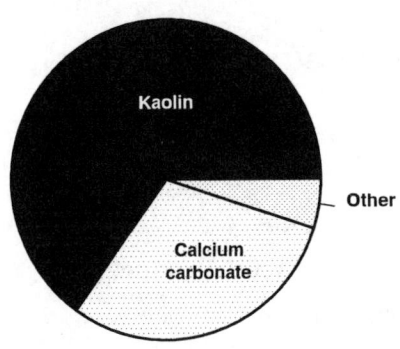

Shares, by type, are shown in percent.

Kaolin 65.0%
Calcium carbonate 30.0
Other 5.0

Source: *Ceramic Industry*, September 1991, p. 17, from Industrial Minerals and Roskill Information Services Ltd.

★ 881 ★

Ceiling Tiles (SIC 3299)

Ceiling Manufacturers

Shares of acoustical mineral fiber ceiling production are shown in percent.

Armstrong 50.0%
USG Corp. 40.0
Celotex 10.0

Source: Investext, Thomson Financial Networks, May 18, 1992, from Kidder, Peabody & Company, Incorporated.

SIC 33 - Primary Metal Industries

★ 882 ★

Metals (SIC 3300)

Metal Producers

Companies are ranked by 1991 sales, shown in millions of dollars. Percent shares are based on a group total of $56,369 million.

	Sales ($ mil.)	% of Group
Aluminum Co. of Amer.	$ 9,981	17.7%
LTV	6,117	10.9
Reynolds Metals	5,785	10.3
Bethlehem Steel	4,318	7.7
Amax	3,772	6.7
Inland Steel Ind.	3,404	6.0
Phelps Dodge	2,461	4.4
National Steel	2,330	4.1
Maxxam	2,317	4.1
Cyprus Minerals	1,659	2.9
Armco	1,624	2.9
Nucor	1,465	2.6
Walter Industries	1,329	2.4
Cyclops Industries	1,056	1.9
Weirton Steel	1,039	1.8
Allegheny Ludlum	1,005	1.8
Wheeling-Pittsburgh	966	1.7
Essex Group	886	1.6
Worthington Ind.	875	1.6
Amsted Industries	817	1.4
Magma Copper	725	1.3
Texas Industries	655	1.2
Lukens	631	1.1
Quanex	589	1.0
Carpenter Technology	562	1.0

Source: *Fortune*, April 20, 1992, p. 276.

★ 883 ★

Nonferrous Metals (SIC 3300)

Nonferrous Metal Producers

Sales by 12 leading nonferrous metals producers worldwide, are shown in billions of dollars, totaling $109.32 billion in 1990. (Data for Noranda excludes sales of forest products). Relative market shares are shown in percent.

	Sales ($ bil.)	% of Group
Preussag	$ 14.99	14.0%
Pechiney	14.12	13.0
Vlag	12.17	11.0
Metallgesellschaft	11.97	11.0
Alcoa	10.87	10.0
Alcan	8.85	8.0
Degussa	8.26	8.0
RTZ	7.20	7.0
Reynolds	6.08	6.0
Mitsubishi Metal	5.58	5.0
Noranda	4.68	4.0
Alusuisse	4.56	4.0

Source: *Business Horizons*, November 1991, p. 16.

★ 884 ★

Nonferrous Metals (SIC 3300)

Nonferrous Metal Sales

Shares of first-quarter nonferrous metal sales by American producers, totaling $9.8929 billion in 1991 and $9.4122 billion in 1992, are shown in percent.

	'91	'92
Alcoa	24.3%	24.4%
Alcan	19.7	19.5
Reynolds	13.9	14.1
Amax	9.4	9.3
Inco	8.5	7.2
Phelps Dodge	6.1	6.3
Kaiser	5.2	4.9

Continued on next page.

★ 884 ★ *Continued*

Nonferrous Metals (SIC 3300)

Nonferrous Metal Sales

Shares of first-quarter nonferrous metal sales by American producers, totaling $9.8929 billion in 1991 and $9.4122 billion in 1992, are shown in percent.

	'91	'92
Asarco	4.7%	4.9%
Cyprus	4.2	4.2
Cominco	2.3	2.9
Magma Copper	1.7	2.1

Source: *Iron Age*, June 1992, p. 33, from company quarterly reports.

★ 885 ★

Steel (SIC 3312)

Continuous Casters - U.S. Market

U.S. Steel Group, USX Corp.

LTV Steel Co. Inc.

WCI Steel Inc.

Cascade Steel Rolling Mills, Inc.

SMI Steel Inc.

Continuous casters ordered and/or installed in 1991 are shown by U.S. steel producer. Relative shares are shown in percent based on a total capacity of 7.4 million tons.

	Tons (mil.)	% of Group
U.S. Steel Group, USX Corp. . .	2.6	35.1%
LTV Steel Co. Inc.	2.0	27.0
WCI Steel Inc.	1.6	21.6
Cascade Steel Rolling Mills, Inc. .	0.7	9.5
SMI Steel Inc.	0.5	6.8

Source: *Iron & Steel Engineer*, February 1992, pp. D-28.

★ 886 ★

Steel (SIC 3312)

Direct Reduced Iron Production

Tons of iron produced worldwide in HYL (Hydroxylysine) and HYL III process plants are shown for 1990. Percent shares are based on a group total of 5,252,730 tons.

	Tons	% of Group
PT Krakatau	1,407,614	26.8%
Sicartsa	754,888	14.4
Sidor 2	706,974	13.5
Hylsa 2P	614,836	11.7
Hylsa 3M5	510,255	9.7
Hylsa 2M5	292,927	5.6
Sidor 1	247,271	4.7
Usiba	243,258	4.6
Tamsa	217,148	4.1
SEIS	166,418	3.2
Hylsa 1M	91,141	1.7

Source: *Iron and Steelmaking*, 1991, p. 305.

★ 887 ★

Steel (SIC 3312)

EAF Capacities - Canada

Electric arc furnace capacities by steel maker, are shown in thousands of short tons per year. Market shares are shown in percent.

	S.t./yr. (000)	Shares
Sidbec-Dosco Inc.	1,730,000	24.2%
IPSCO Inc.	1,090,000	15.2
Lake Ontario Steel Co.	1,000,000	14.0
Stelco Steel	775,000	10.8
Sydney Steel Corp.	600,000	8.4
IVACO Inc.	400,000	5.6
Atlas Specialty Steels	320,000	4.5
Manitoba Rolling Mills Ltd. . .	300,000	4.2
Slater Steels Corp.	300,000	4.2
Courtice Steel Inc.	250,000	3.5
Canadian Steel Wheel Div. . .	166,000	2.3
Atlas Stainless Steels	100,000	1.4
Sorel Forge Inc.	60,000	0.8
Dofasco Inc.	58,000	0.8
ESCO Ltd.	12,800	0.2
Algoma Steel Corp., Ltd. . . .	1,500	0.0

Source: *Iron and Steelmaking*, May 1992, p. 11.

★ 888 ★

Steel (SIC 3312)

EAF Capacities - U.S.

The 25 largest EAF (electric arc furnace) capacities, by steel manufacturer, are shown in thousands of short tons per year. Relative market shares are shown in percent.

	S.t./yr. (000)	% of Group
Nucor Corp.	4,180,000	11.6%
Bethlehem Steel Corp.	3,410,000	9.5
North Star Steel Co.	2,571,000	7.1
Northwestern Steel & Wire Co.	2,570,000	7.1
The Timken Co.	2,000,000	5.6
Armco Inc.	1,785,000	5.0
Florida Steel Corp.	1,700,000	4.7
Nucor-Yamato Steel Corp.	1,600,000	4.4
Birmingham Steel Corp.	1,504,200	4.2
Chaparral Steel Co.	1,500,000	4.2
NS Group Inc.	1,265,000	3.5
MACSTEEL	1,040,000	2.9
U.S. Steel Group	1,000,000	2.8
CMC Steel Group	990,000	2.8
Rouge Steel Co.	750,000	2.1
Georgetown Steel Corp.	900,000	2.5
Laclede Steel Co.	900,000	2.5
Lukens Inc.	880,000	2.4
Cyclops Industries, Inc.	850,000	2.4
CF&I Steel Corp.	800,000	2.2
J&L Specialty Products Corp.	800,000	2.2
LTV Steel Co.	792,000	2.2
Bayou Steel Corp.	786,000	2.2
National Steel Corp.	720,000	2.0
Cascade Steel Rolling Mills, Inc.	700,000	1.9

Source: *Iron and Steelmaking*, May 1992, p. 25.

★ 889 ★

Steel (SIC 3312)

Gulf States Steel Mills

Steel production, by company, is shown in thousands of tons. Relative market shares are shown in percent.

	Tons (000)	% of Group
Chaparral Steel (Midlothian, TX)	1,500	22.1%
North Star (Beaumont, TX)	800	11.8
Bayou Steel (LaPlace, LA)	800	11.8
Nucor-Yamato (Blytheville, AR)	650	9.6
Nucor (Jewett, TX)	550	8.1
CMC Steel (Seguin, TX)	550	8.1
Florida Steel (Jacksonville, TN)	410	6.0
Sheffield Steel (Sand Springs, OK)	400	5.9
Lone Star (Lone Star, TX)	300	4.4
Birmingham Steel (Jackson, MS)	300	4.4
Border Steel (El Paso, TX)	225	3.3
Arkansas Steel (Newport, AR)	220	3.2
Marathon-LeTourneau (Long View, TX)	75	1.1

Source: *Recycling Today*, 15, 1991, p. 62, from AUS Consultants.

★ 890 ★

Steel (SIC 3312)

Steel Industry Profile

Shares of steel sales by American producers are based on first-quarter sales in 1991 and 1992. (Quanex, Roanoke, Northwestern quarters end January 31; Chaparral, Geneva, New Jersey, Commercial quarters end February 29).

	'91	'92
LTV	16.1%	15.6%
U.S. Steel	12.5	13.2
Bethlehem	11.9	11.2
Inland	9.4	10.1
National	5.9	6.3
Timken	5.1	4.7
Nucor	3.9	4.4
Armco	4.6	4.1
Weirton	2.8	3.0
Al Ludlum	3.0	3.0
Commercial Metals	3.1	3.0
Wheeling Pittsburgh Steel Corp.	2.5	2.7
Carpenter	1.6	1.8
Lukens	1.8	1.6

Continued on next page.

★ 890 ★ *Continued*

Steel (SIC 3312)

Steel Industry Profile

Shares of steel sales by American producers are based on first-quarter sales in 1991 and 1992. (Quanex, Roanoke, Northwestern quarters end January 31; Chaparral, Geneva, New Jersey, Commercial quarters end February 29).

	'91	'92
Quanex	1.6%	1.4%
Florida	1.2	1.3
Geneva	1.3	1.2
Birmingham	1.0	1.2
Northwestern	1.3	1.1
Chaparral	1.1	1.1
Acme	1.0	1.1
Lone Star	1.7	1.1
Keystone	0.8	0.9
CF&I	0.8	0.8
Laclede	0.7	0.8
NS	0.6	0.8
Roanoke	0.4	0.4
Bayou Steel	0.3	0.3
New Jersey	0.2	0.2
Steel of W. Wa.	0.2	0.2

Source: *Iron Age*, June 1992, p. 32.

★ 891 ★

Steel (SIC 3312)

Steel Maker Shares

Company shares are shown in percent. 1992 and 1993 shares are based on estimated totals.

	'91	'92	'93
USX	10.0%	9.8%	10.0%
Bethlehem	9.5	8.5	8.3
LTV	7.5	7.1	7.0
National	5.6	5.3	4.9
Inland	4.7	4.5	4.6
Direct importers	17.8	19.1	18.8
Other	44.9	45.7	46.4

Source: Investext, Thomson Financial Networks, April 6, 1992, from Donaldson, Lufkin & Jenrette Securities and annual report.

★ 892 ★

Steel (SIC 3312)

Steel Market

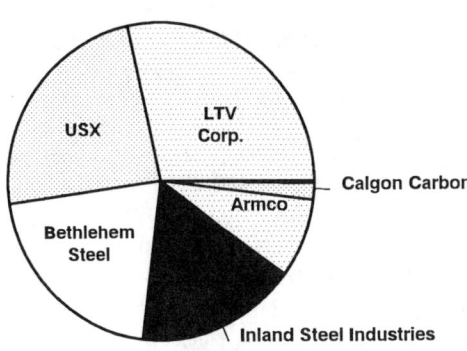

Company shares of steel, coke, and coal-tar chemicals are shown in percent based on a total of $20.4675 billion in sales in 1991.

LTV Corp.	29.2%
USX	23.8
Bethlehem Steel	21.1
Inland Steel Industries	16.6
Armco	7.8
Calgon Carbon	1.5

Source: *Chemicalweek*, May 6, 1992, p. 34, from Standard and Poor's Compustat Services.

★ 893 ★

Steel (SIC 3312)

Steel Mills

Shares of the 1991 market are shown in percent.

USX	11.2%
Bethlehem	10.6
LTV	8.4
National Steel	6.2
Inland	5.3
Armco	5.1
Other	53.2

Source: Investext, Thomson Financial Networks, March 10, 1992, from Paine Webber, Inc.

★ 894 ★

Steel (SIC 3312)

Steel Product Shipments by End Use

Shares, by market classification, are based on total shipments of 78,868,348 short tons in 1991, shown in percent. Sort of data is by industrial sector as reported in the source.

Nonclassified shipments	23.7%
Steel service centers and distributors	21.7
Automotive	11.9
Construction and contractors' products	11.5
Steel for converting and processing	7.8
Export (reporting companies only)	5.7
Containers, packaging and shipping materials	5.4
Electrical equipment	2.6
Machinery, industrial equipment and tools	2.1
Appliances, utensils and cutlery	1.7
Oil and gas	1.3
Rail transportation	1.1
Other domestic and commercial equipment	1.0
Independent forgers (n.e.c.)	0.8
Agricultural	0.6
Mining , quarrying and lumbering	0.4
Shipbuilding and marine equipment	0.3
Industrial fasteners	0.3
Ordnance and other military	0.1
Aircraft and aerospace	0.0

Source: *I&SM*, July 1992, p. 28, from U.S. Department of Commerce and American Iron and Steel Institute.

★ 895 ★

Steel (SIC 3312)

Steel Product Shipments - 1991

Shares, by product type, are based on 1991 total shipments of 78,868,348 short tons, shown in percent.

Sheets and strip	46.5%
Bars	16.9
Shapes and plates	16.2
Semifinished products	8.8
Pipe and tubing	5.8
Tin mill products	5.2
Rails and accessories	0.6

Source: *I&SM*, July 1992, p. 24, from American Iron and Steel Institute.

★ 896 ★

Steel (SIC 3312)

Steel Production by Process - EC

Percent distribution is based on a European Community production total of 137.449 million metric tons in 1991.

Basic oxygen furnace	67.9%
Electric arc furnace	31.6
Open hearth	0.6

Source: *I&SM*, July 1992, p. 19, from International Iron and Steel Institute.

★ 897 ★

Steel (SIC 3312)

Steel Production by Process Worldwide

Percent distribution is based on a 1991 production total of 642.090 million metric tons.

Basic oxygen furnace	58.2%
Electric arc furnace	28.4
Open hearth	13.2
Other	0.1

Source: *I&SM*, July 1992, p. 19, from International Iron and Steel Institute.

★ 898 ★

Steel (SIC 3312)

Steel Production in Eastern Europe

Shares, by process, are based on 1991 Eastern Europe production of 166,023 thousand metric tons, shown in percent.

Open hearth	46.1%
Basic oxygen furnace	39.2
Electric arc furnace	14.7

Source: *I&SM*, July 1992, p. 19, from International Iron and Steel Institute.

★ 899 ★

Steel (SIC 3312)

Steel Scrap Consumption - U.S.

EAF
BOF
Foundry
Export
Other

Shares of steel scrap consumption by steel industry segments reached an estimated 78.9 million metric tons in 1991 and are forecasted to total 80.7 million metric tons in 1992. Segment distribution is shown in percent.

	'91	'92
EAF (electric air furnace)	43.6%	43.4%
BOF (basic oxygen furnace)	20.1	20.8
Foundry	17.8	17.8
Export (net)	12.4	11.8
Other	6.1	6.2

Source: *Iron Age*, June 1992, p. 26, from UCAR Carbon Co.

★ 900 ★

Steel (SIC 3313)

Iron and Steel Industry Leaders - Japan

Companies are ranked by 1991 declared income, shown in millions of Yen. Relative market shares are shown in percent.

	Yen (mil.)	% of Group
Nippon Steel	95,528	26.0%
Tokyo Steel Mfg.	67,496	18.3
Kobe Steel	53,391	14.5
Nisshin Steel	44,186	12.0
Sumitomo Metal Industries	27,982	7.6
Hitachi Metals	23,328	6.3
Kyoei Steel	20,910	5.7
Toa Steel	18,547	5.0
Yodogawa Steel Works	16,547	4.5

Source: *TOKYO Business Today*, July 1992, p. 37.

★ 901 ★

Steel (SIC 3313)

Iron and Steel Leaders

Sales of the 12 leading iron and steel producers worldwide are shown in billions of dollars for 1990. Relative market shares are shown in percent.

	Sales ($ bil.)	% of Group
Thyssen	$ 21.49	15.0%
Nippon Steel	21.16	15.0
Usinor-Sacilor	17.64	12.0
Sumitomo Metal	12.78	9.0
Broken Hill Proprietary	10.83	7.0
NKK	10.25	7.0
Krupp	9.70	7.0
Kobe Steel	9.44	7.0
Kawasaki Steel	8.65	6.0
British Steel	8.45	6.0
Hoesch	7.83	5.0
Pohang Iron & Steel	7.00	5.0

Source: *Business Horizons*, November 1991, p. 16.

★ 902 ★

Conduits (SIC 3317)

Conduit Manufacturers

Shares of sales of steel and plastic conduits for commercial construction are shown in percent.

Kellems	80.0%
Thomas & Betts	20.0

Source: Investext, Thomson Financial Networks, January 30, 1992, from Prudential Securities, Inc.

★ 903 ★

Copper (SIC 3331)

Copper and Copper Alloy End Use

Share by application is shown in percent, based on 1990 total shipments by weight.

Building construction	41.3%
Electrical and electronic products	23.9
Industrial machinery and equipment	13.5
Transportation equipment	11.5
Consumer and general products	9.8

Source: *U.S. Industrial Outlook 1992*, p. 14-7, from Copper Development Association and U.S. Department of Commerce, Bureau of the Census.

★ 904 ★
Aluminum (SIC 3334)

Aluminum Industry Leaders

Companies are ranked by 1991 sales, shown in millions of dollars. Percentages are based on the group total.

	Sales ($ mil.)	% of Group
Aluminum Co. of America . . .	$ 9,884	46.2%
Reynolds Metals	5,730	26.8
Amax	3,772	17.6
Kaiser Aluminum	2,001	9.4

Source: *The 1992 Business Week 1000*, p. 190.

★ 905 ★
Aluminum (SIC 3334)

Aluminum Sheet Market - U.S.

Shares of the aluminum can sheet market, by company, are shown in percent. Shares are based on an estimated industry total of 4.230 billion lbs. in shipments. Figures for Reynolds and Golden Aluminum include internal consumption. Figures for Logan Aluminum are the result of an ARCO/Alcan joint venture.

Alcoa	40.0%
Reynolds	20.0
Alcan	15.0
Kaiser	9.0
Logan Aluminum	5.0
Ravenswood	4.0
Amax	2.0
Golden Aluminum	2.0
Consolidated	2.0
Commonwealth	1.0

Source: Investext, Thomson Financial Networks, March 18, 1992, from The First Boston Corporation.

★ 906 ★
Aluminum (SIC 3334)

Aluminum Smelting - Western Europe

Smelting capacity is shown in tons per annum (tpa) for the leading twenty companies; relative shares are shown in percent.

	Cap. (tpa)	% of Group
Pechiney	615,000	19.0%
Hydro Aluminum	590,000	18.2
VAW	365,000	11.3
Inespal	350,000	10.8
State-owned industry (Yugoslavia)	305,000	9.4
Alusuisse	200,000	6.2
Elkem	190,000	5.9
Hoogovens	180,000	5.6
British Alcan	172,000	5.3
Aluminia Italia	165,000	5.1
Anglesey Aluminum	110,000	3.4

Source: Investext, Thomson Financial Networks, February 5, 1992, from Lehman Brothers Limited.

★ 907 ★
Aluminum (SIC 3334)

Can Sheet Production

Capacity shares of domestic can sheet rolling mills are shown in percent, based on an estimated industry capacity of 5.560 billion lbs. in 1992.

Alcoa	39.6%
Alcan	19.8
Reynolds	14.9
Kaiser	7.9
Arco	5.0
Ravenswood	4.0
Alumax	3.0
Commonwealth	3.0
Golden Aluminum	2.0
Conalco	1.0

Source: Investext, Thomson Financial Networks, February 5, 1992, from Shearson Lehman Brothers, Inc.

★ 908 ★

Titanium Sponge (SIC 3339)

Titanium Sponge Producers Worldwide

Manufacturer shares of global production are shown for selected companies. Data are shown as percent of 119,437.5 tons produced worldwide in 1991.

Osaka Titanium	12.6%
Timet	10.7
RMI Company	9.1
Toho Titanium	9.1
Oremet	5.7
Deeside Titanium	4.2
Showa Denko	2.5
Other	46.1

Source: *JOM*, May 1992, p. 6, from Titanium Development Association.

★ 909 ★

Metals (SIC 3350)

Aluminum Market by Application

Shares by application are shown in percent for 1990 through 1992 (estimated).

	'90	'91	'92
Construction	44.0%	41.0%	40.0%
Primary	12.0	17.0	20.0
Transportation	17.0	14.0	15.0
Packaging	8.0	10.0	10.9
Durables	7.0	6.0	5.0
Others	12.0	12.0	10.0

Source: Investext, Thomson Financial Networks, April 23, 1992, from Nomura Research Institute America, Inc.

★ 910 ★

Copper Tubing (SIC 3351)

Copper Tube Producers - U.K.

Shares are shown in percent based on a total market of 55,000 tons in 1991.

IMI	40.0%
Glynwed	30.0
Other	30.0

Source: Investext, Thomson Financial Networks, February 24, 1992, from Panmure Gordon & Co., Limited.

★ 911 ★

Die Casting (SIC 3364)

Magnesium Die Casters - North America

Estimated shares of the North American market are shown in percent, based on a total of 17.44 million lbs. shipped in 1991.

Magnesium Products Ltd.	43.0%
Diemakers Inc.	26.0
Lunt Manufacturing	13.0
Other	18.0

Source: Investext, Thomson Financial Networks, June 26, 1992, from Midland Walwyn Capital Inc.

SIC 34 - Fabricated Metal Products

★912★

Metal Products (SIC 3400)

Fabricated Metal Products

Value of shipments is shown in millions of dollars for 1991. Shares by type are shown in percent based on a group total of $21,011 million.

	Value ($ mil.)	% of Group
Valves and pipe fittings	$ 8,689	41.4%
Industrial fasteners	4,719	22.5
Ball and roller bearings . . .	4,356	20.7
Screw machine products . . .	3,247	15.5

Source: *U.S. Industrial Outlook 1992*, p. 15-2, from U.S. Department of Commerce, Bureau of the Census.

★913★

Metal Products (SIC 3400)

Metal Product Manufacturers

Companies are ranked by 1991 total sales shown in millions of dollars. Relative market shares are based on a total of $33,349 million.

	Sales ($ mil.)	% of Group
Gillette	$ 4,706	14.1%
Crown Cork & Seal	3,807	11.4
Masco	3,177	9.5
Tyco Laboratories	3,108	9.3
Illinois Tool Works	2,647	7.9
McDermott	2,299	6.9
Ball	2,267	6.8
Stanley Works	1,962	5.9
Harsco	1,956	5.9
Masco Industries	1,502	4.5
Hillenbrand Ind.	1,209	3.6
Newell	1,119	3.4
Snap-on Tools	883	2.6
Danaher	837	2.5
Silgan	679	2.0

	Sales ($ mil.)	% of Group
Robertson-Ceco	$ 651	2.0%
Barnes Group	538	1.6

Source: *Fortune*, April 20, 1992, p. 276.

★914★

Welding Materials (SIC 3400)

Welding-Filler Material Production - Japan

Shares are shown in percent, based on total production of 402,496 tons in 1990.

Solid wire	47.0%
Covered electrode	25.0
Flux-cored wire	16.0
Submerged-arc-welding materials	12.0

Source: *Welding Design & Fabrication*, April 1992, p. 40.

★915★

Metal Cans (SIC 3411)

Beverage Can Manufacturers

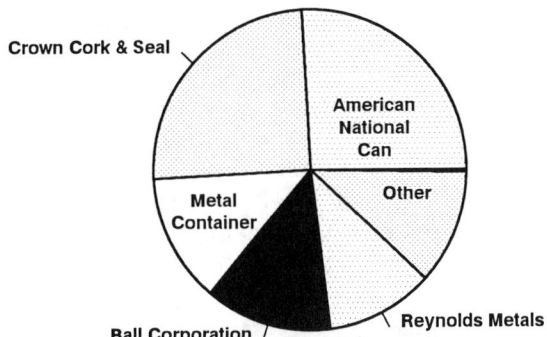

Market shares are shown in percent, based on total unit capacity.

American National Can	26.0%
Crown Cork & Seal	25.0
Metal Container	13.0
Ball Corporation	13.0
Reynolds Metals	11.0
Other	12.0

Source: Investext, Thomson Financial Networks, March 5, 1992, from Paine Webber Inc.

★916★

Razors (SIC 3421)

Gillette Razor and Blade Sales

Market shares, by brand, are shown in percent for November/December 1991.

Gillette Disposables	22.4%
Sensor	14.8
Atra Blades	14.0
Trac II Blades	9.9

Source: Investext, Thomson Financial Networks, March 16, 1992, from Prudential Securities, Inc.

★917★

Plumbing Appliances (SIC 3431)

Plumbing Appliances and Fixtures

Market shares by product type are shown in percent, based on total shipments of 13,451,216 units in 1991.

Bathtubs, cast iron, enameled	2.6%
Bathtubs, plastic and fiberglass	13.7
Bathtubs, steel, enameled	5.7%
Kitchen sinks, cast iron, enameled	4.6
Kitchen sinks, steel, enameled	2.9
Kitchen sinks, stainless steel and other materials	23.7
Lavatories, cast iron, enameled	3.8
Lavatories, steel, enameled	8.7
Lavatories, vitreous china	20.4
Water softener pressure tanks	5.8
Water systems	8.0

Source: *Appliance*, April 1992, p. 54.

★918★

Plumbing Fixtures (SIC 3432)

Faucet Manufacturers

Estimated shares are shown in percent. NA stands for not available.

Masco	33.0%
Moen	NA
Black & Decker	NA
American Standard	NA
Kohler	NA

Source: Investext, Thomson Financial Networks, May 26, 1992, from Kidder, Peabody & Company, Incorporated.

★919★

Architectural Metal Work (SIC 3446)

Industrial Grate and Decking Industry

Market share is shown in percent.

IKG Industries	50.0%
Other	50.0

Source: Investext, Thomson Financial Networks, June 11, 1992, from Donaldson, Lufkin & Jenrette Securities.

★920★

Garage Doors (SIC 3448)

Garage Door Suppliers

Market shares, by company, are shown in percent.

Overhead Door	15.0+ %
Raynor Door	15.0+
Clopay	12.0
Other	58.0

Source: Investext, Thomson Financial Networks, June 10, 1992, from Paine Webber, Inc.

★ 921 ★
Prefabricated Buildings (SIC 3448)

Prefab Building Manufacturers

Shares of the prefabricated building market are shown in percent. "Other" includes American Building, Inland, USA, Gulf States, A&S, and Whirlwind.

Butler Manufacturing	22.0%
United Dominion	20.0
Robertson-Ceco	16.0
Other	42.0

Source: Investext, Thomson Financial Networks, May 7, 1992, from J.C. Bradford & Co.

★ 922 ★
Iron and Steel Forgings (SIC 3462)

Domestic Iron and Steel Mills

Company third-quarter sales are shown in millions of dollars for 1991. Relative shares are based on a group total of $5,734.06 million.

	Sales ($ mil.)	% of Group
U.S. Steel	$ 1,281.00	22.3%
LTV	1,479.90	25.8
Bethlehem	1,121.60	19.6
Inland	860.06	15.0
National	603.90	10.5
Armco	387.60	6.8

Source: *Iron Age*, December 1991, p. 26.

★ 923 ★
Nonferrous Forgings (SIC 3463)

Nonferrous Forging Mills

Relative shares are based on a third quarter group total of $10.0447 billion in sales.

	Sales ($ mil.)	% of Group
Alcoa	$ 2,500.0	24.9%
Alcan	1,951.0	19.4
Reynolds	1,440.0	14.3
Amax	978.0	9.7
Inco	648.0	6.5
Phelps Dodge	617.6	6.1
Kaiser	509.7	5.1
Asarco	493.4	4.9
Cyprus	441.9	4.4

	Sales ($ mil.)	% of Group
Cominco	$ 271.3	2.7%
Magma Copper	193.8	1.9

Source: *Iron Age*, December 1991, p. 27, from company quarterly reports.

★ 924 ★
Cookware (SIC 3469)

Cookware Market by Material

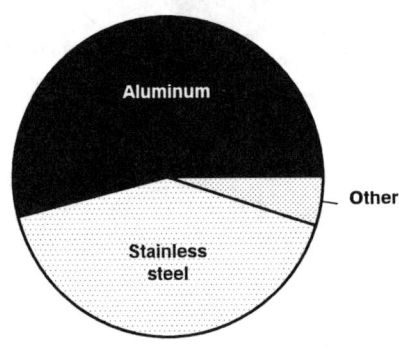

Cookware shares, by material, are shown as a percent of $537 million total in factory billings in 1990. "Other" includes cast iron, copper and porcelain on steel or iron.

Aluminum	54.0%
Stainless steel	41.0
Other	5.0

Source: *HFD*, October 14, 1991, p. 6, from CMA.

★ 925 ★

Weapons (SIC 3484)

Assault Weapons Used in Crime

Figures show leading assault weapons traced after commission of a crime. The number of weapons traced is a small fraction of total. Data are for 1990 or 1991 and show number of weapons in each category.

Tec-9 (Intratec and imitations) 1,546
M-10, M-11 (Various producers) 1,167
Mini-14 (Sturm, Ruger) 884
AR-15 and M-16 (Cold and others) 850
AKS/AKM (Chinese and other
   foreign producers) 802

Source: *The New York Times*, March 10, 1992, p. A22, from Bureau of Alcohol, Tobacco, and Firearms.

★ 926 ★

Weapons (SIC 3484)

Guns by Type

Segment distribution of the firearms market is shown in percent. Figures are based on totals of 2.4 million units in 1965 and 3.7 million units in 1990.

	1965	1990
Handguns	28.0%	48.0%
Rifles	34.0	30.0
Shotguns	38.0	22.0

Source: *USA TODAY*, May 6, 1992, p. 1A, from National Association of Federally Licensed Firearms.

★ 927 ★

Weapons (SIC 3484)

Pistol Production Leaders

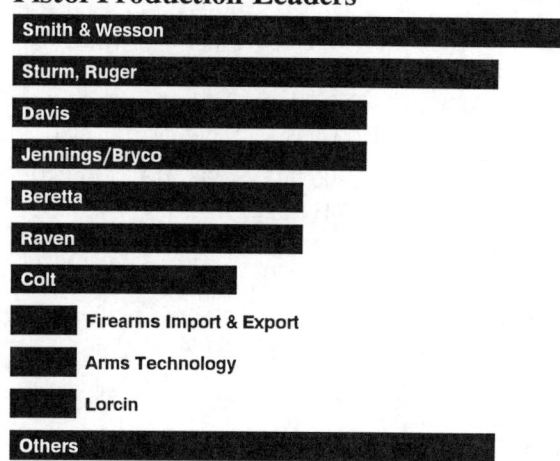

Manufacturers' shares are based on total pistol production of 1.36 million units in 1990, shown in percent.

Smith & Wesson 16.6%
Sturm, Ruger 15.4
Davis 10.5
Jennings/Bryco 10.5
Beretta 9.2
Raven 8.7
Colt 6.9
Firearms Import & Export 2.4
Arms Technology 2.3
Lorcin 2.2
Others 15.3

Source: *The Wall Street Journal*, February 28, 1992, p. A7, from Bureau of Alcohol, Tobacco, and Firearms.

★ 928 ★

Weapons (SIC 3484)

Top Gun Producers

Gun producers' domestic and foreign sales in 1990. Data show units shipped.

	Hand-Guns	Rifles & Shotguns	Total
Sturm, Ruger . . .	328,775	302,318	631,093
Remington Arms . .	1,806	564,609	566,415
Smith & Wesson . .	450,647	-	450,647
Marlin Firearms . .	-	389,990	389,990
O.F. Mossberg . . .	-	308,663	308,663
U.S.			
Repeating Arms .	-	192,782	192,782

Continued on next page.

★ 928 ★ *Continued*

Weapons (SIC 3484)

Top Gun Producers

Gun producers' domestic and foreign sales in 1990. Data show units shipped.

	Hand-Guns	Rifles & Shotguns	Total
Colt	106,997	38,913	145,010
Davis Industries . .	143,252	-	143,252
Beretta U.S.A. . . .	125,027	-	125,027
Raven Arms . . .	119,000	-	119,000

Source: *The New York Times*, March 8, 1992, p. 19, from Bureau of Alcohol, Tobacco, and Firearms.

★ 929 ★

Armaments (SIC 3489)

Arms Manufacturers Worldwide

Sales of the ten leading armament manufacturers are shown in billions of dollars; relative shares are shown in percent. Data are shown for 1989.

	Sales ($ bil.)	% of Group
McDonnell Douglas	$ 8.5	13.8%
General Dynamics	8.4	13.6
Lockheed	7.4	12.0
British Aerospace	6.3	10.2
General Electric	6.3	10.2
General Motors	5.5	8.9
Raytheon	5.3	8.6
Boeing	4.8	7.8
Northrop	4.7	7.6
Rockwell International	4.5	7.3

Source: *Accountancy*, May 1992, from *SIPRI Yearbook 1991*.

★ 930 ★

Armaments (SIC 3489)

Leading Military Equipment Makers Worldwide

Companies are ranked by 1989 sales, shown in billions of dollars. Relative market shares are shown in percent.

	Sales ($ bil.)	% of Group
McDonnell Douglas	$ 8.5	13.8%
General Dynamics	8.4	13.6
Lockheed	7.4	12.0
British Aerospace	6.3	10.2
General Electric	6.3	10.2
General Motors	5.5	8.9
Raytheon	5.3	8.6
Boeing	4.8	7.8
Northrop	4.7	7.6
Rockwell International	4.5	7.3

Source: *Accountancy*, May 1992, p. 67, from *Sipri Yearbook 1991*.

★ 931 ★

Valves (SIC 3491)

Pressure Relief Valve Makers

Company shares are shown in percent.

Crosby	23.0%
DI	21.0
KII	10.0
Other	46.0

Source: Investext, Thomson Financial Networks, January 21, 1992, from Smith Barney, Harris Upham & Co.

★ 932 ★

Valves (SIC 3491)

Quarter-Turn Valve Manufacturers

Shares are shown in percent. "Other" includes Xomox.

	U.S.	World
Duriron	60.0%	40.0%
Other	40.0	60.0

Source: Investext, Thomson Financial Networks, March 12, 1992, from Donaldson, Lufkin & Jenrette Securities.

★ 933 ★
Fabricated Wire (SIC 3496)

Paper Machinery Clothing

Market shares, by company, are shown in percent, based on a global market of $2.8 billion dollars.

Albany	19.0%
Scapa	11.0
BTR	10.0
Other	60.0

Source: Investext, Thomson Financial Networks, June 15, 1992, from Smith New Court Securities plc.

★ 934 ★
Laundry Accessories (SIC 3499)

Laundry Accessories Sales by Category

Ironing board covers and pads

Ironing boards

Individual...

Industry segmentation, by category, is shown in percent, based on a total of $230 million in sales.

Ironing board covers and pads	54.0%
Ironing boards	39.0
Individual dryers and accessories	7.0

Source: *HFD*, February 1992, p. 9.

★ 935 ★
Powder Metallurgy (SIC 3499)

Metal Powder - North America

Segment distribution of shipments in 1990 is shown in percent, based on a total of 268.5 thousand metric tons.

Iron and steel	73.5%
Aluminum	12.2
Copper and copper base	6.4
Nickel	3.4

Tungsten carbide	1.7%
Stainless steel	1.0
Tungsten	0.8
Molybdenum	0.7
Tin	0.3

Source: *U.S. Industrial Outlook 1992*, p. 17-10, from Bureau of Mines and Metal Powder Industries Foundation.

★ 936 ★
Powder Metallurgy (SIC 3499)

Metal Powder - Worldwide

Segment distribution is shown in percent of shipments in 1990, based on a total of 742.5 thousand metric tons. The stainless steel category includes high-speed tool steel. The tungsten category includes tungsten carbide.

Iron and steel	72.7%
Aluminum	12.1
Copper and copper base	5.8
Tungsten	3.6
Stainless steel	3.0
Nickel	2.7

Source: *U.S. Industrial Outlook 1992*, p. 17-10, from Bureau of Mines and Metal Powder Industries Association.

★ 937 ★
Powder Metallurgy (SIC 3499)

Powder Metal Products Use - Australia

Shares, by end use, are shown in percent for fiscal year 1990/91.

Automotive	42.0%
White goods	31.0
General engineering	23.0
Power tools and garden equipment	1.0
Building industry	1.0
Other	2.0

Source: *The International Journal of Powder Metallurgy - Volume 28, NO.3*, 1992, p. 244.

★ 938 ★

Powder Metallurgy (SIC 3499)

Powder Metal Products - Japan

Shares, by product type, are based on a 1991 total production of 91,545 tons.

Powder metal parts	.89.0%
Bearings	9.6
Friction materials	0.6
Electrical collector shoes	0.3
Electrical contacts	0.2
Other	0.3

Source: *The International Journal of Powder Metallurgy*, 1992, p. 227, from Japan Powder Metallurgy Association.

SIC 35 - Industry Machinery and Equipment

★ 939 ★

Industrial and Farm Equipment (SIC 3500)

Industrial and Farm Equipment

Sales by 12 leading industrial and farm equipment manufacturers worldwide are shown in billions of dollars based on a total of $132.86 billion in 1990. Relative market shares are shown in percent.

	Sales ($ bil.)	% of Group
Daewoo	$ 22.26	17.0%
Mitsubishi Heavy Industries	16.40	12.0
Mannesmann	15.09	11.0
Tenneco	14.89	11.0
Caterpillar	11.54	9.0
MAN	10.83	8.0
Deere	7.88	6.0
Hoesch	7.83	6.0
Schneider	6.80	5.0
Kawasaki Heavy Industries	6.53	5.0
Komatsu	6.43	5.0
BICC	6.38	5.0

Source: *Business Horizons*, November 1991, p. 16.

★ 940 ★

Industrial and Farm Equipment (SIC 3500)

Industrial and Farm Equipment Manufacturers

Companies are ranked by 1991 sales, shown in millions of dollars. Relative market shares are based on sales of $85,120 million.

	Sales ($ mil.)	% of Group
Tenneco	$ 14,035	16.5%
Caterpillar	10,182	12.0
Deere	7,055	8.3
Dresser Industries	4,702	5.5
Black & Decker	4,637	5.4
Ingersoll-Rand	3,586	4.2
Cummins Engine	$ 3,406	4.0%
Baker Hughes	2,912	3.4
Parker Hannifin	2,441	2.9
Dover	2,196	2.6
Trinova	1,681	2.0
York International	1,653	1.9
Timken	1,647	1.9
Harnischfeger Ind.	1,624	1.9
NACCO Industries	1,369	1.6
Gt Am. Mgmt. & Invest.	1,330	1.6
Crane	1,303	1.5
Federal-Mogul	1,252	1.5
Figgie International	1,243	1.5
Clark Equipment	1,201	1.4
Tecumseh Products	1,198	1.4
Dresser-Rand	1,192	1.4
Pentair	1,170	1.4
IMO Industries	1,024	1.2
Briggs & Stratton	952	1.1
Nortek	926	1.1
AM International	860	1.0
Lincoln Electric	844	1.0
Terex	803	0.9
Cincinnati Milacron	788	0.9
Interlake	715	0.8
Toro	712	0.8
Blount	673	0.8
Joy Technologies	668	0.8
Pall	663	0.8
Stewart & Stevenson	646	0.8
Applied Materials	644	0.8
Kennametal	619	0.7
Goulds Pumps	569	0.7

Source: *Fortune*, April 20, 1992, p. 274.

★ 941 ★

Farm Machinery (SIC 3520)

European Combine Market

Estimated market shares are shown in percent for 1991. "Other" includes Iseki, Mitsubishi, and Yanmar.

Claas	28.0%
NHGeotech	25.0
Deere	16.0
Massey Ferguson	5.0
J.I. Case	4.0
Other	22.0

Source: Investext, Thomson Financial Networks, May 19, 1992, from The First Boston Corporation.

★ 942 ★

Farm Machinery (SIC 3520)

Farm Equipment Market - Europe

Shares, by company, are shown in percent.

Fiat	17.0%
J. I. Case	12.0-13.0
Deere	10.0
Massey-Ferguson	10.0
Ford-New Holland	10.0
Deutz	10.0
Renault	9.0
Fendt	7.0
SAME	7.0
Steyr	7.0
Other	3.0

Source: Investext, Thomson Financial Networks, June 5, 1992, from The First Boston Corporation.

★ 943 ★

Farm Machinery (SIC 3520)

Farm Equipment Producers Worldwide

Shares of the global market are shown in percent based on a total of $21.3 billion in net sales in 1991.

Deere & Company	19.2%
NHGeotech	16.5
Kubota	15.1
J.I. Case/IH	10.5
Massey Ferguson	5.1
Claas	3.4

Deutz	3.2%
Fendt	2.6
S+L+H	2.0
Renault	1.9
AGCO	1.5
Greenland NV	1.5
Valmet-Volvo	1.5
Gehl Company	0.4
Other	15.5

Source: Investext, Thomson Financial Networks, May 19, 1992, from The First Boston Corporation.

★ 944 ★

Farm Machinery (SIC 3520)

Farm Equipment Producers - 100 HP Tractors

Shares of the North American market for 100-horsepower tractors are shown in percent.

J. I. Case	35.0%
Deere	33.0
NHGeotech	5.0
AGCO	4.0
Massey Ferguson	2.0
Other	21.0

Source: Investext, Thomson Financial Networks, June 5, 1992, from The First Boston Corporation.

★ 945 ★

Farm Machinery (SIC 3520)

Farm Equipment Producers - 40-100 HP

Shares of the North American market for 40-100 horsepower tractors, are shown in percent for 1991.

Deere	30.0%
NHGeotech	25.0
Massey Ferguson	10.0
AGCO	4.0
Other	31.0

Source: Investext, Thomson Financial Networks, June 5, 1992, from The First Boston Corporation.

★ 946 ★

Farm Machinery (SIC 3520)

Farm Equipment Producers - 4-Wheel

Shares of the North American market for 4-wheels, are shown in percent for 1991.

J. I. Case 34.0%
NHGeotech 34.0
Deere 32.0

Source: Investext, Thomson Financial Networks, June 5, 1992, from The First Boston Corporation.

★ 947 ★

Farm Machinery (SIC 3520)

Farm Equipment Producers - Hay Tools

Shares, by company, of the North American market for hay tools, are shown in percent for 1991.

NHGeotech 35.0%
Deere 25.0
J. I. Case 15.0
AGCO 15.0
Gehl 10.0

Source: Investext, Thomson Financial Networks, June 5, 1992, from The First Boston Corporation.

★ 948 ★

Farm Machinery (SIC 3520)

Farm Equipment - Canada

Farm equipment retail sales, by type, are shown in units for 1991. Shares are shown in percent.

	Units	Shares
Balers	2,621	42.5%
Mower conditioners	2,090	33.9
Combines	661	10.7
Swathers	501	8.1
Forage harvesters	287	4.7

Source: *Implement & Tractor*, September 1991, p. 21.

★ 949 ★

Farm Machinery (SIC 3520)

Farm Equipment - U.S.

Data reflect unit sales in July, 1991. Relative market distribution is shown in percent.

	Unit Sales	% of Group
2-wheel-drive tractors	7,919	91.4%
4-wheel-drive tractors	212	2.4
Combines	534	6.2

Source: *Implement & Tractor*, September 1991, p. 4.

★ 950 ★

Farm Machinery (SIC 3520)

Farm Machinery by Type

Number of units sold in 1991 is shown with relative market shares in percent for the same period.

	Units Sold	% of Group
Two-wheel drive tractors	89,905	86.7%
Combines	9,715	9.4
Four-wheel drive tractors	4,069	3.9

Source: *Farm Journal*, February 1992, p. 18, from Equipment Manufacturers Institute.

★ 951 ★

Farm Machinery (SIC 3520)

North American Combine Market

Estimated market shares are shown in percent for 1991.

Deere 50.0%
J.I. Case 35.0
AGCO 5.0
NHGeotech 5.0
Massey Ferguson 4.0
Claas 1.0

Source: Investext, Thomson Financial Networks, May 19, 1992, from The First Boston Corporation.

★ 952 ★

Farm Machinery (SIC 3520)

North American Hay Tool Market

Estimated market shares are shown in percent for 1991.

NHGeotech	35.0%
Deere	25.0
AGCO	15.0
J.I. Case	15.0
Gehl	10.0

Source: Investext, Thomson Financial Networks, May 19, 1992, from The First Boston Corporation.

★ 953 ★

Tractors (SIC 3523)

European Tractor Market (40-100 HP)

Estimated market shares for 40-100 horsepower tractors are shown in percent for 1991. "Other" includes Iseki, Mitsubishi, and Yanmar.

NHGeotech	20.0%
Deere	12.0
Massey Ferguson	12.0
J.I. Case	10.0
Other	44.0

Source: Investext, Thomson Financial Networks, May 19, 1992, from The First Boston Corporation.

★ 954 ★

Tractors (SIC 3523)

North American Four-Wheel Tractor Market

Estimated market shares are shown in percent for 1991.

J.I. Case	34.0%
NHGeotech	34.0
Deere	32.0

Source: Investext, Thomson Financial Networks, May 19, 1992, from The First Boston Corporation.

★ 955 ★

Tractors (SIC 3523)

North American Tractor Market (100 HP)

Estimated market shares for 100-horsepower tractors are shown in percent for 1991. "Other" includes Iseki, Mitsubishi, and Yanmar.

J.I. Case	35.0%
Deere	33.0
NHGeotech	5.0
AGCO	4.0
Massey Ferguson	2.0
Other	21.0

Source: Investext, Thomson Financial Networks, May 19, 1992, from The First Boston Corporation.

★ 956 ★

Tractors (SIC 3523)

North American Tractor Market (40-100 HP)

Estimated market shares for 40-100 horsepower tractors are shown in percent for 1991. "Other" includes Iseki, Mitsubishi, and Yanmar.

Deere	30.0%
NHGeotech	25.0
Massey Ferguson	10.0
AGCO	4.0
Other	31.0

Source: Investext, Thomson Financial Networks, May 19, 1992, from The First Boston Corporation.

★ 957 ★

Tractors (SIC 3523)

Tractor Market (40-100 HP) Worldwide

Estimated market shares for 40-100 horsepower tractors are shown in percent for 1991. "Other" includes Iseki, Mitsubishi, and Yanmar.

NHGeotech	33.0%
Massey Ferguson	22.0
J.I. Case	12.0
Deere	10.0
Other	23.0

Source: Investext, Thomson Financial Networks, May 19, 1992, from The First Boston Corporation.

★958★

Lawn and Garden Equipment (SIC 3524)

Lawn and Garden Equipment Sales

The segmentation of the lawn and garden equipment market is shown in billions of dollars for 1991.

Lawn care	$ 6.9
Landscape	4.8
Flowers	2.3
Vegetables	1.7
Tree care	1.4
Other	5.0

Source: *Chicago Tribune*, April 5, 1992, p. C1, from National Gardening Association.

★959★

Lawn and Garden Equipment (SIC 3524)

Mower and Tiller Shipments

Shares, by type, are based on 6.805 million units shipped in 1991, shown in percent.

Walk-behind mowers	78.4%
Front-engine lawn tractors	12.3
Tillers	4.3
Rear-engine riding mowers	3.1
Riding garden tractors	1.9

Source: *Hardware Age*, July 1992, p. 93, from Outdoor Power Equipment Institute.

★960★

Lawn and Garden Equipment (SIC 3524)

Outdoor Appliances

Market shares by product type are shown in percent, based on total of 73,445,570 units in 1991.

Bug killers	5.7%
Chain saws, gasoline	5.0
Leaf blowers, back pack, gasoline	0.3
Leaf blowers, hand held, gasoline	2.4
Outdoor grills, charcoal	32.2
Outdoor grills, electric	0.6
Outdoor grills, gas	16.0
Power mowers, walk behind	20.4
Riding mowers and lawn tractors	4.0

Riding garden tractors	0.5%
Rotary tillers	1.1
Snowthrowers	1.1
Trimmers, monofilament, gasoline	10.7

Source: *Appliance*, April 1992, p. 54.

★961★

Lawn and Garden Equipment (SIC 3524)

Outdoor Power Equipment

Shares by type are based on unit shipments in 1991 and 1992 (forecast).

	1991	1992
Walk-behind mowers	66.3%	65.1%
Front-engine lawn tractors	10.6	11.3
Rear-engine riding mowers	2.8	3.0
Tillers	3.3	2.8
Riding garden tractors	1.7	1.8
All riding units	15.2	16.0

Source: *Hardware Age*, July 1991, p. 66, from Outdoor Power Equipment Institute, Inc.

★962★

Mining Machinery (SIC 3532)

Coal Mining Machinery Market

Estimated domestic company shares of underground coal mining continuous miners is shown in percent for 1991.

Joy Technologies	63.0%
Jeffery	12.0-15.0
Simmons-Rand	10.0
Eimco	10.0
Other	2.0-5.0

Source: Investext, Thomson Financial Networks, February 11, 1992, from The First Boston Corporation.

★ 963 ★

Oil and Gas Field Machinery (SIC 3533)

Offshore Rigs by Type

Percent distribution of offshore mobile and platform rigs, by type, is based on a total of 1,094 rigs as of December 1990.

Jackup	.39.2%
Self-contained platform	.30.2
Semisubmersible	.15.9
Drillship	.11.2
Other	3.5

Source: *JPT*, March 1992, p. 355.

★ 964 ★

Oil and Gas Field Machinery (SIC 3533)

Oil Well Production

Shares by well type are shown in percent, based on U.S. total of 613,810 oil wells at the end of 1991.

Artificial lift	.93.5%
Flowing	6.5

Source: *World Oil*, February 1992, p. 67.

★ 965 ★

Oil and Gas Field Machinery (SIC 3533)

U.S. Rig Fleet

Shares by type are shown in percent, based on totals of 2,320 rigs available in 1990 and 2,251 rigs available in 1991.

	1990	1991
Diesel	81.5%	79.9%
Electric	17.6	19.5
Gas	0.9	0.7

Source: *World Oil*, October 1992, p. 54.

★ 966 ★

Material Handling (SIC 3535)

Material Handling Forecast

Market segmentation is forecast for 1995, based on a total market of $1.439 billion. AS/RS stands for automatic storage and retrieval systems. AGVs stands for automatic guided vehicle systems.

Services	.24.0%
Conveyors	.22.0
AS/RS	.20.0
Carousels	.11.0
Monorail	9.0
AGVs	8.0
Robots	6.0

Source: *American Machinist*, August 1991, p. 29, from Frost & Sullivan.

★ 967 ★

Construction Equipment (SIC 3537)

Construction Machinery Market

Market segmentation, by company, is shown in percent for 1991.

Caterpillar	.40.0+%
Komatsu	15.0
Other	45.0

Source: Investext, Thomson Financial Networks, May 13, 1992, from Shearson Lehman Brothers, Inc.

★ 968 ★
Machine Tools (SIC 3540)

Leading Machine Tool Makers Worldwide

| Amada |
| Yamazaki Mazak |
| Fanuc |
| Okuma Machinery Works |
| Litton Industries |
| Giddings & Lewis |
| Mori Seiki |
| Komatsu |
| Schuler Group |
| Toyota Mach. |

Companies are ranked by machine tool sales, shown in millions of dollars and as a percent of group total.

	Sales ($ mil.)	% of Group
Amada	$ 1,207	15.8%
Yamazaki Mazak	1,150	15.1
Fanuc	1,100	14.4
Okuma Machinery Works	739	9.7
Litton Industries	721	9.4
Giddings & Lewis	663	8.7
Mori Seiki	661	8.7
Komatsu	470	6.2
Schuler Group	464	6.1
Toyota Mach.	464	6.1

Source: *Ward's Autoworld*, May 1992, p. 55, from *American Machinist* and German Association of Machine Tool Builders.

★ 969 ★
Machine Tools (SIC 3540)

Machine Tool Market

Market shares are shown in percent, based on sales totals of $4,169 million in 1991 (estimate) and $4,962 million in 1992 (forecast).

	'91	'92
Metal cutting machines	65.9%	65.4%
Metal forming machines	34.1	34.6

Source: *U.S. Industrial Outlook 1992*, p. 18-2, from U.S. Census of Commerce, Bureau of the Census.

★ 970 ★
Machine Tools (SIC 3540)

Machine Tool Production Worldwide - 1991

Shares by type are based on world total of $41,524 million dollars in 1991, shown in percent.

| Cutting | 73.2% |
| Forming | 26.8 |

Source: *American Machinist*, February 1992, p. 60.

★ 971 ★
Machine Tools (SIC 3540)

Machine Tool Production - 1991

Shares by type are based on 1991 total production value of $2,740.0 million dollars, shown in percent.

| Cutting | 68.2% |
| Forming | 31.8 |

Source: *American Machinist*, February 1992, p. 60.

★ 972 ★
Machine Tools (SIC 3541)

Machine Tool Market - 1990

Shares by type of machine are shown in percent, based on U.S. consumption value in 1990.

Machining centers	17.1%
Grinding machines	12.6
Station-type	11.7
NC horizontal lathes	10.7
Other metal forming	6.7
Presses	6.6
Milling machines	5.7
Other metal cutting	5.5
Bending and forming	5.1
Boring and drilling	4.9
Punching and shearing	4.4
Non-NC lathes	3.4
Gear cutting	2.1
Forging machines	1.8
NC vertical lathes	1.7

Source: Investext, Thomson Financial Networks, April 28, 1992, from Schroder Securities (Japan) Limited.

★ 973 ★

Machine Tools (SIC 3541)

Machine Tool Production

Distribution, by type, is shown in percent, based on an estimated total of $2.740 billion in 1991.

Cutting 68.2%
Forming 31.8

Source: *American Machinist*, February 1992, p. 60.

★ 974 ★

Machine Tools (SIC 3541)

Machine Tool Production Worldwide

Distribution, by type, is shown in percent, based on an estimated total of $41.524 billion in 1991.

Cutting 73.2%
Forming 26.8

Source: *American Machinist*, February 1992, p. 60.

★ 975 ★

Textile Machinery (SIC 3552)

Textile Machinery - Pakistan

Textile machinery by type are shown with number of units installed in 1990-91 period. Shares are shown in percent.

	Units (000)	Shares
Ring spindles	5,569	98.5%
Rotors	72	1.3
Looms	15	0.3

Source: *Textile World*, June 1992, p. 62.

★ 976 ★

Printing Presses (SIC 3555)

Printing Presses Using Recycled Stock

SF

Web

Both

Recycled paper stock, by type of press, is shown in percent.

SF 40.0%
Web 30.0
Both 30.0

Source: *High Volume Printing*, February 1991, p. 4.

★ 977 ★

Glass Furnaces (SIC 3559)

Glass Furnace Use

Shares, by segment of the glass market, are shown in percent, based on an estimated total of 501 units.

Technical and specialty 36.9%
Container 32.9
Fiber 22.0
Flat 8.2

Source: *Ceramic Industry*, March 1992, p. 50, from F. Tooley.

★ 978 ★

Glass Furnaces (SIC 3559)

Glass Furnaces by Type

Distribution in the U.S. is shown in percent, by type of furnace, based on an estimated total of 501 furnaces.

Regenerative
  Side port 39.9%
  End port 15.4
Recuperative 17.6
Electric 15.7
Direct-fired
  Air/fuel 8.0
  Oxy-fuel 3.4

Source: *Ceramic Industry*, March 1992, p. 50, from F. Tooley.

Pumps (SIC 3561)

Pump Manufacturers

Shares of the domestic market are shown in percent.

Duriron	40.0%
Goulds	40.0
Other	20.0

Source: Investext, Thomson Financial Networks, March 12, 1992, from Donaldson, Lufkin & Jenrette Securities.

Air Filtration (SIC 3564)

Air Filtration Use

Distribution of market applications in the U.S. is shown in percent. The 1991 market was approximately $800 million.

Industrial manufacturing	25.0%
Residential buildings	14.0
Public and commercial buildings	11.0
Health treatment facilities	8.0
Autos	7.0
Power generation	7.0
Fabricated metals	7.0
Electronic manufacturing	5.0
Pharmaceuticals	5.0
Utilities	5.0
Education	3.0
Locomotives	3.0

Source: *Heating/Piping/Air Conditioning*, January 1992, p. 100, from SnyderGeneral Corporation.

Automation (SIC 3569)

AGV and AEM Sales

Market share by application is shown as percentage of sales for 1990, 1991 and 1992. AGV stands for automated guided vehicle. AEM stands for automated electrified monorail.

	'90	'91	'92
Automotive	26.0%	26.4%	26.8%
Consumer prods.	19.7	20.0	20.3
Electronic	11.8	11.9	12.0
Aerospace/defense	12.4	11.8	11.2
Heavy engineering	8.7	8.7	8.7
Other	21.4	21.2	21.0

Source: *Manufacturing Engineering*, April 1992, p. 16, from Market Intelligence Research Company.

Electronic Equipment (SIC 3569)

Electronic Assembly Equipment - Germany

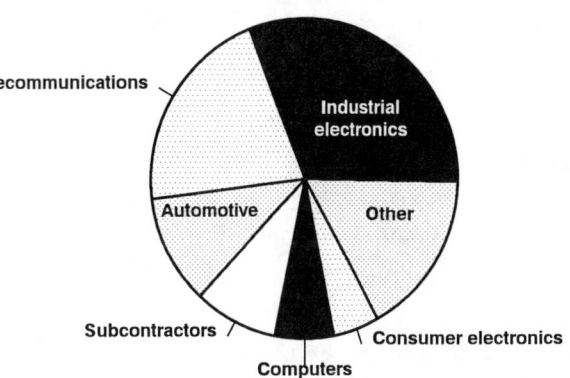

Shares of the German market for pick-and-place equipment, by end-use, are shown in percent for 1990.

Industrial electronics	31.0%
Telecommunications	21.0
Automotive	11.0
Subcontractors	9.0
Computers	6.0
Consumer electronics	5.0
Other	17.0

Source: *Electronic Business*, April 27, 1992, p. 108, from Siemens AG.

★ 983 ★
Robots (SIC 3569)

Robot Applications

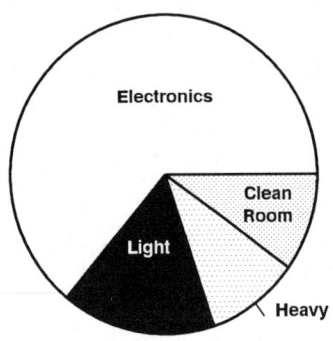

Distribution of robot sales for U.S. assembly applications is shown in percent for 1990 and 1997 (forecasted).

	1990	1997
Electronics	46.0%	64.0%
Light	21.0	16.0
Heavy	17.0	10.0
Clean Room	16.0	10.0

Source: *Manufacturing Engineering*, June 1992, p. 14, from MIRC.

★ 984 ★
Computer-Based Systems (SIC 3570)

Computer-Based Systems - Top Producers

Company sales are shown in millions of dollars for fiscal 1991. Relative market shares are shown in percent.

	($ mil.)	% of Group
Symbol Technologies	$ 319.4	28.0%
Sensormatic Electronics	239.2	20.9
VeriFone	187.9	16.4
BancTec	183.8	16.1
FileNet	122.5	10.7
Landmark Graphics	89.9	7.9

Source: *Electronic Business*, May 18, 1992, p. 91.

★ 985 ★
Computers (SIC 3571)

10 Leading Computer Makers Worldwide

Sales for 1990 are shown in millions of dollars. Percent shares are based on a group total.

	Sales ($ mil.)	% of Group
IBM	$ 64,637	41.8%
Fujitsu	15,998	10.3
Digital Equipment	13,072	8.5
NEC	11,841	7.7
Hitachi	10,843	7.0
Unisys	10,111	6.5
Hewlett-Packard	8,313	5.4
Siemens	6,987	4.5
Olivetti	6,485	4.2
Groupe Bull	6,390	4.1

Source: *Financial World*, January 21, 1992, p. 52, from Gartner Group's Yardstick Top 100 Worldwide; Warner Computer and Services: earnings estimates courtesy of I/B/E/S.

★ 986 ★
Computers (SIC 3571)

3-D Graphics Hardware Market

Market shares are based on total of units sold and revenues in 1991.

	Units	Shares
Silicon Graphics	12,409	29.2%
Hewlett-Packard	9,881	21.8
IBM	6,646	21.5
DEC	4,843	17.0
Stardent	1,843	4.4
Sun	1,179	3.9
Intergraph	836	2.2

Source: *UniForum Monthly*, November 1992, p. 20, from InfoCorp.

	Sales ($ mil.)	% of Group
AST Research	$ 697	0.5%
Bell & Howell	625	0.4

Source: *Fortune*, April 20, 1992, p. 264.

★ 987 ★
Computers (SIC 3571)

Communications - Leading Producers

Company sales are shown in millions of dollars for fiscal 1991. Relative market shares, based on group total sales, are shown in percent.

	Sales ($ mil.)	% of Group
3Com	$ 398.6	26.2%
Inmac	302.8	19.9
SynOptics Communications . . .	248.3	16.3
Cabletron Systems	180.5	11.9
Octel Communications	160.3	10.5
Digital Microwave	136.0	8.9
Proteon	94.7	6.2

Source: *Electronic Business*, May 18, 1992, p. 91.

★ 988 ★
Computers (SIC 3571)

Computer and Office Machine Makers

Companies are ranked by dollar sales in 1991. Percent shares are based on a group total of $140,054 million.

	Sales ($ mil.)	% of Group
IBM	$ 64,792	46.6%
Hewlett-Packard	14,541	10.5
Digital Equipment	14,024	10.1
Unisys	8,696	6.3
Apple Computer	6,309	4.5
Pitney Bowes	3,417	2.5
Compaq Computer	3,271	2.4
Sun Microsystems	3,260	2.3
Seagate Technology	2,691	1.9
Wang Laboratories	2,127	1.5
Tandem Computers	1,940	1.4
Amdahl	1,702	1.2
Storage Technology	1,653	1.2
Conner Peripherals	1,627	1.2
Dr Holdings (Del.)	1,391	1.0
Data General	1,237	0.9
Intergraph	1,205	0.9
SCI Systems	1,129	0.8
Quantum	878	0.6
Maxtor	875	0.6
Cray Research	862	0.6

★ 989 ★
Computers (SIC 3571)

Computer Industry Leaders

Company revenue per employee is shown in dollars and as percent of group total.

	Rev. per employee	% of Group
Apple	$ 451,600	19.1%
Compaq	317,500	13.5
NEC	198,200	8.4
IBM	184,600	7.8
Hitachi	162,400	6.9
Groupe Bull	152,700	6.5
Fujitsu	145,600	6.2
Hewlett-Packard	143,800	6.1
Olivetti	140,600	6.0
Unisys	134,300	5.7
NCR	116,300	4.9
Siemens	106,700	4.5
Digital	105,500	4.5

Source: *Fortune*, July 15, 1991, p. 45.

★ 990 ★
Computers (SIC 3571)

Computer Manufacturers - 1990

Company shares are shown as percent of the global market, based on unit shipments.

IBM	12.9%
Apple	7.2
Commodore	6.4
NEC	5.7
Compaq	3.7
Toshiba	3.1
Tandy/Grid/Victo	2.7

Continued on next page.

★ 990 ★ *Continued*

Computers (SIC 3571)

Computer Manufacturers - 1990

Company shares are shown as percent of the global market, based on unit shipments.

Astrad	2.5%
Seiko/Epson	2.4
Olivetti	2.1
Other	51.3

Source: Investext, Thomson Financial Networks, May 28, 1992, from UBS Phillips & Drew Global Research Group.

★ 991 ★

Computers (SIC 3571)

Computer Market by Type

Market distribution by type is shown in percent, based on total shipments of $59 billion in 1991 and a projected $85 billion in 1995.

	1991	1995
PCs	76.0%	57.0%
Workstations	13.0	24.0
Portables	11.0	19.0

Source: *Systems Integration Business*, May 1992, p. 52, from BIS Strategic Decisions.

★ 992 ★

Computers (SIC 3571)

Computer Use by Category

Computer use in the security field, by category, is shown in precent.

Desktop	78.0%
Network	56.0
Mini	32.0
Portable	26.0
Other	9.0

Source: *Security*, January 1992, p. 9.

★ 993 ★

Computers (SIC 3571)

Computer Workstation Market

Sun
Hewlett-Packard
IBM
Digital
Other

Shares are shown in percent for the past 12 months.

Sun	43.0%
Hewlett-Packard	14.0
IBM	14.0
Digital	13.0
Other	16.0

Source: *Datamation*, November 15, 1991, p. 66, from *Datamation/* Cowen & Co.

★ 994 ★

Computers (SIC 3571)

Computers - Leading Producers

Company sales are shown in millions of dollars for fiscal 1991. Relative market shares, based on group total sales, are shown in percent.

	Sales ($ mil.)	% of Group
Apple Computer	$ 6,308.8	32.0%
Compaq Computer	3,271.4	16.6
Sun Microsystems	3,221.0	16.4
Tandem Computers	1,922.2	9.8
Dell Computer	889.9	4.5
AST Research	688.5	3.5
Silicon Graphics	549.9	2.8
Tandon	461.4	2.3
Stratus Computer	448.6	2.3
Terdata	257.8	1.3
Concurrent Computer	254.9	1.3
Zeos International	230.9	1.2
Advanced Logic Research	228.0	1.2
Pyramid Technology	227.9	1.2
Sequent Computer Systems	213.3	1.1
Convex Computer	198.1	1.0
MIPS Computer Systems	168.5	0.9
Encore Computer	150.0	0.8

Source: *Electronic Business*, May 18, 1992, p. 91.

★ 995 ★
Computers (SIC 3571)

Laptop/Notebook PC Market Leaders

Market shares are shown in percent for the past 12 months.

Toshiba	15.0%
Compaq	14.0
IBM	10.
Zenith	6.0
Dell	3.0
AST	3.0
Other	49.0

Source: *Datamation*, November 15, 1991, p. 65, from *Datamation*/ Cowen & Co.

★ 996 ★
Computers (SIC 3571)

Leading Computer Makers in Czechoslovakia

Company shipments are shown in millions of dollars for 1989. Relative market shares are shown in percent.

	Shipm. ($ mil.)	% of Group
ICL	$ 5.7	46.0%
Siemens	5.7	46.0
Olivetti	1.0	8.1

Source: *Electronics*, July 1991, p. 35.

★ 997 ★
Computers (SIC 3571)

Leading Computer Makers in Hungary

Company shipments are shown in millions of dollars for 1989. Relative market shares are shown in percent.

	Shipm. ($ mil.)	% of Group
Olivetti	$ 2.7	40.3%
IBM	2.5	37.3
ICL	1.5	22.4

Source: *Electronics*, July 1991, p. 35.

★ 998 ★
Computers (SIC 3571)

Leading Computer Makers in Poland

Company shipments are shown in millions of dollars for 1989. Relative market shares are shown in percent.

	Shipm. ($ mil.)	% of Group
IBM	$ 4.8	37.8%
Siemens	4.2	33.1
ICL	3.7	29.1

Source: *Electronics*, July 1991, p. 35.

★ 999 ★
Computers (SIC 3571)

Leading PC Companies in the U.S.

Companies are ranked by 1990 PC revenues, shown in millions of dollars. Relative market shares are shown in percent.

	Rev ($ mil.)	% of Group
IBM	$ 3,760.00	26.4%
Apple Computer Inc.	2,230.00	15.7
Compaq Computer Corp. . . .	1,600.00	11.2
Tandy Corp.	1,000.00	7.0
Toshiba America Information Systems Inc. . . .	800.00	5.6
Unisys Corp.	567.00	4.0
AT&T	560.00	3.9
Zenith Data Systems Inc. . . .	560.00	3.9
Intel Corp.	529.00	3.7

Continued on next page.

★ 999 ★ *Continued*

Computers (SIC 3571)

Leading PC Companies in the U.S.

Companies are ranked by 1990 PC revenues, shown in millions of dollars. Relative market shares are shown in percent.

	Rev ($ mil.)	% of Group
Hewlett-Packard Co.	$ 387.00	2.7%
Dell Computer Corp.	382.00	2.7
Epson America Inc.	300.00	2.1
NEC Technologies Inc.	300.00	2.1
AST Research Inc.	299.40	2.1
Everex Systems Inc.	223.00	1.6
Northgate Computer Systems Inc.	191.00	1.3
Wyse Technology	166.25	1.2
Advanced Logic Research . . .	163.40	1.1
Zeos International Ltd.	120.75	0.8
Club American Technologies Inc.	100.00	0.7

Source: *Datamation*, December 1, 1991, p. 44, from company reports, *Datamation*, and Brand Preference Report.

★ 1000 ★

Computers (SIC 3571)

Magazine Pre-Press Market

Shares of computer use in magazine production (pre-press operations) are shown in percent. Totals may not add to 100% due to rounding.

	Edit. Work	Page Design
Macs	28.5%	70.3%
PCs	58.2	16.4
Other	7.9	9.1
No answer	5.5	4.2

Source: *Folio*, August 1991, p. 58, from survey.

★ 1001 ★

Computers (SIC 3571)

Midrange Computer Market by RISC Supplier

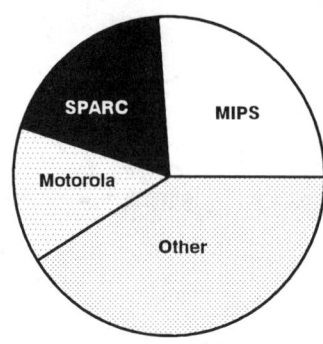

Shares of the midrange market, by RISC (reduced instruction set computer) supplier, are shown in percent.

MIPS	26.0%
SPARC	19.0
Motorola	14.0
Other	41.0

Source: *Datamation*, June 1, 1991, p. 33, from Gather Group.

★ 1002 ★

Computers (SIC 3571)

Multimedia PC Market

Business desktop

Education

Training

Kiosk

Industrial

Market segments are shown in percent, based on a total of 792 units shipped in 1991.

Business desktop	61.4%
Education	17.7
Training	13.5
Kiosk	5.2
Industrial	2.3

Source: *PC Week*, May 25, 1992, p. 113, from Intelco.

★ 1003 ★

Computers (SIC 3571)

Notebook Computer Manufacturers - U.K.

Shares of units and of market value are shown in percent based on indirect shipments of notebook computers in the U.K. for the period from January to October 1991.

	Units	Value
Toshiba	49.4%	39.0%
Compaq	30.8	43.0
Sanyo	7.9	6.4
Commodore	3.2	4.1
Other	8.7	7.5

Source: *Financial Times*, February 17, 1992, p. 3, from ROMTEC.

★ 1004 ★

Computers (SIC 3571)

Notebook Computer Market

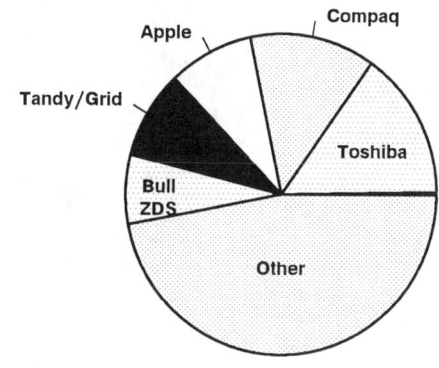

Manufacturer shares of the notebook computer market are shown in percent.

Toshiba	14.6%
Compaq	13.2
Apple	9.3
Tandy/Grid	9.1
Bull ZDS	7.3
Other	46.5

Source: *Infoworld*, June 22, 1992, p. S69, from International Data Corp.

★ 1005 ★

Computers (SIC 3571)

Notebook Computer Market

1991 U.S. sales, by company, are shown in thousands of units. Relative market shares are shown in percent.

	Units (000)	% of Group
Compaq	98.5	22.8%
Toshiba	98.5	22.8
Apple	68.2	15.8
AST Research	60.6	14.0
Tandy/Grid	53.0	12.3
TI	53.0	12.3

Source: *Electronic Business*, May 18, 1992, p. 128, from IDC.

★ 1006 ★

Computers (SIC 3571)

PC Manufacturers Worldwide

The largest PC companies are ranked by PC revenues in 1990, shown in millions of dollars. Relative market shares are based on total PC revenues of $45,230.19 million. NEC includes revenues from NEC Technologies Inc.; Toshiba includes revenues from Toshiba America Information Systems Inc.; Bull includes revenues from Zenith Data Systems; Seiko Epson includes revenues from Epson America Inc.; Acer Inc. includes revenues from Acer America Corp.; Mitac International Corp. includes revenues from American Mitac Corp.

	Rev ($ mil.)	% of Group
IBM	$ 9,644.00	26.6%
Apple Computer Inc.	3,845.80	10.6
NEC Corp.	3,620.00	10.0
Compaq Computer Corp.	3,598.00	9.9
Toshiba Corp.	2,488.30	6.9
Ing. C. Olivetti & Co. SpA	1,791.70	4.9
Fujitsu Ltd.	1,419.60	3.9
Unisys Corp.	1,181.00	3.3
Compagnie De Machines Bull	1,142.90	3.2
Commodore International Ltd.	995.70	2.7
Intel Corp.	980.00	2.7
Tandy Corp.	850.30	2.3
Aser Inc.	739.60	2.0

Continued on next page.

★ 1006 ★ *Continued*

Computers (SIC 3571)

PC Manufacturers Worldwide

The largest PC companies are ranked by PC revenues in 1990, shown in millions of dollars. Relative market shares are based on total PC revenues of $45,230.19 million. NEC includes revenues from NEC Technologies Inc.; Toshiba includes revenues from Toshiba America Information Systems Inc.; Bull includes revenues from Zenith Data Systems; Seiko Epson includes revenues from Epson America Inc.; Acer Inc. includes revenues from Acer America Corp.; Mitac International Corp. includes revenues from American Mitac Corp.

	Rev ($ mil.)	% of Group
Hitachi Ltd.	$ 718.40	2.0%
Siemens Nixdorf Informationssysteme GmbH	709.90	2.0
Tatung Co.	150.20	0.4
Leading Technology Inc. . . .	150.00	0.4
Triad Computing Inc.	144.69	0.4
Zeos International Ltd. . . .	127.10	0.4
Laser Computer Inc.	125.00	0.3
Memorex Telex NV	213.30	0.6
Northgate Computer Systems Inc.	203.40	0.6
Mitsubishi Electric Corp. . . .	201.30	0.6
DTK Computer Inc.	200.00	0.6
Goldstar Co. Ltd.	195.50	0.5
Wyse Technology	175.00	0.5
Advanced Logic Research Inc. .	172.00	0.5
Omron Corp.	167.90	0.5
Matsushita Electric Industrial Co. Ltd.	164.10	0.5
International Computers Ltd. . .	159.00	0.4

Source: *Datamation*, December 1, 1991, p. 42.

★ 1007 ★

Computers (SIC 3571)

PC Market Shares - 1990

Company shares are shown in percent based on 1990 revenues of $23.7 billion.

IBM	16.9%
Apple	12.1
Others	71.0

Source: *Electronics*, August 1991, p. 27, from Dataquest Inc.

★ 1008 ★

Computers (SIC 3571)

PC Market - 1990

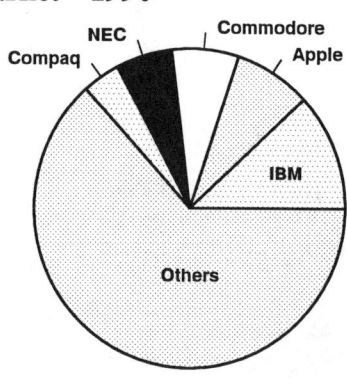

Company shares of 1990 PC (personal computer) market are shown in percent, based on total of 24 million units. All PCs are based on Intel architecture, except Apple's machines.

IBM	11.9%
Apple	7.5
Commodore	7.1
NEC	5.6
Compaq	3.9
Others	64.0

Source: *Electronics*, November 1992, p. 59, from Dataquest Inc.

★ 1009 ★

Computers (SIC 3571)

PC Market - 1991

Manufacturer shares of the 1991 personal computer market (total units 9.4 million) are shown in percent.

IBM	14.4%
Apple	14.0
Packard Bell	4.8
Compaq	4.1
Tandy/Grid	3.7
AST Research	2.8
Gateway 2000	2.6
Other	53.6

Source: *The Wall Street Journal*, July 21, 1992, p. B3, from International Data Corp.

★ 1010 ★

Computers (SIC 3571)

PC Market - Japan

NEC

Fujitsu

Toshiba

Seiko Epson

IBM Japan

Apple Computer Co.

Other

Shares of the 1991 market are shown, by company, in percent.

NEC	52.8%
Fujitsu	8.0
Toshiba	7.9
Seiko Epson	7.7
IBM Japan	6.9
Apple Computer Co.	6.0
Other	10.7

Source: *The Wall Street Journal*, November 19, 1992, p. B4, from Dataquest Japan, Ltd.

★ 1011 ★

Computers (SIC 3571)

Pen-Based Computer Market

Anticipated U.S. pen-based personal computer shipments, by application type, are shown for 1992 and 1993.

	1992	1993
Horizontal	100,000	1,000,000
Vertical	140,000	423,000

Source: *PC Week*, April 13, 1992, p. 6, from Lempesis Research.

★ 1012 ★

Computers (SIC 3571)

Personal Computer Makers

Company sales in 1991 are shown in millions of units. Percent shares of the market are based on a total of 9.8 million units.

	Vol. (mil.)	Shares
IBM	1,490	15.2%
Apple	1,340	13.7
Packard Bell	420	4.3
Compaq Computer Corp.	400	4.1
Tandy Corp.	385	3.9
AST Research	250	2.6
Gateway 2000	235	2.4
Everex Systems	215	2.2
Zenith Data Systems	215	2.2
Toshiba America	200	2.0
Other	4,650	47.4

Source: *Advertising Age*, April 27, 1992, p. 37, from International Data Corp.

★ 1013 ★
Computers (SIC 3571)

Personal Computer Market

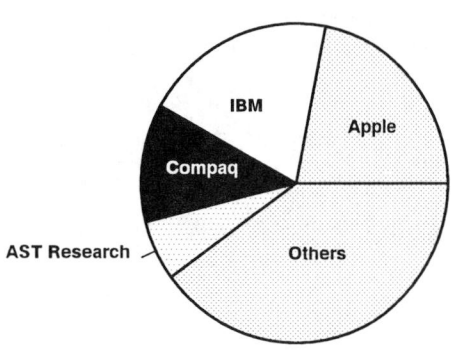

Company shares are shown in percent for 1991 and 1992 based on January sales.

	Jan 1991	Jan 1992
Apple	16.4%	21.5%
IBM	28.5	20.3
Compaq	17.0	12.4
AST Research	4.3	5.6
Others	33.8	40.2

Source: *PC Week*, April 16, 1992, p. 1, from Storeboard.

★ 1014 ★
Computers (SIC 3571)

Portable Computer Manufacturers - U.K.

Shares of units and of market value are shown in percent based on indirect shipments of portable computers in the U.K. for the period from January to October 1991.

	Units	Value
Toshiba	37.0%	30.8%
Compaq	29.2	40.6
Amstrad	12.3	7.2
Sanyo	5.0	3.8
Commodore	2.1	2.4
Other	14.4	15.2

Source: *Financial Times*, February 17, 1992, p. 3, from ROMTEC.

★ 1015 ★
Computers (SIC 3571)

Portable Computer Market - Japan

Manufacturer shares are shown in percent.

NEC and Seiko Epson Corp.	70.0%
Apple Japan	3.0
IBM, Toshiba, and others	27.0

Source: *The Wall Street Journal*, February 11, 1992, p. B7, from Toshiba.

★ 1016 ★
Computers (SIC 3571)

Portable PC Vendors

Shares of the domestic market are shown as percent of portable computers shipped in 1990.

Toshiba	20.9%
Compaq	15.1
Tandy Corp.	10.2
Bull Group	10.1
NEC	5.0
Other	38.7

Source: *The Wall Street Journal*, February 11, 1992, p. B6, from Toshiba.

★ 1017 ★
Computers (SIC 3571)

Supercomputer Producers Worldwide

Shares of the 1991 global market are shown in percent.

Cray Research	36.3%
Fujitsu Ltd.	5.6
Other	58.1

Source: *The Wall Street Journal*, March 4, 1992, p. B5, from Dataquest, Inc.

★ 1018 ★
Computers (SIC 3571)

Unix-Based Hardware Market in France

1990 vendor shares are based on number of machines installed, shown in percent.

Sun	20.4%
HP	17.9

Continued on next page.

★**1018**★ *Continued*

Computers (SIC 3571)

Unix-Based Hardware Market in France

1990 vendor shares are based on number of machines installed, shown in percent.

Bull	7.9%
Altos	4.8
Cetia	3.7
IBM	3.3
TI	2.4
NCR	2.4
Olivetti	2.3
Other	34.9

Source: *UniForum Monthly*, March 1992, p. 32.

★**1019**★

Computers (SIC 3571)

X-Terminal Manufacturers

Shares are shown in percent, based on a total of 118,800 units shipped in 1991.

Network Computing Devices Inc.	25.0%
Hewlett-Packard Co.	17.0
DEC	14.0
IBM	11.0
Tektronix Inc.	7.0
C. Itoh & Co. Ltd.	4.0
Other	22.0

Source: *PC Week*, June 15, 1992, p. 22.

★**1020**★

Workstations (SIC 3571)

Workstation Leaders - 1991

Companies are ranked by number of units shipped in 1991; relative market shares are shown in percent.

	Unit Ship.	% of Group
Sun	215,000	45.5%
Hewlett-Packard	85,000	18.0
DEC	77,000	16.3
IBM	45,000	9.5
NeXT	36,000	7.6
Silicon Graphics	15,000	3.2

Source: *Electronics*, April 1992, p. 33, from International Data Corp.

★**1021**★

Workstations (SIC 3571)

Workstation Manufacturers

Shares are shown in percent based on a total of 401,500 units shipped worldwide in 1991.

Sun Microsystems	46.9%
Hewlett-Packard	20.6
DEC	16.2
IBM	11.5
NeXT	4.8

Source: *PC Week*, May 18, 1992, p. 189, from Dataquest, Inc.

★**1022**★

Workstations (SIC 3571)

Workstation Market by RISC Supplier

Shares of workstation market, by RISC (reduced instruction set computer) supplier, are shown in percent.

SPARC	36.0%
MIPS	24.0
Motorola	11.0
Other	29.0

Source: *Datamation*, June 1, 1991, p. 33, from Gather Group.

★ 1023 ★
Workstations (SIC 3571)

Workstation Market - 1990

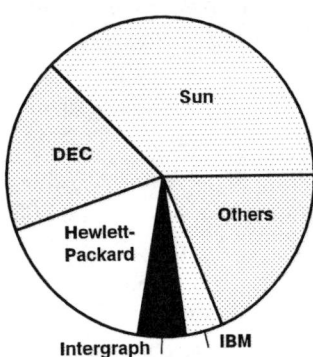

Company shares of the 1990 workstation market are shown in percent, based on a total of 386,000 units. All workstations are based on non-Intel architecture.

Sun (SPARC)	37.5%
DEC (MIPS)	17.5
Hewlett-Packard (HP-PA)	16.7
Intergraph (Clipper)	5.2
IBM (R6000)	4.2
Others	18.8

Source: *Electronics*, November 1992, p. 59, from Dataquest Inc.

★ 1024 ★
Workstations (SIC 3571)

Workstation Market - Worldwide

Company shares of global workstation market, based on 1991 total revenues of $8.8 billion, are shown in percent.

Sun Microsystems	29.0%
Hewlett-Packard	18.8
IBM	16.0
DEC	11.6
Intergraph	5.9
Other	18.7

Source: *Electronic Business*, April 27, 1992, p. 87, from Dataquest Inc..

★ 1025 ★
Workstations (SIC 3571)

Workstation Producers

Producers' shares of the worldwide workstation market are shown in percent, based on factory revenues of $8.8 billion in 1991. Figures did not add to 100% in original source.

Sun Microsystems	29.0%
Hewlett-Packard	18.8
IBM	16.0
Digital	11.6
Others	18.6

Source: *The New York Times*, January 31, 1992, p. C1, from Dataquest and Datastream.

★ 1026 ★
Workstations (SIC 3571)

Workstation Shipments Worldwide

1991 estimated vendor shares of worldwide workstation shipments are shown in percent.

Sun Microsystems	36.0%
Hewlett-Packard	16.0
DEC	13.0
IBM	9.0
Intergraph	4.0
Silicon Graphics	2.0
Other	20.0

Source: *Informationweek*, December 9, 1991, p. 17, from Dataquest.

★ 1027 ★

Workstations (SIC 3571)

Workstation Shipments - Third Quarter

Six leading vendor relative shares of workstation shipments in 1991 third quarter are based on group total of 98,356 units (80% of the total workstation market). Data are shown in number of units shipped and as percent of group total.

	Units	% of Group
Sun Microsystems	43,005	43.7%
Hewlett-Packard	20,850	21.2
DEC	14,150	14.4
IBM	11,635	11.8
Intergraph	5,316	5.4
SGI	3,400	3.5

Source: *Infomationweek*, December 2, 1991, p. 15, from Dataquest.

★ 1028 ★

Workstations (SIC 3571)

Workstation Vendors

Shares are shown as percent of factory revenue in 1990.

Sun Microsystems	29.0%
HP/Apollo	23.0
DEC	18.0
Intergraph	6.0
Silicon Graphics	5.0
IBM	4.0
Other	15.0

Source: *Information Executive*, September 1991, p. 54, from Dataquest.

★ 1029 ★

Workstations (SIC 3571)

Workstation Vendors

Shares of planning sites in 1991 are shown in percent.

IBM	50.0%
Sun Microsystems	22.0
Hewlett-Packard	10.0
DEC	8.0
Silicon Graphics	1.0
Other	9.0

Source: Investext, Thomson Financial Networks, February 26, 1992, from Dean Witter Reynolds.

★ 1030 ★

Workstations (SIC 3571)

Workstation Worldwide Sales - 1991

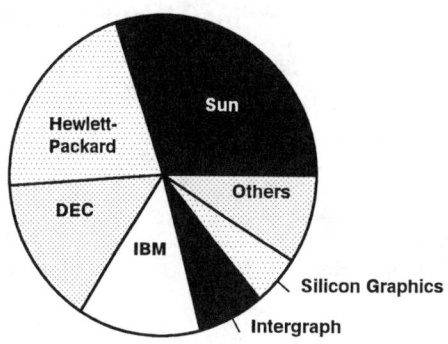

Company shares are based on 1991 worldwide sales of $10.4 billion.

Sun	30.0%
Hewlett-Packard	21.0
DEC	15.0
IBM	13.0
Intergraph	7.0
Silicon Graphics	5.0
Others	9.0

Source: *Electronics*, January 1992, p. 28, from Gartner Group Inc.

★ 1031 ★
Workstations (SIC 3571)

Workstations in the U.S.

Market shares are shown in percent based on sales volumes of 468,187 units in 1991 and 557,144 units in 1992.

	1991	1992
Sun	40.0%	38.0%
Hewlett-Packard	17.0	18.0
DEC	13.0	13.0
IBM	8.0	11.0
Silicon Graphics	3.0	5.0
Other	18.0	14.0

Source: *The Wall Street Journal*, November 10, 1992, p. B4, from Sanford C. Bernstein and company reports.

★ 1032 ★
Computer Storage Devices (SIC 3572)

Disk-Drive Leading Manufacturers

U.S. disk-drive sales totals, by manufacturer, are shown in billions of dollars; shares of group are shown in percent.

	Sales ($ bil.)	% of Group
Seagate	$ 2.68	49.5%
Conner Peripherals	1.60	29.6
Quantum	1.13	20.9

Source: *The Wall Street Journal*, June 1, 1992, p. B4, from Hambrecht & Quist.

★ 1033 ★
Computer Storage Devices (SIC 3572)

Helical-Scan Tape-Drive Market

Market segmentation is shown according to projected worlwide shipments, in thousands of units for 1994.

	Units (000)
DAT	575.0
8mm	200.0
VHS	1.4

Source: *PC Week Hardware*, May 18, 1992, p. 37, from Freeman Associates, Inc.

★ 1034 ★
Computer Peripherals (SIC 3577)

Computer Peripheral Equipment Producers

Company sales are shown in millions of dollars for fiscal 1991. Relative market shares are shown in percent.

	Sales ($ mil.)	% of Group
Seagate Technology	$ 2,677.0	42.9%
Quantum	877.7	14.0
Maxtor	871.3	13.9
Archive	345.6	5.5
QMS	304.3	4.9
Komag	279.2	4.5
EMC	232.4	3.7
Qume	217.5	3.5
Rexon	183.0	2.9
CMS Enhancements	130.1	2.1
Adaptec	128.9	2.1

Source: *Electronic Business*, May 18, 1992, p. 91.

★ 1035 ★
Computer Peripherals (SIC 3577)

Computer Screen Enhancement Device Makers

Company shares are shown in percent, based on total markets of $115.0 million in 1991 and $142.8 million in 1992.

	'91	'92
OCLI	37.8%	36.6%
ODI	9.5	10.2
Polaroid	10.0	9.2
Others	42.8	44.0

Source: Investext, Thomson Financial Networks, April 10, 1992, from Prudential Securities Inc.

★1036★

Computer Printers (SIC 3577)

Computer Printers by Type

Printers are shown with unit sales in 1991. Percentages are based on the group total.

	Sales (Unit)	% of Group
Impact	5,165,000	81.2%
B&W ink jet	1,100,000	17.3
Color ink jet	92,700	1.5

Source: *HFD*, May 18, 1992, p. 128.

★1037★

Computer Printers (SIC 3577)

Desktop Page Printer Manufacturers

Company shares for 1990 and 1991 are shown in percent, based on total shipments for the same periods.

	1990	1991
HP	60.9%	45.0%
Apple	7.4	12.3
IBM/Lexmark	7.0	5.7
Panasonic	3.2	4.6
Others	21.5	32.4

Source: *PC Week*, May 11, 1992, p. 16, from InfoCorp.

★1038★

Computer Printers (SIC 3577)

Ink Jet Printers

Shares for 1991 are shown as percent of total units shipped.

Hewlett-Packard	46.9%
Canon	19.3
Apple	18.5
Kodak	11.0
Others	4.3

Source: *The New York Times*, March 10, 1992, p. C6, from Infocorp.

★1039★

Computer Printers (SIC 3577)

Inkjet Printer Manufacturers

Estimated shares of machine sales are shown in percent for 1991.

Videojet	60.0%
Domino	15.0
Other	25.0

Source: Investext, Thomson Financial Networks, February 25, 1992, from S.G. Warburg Securities.

★1040★

Computer Printers (SIC 3577)

Inkjet Printer Manufacturers - U.K.

Estimated shares of machine placement are shown in percent.

Domino	27.0%
Videojet	26.0
Imaje	17.0
Willett	10.0
Hitachi	9.0
Linx	9.0
Other	2.0

Source: Investext, Thomson Financial Networks, February 25, 1992, from S.G. Warburg Securities.

★1041★

Computer Printers (SIC 3577)

Laser Printer Market

Brand shares of 1990 and 1991 markets are shown in percent based on total shipments of 1,1774,000 printers in 1990 and 1,889,000 printers in 1991.

	1990	1991
PCL5	38.0%	44.0%
PCL4	45.0	35.0
PostScript	14.0	18.0
Other	3.0	3.0

Source: *PC World*, May 1992, p. 78, from BIS Strategic Decisions.

★ 1042 ★

Computer Printers (SIC 3577)

Laser Printers

Company shares are shown as percent of total unit shipments of four-to six-pages-a-minute laser printers in 1991.

Hewlett-Packard	40.5%
Apple	16.2
Okidata	9.4
Epson	7.5
IBM/Lexmark	5.1
Others	21.2

Source: *The New York Times*, March 10, 1992, p. C6, from Infocorp.

★ 1043 ★

Computer Printers (SIC 3577)

Laser Printers

Company shares are shown as percent of total unit shipments of 7-to 14-pages-a-minute laser printers in 1991.

Hewlett-Packard	50.2%
Panasonic	9.9
Apple	7.9
IBM/Lexmark	6.3
Okidata	4.6
Others	21.2

Source: *The New York Times*, March 10, 1992, p. C6, from Infocorp.

★ 1044 ★

Computer Printers (SIC 3577)

Printer Sales by Type

Impact

B&W

Color

Overall printer sales, including daisy wheel, dot matrix, and line printers, are shown in thousands of units sold in 1990 and 1991.

	1990	1991
Impact	5440.0	5165.0
B&W	646.6	1100.0
Color	71.4	92.7

Source: *Dealerscope*, June 1992, p. 114, from BIS Strategic Decisions.

★ 1045 ★

Network Hubs (SIC 3577)

Network Hubs Global Shares

Shares of the world market, by company, are shown in percent for 1990 and 1991.

	1990	1991
SynOptics	28.5%	27.0%
Ungermann-Bass	26.6	21.9
Cabletron	16.1	21.5
BICC	5.1	4.8
Chipcom	1.6	4.0
3 Com	1.9	3.8
David Systems	2.5	3.8
Proteon	3.5	2.8
Other	14.1	10.3

Source: Investext, Thomson Financial Networks, February 18, 1992, from Kidder, Peabody & Company, Incorporated.

★ 1046 ★

Copy Machines (SIC 3579)

Copier Manufacturers - Canada

Shares of the Canadian market are shown as percent of net revenues.

Xerox	39.0%
Canon	15.0
Savin	5.0
Toshiba	5.0
Kodak	4.0
Minolta	4.0
Mita	4.0
Sharp	4.0
Other	20.0

Source: *Report on Business*, February 1992, p. 17.

★1047★

Heating and Cooling (SIC 3585)

Comfort Cooling Manufacturing Leaders

Market shares, by company, are shown in percent for 1991.

Carrier	11.0%
Matsushita	8.0
Other	81.0

Source: Investext, Thomson Financial Networks, March 13, 1992, from Prudential Securities Inc.

★1048★

Heating and Cooling (SIC 3585)

Gas Heat Equipment by Type

Percent distribution, by equipment type, is based on shipments in 1990 and 1991.

	1990	1991
Central heating		
Furnaces	20.6%	21.6%
Boilers	2.2	1.9
Space heating		
Wall furnaces	1.6	1.5
Water heaters		
Gas	41.2	41.3
Electric	34.1	33.3
Oil	0.4	0.3

Source: *National Petroleum News*, June 1992, p. 64, from Gas Appliance Manufacturers Assn. and Statistical Highlights.

★1049★

Deli Equipment (SIC 3589)

Deli Equipment Market Penetration

Market penetration in deli service is shown in percent.

Random weight scales	100.0%
Slicer	100.0
Refrigerator (walk-in)	100.0
Microwave oven	83.0
Fryer	83.0
Freezer	80.0
Oven	78.0
Barbeque system	73.0
Coffee maker	72.0
Stove	72.0

Scales tied to scanners	70.0%
Steam table	67.0
Cold drink dispenser	61.0
Convection oven	52.0
Food processor	50.0
Industrial mixer	34.0
Pressure cooker	33.0
Vacuum packing system	33.0
Pizza oven	28.0
Heated cabinets	26.0
Coffee grinder	22.0
Hot dog grill	22.0

Source: *Supermarket Business*, February 1992.

★1050★

Carburetors (SIC 3592)

Carburetor Manufacturers Worldwide

Shares of the global market for small engine diaphragm carburetors are shown in percent.

Walbro Corp.	70.0%
Other	30.0

Source: Investext, Thomson Financial Networks, January 9, 1992, from Interstate/Johnson Lane.

★1051★

Pneumatics (SIC 3599)

Pneumatic Tool Manufacturers

Market shares, by company, are shown in percent.

Atlas Copco	40.0%
Ingersoll-Rand	40.0
Other	20.0

Source: Investext, Thomson Financial Networks, May 12, 1992, from The First Boston Corporation.

SIC 36 - Electronic and Other Electric Equipment

★1052★

Electrical Equipment (SIC 3600)

Electrical Equipment Market

Segment distribution is based on totals of $22,150 million in 1991 (estimate) and $22,326 million in 1992 (forecast).

	1991	1992
Relays and controls	30.5%	31.2%
Motors and generators	31.2	31.1
Switchgear and apparatus	22.9	22.8
Transformers	15.4	15.0

Source: *U.S. Industrial Outlook 1992*, p. 20-1, from U.S. Department of Commerce, Bureau of the Census.

★1053★

Electrical Products (SIC 3600)

Electrical Product Manufacturers

Sales figures are shown in millions of dollars for 1991. Percent shares are based on a group total of $30,688 million.

	Sales ($ mil.)	% of Group
Westinghouse Electric	$ 12,794	41.7%
Emerson Electric	7,443	24.3
Cooper Industries	6,163	20.1
National Services Industries	1,599	5.2
Raychem	1,273	4.1
Hubbell	756	2.5
Thomas & Betts	566	1.8
American Power Conversion	94	0.3

Source: *The 1992 Business Week 1000*, 1992, p. 172.

★1054★

Electronics (SIC 3600)

Consumer Electronics Market Worldwide

World shares of the electronics consumer market are based on sales of $88.0 billion in 1990.

Color TVs	30.7%
VCRs	13.6
Car audio systems	11.5
Tapes	11.4
Video cameras	6.4
CD players	2.6
Black and white TVs	1.6
Videodisk equipment	0.9
Other	21.4

Source: *Electronic Business*, May 18, 1992, p. 31, from Electronics International Corp.

★1055★

Electronics (SIC 3600)

Consumer Electronics Sales - 1991

Segment distribution of an estimated $27.81 billion in sales is shown in percent.

Color TV and projection TV	25.4%
Car stereos	16.3

Continued on next page.

★1055★ *Continued*

Electronics (SIC 3600)

Consumer Electronics Sales - 1991

Segment distribution of an estimated $27.81 billion in sales is shown in percent.

Home computers	14.5%
VCR decks	8.9
Camcorders	8.6
Audio components	7.0
Portable tape and compact disc players	5.7
Cellular telephones	5.0
Audio systems	4.5
Corded and cordless telephones	4.1

Source: *The New York Times*, February 9, 1992, p. C13, from Electronics Industries Association.

★1056★

Electronics (SIC 3600)

Electrical and Electrical Equipment Producers

Companies are ranked by dollar sales in 1991. Percent shares are based on a group total of $188,298 million.

	Sales ($ mil.)	% of Group
General Electric	$ 69,236	35.1%
Westinghouse Electric	12,794	6.5
Rockwell International	12,028	6.1
Motorola	11,341	5.7
Raytheon	9,356	4.7
Emerson Electric	7,427	3.8
Texas Instruments	6,812	3.5
Whirlpool	6,770	3.4
Cooper Industries	6,163	3.1
North American Philips	6,065	3.1
Litton Industries	5,313	2.7
Intel	4,779	2.4
Teledyne	3,218	1.6
AMP	3,095	1.6
Harris	3,081	1.6
Maytag	2,971	1.5
Loral	2,136	1.1
E-Systems	1,998	1.0
Natl. Semiconductor	1,711	0.9
General Signal	1,620	0.8
Natl. Service Ind.	1,602	0.8
Duracell International	1,524	0.8
Reliance Electric	1,516	0.8

	Sales ($ mil.)	% of Group
Varian Associates	$ 1,381	0.7%
Zenith Electronics	1,322	0.7
Raychem	1,250	0.6
Advanced Micro Dev.	1,227	0.6
Magnetek	1,134	0.6
Western Digital	986	0.5
Pittway	984	0.5
Mark IV Industries	937	0.5
Sunbeam/Oster	886	0.4
Hubbell	768	0.4
Exide	743	0.4
Molex	716	0.4
LSI Logic	713	0.4
Harman Intl. Indus.	587	0.3
Thomas & Betts	573	0.3
Analog Devices	539	0.3

Source: *Fortune*, April 20, 1992, p. 268.

★1057★

Electronics (SIC 3600)

Electrical and Electronics Industry Leaders - Europe

Company 1990 sales are shown in billions of European Currency Units. Shares of the group are shown in percent.

	(ECU bil.)	% of Group
Siemens	30.8	30.2%
Phillips Electronics	24.1	23.6
Alcatel Alsthom	20.8	20.4
Robert Bosch	15.5	15.2
Thomsom	10.9	10.7

Source: *International Management*, April 1992, p. 75.

★ 1058 ★
Electronics (SIC 3600)

Electronic Equipment Leaders - Japan

Companies are ranked by 1991 declared income, shown in millions of Yen. Relative market shares are shown in percent.

	Income (Y mil.)	% of Group
Matsushita Electric Industrial .	303,762	21.8%
Hitachi	209,473	15.0
Toshiba	181,791	13.1
Mitsubishi Electric	138,950	10.0
Sony	117,204	8.4
NEC	112,223	8.1
Fujitsu	97,076	7.0
Matsushita Electric Works . . .	85,509	6.1
Sharp	74,323	5.3
Fanuc	72,671	5.2

Source: *TOKYO Business Today*, July 1992, p. 38.

★ 1059 ★
Electronics (SIC 3600)

Electronic Parts Manufacturers - Japan

The top 10 companies are ranked by 1991 declared income, shown in millions of Yen. Relative market shares are shown in percent.

	Income (Y mil.)	% of Group
Kyocera	55,677	19.7%
Matsushita Electronics	46,234	16.3
TDK	41,227	14.6
Matsushita Communication Ind.	39,785	14.1
Murata Mfg.	24,360	8.6
Matsushita Battery Ind.	23,604	8.3
Futaba Corp.	15,776	5.6
Keyence	13,497	4.8
Nitto Denko	11,996	4.2
Hirose Electric	10,942	3.9

Source: *TOKYO Business Today*, July 1992, p. 39.

★ 1060 ★
Electronics (SIC 3600)

Electronics Exports from the U.S.

Exports of electronics from the U.S., by industry sector, are shown in millions of dollars for 1991. Relative market shares are shown in percent.

	($ mil).	% of Group
Computer/industrial	$ 31.48	53.9%
Solid-state products	11.27	19.3
Communications	6.80	11.6
Passives	6.09	10.4
Consumer electronics	2.21	3.8
Electron tubes	0.55	0.9

Source: *Electronic Business*, March 16, 1992, p. 23, from U.S. Department of Commerce, Electronic Industries Association.

★ 1061 ★
Electronics (SIC 3600)

Electronics Major Markets

Computers and office equipment

Communications

Consumer

Semiconductors

Capital equipment, test, CAD/CAE, bench instruments

Electronics consumption by major market is shown in billions of dollars for 1992 (forecast). Shares are shown in percent.

	($ bil.)	Share
Computers and office equipment .	$ 102.9	49.5%
Communications	35.8	17.2
Consumer	35.0	16.8
Semiconductors	23.8	11.4
Capital equipment, test, CAD/ CAE, bench instruments	10.5	5.0

Source: *Electronics*, January 1992, p. 26.

★1062★

Electronics (SIC 3600)

Electronics Manufacturers

Sales figures are shown in millions of dollars for 1991. Percent shares are based on a group total of $47,058 million.

	Sales ($ mil.)	% of Group
GM Hughes Electronics . . .	$ 11,481	24.4%
Motorola	11,341	24.1
Raytheon	9,274	19.7
Litton Industries	5,463	11.6
Harris	2,997	6.4
Loral	2,870	6.1
E-Systems	1,991	4.2
Varian Associates	1,366	2.9
Sensormatic Electronics . . .	274	0.6

Source: *The 1992 Business Week 1000*, p. 172.

★1063★

Power Generation Equipment (SIC 3612)

Power Generation Equipment Global Shares

Company shares of the world market are shown in percent for 1985-89 combined.

ABB	15.0%
GE	13.0
GEC Alsthom	11.0
Mitsubishi	11.0
Hitachi	7.0
Toshiba	6.0
Siemens	5.0
Westinghouse	2.0
Other	30.0

Source: Investext, Thomson Financial Networks, January 28, 1992, from Credit Suisse First Boston Ltd.

★1064★

Transformers (SIC 3612)

Transformer Industry Shipments

Shares by power rating are shown in percent based on unit shipments in 1991.

501-10,000	72.4%
10,001-30,000	18.7
30,001-100,000	7.2
100,000 and larger	1.7

Source: *U.S. Industrial Outlook 1992*, p. 20-1, from Edison Electric Institute.

★1065★

Industrial Apparatus (SIC 3620)

Machine Control Product Market

Market segment distribution is shown, in percent, based on totals of $1.01 billion in 1988 and $1.9 billion in 1993 (forecast).

	'88	'93
Computer numerical controllers . . .	56.2%	54.7%
Cell controllers	28.7	35.3
Other	15.1	10.0

Source: *FMS Magazine*, October 1989, p. 168, from Frost & Sullivan, Inc.

★1066★

Generators (SIC 3621)

Generator Industry - England and Wales

Market shares, by company, are shown in percent for 1991-1992.

National Power	43.8%
PowerGen	28.0
Nuclear Electric	18.5
Imports	8.5
Independents	0.8
Pumped Storage	0.4

Source: Investext, Thomson Financial Networks, June 1, 1992, from Yamaichi International (Europe) Limited and National Grid Company.

★ 1067 ★

Motors (SIC 3621)

Industrial Motor Manufacturers

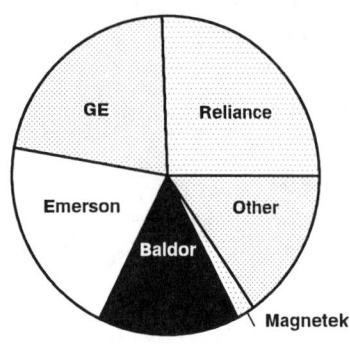

Estimated company shares are shown in percent based on a total market of $1.2 million.

Reliance	26.1%
GE	21.7
Emerson	20.8
Baldor	15.0
Magnetek	1.7
Other	15.8

Source: Investext, Thomson Financial Networks, June 18, 1992, from Prudential Securities Inc.

★ 1068 ★

Motors (SIC 3621)

Motor Manufacturers

Estimated shares of the 1991 market are shown, in percent, based on a total of $5.5 million.

Emerson	29.1%
GE	19.3
Magnetek	8.0
Reliance	5.5
Baldor	4.7
Other	33.5

Source: Investext, Thomson Financial Networks, June 18, 1992, from Prudential Securities Inc.

★ 1069 ★

Control Equipment (SIC 3625)

Control and Instrumentation Market - Western Europe

Market segmentation is shown in percent.

Flow meters	13.5%
Distributed control	11.1
Programmable controllers	7.6
Transmitters & receivers	7.5
Temperature sensors	7.4
Pressure sensors	6.9
Level sensors	5.8
Networks	5.7
Engineering workstations	4.2
Batch controllers	3.1
Supervisory control	2.9
Data acquisition systems	2.8
Micros as terminals	2.8
Data loggers	2.8
Add-on displays	2.0
Single loop controllers	2.0
Load & mass sensors	1.9
Multi-function controllers	1.7
Converters for sensors	1.5
Multi-loop controllers	1.5
Humidity sensors	1.2
Recorders	1.2
Gas & chemical sensors	1.2
Micro front-end I/O	0.9
Position sensors	0.8

Source: *C&I*, November 1992, p. 67.

★ 1070 ★

Appliances (SIC 3630)

Commercial Appliances

Market shares by product type are shown in percent based on total shipments of 2,910,400 units in 1991.

Clothes dryers, coin op.	4.1%
Clothes washers, coin op.	6.6
Duct furnaces, gas	0.5
Electronic video games	5.2
Freezers	0.1
Fryers, deep fat	2.8
Ice makers	4.4
Juke boxes	0.8
Refrigerated display cases	12.0
Refrigerators	6.9
Unit heaters, gas	4.7

Continued on next page.

★1070★ *Continued*
Appliances (SIC 3630)

Commercial Appliances

Market shares by product type are shown in percent based on total shipments of 2,910,400 units in 1991.

Vacuum cleaners	17.2%
Vending machines	22.5
Warmers, food	0.2
Water coolers	8.2
Water heaters, gas	3.1
Water heaters, electric	0.7

Source: *Appliance*, April 1992, p. 53.

★1071★
Household Appliances (SIC 3630)

Appliance Manufacturers

Shares are shown in percent for 1991.

GE	34.0%
Whirlpool	23.0
Electrolux (Frigidaire)	20.0
Maytag (Admiral)	12.0
Other	11.0

Source: Investext, Thomson Financial Networks, April 1, 1992, from Prudential Securities Inc.

★1072★
Household Appliances (SIC 3630)

Comfort Conditioning Houseware

Shares by product type are shown in percent, based on total shipments of 39,433,163 units in 1991.

Air cleaners, electronic	0.8%
Air-conditioners, room	7.5
Air-conditioners, unitary	8.0
Boilers, gas	0.5
Boilers, oil	0.3
Dehumidifiers	2.2
Fans, ceiling	15.5
Fans, desk	12.3
Fans, exhaust	9.4
Fans, floor	4.3
Fans, window	14.6
Furnaces, floor, gas	0.0
Furnaces, wall, gas	0.4
Furnaces, warm air, electric	0.7
Furnaces, warm air, gas	0.7
Furnaces, warm air, oil	0.3

Heat pumps	2.0%
Humidifiers, standard	1.6
Humidifiers, ultrasonic	1.2
Portable heaters, electric, baseboard	0.2
Portable heaters, electric, ceramic	3.2
Portable heaters, electric, fan forced	10.0
Portable heaters, non-fan forced	0.3
Portable heaters, oil-filled	1.3
Portable heaters, electric, quartz	0.2
Portable heaters, kerosene	1.9
Room heaters, vented gas	0.2
Room heaters, unvented gas	0.6

Source: *Appliance*, April 1992, p. 52.

★1073★
Household Appliances (SIC 3630)

Household Appliance Industry

Shares, by appliance type, are shown in percent, based on total shipments of 45.62 million units in 1990 and 43.39 million units in 1991.

	1990	1991
Ranges and microwave ovens	30.4%	29.6%
Washers and dryers	23.0	24.2
Refrigerators and freezers	18.4	20.0
Dishwashers, disposers, compactors	17.4	17.8
Air conditioners and dehumidifiers	10.7	8.4

Source: *Chicago Tribune*, March 8, 1992, p. 7-1, from Association of Home Appliance Manufacturers.

★1074★
Household Appliances (SIC 3630)

Household Appliance Manufacturers

Companies are ranked by 1991 sales, shown in millions of dollars. Percent shares are based on a group total $21,116 million.

	Sales ($ mil.)	% of Group
Whirlpool	$ 6,770	32.1%
Masco	3,141	14.9
Maytag	2,971	14.1
Circuit City Stores	2,628	12.4
Armstrong World Industries	2,439	11.6
Leggett & Platt	1,082	5.1
LA-Z-Boy Chair	610	2.9
Kimball International	553	2.6

Continued on next page.

★ 1074★ *Continued*

Household Appliances (SIC 3630)

Household Appliance Manufacturers

Companies are ranked by 1991 sales, shown in millions of dollars. Percent shares are based on a group total $21,116 million.

	Sales ($ mil.)	% of Group
Heilig-Meyers	$ 487	2.3%
Royal Appliance Mfg.	273	1.3
National Presto Industries . . .	162	0.8

Source: *The 1992 Business Week 1000*, p. 170.

★ 1075★

Household Appliances (SIC 3630)

Household Appliance Production - Japan

Figures are shown in millions of units produced in 1990 and as a percent of the group total production in that year.

	Units	Shares
Air conditioners	7,813,000	26.1%
Vacuum cleaners	6,851,000	22.9
Washing machines	5,576,000	18.6
Refrigerators	5,048,000	16.8
Microwave ovens	4,673,000	15.6

Source: *Business TOKYO*, March 1992, p. 42, from Ministry of Trade and Industry.

★ 1076★

Household Appliances (SIC 3630)

Household Appliances: Major U.S. Manufacturers

Shares, by company, are shown in percent for 1990.

Whirlpool
Compactors	9.7%
Dishwashers	4.4
Dryers, electric	6.9
Dryers, gas	7.1

Freezers	0.8%
Ranges, electric	2.3
Ranges, gas	2.3
Refrigerators	3.1
Washers	6.9

General Electric
Compactors	1.6
Dishwashers	5.4
Dryers, electric	2.3
Dryers, gas	1.9
Ranges, electric	5.4
Ranges, gas	3.4
Refrigerators	4.6
Washers	2.2

Frigidaire
Dishwashers	2.7
Disposers	3.9
Dryers, electric	1.6
Dryers, gas	1.5
Freezers	9.0
Ranges, electric	2.7
Ranges, gas	3.7
Refrigerators	2.7
Washers	1.6

Source: Investext, Thomson Financial Networks, March 25, 1992, from Merrill Lynch Capital Markets.

★ 1077★

Household Cooking Equipment (SIC 3631)

Microwave Uses

Market penetration by use is shown in percent. Figures are the result of a survey of 2,106 adults.

Reheating	93.0%
Warming	79.0
Defrosting	76.0
Making popcorn	74.0
Heating frozen foods	63.0

Source: *Supermarket Business*, May 1992, p. 186, from *Parade*.

★1078★
Hair Care Appliances (SIC 3634)

Hair Care Appliance Market

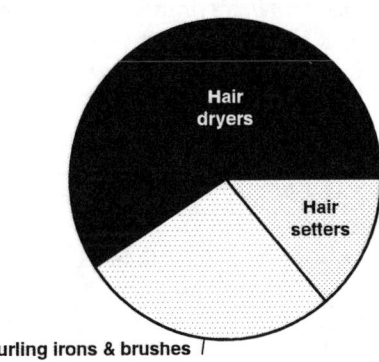

Curling irons & brushes

Market segmentation is shown as percent of 1990 sales, totaling $432.6 million.

Hair dryers	59.0%
Curling irons & brushes	27.0
Hair setters	14.0

Source: *HFD*, January 1992, p. 5.

★1079★
Household Personal Appliances (SIC 3634)

Coffee Maker Market Share

Shares by type are shown in percent for 1990 and 1991.

	1990	1991
Electric drip	67.0%	65.0%
Percolators	17.0	16.0
Drip pot	8.0	11.0
Filter cone	4.0	4.0
Other	2.0	2.0

Source: *HFD*, November 1991, p. 4.

★1080★
Household Personal Appliances (SIC 3634)

Electric Household Appliances

Market shares, by product type, are shown in percent based on total shipments of 171,342,000 units in 1991.

Air purifiers	2.7%
Blenders	4.1
Breadmakers	0.4
Broilers	1.2

Can openers	4.6%
Clocks, alarm	16.6
Clocks, decorative wall	5.1
Clocks, desk/table	1.7
Clocks, kitchen wall	5.4
Coffee grinders	0.6
Coffee makers	11.9
Convection ovens	0.1
Corn poppers, hot air	1.5
Corn poppers, hot oil	0.6
Deep fryers	1.5
Knives	1.0
Mixers, food, portable hand	3.5
Mixers, food, stand type	0.8
Sandwich makers	3.1
Slow cookers	2.9
Smoke detectors	7.3
Toaster ovens	2.1
Toasters	6.5
Vacuums, canister	1.7
Vacuums, handheld electric	2.1
Vacuums, handheld rechargeable	2.5
Vacuums, stick	1.1
Vacuums, upright	5.1
Waffle irons/sandwich grills	1.3
Woks	1.1

Source: *Appliance*, April 1992, p. 53.

★1081★
Household Personal Appliances (SIC 3634)

Massager Sales by Category

Body massagers

Foot massagers

Back massagers

Shares by category are shown in percent for 1990, based on total sales of 4,000,000 units valued at $138 million.

	Sales (unit)	Sales (dollar)
Body massagers	81.0%	58.7%
Foot massagers	35.0	25.4
Back massagers	22.0	15.9

Source: *HFD*, December 1991, p. 5.

★1082★

Household Personal Appliances (SIC 3634)

Men's Razor Manufacturers

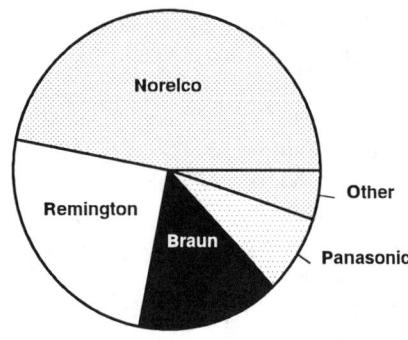

Shares of the domestic market are shown in percent, based on total units shipped.

Norelco	47.0%
Remington	25.0
Braun	15.0
Panasonic	8.0
Other	5.0

Source: *Advertising Age*, October 12, 1992, p. 20.

★1083★

Household Personal Appliances (SIC 3634)

Personal Care Appliances

Market shares, by product type, are shown in percent based on total shipments of 58,758,800 units in 1991.

Curling brushes	3.5%
Curling irons and styling combs/wands/ crimpers	19.2
Hair dryers, bonnet	0.3
Hair dryers, hard top	0.9
Hair dryers, pistol type	26.8
Hair dryers, styling type	7.0
Hair setters	5.0
Heating pads	7.7
Massagers, foot bath	1.7
Massagers, hand-held	3.3
Massagers, shower head	5.8
Shavers, men's	11.7
Shavers, women's	2.9
Toothbrushes	2.7
Water pulsators/bubblers	0.8
Whirlpool baths, portable	0.7

Source: *Appliance*, April 1992, p. 54.

★1084★

Household Personal Appliances (SIC 3634)

Women's Razor Manufacturers

Shares of the domestic market are shown in percent, based on total units shipped.

Remington	35.0%
Norelco	31.0
Panasonic	29.0
Braun	1.0
Other	4.0

Source: *Advertising Age*, October 12, 1992, p. 20.

★1085★

Household Vacuum Cleaners (SIC 3635)

Vacuum Manufacturers

Shares of an estimated $1.9 billion annual domestic market are shown in percent, based on manufacturer shipments in 1990.

Hoover	31.0%
Eureka	24.0
Ryobi (Singer, Kenmore)	11.0
Regina	7.0
Whirlpool (Kenmore)	7.0
Electrolux	5.0
Others	15.0

Source: *The Wall Street Journal*, November 4, 1991, p. B6, from *Appliance Manufacturer*.

★1086★

Sewing Machines (SIC 3639)

Sewing Machine Manufacturers Worldwide

Shares of the free world market for consumer sewing machines are shown in percent.

Singer	34.0%
Brother	10.0
Janome	8.0
Jaguar	5.0
Pfaff	3.0
Husquarna	3.0
Other	38.0

Source: Investext, Thomson Financial Networks, February 10, 1992, from Dillon, Read & Co.

★ 1087 ★
Sewing Machines (SIC 3639)

Sewing Machines by Type

Approximate market segmentation of consumer sewing machines in 1990 is shown in percent, based on a total of 2.75 million units.

Zig zag	93.3%
Straight stitch	5.3
Electronic	1.5

Source: Investext, Thomson Financial Networks, February 10, 1992, from Dillon, Read & Co.

★ 1088 ★
Connectors (SIC 3643)

Automotive Connector Manufacturers - Europe

Shares, by company, are shown as percent of sales. "Other" includes Molex among 500 other companies.

AMP	24.0%
Framatome	10.0
Other	66.0

Source: Investext, Thomson Financial Networks, January 21, 1992, from Prudential Securities Inc.

★ 1089 ★
Lighting (SIC 3648)

Electric Lanterns

Estimated shares of the domestic market are shown in percent, based on a total of $500 million.

Ray o Vac	24.0%
Eveready	17.0
Coleman	6.0
Other	53.0

Source: Investext, Thomson Financial Networks, March 26, 1992, from The First Boston Corporation.

★ 1090 ★
Lighting (SIC 3648)

Gas Lantern and Stove Manufacturers

Estimated shares of the domestic market are shown in percent, based on a total of $45-50 million.

Coleman	94.0%
Mountain Safety Research	5.0
Other	1.0

Source: Investext, Thomson Financial Networks, March 26, 1992, from The First Boston Corporation.

★ 1091 ★
Lighting (SIC 3648)

Propane Lantern and Stove Manufacturers

Estimated shares of the domestic market are shown in percent, based on a total of $50.0 million.

Coleman	83.0%
Century Primus	6.0
Greatlands	5.0
American Camper	4.0
Other	2.0

Source: Investext, Thomson Financial Networks, March 26, 1992, from The First Boston Corporation.

★ 1092 ★
Consumer Audio Equipment (SIC 3651)

Headphone Stereo Manufacturers - Japan

Company shares of Japan's domestic shipments are shown in percent based on a total of 4.7 million units in 1990.

Sony	40.0%
Matsushita	22.0
Aiwa	20.0
Sanyo	6.0
Sharp	5.0
Other	7.0

Source: *Dealerscope Merchandising*, July 1992, p. 10, from Nikkei.

★ 1093 ★
Consumer Audio Equipment (SIC 3651)

Mini-Stereo Manufacturers - Japan

Company shares of Japan's domestic shipments are shown in percent based on a total of 1.95 million units in 1990. Category includes stereos and stereo components.

Sony	23.0%
Pioneer	17.0
Kenwood	14.0
Matsushita	13.5
JVC	12.0
Other	21.0

Source: *Dealerscope Merchandising*, July 1992, p. 10, from Nikkei.

★ 1094 ★
Consumer Audio Equipment (SIC 3651)

Scanner Radio Listeners

Scanner-radio usage, by listening audience, is shown in percent.

Entertainment information listeners	70.0%
Serious hobbyists	18.0
Police, firefighters, emergency volunteers, etc.	12.0

Source: *HFD*, May 25, 1992, p. 5.

★ 1095 ★
Consumer Electronics (SIC 3651)

Audio/Video Sales

Sales figures are shown in terms of units sold to dealers for a 36-week period ended 09/23/91. Shares by type are based on group total.

	Unit Sales	% of Group
Color TV	11,906,305	86.5%
Camcorders	1,675,669	12.2
Projection TV	183,780	1.3

Source: *HFD*, September 23, 1991, p. 84.

★ 1096 ★
Consumer Electronics (SIC 3651)

Camcorder Manufacturers - Japan

Company shares of Japan's domestic shipments are shown in percent based on a total of 1.86 million units in 1990.

Sony	40.0%
Matsushita	28.0
JVC	12.5
Hitachi	3.5
Sharp	3.0
Other	3.5

Source: *Dealerscope Merchandising*, July 1992, p. 10, from Nikkei.

★ 1097 ★
Consumer Electronics (SIC 3651)

Color TV Manufacturers - Japan

Company shares of Japan's domestic shipments are shown in percent based on a total of 9.05 million units in 1990.

Matsushita	23.5%
Toshiba	15.0
Sharp	14.5
Hitachi	10.5
Sony	9.5
Other	27.0

Source: *Dealerscope Merchandising*, July 1992, p. 10, from Nikkei.

★ 1098 ★
Consumer Electronics (SIC 3651)

Consumer Electronics for Home Theaters

Unit-to-dealer sales for home theaters are shown in millions for 1990 and 1991.

	1990	1991
Color TV receivers	20.8	20.9
CD players	9.15	10.0
Hi-Fi stereo VCRs	1.86	2.3
Projection TVs	0.35	0.36
Laser disc players	0.16	0.25

Source: *HFD*, January 1992, p. 5.

★ 1099 ★

Consumer Electronics (SIC 3651)

Consumer Electronics Market

Segment distribution is shown in percent.

Home office equipment	24.72%
Audio equipment	21.34
Televisions	20.94
Videocassette recorders	10.55
Blank videotapes	7.15
Blank audiotapes	6.16
Videogame modules/cartridges	5.64
Miscellaneous	3.52

Source: *Discount Merchandiser*, June 1992, p. 61.

★ 1100 ★

Consumer Electronics (SIC 3651)

Consumer Electronics Sales to Dealers

Unit sales to dealers are shown for the year-to-date (47 weeks). Percent shares are based on group total.

Color TV	17,261,040	58.6%
VCR decks	8,970,108	30.5
Camcorders	2,548,019	8.7
Color TV/VCR combinations	365,038	1.2
Projection TVs	293,637	1.0

Source: *HFD*, December 9, 1991, p. 68.

★ 1101 ★

Consumer Video Equipment (SIC 3651)

Laser Disc Sales in Japan

Production of video disc players in Japan, by company, are shown in percent, based on a total of 137 billion yen in 1991.

Pioneer	55.0%
Sony	35.0
Other	10.0

Source: Investext, Thomson Financial Networks, May 14, 1992, from Sanyo Securities America.

★ 1102 ★

Consumer Video Equipment (SIC 3651)

VCR Manufacturers - Japan

Company shares of Japan's domestic shipments are shown in percent based on a total of 5.71 million units in 1990.

Matsushita	25.0%
JVC	14.0
Toshiba	12.0
Hitachi	11.5
Mitsubishi	11.5
Other	26.0

Source: *Dealerscope Merchandising*, July 1992, p. 10, from Nikkei.

★ 1103 ★

Consumer Video Equipment (SIC 3651)

Video Disk Player Manufacturers - Japan

Company shares of Japan's domestic shipments are shown in percent for 1990.

Pioneer	47.0%
Sony	20.0
Nippon Columbia	13.0
Matsushita	10.0
Funai	2.0
Other	8.0

Source: *Dealerscope Merchandising*, July 1992, p. 10, from Nikkei.

★ 1104 ★

Prerecorded Music (SIC 3652)

Album Producers Worldwide

Shares of the global album market are shown by label in percent for 1991.

EMI	23.8%
Polygram	22.0
Warner Music	13.1
Sony Music	12.0
BMG	5.4

Continued on next page.

★ 1104 ★ *Continued*
Prerecorded Music (SIC 3652)

Album Producers Worldwide

Shares of the global album market are shown by label in percent for 1991.

Telstar	4.4%
MCA	3.9
Dino	1.9
Other	13.5

Source: *Accountancy*, June 1992, p. 72, from *BPI Statistical Handbook, 1992.*

★ 1105 ★
Prerecorded Music (SIC 3652)

Album Sales Worldwide

Percent distribution of the global market by music genre is shown in percent for 1991.

Pop	45.0%
Rock	15.0
Classical	12.0
Middle-of-the-Road	10.0
Dance/soul/reggae	9.0
Country/folk	4.0
Jazz	1.0
Other	4.0

Source: *Accountancy*, June 1992, p. 72, from *BPI Statistical Handbook, 1992.*

★ 1106 ★
Prerecorded Music (SIC 3652)

Music Media by Type

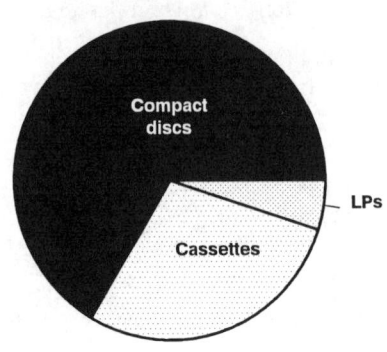

Segment distribution by type of recording media is shown in percent, based on a retail value total of $20.0 billion for 1991.

Compact discs	66.5%
Cassettes	29.0
LPs	4.5

Source: *The Economist*, September 26, 1992, p. 119, from BIS Strategic Decisions.

★ 1107 ★
Prerecorded Music (SIC 3652)

Recorded Music Market

Segment distribution is shown for the first six months of 1991. Percentages are based on a total of 362.4 million units shipped (after returns).

Cassettes	47.0%
CDs	42.5
Cassette singles	9.3
CD singles	0.7
LPs	0.6

Source: *The Wall Street Journal*, January 8, 1992, p. B1, from Recording Industry Assn. of America.

★1108★

Prerecorded Music (SIC 3652)

Recording Industry Sales

1991 recordings sales, by type, are shown in billions of dollars; relative market shares are shown in percent.

	Sales ($ bil.)	% of Group
Compact discs	$ 4.3000	56.6%
Cassettes	3.000	39.5
LP vinyl records	0.300	3.9

Source: *USA TODAY*, July 28, 1992, p. D1, from Recording Industry Association of America.

★1109★

Telecommunications Equipment (SIC 3661)

Cellular System Producers Worldwide

Shares of the global market as of January 1992 are shown in percent, based on total subscribers served.

Ericsson	40.7%
Motorola	18.0
AT&T	17.5
NEC	7.0
Northern Telecom	6.5
Siemens	4.0
Nokia	2.7
Other	3.6

Source: Investext, Thomson Financial Networks, June 30, 1992, from Wood Gundy Inc. and Ericsson Radio Systems AB.

★1110★

Telecommunications Equipment (SIC 3661)

Channel Card Manufacturers

Shares of sales of channel cards for telephone digital switching systems are shown in percent.

AT&T	60.0%
Pulsecom	30.0
Other	10.0

Source: Investext, Thomson Financial Networks, January 30, 1992, from Prudential Securities, Inc.

★1111★

Telecommunications Equipment (SIC 3661)

Communications Equipment

Revenue shares are shown in percent, based on a total of $30.6 billion in 1992.

Local-area networks	20.6%
Central office switches	18.6
Facsimile	16.0
Fiber-optic equipment	11.4
Modems	9.2
Private branch exchanges	9.2
Telephone sets	7.2
Multiplexers	4.2
Key/hybrid phone systems	3.6

Source: *Electronics*, January 1992, p. 34.

★1112★

Telecommunications Equipment (SIC 3661)

Desktop Digital Video Market

Shares, by end use, are shown in percent, based on a total of $1.86 billion in forecasted year 1994.

Business	76.0%
Education	12.0
Government/military	6.0
Medical	4.0
Other	2.0

Source: *Electronics*, August 1991, p. A3.

★1113★

Telecommunications Equipment (SIC 3661)

Digital CO Switching Systems

Top 10 suppliers of digital (CO) central office switching systems are shown with number of ports installed in 1991/92. Shares are based on a group total.

	Ports (mil.)	% of Group
Alcatel	80.55	20.7%
Northern Telecom	71.43	18.3
AT&T	66.31	17.0
Ericsson	49.79	12.8
Siemens/Stromberg-Carlson	45.18	11.6
NEC	21.53	5.5
GPT	20.54	5.3
Fujitsu	14.05	3.6

Continued on next page.

★ 1113 ★ *Continued*

Telecommunications Equipment (SIC 3661)

Digital CO Switching Systems

Top 10 suppliers of digital (CO) central office switching systems are shown with number of ports installed in 1991/92. Shares are based on a group total.

	Ports (mil.)	% of Group
GTE-AG	13.00	3.3%
Hitachi	7.56	1.9

Source: *Telephony*, July 6, 1992, p. 16, from Dittberner Associates Inc.

★ 1114 ★

Telecommunications Equipment (SIC 3661)

Digital Switch Suppliers

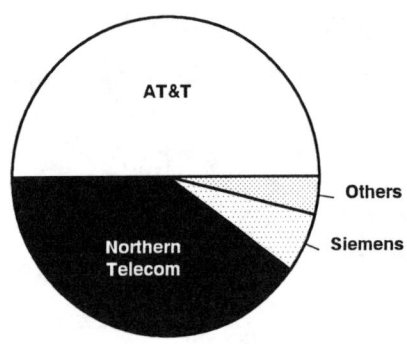

Company shares are based on total of 76 million lines installed in U.S., shown in percent. Siemens is a Germany-based company.

AT&T	50.0%
Northern Telecom	40.0
Siemens	6.0
Others	4.0

Source: *Electronics*, March 1992, p. 25.

★ 1115 ★

Telecommunications Equipment (SIC 3661)

FDDI Card Shipments

1991 shipments of FDDI (Fiber Distributed Data Interface) cards totaled 3,100. Market shares are shown in percent.

	Cards	Share
Interphase Corp.	1,000	32.3%
SMCC	500	16.1
Network Peripherals	500	16.1
Other	1,100	35.5

Source: *UniForum*, August 1992, p. 20, from Dataquest.

★ 1116 ★

Telecommunications Equipment (SIC 3661)

ISDN Lines - 1994

Table shows estimated number and percent of telephone lines available to customers for ISDN (Integrated Services Digital Network) applications by each RBOC (Regional Bell Operating Company). This represents 62 million lines or 54 percent of the country's access lines by year-end 1994.

	ISDN Lines	% of Lines
Bell Atlantic	17.1	87.0%
Ameritech	11.2	70.0
U.S. West	8.0	58.6
Bell South	10.5	52.0
Pacific Telesis	7.5	50.0
NYNEX	5.5	33.4
Southwestern Bell	2.2	16.3

Source: *Networking Management*, March 1992, p. 38, from Bellcore.

★ 1117 ★

Telecommunications Equipment (SIC 3661)

ISDN Users

Distribution by RBOC (Regional Bell Operating Company) of the number of lines (in millions) with access to ISDN (Integrated Services Digital Network) central office switches. Data compare estimated installed lines for 1991 and 1994. 1994 estimated user shares are shown in percent.

	'91	'94	'94 Share
Bell Atlantic	6.9	17.1	25.5%
Ameritech	2.2	16.1	24.0
Bell South	3.1	10.5	15.7
Pacific Bell	3.7	7.5	11.2
US West	3.0	7.3	10.9
Southwestern Bell	1.1	4.4	6.6
NYNEX	2.1	4.1	6.1

Source: *Networking Management*, September 1992, p. 28, from Bellcore.

★ 1118 ★

Telecommunications Equipment (SIC 3661)

ISDN-Capable Telephone Lines

Companies are shown with percent of lines in wire center planned to have ISDN (integrated services digital network) in 1992, 1993, and 1994.

	'92	'93	'94
Bell Atlantic	79.0%	82.0%	87.0%
Ameritech	22.0	51.0	70.0
U.S. West	45.0	55.0	59.0
BellSouth	30.0	41.0	52.0
Pacific Bell	33.0	39.0	50.0
NYNEX	25.0	33.0	33.0
Southwestern Bell	16.0	16.0	16.0

Source: *Telephony*, January 20, 1992, p. 30, from Bellcore.

★ 1119 ★

Telecommunications Equipment (SIC 3661)

PBX and Key System Producers Worldwide

Shares of the global market for (PBX) private branch exchanges and key systems are shown in percent for 1991.

Northern Telecom	11.8%
Siemens/Rolm	11.0
AT&T	9.5
Alcatel	9.2
NEC	5.0
Mitel	2.0
Other	51.5

Source: Investext, Thomson Financial Networks, June 30, 1992, from Wood Gundy Inc.

★ 1120 ★

Telecommunications Equipment (SIC 3661)

PBX Companies - 1991

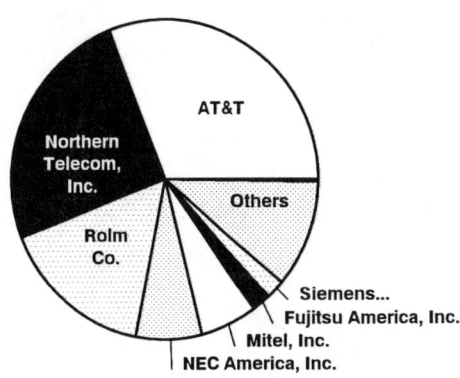

PBX (private branch exchange) lines shipped in 1991 totaled 4.417 million. Company shares are shown in percent.

AT&T	30.9%
Northern Telecom, Inc.	25.2
Rolm Co.	16.1
NEC America, Inc.	6.7
Mitel, Inc.	6.0
Fujitsu America, Inc.	2.4
Siemens Public Switching Systems, Inc.	2.2
Others	10.5

Source: *Network World*, May 18, 1992, p. 27, from Infotech Consulting, Inc.

★ 1121 ★

Telecommunications Equipment (SIC 3661)

PBX Sales by Company

Shares are shown in percent for the first half of 1991 based on a total of 1,899,000 PBX (private branch exchange) lines.

AT&T	28.8%
Northern Telecom	24.5
Rolm	11.8
NEC	6.6
Mitel	6.3
Other	22.8

Source: *Data Communications*, February 1992, p. 18, from Eastern Management Group.

★ 1122 ★

Telecommunications Equipment (SIC 3661)

Set-Top Converter Manufacturers

Manufacturer shares are based on 1991 total market of $650 million.

General Instrument	50.0%
Scientific Atlanta	30.4
Zenith	8.5
Pioneer	8.0
Other	3.1

Source: Investext, Thomson Financial Networks, May 29, 1992, from Wertheim Schroder & Co. Inc.

★ 1123 ★

Telecommunications Equipment (SIC 3661)

Switched Digital Service Networks - Europe

Percent shares by operator and country are based on a European total of 57 switches.

Telecom Denmark & Jutland Telephone Co.	20.0%
Swiss PTT	15.0
Swedish Telecom	10.0
Norwegian Telecom	4.0

Regie des Telegraphes et Telephones (Belgium)	2.0%
Telecom Finland & Helsinki Telephone Co.	2.0
Netherlands PTT	2.0
Mercury Communications Ltd. (U.K.)	2.0

Source: *Data Communications*, December 1991, p. 117.

★ 1124 ★

Telecommunications Equipment (SIC 3661)

T1 Multiplexer Market

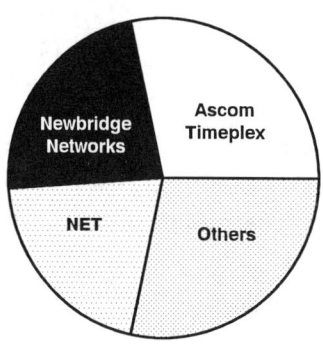

Vendors' shares of the T1 multiplexer market are based on actual revenues, shown in percent. Numbers did not add to 100% in the original source.

Ascom Timeplex	26.0%
Newbridge Networks	20.5
NET	18.9
Others	26.3

Source: *Communications Week*, May 4, 1992, p. 25, from The Yankee Group.

★ 1125 ★

Telecommunications Equipment (SIC 3661)

TDM Companies - Europe

Shares of the 1989 market are shown in percent based on $220.5 million in revenues. TDM stands for time-division multiplexer.

Timeplex	32.1%
Newbridge	14.5
General DataComm	9.4
BT Data Communications	6.8
Dowty (incl. CASE Datatel)	5.8
Infotron	4.9
Craycom Master Systems	3.0

Continued on next page.

★1125★ *Continued*

Telecommunications Equipment (SIC 3661)

TDM Companies - Europe

Shares of the 1989 market are shown in percent based on $220.5 million in revenues. TDM stands for time-division multiplexer.

Telematics	2.7%
Craycom Eurotel	2.5
Motorola	2.4
Racal	2.2
Others	13.7

Source: *Data Communications*, October 1991, p. 24, from Dataquest Ltd.

★1126★

Telecommunications Equipment (SIC 3661)

Technology ECI Revenues

1991 shares of Electronic Communications Index revenues which companies derive from TV and radio technology are shown in millions of dollars. Company shares are shown in percent.

	Revenue	Share
Sony	$ 2,550.0	32.7%
Matsushita	2,100.0	26.9
GI Corp.	745.0	9.6
Ampex	493.3	6.3
Harris Corp.	451.0	5.8
Scientific-Atlanta	355.8	4.6
Tektronix	293.6	3.8
3M	266.8	3.4
PESA Chyron	154.8	2.0
Eastman Kodak	141.5	1.8
Varian	100.7	1.3
Zenith	80.0	1.0
Motorola	34.0	0.4
C-COR	26.2	0.3

Source: *Broadcasting*, June 22, 1992, p. 48, from company estimates, securities analysts, and industry associations.

★1127★

Telecommunications Equipment (SIC 3661)

Telecom Cable Producers - Italy

Shares of the Italian telecommunications cable market are shown in percent, based on a total of 875 billion Lira in 1990. The category includes both copper and optic cable. Alcatel includes Fulgor.

Pirelli	42.9%
Teleco	14.2
Alcatel	13.9
Ceat	13.0
Other	16.0

Source: Investext, Thomson Financial Networks, January 23, 1992, from Paribas Capital Markets Group.

★1128★

Telecommunications Equipment (SIC 3661)

Telemarketing Equipment by Type

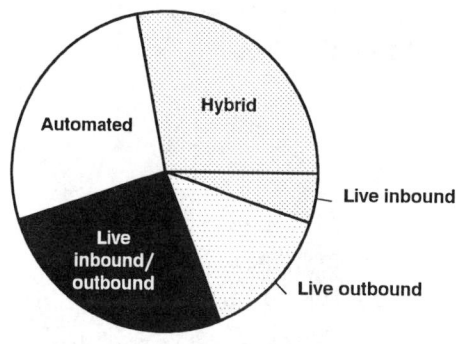

Distribution of lines employed by these segments is shown in percent, based on total of 371,828 lines.

Hybrid	27.8%
Automated	27.1
Live inbound/outbound	26.2
Live outbound	14.0
Live inbound	5.0

Source: *Telephony*, June 15, 1992, p. 110, from *Strategic Telemedia*, 1991.

★ 1129 ★

Telecommunications Equipment (SIC 3661)

T-1 Mux Market - 1991

U.S. vendor shares of the T-1 multiplexer market are shown in percent, based on total revenues of $609 million in 1991.

Ascom Timeplex, Inc.	26.8%
Network Equipment Technologies, Inc.	19.4
Newbridge Networks Corp.	18.6
StrataCom, Inc.	8.5
General DataCom, Inc	5.9
Tellabs, Inc.	5.1
Infotron Systems Corp.	3.9
Racal-Datacom, Inc.	3.9
Netrix Corp.	3.0
Other	4.9

Source: *Network World*, April 27, 1992, p. 25, from The Yankee Group.

★ 1130 ★

Telecommunications Equipment (SIC 3661)

T-1 Mux Vendors

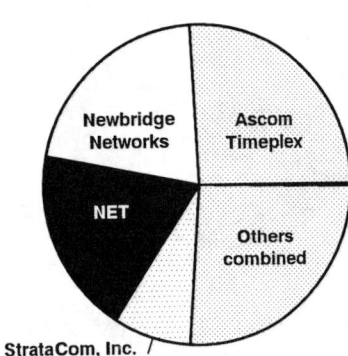

1991 leading vendor shares of the T-1 multiplexer market are shown in percent, based on actual revenues. "Other" includes vendors with shares of less than 6 percent each.

Ascom Timeplex	26.0%
Newbridge Networks	20.5
NET	18.9
StrataCom, Inc.	8.3
Others combined	26.3

Source: *Communications Week*, May 4, 1992, p. 25, from The Yankee Group.

★ 1131 ★

Telecommunications Equipment (SIC 3661)

Universities' PBX Market by Vendor

Vendor shares of universities' PBX market are shown in percent. PBX stands for private branch exchange.

AT&T	34.3%
Northern	14.6
NEC	11.4
Rolm	11.3
Mitel	6.1
Fujitsu	4.5
Siemens	4.1
Other	13.7

Source: *Communications News*, July 1992, p. 6, from Computer Intelligence.

★ 1132 ★

Telecommunications Equipment (SIC 3661)

Video Teleconferencing Equipment Makers

Company shares are shown in percent, based on 1991 sales.

PictureTel Corp.	48%
Compression Labs Inc.	39
Other	13

Source: *PC Week*, April 27, 1992, p. 137, from The Yankee Group Inc.

★ 1133 ★

Telecommunications Equipment (SIC 3661)

VSAT Industry Segment Revenues

Percent shares of VSAT industry revenue by segment are based on totals of $304.68 million in 1991 and $398.37 million in 1996 (forecast). VSAT stands for Very Small Aperture Terminal.

	1991	1996
Unit sales/install	51.4%	39.1%
Space segment	18.0	23.2
Maintenance	18.5	22.4
Shared hubs	12.2	15.3

Source: *Telecommunications*, June 1992, p. 10.

★1134★

Telephones (SIC 3661)

Telephone Sales

Shares of telephone sales value, by type, are shown in percent for 1990, 1991, 1992.

	'90	'91	'92
Cordless phones	36.8%	44.0%	46.5%
Answering machines	36.2	34.0	33.7
Corded phones	27.0	22.0	19.8

Source: *Dealerscope*, June 1992, p. 38, from The Electronic Industries Association.

★1135★

Communications Satellites (SIC 3663)

Satellite Contractors Worldwide

Data represent shares of the market for first-generation (1980-1989) and second-generation (1990-1995) communications satellites. Shares are shown in percent.

	1st Gen.	2nd Gen.
USA	69.7%	59.6%
Hughes	27.7	21.4
GE	16.8	21.3
Ford	18.9	9.6
Europe	23.5	36.0
Matra	4.4	18.9
Aerospatiale	5.2	9.9
British Aerospace	8.2	5.6
Deutsche Aerospace	4.8	2.3
Canada	3.8	2.4
Spar	3.8	2.4
NEC & Japan	3.0	2.0

Source: Investext, Thomson Financial Networks, January 15, 1992, from Sanwa McCarthy Securities Ltd. and Euroconsult.

★1136★

Communications Satellites (SIC 3663)

Telemetry Receiver Market

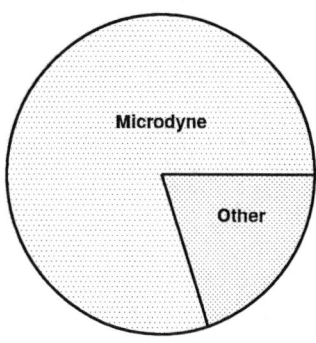

Shares of the domestic market are shown in percent.

Microdyne	80.0%
Other	20.0

Source: Investext, Thomson Financial Networks, March 30, 1992, from Tucker, Anthony & R. L. Day.

★1137★

Data Communications (SIC 3663)

Remote Bridge Makers Worldwide

Company shares are based on a 1990 global market of 21,000 units, shown in percent.

Vitalink Communications	24.5%
Retix	20.7
IBM	18.9
3Com Corp.	14.1
Ungermann-Bass Inc.	11.0
Microcom Inc.	5.6
Others	5.2

Source: *Data Communications*, July 1991, p. 24, from International Data Corp.

★1138★

Portable Communications Equipment (SIC 3663)

Cellular Equipment Manufacturers Worldwide

Company shares of the global market are shown in percent, based on a total of $5.0 billion. The category includes handsets and transmitter equipment. "Other" includes AT&T, Fujitsu, NEC, Nokia, Northern Telecom, Oki, and Toshiba.

Motorola	35.0%
Ericsson (Sweden)	23.0
Other	42.0

Source: *The Globe and Mail*, February 11, 1992, p. B1.

★1139★

Portable Communications Equipment (SIC 3663)

Cellular Phone Sales by Type

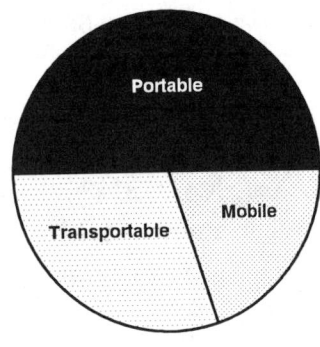

Shares by type are shown in percent.

Portable	50.0%
Transportable	30.0
Mobile	20.0

Source: *HFD*, June 8, 1992, p. 10.

★1140★

Space Commerce (SIC 3663)

U.S. Space Commerce Revenues

Shares by industry segment are shown in percent, based on total revenues of $3,850 million in 1991 and $4,650 million in 1992 (forecast).

	1991	1992
Satellite ground equipment	33.8%	36.6%
Satellite services	31.2	29.0
Commercial satellite	20.8	21.5
Commercial launches	9.9	8.6
Remote sensing data and services	4.4	4.3

Source: *U.S. Industrial Outlook 1992*, p. 41-1.

★1141★

Data Communications (SIC 3669)

Communications Processor Industry - Europe

Shares of the total European communications processor market, by product type, are shown in percent for 1990.

Front-end processors	56.5%
Packet-oriented systems	13.4
LAN controllers	13.4
Network gateways	12.9
Concentrators	2.7
Messaging systems	1.0

Source: *Data Communications*, December 1991, p. 22, from Frost & Sullivan, Inc.

★1142★

Data Communications (SIC 3669)

Data Communications Products - U.S.

Revenues of the data communications products market in the U.S. are shown, by type of product, in millions of dollars for the years 1991 (estimated) and 1992 (projected). Percent shares are based on industry totals of $20,407 million in revenues in 1991 and $22,418 million in revenues in 1992.

	1991	1992
Servers	27.7%	29.0%
LAN cards	13.0	13.0
Facsimile	11.0	10.5
PC LAN operating systems	7.3	7.6
Wiring	7.3	7.6

Continued on next page.

★ 1142 ★ *Continued*
Data Communications (SIC 3669)

Data Communications Products - U.S.

Revenues of the data communications products market in the U.S. are shown, by type of product, in millions of dollars for the years 1991 (estimated) and 1992 (projected). Percent shares are based on industry totals of $20,407 million in revenues in 1991 and $22,418 million in revenues in 1992.

	1991	1992
PBXs and key systems	5.7%	6.4%
Modems	7.5	5.1
Multiplexers	4.6	4.3
Intelligent hubs	2.7	3.1
Front-end processors	2.2	1.9
Network management	1.7	1.8
Routers	1.4	1.8
CSU/DSUS	1.6	1.6
Diagnostic and test equipment . . .	1.6	1.5
Packet-switching gear	1.6	1.4
Bridges	1.3	1.3
Gateways	1.0	1.0
Videoconferencing	0.6	0.8
Matrix switches	0.4	0.3

Source: *Data Communications*, January 1992, p. 62.

★ 1143 ★
Data Communications (SIC 3669)

High-Performance Multiprotocol Routers

Worldwide market shares are shown in percent, based on total market revenues of $320 million in 1991 and $575 million in 1992 (forecasted).

	'91	'92
Cisco	76.0%	68.0%
Wellfleet	18.0	20.0
Others	6.0	12.0

Source: Investext, Thomson Financial Networks, March 2, 1992, from The First Boston Corporation.

★ 1144 ★
Data Communications (SIC 3669)

Intelligent Wiring Hub Global Market

Company shares of global market are based on total shipments of 1.6 million ports in 1991.

SynOptics Communications Inc.	32.0%
Cabletron Systems Inc.	19.0
Ungermann-Bass Inc.	12.0
BICC Data Networks	9.0
Optical Data Systems Inc.	8.0
David Systems Inc.	7.0
Chipcom Corp.	4.0
Hewlett-Packard Co.	4.0
AT&T	3.0
3Com Corp.	3.0
Others	5.5

Source: *Data Communications*, June 21, 1991, p. 12, from International Data Corp.

★ 1145 ★
Data Communications (SIC 3669)

Internetworking Market Penetration - Europe

The most popular internetworking methods are ranked according to responses in a survey of 512 internetworking users in the largest companies in Western Europe. Figures are shown in percent.

Local bridges	55.0%
Remote bridges	41.0
Application gateways	38.0
Host-based routing	29.0
Conversion software	29.0
Single-protocol routers	22.0
Multiprotocol servers	22.0
Multiprotocol routers	19.0
Multiplexers	19.0
Common transport networks	17.0
Manageable hubs	12.0
OSI protocol stacks	12.0
Do not know/no answer given	14.0

Source: *Data Communications*, January 1992, p. 15, from Business Research Group, Newton, Massachusetts.

★1146★

Data Communications (SIC 3669)

LAN and Internetworking Market - Western Europe

Market shares of the total Western European data communications market, by product type, are shown in percent for 1991 (estimated) and 1992 (projected), based on industry totals of $1.580 billion in 1991 and $2.053.4 billion in 1992.

	1991	1992
Adapter cards	45.0%	42.0%
Gateways, bridges, and routers . . .	22.0	26.0
Cabling, hubs, and related LAN components	18.0	17.0
LAN operating systems	12.0	12.0
LAN management software . . .	3.0	3.0

Source: *Data Communications*, January 1992, p. 64.

★1147★

Data Communications (SIC 3669)

Smart Hub Producers

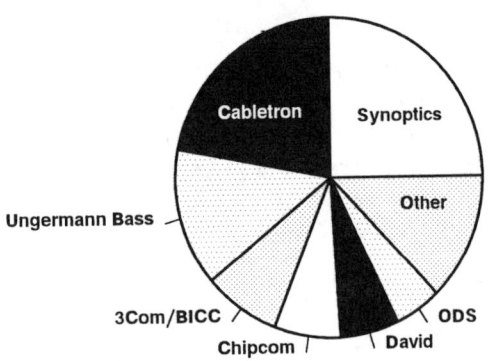

Shares are shown in percent, based on total sales of $526 million in 1991.

Synoptics	25.0%
Cabletron	22.0
Ungermann Bass	14.0
3Com/BICC	8.0
Chipcom	7.0
David	6.0
ODS	5.0
Other	13.0

Source: *The New York Times*, August 23, 1992, p. F9, from The Yankee Group.

★1148★

Data Communications (SIC 3669)

Transmission Media Worldwide

Shares of the worldwide transmission media industry, by medium, are shown in percent for the years 1990 and 1997.

	1990	1997
Fiber	45.7%	59.8%
Satellite	22.7	17.9
Copper	22.8	16.7
Microwave	8.8	5.8

Source: *Data Communications*, December 1991, p. 23, from Market Intelligence Research Corp.

★1149★

Data Communications (SIC 3669)

WAN Market - Western Europe

Market shares of the total WAN (wide area network) products industry in Western Europe, by product type, are shown in percent for 1991 (estimated) and 1992 (projected), based on industry totals of $782.6 million in 1991 and $791.8 million in 1992.

	1991	1992
Multiplexers	53.0%	52.0%
Small packet switches (fewer than 16 ports) and X.25 access products . .	27.0	27.0
Larger packet switches (more than 64 ports)	10.0	11.0
Medium packet switches (16 to 64 ports)	10.0	10.0

Source: *Data Communications*, January 1992, p. 65.

★ 1150 ★
Data Communications (SIC 3669)

Wireless Data and Voice Communications

The wireless communications equipment market is shown with sales, by type of equipment, in millions of dollars for 1991 and 1995.

	1991	1995
Cellular telephones	$ 1,800	$ 3,600
Pagers	1,600	2,700
Wireless PBXs	74	325
Wireless local area networks	10	250
Wireless wide area networks	102	102

Source: *Electronic Business*, February 10, 1992, p. 59, from Dataquest.

★ 1151 ★
Security Equipment (SIC 3669)

CCTV Security System Market

1991 market distribution by type is shown in percent. CCTV stands for Closed Circuit TV.

Multiplexers	20.0%
Video motion detection	15.0
Matrix switchers	13.0
Digital CCTV	13.0
Color CCTV	11.0
Slow scan video	7.0
Other	21.0

Source: *Security*, March, p. 92.

★ 1152 ★
Security Equipment (SIC 3669)

CCTV Security System Market Penetration

Percentages reflect market penetration for CCTV (closed circuit TV) systems.

Sequential switching	77.6%
Slow scan	58.2
Quad, switched quad	46.3
Multiplexed video	44.8
Video motion detection	38.8
Matrix CPU-based video	11.9

Source: *Security*, December 1991, p. 27, from National Guardian Security Services Corp.

★ 1153 ★
Security Equipment (SIC 3669)

Security Equipment Market by Type

Distribution of the security equipment market by type is shown in percent for 1991.

Wireless alarm	23.0%
Guard tour systems	21.0
Remote-monitored access	21.0
CCTV multiplexers	20.0
Others	15.0

Source: *Security*, March 1992, p. 5.

★ 1154 ★
Electronics (SIC 3670)

Computer Component Makers

Company sales are shown in millions of dollars for fiscal year 1991. Relative market shares are shown in percent.

	Sales ($ mil.)	% of Group
Applied Magnetics	$ 455.5	35.8%
Borland International	442.3	34.8
Read-Rite	177.0	13.9
Data Switch	103.0	8.1
American Power Conversion	93.6	7.4

Source: *Electronic Business*, May 18, 1992, p. 91.

★ 1155 ★
Electronics (SIC 3670)

Electronics Forecast - Japan

Leading Japanese consumer electronics companies project their pretax earnings from worldwide operations for the 12 months ending March 31, 1992. Relative market shares are shown in percent.

	Profits ($ mil.)	% of Group
Hitachi	$ 2,773	32.4%
Matsushita Electric	2,656	31.0
Sony	1,289	15.1
Toshiba	859	10.0
NEC	508	5.9
Fujitsu	469	5.5

Source: *Fortune*, March 23, 1992, p. 12.

★ 1156 ★

Electronics (SIC 3670)

Electronics Manufacturers

Sales of 12 leading electronics manufacturers worldwide, are shown in billions of dollars. Relative market shares are shown in percent, based on a total of $405.13 billion in 1990.

	Sales ($ bil.)	% of Group
Hitachi	$ 50.69	13.0%
Samsung	45.04	11.0
GE	44.88	11.0
Matsushita Electric Industrial	43.52	11.0
Siemens	39.23	10.0
Philips	30.87	8.0
Toshiba	30.18	7.0
Asea Brown Boveri	27.71	7.0
Alcatel-CGE	26.46	7.0
NEC	24.39	6.0
Mitsubishi Electric	21.23	5.0
Sony	20.93	5.0

Source: *Business Horizons*, November 1991, p. 17.

★ 1157 ★

Electronics (SIC 3670)

Top Electronics Exporters

The 20 leading U.S. electronics exporters are ranked by export sales in 1990 in millions of dollars. Relative market shares are shown in percent.

	Sales ($ mil.)	% of Group
IBM	$ 6,195	22.6%
Hewlett-Packard	2,816	10.3
Motorola	2,801	10.2
Digital Equipment	2,082	7.6
GM Hughes	1,895	6.9
Unisys	1,707	6.2
Raytheon	1,435	5.2
Intel	1,202	4.4
Sun Microsystems	1,117	4.1
Compaq	1,019	3.7
Xerox	900	3.3
Apple	559	2.0
Tandem Computers	557	2.0
Atari	512	1.9
Western Digital	487	1.8
Tektronix	467	1.7
NCR	466	1.7

	Sales ($ mil.)	% of Group
National Semiconductor	$ 421	1.5%
Varian Associates	397	1.4
Advanced Micro Devices	348	1.3

Source: *Electronic Business*, March 16, 1992, p. 40.

★ 1158 ★

Electronics (SIC 3670)

Top Electronics Sales Worldwide

The 20 leading U.S. electronics manufacturers are ranked by total 1990 sales in millions of dollars. Relative market shares are shown in percent.

	Sales ($ mil.)	% of group
IBM	$ 69,018	33.6%
Xerox	17,973	8.8
Hewlett-Packard	13,233	6.5
Digital Equipment	12,943	6.3
GM Hughes	11,723	5.7
Motorola	10,885	5.3
Unisys	10,111	4.9
Raytheon	9,268	4.5
Texas Instruments	6,567	3.2
Honeywell	6,309	3.1
NCR	6,285	3.1
Apple	5,558	2.7
Tandy	4,500	2.2
Intel	3,921	1.9
Compaq	3,599	1.8
Harris	3,053	1.5
AMP	3,044	1.5
Wang Laboratories	2,497	1.2
Sun Microsystems	2,466	1.2
Amdahl	2,159	1.1

Source: *Electronic Business*, March 16, 1992, p. 40.

★1159★

Television Tubes (SIC 3671)

TV Tube Manufacturers - China

Shares are shown in percent for 1991. Figures are based on the production quota of 7.2 million units set by the Shanghai Instrumentation Bureau.

Xianyang	38.9%
Beijing	25.0
Nanjing	22.2
Shanghai Novel	13.9

Source: Investext, Thomson Financial Networks, January 17, 1992, from Sun Hung Kai Research Ltd.

★1160★

Printed Circuit Boards (SIC 3672)

Ethernet Board Producers Worldwide

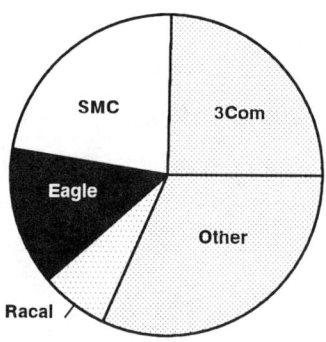

Shares of the global market are shown in percent for 1991.

3Com	25.0%
SMC	23.0
Eagle	13.6
Racal	6.9
Other	31.5

Source: *PC Week*, July 20, 1992, p. 18, from International Data Corp.

★1161★

Printed Circuit Boards (SIC 3672)

PCB Fabricators - North America

Estimated 1992 sales volume of PCBs (Printed circuit boards) is shown in millions of dollars. Shares of the group's sales are shown in percent. Sales figures may include revenue from non-fabricating activities.

	Sales ($ mil.)	% of Group
Tappan West	$ 220.0	12.9%
Rogers Corp., Soladyne Div., Flexible Interconnection Div.	182.0	10.7
Hadco Corp.	152.9	9.0
Zycon Corp.	113.0	6.6
Diceon Electronics Inc.	105.0	6.2
Advance Circuits	90.0	5.3
Sheldahl	85.0	5.0
Circo Craft	80.0	4.7
Sanmina Corp.	66.0	3.9
AMP-AKZO Corp.	65.0	3.8
Continental Circuits Corp.	65.0	3.8
Altron Inc.	62.0	3.6
Tektronix	61.0	3.6
Litton Advanced Circuitry	54.0	3.2
LIKA	51.0	3.0
Circuit Wise Inc.	50.0	2.9
Bureau of Engraving Inc.	50.0	2.9
Praegitzer Industries	41.0	2.4
Automata Inc.	38.0	2.2
Circuit Systems Inc.	35.5	2.1
Advance Quick Circuits	35.0	2.1

Source: *Electronic Packaging & Production*, April 1992, p. 48, from EP&P survey.

★ 1162 ★

Wiring Boards (SIC 3672)

Printed Wiring Boards

Printed wiring board shipment value to the instrument market is shown in millions of dollars. Shares by type are shown in percent, based on a 1990 total of $71.7 million.

	Value ($ mil.)	Share
Multilayers	$ 50.75	70.8 %
Two-sided	20.04	28.0
One-sided	0.89	1.2

Source: *Electronic Packaging & Production*, September 1991, p. 93, from IPC survey.

★ 1163 ★

Microelectronics (SIC 3674)

Chip Microsensor Market

Market shares, by application, are shown in percent, based on a 1991 total of $535 million.

Biomedical	25.6 %
Industrial	25.2
Automotive	20.9
Military/Aerospace	19.6
Consumer	8.6

Source: *Intech*, February 1992, p. 7, from Frost & Sullivan, Inc.

★ 1164 ★

Microelectronics (SIC 3674)

Hybrid Microelectronics Market

Shares by end use are shown in percent, based on a 1990 total market of $6.1 billion.

Communications	27.0 %
Military/aerospace	24.6
Computer/peripheral	23.7
Industrial and instrument	13.6
Automotive/consumer	11.0

Source: *Electronic Packaging & Production*, September 1991, p. 12, from Frost & Sullivan Inc.

★ 1165 ★

Microelectronics (SIC 3674)

Math Coprocessor Market

Company shares are shown in percent, based on 1991 worldwide revenue.

Intel Corp.	74.0 %
Cyrix Corp.	16.0
Integrated Information Technology Inc. . . .	9.0
Other	1.0

Source: *PC Week*, July 6, 1992, p. 15, from Dataquest Inc.

★1166★

Semiconductors (SIC 3674)

386 Microprocessor Global Manufacturers

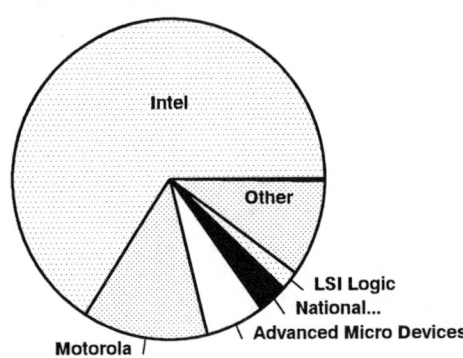

Shares are shown as percent of the global market for 386 and other 32-bit microprocessors in 1991.

Intel	66.0%
Motorola	13.0
Advanced Micro Devices	6.0
National Semiconductor	3.0
LSI Logic	2.0
Other	10.0

Source: *Business Week*, June 1, 1992, p. 87, from Integrated Circuit Engineering Corp., Robertson, Shepards & Co., and Intel Corp.

★1167★

Semiconductors (SIC 3674)

CMOS E2PLD Market by End Use - Worldwide

Worldwide demand for CMOS (complementary metal-oxide semiconductor) programmable logic devices, by end use, is shown in percent for 1990 and 1995.

	1990	1995
Electronic data processing	70.1%	50.5%
Communication	22.6	28.9
Industrial	4.4	10.7
Military	2.2	8.3
Consumer	0.7	1.2
Automotive	0.0	0.0

Source: *Electronic Business*, May 18, 1992, p. 116.

★1168★

Semiconductors (SIC 3674)

CMOS EPLD Market by End Use - Worldwide

Worldwide demand for CMOS (complementary metal-oxide semiconductor) EPLD programmable logic devices), by end use, is shown in percent for 1990 and 1995.

	1990	1995
Electronic data processing	36.8%	28.8%
Industrial	28.1	28.5
Communication	21.0	28.0
Military	12.9	14.0
Consumer	1.0	1.1
Automotive	0.0	0.0

Source: *Electronic Business*, May 18, 1992, p. 116.

★1169★

Semiconductors (SIC 3674)

CMOS FPGA Market Worldwide

Worldwide demand for CMOS (complementary metal-oxide semiconductor) FPGAs (field-programmable gate arrays), by consumer type, is shown in percent for 1990 and 1995.

	1990	1995
Electronic data processing	40.0%	32.5%
Communication	22.5	28.5
Industrial	19.0	19.0
Military	17.0	18.5
Consumer	1.5	1.5
Automotive	0.0	0.0

Source: *Electronic Business*, May 18, 1992, p. 114, from In-Stat, Inc.

★ 1170★
Semiconductors (SIC 3674)

CMOS PLD Market by End Use - Worldwide

Shares of the worldwide CMOS (complementary metal-oxide semiconductor) programmable logic device market, by end use, are shown in percent for 1990 and 1995.

	1990	1995
Electronic data processing	51.5%	32.5%
Communication	21.8	28.5
Industrial	17.5	19.0
Military	8.2	18.5
Consumer	1.0	1.5
Automotive	0.0	0.0

Source: *Electronic Business*, May 18, 1992, p. 116, from In-Stat, Inc.

★ 1171★
Semiconductors (SIC 3674)

DRAM Geographic Market - 1991

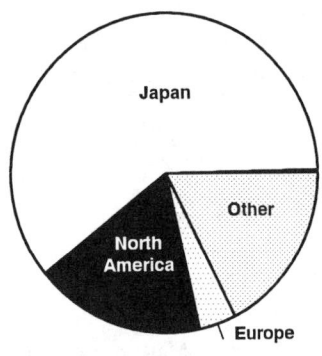

Worldwide geographic shares of DRAM (dynamic random-access memory) computer chip production worth $7 billion are shown in percent. (Data for North America do not include IBM's production, which is consumed internally).

Japan	60.6%
North America	18.1
Europe	3.8
Other	17.5

Source: *The Economist*, July 18, 1992, p. 66.

★ 1172★
Semiconductors (SIC 3674)

DRAM Manufacturers Worldwide

Worldwide manufacturer shares of DRAM (dynamic random-access memory) computer chips worth $7 billion are shown in percent. (Table does not include IBM's production which is consumed internally).

Toshiba	14.0%
Samsung	12.3
Hitachi	10.2
NEC	10.0
Fujitsu	8.8
Texas Instruments	7.6
Mitsubishi	7.0
Oki	5.2
Micron Technology	4.8
Siemens	3.8
Others	16.3

Source: *The Economist*, July 18, 1992, p. 66, from Dataquest.

★ 1173★
Semiconductors (SIC 3674)

DRAM Producers

1991 company shares of the world market for DRAM (dynamic random access memory) chips are shown in percent. IBM's internal DRAM production is not included.

Toshiba	14.0%
Samsung	12.3
Hitachi	10.2
NEC	10.0
Fujitsu	8.8
Texas Instuments	7.6
Mitsubishi	7.0
Oki	5.2
Micron Tech	4.8
Siemens	3.8

Source: *The Wall Street Journal*, July 14, 1992, p. B1, from Dataquest Inc.

★ 1174 ★

Semiconductors (SIC 3674)

Integrated Circuit Industry - Japan

Distribution of integrated circuit sales, by product, is shown in percent based on totals of $80.990 billion in 1989 and $58.354 billion in 1990.

	1989	1990
Linear circuits	3.4%	4.8%
Counter circuits	20.8	26.4
Bipolar	2.0	2.9
Logic	1.7	2.4
Memory	0.4	0.5
MOS	18.0	23.6
Logic	9.2	12.1
Microcomputers	3.9	5.1
Memory	8.2	10.7
RAM	6.6	8.7
ROM	1.6	2.1
Other	24.2	0.7

Source: Electronics, September 1991, p. 70, from Ministry of International Trade and Industry.

★ 1175 ★

Semiconductors (SIC 3674)

Leading Semiconductor Makers

Companies are shown with revenues for the latest four quarters in millions of dollars. Relative market shares are shown in percent.

	Rev. ($ mil.)	% of Group
Motorola	$ 11,341	63.3%
Intel	4,779	26.7
National Semiconductor	1,671	9.3
Brooktree	86	0.5
Vitesse Semiconductor	27	0.2

Source: Fortune, April 6, 1992, p. 38.

★ 1176 ★

Semiconductors (SIC 3674)

Semiconductor Equipment Leaders Worldwide

The leading ten semiconductor equipment manufacturers are ranked according to 1991 sales in millions; relative shares for the same period are shown in percent.

	Sales ($ mil.)	% of Group
Tokyo Electron Ltd.	$ 764	18.1%
Applied Materials	654	15.5
Nikon	616	14.6
Advantest	448	10.6
Canon	360	8.5
Varian	328	7.8
Hitachi	316	7.5
Teradyne	263	6.2
General Signal	243	5.7
Silicon Valley Group	235	5.6

Source: Solid State Technology, May 1992, from VLSI Research Inc.

★ 1177 ★

Semiconductors (SIC 3674)

Semiconductor Leaders Worldwide

Revenue figures are shown in millions of dollars for 1991. Company shares are shown as percent of global market.

	Rev ($ mil.)	Share
NEC	$ 4,898	15.2%
Toshiba	4,843	15.0
Hitachi	3,893	12.1
Intel	3,171	9.8
Motorola	3,694	11.5
Fujitsu	2,880	8.9
Texas Instruments	2,574	8.0
Mitsubishi	2,319	7.2
Philips	2,011	6.2
Matsushita	1,942	6.0

Source: Electronics, February 1992, p. 14, from Dataquest Inc.

★ 1178 ★

Semiconductors (SIC 3674)

Semiconductor Leading Manufacturers

Company sales are shown in millions of dollars for fiscal year 1991. Relative market shares, based on group total sales, are shown in percent.

	Sales ($ mil.)	% of Group
Intel	$ 4,778.6	65.8%
LSI Logic	697.8	9.6
VLSI Technology	413.4	5.7
Cypress Semiconductor	286.8	4.0
Chips and Technologies	225.1	3.1
Integrated Device Technology	198.6	2.7
Micron Technology	149.1	2.1
ATMEL	120.4	1.7
Altera	106.9	1.5
Dallas Semiconductor	103.8	1.4
Linear Technology	94.2	1.3
Brooktree	85.9	1.2

Source: *Electronic Business*, May 18, 1992, p. 91.

★ 1179 ★

Semiconductors (SIC 3674)

Semiconductor Manufacturers

Company sales are shown in millions of dollars for 1991. Percent shares are based on a group total of $19,424 million.

	Sales ($ mil.)	% of Group
Texas Instruments	$ 6,784	34.9%
Intel	4,779	24.6
AMP	3,095	15.9
National Semiconductor	1,656	8.5
Advanced Micro Devices	1,227	6.3
Molex	740	3.8
Micron Technology	457	2.4
Cypress Semiconductor	287	1.5
Xilinx	130	0.7
Linear Technology	107	0.6
Altera	107	0.6
Vicor	56	0.3

Source: *The 1992 Business Week 1000*, p. 174.

★ 1180 ★

Semiconductors (SIC 3674)

Semiconductor Manufacturing Leaders - Japan

The leading semiconductor manufacturers in Japan are ranked according to actual production figures (in billions of yen) for the first half of 1991. Relative shares shown in percent.

	Yen (bil.)	% of Group
Toshiba	780	29.1%
Hitachi	640	23.9
Fujitsu	465	17.4
Mitsubishi	410	15.3
NEC	385	14.4

Source: *Solid State Technology*, January 1992.

★ 1181 ★

Semiconductors (SIC 3674)

Semiconductor Market in Europe

Percent distribution of the European semiconductor market, by category, is shown in millions of ECUs (European currency units) for 1991 and 1995.

	1991	1995
Bipolar digital	428.0	302.0
Memory	43.0	24.0
Logic	386.0	278.0
MOS digital	4,847.0	9,568.0
Memory	1,928.0	3,855.0
Microcomponent	1,669.0	3,635.0
Logic	1,250.0	2,078.0
Analog	1,951.0	2,984.0
Discrete	1,634.0	2,236.0
Optoelectronic	347.0	484.0

Source: *Electronics*, July 1991, from Dataquest, Inc.

★ 1182 ★

Semiconductors (SIC 3674)

Semiconductor Market Worldwide

Companies' shares of 1991 global market are shown in percent.

NEC (Japan)	8.5%
Toshiba (Japan)	8.2
Hitachi (Japan)	6.7
Intel (U.S.)	6.3

Continued on next page.

★1182★ *Continued*

Semiconductors (SIC 3674)

Semiconductor Market Worldwide

Companies' shares of 1991 global market are shown in percent.

Motorola (U.S.)	6.0%
Fujitsu (Japan)	4.8
Texas Instr (U.S.)	4.2
Mitsubishi (Japan)	4.0
Matsushita (Japan)	3.7
Philips (Netherlands)	3.2
Other	44.4

Source: Investext, Thomson Financial Networks, May 28, 1992, from UBS Phillips & Drew Global Research Group.

★1183★

Electronic Sensors (SIC 3679)

Sensors for Manufacturing Use - Suppliers in Japan

Shares, by company, are shown in percent.

Keyence	70.0%
Others	30.0

Source: Investext, Thomson Financial Networks, March 17, 1992, from Merrill Lynch Capital Markets.

★1184★

Hybrid Microelectronics (SIC 3679)

Hybrid Microelectronics Market

Segment distribution is shown in percent, based on a 1990 market of $6.1 billion.

Communications	27.1%
Military/aerospace	24.6
Computer/peripheral	23.7
Industrial & instrument	13.6
Automotive/consumer	11.0

Source: *Solid State Technology*, October 1991, p. 30, from Frost & Sullivan.

★1185★

LCD Equipment (SIC 3679)

LCD Equipment Worldwide

Segment distribution of the 1990 market is shown in percent, based on a total of $1.504 billion worldwide.

Lithography equipment	37.8%
CVD/sputtering equipment	27.0
Etching equipment	21.6
Liquid crystal display equipment	13.5

Source: *Electronic Business*, March 30, 1992, p. 12, from Nomura Research Institute and Sharp.

★1186★

Batteries (SIC 3691)

Aftermarket of Consumer Rechargeables

Percent shares by application for 1991 are based on total market of $655 million. 1995 market shares are based on a projected total of $1 billion. "Other" includes computers, power tools, etc.

	'91	'95
Round cell/chargers	44.0%	48.0%
Camcorder	12.0	9.0
Cordless	11.0	8.0
Cellular	7.0	12.0
Hobby	8.0	7.0
Other	18.0	16.0

Source: *HFD*, January 1992, p. 4.

★1187★

Batteries (SIC 3691)

Alkaline Batteries

Brand shares are shown in percent for January of 1992.

Duracell	43.9%
Eveready	37.3
Ray O Vac	11.5
Kodak	3.1
Other	4.2

Source: Investext, Thomson Financial Networks, March 11, 1992, from The First Boston Corporation.

★ 1188 ★
Batteries (SIC 3691)

Alkaline Battery Manufacturers

Unit shares are shown as percent of the domestic market.

	Sept/Oct '90	Sept/Oct '91
Duracell	45.7%	44.5%
Eveready	37.2	35.2
Ray O Vac	6.7	7.2
Kodak	4.4	7.0
Other	6.0	6.1

Source: Investext, Thomson Financial Networks, January 2, 1992, from Merrill Lynch Capital Markets.

★ 1189 ★
Batteries (SIC 3691)

Alkaline Battery Manufacturers - Europe

Shares, by company, are shown in percent.

Duracell	47.0%
Eveready	21.0
Other	32.0

Source: Investext, Thomson Financial Networks, May 11, 1992, from The First Boston Corporation.

★ 1190 ★
Batteries (SIC 3691)

Alkaline Battery Manufacturers - U.S.

Shares of the domestic alkaline battery market are shown in percent.

Duracell	44.0%
Eveready	36.0
Other	20.0

Source: Investext, Thomson Financial Networks, June 4, 1992, from Merrill Lynch Capital Markets.

★ 1191 ★
Batteries (SIC 3691)

Batteries

Brand shares are shown in percent, based on an industry total of $85.2 million in advertising expenditures in 1991. Manufacturers' names are shown in parentheses.

Eveready Energizer (Ralston Purina Co.)	51.5%
Duracell (Duracell Batteries)	45.8
Millenium Rechargeable Batteries (Gates Corp.)	2.3
Quantum Battery Packs	0.2
Panasonic Rechargeable Batteries (Matsushita)	0.1

Source: Investext, Thomson Financial Networks, April 28, 1992, from Wheat First Butcher & Singer, Inc. and leading national advertisers.

★ 1192 ★
Batteries (SIC 3691)

Battery Consumption

Shares of battery market by application are shown in percent, based on a total of $3 billion.

Portable/audio	40.0%
Toys/games	21.0
Flashlights	17.0
Photo	12.0
Miscellaneous	10.0

Source: *HFD*, January 1992, p. 3.

★ 1193 ★
Batteries (SIC 3691)

Battery Manufacturers - Europe

Market shares, by company, are shown in percent, based on the total market for batteries in Europe.

Duracell	27.0%
Eveready	22.0
Others	51.0

Source: Investext, Thomson Financial Networks, May 11, 1992, from The First Boston Corporation.

★1194★

Batteries (SIC 3691)

Rechargeable Battery Consumption

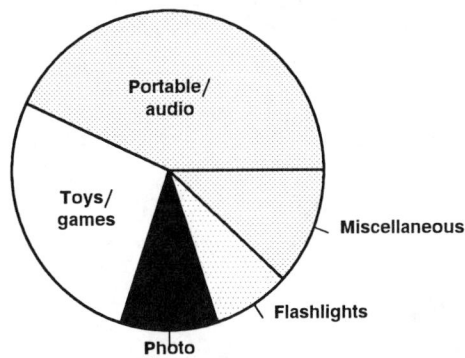

Market shares by application are shown as percent of total consumption.

Portable/audio	43.0%
Toys/games	27.0
Photo	10.0
Flashlights	8.0
Miscellaneous	12.0

Source: *HFD*, January 1992, p. 3.

★1195★

Batteries (SIC 3691)

Retail Battery Market

Shares of the total battery market, by battery type, are shown in percent, based on an industry total of $2.9 billion.

Alkaline	70.0%
Heavy duty	22.0
General purpose	8.0

Source: *DM*, November 1991, p. 44, from RAYOVAC, *NFO*, A.C. Nielsen, and Duracell Research.

★1196★

Motors (SIC 3694)

Leaders of the European Motor Industry

Company 1990 sales are shown in billions of ECUs (European currency units). Percent shares are based on group total.

	ECUs (bil.)	% of Group
Daimler-Benz	41.7	26.2%
Fiat	37.6	23.6
Volkswagen	33.2	20.8
Renault	23.7	14.9
Peugeot	23.1	14.5

Source: *International Management*, April 1992, p. 75.

★1197★

Data Storage Media (SIC 3695)

Floppy Disk Producers

The leading U.S. manufacturers of computer floppy disks are ranked by millions of units sold in 1991. Percentages are based on the group total.

	Units (mil.)	% of Group
3M Co.	418	17.5%
Verbatim	364	15.2
Hitachi Maxell	268	11.2
KAO Infosystems	236	9.9
Sony	268	11.2
Hanny/Dysan	261	10.9
BASF Infosystems	234	9.8
Fuji Photo Film	170	7.1
Megamedia Corp.	169	7.1

Source: *Business America*, June 1, 1992, p. 4.

★ 1198 ★

Data Storage Media (SIC 3695)

Tape Backup Media

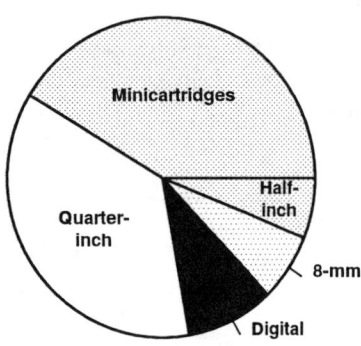

Projected market shares for 1992 are shown in percent.

Minicartridges	41.1%
Quarter-inch	36.3
Digital	9.3
8-mm	6.9
Half-inch	6.4

Source: *PC Week Hardware*, June 15, 1992, p. 34, from Peripheral Strategies Inc.

★ 1199 ★

Recording Media (SIC 3695)

Blank Audio Tape Market by Type

Percentages reflect shares of factory sales of standard size blank audio tapes to retailers.

	Vol. Share	Sales Share
Normal	75.0%	57.0%
High bias	22.0	38.0
Metal	3.0	5.0

Source: *HFD*, March 1992, p. 9.

★ 1200 ★

Recording Media (SIC 3695)

Blank VHS Video Cassette Market

Shares of the blank full-size VHS video cassette market, by tape length, are shown in percent for 1991.

T-120	88.0%
T-160	3.0
Other	9.0

Source: *HFD*, March 1992, p. 7.

★ 1201 ★

Defense Electronics (SIC 3699)

Asian/Canadian/European Defense Electronics Companies

Company sales are shown in millions of dollars for fiscal year 1991. Percent shares are based on the group's total.

	Sales ($ mil.)	% of Group
General Electric Company	$ 11,277.5	34.7%
Thomson-CSF	6,818.7	21.0
Matra S.A.	4,637.6	14.3
Hawker Siddeley Company	3,888.0	12.0
Racal Electronics	3,851.6	11.8
Smiths Industries	1,208.1	3.7
Ferranti International	846.3	2.6

Source: *Aviation Week & Space Technology*, May 25, 1992, p. 51.

★ 1202 ★

Simulators (SIC 3699)

Flight Simulator Suppliers

Shares of commercial flight simulator orders are shown in percent, based on a total of 25 units in 1991. "Other" includes FlightSafety.

CAE	36.0%
Rediffusion	20.0
Thomson CSF	32.0
Other	12.0

Source: Investext, Thomson Financial Networks, February 25, 1992, from Wood Gundy Inc.

★1203★

Simulators (SIC 3699)

Flight Training Device Suppliers

Shares of flight training device orders are shown in percent, based on a total of 23 units in 1991. "Other" includes FlightSafety.

Rediffusion	52.0%
CAE	31.0
Thomson CSF	13.0
Other	4.0

Source: Investext, Thomson Financial Networks, February 25, 1992, from Wood Gundy Inc.

SIC 37 - Transportation Equipment

★1204★

Autos (SIC 3710)

Car and Truck Market Shares

Percent shares of total car and truck market, by brand, are based on total sales of 13,886,918 vehicles in 1990 and 12,335,430 vehicles in 1991. Brands are arranged in alphabetical order.

	'90	'91
Acura	1.0%	1.2%
Alfa Romeo	<0.1	<0.1
Aston Martin	<0.1	<0.1
Audi	0.2	0.1
BMW	0.5	0.4
Buick	3.9	4.4
Cadillac	1.9	1.7
Chevrolet/Geo	18.8	18.1
Chrysler	1.4	1.1
Daihatsu	0.1	0.1
Dodge	6.0	6.3
Eagle	0.4	0.5
Ferrari	<0.1	<0.1
Ford	19.4	18.7
GMC	2.4	2.3
Honda	5.2	5.3
Hyundai	1.0	1.0
Infiniti	0.2	0.3
Isuzu	0.8	0.9
Jaguar	0.1	0.1
Jeep	1.4	1.4
Lamborghini	<0.1	<0.1
Lexus	0.5	0.6
Lincoln	1.7	1.4
Lotus	<0.1	<0.1
Maserati	<0.1	<0.1
Mazda	2.5	2.8
Mercedes-Benz	0.6	0.5
Mercury	2.8	3.0
Mitsubishi	1.4	1.5
Nissan	4.3	4.4
Oldsmobile	3.94	3.7
Peugeot	<0.1	<0.1

	'90	'91
Plymouth	3.1%	3.0%
Pontiac	4.8	4.2
Porsche	0.1	<0.1
Range Rover	<0.1	<0.1
Rolls/Bentley	<0.1	<0.1
Saab	0.2	0.2
Saturn	<0.1	0.6
Sterling	<0.1	<0.1
Subaru	0.8	0.9
Suzuki	0.1	0.2
Toyota	7.2	7.6
Volvo	0.6	0.5
Volkswagen	1.0	0.8
Yugo	<0.1	<0.1

Source: *Automotive News, 1992 Market Data Book*, May 27, 1992, p. 17, from Automotive News Data Center.

★1205★

Autos (SIC 3710)

Car Sales in Canada

Company sales are shown for 1991 as units sold. Percent shares are based on 1991 total sales of 873,203 cars.

	Units	% of Group
General Motors	285,407	32.7%
Ford	147,355	16.9
Chrysler	110,495	12.7
Honda	104,454	12.0
Toyota	76,343	8.7
Mazda	34,486	3.9
Volkswagen	33,457	3.8
Nissan	30,613	3.5
Hyundai	22,011	2.5
Subaru	8,360	1.0
Suzuki	6,662	0.8
BMW	4,304	0.5

Continued on next page.

★ 1205 ★ *Continued*

Autos (SIC 3710)

Car Sales in Canada

Company sales are shown for 1991 as units sold. Percent shares are based on 1991 total sales of 873,203 cars.

	Units	% of Group
Volvo	4,215	0.5%
Mercedes-Benz	3,455	0.4
Jaguar	740	0.1
Lada	694	0.1
Peugeot	152	0.0

Source: *Automotive News, 1992 Market Data Book*, May 27, 1992, p. 31, from Automotive News Data Center.

★ 1206 ★

Autos (SIC 3710)

Vehicle Makers - Japan

Car and truck production shares, by company, are shown in percent, based on totals of 13,486,796 vehicles in 1990 and 13,142,810 vehicles in 1991.

	'90	'91
Toyota	31.2%	30.8%
Nissan	17.9	17.6
Mitsubishi	9.9	10.6
Mazda	10.5	10.5
Honda	10.3	10.3
Suzuki	6.2	6.5
Daihatsu	4.7	5.1
Fuji	3.8	4.0
Isuzu	4.2	3.6
Hino	0.7	0.7
Nissan Diesel	0.5	0.5
Other trucks	0.0	0.0

Source: *Automotive News, 1992 Market Data Book*, May 27, 1992, p. 3, from Automotive Industry Data Ltd.

★ 1207 ★

Autos (SIC 3711)

Auto Manufacturers - Europe

Shares for the first six months of 1991 are shown in percent based on a total market of 7.355 million vehicles.

Volkswagen	16.5%
Fiat	13.3
GM	12.7
Ford	12.2
Peugeot	11.4
Renault	9.7
Japanese automakers	12.2
Other	12.0

Source: *The Detroit News*, August 4, 1991, p. 1D, from *Financial Times* and company reports.

★ 1208 ★

Autos (SIC 3711)

Auto Sales in the U.S.

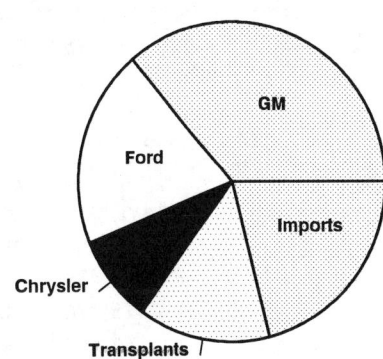

Estimated manufacturer shares of the domestic new car market are shown in percent for 1991. The import category does not include captive imports sold by the Big Three automakers.

GM	36.0%
Ford	20.0
Chrysler	9.0
Transplants	14.0
Imports	21.0

Source: *The Christian Science Monitor*, December 26, 1991, p. 6, from Prudential Securities Inc.

★ 1209 ★
Autos (SIC 3711)

Automakers - Western Europe

Market shares of 1991 passenger car sales are shown in percent based on a total of 13.488 million units.

VW group	.16.5%
Fiat group	.12.8
GM group	.12.1
Peugeot/Citroen	.12.0
Ford group	.11.9
Renault	.10.1
Other	.24.6

Source: *Financial Times*, February 17, 1992, p. 12, from automotive industry provisional estimates.

★ 1210 ★
Autos (SIC 3711)

Automobile Production

Automobile production by U.S. factories is shown in percent for 1990, based on a total of 6,069,030 units. (Data for Mitsubishi, Subaru, and Toyota represent joint ventures with U.S. car makers).

	No. of Autos	Share
General Motors	2,653,391	43.7%
Ford	1,377,351	22.7
Chrysler	726,466	12.0
Honda	435,438	7.2
Toyota	415,416	6.8
Mazda	184,368	3.0
Mitsubishi	148,379	2.4
Nissan	95,844	1.6
Subaru	32,377	0.5

Source: *U.S. Industrial Outlook 1992*, p. 36-4, from *Automotive News* and *Ward's Automotive Reports*.

★ 1211 ★
Autos (SIC 3711)

Car Manufacturers in Germany

German car manufacturers' shares are shown in percent, based on 1991 total sales of 4.2 million cars.

Volkswagen	.26.6%
Opel	.17.2
Mercedes-Benz	7.0
BMW	5.6
Porsche	0.2
Other European	.24.8
Japanese	.14.9
Other	3.7

Source: *The Economist*, May 24, 1992, p. 70, from DRI/McGraw-Hill, VDA, and company reports.

★ 1212 ★
Autos (SIC 3711)

Car Market in Australia

Manufacturers' shares of the 1991 market are shown in percent.

Toyota	.21.5%
Ford	.20.6
General Motors	.16.8
Mitsubishi	.11.3
Nissan	.10.0
Others	.19.8

Source: *Far Eastern Economic Review*, February 20, 1992, p. 42, from Paxus Corp.

★ 1213 ★

Autos (SIC 3711)

Car Market Shares

Percent shares of total market, by brand, are based on total sales of 9,295,841 cars in 1990 and 8,176,014 cars in 1991. Brands are presented in alphabetical order.

	'90	'91
Acura	1.5%	1.8%
Alfa Romeo	<0.1	<0.1
Aston Martin	<0.1	<0.1
Audi	0.2	0.2
BMW	0.7	0.7
Buick	5.8	6.7
Cadillac	2.8	2.6
Chevrolet/Geo	14.7	14.2
Chrysler	2.0	1.5
Daihatsu	0.1	0.1
Dodge	3.9	4.0
Eagle	0.7	0.7
Ferrari	<0.1	<0.1
Ford	14.2	13.2
Honda	7.7	8.1
Hyundai	1.5	1.4
Infinity	0.3	0.4
Isuzu	0.1	0.2
Jaguar	0.2	0.1
Lamborghini	<0.1	<0.1
Lexus	0.7	0.9
Lincoln	2.5	2.2
Lotus	<0.1	<0.1
Maserati	<0.1	<0.1
Mazda	2.4	2.7
Mercedes-Benz	0.8	0.7
Mercury	4.2	4.6
Mitsubishi	1.6	2.0
Nissan	4.5	4.6
Odsmobile	5.5	5.2
Peugeot	<0.1	<0.1
Plymouth	2.7	2.4
Pontiac	6.8	6.0
Porsche	0.1	0.1
Rools/Bentley	<0.1	<0.1
Saab	0.3	0.3
Saturn	<0.1	0.9
Sterling	<0.1	-
Subaru	1.2	1.3
Suzuki	0.1	0.1
Toyota	7.7	8.2
Volvo	1.0	0.8

	'90	'91
Volkswagen	1.4%	1.1%
Yugo	0.1	<0.1

Source: *Automotive News, 1992 Market Data Book*, May 27, 1992, p. 17, from Automotive News Data Center.

★ 1214 ★

Autos (SIC 3711)

Car Production in Canada

Market shares, by company, are shown as percent of production in 1991.

General Motors	46.7%
Ford	31.0
Honda	9.4
Toyota	6.5
Hyundai	2.7
Chrysler	1.7
Volvo	0.8

Source: Investext, Thomson Financial Networks, March 17, 1992, from Smith, Barney, Harris Upham & Company.

★ 1215 ★

Autos (SIC 3711)

Car Production in Mexico

Company shares are shown as percent of total production in 1990 and 1991.

	1990	1991
VW de Mexico	30.6%	27.4%
Ford	22.5	23.2
Chrysler	18.1	18.4
GM de Mexico	12.3	17.4
Nissan Mexicana	16.5	13.6

Source: *Ward's Auto World*, April 1992, p. 16, from AMIA.

★ 1216 ★
Autos (SIC 3711)

Car Sales in Canada

Market shares, by company, are shown in percent for 1991.

General Motors	44.9%
Ford	25.1
Chrysler	17.0
Honda	5.5
Toyota	3.5
Hyundai	0.9
Volvo	0.3

Source: Investext, Thomson Financial Networks, March 17, 1992, from Smith, Barney, Harris Upham & Company.

★ 1217 ★
Autos (SIC 3711)

Car Sales - Western Europe

Company shares are shown as percent of total sales of 13,428,946 cars in 1990 and 13,460,608 cars in 1991.

	1990	1991
VW Group	16.2%	15.7%
Fiat Group	12.6	13.9
Peugeot Group	12.1	12.9
Ford	12.0	11.5
GM (Opel/Vaux.)	11.7	11.6
Renault	10.1	9.9
Mercedes-Benz	3.5	3.3
Nissan	3.4	3.1
BMW	3.2	2.8
Toyota	2.8	2.8
Rover Group	2.7	3.0
Mazda	2.1	2.2
Other Japan	1.6	1.4
Volvo	1.5	1.7
Mitsubishi	1.4	1.4
Honda	1.3	1.2
Saab	0.4	0.4
Jaguar	0.1	0.1
GM (Isuzu)	0.1	0.1
Others	1.0	1.2

Source: *Ward's Auto World*, March 1992, p. 97.

★ 1218 ★
Autos (SIC 3711)

Carmakers Worldwide

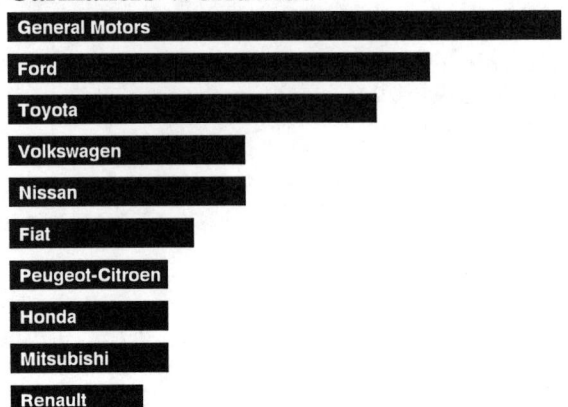

The world's 10 biggest carmakers produced 33.496 million cars in 1991. Relative shares are shown in percent.

	Cars (mil.)	% of Group
General Motors	7,015	20.9%
Ford	5,359	16.0
Toyota	4,719	14.1
Volkswagen	3,128	9.3
Nissan	3,082	9.2
Fiat	2,461	7.3
Peugeot-Citroen	2,058	6.1
Honda	1,975	5.9
Mitsubishi	1,908	5.7
Renault	1,791	5.3

Source: *The Economist*, August 1, 1992, p. 60, from *Automotive News*.

★ 1219 ★

Autos (SIC 3711)

Changing Auto Market

Shares by model for the first five months of 1991 and 1992 are shown as percent of the total U.S. auto market. Producers are shown in parentheses.

	Jan-May 1991	Jan-May 1992
Accord (Honda)	5.0%	4.5%
Taurus (Ford)	3.8	4.3
Camry (Toyota)	3.0	3.4
Grand Am (Pontiac)	2.3	2.9
Other	85.9	84.9

Source: *The Wall Street Journal*, June 11, 1992, p. B1, from Furzman Selz Inc.

★ 1220 ★

Autos (SIC 3711)

Domestic and Imported Subcompact Car Sales

Subcompact car sales are shown, by brand, as units sold in 1991. Percent brand shares are based on group total.

	Units	% of Group
Ford Escort	247,864	14.9%
Honda Civic	232,690	14.0
Toyota Corolla	199,083	11.9
Nissan Sentra	146,618	8.8
Toyota Tercel	102,043	6.1
Geo Prizm	98,433	5.9
Geo Metro	90,373	5.4
Dodge Shadow	77,191	4.6
Geo Storm	77,186	4.6
Saturn	74,493	4.5
Hyundai Excel	66,376	4.0
Plymouth Sundance	53,818	3.2
Mazda Protege	53,474	3.2
Mitsubishi Eclipse	49,278	3.0
Mercury Tracer	45,422	2.7
Nissan NX	8,211	0.5
Subaru Justy	6,741	0.4
Daihatsu Charade	6,202	0.4
Suzuki Swift	5,530	0.3
Volkswagen Cabriolet	5,401	0.3
Mazda MX-3	4,667	0.3
Volkswagen Corrado	4,331	0.3
Mitsubishi Precis	3,329	0.2
Yugo	3,092	0.2%
Izusu Impulse	3,059	0.2
Mitsubishi Expo LRV	1,773	0.1
Dodge Omni	561	0.0
Plymouth Horizon	505	0.0
Isuzu I-Mark	99	0.0
Nissan Pulsar	33	0.0

Source: *Automotive News, 1992 Market Data Book*, May 27, 1992, p. 30, from Automotive News Data Center.

★ 1221 ★

Autos (SIC 3711)

European Luxury-Car Market in U.S.

European luxury cars are ranked according to the number of units sold in the U.S. during 1992.

Volvo	64,893
BMW	63,870
Mercedes-Benz	62,903
Saab	25,637
Audi	13,905
Porsche	4,209
Jaguar	3,506
Alfa-Romeo	2,941
Ferrari	552

Source: *USA TODAY*, November 9, 1992, p. 5B, from Autodata.

★ 1222 ★

Autos (SIC 3711)

Intermediate Car Sales

Car sales are shown by brand based on units sold in 1991. Percent shares are based on group total. Imported car sales are included.

	Units	% of Group
Honda Accord	399,297	12.9%
Ford Taurus	299,659	9.7
Toyota Camry	263,818	8.5
Chevrolet Lumina	217,555	7.0
Pontiac Grand Am	143,774	4.6
Odsmobile Cutlass Ciera	135,670	4.4
Buick Century	128,904	4.2
Dodge Dynasty	105,651	3.4

Continued on next page.

★ 1222 ★ *Continued*

Autos (SIC 3711)

Intermediate Car Sales

Car sales are shown by brand based on units sold in 1991. Percent shares are based on group total. Imported car sales are included.

	Units	% of Group
Buick Regal	104,802	3.4%
Pontiac Grand Prix	103,203	3.3
Mercury Sable	100,331	3.2
Nissan Maxima	99,026	3.2
Plymouth Acclaim	92,352	3.0
Oldsmobile Cutlass Supreme	87,540	2.8
Dodge Spirit	81,222	2.6
Ford Thunderbird	74,189	2.4
Nissan Stanza	73,475	2.4
Mazda 626	68,369	2.2
Subaru Legacy	64,937	2.1
Buick Skylark	60,327	1.9
Mercury Cougar	55,148	1.8
Chevrolet Camaro	54,383	1.8
Oldsmobile Calais	47,666	1.5
Mitsubishi Galant	38,742	1.3
Chrysler LeBaron J	35,274	1.1
Chrysler LeBaron A	25,587	0.8
Pontiac Firebird	24,035	0.8
Pontiac 6000	21,624	0.7
Hyundai Sonata	20,966	0.7
Volkswagen Passat	16,134	0.5
Infinity G20	13,929	0.4
Eagle Premier	11,283	0.4
Dodge Monaco	7,822	0.3
Saab 900S	6,874	0.2
Saab 900 Turbo	4,733	0.2
Saab 900	4,646	0.1
Peugeot 405-505	3,575	0.1
Chevrolet Celebrity	615	0.0
Mitsubishi Sigma	150	0.0
Oldsmobile Achieva	83	0.0

Source: *Automotive News, 1992 Market Data Book*, May 27, 1992, p. 30, from Automotive News Data Center.

★ 1223 ★

Autos (SIC 3711)

Japanese Automobile Sales

Company shares, shown in percent, are based on total sales of 5,102,663 cars in 1990 and 4,868,053 cars in 1991.

	1990	1991
Toyota	37.1%	35.5%
Nissan	20.7	20.5
Honda	10.1	10.6
Mazda	7.8	7.4
Mitsubishi	6.2	6.9
Daihatsu	4.9	5.6
Suzuki	4.9	5.6
Fuji/Subaru	3.2	3.2
Mercedes-Benz	0.8	0.7
BMW	0.7	0.7
VW	0.8	0.6
Isuzu	0.7	0.6
Audi	0.3	0.3
Rover	0.3	0.3
Volvo	0.2	0.2
General Motors	0.2	0.2
Others	1.1	1.1

Source: *Ward's Auto World*, May 1992, p. 7, from Japanese industry sources.

★ 1224 ★

Autos (SIC 3711)

Japanese Luxury-Car Market in U.S.

Japanese luxury cars are ranked according to number of units sold in the U.S. during 1992.

Lexus	91,195
Acura (excluding Integra)	71,843
Infiniti	39,945

Source: *USA TODAY*, November 9, 1992, p. 5B, from Autodata.

★1225★

Autos (SIC 3711)

Luxury Car Sales

Car sales are shown in units sold, by brand, in 1991; relative market shares are shown in percent for the same period.

	Units	% of Group
Cadillac DeVille	146,636	23.4%
Lincoln Town Car	116,900	18.7
Acura Legend	65,689	10.5
Lincoln Continental	52,450	8.4
Lexus LS400	36,955	5.9
Cadillac Seville	26,688	4.3
Cadillac Brougham	22,017	3.5
Mercedes-Benz 300 class	18,916	3.0
Mercedes-Benz S class	17,972	2.9
BMW 5 series	16,655	2.7
Cadillac Eldorado	15,304	2.4
Infinity Q45	14,622	2.3
Volvo 940 series	14,032	2.2
Mercedes-Benz 190 class	13,750	2.2
Lexus SC400/300	11,775	1.9
Lincoln Mark VII	9,351	1.5
Audi 100/200	7,166	1.1
Jaguar XJ6	6,638	1.1
BMW 7 series	5,508	0.9
Sterling	2,744	0.4
BMW 850i	1,711	0.3
Audi 100/200 Quattro	1,125	0.2
Rolls-Royce/Bentley	447	0.1
Audi V8 Quattro	527	0.1
BMW M5	455	0.1
Audi Coupe Quattro	364	0.1
Maserati	240	0.0
Aston Martin	60	0.0
BMW 635CSi	12	0.0

Source: *Automotive News, 1992 Market Data Book*, May 27, 1992, p. 30, from Automotive News Data Center.

★1226★

Autos (SIC 3711)

Mexican Car Exports

Ford
GM de Mexico
Chrysler
VW de Mexico
Nissan Mexicana

Company shares are shown as percent of total car exports in 1990 and 1991.

	1990	1991
Ford	35.1%	32.8%
GM de Mexico	16.2	25.4
Chrysler	22.1	19.9
VW de Mexico	19.2	16.0
Nissan Mexicana	7.3	6.0

Source: *Ward's Auto World*, April 1992, p. 16, from AMIA.

★1227★

Autos (SIC 3711)

Near Luxury Car Sales

Car sales are shown in units sold, by brand, in 1991; relative market shares are shown in percent for the same period. Data include imports.

	Units	% of Group
Buick Electra	83,831	25.9%
Oldsmobile Ninety Eight	59,828	18.5
Volvo 700 series	29,198	9.0
BMW 3 series	28,618	8.8
Lexus ES250/300	22,476	6.9
Mazda 929	16,148	5.0
Mitsubishi Diamante	15,595	4.8
Buick Riviera	12,947	4.0
Acura Vigor	11,324	3.5
Chrysler Imperial	10,625	3.3
Toyota Cressida	9,547	2.9
Oldsmobile Toronado	6,339	2.0
Infinity M30	4,392	1.4
Saab 9000S	3,042	0.9
Saab 9000CD	2,294	0.7
Saab 9000 Turbo	2,294	0.7

Continued on next page.

★ 1227 ★ *Continued*

Autos (SIC 3711)

Near Luxury Car Sales

Car sales are shown in units sold, by brand, in 1991; relative market shares are shown in percent for the same period. Data include imports.

	Units	% of Group
Alfa Romeo 164	2,155	0.7%
Audi 80	1,965	0.6
Audi 90	1,136	0.4
BMW M3	384	0.1

Source: *Automotive News, 1992 Market Data Book*, May 27, 1992, p. 30, from Automotive News Data Center.

★ 1228 ★

Autos (SIC 3711)

Specialty Car Sales

Car sales are shown in units sold, by brand, in 1991; relative market shares are shown in percent for the same period. Data include imports.

	Units	% of Group
Mazda MX-5 Miata	31,240	19.6%
Mercury Capri	21,200	13.3
Dodge Stealth	18,352	11.5
Chevrolet Corvette	17,480	11.0
Nissan 300ZX	14,903	9.4
Mitsubishi 3000GT	11,777	7.4
Toyota MR2	9,676	6.1
Mercedes-Benz SL	7,446	4.7
Toyota Supra	6,986	4.4
Jaguar XJS	3,623	2.3
Cadillac Allante	2,738	1.7
Buick Reatta	2,643	1.7
Porsche 911 Carrer2	2,304	1.4
Acura NSX	2,101	1.3
Alfa Romeo Spider	1,940	1.2
Chrysler TC by Maserati	1,077	0.7
Ferrari	960	0.6
Porsche 944S/Cabriolet . . .	862	0.5
Porsche 911 Carrera 4	748	0.5

	Units	% of Group
Porsche 911 Turbo	415	0.3%
Lotus	324	0.2
Porsche 928S4-GT	262	0.2
Lamborghini	156	0.1

Source: *Automotive News, 1992 Market Data Book*, May 27, 1992, p. 30, from Automotive News Data Center.

★ 1229 ★

Autos (SIC 3711)

Top-Selling Cars

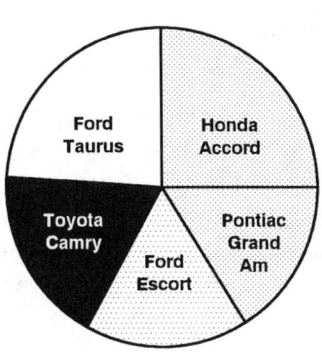

Top-selling car brands for the first half of 1992 are shown in number of units sold. Relative shares are shown in percent.

	Units sold	% of Group
Honda Accord	191,662	25.4%
Ford Taurus	181,189	24.0
Toyota Camry	137,906	18.3
Ford Escort	124,212	16.5
Pontiac Grand Am	120,059	15.9

Source: *USA TODAY*, July 14, 1992, p. 1B, from Autodata.

★1230★

Autos (SIC 3711)

Truck Manufacturers

Shares are shown in percent, based on totals of 4,847,354 units in 1990 and 4,366,989 units in 1991.

	1990	1991
General Motors	34.3%	32.9%
Ford	29.3	28.9
Dodge/Plymouth	13.2	14.4
Jeep	4.1	4.1
Non-captive imports	12.1	12.0
Other	7.0	7.7

Source: Investext, Thomson Financial Networks, February 25, 1992, from Paine Webber Inc.

★1231★

Autos (SIC 3711)

Truck Market Shares

Percent shares of total light-truck market, by brand, are based on total sales of 4,591,077 trucks in 1990 and 4,159,416 trucks in 1991.

	'90	'91
Chevrolet/Geo	27.1%	25.6%
Chrysler	0.1	0.1
Daihatsu	0.1	0.1
Dodge	10.1	10.8
Ford	29.9	29.5
GMC	7.1	6.9
Isuzu	2.3	2.3
Jeep	4.3	4.3
Mazda	2.7	2.9
Mitsubishi	0.9	0.7
Nissan	3.8	4.1
Oldsmobile	0.6	0.8
Plymouth	3.7	4.2
Pontiac	0.7	0.6
Range Rover	0.1	0.1
Suzuki	0.3	0.4
Toyota	6.1	6.5
Volkswagen	0.1	0.1

Source: *Automotive News, 1992 Market Data Book*, May 27, 1992, p. 17, from Automotive News Data Center.

★1232★

Autos (SIC 3711)

U.S. Car Market

Manufacturer shares are shown in percent for 1990 and 1991.

	'90	'90
General Motors	35.4%	35.4%
Ford	20.8	19.9
Honda	9.1	9.8
Toyota	8.3	9.0
Chrysler	9.2	8.5
Nissan	4.9	5.0
Mazda	2.9	3.3
Mitsubishi	1.7	2.1
Other	7.7	7.0

Source: *The Wall Street Journal*, January 7, 1992, p. B1.

★1233★

Autos (SIC 3713)

Light-Truck Sales - Compact Pickups

Sales figures are shown by brand as units sold in 1991. Percent shares are based on group total.

	Units sold	% of Group
Ford Ranger	233,503	23.8%
Chevrolet S10	200,247	20.4
Toyota pickup	162,972	16.6
Nissan pickup	129,972	13.2
Dodge Dakota	82,336	8.4
Mazda pickup	62,421	6.4
GMC S150 Sonoma	44,109	4.5
Isuzu pickup	35,911	3.7
Mitsubishi pickup	18,247	1.9
Jeep Comanche	6,663	0.7
Dodge Ram 50	4,671	0.5

Source: *Automotive News, 1992 Market Data Book*, May 27, 1992, p. 30, from Automotive News Data Center.

★ 1234 ★

Autos (SIC 3713)

Light-Truck Sales - Compact Sport-Utilities

Sales figures are shown by brand as units sold in 1991. Percent shares are based on group total.

	Units sold	% of Group
Ford Explorer	250,059	31.8%
Chevrolet S10 Blazer	123,346	15.7
Jeep Cherokee	121,461	15.4
Jeep Wrangler	46,478	5.9
Toyota 4Runner	44,881	5.7
Nissan Pathfinder	39,500	5.0
Geo Tracker	30,702	3.9
GMC S15 Jimmy	29,994	3.8
Isuzu Trooper	26,776	3.4
Isuzu Rodeo	24,612	3.1
Suzuki Sidekick	11,749	1.5
Mazda Navajo	11,404	1.4
Mitsubishi Montero	10,606	1.3
Isuzu Amigo	7,829	1.0
Suzuki Samurai	4,378	0.6
Daihatsu Rocky	2,761	0.4

Source: *Automotive News, 1992 Market Data Book*, May 27, 1992, p. 30, from Automotive News Data Center.

★ 1235 ★

Autos (SIC 3713)

Light-Truck Sales - Minivans

Sales figures are shown by brand as units sold in 1991. Percent shares are based on group total.

	Units sold	% of Group
Dodge Caravan	207,919	23.7%
Plymouth Voyager	173,373	19.8
Ford Aerostar	147,373	16.8
Chevrolet Astro	105,808	12.1
Toyota Previa	52,099	5.9
Mazda MPV	48,144	5.5
Chevrolet Lumina APV	48,117	5.5
GMC Safari	33,600	3.8
Pontiac Trans Sport	23,682	2.7
Oldsmobile Silhouette	23,004	2.6
Dodge Caravan C/V	8,591	1.0
Chrysler Town & Country	5,236	0.6
Nissan Axxess	334	0.0

	Units sold	% of Group
Mitsubishi Van	59	0.0%
Nissan Van	6	0.0

Source: *Automotive News, 1992 Market Data Book*, May 27, 1992, p. 30, from Automotive News Data Center.

★ 1236 ★

Autos (SIC 3713)

Minivan Manufacturer Shares

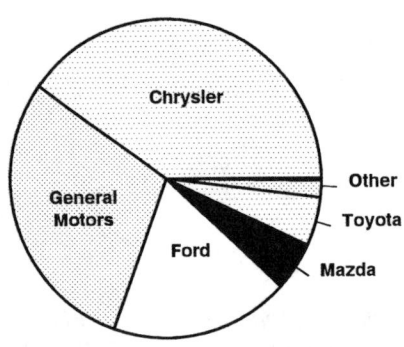

Company shares, shown in percent, are based on the 1990 market.

Chrysler	40.8%
General Motors	29.5
Ford	19.0
Mazda	4.6
Toyota	4.5
Other	1.6

Source: *Fortune*, July 1, 1991, p. 12, from *Automotive News*.

★ 1237 ★

Autos (SIC 3713)

Truck Sales in Canada

Company sales are shown for 1991 as units sold. Percent shares are based on 1991 total sales of 399,673 trucks.

	Units sold	% of Group
General Motors	137,173	34.3%
Ford	101,329	25.4
Chrysler	97,076	24.3
Mazda	21,391	5.4

Continued on next page.

★ 1237 ★ *Continued*

Autos (SIC 3713)

Truck Sales in Canada

Company sales are shown for 1991 as units sold. Percent shares are based on 1991 total sales of 399,673 trucks.

	Units sold	% of Group
Toyota	21,051	5.3%
Nissan	12,862	3.2
Suzuki	7,427	1.9
Volkswagen	1,011	0.3
Lada	192	0.0
Land Rover	161	0.0

Source: *Automotive News, 1992 Market Data Book*, May 27, 1992, p. 31, from Automotive News Data Center.

★ 1238 ★

Trucks (SIC 3713)

Class 8 Truck Industry - U.S.

Market shares for Class 8 trucks in the U.S., by company, are shown in percent.

	1990	1991
Navistar	23.3%	23.1%
Freightliner	20.6	20.6
Kenworth	12.3	11.6
Volvo/GM	11.2	11.5
Peterbilt	10.7	10.3
Mack	11.8	10.0
Ford	9.9	8.1
Other	3.1	4.8

Source: Investext, Thomson Financial Networks, June 11, 1992, from Bear, Stearns & Co., Inc.

★ 1239 ★

Trucks (SIC 3713)

Class 8 Trucks - North America

Market shares of Class 8 heavy-duty trucks are shown in percent for 1989, 1990, and 1991.

	'89	'90	'91
Navistar	23.0%	22.7%	22.7%
Freightliner	16.0	18.3	22.5
Kenworth	12.8	12.3	12.2
White	11.7	11.8	11.9
Mack	13.2	12.7	11.0

	'89	'90	'91
Peterbilt	11.5%	9.5%	9.7%
Ford	10.0	10.8	8.4
General Motors	0.1	0.0	0.0
Other	1.8	1.8	1.4

Source: Investext, Thomson Financial Networks, June 4, 1992, from Robert W. Baird & Co., Incorporated.

★ 1240 ★

Trucks (SIC 3713)

Heavy-Duty-Truck Makers

Company shares of U.S. heavy-duty-truck sales are shown in percent, based on sales totals of 121,324 trucks in 1990 and 98,730 trucks in 1991. Kenworth and Peterbilt are divisions of PACCAR Inc.

	1990	1991
Navistar	22.9%	23.1%
Freightliner	19.0	22.9
Volvo GM	12.2	12.3
Kenworth	12.1	11.9
Mack	11.8	10.6
Peterbilt	9.9	9.5
Ford	10.8	8.6
Western-Star	0.8	0.6
Scania	0.1	0.1
Others	0.5	0.4

Source: *Ward's Auto World*, March 1992, p. 111, from MVMA.

★ 1241 ★

Trucks (SIC 3713)

Heavy-Truck Manufacturers

Shares of the heavy-truck market in the first eleven months of 1991 are shown in percent.

Freightliner	23.3%
Navistar	22.8
Volvo-White	12.0
Kenworth	11.8
Mack	10.7
Peterbilt	9.6
Ford	8.6
Other	1.1

Source: Investext, Thomson Financial Networks, January 24, 1992, from Prudential Securities, Inc and Motor Vehicle Manufacturers Assn.

★ 1242 ★

Trucks (SIC 3713)

Truck Manufacturers - Germany

Shares are shown in percent, based on total registrations of 75,831 vehicles in 1990 and 85,728 vehicles in 1991. Category includes commercial vehicles over 3.5 tons, excluding buses.

	1990	1991
Mercedes-Benz	58.6%	57.8%
MAN	19.4	18.8
Iveco	12.2	12.0
Scania	3.0	3.7
Volvo	2.5	3.0
Other	4.3	4.7

Source: Investext, Thomson Financial Networks, February 24, 1992, from UBS Phillips & Drew Global Research Group and AID.

★ 1243 ★

Trucks (SIC 3713)

Truck Sales in Canada

Market shares, by company, are shown as percent of quarterly production in 1991.

Chrysler	47.4%
General Motors	39.9
Ford	12.7

Source: Investext, Thomson Financial Networks, March 17, 1992, from Smith, Barney, Harris Upham & Company.

★ 1244 ★

Trucks (SIC 3713)

Trucks Sales in Canada

Market shares, by company, are shown as percent of quarterly retail sales in 1991.

General Motors	40.9%
Ford	30.8
Chrylser	28.9

Source: Investext, Thomson Financial Networks, March 17, 1992, from Smith, Barney, Harris Upham & Company.

★ 1245 ★

Air Bags (SIC 3714)

Driver's Side Airbag Manufacturers

Estimated shares of the domestic market for sodium azide inflators are shown in percent for 1992.

Morton	65.0%
TRW	35.0

Source: Investext, Thomson Financial Networks, June 30, 1992, from Wertheim Schroeder & Co. Inc.

★ 1246 ★

Air Bags (SIC 3714)

Electrically Controlled Transmissions

Percentages reflect the number of cars with electrically controlled transmissions, by company, based on a total of 951,254 cars in 1991.

Ford	43.5%
Chrysler	31.7
GM	24.8

Source: *Ward's Auto World*, June 1992, p. 57.

★ 1247 ★

Auto Parts (SIC 3714)

Antilock Brake Systems

North American 4-wheel ABS (antilock brake system) market shares, shown in percent, are based on total production of 1,508 thousand units in 1991 and projected production of 10,820 thousand units in 1996.

	'91	'96
Kelsey-Hayes	4.0%	29.0%
Delco	15.0	24.0
Bosch	23.0	18.0
Teves	41.0	17.0
Bendix	12.0	5.0
Honda	3.0	3.0
Sumitomo	1.0	2.0
Unknown	1.0	2.0

Source: *Ward's Auto World*, April 1992, p. 58, from Tier One.

★1248★

Auto Parts (SIC 3714)

Auto Parts

Segment distribution is shown in percent. This category does not include tires or outside sales.

Motor oil	22.75%
Accessories	13.25
Parts	11.05
Car stereos	10.83
Filters	7.37
Batteries	6.81
Antifreeze	5.82
Ignition/electrical	5.79
Waxes and polishes	5.75
Chemicals/additives	3.85
Do-It-Yourself books	0.49
Miscellaneous	6.24

Source: *Discount Merchandiser*, June 1992, p. 60, from survey.

★1249★

Auto Parts (SIC 3714)

Automotive Suppliers

Company shares are shown in percent, based on total sales of $367.13 billion in 1990 and $367.52 billion in 1991.

	'90	'91
Exxon	31.8%	31.7%
GE	15.9	16.4
DuPont	11.0	10.5
United Technologies	5.9	5.8
Digital	2.2	3.8
Phillips	3.8	3.6
Rockwell	3.4	3.2
Allied-Signal	3.4	3.2
Motorola	3.0	3.1
Goodyear	3.1	3.0
TRW	2.2	2.2
Alcan	2.4	2.1
Cooper	1.7	1.7
PPG	1.6	1.6
Johnson Controls	1.2	1.2
Dana	1.3	1.2
Inland Steel	1.1	0.9
Eaton	1.0	0.9
Amp	0.8	0.8
ARCO	0.8	0.8
Owens-Corning	0.8	0.8

	'90	'91
Magna	0.4%	0.5%
Timken	0.5	0.4
Masco Industries	0.4	0.4
Federal-Mogul	0.3	0.3

Source: *Ward's Auto World*, April 1992, p. 64.

★1250★

Auto Parts (SIC 3714)

Initiators for Automotive Air Bags

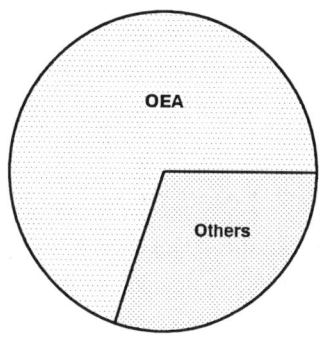

Shares are shown in percent, based on the 1990 market.

OEA	70.0%
Others	30.0

Source: Investext, Thomson Financial Networks, March 4, 1992, from Nomura Research Institute America, Inc.

★1251★

Auto Parts (SIC 3714)

Passenger's Side Airbag Manufacturers

Estimated shares of the domestic market for sodium azide and hybrid inflators are shown in percent for 1992. "Other" includes Takata/Olin, Bayern Chemie, and Bendix/Atlantic Research.

Morton/OEA	55.0%
TRW	40.0
Other	5.0

Source: Investext, Thomson Financial Networks, June 30, 1992, from Wertheim Schroeder & Co. Inc.

★ 1252★

Aircraft Parts (SIC 3720)

Aircraft Parts Overhauls in Japan

Market shares by type of product are shown in percent based on a 1991 total of 934 units.

Airframe	54.7%
Engine	22.9
Instrument	8.2
Propeller/rotor	14.1

Source: *Aviation Week & Space Technology*, May 11, 1992, p. 56, from Society of Japanese Aerospace Companies.

★ 1253★

Aircraft Parts (SIC 3720)

Aircraft Parts Production in Japan

Shares by type are shown in percent, based on a 1991 total of 5,417 units.

Airframe	58.5%
Engine	19.5
Instrument	6.8
Propeller/rotor	8.0
Comm. equip	1.9
Other airborne equip.	3.3
Radars	1.9
Tire	0.2

Source: *Aviation Week & Space Technology*, May 11, 1992, p. 56, from Society of Japanese Aerospace Companies.

★ 1254★

Aircraft Parts (SIC 3720)

Japanese Aviation Production

Distribution of aviation production, by major market, is shown in percent, based on a 1991 total of 6,351 units (including overhauls).

Defense	74.9%
Civil	10.9
Export	14.0
U.S. Military	0.2

Source: *Aviation Week & Space Technology*, May 11, 1992, p. 56, from Society of Japanese Aerospace Companies.

★ 1255★

Aircraft (SIC 3721)

Aerospace Companies

Aerospace company sales are shown in millions of dollars for fiscal 1991. Percent shares are based on the group total.

	Sales ($ mil.)	% of Group
Boeing Co.	$ 29,314.0	20.0%
United Technologies Corp.	20,953.0	14.3
McDonnell Douglas Corp.	18,432.0	12.6
Allied Signal Inc.	11,831.0	8.1
Lockheed Corp.	9,809.0	6.7
General Dynamics Corp.	8,751.0	6.0
Textron Inc.	7,840.1	5.3
Martin Marietta Corp.	6,075.4	4.1
LTV Corp.	5,986.4	4.1
Northrop Corp.	5,694.2	3.9
Grumman Corp.	4,037.9	2.8
Hercules Inc.	2,928.9	2.0
BFGoodrich Co.	2,471.6	1.7
Parker-Hannifin Corp.	2,440.8	1.7
Gencorp Inc.	1,993.0	1.4
Sundstrand Corp.	1,669.2	1.1
Rohr Inc.	1,385.1	0.9
Thkokol Corp.	1,255.4	0.9
Alliant Techsystems Inc.	1,247.7	0.9
Precision Castparts Corp.	538.3	0.4
Fairchild Corp.	515.7	0.4
Hexcel Corp.	386.6	0.3
UNC Inc.	360.6	0.2
Wyman-Gordon Co.	355.4	0.2
Fansteel Inc.	134.9	0.1
Eldec Corp.	123.0	0.1
Hi-Shear Industries	104.9	0.1
OEA Inc.	83.7	0.1
Oregon Metallurgical Corp.	54.2	0.0

Source: *Aviation Week & Space Technology*, May 25, 1992, p. 40.

★1256★
Aircraft (SIC 3721)

Aerospace Companies

Aerospace company sales are shown in millions of dollars for fiscal 1991. Percent shares are based on group total.

	Sales ($ mil.)	% of Group
Boeing Co.	$29,314.0	20.0%
United Technologies Corp.	20,953.0	14.3
McDonnell Douglas Corp.	18,432.0	12.6
Allied Signal Inc.	11,831.0	8.1
Lockheed Corp.	9,809.0	6.7
General Dynamics Corp.	8,751.0	6.0
Textron Inc.	7,840.1	5.3
Martin Marietta Corp.	6,075.4	4.1
LTV Corp.	5,986.4	4.1
Northrop Corp.	5,694.2	3.9
Grumman Corp.	4,037.9	2.8
Hercules Inc.	2,928.9	2.0
BFGoodrich Co.	2,471.6	1.7
Parker-Hannifin Corp.	2,440.8	1.7
Gencorp Inc.	1,993.0	1.4
Sundstrand Corp.	1,669.2	1.1
Rohr Inc.	1,385.1	0.9
Thiokol Corp.	1,255.4	0.9
Alliant Techsystems Inc.	1,247.7	0.9
Precision Castparts Corp.	538.3	0.4
Fairchild Corp.	515.7	0.4
Hexcel Corp.	386.6	0.3
UNC Inc.	360.6	0.2
Wyman-Gordon Co.	355.4	0.2
Fansteel Inc.	134.9	0.1
Eldec Corp.	123.0	0.1
Hi-Shear Industries	104.9	0.1
OEA Inc.	83.7	0.1
Oregon Metallurgical Corp.	54.2	0.0

Source: *Aviation Week & Space Technology*, May 25, 1992, p. 40.

★1257★
Aircraft (SIC 3721)

Aerospace/Defense Shares

Shares for 1991 are shown in percent.

Boeing	56.0%
McDonnell Douglas	22.5
Airbus Industries	21.5

Source: Investext, Thomson Financial Networks, February 3, 1992, from Shearson Lehman Brothers, Inc.

★1258★
Aircraft (SIC 3721)

Aircraft by Type - 1991

Shares, based on flight hours, are shown in percent.

Single-engine piston	77.8%
Multiengine piston	10.7
Rotorcraft	3.5
Turboprop	2.6
Turbojet	2.0
Other	3.3

Source: *Business & Commercial Aviation*, May 1992, p. 31.

★1259★
Aircraft (SIC 3721)

Aircraft - Leading Producers

Companies are ranked by 1991 sales, shown in millions of dollars. Percent shares are based on a group total of $137,773 million.

	Sales ($ mil.)	% of Group
Boeing	$29,314	21.3%
United Technologies	21,262	15.4
McDonnell Douglas	18,718	13.6
Allied-Signal	11,882	8.6
Lockheed	9,809	7.1
General Dynamics	9,548	6.9
Textron	7,840	5.7
Martin Marietta	6,107	4.4
Northrop	5,706	4.1
Grumman	4,038	2.9
Sequa	2,137	1.6
Gencorp	1,993	1.4
Sundstrand	1,709	1.2
Rohr	1,386	1.0
Coltec Industries	1,373	1.0

Continued on next page.

★ 1259★ *Continued*
Aircraft (SIC 3721)

Aircraft - Leading Producers

Companies are ranked by 1991 sales, shown in millions of dollars. Percent shares are based on a group total of $137,773 million.

	Sales ($ mil.)	% of Group
Thiokol	$ 1,270	0.9%
Alliant Techsystems	1,047	0.8
Kaman	780	0.6
Henley Group	704	0.5
Fairchild	612	0.4
Precision Castparts	538	0.4

Source: *Fortune*, April 20, 1992, p. 259.

★ 1260★

Aircraft (SIC 3721)

Airplane Shipments - GAMA

| **Turbojets** |
| **Turboprops** |
| **Piston** |

General Aviation Manufacturers Association shipments totaled 1,021 business planes and $1.968 billion in 1991. Product shares based on billings are shown in percent.

	Planes	($ mil.)	Share
Turbojets	186	$ 1,348	68.5%
Turboprops	222	527	26.8
Piston	613	93	4.7

Source: *Business Aviation*, January 20, 1992, p. 33.

★ 1261★

Aircraft (SIC 3721)

Asian/Canadian/European Aerospace Companies

Company sales are shown in millions of dollars for fiscal year 1991. Relative shares are shown in percent.

	Sales ($ mil.)	% of Group
British Aerospace plc.	$ 19181.1	41.0%
Rolls-Royce plc.	6551.4	14.0
Saab-Scania AB	4913.3	10.5

	Sales ($ mil.)	% of Group
Lucas Industries plc.	$ 4375.5	9.3%
Dassault Aviation	3682.4	7.9
Bombardier Inc.	2434.1	5.2
Fokker Aircraft B.V.	1781.1	3.8
Dowty Group plc.	1420.7	3.0
CAE Industries Ltd.	946.3	2.0
Westland Group plc.	852.7	1.8
Intertechnique S.A.	279.8	0.6
Hong Kong Aircraft Engr. Co. .	205.5	0.4
Sabca	166.7	0.4
Ipeco Holdings plc.	32.2	0.1

Source: *Aviation Week & Space Technology*, May 25, 1992, p. 51.

★ 1262★

Aircraft (SIC 3721)

Business Aircraft Worldwide

Business aircraft shipments of the 21 largest manufacturers worldwide totaled 1,548 in 1991. Relative shares are shown in percent.

	No. of Planes	% of Group
Beech	402	26.0%
Aerospatiale	203	13.1
Cessna	176	11.4
British Aerospace	103	6.7
Mooney	88	5.7
Embraer	87	5.6
American General	82	5.3
Aviat	71	4.6
Maule Air	66	4.3
De Havilland	58	3.7
Piper	41	2.6
Gulfstream	29	1.9
Dassault	26	1.7
Learjet	25	1.6
TBM	23	1.5
Canadair	18	1.2
Britten-Norman	12	0.8
Israel	11	0.7
Lake	11	0.7
Fairchild	10	0.6
Piaggio Avanti	6	0.4

Source: *Business Aviation*, January 20, 1992, p. 28.

★ 1263 ★

Aircraft (SIC 3721)

Commercial Jet Transport Orders - 1990

Shares, by company, are shown in percent for 1990.

Boeing	47.0%
Airbus	31.0
McDonnell Douglas	15.0
Fokker	4.0
British Aerospace	3.0

Source: Investext, Thomson Financial Networks, February 18, 1992, from Morgan Stanley & Co., Inc.

★ 1264 ★

Aircraft (SIC 3721)

Commercial Jet Transport Unit Deliveries

Shares, by company, are shown in percent for 1988 and 1989.

	1988	1989
Boeing	56.0%	50.0%
McDonnell Douglas	25.0	21.0
Airbus	12.0	18.0
British Aerospace	4.0	6.0
Fokker	2.0	4.0

Source: Investext, Thomson Financial Networks, February 18, 1992, from Morgan Stanley & Co., Inc.

★ 1265 ★

Aircraft (SIC 3721)

Commercial Jets

New orders of commercial jets amounted to $82 billion in 1990. Manufacturer shares are shown in percent.

Boeing	62.0%
Airbus	21.0
McDonnell Douglas	15.0
Other	2.0

Source: *Industrial Distribution*, December 1991, p. 28, from Boeing Commercial Airplane Group.

★ 1266 ★

Aircraft (SIC 3721)

Complete U.S. Aircraft

Shipment value shares are based on totals of $41,920 million in 1990 and $44,989 million in 1991.

	1990	1991
Civil large transportation	53.0%	59.2%
Civil general aviation	4.8	4.2
Civil rotorcraft	0.6	0.4
Military aircraft	41.6	36.2

Source: *U.S. Industrial Outlook 1992*, p. 21-6, from U.S. Department of Commerce, International Trade Administration, General Aviation Manufacturers Association, and Aerospace Industries Association.

★ 1267 ★

Aircraft (SIC 3721)

GA Aircraft Manufacturers

Percent shares of GA (general aviation) aircraft are based on net billings of $1.968 billion by the General Aviation Manufacturers Assn. in 1991.

Gulfstream	32.0%
Cessna	30.0
Beech	28.0
Learjet	6.0
Fairchild	2.0
Piper	1.0
Other	1.0

Source: Investext, Thomson Financial Networks, April 27, 1992, from Morgan Stanley & Co. Inc.

★ 1268 ★

Aircraft (SIC 3721)

Jet Transport Orders

Companies and brands are shown with numbers of planes ordered in 1990 and 1991. Numbers in parentheses indicate a canceled order.

	'90	'91
Airbus		
A300	31	40
A310	40	12
A320	183	15
A321	117	3
A330	25	5
A340	8	26

Continued on next page.

★ 1268 ★ *Continued*
Aircraft (SIC 3721)

Jet Transport Orders

Companies and brands are shown with numbers of planes ordered in 1990 and 1991. Numbers in parentheses indicate a canceled order.

	'90	'91
Boeing		
737-300/400/500	162	71
747	172	38
757	97	49
767	52	72
777	49	27
British Aerospace		
BAe 146	7	23
Canadair		
RJ	44	23
Fokker		
Fokker 100	116	13
McDonnell Douglas		
MD-80/MD-90	116	0 (27)
MD-11	52	3 (9)

Source: *Air Transport World*, March 1992, p. 9, from *ATW*.

★ 1269 ★
Aircraft (SIC 3721)

Naval Aircraft Procurement

Distribution, by model, is shown as percent of 119 aircraft in 1992.

F/A-18	30.3%
CH/MH-53E	16.8
AH-1W	10.1
SH-60B	10.1
SH-60F	10.1
T-45TS	10.1
HH-60H	7.6
E-2C	5.0

Source: *Armed Forces Journal International*, March 1991, p. 22.

★ 1270 ★
Aircraft (SIC 3721)

Small Plane Manufacturers

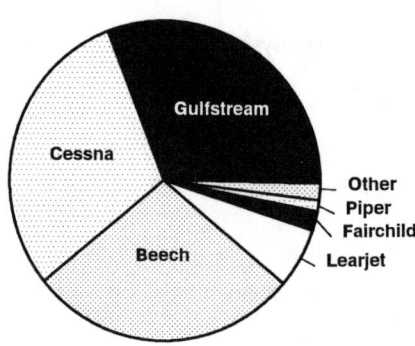

Company shares are shown in percent, based on billings of $1.3 billion in 1991. The figure for Gulfstream was based on a billing total that combined actual dollars for the first three quarters with an estimate of the fourth quarter.

Gulfstream	31.1%
Cessna	29.9
Beech	27.9
Learjet	5.8
Fairchild	2.0
Piper	0.9
Other	2.4

Source: *The New York Times*, January 18, 1992, p. 17, from General Aviation Manufacturers Assn.

★ 1271 ★
Aircraft Engines (SIC 3724)

Engine Manufacturers - U.K.

Shares are shown in percent, based on a total of 1,812 units ordered in 1992.

Pratt & Whitney	35.0%
CFM International	31.0
General Electric	18.0
Rolls-Royce	15.0
IAE	1.0

Source: Investext, Thomson Financial Networks, February 1, 1992, from Charterhouse Tilney.

★ 1272 ★

Shipbuilding (SIC 3731)

Military Ships under Construction by Type

Number of military ships under construction are shown by type as of October 1, 1991. Shares are based on a total of 83 military ships, shown in percent.

	No.	%
Guided missile destroyer, DDG . . .	16	19.3%
Attack submarine, SSN-688	15	18.1
Oiler, T-AO	10	12.0
Guided missile cruiser, CG	7	8.4
Ballistic missile submarine, SSBN . . .	6	7.2
Mine countermeasures ships, MCM . .	6	7.2
Dock landing ship, LSD	4	4.8
Fast combat support ship, ADE . . .	3	3.6
Aircraft carrier, CVN	3	3.6
Amphibious assault ship, LHD	3	3.6
Ocean surveillance ship (SWATH), T-AGOS	3	3.6
Ocean survey ship, T-AGS-60	2	2.4
Coastal hydrographic ship, T-AGS-51 .	2	2.4
Attack submarine, SSN-21	1	1.2
Ocean surveillance ship, T-AGOS-23 .	1	1.2
Ocean survey ship, T-AGOS-45 . . .	1	1.2

Source: *U.S. Industrial Outlook 1992*, p. 22-2, from U.S. Department of the Navy.

★ 1273 ★

Boats (SIC 3732)

Auxiliary Inboard-Engine Sailboat Sales

Shares, by engine type, are shown in percent, based on total sales of 4,850 units in 1989, 3,625 units in 1990 and 2,475 units in 1991.

	'89	'90	'91
9-18 Horsepower	31.4%	38.6%	39.4%
19-40 Horsepower	38.1	35.2	34.3
Over-40 Horsepower	30.4	26.2	26.3

Source: *Boating Registration Statistics 1990*, p. 8, from Power Systems Research.

★ 1274 ★

Boats (SIC 3732)

Boat, Trailer, and Motor Sales in 1991

Boats, trailers, and motors are ranked according to their wholesale unit sales for model year August 1, 1990 to July 31, 1991. Relative market shares are shown in percent for that period.

	No. of Units	% of Group
Outboard motors	289,000	32.4%
Outboard boats	195,000	21.9
Trailers	133,000	14.9
Inboard/outdrive boats	73,000	8.2
Canoes	72,300	8.1
Personal watercraft	68,000	7.6
Pontoon boats	21,500	2.4
Inflatable boats	21,200	2.4
Sailboats	8,468	1.0
Inboard runabouts	6,200	0.7
Inboard cruisers	3,600	0.4

Source: *Boating Registration Statistics 1990*, p. 3, from National Marine Manufacturers Association.

★ 1275 ★

Boats (SIC 3732)

Diesel Inboard-Engine Sales

Shares, by engine type, are shown in percent, based on total sales of 8,725 units in 1989, 7,780 units in 1990 and 4,680 units in 1991.

	'89	'90	'91
201-500 Horsepower	56.6%	56.9%	56.1%
75-200 Horsepower	22.7	19.5	21.6
501-1,000 Horsepower	15.1	18.8	18.3
Greater than 1,000 Horsepower	5.6	4.8	4.1

Source: *Boating Registration Statistics 1990*, p. 7, from Power Systems Research.

★ 1276 ★
Boats (SIC 3732)

Gasoline Inboard-Engine Sales

Shares, by engine type, are shown in percent, based on total sales of 32,150 units in 1989, 24,500 units in 1990 and 19,000 units in 1991.

	'89	'90	'91
130-250 Horsepower	38.2%	39.5%	45.0%
251-300 Horsepower	20.9	21.8	25.0
Greater than 300 Horsepower	40.9	38.7	30.0

Source: *Boating Registration Statistics 1990*, p. 7, from Power Systems Research.

★ 1277 ★
Boats (SIC 3732)

Inboard-Boat Registrations in 1990

Registrations of inboard boats, by hull materials, are ranked by numbers of units registered. Market shares are shown in percent, based on total registration of 10,996,253 boats in 1990.

	Units	Share
Fiberglass	1,959,935	88.5%
Metal	130,875	5.9
Wood	103,225	4.7
Inflatable	1,904	0.1
Other	18,586	0.8

Source: *Boating Registration Statistics 1990*, p. 7, from National Marine Manufacturers Association.

★ 1278 ★
Boats (SIC 3732)

Outboard-Boat Registrations in 1990

Outboard-boat registrations, by hull materials, are ranked according to number of units. Relative market shares are shown in percent. The 1990 registered recreational boat total was 10,996,253.

	Units	Share
Metal	3,875,643	49.2%
Fiberglass	3,541,891	44.9
Wood	221,634	2.8
Inflatable	54,533	0.7
Other	191,116	2.4

Source: *Boating Registration Statistics 1990*, p. 7, from National Marine Manufacturers Association.

★ 1279 ★
Railroad Equipment (SIC 3743)

Rail Intermodal Transportation Equipment

Trailers

Containers

Percent shares by type of equipment are based on total intermodal volume in 1990 and 1991.

	'90	'91
Trailers	55.6%	51.4%
Containers	44.4	48.6

Source: *Transportation & Distribution*, May 1992, p. 13, from AAR.

★ 1280 ★
Railroad Equipment (SIC 3743)

Rail Transport Global Shares

Manufacturer shares of the world market are shown in percent.

GEC Alsthom	9.0%
ABB	8.5
AEG	7.5
GE	5.5
Bombardier	3.8
Siemens	3.2
Ansaldo	2.0
Other	60.5

Source: Investext, Thomson Financial Networks, January 28, 1992, from Credit Suisse First Boston Ltd.

★ 1281 ★
Bicycles (SIC 3751)

Bicycles by Hub Type

Domestic shipment shares are shown in percent.

	'89	'90
10-speed	51.0%	57.0%
Coaster brake	42.0	37.0
5-speed	6.0	5.0
2/3-speed	1.0	1.0

Source: *The 1990 Bicycle Market in Review*.

★ 1282 ★

Bicycles (SIC 3751)

Bicycles by Type

Shares, by major category, are shown in percent. Figures include both domestic market and imports.

	'89	'90
20-inch	35.9%	32.7%
Lightweight	32.0	17.4
Other	32.1	49.9

Source: *The 1990 Bicycle Market in Review.*

★ 1283 ★

Motorcycles (SIC 3751)

Motorcycle Manufacturers

Shares, by company, of the U.S. market are shown in percent.

Harley-Davidson	63.7%
Honda	16.5
Yamaha	6.8
Kawasaki	6.5
Suzuki	4.0
Other	2.5

Source: Investext, Thomson Financial Networks, March 18, 1992, from Morgan Stanley & Co., Inc.

★ 1284 ★

Motorcycles (SIC 3751)

Motorcycle Market Shares

Market shares, by company, are shown in percent.

Harley-Davidson	62.9%
Honda	16.4
Other	20.7

Source: Investext, Thomson Financial Networks, March 18, 1992, from Morgan Stanley & Co., Inc.

★ 1285 ★

Aerospace Equipment (SIC 3761)

Aerospace Contractors

Shares of satellite and spacecraft contracts as of mid-1991 are shown in percent.

	Civil	Military	NASA
GE Aerospace	51.5%	25.0%	31.8%
Ford Aerospace	6.1	5.0	-
GM Hughes	42.4	15.0	9.1
Rockwell	-	5.0	9.1
TRW	-	15.0	9.1
Other	-	35.0	40.9

Source: Investext, Thomson Financial Networks, January 15, 1992, from Sanwa McCarthy Securities Ltd.

★ 1286 ★

Aerospace Equipment (SIC 3761)

Aerospace Contractors - Europe

Shares of ESA (European Space Agency) as of mid-1991 are shown in percent.

Matra	30.0%
Aerospatiale	20.0
British Aerospace	20.0
Deutsche Aerospace	6.7
Other	23.3

Source: Investext, Thomson Financial Networks, January 15, 1992, from Sanwa McCarthy Securities Ltd.

★ 1287 ★

Trailers (SIC 3792)

Towable RV Manufacturers

Manufacturer shares for 1991 are shown in percent, based on sales.

Fleetwood Enterprises Inc.	19.5%
Fleetwood Folding Trailers Inc.	9.5
Jayco Inc.	9.2
Dutchmen Mfg. Inc.	5.6
Cobra/Van American Inc.	5.5
Skyline Corp.	5.4
Coachmen Industries Inc.	5.2
Starcraft RV Inc.	4.0
Kit Mfg. Co.	3.2
Mallard Coach Co. Inc.	3.0
Other	29.9

Source: *RVBusiness*, April 1992, p. 9.

SIC 38 - Instruments and Related Products

★ 1288 ★

Instruments (SIC 3800)

Instrument Manufacturers

Sales figures are shown in millions of dollars for 1991. Percent shares are based on group total of $18,661 million.

	Sales ($ mil.)	% of Group
Honeywell	$ 6,193	33.2%
Johnson Controls	4,626	24.8
Henley Group	1,689	9.1
Tektronix	1,311	7.0
Perkin-Elmer	868	4.7
Beckman Instruments	858	4.6
Thermo Electron	805	4.3
Millipore	748	4.0
Ametek	715	3.8
Teradyne	509	2.7
Thermo Instrument Systems . .	339	1.8

Source: *The 1992 Business Week 1000*, p. 172.

★ 1289 ★

Control Equipment (SIC 3823)

Controller Shipments - U.S.

Shipments of IBM and compatible cluster controllers by U.S. vendor in 1991. Market shares are shown in percent.

	Units	Shares
IBM	22,500	53.1%
Memorex Telex Corp	11,500	27.2
IDEA	2,100	5.0
Harris Adacom Corp	1,500	3.5
Lee Data Corp	550	1.3

	Units	Shares
Apertus Technologies, Inc . . .	490	1.2%
McDATA Corp		
Direct	1,640	3.9
OEM	2,060	4.9

Source: *Network World*, April 20, 1992, p. 13, from International Data Corp.

★ 1290 ★

Control Equipment (SIC 3823)

Process Control Instrument Makers

Company shares are shown in percent, based on an estimated industry total of $710 million in sales in 1991.

Lightnin	29.6%
Leeds & Northrup	26.8
Dezurik	18.3
Aurora Pump	12.7
Lindberg	9.9
Kinnet Vacuum	2.8

Source: Investext, Thomson Financial Networks, April 10, 1992, from Prudential Securities Inc.

★ 1291 ★

Industrial Instruments (SIC 3823)

Industrial Mixing Market

Company shares are shown in percent.

Lightnin	33.0%
Philadelphia Gear	9.0
Chemineer	9.0
Ekato	8.0
Others, identified	10.0
Others, not identified	31.0

Source: Investext, Thomson Financial Networks, April 10, 1992, from Prudential Securities Inc.

★ 1292 ★

Test and Measurement Equipment (SIC 3825)

Test and Measurement Equipment - Japan

IC/LSI testers

Oscilloscopes

AV measuring

Digital multimeters

Spectrum analyzers

Board testers

MPU development

Logic analyzers

FFT analyzers

Distortion testers

Analog multimeters

Segment distribution is shown in percent for 1990, based on a total of $1.293 billion in sales.

IC/LSI testers	56.5%
Oscilloscopes	11.8
AV measuring	6.7
Digital multimeters	6.4
Spectrum analyzers	5.1
Board testers	3.8
MPU development	3.6
Logic analyzers	2.1
FFT analyzers	1.9
Distortion testers	1.2
Analog multimeters	1.1

Source: *Electronics*, September 1991, p. 74, from Nomura Research Institute.

★ 1293 ★

Catheters (SIC 3841)

Angioplasty Catheter Market

Company shares are shown in percent, based on total sales of $550 million for the year ended April 1992. "ACS" is a division of Eli Lilly. "Schneider" is a division of Pfizer, Inc.

ACS	51.0%
SciMed Life Systems	28.0
Schneider	8.0
C.R. Bard	7.0
Cordis Corporation	3.0
Medtronic, Inc.	2.0
Other	1.0

Source: Investext, Thomson Financial Networks, April 24, 1992, from Smith Barney, Harris Upham & Co.

★ 1294 ★

Catheters (SIC 3841)

Fixed-Wire Angioplasty Catheter Market

Company shares are shown in percent, based on total sales of $66 million for the year ended April 1992. "ACS" is a division of Eli Lilly.

C.R. Bard	35.0%
SciMed Life Systems	29.0
ACS	25.0
Cordis Corporation	10.0
Medtronic, Inc.	1.0

Source: Investext, Thomson Financial Networks, April 24, 1992, from Smith Barney, Harris Upham & Co.

★ 1295 ★

Catheters (SIC 3841)

Over-the-Wire Angioplasty Catheter Market

Company shares are shown in percent, based on total sales of $308 million for the year ended April 1992. "ACS" is a division of Eli Lilly. "Schneider" is a division of Pfizer, Inc.

ACS	64.0%
SciMed Life Systems	20.0
C.R. Bard	5.0
Medtronic, Inc.	4.0
Cordis Corporation	3.0
Scheider	2.0
Other	3.0

Source: Investext, Thomson Financial Networks, April 24, 1992, from Smith Barney, Harris Upham & Co.

★ 1296 ★

Catheters (SIC 3841)

Rapid Exchange Angioplasty Catheter Market

Company shares are shown in percent, based on total sales of $176 million for the year ended April 1992. "ACS" is a division of Eli Lilly. "Schneider" is a division of Pfizer, Inc.

ACS	37.0%
SciMed Life Systems	43.0
Schneider	20.0

Source: Investext, Thomson Financial Networks, April 24, 1992, from Smith Barney, Harris Upham & Co.

★ 1297 ★

Medical Equipment (SIC 3841)

Medical Technology in Canada

Data reflect access to modern medical technology in Canada in terms of units per million people by type of medical procedure in 1989.

Open heart surgery	1.23
Cardiac catheterization	1.50
Organ transplantation	1.08
Radiation therapy	0.54
Magnetic resonance imaging	0.46
Extracorporeal shock wave lithotripsy	0.16

Source: *Successful Farming*, April 1992, p. 54.

★ 1298 ★

Medical Equipment (SIC 3841)

Surgical Clip Manufacturers

Market shares, by company, are shown in percent for the fourth quarters of 1990 and 1991.

	4Q. '90	4Q '91
U.S. Surgical	85.2%	87.7%
Ethicon	13.4	11.1
Other	1.4	1.2

Source: Investext, Thomson Financial Networks, March 27, 1992, from Kidder, Peabody & Company, Incorporated.

★ 1299 ★

Orthopedic Appliances (SIC 3842)

Hip and Knee Implant Manufacturers

Company shares are shown in percent, based on total domestic sales of $1,194 million in 1991 and estimated domestic sales of $1,372 million in 1992.

	1991	1992
Zimmer	27.2%	26.1%
Howmedica	21.2	20.9
De Puy	17.5	17.5
Richards	7.5	7.9
Biomet	7.1	7.9
Stryker	7.5	7.8
J & J	6.1	6.6
Others	5.8	5.4

Source: Investext, Thomson Financial Networks, March 17, 1992, from Shearson Lehman Brothers, Inc.

★ 1300 ★

Orthopedic Appliances (SIC 3842)

Orthopedics Manufacturers

Market shares, by company, are shown in percent for 1991.

Zimmer	30.2%
Howmedica	19.2
Richards	12.5
DePuy	11.5
Stryker	9.6

Continued on next page.

★ 1300 ★ *Continued*

Orthopedic Appliances (SIC 3842)

Orthopedics Manufacturers

Market shares, by company, are shown in percent for 1991.

Biomet	8.0%
J&J	6.6
Kirschner	2.3
Concept	0.0

Source: Investext, Thomson Financial Networks, March 17, 1992, from Shearson Lehman Brothers, Inc.

★ 1301 ★

Orthopedic Appliances (SIC 3842)

Orthopedics World Market

Shares of the total world orthopedic market in 1991 are shown by segment.

Arthroscopy	30.0%
Rehabilitation	25.0
Fracture fixation	16.8
Post-surgical bracing	14.0
Hip and knee implants	6.3
Spinal implants	4.0
Soft goods	3.0
Synthetic casting	1.0

Source: Investext, Thomson Financial Networks, February 14, 1992, from Lehman Brothers Limited.

★ 1302 ★

Prosthetic Appliances (SIC 3842)

Prosthetic Heart Valve Manufacturers

Market shares, by manufacturer, are shown in percent.

St. Jude Medical	46.0%
Baxter	24.0
Other	30.0

Source: Investext, Thomson Financial Networks, May 12, 1992, from Raymond James & Associates, Inc.

★ 1303 ★

Surgical Supplies (SIC 3842)

Surgical Clip Manufacturers

Shares of the domestic market for small, medium, and large clips are shown in percent for the fourth quarter of 1991.

U.S. Surgical	86.0%
Ethicon	12.5
Other	1.5

Source: Investext, Thomson Financial Networks, January 28, 1992, from Kidder, Peabody & Company, Incorporated.

★ 1304 ★

Surgical Supplies (SIC 3842)

Surgical Table Manufacturers

Shares of the domestic market are shown in percent.

AMSCO	50.0%
Other	50.0

Source: Investext, Thomson Financial Networks, March 11, 1992, from Louis Nicoud & Associates.

★ 1305 ★

Wheelchairs (SIC 3842)

Wheelchair Manufacturers

Estimated shares of the $80.0 million domestic market for standard wheelchairs in 1991 are shown in percent.

Invacare	60.0%
Other	40.0

Source: Investext, Thomson Financial Networks, May 20, 1992, from Robert W. Baird & Co. Incorporated.

★ 1306 ★

Wound Closures (SIC 3842)

External Stapling Products

Shares of the domestic market are shown in percent for the fourth quarter of 1991.

U.S. Surgical	52.0%
Ethicon	30.0
Other	17.0

Source: Investext, Thomson Financial Networks, January 28, 1992, from Kidder, Peabody & Company, Incorporated.

★ 1307 ★

Wound Closures (SIC 3842)

Internal Stapling Products

Shares of the domestic market are shown in percent for the fourth quarter of 1991.

U.S. Surgical	78.0%
Ethicon	20.0
Other	2.0

Source: Investext, Thomson Financial Networks, January 28, 1992, from Kidder, Peabody & Company, Incorporated.

★ 1308 ★

Wound Closures (SIC 3842)

Surgical Sutures Market

Johnson & Johnson

American Cyanamid

U.S. Surgical

Other

Manufacturer shares of the $1.3 billion surgical sutures market are shown in percent.

Johnson & Johnson	80.0%
American Cyanamid	15.0
U.S. Surgical	1.0
Other	4.0

Source: *USA TODAY*, July 20, 1992, p. 5B.

★ 1309 ★

Dental Equipment (SIC 3843)

Amalgam Alloy Market

Shares of the domestic market for amalgam alloy materials are shown in percent for fiscal 1991.

Kerr	35.0-37.0%
Other	63.0-65.0

Source: Investext, Thomson Financial Networks, June 3, 1992, from Donaldson, Lufkin & Jenrette Securities.

★ 1310 ★

Electromedical Equipment (SIC 3845)

Acute-Care Monitoring Market

Market shares, by company, are shown in percent, based on an industry total of approximately $1.2 billion.

SpaceLabs	35.0%
Hewlett-Packard	30.0-35.0
Other	30.0-35.0

Source: Investext, Thomson Financial Networks, June 1, 1992, from Ragen Mackenzie.

★ 1311 ★

Electromedical Equipment (SIC 3845)

Critical-Care Monitoring Worldwide

Global shares of the critical care monitoring equipment market are shown in percent, based on sales of $995 million in 1989, $1.095 billion in 1990, and $1.20 billion in 1991.

	'89	'90	'91
SpaceLabs	17.0%	18.0%	19.0%
Hewlett-Packard	17.0	17.0	18.0
Siemens	11.0	11.0	11.0
Marquette	9.0	9.0	9.0
Nihon Kohden	9.0	9.0	9.0
Other	37.0	35.0	33.0

Source: Investext, Thomson Financial Networks, April 21, 1992, from The First Boston Corporation.

★1312★
Electromedical Equipment (SIC 3845)

Patient Monitoring Market Worldwide

Shares by segment are shown in percent, based on total market of $1,100 million.

Systems	49.5%
Stand-alone bedside	31.5
Telemetry	13.5
Transport	5.4

Source: Investext, Thomson Financial Networks, April 24, 1992, from The First Boston Corporation.

★1313★
Electromedical Equipment (SIC 3845)

PET Use by Specialty

Percentages reflect national forecast of PET (positron emission tomography) scanner use by specialty for short term of 2-3 years and long term of 7-8 years.

	Short Term	Long Term
Cardiology	64.0%	66.0%
Neurology/psychiatry	31.0	21.0
Oncology	5.0	13.0

Source: *Hospitals*, May 5, 1992, p. 60, from AHA survey, 1991.

★1314★
Cameras (SIC 3861)

Camera Sales by Category - U.S.

Camera sales, by category, are shown in percent based on a total maket of 15.6 million units sold in 1991.

Lens shutter	58.0%
Cartridge	24.0
Instant	9.0
Single-lens reflex	7.0
Disc	1.0
Other	1.0

Source: *U.S. Industrial Outlook 1992*, p. 24, from Photo Marketing Association International.

★1315★
Cameras (SIC 3861)

Cameras by Type

Shares are shown in percent for 1990.

Lens shutter	57.7%
110	23.7
Instant	10.3
SLR	7.1
Disc	1.2

Source: *DM*, February 1992, p. 54, from PMA Marketing Research.

★1316★
Cameras (SIC 3861)

Cardboard Camera Manufacturers

Shares of the domestic market are shown in percent. In 1991 approximately 15 million units were sold in the U.S.

Kodak	80.0%
Fuji and other	20.0

Source: *The Wall Street Journal*, February 11, 1992, p. B1, from Photo Marketing Association.

★1317★
Cameras (SIC 3861)

Professional-Use Video Equipment Worldwide

Manufacturers' shares of the global market are shown in percent.

	News Cameras	Studio Cameras
Sony	90.0%	50.0%
Other	10.0	50.0

Source: Investext, Thomson Financial Networks, June 22, 1992, from County Natwest Securities Japan Ltd.

★ 1318 ★

Film (SIC 3861)

Film Sales by Category

Film sales, by category, are shown in percent, based on a total of 848 million rolls sold in the U.S. in 1990.

35mm	71.0%
Cartridge	12.0
Instant	10.0
Disc	6.0
Other	1.0

Source: *U.S. Industrial Outlook 1992*, p. 24, from Photo Marketing Association International.

★ 1319 ★

Photographic Goods (SIC 3861)

Photographic Goods

Segment distribution is shown in percent.

Film	42.28%
Cameras	29.06
Photofinishing	21.34
Lenses	1.50
Miscellaneous	5.82

Source: *Discount Merchandiser*, June 1992, p. 60, from survey.

SIC 39 - Miscellaneous Manufacturing Industries

★1320★

Juvenile Products (SIC 3940)

Juvenile Products Sales

Juvenile product sales are shown in millions of dollars for 1991. Shares by category are shown in percent.

	($ mil.)	Share
Cribs	$ 300	27.0%
Swingers/jumpers	240	21.6
Child restraints	200	18.0
Strollers (full size)	112	10.1
Infant restraint	90	8.1
Strollers (portable)	90	8.1
Walkers	80	7.2

Source: *Discount Stores News*, May 18, 1992, p. 98, from Juvenile Products Manufacturers Association.

★1321★

Toys and Games (SIC 3940)

Infant and Preschool Toy Sales

Toy sales, shown in millions of dollars, totaled $1.086 billion in 1991. Shares by type are shown in percent, based on the total.

	($ mil.)	Share
Infant toys	$ 356	32.8%
Learning toys	121	11.1
Musical toys	94	8.7
Talking/sound toys	59	5.4
Blocks/accessories	26	2.4
Other	430	39.6

Source: *Discount Stores News*, May 18, 1992, p. 98, from Toy Manufacturers of America.

★1322★

Toys and Games (SIC 3940)

Toyland Giants

Companies are ranked by 1991 revenues, shown in millions of dollars; percent shares are based on group total. Fisher-Price figures are shown for trailing four quarters.

	Rev. ($ mil.)	% of Group
Hasbro	$ 2,141	41.7%
Mattel	1,622	31.6
Fisher-Price	663	12.9
Tyco	549	10.7
SLM Intl.	164	3.2

Source: *Fortune*, June 1, 1992, p. 28.

★1323★

Toys and Games (SIC 3940)

Toys and Games Sales in the U.K. by Category

Shares of U.K. retail sales of toys and games, by category, are shown in percent.

	1988	1989
Toy specialists		
Toys "R" Us.	8.9%	10.4%
Other	18.1	17.9
Mail order	26.7	26.2
Variety stores	10.7	11.7
Supermarkets	9.3	8.1
Department stores	5.4	4.4
Other	21.1	21.3

Source: Investext, Thomson Financial Networks, February 20, 1992, from Prudential Securities, Inc., *Euromonitor*, and British Toy & Hobby Mfrs. Assn.

★1324★

Toys and Games (SIC 3940)

Toys & Games Market

Segment distribution of the domestic market is shown in percent.

Video games	26.0%
Dolls/stuffed animals	15.0
Vehicles	11.0
Infant	9.0
Activity toys	9.0
Games/puzzles	8.0
Other	22.0

Source: *USA TODAY*, February 17, 1992, p. 1D, from Toy Manufacturers of America.

★1325★

Toys and Games (SIC 3940)

Toys & Games Market Segments

Segment distributon is shown in percent.

Dolls, accessories, houses	16.41%
Action figures, accessories, robots	15.06
Games, puzzles	12.49
Plush toys	10.45
Infants, pre-school	9.19
Educational	4.34
Crafts	4.30
Kids' sporting goods	3.96
Kids' riding vehicles	3.11
Books	3.02
Playground equipment	1.36
Miscellaneous	16.31

Source: *Discount Merchandiser*, June 1992, p. 61.

★1326★

Games (SIC 3944)

Leading Adult Games

Volume of sales in 1990 is shown in thousands of units; relative market shares are shown in percent. Milton Bradley and Parker Brothers are owned by Hasbro.

	Units (000)	% of Group
Sacttergories (Milton Bradley) . .	1,772	41.9%
Taboo (Milton Bradley)	740	17.5
Outburst (Western Publishing) . .	664	15.7
Adverteasing (Cadaco)	439	10.4
Pictionary (Games Gang)	319	7.5
Trivial Pursuit 1980's (Parker Brothers)	295	7.0

Source: *The New York Times*, July 4, 1991, p. 30, from N.P.D. Group.

★1327★

Toys (SIC 3944)

Water Guns by Brand

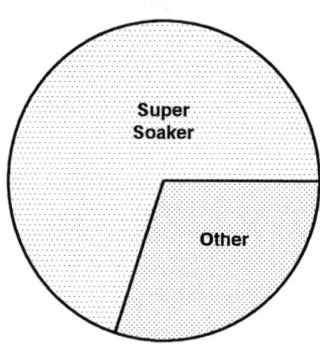

Estimated shares as of June 1992 are shown in percent. Manufacturers are shown in parentheses; "other" includes Tyco's Super Saturator.

Super Soaker (Larami)	70.0%
Other	30.0

Source: *The Wall Street Journal*, June 11, 1992, p. B2, from Gerard Klauer Mattison & Co.

★ 1328 ★
Video Games (SIC 3944)

Video Game Hardware

Estimated shares of the 1992 domestic market are shown in percent, based on total hardware sales of $1.236 billion.

Super Nintendo 16 BIT system	36.1%
Sega Genesis 16 BIT system	26.0
Game Boy portable system	16.3
Nintendo 8 BIT system	14.6
Game Gear portable system	6.5
Other	0.5

Source: Investext, Thomson Financial Networks, April 16, 1992, from Johnson, Rice & Co.

★ 1329 ★
Video Games (SIC 3944)

Video Game Makers

Shares are shown in percent, based on an estimated total market of $5.80 billion in 1992. The category includes both hardware and software (8-BIT and 16-BIT).

Nintendo Entertainment Systems	79.0%
SEGA	1.7
Other	19.3

Source: Investext, Thomson Financial Networks, April 13, 1992, from Dean Witter Reynolds.

★ 1330 ★
Sporting Goods (SIC 3949)

Golf Market Shares

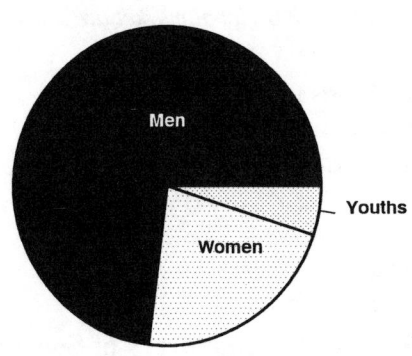

Percent shares of golf market for 1990 and 1991.

	1990	1991
Men	77.2%	73.3%
Women	17.6	21.6
Youths	5.2	5.1

Source: *Sporting Goods Business*, December 1991.

★ 1331 ★
Sporting Goods (SIC 3949)

Golf-Ball Sales

Revenues from golf ball sales in the United States are shown in millions of dollars for 1991.

Titleist	$ 201.0
Spalding	182.0
Wilson	66.0
Maxfli	56.0
Slazenger	13.0
Ram	12.0
Bridgestone	6.2
Hogan	5.0
Bullet	4.5

Source: *USA TODAY*, November 20, 1992, p. B-1, from Golf Pro Merchandiser.

★1332★
Sporting Goods (SIC 3949)

Hockey Helmet Manufacturers

Shares of the 1990 global market are shown in percent.

Canstar Sports Inc. 50.0%
Other 50.0

Source: *The Globe and Mail*, February 10, 1992, p. B1.

★1333★
Sporting Goods (SIC 3949)

Preferred Manufacturers of Soccer Products

Percentages are based on replies of 148 dealers who named a company as the best overall marketer.

Umbro 73.6%
Adidas 11.5
Brine 4.1
Kwik Goal 2.0
Mitre 2.0

Source: *Sporting Goods Business*, March 1992, p. 49.

★1334★
Sporting Goods (SIC 3949)

Soccer Hand-Sewn/Stitched Ball Market by Price

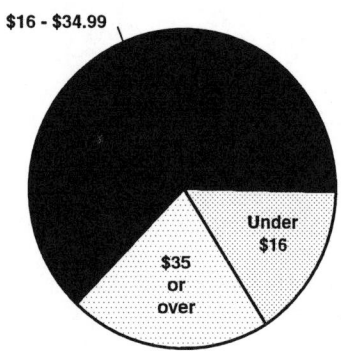

Figures represent percent shares of soccer hand-sewn/stitched ball market by price.

$16 - $34.99. . . . . 63.4%
$35 or over 21.0
Under $16 . . . . 15.6

Source: *Sporting Goods Business*, April 1992, p. 48.

★1335★
Sporting Goods (SIC 3949)

Soccer Molded/Laminated Ball Market by Price

Figures represent percent shares of soccer molded/laminated ball market by price.

Under $16 . . . . 46.3%
$16 - $34.99. . . . . 45.9
$35 or over 7.8

Source: *Sporting Goods Business*, April 1992, p. 48.

★1336★
Sporting Goods (SIC 3949)

Sporting Goods Market

Segment distribution is shown in percent.

Fishing and camping supplies 32.41%
Firearms and supplies 15.95
Team sports goods 11.57
Marine supplies/water sports 9.76
Bicycles 7.08
Sports apparel and footwear 7.05
Racquet and golf goods 4.71
Exercise equipment 3.93
Miscellaneous 7.54

Source: *Discount Merchandiser*, June 1992, p. 61.

★1337★
Writing Instruments (SIC 3951)

Pen Makers - U.K.

Company shares are shown as percent of the U.K. market.

Parker 53.0%
Schaeffer 7.0
Cross 6.0
Mont Blanc 6.0
Other 28.0

Source: *Financial Times*, February 11, 1992, p. 11.

★1338★

Writing Instruments (SIC 3951)

Writing Instrument Industry

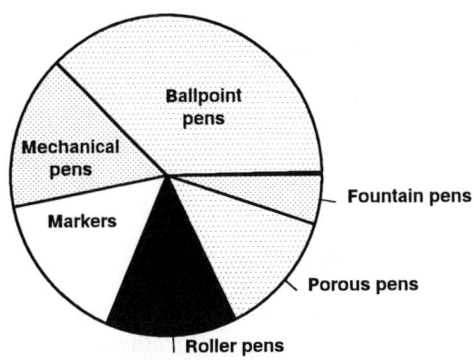

Shares of manufacturers' sales by type of writing instrument are shown in percent for 1990.

Ballpoint pens	38.0%
Mechanical pens	16.0
Markers	15.5
Roller pens	13.5
Porous pens	12.5
Fountain pens	4.5

Source: *Jewelers' Circular-Keystone*, January 1992, p. 36.

★1339★

Costume Jewelry (SIC 3961)

Costume Jewelry Manufacturers - Leaders

Sales for 1990 are shown in millions of dollars; relative market shares are shown in percent for the same period.

	Sales ($ mil.)	% of Group
Artra Group Inc.	$ 210.1	20.8%
Lori Corp.	105.4	10.4
1928 Jewelry Co.	100.0	9.9
Kerr Manufacturing Co.	85.0	8.4
Napier Co.	70.0	6.9
Trifari, Krussman and Fishel Inc.	63.0	6.2
R. N. Koch Inc.	61.0	6.0
Ace Novelty Co.	58.0	5.7
Victoria Creations Inc.	56.9	5.6
Textron Inc. (Speidel)	42.0	4.2
Swarovski Jewelry U.S. Ltd. . .	40.0	4.0

	Sales ($ mil.)	% of Group
Weingeroff Enterprises Co. . . .	$ 35.0	3.5%
K and M Associates	30.0	3.0
Monet	30.0	3.0
Accessories Associates Inc. . . .	25.0	2.5

Source: *Infotrak*, 1991, p. 20, from Fairchild Fashion & Merchandising Group 1991.

★1340★

Toothbrushes (SIC 3991)

Toothbrushes

Shares of the $309.2 million market are shown in percent, by brand. Manufacturers' names are shown in parentheses.

Oral-B (Gillette Co.)	29.4%
Reach (Johnson & Johnson)	21.9
Colgate Plus (Colgate)	15.3
Aquafresh Flex (SmithKline Beecham) . . .	7.4
Other	26.0

Source: *The Wall Street Journal*, November 10, 1992, p. B1, from Towne Oller & Associates.

★1341★

Video Lottery Terminals (SIC 3999)

Lottery Video Game Vendors - Canada

Market shares, by vendor, are shown in percent. Shares are based on sales to the four provinces participating in the Atlantic Lottery as of January 31, 1992, by which time a total of 5,101 terminals had been installed.

Video Lottery Technologies	44.3%
International Game Technology	23.2
Spielo	18.8
Bally Gaming	6.4
Merit Industries	5.4
SMS/Premier	1.5
Universal	0.1
Aries	0.1

Source: Investext, Thomson Financial Networks, March 18, 1992, from Raymond James & Associates, Inc.

SIC 40 - Railroad Transportation

★ 1342 ★
Railroads (SIC 4011)

Chemical Shippers

Union Pacific	
CSX Transportation	
Southern Pacific	
Santa Fe	
Norfolk Southern	
Burlington Northern	
Illinois Central	
Conrail	
Other Class I railroads	
Total other railroads	

Number of rail carloads of chemicals originated in 1991 is distributed by carrier. Market shares are shown in percent.

	Car-Loads	Share
Union Pacific	382,766	26.5%
CSX Transportation	291,640	20.2
Southern Pacific	176,643	12.2
Santa Fe	120,007	8.3
Norfolk Southern	102,274	7.1
Burlington Northern	91,737	6.3
Illinois Central	75,493	5.2
Conrail	71,808	5.0
Other Class I railroads	89,199	6.2
Total other railroads	45,484	3.1

Source: *Chemicalweek*, February 19, 1992, p. 44, from American Association of Railroads.

★ 1343 ★
Railroads (SIC 4011)

Class 1 Railroads

Net railway operating income, by railroad, is shown in thousands of dollars. Relative shares are shown in percent.

	($000)	%
Union Pacific	$ 548,420	19.9%
Norfolk Southern	502,551	18.2
Burlington Northern	414,082	15.0
CSX Transportation	370,098	13.4
Consolidated Rail	295,265	10.7
Atchison, Topeka & Santa Fe	278,205	10.1
Illinois Central	111,324	4.0
Chicago & North Western	68,472	2.5
Soo Line	44,952	1.6
Southern Pacific	42,882	1.6
Kansas City Southern	36,731	1.3
Denver & Rio Grande	26,042	0.9
Grand Trunk	10,423	0.4
Florida East Coast	5,421	0.2

Source: *Railroad Facts*, 1991.

★ 1344 ★
Railroads (SIC 4011)

Largest U.S. Railroads

Percent shares by company are based on 1990 operating revenue.

Burlington Northern	16.5%
Union Pacific	16.2
CSX Transportation	15.6
Norfolk Southern	13.4
Consolidated Rail	11.6

Continued on next page.

★ 1344 ★ *Continued*

Railroads (SIC 4011)

Largest U.S. Railroads

Percent shares by company are based on 1990 operating revenue.

Southern Pacific/DRGW Cos.	9.7%
Atchison, Topeka & Santa Fe	7.4
Chicago & North Western	2.9
Other	6.7

Source: *The Wall Street Journal*, February 26, 1992, p. B4, from Association of American Railroads.

★ 1345 ★

Railroads (SIC 4011)

Major U.S. Railroads - Eastern District

Shares of year-to-date 1991 freight revenues for the Eastern District, by railroad, are shown in percent, based on a total of $8.70 billion. The figure for Grand Trunk Western includes special charges taken in the second and third quarters of 1991.

CSX Transportation	35.9%
Norfolk Southern	30.4
Consolidated Rail	26.0
Illinois Central	4.4
Grand Trunk Western	2.2
Florida East Coast	1.1

Source: *Railroad Revenues, Expenses, and Income: Class 1 Railroads (Association of American Railroads)*, 1991.

★ 1346 ★

Railroads (SIC 4011)

Major U.S. Railroads - Eastern District

Shares of third-quarter freight revenues for the Eastern District, by railroad, are shown in percent, based on a total of $2.99 billion.

CSX Transportation	35.7%
Norfolk Southern	30.5
Consolidated Rail	26.4
Illinois Central	4.3
Grand Trunk Western	2.1
Florida East Coast	1.1

Source: *Railroad Revenues, Expenses, and Income: Class 1 Railroads (Association of American Railroads)*, 1991.

★ 1347 ★

Railroads (SIC 4011)

Major U.S. Railroads - Western District

Shares of year-to-date 1991 freight revenues for the Western District, by railroad, are shown in percent, based on a total of $11.39 billion. The figures provided for Burlington Northern and Union Pacific include special charges taken in the second and third quarters of 1991.

Union Pacific	30.0%
Burlington Northern	28.8
Southern Pacific	14.6
Atchison Topeka & Santa Fe	13.8
Chicago & North Western	4.5
Soo Line	3.8
Denver & Rio Grande Western	2.5
Kansas City Southern	2.0

Source: *Railroad Revenues, Expenses, and Income: Class 1 Railroads (Association of American Railroads)*, 1991.

★ 1348 ★

Railroads (SIC 4011)

Major U.S. Railroads - Western District

Shares of third-quarter freight revenues for the Western District, by railroad, are shown in percent, based on a total of $3.88 billion. During this period, Union Pacific recorded a special charge of $745 million in operating expenses, resulting in a reduction of $492 million in its ordinary income and net railway operating income.

Union Pacific	29.6%
Burlington Northern	29.1
Southern Pacific	14.7
Atchison Topeka & Santa Fe	14.2
Chicago & North Western	4.5
Soo Line	3.8
Kansas City Southern	2.0
Denver & Rio Grande Western	2.0

Source: *Railroad Revenues, Expenses, and Income: Class 1 Railroads (Association of American Railroads)*, 1991.

★ 1349 ★

Railroads (SIC 4011)

Rail Freight

Percent of freight trains that carry each commodity shown. Data shown are for 1990.

Pulp & paper products	68.0%
Transportation equipment	67.0
Coal	60.0
Lumber	53.0
Food products	45.0

Source: *Journal of Commerce*, June 25, 1992, p. 1A, from Association of American Railroads.

★ 1350 ★

Railroads (SIC 4011)

Railroad Freight Cars by Type

Shares by type of freight car are shown in percent, based on a total fleet size of 1,197,419 cars in 1990 and 1,218,197 cars in 1991.

	'90	'91
Covered hopper	27.9%	24.6%
Hopper	21.7	18.3
Tank	17.9	15.8
Box	1.8	14.8
Gondola	12.7	11.5
Flat	12.5	10.7
Refrigerator	4.1	3.3
All other	1.4	1.1

Source: *Railway Age*, September 1991, p. 15, from Economics and Finance Department, Assn. of American Railroads and AAR's Operation and Maintenance Department.

SIC 41 - Local and Interurban Passenger Transit

★ 1351 ★

Commuter Rail Lines (SIC 4111)

Commuter Railroad Systems

New and prospective railroad commuter systems are ranked according to number of trips per day (estimated) during the first year of operation.

Los Angeles	23,000
Seattle-Tacoma	13,000
Dallas-Fort Worth	12,000
Northern Virginia	9,000
Miami-West Palm Beach	7,000
San Diego	3,800
Atlantic City	1,600
New Haven-Old Saybrook	1,050
Sacramento	800

Source: *The Wall Street Journal*, October 1, 1991, p. B1.

★ 1352 ★

Bus Transportation (SIC 4131)

Motorcoach Fleet - 1992

Top 25 companies' rankings in 1992 are based on number of motorcoaches. Shares of group are shown in percent.

	Total Coach	% of Group
Greyhound Lines Inc. (Dallas, TX)	2381	32.6%
Academy Lines Inc. (Hoboken, NJ)	455	6.2
Robert's Hawaii Inc. (Honolulu, HI)	421	5.8
Greyhound Lines of Canada Ltd. (Calgary, AB)	395	5.4
Shortline Companies (Mahwah, NJ)	325	4.5
Diversified Transportation Ltd. (Edmonton, AB)	300	4.1
Suburban Transit Corp. (New Brunswick, NJ)	264	3.6%
Holland America Line-Westours Inc. (Seattle, WA)	262	3.6
Kerrville Bus Co. Inc (Kerrville, TX)	230	3.2
Grey Line of Fort Lauderdale (Fort Lauderdale, FL)	191	2.6
Blue Bird Coach Lines Inc. (Olean, NY)	185	2.5
Rockland Coaches Inc. (Bergenfield, NJ)	176	2.4
EG&G Idaho Inc. (Idaho Falls, ID)	161	2.2
Lake Front Lines (Brook Park, OH)	157	2.2
Voyageur Colonial Ltd. (Ottawa, ON)	155	2.1
Peter Pan Bus Lines Inc. (Springfield, MA)	150	2.1
Command Bus Co. Inc. (Brooklyn, NY)	142	1.9
Leisure Time Tours (Mahwah, NJ)	139	1.9
Antelope Valley Bus Inc. (Lancaster, CA)	135	1.9
ATE Management & Service Co. Inc. (Houston, TX)	122	1.7
Pacific Western Transportation (Calgary, AB)	120	1.6
Shoup Buses Inc. (Middlebury, IN)	112	1.5
K-T Contract Services Inc. (Las Vegas, NV)	110	1.5
TransHawaiian Services (Honolulu, HI)	103	1.4
Tour Coach Inc. (Los Angeles, CA)	103	1.4

Source: *METRO* Magazine, January 1992, p. 18.

★ 1353 ★

School Buses (SIC 4151)

School Bus Fleets

*The largest 26 school bus fleets are shown with
number of buses in 1991 and relative market shares
in percent.*

	Fleet Size	% of Group
Laidlaw Transit, Ltd. (Burlington, ON)	19,719	35.3%
Mayflower Contract Services (Overland Park, KS) . .	7,558	13.5
Ryder Student Transportation (Miami, FL) . .	6,867	12.3
National School Bus Service (Palatine, IL)	3,221	5.8
Vancom Inc. (South Holland, IL)	2,730	4.9
Durham Transportation, Inc. (Rosemead, CA)	2,478	4.4
Charterways Transportation (London, ON) .	2,240	4.0
Atlantic Express (Staten Island, NY)	1,485	2.7
School Services & Leasing (Shawnee, KS)	1,243	2.2
Cook-Illinois Corp. (Oak Forest, IL)	1,200	2.1
ICBM/Transcom (Mattapan, MA)	1,047	1.9
Mark IV Charter/Embree (Gardena, CA)	825	1.5
Stock Transp. Ltd. (Richmond Hill, ON)	710	1.3
Septran, Inc. (Bloomington, MN)	690	1.2
Towne Bus/WE Transp. (Hicksville, NY)	635	1.1
George Krapf Jr. and Sons, Inc. (Glenmoore, PA) . .	472	0.8
Briggs Bus Lines (Edmonton, AB)	440	0.8
School Bus Services, Inc. (Gresham, OR)	400	0.7
Logan Bus Co. (Ozone Park, NY)	350	0.6
Reliable Bus Co. (Chicago, IL) . .	325	0.6
Riteway Bus Service (Richfield, WI)	275	0.5
Medicine Lake Bus Co. (St. Paul, MN)	265	0.5

	Fleet Size	% of Group
Action Transit (Pittsburgh, PA) .	250	0.4%
Dean Transportation, Inc. (Lansing, MI)	250	0.4
Kobussen Buses, Ltd. (Kaukauna, WI)	125	0.2
Beck Bus Transportation Corp. (Mt. Vernon, IL)	125	0.2

Source: *School Bus Fleet*, December 1992, p. 38.

★ 1354 ★

School Buses (SIC 4151)

School Transportation

*Shares by type of ownership are shown in percent,
based on a total of 392,179 buses in the 1989-1990
school year.*

District-owned buses	69.6%
Contractor-owned buses	28.2
Other	2.2

Source: *School Bus Fleet*, April 1992, p. 46.

SIC 42 - Trucking and Warehousing

★ 1355 ★

Trucking (SIC 4200)

Trucking Services by Type

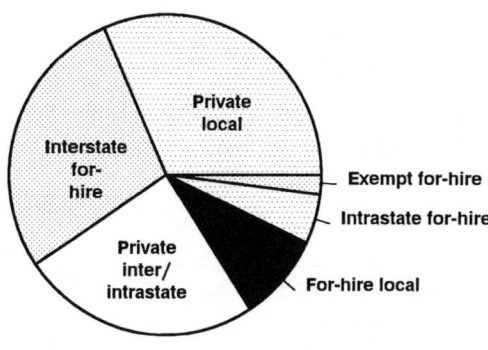

Shares by type of fleet are shown in percent, based on total revenue of $266.7 billion in the year-to-date.

Private local	. 32.1%
Interstate for-hire	. 27.7
Private inter/intrastate	. 24.9
For-hire local	. 8.7
Intrastate for-hire	. 4.5
Exempt for-hire	. 2.1

Source: *Transportation & Distribution*, April 1992, p. T2, from NPTC.

★ 1356 ★

Trucking (SIC 4213)

LTL Carrier Operating Ratios

Nation's largest LTL (less-than-truckload) carriers (listed alphabetically) are shown with 1991 operating ratios.

AAA Cooper Transportation	90.3
ABF Freight System	95.7
ANR Freight Systems	128.9
A-P-A Transport Inc.	94.7
Carolina Freight Carriers	98.2
Central Freight Lines	96.2

Central Transport (Michigan)	98.3
Churchill Truck Lines	98.9
Consolidated Freightways	97.5
Con-Way Transport Services	91.4
Northwest Transport Services	94.1
Overnite Transportation	95.9
Preston Trucking Co.	99.9
Roadway Express	95.5
St. Johnsbury Trucking Co.	100.4
TNT Holland Motor Express	89.9
TNT Red Star Express Lines	99.4
Viking Freight System	93.6
Watkins Motor System	94.2
Yellow Freight System	98.5

Source: *Traffic Management*, February 1992, p. 17.

★ 1357 ★

Chemical Terminals (SIC 4226)

Chemical Storage - Canada

Chemical storage terminals, by company, are ranked by cubic meters of capacity. Shares are shown in percent.

	Capacity (cu. m.)	Share
Vancouver Wharves Ltd. . . .	1,038,000	80.7%
Intertank - IMTT Inc.	123,400	9.6
Montank Transit Inc.	103,000	8.0
Valleytank Inc.	22,370	1.7

Source: *ECN* Supplement, September 1991, p. 43.

★ 1358 ★
Chemical Terminals (SIC 4226)

Chemical Storage - Japan

Chemical storage terminals, by company, are ranked by cubic meters of capacity. Shares are shown in percent.

	Capacity (cu. m.)	Share
MC Terminal Co. Ltd.	1,418,800	85.2%
Showa-GATX Co. Ltd.	93,550	5.6
Nippon GATX Co. Ltd.	56,530	3.4
Toyo Gosei Kogyo Co. Ltd.	52,925	3.2
Maruzen Co. Ltd.	36,100	2.2
Fuji Tank Service KK	7,000	0.4

Source: *ECN* Supplement, September 1991, p. 14.

★ 1359 ★
Chemical Terminals (SIC 4226)

Chemical Storage - U.K.

Chemical storage terminals, by company, are ranked by cubic meters of capacity. Shares are shown in percent.

	Capacity (cu. m.)	Share
GATX Terminals Ltd.	899,890	19.5%
Immingham Terminals	612,000	13.3
Powell Duffryn Terminals Ltd.	563,000	12.2
London and Coastal Oil Wharves Ltd.	461,000	10.0
Thames Matex	348,000	7.5
Carless Refining & Marketing	263,535	5.7
Tees Storage Co. Ltd.	255,000	5.5
United Molasses	213,900	4.6
Seal Sands Terminal	196,400	4.3
BTP Storage Ltd.	150,000	3.3
Panocean Storage and Transport Ltd.	128,750	2.8
Felixstowe Tankstore	105,500	2.3
The Ross Chemical & Storage Co. Ltd.	100,000	2.2
Tyne Terminal	54,700	1.2
Wymondham Oil Storage Co. Ltd.	39,200	0.8
Sunderland Tank Storage Ltd.	36,000	0.8
Hamber Tankstore	32,000	0.7
Cumbrian Terminal	31,500	0.7
Oil Rail Terminals Ltd.	21,000	0.5
PL Transtore Ltd.	20,000	0.4

	Capacity (cu. m.)	Share
Kuwait Petroleum	16,500	0.4%
Panocean Hull Ltd.	14,500	0.3
Cargo Fleet Chemical Co. Ltd.	14,000	0.3
Shannon Terminal	13,000	0.3
MP Storage & Blending Ltd.	12,169	0.3
Henry Diaper & Co. Ltd.	8,530	0.2
King's Lynn Storage Ltd.	4,000	0.1

Source: *ECN* supplement, September 1991, p. 30.

★ 1360 ★
Chemical Terminals (SIC 4226)

Chemical Storage - U.S.

Chemical storage terminals, by company, are ranked by cubic meters of capacity. Shares are shown in percent.

	Capacity (cu. m.)	Share
GATX Terminals Corp.	7,919,000	48.3%
Intercontinental Terminals Co.	825,000	5.0
Marysville Underground Storage Terminal	794,919	4.8
Stolt-Nielsen Inc.	694,906	4.2
Oiltanking Inc.	686,000	4.2
Seaview Oil Co.	641,000	3.9
Ergon Inc.	625,326	3.8
Time Oil Co.	415,793	2.5
Powell Duffryn Terminals Inc.	358,000	2.2
Colonial Terminals Inc.	338,350	2.1
ST Services	331,946	2.0
Westway Trading Corp.	308,318	1.9
Independent Terminal & Pipeline Co.	284,451	1.7
Stan Trans Inc.	281,000	1.7
Wyco Pipeline Co.	269,794	1.6
Delta Commodities Inc.	243,270	1.5
Panocean Southland Inc.	243,000	1.5
Delaware Terminal Co.	190,780	1.2
Statia Terminals	175,000	1.1
Tidewater Terminal Co.	159,294	1.0
Baytank Inc.	154,000	0.9
Lake River Corp.	146,000	0.9
Ashland Petroleum	119,250	0.7
Hudson Tank Terminals Corp.	113,658	0.7
River Transportation Co.	31,800	0.2
Columbia Terminals Inc.	29,415	0.2

Continued on next page.

★ 1360 ★ *Continued*

Chemical Terminals (SIC 4226)

Chemical Storage - U.S.

Chemical storage terminals, by company, are ranked by cubic meters of capacity. Shares are shown in percent.

	Capacity (cu. m.)	Share
Norfolk Oil Transit Inc.	12,136	0.1%
Advance Chemical Distribution Inc.	6,797	0.0
LA Terminals Inc.	6,356	0.0
3 Rivers Terminal	3,975	0.0

Source: *ECN* Supplement, September 1991, p. 43.

SIC 44 - Water Transportation

★ 1361 ★

Water Transportation (SIC 4400)

Top 10 Shipping Companies - Japan

Companies are ranked by 1991 declared income, shown in millions of Yen. Relative market shares are shown in percent.

	Income (Y mil.)	% of Group
Nippon Yusen	20,062	40.0%
Mitsui O.S.K. Lines	8,792	17.5
Kawasaki Kisen	7,926	15.8
Tonen Tanker	2,434	4.8
Shin-Nihonkai Ferry	2,299	4.6
Awaji Ferryboat	2,268	4.5
Daiichi Chuo Kisen	1,839	3.7
Tatsumi Shokai	1,541	3.1
Azuma Shipping	1,539	3.1
Tabuchi Kaiun	1,513	3.0

Source: *TOKYO Business Today*, July 1992, p. 40.

★ 1362 ★

Water Transportation (SIC 4400)

U.S. Flag Merchant Fleet Vessels - Deep Sea

Shares, as of May 1, 1991, are shown by vessel type in percent, based on totals of 630 vessels and 24,030 thousand tons.

	% of Vessels	% of Freight
Tankers	36.2%	64.2%
Intermodal	26.7	19.6
General cargo	31.4	10.6
Bulk carriers	4.1	5.3
Passenger and cargo	1.6	0.4

Source: *U.S. Industrial Outlook 1992*, p. 40-16.

★ 1363 ★

Shipping (SIC 4412)

Biggest Barge Fleets - U.S.

| Ashland |
| National |
| Hollywood |
| ACBL |
| Dixie |
| Ingram |
| Union Carbide |
| Other |

Shares of major barge fleets are shown as percent of U.S. totals in 1991 and 1992. Major barge fleets are those operators with more than 100 barges as of January 1, 1992. Ashland and Union Carbide are captive fleets. The total market for 1991 was 2,959 units. The total market for 1992 is 2,972 units.

	1991	1992
Ashland	8.4%	8.4%
National	8.3	8.3
Hollywood	7.3	7.4
ACBL	6.3	6.7
Dixie	6.4	6.6
Ingram	6.2	6.4
Union Carbide	5.7	5.1
Other	51.3	51.0

Source: *Chemicalweek*, February 19, 1992, p. 34, from Lambert & Lambert.

★ 1364 ★

Shipping (SIC 4412)

Container Ports

The ten largest ports in the U.S. are shown with cargo shipment value in billions of dollars for 1991. Relative shares are shown in percent for the same period.

	Cargo Value	% of Group
Los Angeles	$ 57.4	19.3 %
New York/New Jersey	49.6	16.6
Long Beach	48.9	16.4
Seattle	26.0	8.7
Houston	24.9	8.4
Tacoma, WA	23.5	7.9
Hampton Roads, VA	19.2	6.4
Oakland	18.4	6.2
Baltimore	16.6	5.6
Charleston, SC	13.6	4.6

Source: *The New York Times*, October 13, 1992, p. C16, from American Association of Port Authorities.

★ 1365 ★

Shipping (SIC 4412)

Shipping Trade: U.S. - Mediterranean

Distribution of waterborne cargo between the U.S. and the Mediterranean is based on total of 50.550 million TEU (20-foot equivalent units) for the first quarter of 1992, shown by carrier. Shipping shares are shown in percent.

Sea-Land Service	19.3 %
Zim Israel Navigation	15.4
Transatlantica	8.8
Italia di Navigazione	8.3
Farrell Lines	7.0
P&O Containers	5.9
Nedlloyd Lines	5.3
Croatia Line	5.1
Evergreen Line	5.0
Lykes Lines	4.7
DB Turkish Cargo Lines	3.3
Cle. Generale Maritime	3.1
British Continental	2.9

Maersk Line	2.4 %
Nordana Lines	1.8
Levant Line	1.0
Contship Containerlines	0.6

Source: *The Journal of Commerce*, June 30, 1992, p. 1A, from Port Import/Export Reporting Service and Doug Pinkerton - *Journal of Commerce*.

★ 1366 ★

Water Transportation Services (SIC 4490)

Water Transportation Facilities

Shares, by type of marine facility, are shown in percent for 1991. Total exceeds 100 percent according to source.

Marinas	92.0 %
Boatyards	11.0
Yacht clubs	7.0
Dryland marinas	2.0
Dockominiums	1.0

Source: *Boating Registration Statistics 1990*, 1990, p. 3, from National Marine Manufacturers Association.

SIC 45 - Transportation by Air

★ 1367 ★

Air Transport (SIC 4510)

Airline Operating Revenue

Shares by industry segment are shown in percent, based on a 1990 total operating revenue of $80.0 billion.

Scheduled passenger revenue	60.9%
Cargo revenue	8.9
Charter passenger revenue	1.3
Other revenue	8.9

Source: *U.S. Industrial Outlook 1992*, p. 40-1, from U.S. Department of Transportation.

★ 1368 ★

Air Transport (SIC 4510)

Airline Traffic - World

Distribution of 1992 world airline traffic is shown in thousands of RPKs (revenue passenger kilometers) and FTKs (freight ton kilometers).

	RPKs (000)	FTKs (000)
Adria	18,428	171
Aerlen	81,448	-
Aeromexico	1,280,604	10,274
Air Atlantis	191,523	-
Air Caledonie	13,045	1,106
Air Canada	4,971,810	-
Air Europa	393,680	-
Air Jamaica	313,995	6,361
AirLanka	1,363,975	37,243
Air Littoral	64,939	49,100
Air New Zealand	1,693,873	54,199
Air Niugini	85,627	2,966
Air UK	213,120	-
All Nippon	1,779,339	133,199
Ariana Afghan 2	26,790	2,485
Royal Brunei	81,069	2,269
Sabena	1,349,957	99,023
SAS	2,025,000	58,668

	RPKs (000)	FTKs (000)
Saudia	2,877,894	106,135
Singapore	11,738,000	684,379
South African	859,327	18,740
Spanair	1,299,658	-
Swissair	4,713,147	329,920
Syrian	152,937	3,162
TAP-Air Portugal	1,522,978	39,214
Thai Int'l	5,121,232	79,497
Transbrasil	1,005,551	36,271
Varig	4,169,670	198,123
Vasp	1,324,653	32,234
Windward Islands	764	-

Source: *Air Transport World*, July 1992, p. 101, from direct airline reports and OAA.

★ 1369 ★

Air Transport (SIC 4510)

Federal Planes

Approximate operating costs of each federal fleet in fiscal year 1989. The Department of Commerce and Health and Human Services (HHS) own no planes but charter or lease all necessary aircraft. Department shares are shown in percent, based on aviation cost. "Other" includes the National Science Foundation and the Tennessee Valley Authority.

	Costs ($ mil.)	% of Group
Department of Transportation	$ 446.0	59.0%
Department of the Treasury	74.5	9.9
Department of Agriculture	64.2	8.5
Department of the Interior	54.7	7.2
Department of Justice	41.0	5.4
Department of Energy	35.0	4.6
Department of State	23.0	3.0
Department of Commerce	7.2	1.0
NASA	6.0	0.8

Continued on next page.

★1369★ *Continued*

Air Transport (SIC 4510)

Federal Planes

Approximate operating costs of each federal fleet in fiscal year 1989. The Department of Commerce and Health and Human Services (HHS) own no planes but charter or lease all necessary aircraft. Department shares are shown in percent, based on aviation cost. "Other" includes the National Science Foundation and the Tennessee Valley Authority.

	Costs ($ mil.)	% of Group
Department of Health and Human Services	$ 3.5	0.5%
Other	1.004	0.1

Source: *Government Executive*, June 1991, p. 51, from *Washington Post*.

★1370★

Air Transport (SIC 4512)

U.S. Airlines Worldwide - 1991

Company shares are shown in percent based on a group total of 149.124 million RPKs (revenue passenger kilometers). Figures for Northwest were not available. Pan Am ceased operation in December of 1991.

United	27.6%
American	19.4
Pan Am	15.3
Continental	12.7
Delta	11.6
TWA	11.1
USAir	1.3
Federal Express	0.6
America West	0.4

Source: *Air Transport World*, April 1992, p. 123, from Department of Transportation.

★1371★

Airlines (SIC 4512)

African Airlines

Airlines are ranked by RPKs (revenue passenger kilometers) in 1991 shown in millions. Percent shares are based on regional total of 24,741 million RPKs.

	RPK (mil.)	Share
South African	8,410	34.0%
EgyptAir	3,722	15.0
Royal Swazi	3,606	14.6
Air Algerie	2,801	11.3
Tunis Air	1,802	7.3
Others	4,400	17.8

Source: *Air Transport World*, June 1992, p. 79, from direct airline reports.

★1372★

Airlines (SIC 4512)

Air Passenger Leaders

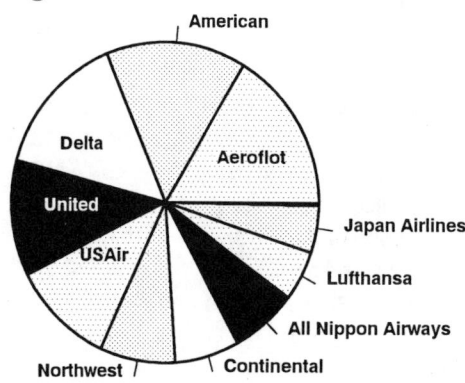

Biggest air carriers worldwide in 1991 are ranked by millions of passengers. Shares of group are shown in percent.

	Pass. (mil.)	% of Group
Aeroflot	85.6	16.7%
American	75.9	14.8
Delta	74.3	14.5
United	61.9	12.1
USAir	55.6	10.8
Northwest	41.1	8.0
Continental	37.0	7.2
All Nippon Airways	34.4	6.7

Continued on next page.

★ 1372 ★ *Continued*

Airlines (SIC 4512)

Air Passenger Leaders

Biggest air carriers worldwide in 1991 are ranked by millions of passengers. Shares of group are shown in percent.

	Pass. (mil.)	% of Group
Lufthansa	24.1	4.7%
Japan Airlines	23.1	4.5

Source: *USA TODAY*, July 22, 1992, p. 2B, from International Air Transport Association.

★ 1373 ★

Airlines (SIC 4512)

Air Passenger Leaders - International

Biggest air carriers worldwide in 1991 are ranked by millions of international passengers. (Data for Aeroflot has been divided among smaller airlines). Company shares of group are shown in percent.

	Pass. (mil.)	% of Group
British Airways	17.9	18.0%
Lufthansa	13.4	13.5
American	12.2	12.2
Air France	11.1	11.1
Scandinavian Airlines System (SAS)	7.9	7.9
Japan Airlines	7.8	7.8
Singapore Airlines	7.7	7.7
United	7.3	7.3
Cathay Pacific	7.2	7.2
KLM	7.1	7.1

Source: *USA TODAY*, July 22, 1992, p. 2B, from International Air Transport Association.

★ 1374 ★

Airlines (SIC 4512)

Air Travel - Transatlantic

Transatlantic air carrier market shares are shown as percent of revenue passenger kilometers in 1991. (At this writing, TWA has been withdrawn from many routes and Pan Am has been liquidated). Distribution is shown in percent.

BA	13.6%
TWA	9.9

American	8.8%
Lufthansa	8.5
Pan Am	8.3
Delta	6.9
KLM	6.7
United	5.2
Air France	4.6
Northwest	4.2

Source: *The Economist*, July 18, 1992, p. 68, from Avitas and Association of European Airlines.

★ 1375 ★

Airlines (SIC 4512)

Air Travel: U.S. - Japan

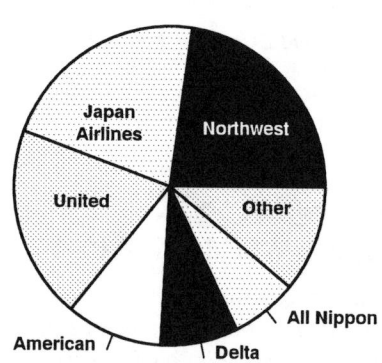

U.S.- Japan air-traffic market shares, by carrier, are based on the number of weekly seats on U.S.- to-Japan flights in the months of August and December 1991, shown in percent.

Northwest	23.0%
Japan Airlines	22.0
United	19.5
American	10.0
Delta	7.5
All Nippon	7.0
Other	11.0

Source: *Business TOKYO*, February 1992, p. 30, from Simat, Helliesen & Eichne, Inc. and ABC Schedule Tapes.

★ 1376 ★

Airlines (SIC 4512)

Airline Domestic Shares - 1991

Company shares are shown in percent based on a group total of 613.678 million RPKs (revenue passenger kilometers). Figures for Northwest were not available. Pan Am ceased operation in December 1991.

United	21.6%
American	21.4
Delta	17.6
Continental	11.1
USAir	9.0
TWA	7.5
Pan Am	5.1
America West	3.4
Southwest	3.0
Federal Express	0.2

Source: *Air Transport World*, April 1992, p. 123, from Department of Transportation.

★ 1377 ★

Airlines (SIC 4512)

Airline Fleet Size - 1990

Airlines are shown with number of planes and relative market share in percent. The figure for Aeroflot is estimated.

	No. of Planes	% of Group
Aeroflot	1,437	23.9%
American	622	10.3
Delta	538	8.9
United	487	8.1
USAir	429	7.1
Northwest	356	5.9
Continental	350	5.8
British Airways	235	3.9
Lufthansa	224	3.7
TWA	196	3.3
SAS	132	2.2
Southwest	123	2.0
Air France	120	2.0
America West	120	2.0
All Nippon	119	2.0
Iberia	114	1.9
JAL	113	1.9
Saudi Arabian	110	1.8

	No. of Planes	% of Group
Air Canada	103	1.7%
Alitalia	96	1.6

Source: *The Wall Street Journal*, January 14, 1992, p. A8, from Global Aviation Associates Ltd. and airlines.

★ 1378 ★

Airlines (SIC 4512)

Airline Passengers - 1990

Number of passengers is shown in millions; relative market share is shown in percent.

	Pass. (mil.)	% of Group
Aeroflot	137.7	19.0%
American	73.3	10.1
Delta	65.8	9.1
USAir	60.1	8.3
United	57.6	8.0
Northwest	41.0	5.7
Continental	35.5	4.9
All Nippon	33.1	4.6
British Airways	25.2	3.5
TWA	24.5	3.4
JAL	23.4	3.2
Lufthansa	22.4	3.1
Alitalia	18.2	2.5
Air Inter	17.1	2.4
Iberia	16.2	2.2
Air France	15.7	2.2
America West	15.6	2.2
SAS	14.9	2.1
Japan Air System	13.4	1.9
Korean Air	12.3	1.7

Source: *The Wall Street Journal*, January 14, 1992, p. A8, from Global Aviation Associates Ltd. and Orient Airlines Association.

★ 1379 ★

Airlines (SIC 4512)

Airline RPKs - 1990

RPKs (revenue passenger kilometers) are shown in billions; relative market share is shown in percent.

	RPK (bil.)	% of Group
Aeroflot	243.8	19.4%
American	123.8	9.8
United	122.5	9.7
Delta	95.0	7.5
Northwest	83.9	6.7
British Airways	65.9	5.2
Continental	63.0	5.0
USAir	57.2	4.5
TWA	55.7	4.4
JAL	55.3	4.4
Lufthansa	41.5	3.3
Air France	36.8	2.9
All Nippon	33.1	2.6
Singapore	31.5	2.5
Qantas	27.8	2.2
Air Canada	26.7	2.1
KLM	26.7	2.1
Cathay Pacific	23.6	1.9
Alitalia	22.8	1.8
Iberia	22.1	1.8

Source: *The Wall Street Journal*, January 14, 1992, p. A8, from Global Aviation Associates Ltd. and Orient Airlines Association.

★ 1380 ★

Airlines (SIC 4512)

Airline Sales - 1991

Company sales are shown in millions of dollars for fiscal 1991. Percent shares are based on group total.

	Sales ($ mil.)	% of Group
AMR Corp.	$ 12,887.0	20.9%
UAL Corp.	11,662.6	18.9
Delta Air Lines Inc.	9,170.6	14.8
Federal Express Corp.	7,688.3	12.4
USAir Group	6,514.1	10.5
Trans World Airlines	3,660.0	5.9
PHH Corp.	2,031.1	3.3
America West Airlines Inc.	1,413.9	2.3
Airborne Freight Corp.	1,367.0	2.2
Southwest Airlines	1,313.6	2.1

	Sales ($ mil.)	% of Group
Alaska Airgroup Inc.	$ 1,104.0	1.8%
Air Express International	601.9	1.0
AAR Corp.	466.5	0.8
HAL Inc.	365.0	0.6
PS Group Inc.	284.1	0.5
FlightSafety International	280.4	0.5
Worldcorp Inc.	280.3	0.5
Atlantic Southeast Airlines	221.9	0.4
Comair Holdings Inc.	201.7	0.3
Curtiss-Wright Corp.	191.3	0.3
Flight International Group	47.7	0.1
National Technical Sys. Inc.	35.5	0.1
Braniff Inc.	0.2	0.0

Source: *Aviation Week & Space Technology*, May 25, 1992, p. 49.

★ 1381 ★

Airlines (SIC 4512)

Airlines Global Market

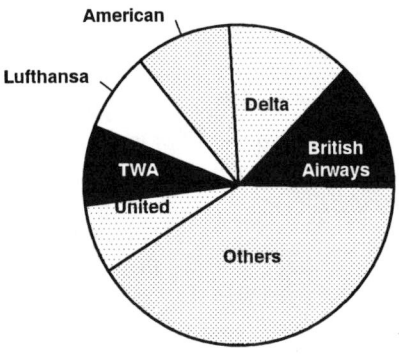

Shares of the global market, by company, are shown in percent for the period from 1990 to 1992.

British Airways	13.33%
Delta	12.93
American	10.46
Lufthansa	7.95
TWA	7.68
United	6.64
Others	41.01

Source: Investext, Thomson Financial Networks, March 16, 1992, from The First Boston Corporation.

★1382★

Airlines (SIC 4512)

Airlines - Canada

Shares of the Canadian industry are shown in percent for December 1990 and December 1991.

	Dec. 1990	Dec. 1991
PWA Corp.	47.5%	50.7%
Air Canada	52.5	49.3

Source: Investext, Thomson Financial Networks, February 12, 1992, from Midland Walwyn Capital Inc.

★1383★

Airlines (SIC 4512)

Airlines - Federal Travel Vendors

Airlines are shown as federal travel vendors whose market share in 1990 was greater than 5 percent, as measured in billings through the government's travel card program, administered by Citibank/Diners Club. Data represent fiscal 1990 sales in thousands of dollars which were only one-fifth of the government's travel expenses. Market share is shown in percent.

	Sales ($ 000)	Share
Delta	$ 125,783	18.7%
United	105,553	15.7
American	97,619	14.6
USAir	90,136	13.4
Northwest	64,029	9.5
TWA	54,392	8.1
Continental	42,453	6.3

Source: *Government Executive*, August 1991, p. 50, from General Services Administration.

★1384★

Airlines (SIC 4512)

Asian/Canadian/European Airlines

Airline sales are shown in millions of dollars for fiscal 1991. Percent shares are based on group total.

	Sales ($ mil.)	% of Group
Lufthansa	$ 9819.4	15.4%
Japan Air Lines Co. Ltd	9635.9	15.1
British Airways plc.	9123.1	14.3
Federal Express Corp.	7688.3	12.1

	Sales ($ mil.)	% of Group
All Nippon Airways Co. Ltd. . .	$ 5720.0	9.0%
Alitalia Spa.	4612.7	7.2
KLM	3700.9	5.8
Swissair AG	3402.0	5.3
Air Canada	3115.3	4.9
Singapore Airlines Ltd.	2786.3	4.4
Cathay Pacific Airways Ltd . . .	2544.0	4.0
Air New Zealand Ltd	1458.4	2.3
Crossair AG	133.4	0.2

Source: *Aviation Week & Space Technology*, May 25, 1992, p. 51.

★1385★

Airlines (SIC 4512)

Asian-Pacific Airlines

Airlines are ranked by RPKs (revenue passenger kilometers) in 1991, shown in millions. Percent shares are based on a regional total of 307,312 million RPKs.

	RPK (mil.)	Share
Japan Airlines	51,524	16.8%
All Nippon	35,692	11.6
Singapore	32,594	10.6
Royal Nepal	26,638	8.7
Cathay Pacific	24,433	8.0
Others	136,431	44.4

Source: *Air Transport World*, June 1992, p. 80, from direct airline reports.

★1386★

Airlines (SIC 4512)

Australasian Airlines

Australasian carriers' operating results are shown in thousands of revenue passenger kilometers (RPK) as of November 1991. Percent shares are based on the group total.

	RPK (000)	% of Group
Japan Airlines	3,270,888	17.5%
Singapore Airlines	2,867,900	15.4
Qantas	2,398,561	12.8
Cathay Pacific	2,104,388	11.3
Thai International	1,504,231	8.1

Continued on next page.

★ 1386 ★ *Continued*

Airlines (SIC 4512)

Australasian Airlines

Australasian carriers' operating results are shown in thousands of revenue passenger kilometers (RPK) as of November 1991. Percent shares are based on the group total.

	RPK (000)	% of Group
Korean Airlines	1,266,124	6.8%
Malaysia Airlines	979,333	5.2
Garuda Indonesia	953,679	5.1
China Airlines	942,553	5.0
Philippine Airlines	805,285	4.3
Air New Zealand	777,779	4.2
All Nippon Airways	739,392	4.0
Royal Brunei	62,962	0.3

Source: *Aviation Week & Space Technology*, February 24, 1992, p. 57, from Orient Airlines Association.

★ 1387 ★

Airlines (SIC 4512)

Canadian Airlines

Airlines are ranked by RPKs (revenue passenger kilometers), shown in millions. Percent shares are based on national total of 43,618 million RPKs.

	RPK (mil.)	Share
Air Canada	21,975	50.4%
Canadian	20,391	46.7
Air Nova	471	1.1
Air Ontario	326	0.7
Ontario Express	212	0.5
Others	243	0.6

Source: *Air Transport World*, June 1992, p. 81, from direct airline reports.

★ 1388 ★

Airlines (SIC 4512)

Commercial Airlines Flights to Central and South America

Shares, by company, are shown in percent for the period from 1990 to 1992.

American	22.58%
Mexicana	13.13
United	9.29
Varig	8.57
Other	46.43

Source: Investext, Thomson Financial Networks, March 16, 1992, from The First Boston Corporation.

★ 1389 ★

Airlines (SIC 4512)

Commercial Airlines Flights to France

Shares, by company, are shown in percent for the period from 1990 to 1992.

Air France	29.11%
TWA	17.24
American	11.79
Delta	11.17
Other	30.69

Source: Investext, Thomson Financial Networks, March 16, 1992, from The First Boston Corporation.

★ 1390 ★

Airlines (SIC 4512)

Commercial Airlines Flights to Germany

Shares, by company, are shown in percent for the period from 1990 to 1992.

Lufthansa	39.11%
Delta	27.48
American	7.95
United	5.45
Other	20.01

Source: Investext, Thomson Financial Networks, March 16, 1992, from The First Boston Corporation.

★ 1391 ★

Airlines (SIC 4512)

Commercial Airlines Flights to Italy

Shares, by company, are shown in percent for the period from 1990 to 1992.

Alitalia	56.55%
TWA	25.30
Delta	11.74
American	6.42

Source: Investext, Thomson Financial Networks, March 16, 1992, from The First Boston Corporation.

★ 1392 ★

Airlines (SIC 4512)

Commercial Airlines Flights to Spain

Shares, by company, are shown in percent for the period from 1990 to 1992.

Iberia	38.73%
American	17.92
TWA	14.76
United	10.56
Other	18.03

Source: Investext, Thomson Financial Networks, March 16, 1992, from The First Boston Corporation.

★ 1393 ★

Airlines (SIC 4512)

Commercial Airlines Flights to Switzerland

Shares, by company, are shown in percent for the period from 1990 to 1992.

Swissair	76.36%
American	15.50
Delta	8.14

Source: Investext, Thomson Financial Networks, March 16, 1992, from The First Boston Corporation.

★ 1394 ★

Airlines (SIC 4512)

Commercial Airlines Flights to the Far East

Shares, by company, are shown in percent for the period from 1990 to 1992.

Northwest	22.19%
Japan Airlines	19.14
United	19.08
All Nippon	5.08
Korean	4.12
Singapore	4.06
Other	26.33

Source: Investext, Thomson Financial Networks, March 16, 1992, from The First Boston Corporation.

★ 1395 ★

Airlines (SIC 4512)

Commercial Airlines Flights to the Netherlands

Shares, by company, are shown in percent for the period from 1990 to 1992.

KLM	69.11%
Delta	8.90
Northwest	5.79
TWA	5.63
Other	10.70

Source: Investext, Thomson Financial Networks, March 16, 1992, from The First Boston Corporation.

★ 1396 ★

Airlines (SIC 4512)

Commercial Airlines Flights to the U.K.

Shares, by company, are shown in percent for the period from 1990 to 1992.

British Airways	40.44%
American	14.35
United	11.32
Virgin Atlantic	9.99
Other	23.90

Source: Investext, Thomson Financial Networks, March 16, 1992, from The First Boston Corporation.

★ 1397 ★
Airlines (SIC 4512)

Commercial Airlines Flights - Intra Far East

Shares, by company, are shown in percent for the period from 1990 to 1992.

Japan Airlines	12.22%
All Nippon	12.12
Thai Airways	6.28
Singapore	6.11
Cathay Pacific	5.61
Other	57.66

Source: Investext, Thomson Financial Networks, March 16, 1992, from The First Boston Corporation.

★ 1398 ★
Airlines (SIC 4512)

Domestic Air Shares

Company shares are shown in percent based on revenue passenger miles from January through April 1992. TWA is operating under Chapter 11 as of this writing.

American	20.6%
United	18.9
Delta	17.2
Northwest	12.5
Continental	10.0
USAir	7.7
TWA	7.1
Southwest	3.1
America West	2.9

Source: *The Economist*, June 6, 1992, p. 76, from Avitas.

★ 1399 ★
Airlines (SIC 4512)

Domestic Airline Shares

Carrier shares for the year ending June 30, 1991 are shown in percent based on a total of 369,529,008 passengers.

Delta	17.8%
American	17.8
USAir	15.4
United	14.7
Northwest	9.4

Continental	8.5%
Southwest	6.3
TWA	5.1
America West	4.6
Trump	0.5

Source: *The New York Times*, January 12, 1992, p. 3, from *Avmark*.

★ 1400 ★
Airlines (SIC 4512)

Domestic Regional/Specialty Carriers

Airlines are ranked by RPKs (revenue passenger kilometers), shown in thousands. Percent shares are based on total of 10,109,143 thousand RPKs.

	RPK (000)	Share
Sun Country	2,418,967	23.9%
Atlantic Southeast	806,900	8.0
Carnival	795,129	7.9
Key	756,941	7.5
Comair	695,700	6.9
Others	4,635,506	45.9

Source: *Air Transport World*, June 1992, p. 88, from direct airline reports.

★ 1401 ★
Airlines (SIC 4512)

Domestic Scheduled Airlines - Australia

Airline activity is shown with percent share, based on a total of 16,725,652 passengers.

Ansett	39.3%
Australian	39.2
Compass	8.3
Eastwest	5.8
Ansett Express	3.3
Ansett WA	3.2
Australian Airlink	0.6
Ansett NT	0.2

Source: *Air Transport World*, April 1992, p. 124, from Australian Department of Transport and Communications.

★ 1402 ★

Airlines (SIC 4512)

European Airlines

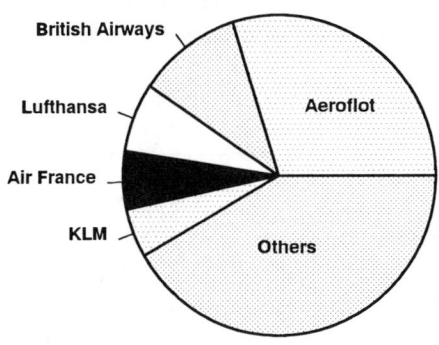

Airlines are ranked by RPKs (revenue passenger kilometers), shown in millions. Percent shares are based on regional total of 589,821 million RPKs.

	RPK (mil.)	Share
Aeroflot	175,925	29.8%
British Airways	63,186	10.7
Lufthansa	42,261	7.2
Air France	33,781	5.7
KLM	27,307	4.6
Others	247,361	41.9

Source: *Air Transport World*, June 1992, p. 81, from direct airline reports.

★ 1403 ★

Airlines (SIC 4512)

International Air Travel

Passengers carried by U.S. and international airlines operating abroad. Data are shown in millions of passengers in 1990.

	Pass. (mil.)
British Airways	19.68
Lufthansa	13.33
Air France	12.42
Pan Am	10.10
Japan Airlines	8.35
American Airlines	8.34
S.A.S.	8.34
Cathay Pacific	7.38
Alitalia	7.11
Singapore Airlines	7.09

	Pass. (mil.)
Swissair	7.02
KLM	6.86
United Airlines	6.09
Iberia	5.91
Continental	4.72

Source: *The New York Times*, March 11, 1992, p. C1, from International Air Transport Association.

★ 1404 ★

Airlines (SIC 4512)

International Carriers - 1990

Number of passengers carried by each airline is shown in millions for 1990; relative market shares are shown in percent.

	Pass. (mil.)	% of Group
British Airways	19.68	14.8%
Lufthansa	13.33	10.0
Air France	12.42	9.4
Pan Am	10.10	7.6
Japan Airlines	8.35	6.3
American Airlines	8.34	6.3
SAS	8.34	6.3
Cathay Pacific	7.38	5.6
Alitalia	7.11	5.4
Singapore Airlines	7.09	5.3
Swissair	7.02	5.3
KLM	6.86	5.2
United Airlines	6.09	4.6
Iberia	5.91	4.5
Continental	4.72	3.6

Source: *The Globe and Mail*, March 18, 1992, p. D4, from International Air Transport Association.

★ 1405 ★

Airlines (SIC 4512)

Latin American-Caribbean Airlines

Airlines are ranked by RPKs (revenue passenger kilometers), shown in millions. Percent shares are based on regional total of 64,259 million RPKs.

	RPK (mil.)	Share
Varig	16,403	25.5%
Mexicana	10,743	16.7
Aeromexico	7,540	11.7
Transbrasil	3,584	5.6
Avianca	3,421	5.3
Others	22,568	35.1

Source: *Air Transport World*, June 1992, p. 85, from direct airline reports.

★ 1406 ★

Airlines (SIC 4512)

Leading Airlines

| American Airlines |
| United Airlines |
| Delta |
| Northwest |
| Continental |
| USAir |
| TWA |

Major carriers are shown with miles flown by paying passengers in 1991. Relative market shares are shown in percent.

	Miles (bil.)	% of Group
American Airlines	82.2	21.2%
United Airlines	81.9	21.1
Delta	67.3	17.3
Northwest	53.2	13.7
Continental	41.4	10.7
USAir	34.1	8.8
TWA	28.0	7.2

Source: *The New York Times*, February 1, 1992, p. 324, from Air Transport Association.

★ 1407 ★

Airlines (SIC 4512)

Leading Airlines - Japan

Companies are ranked by 1991 declared income, shown in millions of Yen. Relative market shares are shown in percent.

	Income (Y mil.)	% of Group
All Nippon Airways	21,978	45.4%
Japan Airlines	8,480	17.5
Japan Air System	6,908	14.3
PASCO	3,331	6.9
Kokusai Kogyo	2,818	5.8
Japan	1,992	4.1
Asia Air Survey	869	1.8
Air Nippon	827	1.7
Nakanigon Air Service	664	1.4
Hasshu	547	1.1

Source: *TOKYO Business Today*, July 1992, p. 40.

★ 1408 ★

Airlines (SIC 4512)

Mexican Airlines

Shares of traffic in or out of Mexico are estimated and shown in percent. Figures are based on revenue ton miles in the year ended October 1992. Data refer to scheduled flights of both passengers and cargo.

Mexicana	21.6%
Aeromexico	17.8
Taesa	8.6
Non-Mexican carriers	52.0

Source: *The New York Times*, November 13, 1992, p. C1, from Aviation Management Services.

★1409★

Airlines (SIC 4512)

Middle East Airlines

Airlines are ranked by RPKs (revenue passenger kilometers), shown in millions. Percent shares are based on regional total of 42,450 million RPKs.

	RPK (mil.)	Share
Saudia	15,585	36.7%
El Al	7,747	18.2
Gulf Air	6,703	15.8
Iran Air	6,432	15.2
Emirates	2,204	5.2
Others	3,779	8.9

Source: *Air Transport World*, June 1992, p. 86, from direct airline reports.

★1410★

Airlines (SIC 4512)

National Air Carriers

U.S. national carrier market shares are based on total of 23.403 million RPKs (revenue passenger kilometers), shown in percent for 1991. Figures are not available for American Trans Air or UPS. Figures for WestAir are estimated due to sale of its Atlantic coast division. Midway Express ceased operation in November 1991.

Alaska	34.0%
Tower	17.3
Hawaiian	17.0
World	7.0
Aloha	4.6
Midwest Express	4.3
WestAir	4.4
Trump	3.9
Air Wisconsin	3.4
Horizon	2.8
MarkAir	1.2

Source: *Air Transport World*, April 1992, p. 125, from Department of Transportation.

★1411★

Airlines (SIC 4512)

Regional Airlines

Company shares of the 1991 U.S. market are shown as percent of total passengers (15,190,619) and as percent of total of 4,005,141,433 revenue passenger miles.

	Pass.	RPMs
Air Sedona	0.0%	0.0%
Alpine	0.0	0.0
ASA	14.8	12.5
Big Sky	0.2	0.1
Business Express	8.8	6.6
Carnival	4.2	11.4
Casino Express	0.8	2.9
CCAir	5.0	2.6
Chautauqua	3.1	1.8
Christman	0.0	0.0
Comair	13.3	10.8
Empire	0.1	0.1
Executive	6.2	3.2
Flamenco	0.3	0.0
Great American	0.6	1.0
Key	2.7	11.7
Las Vegas	0.2	0.2
Mesa	7.1	5.7
Mesaba	6.9	5.3
Metro	10.6	9.4
MGM Grand Air	0.3	3.2
Paradise Island	1.9	1.3
Reeve	0.4	1.3
Scenic	1.9	1.3
SkyWest	8.3	6.0
StatesWest	2.3	1.5

Source: *Air Transport World*, April 1992, p. 119, from Department of Transportation and company reports.

★1412★

Airlines (SIC 4512)

Top Airlines in the World

Airlines are ranked by number of RPKs (revenue passenger kilometers) in 1991. Percent shares are based on group total.

	RPK (mil.)	% of Group
Aeroflot	175,925	13.4%
American	132,477	10.1
United	132,405	10.1

Continued on next page.

★ 1412 ★ *Continued*

Airlines (SIC 4512)

Top Airlines in the World

Airlines are ranked by number of RPKs (revenue passenger kilometers) in 1991. Percent shares are based on group total.

	RPK (mil.)	% of Group
Delta	108,234	8.2%
Northwest	85,599	6.5
Continental	68,151	5.2
British Airways	63,186	4.8
USAir	54,899	4.2
Japan Airlines	51,524	3.9
TWA	46,115	3.5
Lufthansa	42,261	3.2
All Nippon	35,692	2.7
Air France	33,781	2.6
Singapore	32,594	2.5
Pan Am	31,608	2.4
KLM	27,307	2.1
Qantas	26,638	2.0
Cathay Pacific	24,433	1.9
Air Canada	21,975	1.7
Alitalia	21,710	1.6
America West	20,917	1.6
Iberia	20,473	1.6
Canadian	20,391	1.5
Korean	19,956	1.5
Thai Int'l	18,295	1.4

Source: *Air Transport World*, June 1992, p. 70.

★ 1413 ★

Airlines (SIC 4512)

Top Airlines - 1991

American
Delta
United
USAir
Northwest
Continental
British Airways

Biggest airlines worldwide are ranked by number of passengers in calendar year 1991, shown in millions. Relative shares are shown in percent.

	Pass. (mil.)	% of Group
American	76.0	20.6%
Delta	74.3	20.1
United	61.9	16.8
USAir	55.6	15.1
Northwest	41.1	11.1
Continental	37.0	10.0
British Airways	22.9	6.2

Source: *The Wall Street Journal*, July 22, 1992, p. A3, from Global Aviation Research and Airclaims Ltd.

★ 1414 ★

Airlines (SIC 4512)

Top Five City-Pair Airlines

Top five airlines, contracted by the General Services Administration to supply federal government employees with flights to certain city-pair destinations, are shown in number of city-pairs. An approximate value of contracts, by carrier, is shown in millions of dollars.

	No. of pairs	Value ($ mil.)
USAir	730	$ 218
Delta	625	213
United	476	208
American	442	184
Continental	399	101

Source: *Government Executive*, February 1992, p. 36.

★1415★

Airlines (SIC 4512)

Trans-Atlantic Route Shares

Carrier shares for the year ending June 30, 1991 are shown in percent based on a total of 8,813,167 passengers.

TWA	38.1%
American	18.8
Delta	14.4
Northwest	12.3
United	7.1
Continental	6.9
USAir	2.4

Source: *The New York Times*, January 12, 1992, p. 3, from *Avmark*.

★1416★

Airlines (SIC 4512)

Trans-Pacific Route Shares

Carrier shares for the year ending June 30, 1991 are shown in percent based on a total of 12,457,666 passengers.

United	38.4%
Northwest	36.4
Continental	20.4
Delta	2.9
American	1.6
America West	0.3

Source: *The New York Times*, January 12, 1992, p. 3, from *Avmark*.

★1417★

Airlines (SIC 4512)

U.S. Major Airlines

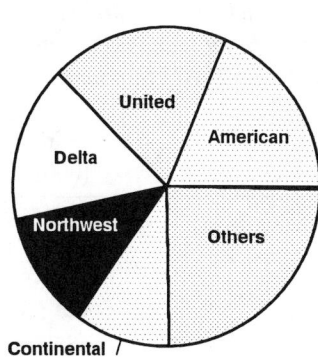

Airlines are ranked by RPKs (revenue passenger kilometers), shown in millions. Percent shares are based on total of 699,938 million RPKs.

	RPK (mil.)	Share
American	132,477	18.9%
United	132,405	18.9
Delta	108,234	15.5
Northwest	85,599	12.2
Continental	68,151	9.7
Others	173,072	24.7

Source: *Air Transport World*, June 1992, p. 86, from direct airline reports.

★1418★

Airlines (SIC 4512)

U.S. National Airlines

Airlines are ranked by RPKs (revenue passenger kilometers), shown in millions. Percent shares are based on a total of 36,552 million RPKs.

	RPK (mil.)	% of Group
Alaska	7,961	21.8%
American Trans Air	7,417	20.3
Hawaiian	5,500	15.0
Midway	4,150	11.4
Tower	4,051	11.1
Others	7,473	20.4

Source: *Air Transport World*, June 1992, p. 86, from direct airline reports.

★ 1419 ★

Air Cargo (SIC 4513)

Cargo Carriers - U.S.

Companies are ranked by FTKs (freight ton kilometers), shown in thousands. Percent shares are based on total of 12,174,807 thousand FTKs.

	FTK (000)	% of Group
Federal Express	6,000,599	49.3%
UPS	2,857,871	23.5
Flagship Express	605,853	5.0
Millon	544,067	4.5
Evergreen	455,300	3.7
Others	1,711,117	14.1

Source: *Air Transport World*, June 1992, p. 88, from direct airline reports.

★ 1420 ★

Air Cargo (SIC 4513)

Cargo Specialist Traffic

U.S. cargo specialist traffic is shown in thousands of FTKs (freight ton kilometers) traveled by airlines in calendar year 1991. Percent shares, by company, are based on a total of 7,957,204 FTKs.

	FTKs (000)	Share
Federal Express	6,000,601	74.8%
Evergreen	422,893	5.3
Southern Air Transport	344,715	4.3
Arrow	326,963	4.1
Challenge	192,083	2.4
American Int'l	185,696	2.3
Florida West	166,510	2.1
Zantop	88,510	1.1
Mountain Air Cargo	64,827	0.8
Amerijet	61,044	0.8
Millon	54,303	0.7
Buffalo	45,770	0.6
Trans Continental	34,335	0.4
Northern Air Cargo	16,240	0.2
Trans Air Link	7,931	0.1
Aerial	5,088	0.1
Wrangler	4,523	0.1

Source: *Air Transport World*, April 1992, p. 122, from U.S. DOT and direct airline reports.

★ 1421 ★

Air Cargo (SIC 4513)

Courier Services in the EC

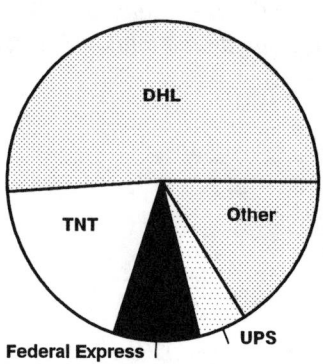

Estimated shares of the European Community market in 1989 are shown in percent.

DHL	51.0%
TNT	19.0
Federal Express	9.0
UPS	5.0
Other	16.0

Source: *Advertising Age*, April 27, 1992, pp. I-6.

★ 1422 ★

Air Cargo (SIC 4513)

Largest Cargo Airlines

Largest cargo-carrying airlines ranked by 1990 cargo revenues worth $6.629 million. Group shares are shown in percent.

	Cargo ($ 000)	% of Group
Federal Express	$ 2,746,259	41.4%
United Parcel Service	887,656	13.4
Northwest	647,517	9.8
United	592,872	8.9
Delta	432,525	6.5
American	428,984	6.5
Pan American	250,187	3.8
Continental	245,605	3.7
TransWorld Airlines	222,807	3.4
Evergreen	173,355	2.6

Source: *T&D*, December 1991, p. 33.

★1423★

Air Cargo (SIC 4513)

Parcel Carriers - U.K.

Shares of the United Kingdom domestic parcel service are shown as percent of independent carriers.

	1989	1990
Parcelforce	34.8%	35.0%
Securicor (OMEGA)	10.5	11.2
TNT	9.6	9.7
Federal Express	4.7	5.5
Redstar	4.6	4.7
Other	35.8	33.9

Source: Investext, Thomson Financial Networks, January 13, 1992, from Nomura Research Institute Europe Ltd.

★1424★

Airports (SIC 4581)

Cargo Airport Leaders

Top 25 airport shares are based on total cargo for this group.

	Cargo	% of Group
New York, J.F. Kennedy Int'l .	1,257,069	10.7%
Los Angeles Int'l	1,141,196	9.7
Chicago O'Hare Int'l . . .	987,281	8.4
Miami Int'l	967,241	8.2
San Francisco Int'l	606,008	5.1
Atlanta Hartsfield Int'l	599,674	5.1
Anchorage Int'l	587,817	5.0
Dallas/Fort Wodrth Int'l . . .	547,008	4.6
Newark Int'l	483,622	4.1
Dayton Int'l	441,418	3.7
Indiannapolis Int'l	394,162	3.3
Honolulu Int'l	382,168	3.2
Philadelphia Int'l	351,059	3.0
Boston Logan Int'l	347,735	3.0
Seattle-Tacoma Int'l	326,569	2.8
Memphis Int'l	312,016	2.6
Denver, Stapleton Int'l . . .	292,625	2.5
Minneapolis-St Paul Int'l . . .	268,114	2.3
Ontario Int'l	256,280	2.2
Oakland Int'l	252,855	2.1
Houston Intercontinental . . .	230,304	2.0
Detroit Metro Wayne County	210,785	1.8
San Juan, Luis Munoz Marin .	206,471	1.8

	Cargo	% of Group
Washington Dulles Int'l . . .	163,823	1.4%
Cincinnati/North Kentucky Int'l	162,553	1.4

Source: *Traffic World*, July 20, 1992, p. 36, from Airports Association Council Inernational.

SIC 46 - Pipelines, Except Natural Gas

★1425★

Pipeline Construction (SIC 4600)

Pipeline Construction Mileage Worldwide

Shares, by construction type, are based on world totals of 19,641 miles for 1991 and planned 19,512 miles for 1992. NGL stands for natural gas liquid.

	'91	'92
Gas lines		
Transmission	56.7%	55.9%
Gathering	4.7	4.5
Crude lines		
Trunklines	7.5	10.8
Gathering	2.3	2.2
Product lines		
Refined products	18.0	18.3
Other	1.9	0.9
Offshore Gas	7.3	
Offshore Oil, NGL	1.7	5.8

Source: *Pipeline Industry*, p. 19.

★1426★

Pipeline Construction (SIC 4600)

Pipeline Construction Mileage - U.S.

Shares, by construction type, are based on U.S. totals of 7,446 miles for 1991 and planned 7,529 miles for 1992. NGL stands for natural gas liquid.

	'91	'92
Gas lines		
Transmission	67.9%	70.2%
Gathering	3.9	1.4
Crude lines		
Trunklines	5.3	6.0
Gathering	4.8	2.7

	'91	'92
Refined product lines	13.6%	15.7%
Offshore		
Gas	3.3	2.7
Oil, NGL	1.2	1.2

Source: *Pipeline Industry*, January 1992, p. 19.

★1427★

Pipelines (SIC 4610)

Petroleum Distribution Companies - Japan

Top 10 companies are ranked by 1991 declared income, shown in millions of Yen. Relative market shares are shown in percent.

	Income (Y mil.)	% of Group
Nippon Oil	70,921	28.4%
Caltex Oil Japan	26,380	10.6
Esso Sekiyu	25,960	10.4
Idemitsu Kosan	25,712	10.3
General Sekiyu	24,313	9.7
Kyodo Oil	23,484	9.4
Mobil Sekiyu	22,635	9.1
Cosmo Oil	18,123	7.3
Kyushi Oil	6,384	2.6
C. Itoh Fuel	6,017	2.4

Source: *TOKYO Business Today*, July 1992, p. 40.

SIC 47 - Transportation Services

★1428★

Transportation Services (SIC 4700)

Coach and Tour Bus Market

Market segmentation is shown in percent.

Dial	65.0+%
Other	35.0

Source: Investext, Thomson Financial Networks, June 18, 1992, from Prudential Securities, Inc.

★1429★

Transportation Services (SIC 4700)

Transportation Services Leaders

Companies are ranked by 1991 sales, shown in millions of dollars. Shares of the group are shown in percent.

	Sales ($ mil.)	% of Group
Federal Express	$7,548	43.3%
Ryder System	5,061	29.0
PHH	1,997	11.4
Airborne Freight	1,367	7.8
Trinity Industries	1,206	6.9
Flightsafety International	268	1.5

Source: *The 1992 Business Week 1000*, p. 190.

★1430★

Tourism (SIC 4720)

International Visitor Arrivals to U.S.

Figures reflect number of visitor arrivals to the United States in 1991 and 1992. Percent shares are based on 1991 total of 41,543 visitors and 1992 total of 44,449 visitors.

	1991	1992
Canada	45.3%	45.7%
Mexico	17.3	17.4
Europe	16.4	16.1
Asia/Middle East	11.7%	11.6%
South America	3.4	3.4
Caribbean	2.8	2.8
Oceania	1.7	1.7
Central America	1.0	0.9
Africa	0.3	0.3

Source: *Hotel & Motel Management*, July 8, 1991, p. 1, from U.S. Travel and Tourism Administration.

★1431★

Tourism (SIC 4720)

Vacation Destinations in the U.S.

Percent distribution of travel is shown for 1990.

Ocean/beach	27.0%
Cities	20.0
Small towns/rural areas	13.0
Mountains	12.0
Lakes	11.0
Amusement/theme parks	10.0
State/national parks	7.0
Other	2.0

Source: *USA TODAY*, June 11, 1992, p. 7A, from *U.S. Travel Data Calendar 1990*.

★ 1432 ★

Travel (SIC 4720)

Travel Industry

Market segmentation is shown in percent.

Airfares 43.0%
Lodging 21.0
Meals 15.0
Entertainment 10.0
Car rental 8.0
Other 3.0

Source: *USA TODAY*, October 13, 1992, from American Express Travel Management Services.

★ 1433 ★

Travel (SIC 4724)

Business Travel

| Outside vendor/travel agency |
| Individual |
| In-house travel department |
| Staff person |

Shares of the business travel market, by segment, are shown in percent. Numbers may not add up to 100% due to rounding.

Outside vendor/travel agency 61.0%
Individual 37.0
In-house travel department 10.0
Staff person 10.0

Source: *Sales & Marketing Management*, June 1992, p. 140.

★ 1434 ★

Travel (SIC 4724)

Federal Travel by Industry Segment

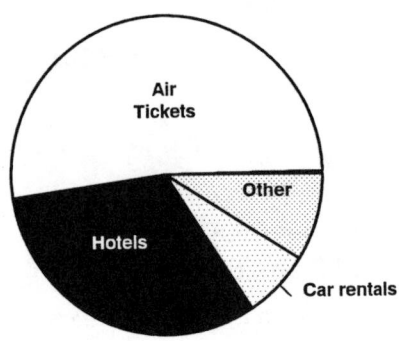

A total of $1.3 billion was charged by federal travelers on their Diners Club cards in 1990. Data represent one-fifth of the 1990 federal travel budget of $6.8 billion. Expenditures by industry segment are shown as percent of a total.

Air Tickets 52.0%
Hotels 32.0
Car rentals 7.0
Other 9.0

Source: *Government Executive*, August 1991, p. 50, from General Services Administration.

★ 1435 ★

Tunnel Operation (SIC 4785)

Chunnel Traffic Shares

Estimated traffic flow shares for the Eurotunnel (between the U.K. and France) in 1993 are shown in percent based on total projected transportation of 84.2 million passengers and 89.2 million tons of goods.

	% of Pass.	% of Goods
Eurotunnel	34.0%	18.2%
Other	66.0	81.8

Source: Investext, Thomson Financial Networks, May 19, 1992, from Meeschaert-Rousselle.

SIC 48 - Communications

★1436★

Data Communications (SIC 4800)

Projections for ISDN Implementation

Company implementation of ISDN (information system data network) are shown with the number of anticipated deployment lines in 1991, 1992, and 1993.

	'91	'92	'93
Ameritech	2.2	3.4	8.0
Bell Atlantic	6.9	14.8	15.8
Bell South	3.1	5.6	8.0
NYNEX	1.3	3.9	5.3
Pacific Bell	4.1	4.7	5.8
Southwestern Bell	1.6	2.0	2.1
U.S. West	3.7	6.7	7.6

Source: *Telecommunications*, April 1992, p. 11.

★1437★

Cellular Phone Service (SIC 4812)

Cellular Services

AT&T

Ericcson

Motorola

Northern Telecom

Other

Shares are shown in percent, based on total subscribers in 1991.

AT&T	47.2%
Ericcson	25.8
Motorola	14.1
Northern Telecom	5.2
Other	7.7

Source: Investext, Thomson Financial Networks, February 1, 1992, from Donaldson, Lufkin & Jenrette Securities.

★1438★

Cellular Services (SIC 4812)

Cellular Services - U.K.

Cumulative market shares as of 1991 are shown in percent, based on a total of 1.184 million subscribers.

Vodafone	57.0%
Cellnet	43.0

Source: Investext, Thomson Financial Networks, February 6, 1992, from UBS Phillips & Drew Global Research Group.

★1439★

Cellular Services (SIC 4812)

Cellular Shares

Shares are shown in percent, based on the total population served (382,399,613). The category includes both wireline and non-wireline services.

AT&T	41.5%
Ericcson	22.6
Motorola	21.6
Northern Telecom	10.9
Novatel	1.6
Astronet	1.5
NEC	0.2
Plexsys	0.0

Source: Investext, Thomson Financial Networks, January 27, 1992, from Kidder, Peabody & Company, Incorporated.

★ 1440 ★

Telecommunications (SIC 4813)

Foreign Telecom Companies Worldwide

Public network operators are shown with 1989 revenue in millions of dollars. Relative market shares are shown in percent.

	Rev. ($ mil.)	% of Group
DBP Telekom (Germany)	$ 20,247	17.2%
BT (United Kingdom)	20,174	17.1
France Telecom (France)	16,449	14.0
SIP (Italy)	11,030	9.4
Telecom (Canada)	10,415	8.8
Telecom Australia (Australia)	6,925	5.9
Telefonica (Spain)	5,978	5.1
Swedish Telecom (Sweden)	4,377	3.7
PTT Nederland N.V. (Netherlands)	4,000	3.4
PTT (Switzerland)	3,935	3.3
PTV (Austria)	2,342	2.0
RTT (Belgium)	2,123	1.8
Norwegian Telecom (Norway)	2,061	1.7
OTE (Greece)	1,008	0.9
Telecom Ireland (Ireland)	992	0.8
Telecom Finland (Finland)	971	0.8
KTAS (Denmark)	969	0.8
MCL (United Kingdom)	807	0.7
Telecom Portugal (Portugal)	719	0.6
JTAS (Denmark)	702	0.6
TD (Denmark)	493	0.4
Italcable (Italy)	479	0.4
HTC (Finland)	305	0.3
TLP (Portugal)	282	0.2
P&T (Luxembourg)	1.20	0.0

Source: *Data Communications*, October 1991, p. 140, from Logica Plc.

★ 1441 ★

Telecommunications (SIC 4813)

Long Distance Market

Company shares are shown in percent, based on a 1990 market of $52.1 million.

AT&T	65.0%
MCI	14.2
Sprint	9.7
Others	11.1

Source: Investext, Thomson Financial Networks, April 13, 1992, from UBS Phillips & Drew Global Research Group.

★ 1442 ★

Telecommunications Services (SIC 4813)

900-Lines by Application

Distribution of calls made to 900 numbers is shown in percent for 1991 and estimated for 1992.

	1991	1992
Information	35.6%	32.5%
Entertainment	20.1	18.4
Ordering	7.1	8.6
Messaging	11.6	8.4
Fund-raising	5.4	6.4
Sweepstakes	5.9	6.0
Polling/surveying	3.5	4.6
Lead generation	2.9	3.4
Couponing	2.1	3.2
Dealer locators	1.6	1.8
Customer services	0.9	1.1
Other	3.3	5.6

Source: *Advertising Age*, February 17, 1992, p. S-6, from Strategic Telemedia.

★ 1443 ★

Telecommunications Services (SIC 4813)

Biggest Telephone Companies

Shares of telephone service by largest telephone companies are shown in number of access lines as of December 1989. (GTE acquired Contel in 1990 to become the nation's fourth largest telephone company.) Relative shares are shown in percent.

	No. of Lines	% of Group
Bell Atlantic Corp.	17,056,802	13.2%
BellSouth Corp.	16,720,367	13.0
Ameritech Corp.	15,899,000	12.3
NYNEX	14,960,953	11.6
Pacific Telesis Group	14,202,949	11.0
U.S. West Communications	12,306,536	9.5
GTE Corp.	12,300,000	9.5
Southwestern Bell Corp.	11,444,061	8.9
United Communications, Inc.	3,811,980	3.0
Contel Service Corp.	2,591,090	2.0
Southern New England Telephone Co.	1,875,000	1.5
Centel Corp.	1,590,716	1.2
Alltel Corp.	1,123,590	0.9
Puerto Rico Telephone Co.	803,713	0.6
Cincinnati Bell Telephone Co.	781,064	0.6
Rochester Telephone Enterprises, Inc.	610,338	0.5
Century Telephone Enterprises	296,034	0.2
Telephone & Data Systems, Inc.	263,914	0.2
Pacific Telecom, Inc.	252,732	0.2
Lincoln Telephone & Telegraph Co.	185,338	0.1

Source: *U.S. Industrial Outlook 1992*, p. 28-3, from United States Telephone Association.

★ 1444 ★

Telecommunications Services (SIC 4813)

Federal Telecom Services

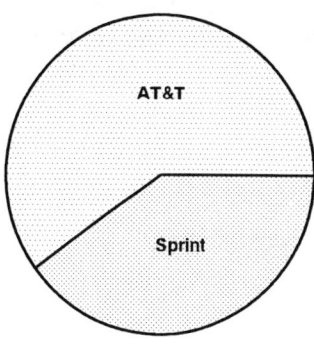

FTS 2000 (Federal Telecommunications Systems 2000) contract revenue shares by long-distance service providers are shown in percent. Providers bill the GSA (General Service Administration) $300 million a year.

AT&T	60.0%
Sprint	40.0

Source: *Government Executive*, July 1991, p. 34, from General Services Administration.

★ 1445 ★

Telecommunications Services (SIC 4813)

Leading Telephone Companies

Revenues of selected companies are shown in millions of dollars; relative market shares are shown in percent.

	Rev. ($ mil.)	% of Group
AT&T	$ 63,089	33.9%
GTE Corp.	19,621	10.5
BellSouth	14,446	7.8
NYNEX	13,229	7.1
Bell Atlantic	12,280	6.6
Ameritech	10,818	5.8
US West	10,577	5.7
Pacific Telesis	9,895	5.3
Southwestern Bell	9,332	5.0
Sprint	8,780	4.7
MCI Communications	8,433	4.5
Alltel	1,748	0.9
Southern New England Tel	1,633	0.9

Continued on next page.

★ 1445 ★ *Continued*

Telecommunications Services (SIC 4813)

Leading Telephone Companies

Revenues of selected companies are shown in millions of dollars; relative market shares are shown in percent.

	Rev. ($ mil.)	% of Group
Centel	$ 1,181	0.6%
Cincinnati Bell	1,087	0.6

Source: *Forbes*, May 25, 1992, p. 69.

★ 1446 ★

Telecommunications Services (SIC 4813)

Long Distance Carriers

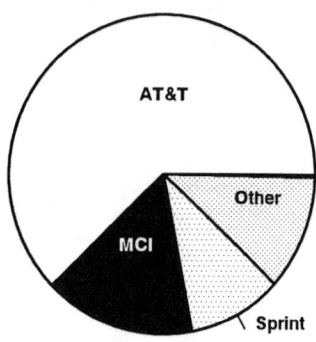

Company shares are shown in percent for 1990 and 1991.

	1990	1991
AT&T	65.0%	63.0%
MCI	14.2	16.0
Sprint	9.7	9.5
Other	11.1	11.5

Source: *USA TODAY*, May 8, 1992, p. 1B, from Federal Communications Commission and LNA/Arbitron Multimedia Service.

★ 1447 ★

Telecommunications Services (SIC 4813)

Long Distance Companies - 1991

Percent shares are based on revenue from long-distance and international calls.

AT&T	66.0%
MCI	15.0

Sprint	9.0%
Alascom	1.0
Allnet	1.0
ATC	1.0
Cable & Wireless	1.0
Metromedia/ITT	1.0
Williams	1.0
Wiltel/Telesphere	1.0

Source: *The Economist*, June 6, 1992, p. 74, from North American Telecommunications Assn., FCC, and company reports.

★ 1448 ★

Telecommunications Services (SIC 4813)

Long Distance Shares

Shares of the $65.0 billion industry are shown in percent.

AT&T	62.0%
MCI	15.0
Sprint	9.0
Other	14.0

Source: *Advertising Age*, April 6, 1992, p. 3, from industry sources.

★ 1449 ★

Telecommunications Services (SIC 4813)

Long Distance Telecom Service

Revenues, by segment, are shown in billions of dollars; relative market shares are shown in percent.

	Rev. ($ bil.)	% of Group
Domestic voice: outbound	$ 27.0	46.6%
International	12.0	20.7
Data	8.0	13.8
Domestic voice: inbound	7.0	12.1
Private line	4.0	6.9

Source: Investext, Thomson Financial Networks, June 24, 1992, from S. G. Warburg & Co., Inc.

★ 1450 ★
Telecommunications Services (SIC 4813)

Long-Distance Phone Companies

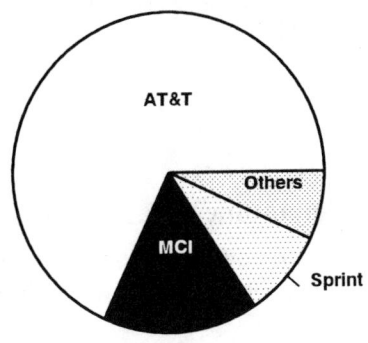

Company shares of long-distance market are shown in percent.

AT&T	68.0%
MCI	16.0
Sprint	9.0
Others	7.0

Source: *Advertising Age*, July 13, 1992, p. 4.

★ 1451 ★
Telecommunications Services (SIC 4813)

Telecom Network Companies - Italy

Estimated shares of the 1991 long distance and local telecommunications network markets are shown in percent. Parent companies are shown in parentheses.

	Long Distance	Local
Sirti (Stet)	59.0%	11.1%
Sielte (Ericsson)	19.0	10.0
Siette (Alcatel)	14.0	13.0
AET (Stet)	8.0	6.0
Other	0.0	60.0

Source: Investext, Thomson Financial Networks, January 14, 1992, from UBS Phillips & Drew Global Research Group.

★ 1452 ★
Telecommunications Services (SIC 4813)

Telecom Service Customers

Revenues, by customer type, are shown in billions of dollars; relative shares are shown in percent.

	Rev. ($ bil.)	% of Group
Residential/small business . . .	$ 29.0	50.0%
Large	15.0	25.9
National	9.0	15.5
General	5.0	8.6

Source: Investext, Thomson Financial Networks, June 24, 1992, from S. G. Warburg & Co., Inc.

★ 1453 ★
Telecommunications Services (SIC 4813)

Toll-Free Business Services

Company shares of toll-free business market are shown in percent.

AT&T	68.0%
MCI	13.0
Sprint	7.0
Others	12.0

Source: *The Wall Street Journal*, May 18, 1992, p. B18, from Sanford C. Bernstein & Co.

★ 1454 ★
Data Communications (SIC 4822)

Cable Information Processors

Company shares of the estimated $200 million market are shown in percent, based on the number of subscriber accounts.

Cable Data	47.0%
Cable Services Group	24.2
Other	28.9

Source: Investext, Thomson Financial Networks, June 30, 1992, from The First Boston Corporation.

★1455★

Data Communications (SIC 4822)

Data Communications Services - U.S.

Revenues of the data communications services market in the U.S., by type of service, are shown, by type of product, in millions of dollars for the years 1991 (estimated) and 1992 (projected). Percent shares are based on an industry total of $29,368 million in 1991 and $32,284 million in 1992.

	1991	1992
Telephone carriers		
Packet switching	$ 77.1	$ 73.0
Frame relay	0.0	2.6
SMDS	0.0	0.3
Alternative (incl. satellite, local fiber, VSAT)	22.9	24.1

Source: *Data Communications*, January 1992, p. 62.

★1456★

Data Communications (SIC 4822)

Information by Telephone

Shares of households obtaining information via telephone, by type of telephone, are shown in percent.

Touch tone	69.0%
Rotary dial	31.0

Source: *USA TODAY*, June 17, 1992, p. 1B, from The Yankee Group, *USA TODAY* research.

★1457★

Data Communications (SIC 4822)

Information Services Market

Market segmentation of services provided via telephone is shown in percent, based on totals of $19.5 billion in 1990 and $31.6 billion projected for 1995.

	1990	1995
Database services	47.0%	48.0%
Transaction processing	13.9	15.1
Home alarm monitoring	12.4	13.8
900 & 976 numbers	5.9	5.8
Telephone answering services	5.4	4.9
Public data networks	4.0	3.7
Customer on-line services	7.9	2.8
Voice messaging	1.0	2.8

	1990	1995
Electronic mail	2.0%	1.8%
Electronic data interchange	0.5	1.2

Source: *The New York Times*, June 7, 1992, p. F10, from LINK Resources, Inc.

★1458★

Data Communications (SIC 4822)

Network Communications Shares

Companies are ranked by estimated revenues, in millions of dollars for 1992; relative market shares are shown in percent.

	Rev. ($ mil.)	% of Group
SynOptics Comm.	$ 278.4	45.3%
Cabletron Systems	269.0	43.7
Chipcom	67.6	11.0

Source: Investext, Thomson Financial Networks, February 18, 1992, from Kidder, Peabody & Company, Incorporated.

★1459★

Message Communications (SIC 4822)

Electronic Mail Services Providers

Shares by company are shown in percent, based on a total of 27.8 million messages monthly in 1990.

AT&T Easylink	31.0%
Prodigy	13.9
SprintMail	10.5
GE Information Services	10.1
BT Dialcom	8.4
MCI Mail	7.0
AT&T Mail	7.0
CompuServe	3.5
Other	8.7

Source: *Data Communications*, August 1991, p. 23, from Electronic Mail & Micro Systems.

★1460★

Message Communications (SIC 4822)

Telephone Answering Service Providers

Top 25 telephone answering service (TAS) providers are shown with number of lines or positions. Relative shares are shown in percent.

	No. of Lines	% of Group
Lo-Ad Communications	27,000	19.1%
HSN 800/900 Corp.	20,000	14.2
American Communications & Engineering	14,000	9.9
Call Interactive	10,000	7.1
Audio Communications Inc. . . .	5,400	3.8
JC Penney Telemarketing Inc. . .	5,000	3.5
Pioneer TeleTechnologies Inc. . .	4,890	3.5
Network Telephone Services Inc.	4,578	3.2
National Data Corp.	4,100	2.9
AT&T American TransTech . . .	4,000	2.8
Sprint TeleMedia	3,700	2.6
The Gateway Group	3,500	2.5
Ameritech Audiotex Services Inc.	3,500	2.5
MCI/Telecom USA Direct . . .	3,425	2.4
Phoneworks	3,000	2.1
Source Communications	3,000	2.1
AT&T-InfoWorx	3,000	2.1
DialAmerica Marketing Inc. . . .	2,900	2.1
West Telemarketing Corp. . . .	2,755	1.9
Interactive Telemedia Inc. . . .	2,688	1.9
Scherers Communications . . .	2,400	1.7
Idelman Telemarketing	2,214	1.6
MATRIXX Message Centers . .	2,150	1.5
MATRIXX Marketing Inc. . . .	2,094	1.5
Bellatrix Communications	2,000	1.4

Source: *Telephony*, June 15, 1992, p. 108, from *Strategic Telemedia 1991*.

★1461★

Message Communications (SIC 4822)

Voice Mail Companies

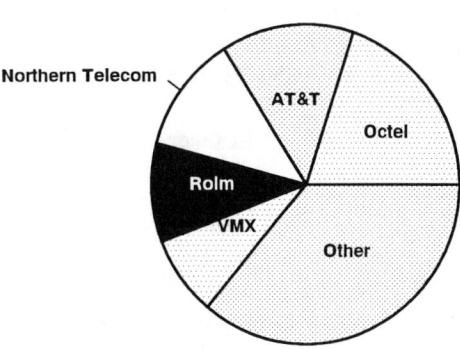

Company shares are shown in percent, based on an annual voice-mail market of $1.0 billion.

Octel	20.0%
AT&T	14.0
Northern Telecom	12.0
Rolm	10.0
VMX	8.0
Other	36.0

Source: *USA TODAY*, March 2, 1992, p. 1B, from Vanguard Communications Corp.

★1462★

Radio Broadcasting (SIC 4832)

15 Leading Radio Networks

Data reflect number of listeners in thousands and percent share of the group. Results are based on a survey of listeners from November 1990 through October 1991.

	Listeners (000)	% of Group
Prime (ABC)	5,389	17.1%
Mutual (Westwood One) . . .	3,242	10.3
Platinum (ABC)	2,849	9.0
Spectrum (CBS)	2,408	7.6
Genesis (ABC)	2,352	7.4
Super (UniStar)	2,239	7.1
Ultima (UniStar)	2,045	6.5
CBS (CBS)	1,753	5.5
WONE (Westwood One) . . .	1,698	5.4
NBC (Westwood One)	1,614	5.1
Source (Westwood One) . . .	1,484	4.7
Power (UniStar)	1,388	4.4

Continued on next page.

★ 1462 ★ *Continued*
Radio Broadcasting (SIC 4832)

15 Leading Radio Networks

Data reflect number of listeners in thousands and percent share of the group. Results are based on a survey of listeners from November 1990 through October 1991.

	Listeners (000)	% of Group
Excel (ABC)	1,107	3.5%
Galaxy (ABC)	1,028	3.3
American Urban (AUR) . . .	998	3.2

Source: *Advertising Age*, March 2, 1992, p. 20, from Statistical Research Inc. and *Radio Audience Measurement*.

★ 1463 ★
Radio Broadcasting (SIC 4832)

FM and AM Radio

Market penetration of radio listening is shown in percent, based on a survey of 2,000 adults.

	1986	1991
FM	31.0%	50.0%
AM	36.0	19.0

Source: *USA TODAY*, June 10, 1992, p. 1D, from The Roper Organization.

★ 1464 ★
Radio Broadcasting (SIC 4832)

Radio Broadcasters

Revenues of top radio broadcasters in 1991 totaled $1.3616 billion. Relative shares are shown in percent.

	Rev. ($ mil.)	% of Group
Capital Cities/ABC	$ 317.0	23.3%
CBS Inc.	245.6	18.0
Westinghouse Electric Corp. . .	171.0	12.6
Westwood One	144.4	10.6
Cox Enterprises	94.0	6.9
Viacom International	79.0	5.8
Great American Communications	75.5	5.5
Gannett Co.	65.3	4.8
Tribune Co.	49.0	3.6
Hearst Corp.	22.2	1.6
Heritage Media Corp.	15.9	1.2

	Rev. ($ mil.)	% of Group
Journal Communications . . .	$ 15.1	1.1%
Multimedia Inc.	13.5	1.0
Pulitzer Publishing Co.	13.0	1.0
E.W. Scripps	12.7	0.9
Ackerley Communications . .	11.5	0.8
New York Times Co.	6.5	0.5
Gaylord Entertainment Co. . . .	5.0	0.4
Dispatch Printing Co.	2.3	0.2
Landmark Communications . .	2.0	0.1
Gillett Holdings	0.6	0.0
Crain Communications	0.5	0.0

Source: *Advertising Age*, August 10, 1992, p. S-10, from *Advertising Age* estimates.

★ 1465 ★
Radio Broadcasting (SIC 4832)

Radio Formats

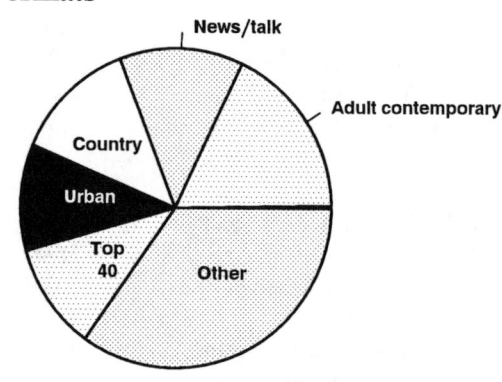

Audience share of radio listening in the U.S. is shown in percent.

Adult contemporary	18.2%
News/talk	13.4
Country	12.7
Urban	10.7
Top 40	10.5
Other	34.5

Source: *USA TODAY*, September 30, 1992, p. 5D, from Arbitron.

★ 1466 ★

Radio Broadcasting (SIC 4832)

Radio Program Formats

The most popular radio program formats are ranked according to size of listening audience, shown in percent.

Adult contemporary	18.1%
News/talk	13.8
Country	12.2
Top 40	10.8
Album rock	9.9
Other	35.2

Source: *USA TODAY*, March 11, 1992, p. 1D, from The Arbitron Company and Billboard Magazine.

★ 1467 ★

Television (SIC 4833)

Children's Television Programs

Programs are shown with hours broadcast per week in Fall 1991 and Fall 1992. Shares are based on 1992 total of 43.5 hours.

	'91	'92	'92 %
Fox	10.5	19.0	43.7%
Disney	10.0	12.5	28.7
ABC	5.0	5.0	11.5
CBS	5.0	5.0	11.5
NBC	4.5	2.0	4.6

Source: *Broadcasting*, May 2, 1992, p. 40.

★ 1468 ★

Television Broadcasting (SIC 4833)

Broadcasting ECI Revenues

1991 shares of Electronic Communications Index revenues which companies derive from broadcasting activities are shown in millions of dollars. Company shares are shown in percent.

	Rev. ($ mil.)	Share
Capital Cities/ABC	$ 4,329.7	26.4%
General Electric	3,121.0	19.0
CBS	3,035.0	18.5
News Corp.	1,300.0	7.9
Westinghouse	707.0	4.3
Tribune	617.5	3.8
Multimedia	395.4	2.4
Gannett Co.	357.4	2.2

	Rev. ($ mil.)	Share
Scripps Howard	$ 348.5	2.1%
Washington Post	323.0	2.0
BHC Communications	262.6	1.6
Great American Commun.	211.5	1.3
SCI Television	208.8	1.3
A.H. Belo	181.8	1.1
Pinelands Inc.	166.2	1.0
Renaissance Commun.	88.9	0.5
Liberty Corp.	71.4	0.4
Lee Enterprises	69.7	0.4
Park Communications	67.0	0.4
Ackerley Communications	66.6	0.4
American Family	64.4	0.4
Clear Channel	64.3	0.4
Jacor Communications	64.2	0.4
Heritage Media	51.2	0.3
The New York Times Co.	47.9	0.3
Outlet Communications	39.4	0.2
Granite Broadcasting	33.4	0.2
Gillett Holdings	30.9	0.2
Northstar Televison	30.3	0.2
Fairmont Communications	29.2	0.2

Source: *Broadcasting*, June 22, 1992, p. 46, from company estimates, securities analysts, and industry associations.

★ 1469 ★

Television Broadcasting (SIC 4833)

Closed-Caption Television Broadcasting

Distribution by category of closed-caption television programming is shown in percent.

Major commercial network	68.0%
HBO and other pay cable	36.0
Local news	20.0
Syndicated television	16.0
Basic cable	1.2

Source: *The Christian Science Monitor*, December 23, 1991, p. 19.

★ 1470 ★

Television Broadcasting (SIC 4833)

Major Television Networks

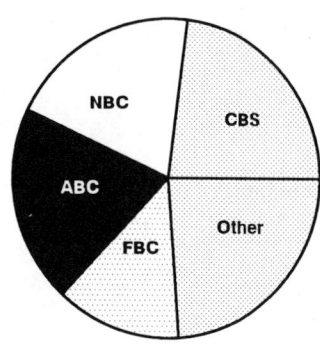

Network shares for the 1991/92 television season are based on prime time viewing and shown in percent.

CBS	22.6%
NBC	20.2
ABC	19.9
FBC	13.0
Other	24.3

Source: Investext, Thomson Financial Networks, April 23, 1992, from Oppenheimer & Co., Inc.

★ 1471 ★

Television Broadcasting (SIC 4833)

Network TV Broadcasters

Revenues of leading television broadcasting companies in 1991 totaled $14.0657 billion. Relative shares are shown in percent.

	($ mil.)	% of Group
Capital Cities/ABC	$ 3,395.0	24.1%
General Electric Co.	3,086.0	21.9
CBS Inc.	2,789.4	19.8
News Corp.	964.0	6.9
Westinghouse Electric Corp. . .	502.0	3.6
Tribune Co.	446.0	3.2
Cox Enterprises	315.0	2.2
Gannett Co.	294.8	2.1
Gillett Holdings	275.0	2.0
Chris-Craft Industries	262.6	1.9
Hearst Corp.	243.0	1.7
E.W. Scripps	232.7	1.7
Paramount Communications . .	184.6	1.3
A.H. Belo Corp.	181.9	1.3

	($ mil.)	% of Group
Pinelands	$ 166.2	1.2%
Univision Holdings	164.0	1.2
Washington Post Co.	163.5	1.2
Multimedia Inc.	137.1	1.0
Gaylord Entertainment Co. . . .	133.4	0.9
McCaw Cellular Communications	129.5	0.9

Source: *Advertising Age*, August 10, 1992, p. S-8, from *Advertising Age* estimates.

★ 1472 ★

Television Broadcasting (SIC 4833)

Television Networks Ratings

Ratings are shown by network. Market shares are shown in percent. Figures reflect the prime-time season through March 15, 1992.

	Rating	Share
CBS	14.0	23.0%
NBC	12.5	20.0
ABC	12.1	20.0

Source: Investext, Thomson Financial Networks, March 30, 1992, from Oppenheimer & Co., Inc.

★ 1473 ★

Television Broadcasting (SIC 4833)

TV Broadcasters - U.K.

Shares of net advertising revenue are shown in percent.

Thames	45.22%
Central	14.42
LWT	11.69
TVS	11.52
Granada	10.82
Yorkshire	8.62
Anglia	6.72
HTV	6.25
STV	5.52
Tyne Tees	3.33
TSW	2.51

Continued on next page.

★ 1473 ★ *Continued*

Television Broadcasting (SIC 4833)

TV Broadcasters - U.K.

Shares of net advertising revenue are shown in percent.

Ulster	1.47%
Grampian	1.12
Border	0.61
Channel	0.16

Source: Investext, Thomson Financial Networks, January 2, 1992, from Rowan, Dartington, & Co. Securities Ltd.

★ 1474 ★

Cable Broadcasting (SIC 4841)

Baby Bell Cable Franchises - U.K.

Data show number of British cable TV franchises in which North American phone companies hold a stake. Data are current as of July 1992.

US West	16
Bell Canada	16
NYNEX	11
Southwestern Bell	8
Pacific Telesis	8

Source: *The Economist*, July 25, 1992, p. 69, from company reports and PA Consulting.

★ 1475 ★

Cable Broadcasting (SIC 4841)

Cable Broadcasting

Revenues of the biggest cable TV broadcasting companies totaled $16.1377 billion in 1991. Relative shares are shown in percent.

	($ mil.)	% of Group
Time Warner	$ 3,301.0	20.5%
Tele-Communications Inc.	3,206.0	19.9
Viacom International	1,300.2	8.1
Turner Broadcasting System	1,190.7	7.4
Continental Cablevision	1,127.0	7.0
Comcast Corp.	647.1	4.0
SCI Holdings	606.7	3.8
Cablevision Systems Corp.	603.3	3.7
Cox Enterprises	596.0	3.7
Capital Cities/ABC	489.4	3.0
Advance Publications	440.0	2.7
Times Mirror Co.	403.8	2.5

	($ mil.)	% of Group
Cablevision Industries Corp.	$ 334.7	2.1%
USA Network	315.0	2.0
Sammons Communications	284.6	1.8
Paragon Communications	284.0	1.8
Adelphia Communications Corp.	276.7	1.7
Century Communications Corp.	257.3	1.6
TeleCable Corp.	249.0	1.5
E.W. Scripps	225.2	1.4

Source: *Advertising Age*, August 10, 1992, p. S-8.

★ 1476 ★

Cable Broadcasting (SIC 4841)

Cable ECI Revenues

1991 shares of Electronic Communications Index revenues which companies derive from cable broadcasting are shown in millions of dollars. Company shares are shown percent.

	Revenue	Share
Time Warner	$ 4,731.0	36.5%
TCI	3,206.0	24.8
Continental	1,039.2	8.0
Comcast	647.1	5.0
SCI Holdings	606.7	4.7
Cablevision Systems	603.3	4.7
Times Mirror	498.0	3.8
Cablevision Industries	334.6	2.6
Century	257.0	2.0
Adelphia	250.2	1.9
Media General	159.6	1.2
TKR Cable	130.0	1.0
TCA Cable	127.0	1.0
ML Media	99.2	0.8
Jones Intercable	98.9	0.8
C-TEC	76.1	0.6
Falcon	45.9	0.4
ML Opportunity	42.0	0.3

Source: *Broadcasting*, June 22, 1992, p. 47, from company estimates, securities analysts, and industry associations.

★ 1477 ★
Cable Broadcasting (SIC 4841)

Cable Networks

Number of subscribers to basic cable services is shown in millions for each network; relative market shares are shown in percent. Context of the original article was a report on the falling stock prices of Black Entertainment Television (BET). Therefore, an artificial gap occurs between The Nashville Network and BET.

	Subscr. (mil.)	% of Group
ESPN	59.2	10.0%
CNN	58.9	9.9
USA Network	58.0	9.8
TBS Super Station	57.2	9.7
MTV	56.6	9.6
The Discovery Channel	56.0	9.5
Nickelodeon	55.4	9.4
TNT	54.2	9.1
C-Span	54.0	9.1
The Nashville Network . . .	53.9	9.1
Black Entertainment Television	29.0	4.9

Source: *The New York Times*, December 22, 1991, p. F13, from *Bloomberg Business News* and Salomon Brothers.

★ 1478 ★
Cable Broadcasting (SIC 4841)

Cable Television Programs for Children

Programs are shown with hours broadcast weekly in Fall 1991 and Fall 1992. Shares are based on 1992 total of 369.5 hours weekly.

	'91	'92	'92%
Cartoon Network	-	168.0	45.5%
Nickelodeon	126.0	126.0	34.1
TNT	32.0	32.0	8.7
USA Network	26.0	26.0	7.0
WTBS	17.5	17.5	4.7

Source: *Broadcasting*, May 2, 1992, p. 40.

★ 1479 ★
Cable Broadcasting (SIC 4841)

Cable TV Penetration

TV audience penetration by leading basic-cable networks (ESPN, CNN) and premium subscription networks (HBO, Showtime/The Movie Channel) is shown in millions of viewers.

ESPN	59.3
CNN	58.9
HBO	17.3
Showtime/The Movie Channel	10.0

Source: *USA TODAY*, August 24, 1992, p. 1D, from National Cable TV Association and premium networks.

★ 1480 ★
Cable Broadcasting (SIC 4841)

Full Day Cable TV Ratings

Full day cable TV ratings by network are shown in number of viewing households (2Q-1991: 5.437 million; 2Q-1992: 5.734 million). 1992 relative shares are shown in percent.

	2Q '91	2Q '92	% '92
WTBS	708,000	715,000	12.5%
USA	637,000	670,000	11.7
Nickelodeon	573,000	591,000	10.3
TNT	496,000	544,000	9.5
ESPN	450,000	480,000	8.4
Nick at Nite	347,000	402,000	7.0
CNN	322,000	345,000	6.0
Family	319,000	336,000	5.9
Lifetime	321,000	308,000	5.4
Nashville	287,000	294,000	5.1
Discovery	268,000	289,000	5.0
MTV	277,000	264,000	4.6
A&E	215,000	228,000	4.0
Headline News	132,000	171,000	3.0
VH-1	85,000	97,000	1.7

Source: *Broadcasting*, July 13, 1992, p. 24, from network estimates and Nielsen Media Research.

Cable Broadcasting (SIC 4841)

Leading Cable TV Providers

Companies are shown with number of subscribers.
Percent shares are based on a total of 55 million
cable subscribers in the U.S.

	Subscr. (mil.)	Share
Tele-Communications Inc. . . .	11.3	20.5%
Time Warner Inc.	6.7	12.2
Comcast Corporation	2.8	5.1
Jones Intercable	1.7	3.1
Cablevision Systems Corp. . . .	1.6	2.9
Others	30.9	56.2

Source: *Forbes*, April 13, 1992, p. 84, from Moran & Associates.

★ 1482 ★

Cable Broadcasting (SIC 4841)

Multiple System Operators

Top 25 operators are ranked by number of basic
subscribers, shown with relative market shares in
percent.

	No. of Subscr.	% of Group
Tele-Communications Inc. . .	12,333,682	29.2%
American Television & Communications Corp. . .	4,700,000	11.1
Continental Cablevision . . .	2,800,000	6.6
Warner Cable Communications	1,677,260	4.0
Comcast	1,665,000	3.9
Cox Cable Communications .	1,661,277	3.9
Cablevision Systems . . .	1,635,633	3.9
Storer Cable Communications	1,616,000	3.8
Jones Intercable/Spacelink . .	1,506,132	3.6
Newhouse Broadcasting . .	1,267,200	3.0
Adelphia Communications . .	1,146,300	2.7
Cablevision Industries	1,131,677	2.7
Times Mirror Cable TV . . .	1,126,220	2.7
Viacom Cable	1,083,600	2.6
Sammons Communications .	919,411	2.2
Century Communications . .	884,000	2.1
Falcon Cable TV	873,572	2.1
Paragon Communications . .	838,341	2.0
TeleCable	640,600	1.5
Scripps-Howard	629,500	1.5

	No. of Subscr.	% of Group
KBLCOM	558,850	1.3%
Cencom Cable	552,200	1.3
Tele-Media	530,571	1.3
Lenfast Group	510,000	1.2
MultiVision Cable TV		

Source: *Adweek*, April 6, 1992, p. 12, from Cabletelevision Advertising Bureau.

★ 1483 ★

Cable Broadcasting (SIC 4841)

Prime Time Cable TV Ratings

Data show number of viewing households (2Q-1991:
8.318 million; 2Q-1992: 8.897 million). 1992 relative
network shares are shown in percent. Ratings are
based on coverage area of each network; prime times
vary by network.

	2Q '91	2Q '92	% '92
USA	1,035,000	1,236,000	13.9%
WTBS	1,047,000	1,165,000	13.1
TNT	1,042,000	1,127,000	12.7
ESPN	990,000	940,000	10.6
Lifetime	658,000	627,000	7.0
Nashville	630,000	595,000	6.7
CNN	498,000	584,000	6.6
Nick at Nite	551,000	574,000	6.5
Discovery	502,000	516,000	5.8
Family	404,000	483,000	5.4
A&E	359,000	392,000	4.4
MTV	332,000	341,000	3.8
Headline News . . .	142,000	164,000	1.8
VH-1	128,000	153,000	1.7

Source: *Broadcasting*, July 13, 1992, p. 24, from network estimates and Nielsen Media Research.

★ 1484 ★

Cable Broadcasting (SIC 4841)

Successful Basic-Cable Networks

Basic-cable networks are ranked by number of subscribers; relative market shares are shown in percent.

	Subscr. (mil.)	% of Group
Cable News Network	58.9	10.1%
TBS	57.7	9.9
The Discovery Channel	56.0	9.6
Nickelodeon	55.5	9.5
MTV	54.9	9.4
TNT	54.9	9.4
Headline News	47.3	8.1
VH-1	43.2	7.4
QVC	42.1	7.2
Black Entertainment Television	31.9	5.5
Comedy Central	22.0	3.8
E! Entertainment Television . .	21.0	3.6
Sports Channel America	18.0	3.1
The Learning Channel	15.6	2.7
Court TV	5.8	1.0

Source: *Adweek*, April 6, 1992, p. 8, from National Cable Television Assn. and Television Critics Assn.

SIC 49 - Electric, Gas, and Sanitary Services

★1485★

Energy (SIC 4900)

Energy Consumption by Source - U.S.

Consumption of energy in the U.S., by energy source, is shown in millions of barrels per day (petroleum products), trillions of cubic feet (natural gas), millions of short tons (coal), and quadrillions of Btus (nuclear power) for 1990, 1991, and 1992. Btus are British thermal units.

	'90	'91	'92
Petroleum products	16.99	16.58	16.92
Natural gas	18.83	18.78	19.36
Coal	894.6	896.9	928.3
Nuclear power	6.186	6.250	6.230

Source: *U.S. Industrial Outlook 1992*, p. 3, from U.S. Department of Energy, Energy Information Administration.

★1486★

Energy (SIC 4900)

Energy Production by Source - U.S.

Production of energy by source in the U.S. is shown in millions of barrels per day (crude oil, plant liquids), trillions of cubic feet (natural gas), millions of short tons (coal), and billions of kilowatthours (natural hydroelectric power, nuclear electric power, other) for 1990, 1991, and 1992. The figures for 1991 are estimated; those for 1992 are forecast. The figures for crude include lease condensate. Natural gas is defined in this table as dry natural gas.

	'90	'91	'92
Crude oil	7.355	7.367	7.088
Natural gas	17.61	17.43	17.69
Plant liquids	1.559	1.627	1.617
Coal	1,029.0	1,001.9	1,026.9
Natural hydroelectric power	279.8	291.0	299.3
Nuclear electric power	576.9	582.7	580.9
Other	10.7	11.6	12.9

Source: *U.S. Industrial Outlook 1992*, p. 3, from U.S. Department of Energy, Energy Information Administration.

★1487★

Electric Services (SIC 4911)

Electric Companies - Hong Kong

Company shares of total electricity consumption in Hong Kong are shown in percent.

China Light	75.0%
HK Electric	25.0

Source: Investext, Thomson Financial Networks, January 2, 1992, from Barclays de Zoete Wedd Securities.

★ 1488 ★
Electric Services (SIC 4911)

Electric Power Generation by Source

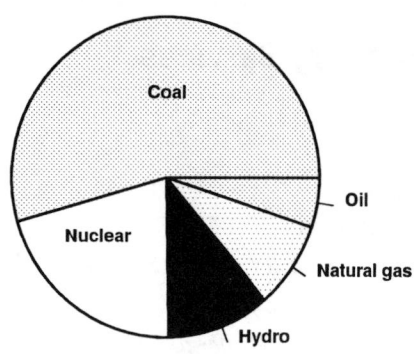

Energy sources are shown as a percent of electric power generation for 1990 and 1991.

Coal	49.3%	54.5%
Nuclear	10.7	20.5
Hydro	10.7	11.0
Natural gas	14.7	9.0
Oil	14.7	4.7

Source: *JPT*, January 1992, p. 52, from *World Energy Update*.

★ 1489 ★
Electric Services (SIC 4911)

Electric Power Sources

1991 shares of net electricity generation by fuel source are shown in percent.

Coal	54.9%
Nuclear	21.7
Hydro	9.7
Natural gas	9.4
Oil	3.9

Source: *The Wall Street Journal*, August 20, 1992, p. A4, from Arthur Andersen & Co.

★ 1490 ★
Electric Services (SIC 4911)

Niagara Hydroelectric Plants

Niagara hydroelectric plants are shown with generating capacity in megawatts. Percent shares are based on a total generating capacity of 4,470 megawatts.

	(MW)	Share
Robert Moses (USA)	1950+	43.6%
Sir Adam Beck No.2 (Canada)	1312	29.4
Sir Adam Beck No.1 (Canada)	488	10.9
Lewiston PGS (USA)	240	5.4
DeCew No.2 (Canada)	144	3.2
Sir Adam Beck PGS (Canada)	122	2.7
Ontario Power (Canada)	104	2.3
Rankine (CNP) (Canada)	75	1.7
DeCew No.1 (Canada)	35	0.8

Source: *IEE Review*, October 1991, p. 342.

★ 1491 ★
Electric Services (SIC 4911)

Power Industry Worldwide

Shares of the global power industry, which comprises generation, transmission, and distribution, are shown in percent, based on a total turnover of $140.0 billion.

ABB	10.0%
Mitsubishi	5.0
Hitachi	5.0
Siemens	5.0
General Electric	5.0
GEC Alsthom	4.0
Toshiba	3.0
Westinghouse	2.0
Other	61.0

Source: Investext, Thomson Financial Networks, May 1, 1992, from Svenska International PLC.

★ 1492 ★

Electricity (SIC 4911)

Electric Company Shares of SCADA/EMS Market

Company shares of Scada/EMS (supervisory control and data acquisition systems and energy management systems) market are shown in percent based on a total of $157 million.

Harris Corp.	36,4%
Landis & Gyr Inc.	17.5
Empros System International	11,9
ESCA Corp.	7.6
Advanced Control Systems	4.5
Stagg Systems	4.4
CAE Electronics	4.1
Others	13.6

Source: *Electrical World*, December 1991, p. 62, from CSR Inc.

★ 1493 ★

Gas Distribution (SIC 4922)

Natural Gas Distributors - Spain

Shares of sales to the residential-commercial sector are shown in percent.

Gas Natural	96.0%
Other	4.0

Source: Investext, Thomson Financial Networks, February 26, 1992, from Schroder Securities UK Ltd.

★ 1494 ★

Utilities (SIC 4939)

Utilities Industry in Spain

Market shares, by company, are shown in percent for 1991.

Sevillana	21.2%
Fenosa	14.0
Iberdrola	12.7
Fecsa	8.2
Endesa Group (except Sevillana & Fecsa)	3.0
Other	40.9

Source: Investext, Thomson Financial Networks, March 13, 1992, from Schroder Securities U.K. Ltd.

SIC 50 - Wholesale Trade - Durable Goods

★ 1495 ★

Wholesale - Industrial Machinery (SIC 5084)

Top Distributors of Industrial Machinery and Equipment

Companies are ranked by 1991 sales, shown in millions of dollars. Percent shares are based on group total.

	Sales ($ mil.)	% of Group
W.W. Grainger, Inc	$ 2,077.0	22.1%
Bearings, Inc.	814.0	8.6
Motion Industries, Inc.	655.0	7.0
Sun Distributors L.P.	596.0	6.3
McJunkin Corp.	515.0	5.5
Guilevin International, Inc. . . .	479.0	5.1
Kaman Industrial Technologies Corp.	400.0	4.2
Berry Bearing Co., Inc.	350.0	3.7
Acklands Limited	343.5	3.6
Cameron & Barkley Co.	318.0	3.4
Fairmont Supply Co.	260.0	2.8
Briggs-Weaver, Inc.	222.0	2.4
Bowman Distribution/ Barnes Group, Inc.	212.4	2.3
Invetech Co.	210.0	2.2
The Bovaird Supply Co.	200.0	2.1
Lawson Products, Inc.	181.7	1.9
The Gage Co.	150.0	1.6

	Sales ($ mil.)	% of Group
Safety Supply America	$ 150.0	1.6%
Vallen Corp.	150.0	1.6
Lucas Fluid Power North America	135.0	1.4
DoAll Co.	129.0	1.4
MSC Industrial Supply Co./ Sid Tool Co.	118.9	1.3
Production Tool Supply	110.0	1.2
Noland Company	100.0	1.1
IBT, Inc.	96.0	1.0
Sepco Industries	93.0	1.0
Bearing Headquarters Co. . . .	92.0	1.0
Hub, Inc.	90.0	1.0
Bearing Distributors, Inc. . . .	86.0	0.9
J.N. Fauver Co.	85.0	0.9

Source: *Industrial Distribution*, June 15, 1992, p. 38.

SIC 51 - Wholesale Trade - Nondurable Goods

★1496★

Warehouse Clubs (SIC 5100)

1991 Wholesale Club Sales

Sales, by company, are shown in millions of dollars.

Sam's Club	$ 9,280
The Price Company	6,598
Costco Wholesale Club	4,725
PACE Membership Warehouse	3,900
BJ's Wholesale Club	1,547
The Warehouse Club	287
Wholesale Depot	53

Source: *Dealerscope Merchandising*, November 1991, p. 33.

★1497★

Warehouse Clubs (SIC 5100)

Warehouse Club Market - 1991

Company shares are based on total market of $28 billion in sales in 1991.

Sam's	36.0%
Price	24.0
Costco	19.0
Pace	15.0
Other	6.0

Source: *Chain Store Age Executive*, May 1992, p. 50, from McKinsey & Co.

★1498★

Warehouse Clubs (SIC 5100)

Warehouse Clubs

Warehouse club shares are based on sales totals of $4,197 million in 1985, $21,680 million in 1990 and $27,900 million in 1991.

	'85	'90	'91
Sam's	18.5%	29.9%	33.3%
Price Club	50.2	25.8	25.4

	'85	'90	'91
Costco	12.7%	19.7%	20.0%
Pace	6.6	10.4	14.7
BJ's	3.1	5.5	5.7
Price Savers	2.8	4.0	0.0
Wholesale Club	1.8	3.5	0.0
Super Savers	1.9	0.0	0.0
Warehouse Club	2.5	1.2	0.8

Source: *Grocery Marketing*, October 24, 1991, p. 6, from Tiger Management.

★1499★

Warehouse Clubs (SIC 5100)

Warehouse Clubs

Shares are shown in percent, based on a total warehouse sales of $28.869 billion in 1991.

Sam's	32.7%
Price Co.	25.9
Costco	23.6
Pace	12.9
BJ's	5.0

Source: Investext, Thomson Financial Networks, April 21, 1992, from Paine Webber Inc.

★1500★

Warehouse Clubs (SIC 5100)

Wholesale Club Industry

The eight wholesale club contenders' shares are based on an estimated $31.897 billion volume in 1992.

Sam's Club	36.1%
The Price Company	24.8
Costco Wholesale Club	19.1
PACE Membership Warehouse	13.5
BJ's Wholesale Club	5.2
The Warehouse Club	0.8

Continued on next page.

★ 1500 ★ *Continued*

Warehouse Clubs (SIC 5100)

Wholesale Club Industry

The eight wholesale club contenders' shares are based on an estimated $31.897 billion volume in 1992.

Wholesale Depot	0.4%
SourceClub	0.2

Source: *DM*, June 1992, p. 66.

★ 1501 ★

Wholesale - Drugs (SIC 5122)

Drug Distribution Companies

Company sales are shown in millions of dollars for 1991. Percent shares are based on a group total of $30,665 million.

	Sales ($ mil.)	% of Group
McKesson	$ 9,711	31.7%
Walgreen	6,901	22.5
Bergen Brunswig	4,961	16.2
Rite Aid	3,670	12.0
Longs Drug Stores	2,366	7.7
Medco Containment Services	1,551	5.1
Cardinal Distribution	1,506	4.9

Source: *The 1992 Business Week 1000*, p. 180.

★ 1502 ★

Wholesale - Food (SIC 5140)

Food Distribution Companies

Sales figures are shown in millions of dollars for 1991. Percent shares are based on a group total of $37,862 million.

	Sales ($ mil.)	% of Group
Fleming	$ 12,902	34.1%
Super Value Stores	10,744	28.4
Wetterau	8,469	22.4
Sysco	5,747	15.2

Source: *The 1992 Business Week 1000*, p. 174.

★ 1503 ★

Wholesale - Food (SIC 5140)

Foodservice Distribution Industry

Company shares of the foodservice distribution market are shown in percent, based on 1991 sales total of $110,000 million.

Sysco Corp.	7.6%
Kraft Foodservice	3.0
Rykoff-Sexton, Inc.	1.4
PYA/Monarch, Inc.	1.2
JP Foodservice, Inc.	1.0
White Swan, Inc.	0.7
Food Services of America	0.7
Gordon Food Service	0.7
Unifax, Inc.	0.7
Consolidated Foodservice Companies	0.4
Shamrock Foods Co.	0.4
Clark Foodservice	0.3
Woodhaven Foods	0.3
Reinhart Institutional Food Inc.	0.2
Maines Paper & Food	0.2
Others	81.2

Source: Investext, Thomson Financial Networks, April 10, 1992, from Brown Brothers Harriman & Co.

★ 1504 ★

Wholesale - Groceries (SIC 5141)

Wholesale Distribution of Foodservice Products

Shares by type of wholesaler are shown in percent..

Foodservice distributors	81.0%
Store inventories	13.0
Grocery wholesalers	6.0

Source: *Supermarket Business*, July 1991, p. 58.

★ 1505 ★
Wholesale - Confectionery (SIC 5145)

Distributors' Sales - Chewing Gum

| Sugared stick gum |
| Sugar-free gum |
| Sugared chunk bubble gum |
| All other gum |

Wholesale distribution of chewing and bubble gum to convenience stores totaled $541 million for the year ending in February 1991 and $592 million for the year ending in February 1992. Segment distribution by type is shown in percent.

	'91	'92
Sugared stick gum	39.3%	37.8%
Sugar-free gum	31.9	34.8
Sugared chunk bubble gum	15.9	15.4
All other gum	13.0	12.0

Source: *Candy Industry*, July 1992, p. H 9, from ICC/ Accutracks Convenience Store Report.

★ 1506 ★
Wholesale - Confectionery (SIC 5145)

Distributors' Sales - Confectionery

Confectionery distribution to convenience stores totaled $1.704 billion for the year ending in February 1991 and $1.890 billion for the year ending in February 1992. Segment distribution by type is shown in percent. Nsk stands for not specified by kind.

	'91	'92
Chocolate bars	56.0%	55.9%
Non-chocolate bars	12.8	12.9
Mints and hard rolls	8.9	9.1
Non-chocolate other packs	8.3	9.0
Chocolate other packs	5.6	5.5
Chocolate changemakers	2.8	2.4
Cough suppressants/throat drops . . .	2.0	2.2
Lollipops	2.5	2.2
Non-chocolate nsk	0.8	0.7
Granola bars	0.3	0.3

Source: *Candy Industry*, July 1992, p. H 9, from ICC/ Accutracks Convenience Store Report.

SIC 52 - Building Materials and Garden Supplies

★ 1507 ★
Retailing - Home Supplies (SIC 5200)

Leading Home Centers

Home Depot	
Lowe's	
Hechinger	
Grossman	
Wolohan Lumber	

Company revenues are shown in thousands of dollars. Percent shares are based on group total.

	Rev. ($ 000)	% of Group
Home Depot	$ 5,136,674	47.0%
Lowe's	3,056,247	28.0
Hechinger	1,615,440	14.8
Grossman	806,636	7.4
Wolohan Lumber	303,715	2.8

Source: *Chain Store Age Executive*, April 1992, p. 72, from company reports.

★ 1508 ★
Retailing - Paint, Glass, Wallpaper (SIC 5231)

Paint, Glass, Wallpaper Sales by Outlet

Shares of 1991 sales by outlet are shown in percent, based on a total of $9.043 million.

Paint, glass, wallpaper stores	51.9%
Home centers	19.3
Hardware stores	15.5
Discount stores	12.2
Misc. general merchandise stores	0.8
Variety stores	0.3

Source: *DM*, June 1992, p. 76.

★ 1509 ★
Retailing - Stores (SIC 5231)

Paint Industry

Shares of the total paint and paint accessories market, by store type, are shown in percent.

Paints and wallcoverings	45.0%
Building materials centers	25.3
Hardware stores	14.8
Department stores	11.5
Other	3.4

Source: *DM*, March 1992, p. 74, from National Decorating Products Association.

★ 1510 ★
Retailing - Batteries (SIC 5251)

Battery Sales by U.S. Retail Outlet

Shares of U.S. battery sales, by retail outlet, are shown in percent.

Mass-merchandisers	34.0%
Food stores	22.0
Drugstores	18.0
Department/variety stores	8.0
Hardware stores	4.0
Photo/electronics stores	2.0
Other	12.0

Source: *DM*, November 1991, p. 44, from RAYOVAC/ NFO/A.C. Nielsen and Duracell Research/NPD/ Nielsen.

★ 1511 ★
Retailing - Hardware (SIC 5251)

Hardware and Tool Sales by Outlet

Shares of 1991 sales by outlet are shown in percent, based on a total of $21.096 million.

Hardware stores	38.4%
Home centers	20.3

Continued on next page.

★ 1511 ★ *Continued*
Retailing - Hardware (SIC 5251)

Hardware and Tool Sales by Outlet

Shares of 1991 sales by outlet are shown in percent, based on a total of $21.096 million.

Discount stores	16.8%
Wholesale clubs	6.1
Department stores	6.1
Supermarkets and grocery stores	3.3
Drug and proprietary stores	2.1
Auto and home supply stores	1.9
Mail order	1.8
Misc. general merchandise stores	1.4
Variety stores	1.1
Household appliance stores	0.7

Source: *DM*, June 1992, p. 76.

★ 1512 ★
Retailing - Hardware (SIC 5251)

Home Improvement Leaders

Sales of 10 leading home improvement chains totaled $19.694 million in 1991. Relative market shares are shown in percent.

	Sales ($ 000)	% of Group
Home Depot	$ 5,136,674	26.1%
Lowe's	3,056,247	15.5
Payless Cashways	2,391,830	12.1
Builders Square	2,049,000	10.4
Hechinger	1,607,727	8.2
Sherwin-Williams	1,495,000	7.6
HomeBase	1,400,000	7.1
Menard's	950,000	4.8
Grossman's	806,636	4.1
Wickes Lumber	800,000	4.1

Source: *Stores*, July 1992, p. 36.

★ 1513 ★
Retailing - Garden Supplies (SIC 5261)

Lawn and Garden Supply Sales by Outlet

Shares of 1991 sales by outlet are shown in percent, based on a total of $12.940 million.

Garden supply stores	29.7%
Discount stores	19.1
Florists	12.4
Home centers	11.3
Hardware stores	10.3
Supermarkets and grocery stores	5.4
Drug and proprietary stores	3.4
Auto and home supply stores	3.1
Mail order	2.4
Variety stores	1.4
Misc. general merchandise stores	1.0
Department stores	0.5

Source: *DM*, June 1992, p. 76.

SIC 53 - General Merchandise Stores

★1514★

General Merchandising (SIC 5300)

Bath Accessory Sales by Outlet

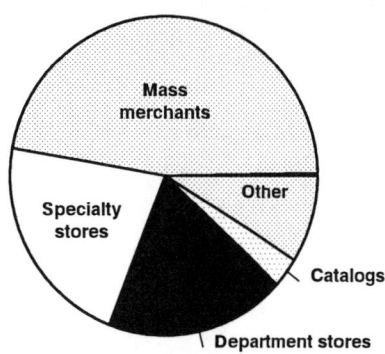

Market shares by retail class are shown as percent of sales totaling $175 million in 1990 and $182 million in 1991.

	1990	1991
Mass merchants	44.0%	47.0%
Specialty stores	22.0	22.0
Department stores	22.0	19.0
Catalogs	3.0	3.0
Other	9.0	9.0

Source: *HFD*, February 24, 1992, p. 4A.

★1515★

General Merchandising (SIC 5300)

Bath Rug Sales by Outlet

Market shares by retail class are shown as percent of sales totaling $455 million in 1990 and $460 million 1991.

	1990	1991
Mass merchants	48.0%	50.0%
Department stores	23.0	20.0
Specialty stores	17.0	18.0
Catalogs	7.0	6.0
Other	5.0	6.0

Source: *HFD*, February 24, 1992, p. 4A.

★1516★

General Merchandising (SIC 5300)

Bath Towel Sales by Outlet

Shares by retail class are shown in percent, based on sales of $1.45 billion in 1990 and $1.39 billion in 1991.

	1990	1991
Mass merchants	44.0%	45.0%
Department stores	28.0	25.0
Specialty stores	10.0	10.0
Catalogs	3.0	3.0
Other	15.0	17.0

Source: *HFD*, February 24, 1992, p. 4A.

★ 1517 ★

General Merchandising (SIC 5300)

Beach Towel Sales by Outlet

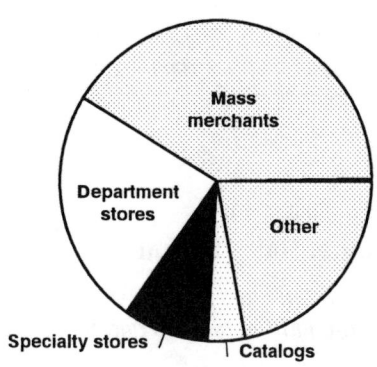

Shares by retail class are shown in percent, based on $238 million market in 1990 and $234 million market in 1991.

	1990	1991
Mass merchants	41.0%	41.0%
Department stores	26.0	24.0
Specialty stores	9.0	9.0
Catalogs	4.0	4.0
Other	20.0	22.0

Source: *HFD*, February 24, 1992, p. 4A.

★ 1518 ★

General Merchandising (SIC 5300)

Bed Pillow Sales by Outlet

Market shares by retail class are shown as percent of sales totaling $447 million in 1990 and $464 million in 1991.

	1990	1991
Mass merchants	40.0%	42.0%
Specialty stores	20.0	21.0
Department stores	18.0	16.0
Catalogs	9.0	8.0
Other	13.0	13.0

Source: *HFD*, February 24, 1992, p. 8A.

★ 1519 ★

General Merchandising (SIC 5300)

Chair Pad Sales by Outlet

Market shares by retail class are shown as percent of sales totaling $70 million in 1990 and $71 million in 1991.

	1990	1991
Mass merchants	66.0%	66.0%
Department stores	15.0	13.0
Specialty stores	12.0	12.0
Catalogs	3.0	3.0
Other	4.0	6.0

Source: *HFD*, February 24, 1992, p. 6A.

★ 1520 ★

General Merchandising (SIC 5300)

Conventional Blanket Sales by Outlet

Market shares by retail class are shown as percent of sales totaling $360 million in 1990 and $368 million in 1991.

	1990	1991
Mass merchants	54.0%	56.0%
Specialty stores	20.0	21.0
Department stores	19.0	16.0
Catalogs	5.0	5.0
Other	2.0	2.0

Source: *HFD*, February 24, 1992, p. 8A.

★ 1521 ★

General Merchandising (SIC 5300)

Decorative Pillow Sales by Outlet

Market shares by retail class are shown as percent of sales totaling $227 million in 1990 and $234 million in 1991.

	1990	1991
Mass merchants	47.0%	48.0%
Department stores	24.0	23.0
Specialty stores	15.0	15.0
Catalogs	6.0	6.0
Other	8.0	8.0

Source: *HFD*, February 24, 1992, p. 6A.

★ 1522 ★

General Merchandising (SIC 5300)

Department and Discount Stores

Sales figures are shown in millions of dollars for 1991. Percent shares are based on group total.

	Sales ($ mil.)	% of Group
Sears, Roebuck	$ 57,242	20.2%
Wal-Mart Stores	43,887	15.5
KMart	34,969	12.4
J.C. Penney	17,295	6.1
Dayton Hudson	16,115	5.7
May Department Stores	10,615	3.8
Woolworth	9,914	3.5
Melville	9,886	3.5
Price	7,056	2.5
The Limited	6,149	2.2
Toys "R" Us	6,124	2.2
Costco Wholesale	5,614	2.0
Home Depot	5,137	1.8
Dillard Department Stores	4,036	1.4
Service Merchandise	3,400	1.2
Nordstrom	3,180	1.1
Lowe's	3,056	1.1
Waban	2,784	1.0
TJX	2,758	1.0
U.S. Shoe	2,737	1.0
Fred Meyer	2,703	1.0
The Gap	2,519	0.9
Mercantile Stores	2,442	0.9
Spiegel	1,976	0.7
Neiman Marcus Group	1,755	0.6
Hechinger	1,608	0.6
ShopKo Stores	1,586	0.6
Venture Stores	1,522	0.5
Fingerhut	1,428	0.5
Edison Brothers Stores	1,367	0.5
Petrie Stores	1,343	0.5
Home Shopping Network	1,079	0.4
Family Dollar Stores	1,029	0.4
Charming Shoppes	1,021	0.4
Pep Boys-Manny, Moe & Jack	971	0.3
Autozone	868	0.3
Consolidated Stores	753	0.3
Merry-Go-Round Enterprises	732	0.3
Dollar General	713	0.3
Lands' End	641	0.2
Value City Department Stores	639	0.2
Pic 'N' Save	545	0.2
Tiffany	492	0.2
Filene's Basement	444	0.2

	Sales ($ mil.)	% of Group
CML Group	$ 402	0.1%
Diagnostek	278	0.1
Duty Free International	188	0.1

Source: *The 1992 Business Week 1000*, 1992, p. 171.

★ 1523 ★

General Merchandising (SIC 5300)

Electric Blanket Sales by Outlet

Market shares by retail class are shown as percent of sales totaling $130 million in 1990 and $122 million in 1991.

	1990	1991
Mass merchants	60.0%	59.0%
Department stores	17.0	18.0
Specialty stores	13.0	13.0
Catalogs	6.0	6.0
Other	4.0	4.0

Source: *HFD*, February 24, 1992, p. 8A.

★ 1524 ★

General Merchandising (SIC 5300)

Embellish Towel Sales by Outlet

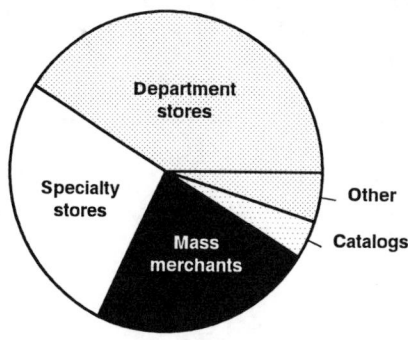

Market shares by retail class are shown as percent of sales totaling $93 million in 1990 and $99 million in 1991.

	1990	1991
Department stores	44.0%	41.0%
Specialty stores	28.0	27.0
Mass merchants	20.0	23.0
Catalogs	4.0	4.0
Other	4.0	5.0

Source: *HFD*, February 24, 1992, p. 4A.

★ 1525 ★

General Merchandising (SIC 5300)

Home Fragrance Sales by Outlet

Market shares by retail class are shown as percent of sales totaling $245 million in 1990 and $243 million in 1991.

	1990	1991
Department stores	39.0%	40.0%
Mass merchants	33.0	35.0
Specialty stores	13.0	10.0
Catalogs	5.0	50.0
Other	10.0	10.0

Source: *HFD*, February 24, 1992, p. 4A.

★ 1526 ★

General Merchandising (SIC 5300)

Kitchen Textile Sales by Outlet

Market shares by retail class are shown as percent of sales totaling $411 million in 1990 and $423 million in 1991.

	1990	1991
Mass merchants	60.0%	61.0%
Specialty stores	10.0	10.0
Department stores	12.0	8.0
Catalogs	6.0	5.0
Other	12.0	16.0

Source: *HFD*, February 24, 1992, p. 6A.

★ 1527 ★

General Merchandising (SIC 5300)

Mattress Sales by Outlet

Market shares by retail class are shown as percent of sales totaling $359 million in 1990 and $361 million in 1991.

	1990	1991
Mass merchants	46.0%	47.0%
Department stores	24.0	22.0
Specialty stores	13.0	14.0
Catalogs	8.0	8.0
Other	9.0	9.0

Source: *HFD*, February 24, 1992, p. 8A.

★ 1528 ★

General Merchandising (SIC 5300)

Sheets and Pillowcases - Sales by Outlet

Market shares by retail class are shown as percent of sales totaling $1.75 billion in 1990 and $1.68 billion in 1991.

	1990	1991
Mass merchants	56.0%	58.0%
Department stores	23.0	21.0
Specialty stores	12.0	11.0
Catalogs	4.0	5.0
Other	5.0	5.0

Source: *HFD*, February 24, 1992, p. 6A.

★ 1529 ★

General Merchandising (SIC 5300)

Shower Curtain Sales by Outlet

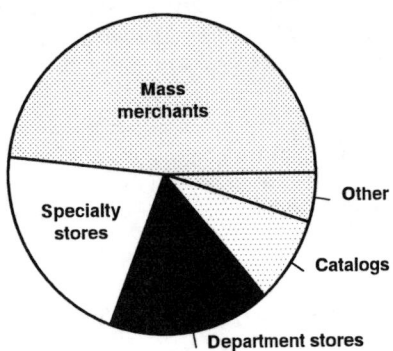

Market shares by retail class are shown as percent of sales totaling $364 million in 1990 and $376 million in 1991.

	1990	1991
Mass merchants	47.0%	48.0%
Specialty stores	21.0	21.0
Department stores	18.0	17.0
Catalogs	9.0	9.0
Other	5.0	5.0

Source: *HFD*, February 24, 1992, p. 4A.

★ 1530 ★

General Merchandising (SIC 5300)

Table Linen Sales by Outlet

Market shares by retail class are shown as percent of sales totaling $467 million in 1990 and $458 million in 1991.

	1990	1991
Mass merchants	36.0%	44.0%
Department stores	25.0	26.0
Specialty stores	18.0	22.0
Catalogs	15.0	-
Other	6.0	8.0

Source: *HFD*, February 24, 1992, p. 6A.

★ 1531 ★

General Merchandising (SIC 5300)

Throw Sales by Outlet

Market shares by retail class are shown as percent of sales totaling $90 million in 1990 and $110 million in 1991.

	1990	1991
Mass merchants	33.0%	25%
Department stores	33.0	25
Specialty stores	20.0	20
Catalogs	8.0	17
Other	6.0	13

Source: *HFD*, February 24, 1992, p. 8A.

★ 1532 ★

Specialty Stores (SIC 5300)

Top Specialty Stores

Companies are ranked by 1991 volume, shown in thousands of dollars. Shares of the group are shown in percent.

	Volume ($ 000)	% of Group
The Limited	$ 6,149,218	8.9%
Toys "R" Us	6,124,209	8.9
Melville	5,182,230	7.5
Woolworth	3,894,400	5.6
Tandy	3,383,089	4.9
Circuit City	2,790,000	4.0
TJX Cos.	2,757,715	4.0
The Gap	2,518,893	3.6
U.S. Shoe	2,270,000	3.3
KMart	1,626,000	2.4
Volume Shoe	1,548,000	2.2
Amcena	1,500,000	2.2
Edison Bros.	1,385,400	2.0
B. Dalton/Barnes & Noble	1,375,000	2.0
Petrie Stores	1,354,525	2.0
Office Depot	1,300,847	1.9
Zale Jewelry	1,156,000	1.7
Charming Shoppes	1,020,656	1.5
Silo Elictronics	1,005,000	1.5
Brown Group	982,000	1.4
Musicland	932,231	1.3
Kohl's Dept. Stores	930,537	1.3
Best Buy	929,692	1.3
Ross Stores	929,661	1.3
Burlington Coat	905,857	1.3
Levitz Furniture	895,000	1.3

Continued on next page.

★ 1532 ★ *Continued*

Specialty Stores (SIC 5300)

Top Specialty Stores

Companies are ranked by 1991 volume, shown in thousands of dollars. Shares of the group are shown in percent.

	Volume ($ 000)	% of Group
Sterling	$ 883,000	1.3%
Merry-Go-Round	761,163	1.1
Conslidated Stores	752,581	1.1
Eddie Bauer	720,000	1.0
Pearl Vision	690,000	1.0
Lechmere	672,000	1.0
Hartmarx	637,300	0.9
Egghead Software	625,000	0.9
Tower Records	600,000	0.9
Herman's	600,000	0.9
Pier 1	586,659	0.8
Value City	586,400	0.8
Child World	580,000	0.8
Highland Superstores . . .	572,200	0.8
Staples	547,080	0.8
Pic'N Save	542,578	0.8
Talbots	521,200	0.8
Heilig-Meyers	519,893	0.8
House of Fabrics	493,062	0.7
Tiffany	491,906	0.7
Fabri-Centers of America . . .	468,904	0.7
Filene's Basement	465,350	0.7
Wherehouse Entertainment . .	457,000	0.7
Specialty Retailers	447,000	0.6

Source: *Stores*, July 1992, p. 32.

★ 1533 ★

Department Stores (SIC 5311)

Biggest Department Stores

Sales of seven leading department store chains totaled $51.820 million in 1991. Shares of the group are in percent.

	Sales ($ mil.)	% of Group
J.C. Penney	$ 12,007,000	23.2%
May Department Stores . . .	8,854,000	17.1
Federated	6,932,300	13.4
R.H. Macy	6,760,000	13.0
Dillard	4,036,392	7.8
Nordstrom	3,179,820	6.1
Dayton Hudson Department Stores	2,931,000	5.7
Belk Stores	2,550,000	4.9
Mercantile Stores	2,442,425	4.7
Carter Hawley Hale	2,127,917	4.1

Source: *Stores*, July 1992, p. 35.

★ 1534 ★

Department Stores (SIC 5311)

Department Store Christmas Sales - 1991

Department store Christmas sales are shown in millions of dollars for 1991. Percent shares are based on group total.

	Sales ($ mil.)	% of Group
Wal-Mart	$ 5,862.0	23.6%
KMart	4,708.2	19.0
Sears	3,301.2	13.3
Dayton Hudson	2,448.9	9.9
J.C. Penney	1,984.0	8.0

Continued on next page.

Department Stores (SIC 5311)

Department Store Christmas Sales - 1991

Department store Christmas sales are shown in millions of dollars for 1991. Percent shares are based on group total.

	Sales ($ mil.)	% of Group
May Dept. Stores	$ 1,684.3	6.8 %
Melville Corp.	1,356.1	5.5
Limited Inc.	996.6	4.0
Woolworth	826.0	3.3
Gap	398.0	1.6
TJX Cos.	340.0	1.4
Waban Inc.	255.1	1.0
Mercantile Stores	388.0	1.6
Charming Shoppes	133.5	0.5
Jamesway	120.9	0.5

Source: *Hardware Age*, February 1992, p. 19, from *The Wall Street Journal*.

★ 1535 ★
Department Stores (SIC 5311)

Department Store Leaders

Volume for the 20 largest department stores totaled $46.120 billion in 1990. Relative shares are shown in percent.

	($ mil.)	% of Group
J.C. Penney	$ 14,616	31.6 %
Mervyn's	4,055	8.8
Dillard's	3,606	7.8
Macy's Northeast	3,090	6.7
Nordstrom	2,894	6.3
Dayton Hudson	1,880	4.1
Macy's South/Bullock's	1,872	4.0
Macy's California	1,520	3.3
Saks Fifth Avenue	1,280	2.8
Neiman Marcus	1,245	2.7
Bloomingdale's	1,166	2.5
Foley's	1,150	2.5
Lord & Taylor	1,147	2.5
The Broadway	1,105	2.4
Marshall Field	1,025	2.2
May Company California	987	2.1
Lazarus	951	2.1
Hecht's	940	2.0

	($ mil.)	% of Group
Woodward & Lathrop	$ 873	1.9 %
Kohl's	840	1.8

Source: *Stores*, July 1991, p. 35.

★ 1536 ★
Department Stores (SIC 5311)

Military Exchanges

1991 sales of U.S. military exchanges worldwide totaled $7,427,573. (Navy sales include concession volume but not ship store volume. Mail order sales include consolidated sales for all services including Coast Guard. AAFES stands for Army & Air Force Exchange Service. CONUS stands for Continental United States). Shares are shown in percent.

	Sales ($ 000)	Share
AAFES		
CONUS	$ 3,125,455	42.1 %
Overseas	2,359,603	31.8
Navy		
CONUS	1,017,199	13.7
Overseas	459,813	6.2
Marine Corps		
CONUS	288,599	3.9
Overseas	46,900	0.6
Coast Guard		
CONUS	87,239	1.2
Overseas	6,674	0.1
Mail order		
CONUS	13,364	0.2
Overseas	22,727	0.3

Source: *Military Market*, January 1992, p. 4, from U.S. Department of Commerce.

★ 1537 ★
Department Stores (SIC 5311)

Nation's Largest Retailers

Company sales are shown in thousands of dollars. Percent shares are based on group total.

	Sales ($ 000)	% of Group
Wal-Mart	$ 11,650,000	23.1 %
KMart	8,266,000	16.4
Sears	7,673,071	15.2

Continued on next page.

★ 1537 ★ *Continued*

Department Stores (SIC 5311)

Nation's Largest Retailers

Company sales are shown in thousands of dollars. Percent shares are based on group total.

	Sales ($ 000)	% of Group
J.C. Penney	.$ 3,793,000	7.5%
Dayton Hudson	3,650,000	7.2
Melville	3,021,425	6.0
May	2,296,900	4.5
Walgreen	2,454,495	4.9
Federated	1,571,000	3.1
The Limited	1,416,000	2.8
Neiman Marcus Group . . .	1,392,500	2.8
Mercantile	594,400	1.2
The Gap	589,000	1.2
Rose's	391,036	0.8
Venture Stores	364,000	0.7
Edison Brothers	326,900	0.6
Charming Shoppes	262,500	0.5
Ross	222,000	0.4
Dollar General	187,500	0.4
Jamesway	182,472	0.4
Best Buy	168,000	0.3
Gottschalks	67,200	0.1

Source: *Chain Store Age Executive*, June 1992, p. 71.

★ 1538 ★

Department Stores (SIC 5311)

Top 10 Department Stores - Japan

Companies are ranked by 1991 declared income, shown in millions of Yen. Relative market shares are shown in percent.

	Income (Y mil.)	% of Group
Marui	59,302	31.5%
Takashimaya & Co.	23,223	12.3
Mitsukoshi	17,531	9.3
Matsuzakaya	17,176	9.1
Isetan	16,601	8.8
Yokohama Takashimaya . . .	11,717	6.2
SOGO	11,559	6.1
Tokyu Department Store . . .	10,860	5.8
Daimaru	10,193	5.4
Hankyu Department Stores . .	10,017	5.3

Source: *TOKYO Business Today*, July 1992, p. 40.

★ 1539 ★

Variety Stores (SIC 5311)

Top Discount Department Stores

Sales of the top three discount department store retailers in 1991 are shown in billions of dollars. Percent shares are based on group total. Figures for Wal-Mart and KMart include specialty store sales.

	Sales ($ bil.)	% of Group
Wal-Mart stores	$ 43.9	50.0%
KMart stores	34.9	39.7
Target stores	9.0	10.3

Source: *Drug Topics*, April 6, 1992, p. 60.

★ 1540 ★

Variety Stores (SIC 5331)

Discount Retailers in Mexico

Sales figures are shown in millions of dollars for 1991. NA stands for not available.

	($ mil.)
Grupo Cifra	2,765
Alamances Aurrera	1,199
Gran Bazar	NA
Club Aurrera	NA
Bodegaurrera	559
Grupo Gigante	1,661
Gigante	1,620
Grupo Comercial Mexicana	1,414
Comercial Mexicana	1,185
Bodega Comercial	110
Price Club de Mexico	NA
Blanco	555
Soriana	515
Woolworth Mexicana	NA
Woolworth	NA
Mini Woolworth (tourist shops)	NA
Oshman's Sporting Goods	NA

Source: *Discount Store News*, May 18, 1992, p. 43.

★ 1541 ★
Variety Stores (SIC 5331)

Leading Retailers

Sales are shown in billions of dollars.

	1991	1990
Wal-Mart	$ 43.9	$ 32.6
KMart	34.6	32.0
Sears Merchandise Group	31.4	32.0

Source: *Advertising Age*, April 20, 1992, p. 42, from Annual reports.

★ 1542 ★
Variety Stores (SIC 5331)

Mass Merchant Leaders

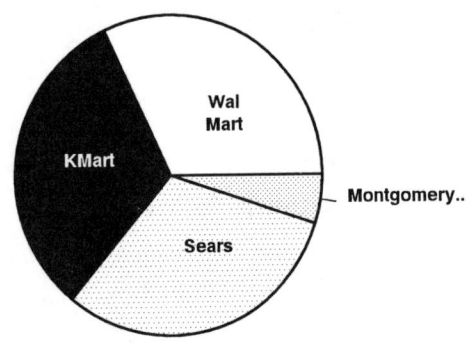

1990 sales of the four largest mass merchandisers totaled to $101.758 million. (Data for Wal-Mart include Sam's Wholesale Clubs and other retail operations. Data for KMart include foreign and nonretail operations. Data for Sears refer to the Sears Merchandise Group. The figure for Montgomery Ward is a "Stores" estimate.) Relative shares are shown in percent.

	($ mil.)	% of Group
Wal Mart	.$ 32,602	32.0%
KMart	32,070	31.5
Sears	31,986	31.4
Montgomery Ward	5,100	5.0

Source: *Stores*, July 1991, p. 32.

★ 1543 ★
Variety Stores (SIC 5331)

One-Price Stores

Sales figures are shown in millions of dollars.
Percent shares are based on group total.

	Sales ($ mil.)	% of Group
One Price Clothing Stores Inc.	. $ 130.2	31.2%
Everything's $1.00 (Value Merchants Inc.)	127.7	30.6
Dollar Tree/Only One Dollar	100	23.9
Simply 6 (Simply Fashion Stores Ltd.)	60	14.4

Source: *The Wall Street Journal*, June 30, 1992, p. B1.

★ 1544 ★
Variety Stores (SIC 5331)

Self Service Stores in Mexico

Company shares are shown as a percent of 24.7 million sq. feet in total self service market.

Comercial Mexicana	. 21.0%
Gigante	. 18.0
Cifra	. 14.0
Blanco	. 14.0
Soriana	. 6.0
Others	. 27.0

Source: *Discount Store News*, May 18, 1992, p. 48, from ANTAD.

★ 1545 ★
Variety Stores (SIC 5331)

Top Discount Retailers

Top 25 discount retailers of general merchandise are shown with number of discount stores. 1991 sales (figures apply only to the sales through discount stores including lessee sales without regard to total company sales) are shown in millions of dollars and as a percent of group total sales.

	No. of Stores	Sales ($ mil.)	% of Group
Wal-Mart	1,699	$ 28,500	32.1%
KMart	2,375	25,550	28.7
Target	463	9,041	10.2
Meijer Thrifty Acres	62	2,820	3.2
Ames	371	2,819	3.2
Marshalls	405	2,358	2.7

Continued on next page.

★1545★ *Continued*

Variety Stores (SIC 5331)

Top Discount Retailers

Top 25 discount retailers of general merchandise are shown with number of discount stores. 1991 sales (figures apply only to the sales through discount stores including lessee sales without regard to total company sales) are shown in millions of dollars and as a percent of group total sales.

	No. of Stores	Sales ($ mil.)	% of Group
Caldor	128	$ 1,914	2.2%
Bradlees	129	1,772	2.0
Hills	154	1,680	1.9
ShopKo	109	1,645	1.9
Venture	84	1,520	1.7
Rose's	231	1,423	1.6
Jamesway	122	835	0.9
Smitty's	24	760	0.9
Consolidated Stores . .	350	748	0.8
Schottenstein (Value City) . . .	55	685	0.8
Fedco	9	680	0.8
Fisher's Big Wheel . .	85	680	0.8
Lechmere	20	673	0.8
Pamida	178	636	0.7
Pic'N'Save	193	542	0.6
Alexander's	11	460	0.5
Clover	25	400	0.4
Bigg's	6	400	0.4
Lanes	26	374	0.4

Source: *DM*, June 1992, p. 64.

★1546★

Variety Stores (SIC 5331)

Top Discount Store Sales

Sales of top 10 discount stores totaled $81.721 million in 1991. Relative market shares are shown in percent.

	Sales ($ mil.)	% of Group
Wal-Mart	$ 31,741,902	38.8%
KMart	25,548,000	31.3
Target	9,041,000	11.1
Meijer	2,900,000	3.5
Ames	2,819,435	3.5
Fred Meyer	2,702,721	3.3
Caldor	1,867,551	2.3
Bradlees	1,771,572	2.2
Hills	1,679,866	2.1
ShopKo	1,648,427	2.0

Source: *Stores*, July 1992, p. 34.

★1547★

General Merchandising (SIC 5399)

Leading Non-Store Retailers

Company revenues are shown in thousands of dollars. Percent shares are based on group total.

	Rev. ($ 000)	% of Group
Spiegel	$ 1,733,521	33.5%
Fingerhut	1,428,428	27.6
QVC Network	921,804	17.8
Lands' End	682,863	13.2
Home Shopping Network . . .	291,800	5.6
Lillian Vernon	116,963	2.3

Source: *Chain Store Age Executive*, April 1992, p. 72, from company reports.

SIC 54 - Food Stores

★1548★

Retailing - Food (SIC 5411)

Food Retailers

Company sales are shown in millions of dollars for 1991. Percent shares are based on a group total of $124,363 million.

	Sales ($ mil.)	% of Group
Kroger	.$ 21,351	17.2%
American Stores	20,823	16.7
Safeway	15,119	12.2
Great Atlantic & Pacific Tea . .	11,624	9.3
Winn-Dixie Stores	10,203	8.2
Albertson's	8,680	7.0
Southland	7,717	6.2
Food Lion	6,439	5.2
Vons	5,350	4.3
Stop & Shop	5,088	4.1
Giant Food	3,397	2.7
Bruno's	2,658	2.1
Smith's Food & Drug Centers . .	2,217	1.8
Hannaford Brothers	2,008	1.6
Weis Markets	1,294	1.0
Quality Food Centers	395	0.3

Source: *The 1992 Business Week 1000*, p. 176.

★1549★

Retailing - Food (SIC 5411)

Food Retailers - Belgium

Shares are shown in percent for 1990.

GIB	18.3%
Delhaize	13.5
Aldi	7.6
Colruyt	6.7
Cora	2.7
Match	2.5
Other	51.3

Source: Investext, Thomson Financial Networks, March 9, 1992, from UBS Phillips & Drew Global Research Group.

★1550★

Retailing - Food (SIC 5411)

Food Retailers - France

Estimated shares of food sales are shown in percent for 1991.

Intermarche	12.2%
Leclerc	11.7
Carrefour	9.9
Promodes	6.7
Casino	4.3
Auchan	4.1
Systeme U	4.0
Docks de France	3.8
Cora	3.2
Other	40.1

Source: Investext, Thomson Financial Networks, March 9, 1992, from UBS Phillips & Drew Global Research Group.

★1551★

Retailing - Food (SIC 5411)

Food Retailers - Germany

Shares are shown in percent for 1990.

Metro	12.2%
Rewe	10.9
Aldi	9.6
Asko-Schaper-Coop	6.4
Karstadt	6.4
Tengelmann	6.0
Spar	5.2
Other	43.3

Source: Investext, Thomson Financial Networks, March 9, 1992, from UBS Phillips & Drew Global Research Group.

★1552★

Retailing - Food (SIC 5411)

Food Retailers - Netherlands

Shares are shown in percent for 1990.

Albert Heijn	26.0%
Edah	7.0
Super	6.0
C1000	6.0
Aldi	5.0
Herman's	3.0
De Boer	3.0
Other	44.0

Source: Investext, Thomson Financial Networks, March 9, 1992, from UBS Phillips & Drew Global Research Group.

★1553★

Retailing - Food (SIC 5411)

Food Retailers - U.K.

Shares are shown in percent for 1991.

Sainsbury	17.0%
Tesco	16.3
Argyll	11.3
Asda	10.5

Gateway	7.0%
Kwik Save	4.4
Morrisons	2.4
Other	31.1

Source: Investext, Thomson Financial Networks, March 9, 1992, from UBS Phillips & Drew Global Research Group.

★1554★

Retailing - Food (SIC 5411)

Frozen Yogurt Sales by Segment

Shares of total frozen yogurt sales by retail class are shown for 1991.

Retail	33.0%
Frozen yogurt shops	30.0
Ice cream shops	16.0
Other foodservice	21.0

Source: *Restaurant Business*, May 1992, p. 216, from Find/SVP Inc.

★ 1555★
Retailing - Food (SIC 5411)

Largest Convenience Store Chains

Company revenues are shown in thousands of dollars. Percent shares are based on group total.

	(S 000)	% of Group
Southland	$ 6,162,897	67.4%
Circle K	1,495,369	16.4
National Convenience	507,641	5.6
Dairy Mart	462,100	5.1
Casey's General Store . . .	439,496	4.8
Uni-Marts	71,816	0.8

Source: *Chain Store Age Executive*, April 1992, p. 72, from company reports.

★ 1556★
Retailing - Food (SIC 5411)

Largest Supermarkets

Sales of nine leading supermarkets totaled $107,300 million in 1991. Shares of the group are shown in percent.

	Sales ($ 000)	% of Group
Kroger	$ 21,350,000	19.9%
American Stores	17,092,956	15.9
Safeway Stores	15,119,200	14.1
A&P	11,590,991	10.8
Winn-Dixie	10,074,331	9.4
Albertson's	8,680,467	8.1
Food Lion	6,438,507	6.0
Publix	6,100,000	5.7
Ahold USA	5,500,000	5.1
Vons	5,350,000	5.0

Source: *Stores*, July 1992, p. 34.

★ 1557★
Retailing - Food (SIC 5411)

Leading Supermarket Chains

Company revenues are shown in thousands of dollars. Percent shares are based on group total.

	($ 000)	% of Group
Kroger	$ 21,350,530	22.8%
American	20,822,956	22.2
Albertson's	8,680,467	9.3
A&P	8,851,047	9.4
Food Lion	6,438,507	6.9
Winn Dixie	5,500,000	5.9
Vons	5,350,200	5.7
Stop & Shop	5,009,581	5.3
Smith's Food & Drug	2,217,437	2.4
Pen Traffic	2,025,273	2.2
Hannaford Bros.	2,007,960	2.1
Bruno's	1,339,488	1.4
Weis Markets	1,294,332	1.4
Ingles Markets	1,044,452	1.1
Marsh	879,972	0.9
Delchamps	468,094	0.5
Quality Food	395,151	0.4
Seaway Food Town	135,260	0.1

Source: *Chain Store Age Executive*, April 1992, p. 72, from company reports.

★ 1558★
Retailing - Food (SIC 5411)

Military Commissaries

1991 sales of U.S. military commissaries worldwide totaled $4,763,971. (Sales include appropriate surcharges. Figures do not include sales tax. CONUS stands for Continental United States). Shares are shown in percent.

	Sales ($ 000)	Share
Air Force		
CONUS	$ 1,760,009	36.9%
Overseas	370,867	7.8
Army		
CONUS	1,246,870	26.2
Overseas	417,485	8.8
Navy		
CONUS	732,654	15.4
Overseas	81,434	1.7
Marine Corps		

Continued on next page.

★ **1558** ★ *Continued*

Retailing - Food (SIC 5411)

Military Commissaries

1991 sales of U.S. military commissaries worldwide totaled $4,763,971. (Sales include appropriate surcharges. Figures do not include sales tax. CONUS stands for Continental United States). Shares are shown in percent.

	Sales ($ 000)	Share
CONUS	$ 146,179	3.1%
Overseas	2,855	0.1
Coast Guard		
CONUS	2,927	0.1
Overseas	2,691	0.1

Source: *Military Market*, January 1992, p. 4, from U.S. Department of Commerce.

★ **1559** ★

Retailing - Food (SIC 5411)

Top 10 Grocery Stores - Japan

Companies are ranked by 1991 declared income, shown in millions of Yen. Relative market shares are shown in percent.

	Income (Y mil.)	% of Group
Ito-Yokado	88,857	29.7%
Seven-Eleven Japan	67,553	22.6
Jusco	30,197	10.1
Nichii	24,460	8.2
Daiei	20,612	6.9
Uny	18,272	6.1
Izumiya	15,439	5.2
FamilyMart	12,825	4.3
Consumers Co-operative Kobe	10,775	3.6
Seiyu	10,239	3.4

Source: *TOKYO Business Today*, July 1992, p. 40.

★ **1560** ★

Retailing - Candy (SIC 5441)

Candy Sales by Outlet

Candy market shares, by outlet, are shown in percent.

Supermarkets	33.0%
Independents/other	17.0
Convenience stores	12.0%
Chain drugstores	12.0
Discounters	8.0
Vending/theater	6.5
Variety stores	5.5
Department stores	3.0
Warehouse clubs	3.0

Source: *DM*, September 1991, p. 54, from National Confectioners Association.

★ **1561** ★

Bakeries (SIC 5461)

In-Store Bakeries

Supermarket companies are ranked by number of in-store bakeries. Percent shares are based on group total. Relative market shares are shown in percent.

	No. of Units	% of Group
Winn-Dixie Stores, Inc.	1,117	21.4%
Kroger Food Stores	946	18.1
Great A&P Food Stores	716	13.7
Safeway Stores, Inc.	575	11.0
American Stores Companies	513	9.8
Albertson's, Inc.	447	8.6
Publix Supermarkets, Inc.	336	6.4
Food Lion, Inc.	255	4.9
Grand Union, Inc.	155	3.0
Vons Companies, Inc.	154	3.0

Source: *Food Review*, April 1991, p. 42, from *Bakery Production and Marketing*.

SIC 55 - Automotive Dealers and Service Stations

★1562★

Retailing - Auto Supplies (SIC 5531)

Auto Supply Sales by Outlet

Shares of 1991 sales of automotive supplies, fuels, and lubricants, by outlet, are shown in percent, based on a total of $34.605 million.

Auto and home supply stores	74.9%
Discount stores	11.8
Wholesale clubs	3.3
Supermarkets and grocery stores	3.0
Department stores	2.1
Mail order	1.3
Drug and proprietary stores	1.1
Home centers	0.8
Hardware stores	0.8
Misc. general merchandise stores	0.7
Variety stores	0.2

Source: *DM*, June 1992, p. 77.

★1563★

Retailing - Auto Supplies (SIC 5531)

Car Radar-Detector Sales by Outlet

Shares by outlet type are shown in percent, based on approximately $200 million in sales in 1991.

Mail order	21.0%
Wal Mart	8.0
Superstores	8.0
Radio Shack	7.5
Discount department stores	6.7
TV shopping programs	6.7
KMart	5.0
Other	37.0

Source: *HFD*, January 1992, p. 4, from Industrial Market Research.

★1564★

Retailing - Tires (SIC 5531)

Tire Sales by Outlet

Shares of tire sales in the U.S., by outlet, are shown in percent for 1992.

Traditional multibrand	44.0%
Discount multibrand	15.0
Mass merchandisers	14.0
Company owned	9.0
Service stations	8.0
Warehouse clubs	6.0
Other	4.0

Source: *Business Week*, March 16, 1992, p. 42, from Goodyear Tire & Rubber Company.

★1565★

Retailing - Gasoline (SIC 5541)

Gasoline Retail Market Shares

Market shares by type of outlet are shown in percent, based on total 1991 volume.

Pumpers	53.6%
Service stations	35.6
Convenience food stores	8.4
Other	2.4

Source: *National Petroleum News*, June 1992, p. 120, from MPSI Inc.

★ 1566 ★

Retailing - Gasoline (SIC 5541)

Service Stations - Canada

Imperial Oil	
Petro-Canada	
Shell Canada	
	Suncor
Other	

Shares of the Canadian petroleum product market as of Dec. 31, 1991 are shown in percent.

Imperial Oil	31.7%
Petro-Canada	18.5
Shell Canada	16.0
Suncor	4.4
Other	29.4

Source: Investext, Thomson Financial Networks, April 30, 1992, from Loewen, Ondaatje, McCutcheon & Co. Ltd.

SIC 56 - Apparel and Accessory Stores

★1567★

Retailing - Apparel (SIC 5600)

Clothing Retailers - U.K.

Company shares are shown in percent for 1991.

Marks & Spencer	15.4%
Burton (inc. Debenhams)	8.8
C&A	4.4
Storehouse	3.7
Sears	3.3
BhS	2.3
Littlewoods	1.9
Next	1.6

Source: Investext, Thomson Financial Networks, March 1, 1992, p. 10, from S.G. Warburg Securities.

★1568★

Retailing - Apparel (SIC 5600)

Largest Apparel Chains

Sales of leading apparel chains totaled $21,302 million in 1991. (Data for Woolworth Apparel include some non-apparel specialty stores.) Relative market shares are shown in percent.

	Sales ($ 000)	% of Group
The Limited	$ 6,149,218	28.9%
Melville Apparel	3,243,159	15.2
TJX Cos.	2,757,715	12.9
The Gap	2,518,893	11.8

	Sales ($ 000)	% of Group
U.S. Shoe Apparel	$ 1,364,000	6.4%
Petrie Stores	1,354,525	6.4
Woolworth Apparel	1,058,000	5.0
Charming Shoppes	1,020,656	4.8
Ross Stores	929,661	4.4
Burlington Coat	905,857	4.3

Source: *Stores*, July 1992, p. 36.

★1569★

Retailing - Apparel (SIC 5611)

Fashion Dress Shirt Sales

Shares, by retail outlet, are shown in percent, based on 1991 total sales of 167.2 million units with value of $2,557.4 million.

	% of Units	% of Sales
Department stores	28.1%	32.6%
Chains	19.6	18.7
Specialty stores	11.5	15.5
Discounters	19.6	12.1
Off-pricers	9.0	8.1
Other	12.3	12.9

Source: *Discount Store News*, May 18, 1992, p. A38, from NPD research.

★1570★

Retailing - Apparel (SIC 5611)

Men's and Boys' Wear Sales by Outlet

Shares of 1991 sales by outlet are shown in percent, based on a total of $43,792 million.

Department stores	30.4%
Discount stores	20.0
Men's and boys' wear stores	18.0

Continued on next page.

★ 1570★ *Continued*

Retailing - Apparel (SIC 5611)

Men's and Boys' Wear Sales by Outlet

Shares of 1991 sales by outlet are shown in percent, based on a total of $43,792 million.

Family apparel stores	17.1%
Off-price apparel	5.1
Sporting goods stores	2.6
Mail order	2.1
Women's ready-to-wear stores	1.1
Variety stores	1.1
Misc. general merchandise stores	1.0
Supermarkets and grocery stores	0.8
Drug and proprietary stores	0.7

Source: *DM*, June 1992, p. 74.

★ 1571★

Retailing - Apparel (SIC 5611)

Men's Wear Retailers - U.K.

Company shares are shown in percent for 1991.

Marks & Spencer	16.3%
Burton (inc. Debenhams)	13.5
Sears	4.9
C&A	4.1
Storehouse	2.2
Next	2.0
BhS	1.9
Littlewoods	1.7

Source: Investext, Thomson Financial Networks, March 1, 1992, from S.G. Warburg Securities.

★ 1572★

Retailing - Apparel (SIC 5621)

Women's and Girls' Wear Sales by Outlet

Shares of 1991 sales by outlet are shown in percent, based on a total of $94,115 million.

Department stores	30.3%
Women's ready-to-wear stores	29.5
Discount stores	14.2
Family apparel stores	10.6
Off-price apparel stores	8.4
Mail order	2.0
Supermarkets and grocery stores	1.5
Variety stores	1.3
Sporting goods stores	0.7
Misc. general merchandise stores	0.7
Drug and proprietary stores	0.5
Men's and boys' wear stores	0.3

Source: *DM*, June 1992, p. 74.

★ 1573★

Retailing - Apparel (SIC 5621)

Women's Wear Retailers - U.K.

Company shares are shown in percent for 1991.

Marks & Spencer	18.6%
Burton (inc. Debenhams)	10.2
C&A	4.4
Storehouse	3.7
Sears	2.4
BhS	2.3
Littlewoods	2.0
Next	1.8

Source: Investext, Thomson Financial Networks, March 1, 1992, from S.G. Warburg Securities.

★ 1574★

Retailing - Lingerie (SIC 5632)

Lingerie Sales by Outlet

Shares, by outlet, are based on a total of $6,792 million in 1990 and $6,900 million in 1991.

	1990	1991
Department store	28.2%	27.0%
Discount store	23.5	24.6
Specialty store	12.6	12.7
J.C. Penney	10.3	9.3

Continued on next page.

★1574★ *Continued*

Retailing - Lingerie (SIC 5632)

Lingerie Sales by Outlet

Shares, by outlet, are based on a total of $6,792 million in 1990 and $6,900 million in 1991.

	1990	1991
Sears	7.7%	8.5%
Factory outlets	3.9	3.9
Off price	3.2	2.8
Montgomery Ward	1.7	1.9
All others	8.8	9.1

Source: *Discount Store News*, May 18, 1992, p. A28, from The NPD Group, Inc.

★1575★

Retailing - Lingerie (SIC 5632)

Panty Sales by Outlet

Outlet shares are based on total sales of $1,186 million in 1990 and $1,257 million in 1991.

	1990	1991
Discount store	35.3%	36.8%
Department store	23.3	23.7
Specialty store	9.9	8.3
J.C. Penney	8.7	8.1
Sears	7.2	7.1
Factory outlets	3.8	4.5
Off price	2.8	2.6
Montgomery Ward	0.9	1.3
All other	8.2	7.7

Source: *Discount Store News*, May 18, 1992, p. A28, from The NPD Group, Inc.

★1576★

Retailing - Underwear (SIC 5632)

Bra Sales by Outlet

Shares, by outlet, are based on total sales of $2,361 million in 1990 and $2,414 million in 1991.

	1990	1991
Department stores	31.6%	29.5%
Discount stores	21.2	24.5
J.C. Penney	12.0	10.8
Sears	8.0	9.7
Specialty store	9.7	9.2
Factory outlets	3.5	3.4
Montgomery Ward	2.4	2.6

	1990	1991
Off price	1.9%	2.0%
All other	9.7	8.3

Source: *Discount Store News*, May 18, 1992, p. A28, from The NPD Group, Inc.

★1577★

Retailing - Underwear (SIC 5632)

Sleepwear Sales by Outlet

Shares, by outlet, are based on total sales of $1,761 million in 1990 and $1,797 million in 1991.

	1990	1991
Department store	27.5%	27.0%
Discount store	24.1	22.1
Specialty store	15.6	17.3
Sears	7.6	7.7
J.C. Penney	8.0	7.6
Off price	4.2	3.8
Factory outlets	4.1	3.8
Montgomery Ward	1.4	1.5
All others	7.6	9.0

Source: *Discount Store News*, May 18, 1992, p. A28, from The NPD Group, Inc.

★1578★

Retailing - Children's Clothing (SIC 5641)

Children's Wear Retailers - U.K.

Company shares are shown in percent for 1991.

Marks & Spencer	9.4%
Storehouse	8.9
Sears	5.5
C&A	5.0
BhS	4.6
Littlewoods	2.7
Next	0.9

Source: Investext, Thomson Financial Networks, March 1, 1992, from S.G. Warburg Securities.

★1579★

Retailing - Children's Clothing (SIC 5641)

Infants' Wear Sales by Outlet

Shares of 1991 sales by outlet are shown in percent,
based on a total of $8.552 million.

Department stores	40.8%
Discount stores	31.1
Children's and infants' wear stores	14.0
Family apparel stores	8.6
Women's ready-to-wear stores	5.5

Source: *DM*, June 1992, p. 74.

SIC 57 - Furniture and Homefurnishings Stores

★ 1580 ★

Retailing - Housewares (SIC 5700)

Houseware Sales by Outlets

Shares of 1991 sales by outlet are shown in percent, based on a total of $29,403 million.

Discount stores	27.1%
Supermarkets and grocery stores	16.6
Department stores	12.9
Gifts, novelty and souvenir shops	10.5
Wholesale clubs	5.7
Home furnishing stores	4.7
Drug and proprietary stores	4.0
Variety stores	3.2
Catalog showrooms	2.7
Furniture stores	2.7
Mail order	2.6
Hardware stores	2.2
Misc. general merchandise stores	2.1
Jewelry stores	1.5
Home centers	1.5

Source: *DM*, June 1992, p. 75.

★ 1581 ★

Retailing - Furniture (SIC 5712)

Furniture Gallery Leaders

Sales of top furniture retail chains are shown with relative market share in percent.

	Sales ($ mil.)	% of Group
Ethan Allen Home Interiors	$ 675.0	45.9%
La-Z-Boy Showcases/Galleries	283.8	19.3
Drexel Heritage Showcase	205.0	13.9
Thomasville Furniture Galleries	110.0	7.5

	Sales ($ mil.)	% of Group
Norwalk Galleries	$ 64.0	4.4%
Pennsylvania House Galleries	51.0	3.5
Expressions	43.0	2.9
Roche Bobois USA	38.0	2.6

Source: *Furniture/Today*, May 18, 1992, p. 47.

★ 1582 ★

Retailing - Furniture (SIC 5712)

Furniture Manufacturer Retailers

Leading furniture manufacturer retail chains had sales of $1.34 billion in 1990. These stores sell a single manufacturer's merchandise, but are typically owned or operated by individual retailers rather than manufacturer. Sales are shown in millions of dollars; relative market shares are shown in percent.

	Sales ($ mil.)	% of Group
Ethan Allen Galleries	$ 650.0	48.5%
La-Z-Boy Showcase Shoppes	302.5	22.6
Drexel Heritage Showcase	200.0	14.9
Thomasville Furniture Galleries	90.0	6.7
Pennsylvania House Galleries	63.0	4.7
Choice Seating	34.5	2.6

Source: *Furniture/Today's Survey of America's Top 100 Furniture Retailers*, 1992, p. 62, from market research.

★1583★

Retailing - Furniture (SIC 5712)

Furniture Retail Profile - 1991

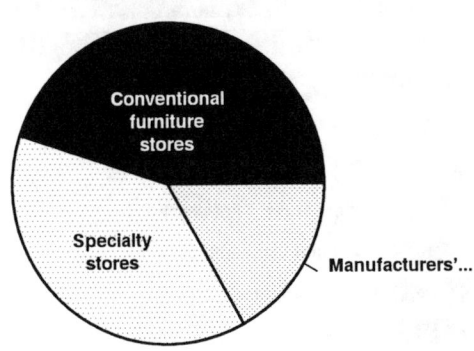

Share of the top 100 furniture stores' unit and dollar sales is shown by type of outlet. Percent distribution includes furniture, bedding, and decorative accessories.

	Vol.	Sales
Conventional furniture stores	67.0%	45.0%
Specialty stores	19.0	38.0
Manufacturers' gallery stores	15.0	17.0

Source: *Furniture/Today*, May 18, 1992, p. 45, from market research.

★1584★

Retailing - Furniture (SIC 5712)

Furniture Retailers - Canada

Shares of the 1991 market are shown in percent based on a total of C$1.2 billion in sales of furniture, bedding, and accessories.

Leon's Furniture	22.2%
The Brick	21.3
Ikea	15.5
BMTC Group	9.1
Pascal	5.8
United Buy and Sell Furniture Warehouse	5.2
Home Furniture Stores	5.2
Le Meubleur	5.0
Great Universal Stores Canada	4.2
Meubles Selection	3.3
Other	3.3

Source: *Furniture/Today*, June 8, 1992, p. 17, from market research and company reports.

★1585★

Retailing - Furniture (SIC 5712)

Furniture Retailers - North America

Sales of the top 25 North American furniture outlets are shown in equivalent U.S. dollar volume for 1991. Relative market shares are shown in percent.

	Sales ($ mil.)	% of Group
Levitz	$885.6	14.4%
Ethan Allen Home Interiors	675.0	10.9
Ikea	396.0	6.4
Pier 1 Imports	344.4	5.6
Heilig-Meyers	294.4	4.8
La-Z-Boy	283.8	4.6
Rhodes	265.9	4.3
Value City	260.0	4.2
Seaman Furniture	250.0	4.1
Haverty's	246.4	4.0
Leon's Furniture	230.9	3.7
The Brick	221.0	3.6
Wickes Furniture	220.0	3.6
Art Van	210.0	3.4
Drexel Heritage	205.0	3.3
W.S. Badcock	197.8	3.2
The Bombay Co.	156.2	2.5
Breuners	123.4	2.0
Thomasville Furniture Galleries	110.0	1.8
BMTC Group	104.7	1.7
Finger Furniture	102.0	1.7
Mattress Discounters	101.0	1.6
RB Furniture	95.3	1.5
Homestead House	95.0	1.5
Reliable Stores	91.5	1.5

Source: *Furniture/Today*, May 18, 1992, p. 50.

★1586★

Retailing - Furniture (SIC 5712)

Furniture Retailers - U.K.

Estimated shares are shown in percent for 1990.

MFI	9.80%
Allied Maples	3.20
Lowndes	2.70
Kingfisher (B&Q)	2.00
Magnet	2.00
Courts	1.60
GUS	1.25
Cantors	1.00

Continued on next page.

★ 1586 ★ *Continued*

Retailing - Furniture (SIC 5712)

Furniture Retailers - U.K.

Estimated shares are shown in percent for 1990.

Argos	0.75%
Sears	0.75
Habitat	0.70
Saxon Hawk	0.70
Storehouse (Habitat)	0.50
Perrings	0.40
Other	72.65

Source: Investext, Thomson Financial Networks, April 30, 1992, from S.G. Warburg Securities and Verdict.

★ 1587 ★

Retailing - Furniture (SIC 5712)

Furniture Sales by Outlet - U.K.

Shares, by type of retailer, are shown in percent, based on total sales of 4.70 billion pounds in 1990.

Furniture specialists	67.0%
Department stores	11.0
DIY retailers	10.0
Home shopping	4.0
Carpet retailers	4.0
Other	4.0

Source: Investext, Thomson Financial Networks, April 30, 1992, from S.G. Warburg Securities.

★ 1588 ★

Retailing - Furniture (SIC 5712)

Specialty Furniture Retailers

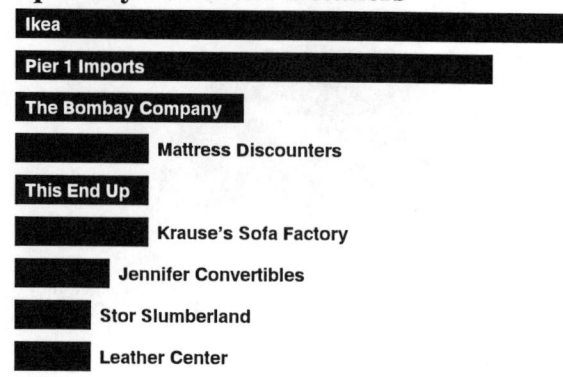

The top ten specialty furniture outlet sales are shown in millions of dollars for 1991. Relative market share is shown in percent. (Specialty outlets include furniture, bedding, and decorative accessories.)

	Sales ($ mil.)	% of Group
Ikea	$ 396.0	29.1%
Pier 1 Imports	344.4	25.3
The Bombay Company	156.2	11.5
Mattress Discounters	101.0	7.4
This End Up	89.9	6.6
Krause's Sofa Factory	89.0	6.5
Jennifer Convertibles	73.0	5.4
Stor Slumberland	56.0	4.1
Leather Center	54.4	4.0

Source: *Furniture/Today*, May 18, 1992, p. 45, from market research.

★ 1589 ★

Retailing - Mattresses (SIC 5712)

Mattress Sales by Outlet

Shares of mattress sales, by outlet, are shown in percent for the first quarter of 1991. The "National Chains" category includes Sears, Roebuck & Co., Montgomery Ward, and J.C. Penney.

Furniture stores	24.7%
Sleep shops	19.8
Department stores	13.0
Discount department store	11.9
National chains	8.5

Continued on next page.

★ 1589 ★ *Continued*
Retailing - Mattresses (SIC 5712)

Mattress Sales by Outlet

Shares of mattress sales, by outlet, are shown in percent for the first quarter of 1991. The "National Chains" category includes Sears, Roebuck & Co., Montgomery Ward, and J.C. Penney.

Factory outlet	4.2%
Home centers	2.8
Warehouse clubs	2.5
Other	12.6

Source: *HFD*, March 1992, p. 4, from IMR.

★ 1590 ★

Retailing - Window Treatments (SIC 5714)

Window Treatments Retail Industry

The leading retailers of window treatments are shown with revenue in millions of dollars for 1991.

J.C. Penney	$ 3,100
Sears	2,300
Montgomery Ward	296

Source: *USA TODAY*, November 2, 1992, p. 3B, from Barbard's Retail Consulting Group, *The Weekly Home Furnishings Newspaper*, and Superbrands Best and Worst 1990.

★ 1591 ★

Retailing - Bakeware (SIC 5719)

Bakeware Sales

Nonstick

Uncoated

Segment distribution of the bakeware market is shown in millions of dollars for 1981 and 1990. The industry totals for 1981 and 1990 are $126 million and $177 million, respectively.

	1981	1990
Nonstick	$ 50	$ 100
Uncoated	76	77

Source: *HFD*, September 1991.

★ 1592 ★

Retailing - Bedding (SIC 5719)

Bed Ensembles Retail Market

The bed ensembles retail market shares, by outlet, are shown in percent, based on total of $1.02 billion in sales for 1991.

Department stores	43.0%
Mass merchants	24.0
Specialty stores	19.0
Catalogs	13.0
Other	1.0

Source: *HFD*, February 24, 1992, p. 10A.

★ 1593 ★

Retailing - Bedding (SIC 5719)

Comforters Retail Market

The comforters market shares, by retail outlet, are shown in percent, based on total of $948 million in 1991.

Mass merchants	47.0%
Department stores	26.0
Specialty stores	16.0
Catalogs	8.0
Other	3.0

Source: *HFD*, February 24, 1992, p. 10A.

★ 1594 ★

Retailing - Cutlery (SIC 5719)

Cutlery Sales by Outlet

Shares of sales volume by retail outlet is shown in percent for 1989 and 1990.

	1989	1990
Mass merchants	24.0%	24.0%
Department stores	22.0	22.0
Catalog-showrooms	9.0	8.0
Specialty stores	8.0	8.0
Warehouse clubs	6.0	7.0
Other	31.0	31.0

Source: *HFD*, March 1992, p. 4, from HFD Research.

★ 1595 ★

Retailing - Home Textiles (SIC 5719)

Home Textiles Retail Industry

Companies are ranked according to 1991 revenue in millions of dollars.

J.C. Penney	$ 3,100
Sears	. 2,300
Wal-Mart	. 1,900
Kmart	. 1,500
Target	602

Source: *USA TODAY*, November 2, 1992, p. 3B, from Barnard's Retail Consulting Group, The Weekly Home Furnishings Newspaper, and Superbrands Best and Worst 1990.

★ 1596 ★

Retailing - Lighting (SIC 5719)

Leading Lighting Retailers

Top 10 furniture stores are shown with lighting sales volume in millions of dollars. Shares are based on group total.

	Sales ($ mil.)	% of Group
Levitz	$ 48.5	39.5%
Breuner's	14.0	11.4
Gabberts	12.5	10.2
W.S. Babcock	10.5	8.6
Wickes	8.0	6.5
Rhodes	7.0	5.7
Haverty's	6.5	5.3
Heilig-Meyers	6.0	4.9
Nebraska Furniture Mart . . .	5.0	4.1
Smyth Homemakers	4.8	3.9

Source: *HFD*, April 6, 1992, p. 65.

★ 1597 ★

Retailing - Lighting (SIC 5719)

Top Lighting Retailers in 1991

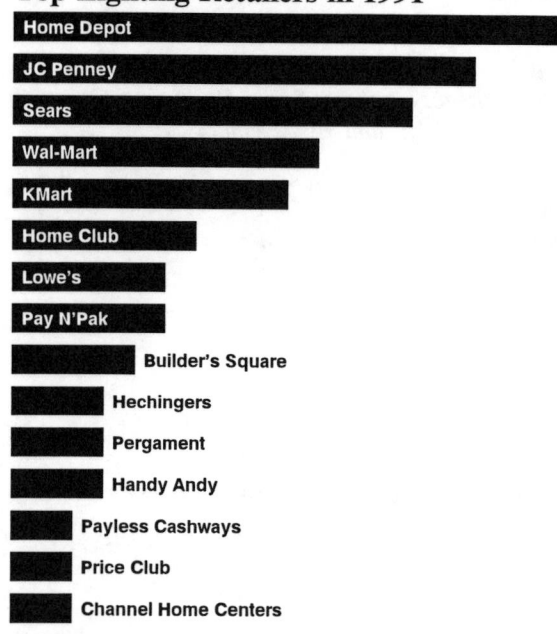

Sales figures are shown in millions of dollars; percent shares are based on group total sales in 1991.

	Sales ($ mil.)	% of Group
Home Depot	$ 150	17.5%
JC Penney	130	15.1
Sears	110	12.8
Wal-Mart	88	10.2
KMart	75	8.7
Home Club	55	6.4
Lowe's	45	5.2
Pay N'Pak	40	4.7
Builder's Square	35	4.1
Hechingers	27	3.1
Pergament	25	2.9
Handy Andy	23	2.7
Payless Cashways	20	2.3
Price Club	19.5	2.3
Channel Home Centers	17	2.0

Source: *HFD*, May 18, 1992, p. 49.

★ 1598 ★
Retailing - Misc. Homefurnishings (SIC 5719)

Curtain Market

Market shares, by outlet, are shown in percent, based on total of $695 million for 1991. The industry total for 1990 was $724 million.

Mass merchants	50.0%
Department stores	28.0
Specialty stores	11.0
Catalogs	9.0
Other	2.0

Source: *HFD*, February 24, 1992, p. 14A.

★ 1599 ★
Retailing - Misc. Homefurnishings (SIC 5719)

Drapery Retail Market

Market shares, by outlet, are shown in percent, based on a total of $723 million for 1991. The industry total for 1990 was $762 million.

Mass merchants	51.0%
Department stores	31.0
Specialty stores	13.0
Catalogs	4.0
Other	1.0

Source: *HFD*, February 24, 1992, p. 14A.

★ 1600 ★
Retailing - Misc. Homefurnishings (SIC 5719)

Free-Standing Curtain Market

Market shares, by outlet, are shown in percent, based on a total of $109 million for 1991. The industry total for 1990 was $91 million.

Mass merchants	45.0%
Specialty stores	23.0
Department stores	22.0
Catalogs	6.0
Other	4.0

Source: *HFD*, February 24, 1992, p. 14A.

★ 1601 ★
Retailing - Misc. Homefurnishings (SIC 5719)

Mini Blind Retail Market

Shares of the mini blind market, by outlet, are shown in percent, based on a total of $1.200 billion for 1991. The industry total for 1990 was $1.22 billion.

Mass merchants	30.0%
Department stores	13.0
Specialty stores	8.0
Catalogs	6.0
Other	43.0

Source: *HFD*, February 24, 1992, p. 12A.

★ 1602 ★
Retailing - Misc. Homefurnishings (SIC 5719)

Roller Shade Retail Market

Market shares, by outlet, are shown in percent, based on sales a total of $186 million for 1991. The industry total for 1990 was $195 million.

Mass merchants	49.0%
Department stores	15.0
Specialty stores	6.0
Catalogs	2.0
Other	28.0

Source: *HFD*, February 24, 1992, p. 14A.

★ 1603 ★
Retailing - Plastic Wrap (SIC 5719)

Plastic Wrap Sales by Distribution Point

Plastic wrap sales, by point of distribution, are shown as a percent of total retail market.

Food stores	70.0%
Discounters	13.0
Club	10.0
Drug stores	6.0
Military	1.0

Source: Investext, Thomson Financial Networks, June 2, 1992, from Shearson Lehman Brothers, Inc.

★ 1604 ★
Retailing - Cookware (SIC 5722)

Cookware Sales by Outlet Type

Shares by class of trade are shown in percent for 1987 and 1990, based on total sales. The category "Specialty/other" includes gourmet stores, factory outlets, supermarkets, hardware stores and premium. Discount department stores include Sears, JC Penney and Montgomery Ward.

	1987	1990
Department stores	18.0%	20.2%
Mass merchandise	22.2	19.9
Discount department stores	18.6	12.5
Catalog/show room	7.8	8.2
Mail order	4.5	6.4
Warehouse club	3.7	4.9
Specialy/other stores	25.2	27.9

Source: *HFD*, October 14, 1991, p. 7, from Independent Nationally Based Study.

★ 1605 ★
Retailing - Electric Housewares (SIC 5722)

Coffee Maker Sales by Outlet

Shares of sales by outlet type are shown in percent for 1989 and 1990.

	1989	1990
Mass merchandisers	52.0%	52.0%
Department stores	13.0	13.0
Catalog-showrooms	9.0	9.0
National chains	6.0	6.0
Warehouse clubs	4.0	4.0
Mail/television order	2.0	3.0
Specialty stores	1.0	1.0
Other	13.0	12.0

Source: *HFD*, November 1991, p. 5.

★ 1606 ★
Retailing - Household Appliances (SIC 5722)

Appliance Stores - U.K.

Shares, by retailer, of the electrical product market, are shown in percent.

Currys/Dixons	16.0%
Electricity Boards	10.0
Comet	7.0
Other specialist electrical multiples	3.0
Other	64.0

Source: Investext, Thomson Financial Networks, June 2, 1992, from Charterhouse Tilney.

★ 1607 ★
Retailing - Household Appliances (SIC 5722)

Household Electronics and Appliances Retail Industry

Companies are ranked according to 1991 revenues in billions of dollars.

Radio Shack	$ 23.1
KMart	23.1
Sears Brand Central	22.2
Circuit City	19.7
Service Merchandise	12.0

Source: *USA TODAY*, November 2, 1992, p. 3B, from Barnard's Retail Consulting Group, The Weekly Home Furnishings Newspaper, and Superbrands Best and Worst 1990.

★ 1608 ★
Retailing - Household Appliances (SIC 5722)

Small Appliance Sales by Outlet

Shares of 1991 sales by outlet are shown in percent, based on a total of $7.662 million.

Discount stores	31.1%
Drug and proprietary stores	15.4
Wholesale clubs	14.3
Department stores	14.0
Misc. general merchandise stores	4.9
Supermarkets and grocery stores	4.5
Catalog showrooms	4.3

Continued on next page.

★1608★ *Continued*
Retailing - Household Appliances (SIC 5722)

Small Appliance Sales by Outlet

Shares of 1991 sales by outlet are shown in percent, based on a total of $7.662 million.

Hardware stores	3.7%
Household appliance stores	3.1
Auto and home supply stores	3.0
Variety stores	1.7

Source: *DM*, June 1992, p. 75.

★1609★
Retailing - Household Appliances (SIC 5722)

Vacuum Cleaner Retailers

Sears
KMart
Wal-Mart
Montgomery Ward
Service Merchandise
Target
Best Products
Cotter
Price Club
Venture
Other

Variety stores are shown with number of full-sized vacuum cleaners sold in 1991. Company shares are shown as a percent of total market.

	Units	Share
Sears	1,785,990	16.0%
KMart	1,100,000	10.0
Wal-Mart	971,250	8.75
Montgomery Ward	469,641	4.23
Service Merchandise	416,250	3.75
Target	349,650	3.15
Best Products	305,250	2.75
Cotter	205,350	1.85
Price Club	199,800	1.8
Venture	194,250	1.75
Other	5,102,670	45.97

Source: *HGD*, January 6, 1992, p. 2A.

★1610★
Retailing - Household Appliances (SIC 5722)

Vacuum Cleaners Top Five Retailers

Stores are ranked by 1991 estimated sales, shown in millions of dollars. Shares are shown as a percent of total market.

	Sales	Share
Sears	$ 293.25	13.3%
KMart	121.33	5.5
Wal-Mart	106.54	4.84
Montgomery Ward	71.5	3.25
Service Merchandise	61.31	2.78
Other	1,550.39	70.30

Source: *HGD*, January 6, 1992, p. 2A.

★1611★
Retailing - Household Appliances (SIC 5722)

Vacuum Shares by Retail Outlet

Vacuum shares by retail outlet for 1988 and 1991 are shown in percent, based on unit sales.

	1988	1991
Mass., discount dept. stores	19.0%	25.0%
Sears	20.0	16.0
Department stores	16.0	11.0
Independent vac. dealers	10.0	10.0
Catalogs-showrooms	6.0	10.0
Door-to-door	9.5	8.0
Membership clubs	5.0	7.5
Appliance stores	8.0	7.0
Hardware	5.0	3.0
Others	5.0	2.5

Source: *HGD*, January 1992, p. 13, from *VDT*.

★1612★
Retailing - Cameras (SIC 5731)

Camera Sales by Outlet - 1990

Shares of camera sales, by outlet type, are shown in percent for 1990.

Discount department stores	39.5%
Camera stores/one-hour labs	16.9
Catalog showroom	12.7
Drugstore/pharmacy	7.3
Department store	7.0
Mail order	6.5
Combination hypermarket/supermarket	5.3

Continued on next page.

★ 1612 ★ *Continued*

Retailing - Cameras (SIC 5731)

Camera Sales by Outlet - 1990

Shares of camera sales, by outlet type, are shown in percent for 1990.

Electronics/video Store	2.4%
Electronic shopping	1.7
Other	0.7

Source: *DM*, September 1992, p. 66, from PMA U.S. Consumer Photographic Survey 1990 Camera Study.

★ 1613 ★

Retailing - Consumer Electronics (SIC 5731)

Blank Audio Tape Market by Outlet

Shares of blank audio tape market by outlet type are shown in percent for 1991.

Discount department stores	42.0%
Warehouse clubs	14.0
Record stores	11.0
Drugstores	6.0
Electronics stores	5.0
Mail order	4.0
Grocery stores	2.0
Other	16.0

Source: *HFD*, March 1992, p. 8.

★ 1614 ★

Retailing - Consumer Electronics (SIC 5731)

Blank Video Cassette Tape Market

Shares of blank full-size video cassette tape market, by type of outlet, are based on total sales in 1991.

Discount department stores	52.0%
Warehouse clubs	13.0
Drugstores	8.0
Grocery stores	5.0
Other	22.0

Source: *HFD*, March 1992, p. 6.

★ 1615 ★

Retailing - Consumer Electronics (SIC 5731)

Cellular Phone Sales

Channel distribution of cellular phone sales is shown in percent.

Retailers	60.0%
Carriers	39.0
Other (auto parts, etc.)	1.0

Source: *HFD*, June 8, 1992, p. 10.

★ 1616 ★

Retailing - Consumer Electronics (SIC 5731)

Consumer Electronics Sales by Outlet - 1990

Consumer electronics sales by outlet are shown in billions of dollars for 1990. Market shares are based on total of $ 30.177 billion.

	Sales ($ bil.)	Share
Mass merchants	$ 9.14	30.3%
Electronics/appliance chains	7.552	25.0
Electronics chains	5.661	18.8
Catalog-showrooms	2.240	7.4
Miscellaneous	2.052	6.8
Warehouse clubs	1.935	6.4
Department stores	1.597	5.3

Source: *HFD*, September 23, 1991, p. 79.

★ 1617 ★

Retailing - Consumer Electronics (SIC 5731)

Consumer Electronics Sales by Outlet - 1991

Shares of 1991 sales by outlet are shown in percent, based on a total of $36.53 million.

TV, radio stores	54.6%
Discount stores	10.2
Department stores	10.1
Wholesale clubs	6.8
Household appliance stores	4.5
Mail order	2.5
Auto and home supply stores	2.4
Catalog showrooms	2.1
Furniture stores	2.0
Misc. general merchandise stores	1.9
Drug and proprietary stores	1.6

Continued on next page.

★ 1617 ★ *Continued*

Retailing - Consumer Electronics (SIC 5731)

Consumer Electronics Sales by Outlet - 1991

Shares of 1991 sales by outlet are shown in percent, based on a total of $36.53 million.

Home centers	0.5%
Variety stores	0.5
Hardware stores	0.3

Source: *DM*, June 1992, p. 77.

★ 1618 ★

Retailing - Consumer Electronics (SIC 5731)

Fire Extinguisher Sales by Outlet

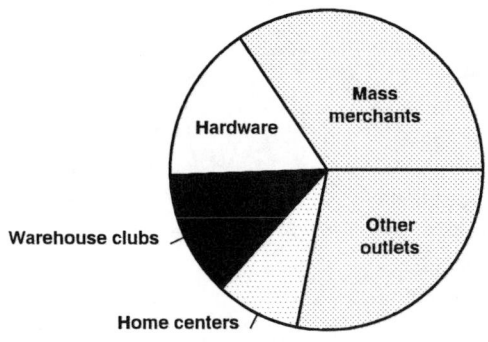

Distribution of sales by retail outlet is shown in percent for 1991.

Mass merchants	31.7%
Hardware	15.2
Warehouse clubs	12.3
Home centers	7.9
Other outlets	26.2

Source: *HFD*, May 18, 1992, p. 8.

★ 1619 ★

Retailing - Consumer Electronics (SIC 5731)

Smoke Detector Sales by Outlet

Distribution of sales by retail outlet is shown in percent for 1991.

Mass merchant	34.4%
Hardware	18.5
Home center	11.6
Warehouse clubs	5.8
Other outlets	24.7

Source: *HFD*, May 18, 1992, p. 8.

★ 1620 ★

Retailing - Electronics (SIC 5731)

Top 50 Electronics Retailers

Top 50 retailers' sales ($25.0335 billion) are shown with percentages for the group.

	Sales ($ mil.)	% of Group
Radio Shack	$ 2,945.0	12.1%
KMart	2,600.0	10.7
Sears Brand Central	2,500.0	10.3
Circuit City	1,900.0	7.8
Service Merchandise	1,400.0	5.8
Wal-Mart Stores	1,100.0	4.5
Montgomery Ward	867.0	3.6
Target	800.0	3.3
Silo	775.0	3.2
Highland Superstores	692.5	2.9
Sam's Wholesale	690.0	2.8
Price Club	650.0	2.7
Best Buy	600.0	2.5
Best Products	600.0	2.5
Toys "R" Us	600.0	2.5
Tandy Name Brand	150.0	0.6
The Good Guys!	150.0	0.6
Office Depot	150.0	0.6
Costco	145.0	0.6
Lechmere	290.0	1.2
Curtis Mathes	288.0	1.2
Macy's Northeast	260.0	1.1
Ames/Zayre	250.0	1.0
The Wiz	250.0	1.0
Pace Membership	230.0	0.9
Caldor	220.0	0.9
Tops Appliance City	175.0	0.7
Newmark & Lewis	173.4	0.7
American of Madison	168.0	0.7

Continued on next page.

Retailing - Electronics (SIC 5731)

Top 50 Electronics Retailers

Top 50 retailers' sales ($25.0335 billion) are shown with percentages for the group.

	Sales ($ mil.)	% of Group
Trader Horn	$ 160.0	0.7%
Fred Meyer	150.0	0.6
Macy's California	150.0	0.6
Venture Stores	150.0	0.6
Child World	145.0	0.6
Audio/Video Affiliates	143.7	0.6
Fretter	140.0	0.6
Sun TV	135.0	0.6
Navy Resale & Services	132.3	0.5
Adray's	130.0	0.5
Dillard's	130.0	0.5
P.C. Richard & Son	130.0	0.5
Lowe's Inc.	120.0	0.5
ABC Appliance Center	118.0	0.5
Sound Advice	110.0	0.5
The Appliance Store	102.0	0.4
Brands Mart	100.5	0.4
Rose's Stores	100.0	0.4
SaveMart	100.0	0.4
Staples	100.0	0.4
BizMart	97.0	0.4

Source: *HFD*, September 23, 1991, p. 89.

★ 1621 ★

Retailing - Computers (SIC 5734)

Computer Retailers

Sales of the leading computer retailers are shown in millions of dollars, with relative market shares in percent. The figure for Egghead refers to software only.

	Sales ($ mil.)	% of Group
Tandy	$ 3,000	44.1%
Intelligent Electronics	1,100	16.2
Computerland	750	11.0
Inacom	680	10.0
Microage	650	9.5

	Sales ($ mil.)	% of Group
Egghead	$ 400	5.9%
Sears Business Centers	110	1.6
Compucon	68	1.0
JWP/Businessland	50	0.7

Source: *The New York Times*, November 13, 1991, p. C4, from Dataquest.

★ 1622 ★

Retailing - Computers (SIC 5734)

Computer Sales by Outlet

Market share by computer reseller segment is shown in percent, based on totals of $41.5 billion in 1991 and $47.6 billion in 1992 (forecast). VAR stands for value-added reseller.

	1990	1991
Outbound dealers	32.5%	32.1%
Computer retailers	18.1	16.0
Boutiques (VARs)	19.0	14.7
Superstores	6.7	13.4
Telemarketing/outbound	5.1	5.0
Warehouse clubs	4.3	4.8
Mail order dealers	4.3	4.2
Office prod. superstores	1.0	2.5
Software stores	3.1	1.7
Catalog dealers	3.0	1.5
Electronics stores	0.6	0.8
Discount dept. stores	0.6	0.8
Specialty merchandisers	0.5	0.8
Other	1.3	1.7

Source: *Dealerscope Merchandising*, September 1991, p. 60.

SIC 58 - Eating and Drinking Places

★ 1623 ★

Catering (SIC 5812)

Airline Catering Services

CaterAire	
Dobbs International	
Onyx	
UAL Services	
Other	

Shares of the global market for in-flight food service are shown in percent.

CaterAire	26.0%
Dobbs International	19.0
Onyx	19.0
UAL Services	15.0
Other	21.0

Source: Investext, Thomson Financial Networks, June 30, 1992, from Shearson Lehman Brothers, Inc.

★ 1624 ★

Catering (SIC 5812)

In-Flight Food Service Market Shares

Market shares are shown in percent for 1991.

Caterair	27.0%
Dobbs	18.0
Skychef	17.0
United	15.0
Ogden	6.0
Chelsea	6.0
Other regional	12.0

Source: Investext, Thomson Financial Networks, June 18, 1992, from Prudential Securities, Inc.

★ 1625 ★

Food Service (SIC 5812)

Food Service Industry

Market segmentation of the food service industry is shown in percent for 1990 and 1991.

	1990	1991
Eating and drinking places	63.0%	62.9%
Business and industry	6.5	6.5
Vending market	6.1	6.1
Student market	5.9	5.9
Hotel/motel market	5.6	5.5
Retail market	4.2	4.3
Health care market	4.2	4.1
Leisure market	3.0	3.1
Airline market	1.6	1.7

Source: *Restaurant Business*, September 20, 1991, p. 74.

★ 1626 ★

Food Service (SIC 5812)

Food Service Market

Food service industry sales by segment are shown in billions of dollars for 1992. Market shares are shown in percent based on industry total.

	Sales ($ bil)	Share
Full service	$ 83.99	32.2%
Fast food	78.38	30.1
Employee feeding	17.7	6.8
Schools	14.8	5.7
Hospitals	11.7	4.5
Lodging	9.6	3.7
Colleges & Universities	7.9	3.0
Military	6.3	2.4
Recreation	4.4	1.7
Nursing homes	4.3	1.6
Supermarkets	3.9	1.5
Transportation	3.4	1.3
Caterers	3.0	1.2

Continued on next page.

★ 1626 ★ *Continued*
Food Service (SIC 5812)

Food Service Market

Food service industry sales by segment are shown in billions of dollars for 1992. Market shares are shown in percent based on industry total.

	Sales ($ bil)	Share
Convenience stores	$ 2.9	1.1%
Child care	2.7	1.0
Retail	2.1	0.8
Life care & elder care	1.1	0.4
Other	2.4	0.9

Source: *Restaurants & Institutions*, January 3, 1992, p. 38.

★ 1627 ★
Food Service (SIC 5812)

Food Service Sales

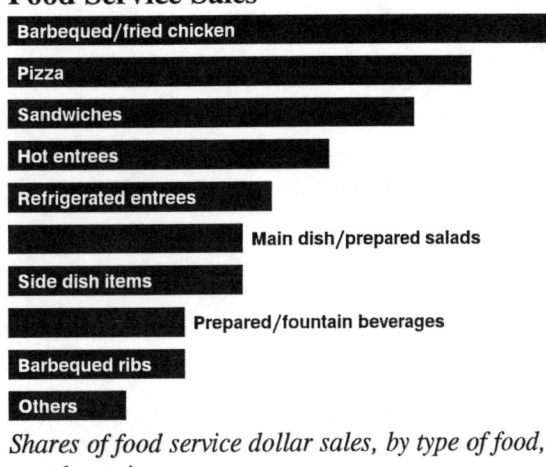

Shares of food service dollar sales, by type of food, are shown in percent.

Barbequed/fried chicken	18.6%
Pizza	15.8
Sandwiches	14.2
Hot entrees	10.6
Refrigerated entrees	9.0
Main dish/prepared salads	8.2
Side dish items	8.0
Prepared/fountain beverages	6.0
Barbequed ribs	5.6
Others	4.0

Source: *Supermarket Business*, July 1991, p. 57.

★ 1628 ★
Food Service (SIC 5812)

Takeout Market by Segment

Shares of 1994 projected takeout sales by segment are shown in percent, based on total sales of $89 billion.

Fast food outlets	62.0%
Supermarkets	17.0
Other restaurants	13.0
Convenience stores	9.0

Source: *Restaurants & Institutions*, August 1991, p. 48, from Find/SVP Inc.

★ 1629 ★
Restaurants (SIC 5812)

Biggest Fast Food Franchises

Franchised fast food companies are ranked by number of units. Shares of the group are shown in percent.

	Total Units	% of Group
McDonald's Corp.	11,000	32.2%
Subway Sandwiches	5,600	16.4
Burger King Corp.	5,147	15.0
KFC Corp.	3,404	10.0
Wendy's International Inc.	2,657	7.8
Arby's Inc.	2,166	6.3
Taco Bell Corp.	1,360	4.0
Hardees Food Systems Inc.	1,315	3.8
Al Copeland Enterprises Inc.	1,128	3.3
Astor Restaurant Group	425	1.2

Source: *Black Enterprise*, September 1991, p. 67.

★1630★
Restaurants (SIC 5812)

Biggest Steakhouse Chains

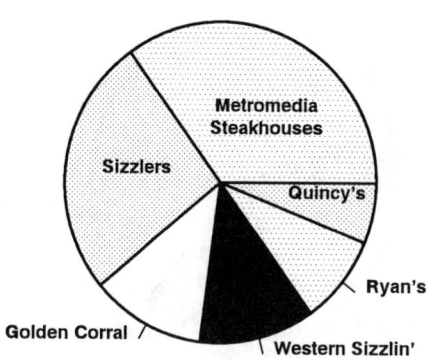

1990 systemwide sales at major steakhouse chains, shown in millions of dollars. Relative shares are shown in percent.

	Sales ($ mil.)	% of Group
Metromedia Steakhouses . . .	$ 1,300	35.1%
Sizzlers	971	26.3
Golden Corral	450	12.2
Western Sizzlin'	445	12.0
Ryan's	331	8.9
Quincy's	202	5.5

Source: *Restaurant Business*, July 20, 1991, p. 172.

★1631★
Restaurants (SIC 5812)

Burger Joints - U.K.

McDonald's
Burger King
Wimpy
Other

Shares are shown in percent, based on a market of 820 million pounds.

McDonald's	39.0%
Burger King	19.0
Wimpy	14.0
Other	28.0

Source: *Accountancy*, February 1992, p. 86.

★1632★
Restaurants (SIC 5812)

Fast Food Chains

U.S. fast food leaders with the largest presence abroad are ranked by number of restaurant units (including international units). Company shares are based on group total.

	No. of Units	% of Group
McDonald's	11,803	29.9%
KFC	8,187	20.8
Pizza Hut	8,040	20.4
Burger King	6,200	15.7
Dairy Queen	5,207	13.2

Source: *Restaurants & Institutions*, July 10, 1991, p. 116, from company reports.

★1633★
Restaurants (SIC 5812)

Household Market Penetration - Restaurants

Average household market penetration, by restaurant, is shown in percent for 1991.

McDonald's	21.7%
Burger King	10.6
Pizza Hut	8.0
Wendy's	7.2

Source: Investext, Thomson Financial Networks, June 5, 1992, from Shearson Lehman Brothers, Inc.

★1634★
Restaurants (SIC 5812)

Ice Cream and Yogurt Chains

Largest ice cream and yogurt chains are shown in terms of millions of dollars in sales in 1991. Relative shares are shown in percent.

	Sales ($ mil.)	% of Group
Dairy Queen	$ 2,105	52.1%
Carvel	582	14.4
Friendly Restaurants	519	12.8
Baskin-Robbins	510	12.6
TCBY	323	8.0

Source: *Restaurant Business*, May 1, 1992, p. 218.

★ 1635 ★
Restaurants (SIC 5812)

International Restaurant Chains

30 international restaurant chains are ranked by number of units. Percent shares are based on group total.

	# of Units	% of Group
McDonald's Corp.	12,418	14.5%
Pizza Hut Inc.	8,500	10.0
Kentucky Fried Chicken	8,480	9.9
Burger King Corp.	6,400	7.5
Subway Sandwiches & Salads . .	6,178	7.2
Dominoes Ann Arbor	5,500	6.4
Dairy Queen	5,308	6.2
Wendy's Intl. Inc.	3,804	4.5
Hardee's	3,673	4.3
Little Caesar's Pizza	3,650	4.3
Taco Bell	3,500	4.1
Baskin-Robbins	3,413	4.0
Dunkin Donuts	2,563	3.0
Arby's Roast Beef	2,500	2.9
Denny's.	1,391	1.6
Church's Fried Chicken . . .	1,135	1.3
Jack-in-the-Box	1,100	1.3
Skylark/Japan	1,095	1.3
Popeye's Famous Fried & Biscuits	823	1.0
Lotteria Co. Ltd./Japan	756	0.9
Sizzler International Inc.	710	0.8
Orange Julius	562	0.7
Shakey's Pizza Restaurants . . .	430	0.5
White Castle Systems Inc. . . .	268	0.3
Chi-Chi's Inc.	230	0.3
Country Kitchen International . .	230	0.3
Quick Hamburger Restaurants/ Belgium	200	0.2
Grandy's Inc.	198	0.2
T.G.I. Friday's	190	0.2
Nordsee Restaurants/Germany .	150	0.2

Source: *Hotels*, May 1992, p. 82.

★ 1636 ★
Restaurants (SIC 5812)

Largest Restaurants - U.S.

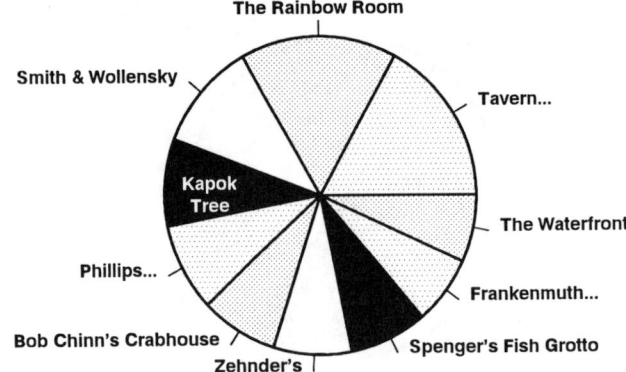

1990 sales of the 10 largest restaurants in the U.S., distributed in thousands of dollars. Restaurant locations are shown in parentheses. Group shares are converted to percent.

	Sales ($000)	% of Group
Tavern on the Green (New York, NY)	$ 27,025	16.8%
The Rainbow Room (New York, NY)	25,500	15.9
Smith & Wollensky (New York, NY)	17,835	11.1
Kapok Tree (Clearwater, FL) . .	15,170	9.4
Phillips Harborplace (Ocean City, MD)	14,988	9.3
Bob Chinn's Crabhouse (Wheeling, IL)	12,805	8.0
Zehnder's (Frankenmuth, MI) . .	12,687	7.9
Spenger's Fish Grotto (Berkeley, CA)	12,000	7.5
Frankenmuth Bavarian Inn (Frankenmuth, MI)	11,703	7.3
The Waterfront (Covington, KY)	11,000	6.8

Source: *Restaurant Hospitality*, 1992.

★ 1637 ★

Restaurants (SIC 5812)

Leading Restaurant Franchisees

Top 20 franchisees (companies that have been granted franchises) are ranked by 1990 sales, shown in millions of dollars. Group shares are converted to percent. (Figures for National Restaurant Management are an R&I estimate).

	Sales ($ mil)	% of Group
Spartan Food Systems	$ 510.5	16.6%
Boddie-Noell Ent.	298.0	9.7
TPI Restaurants	239.4	7.8
National Pizza Co.	198.0	6.4
Harman Mgmt. Co.	190.0	6.2
National Restaurant Mgmt.	185.0	6.0
RTM	169.5	5.5
RPM Pizza	153.9	5.0
Pizza Mgmt.	150.0	4.9
Carrols	149.5	4.9
Collins Foods Intl.	140.0	4.5
Restaurant Mgmt. Services	104.0	3.4
Sybra	103.6	3.4
Consul Restaurants	88.3	2.9
Restaurant Mgmt.	72.1	2.3
Forbco Mgmt.	68.5	2.2
U.S. Restaurants	68.1	2.2
Buehler-Ruckriegel	67.1	2.2
Atlanta Family Restaurants	65.0	2.1
Marcus Restaurants	60.0	1.9

Source: *Restaurants & Institutions*, August 21, 1991, p. 86.

★ 1638 ★

Restaurants (SIC 5812)

Pizza Delivery Shares

Shares are shown in percent based on a total pizza delivery market of $6.0 billion in 1991.

Domino's	44.0%
Pizza Hut	25.0
Others	31.0

Source: *Advertising Age*, June 15, 1992, p. 44, from Domino's.

★ 1639 ★

Restaurants (SIC 5812)

Restaurant Capacity and Efficiency - Leaders

The leading restaurants are ranked according to the number of customers served per day.

Cracker Barrel	1696
Ryan's	1292
Shoney's	1166
Buffets	1005
Spaghetti Warehouse	989
Regas Grill	959
Quincy's	950
Bakers Square	923
Village Inn	869
Denny's	823
Chili's	753
Macaroni Grill	738
Sizzler	734
Pizzeria Uno	698
IHOP	660
Bertucci's	623
Applebee's	621
Outback Steakhouse	442
Chart House	233

Source: *Restaurant Hospitality*, December 1991, p. 67, from Montgomery Securities.

★ 1640 ★

Restaurants (SIC 5812)

Restaurant Off-Premise Purchases

Shares of off-premise purchases from restaurants are shown in percent.

Takeout	60.8%
Drive-through	31.0
Delivery	8.2

Source: *The Wall Street Journal*, June 18, 1992, p. B1, from National Restaurant Association and Crest Report of NPD Group.

★ **1641** ★
Restaurants (SIC 5812)
Restaurant Pizza Sales by Type

Shares, by type, are shown as percent of the total market.

	1987	1990
Thin	59.0%	53.0%
Thick	25.0	23.0
Pan	14.0	22.0
Stuffed	2.0	2.0

Source: *Restaurant Hospitality*, December 1991, p. 67.

★ **1642** ★
Restaurants (SIC 5812)
Shares of Breakfast Traffic

Shares of breakfast traffic by type of service are shown in percent for the 12 months ended August, 1991.

Quick-service	60.0%
Midscale	36.0
Upscale	4.0

Source: *Restaurant Business*, March 1992, p. 184.

★ **1643** ★
Restaurants (SIC 5812)
Take-Out Food Outlets

The take-out food market is shown, by type of outlet, in percent.

	1990	1991
Fast-food restaurants	46.0%	51.0%
Table-service restaurants	27.0	23.0
Supermarkets	14.0	14.0
Other	8.0	12.0

Source: *Restaurant Business*, July 1, 1991, p. 2, from Food Marketing Institute.

★ **1644** ★
Restaurants (SIC 5812)
Top Chicken Restaurants

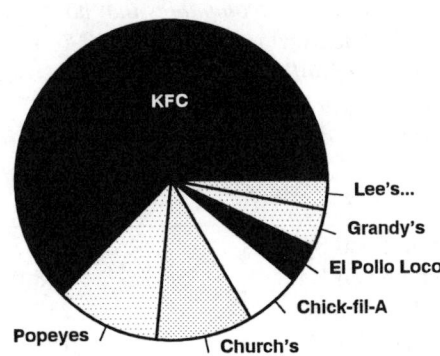

Leading chicken restaurant chains shown with sales in millions of dollars. Relative sales shares are shown in percent.

	Sales ($ mil.)	% of Group
KFC	$ 3200	63.3%
Popeyes	547	10.8
Church's	514	10.2
Chick-fil-A	294	5.8
El Pollo Loco	180	3.6
Grandy's	180	3.6
Lee's Famous Recipe	144	2.8

Source: *Restaurant Business*, August 10, 1991, p. 160.

★ **1645** ★
Restaurants (SIC 5812)
Top Hamburger Chains

Top 10 hamburger chains are ranked by 1990 U.S. systemwide sales, shown in thousands of dollars. Shares are based on group total.

	Sales ($000)	% of Group
McDonald's	$ 12,251,600	46.3%
Burger King	5,250,000	19.8
Hardee's/Roy Rogers	3,360,000	12.7
Wendy's	2,835,000	10.7
Jack in the Box	944,000	3.6
Carl's Jr	575,000	2.2

Continued on next page.

★ 1645 ★ *Continued*

Restaurants (SIC 5812)

Top Hamburger Chains

Top 10 hamburger chains are ranked by 1990 U.S. systemwide sales, shown in thousands of dollars. Shares are based on group total.

	Sales ($000)	% of Group
Sonic Drive-Ins	$ 454,579	1.7%
Whataburger	319,000	1.2
White Castle	291,277	1.1
Rally's	203,043	0.8

Source: *Restaurant Business*, January 1, 1992, p. 124.

★ 1646 ★

Restaurants (SIC 5812)

Top Restaurant Chains - U.S.

1990 sales of the top 10 restaurant chains in the U.S., distributed in millions of dollars. Parent companies are in parentheses. Group shares are converted to percent.

	Sales ($ mil.)	% of Group
McDonald's (McDonald's) . . .	.$ 12,251	30.0%
Burger King (Grand Metropolitan)	6,100	14.9
Hardee's (Imasco)	4,101	10.0
Pizza Hut (Pepsico)	4,000	9.8
KFC (Pepsico)	3,200	7.8
Wendy's (Wendy's International)	2,762	6.8
Domino's Pizza (Domino's Pizza)	2,486	6.1
Taco Bell (Pepsico)	2,461	6.0
Dairy Queen (American Dairy Queen)	1,980	4.9
Denny's (TW Holdings)	1,480	3.6

Source: *Nation's Restaurant News*, 1992, p. 65.

★ 1647 ★

Restaurants (SIC 5812)

Top Restaurant Franchisers

Leading franchisers are shown with numbers of units (including foreign franchised units). Shares of the group are shown in percent.

	Units	% of Group
McDonald's	9,160	15.7%
Kentucky Fried Chicken	6,380	11.0
Subway	5,354	9.2
Dairy Queen	5,204	8.9
Burger King	5,112	8.8
Pizza Hut	4,600	7.9
Domino's Pizza	4,208	7.2
Baskin-Robbins Ice Cream . . .	3,183	5.5
Hardee's	2,670	4.6
Wendy's	2,657	4.6
Arby's	2,166	3.7
TCBY	1,677	2.9
Taco Bell	1,394	2.4
Sonic Industries	949	1.6
Big Boy	802	1.4
A&W Restaurants	740	1.3
Popeye's Chicken & Biscuits . . .	657	1.1
Carvel Ice Cream Bakery	652	1.1
Orange Julius	614	1.1
Round Table Pizza	3	0.0

Source: *Restaurants & Institutions*, August 21, 1991, p. 86, from *R&I* 400 data.

SIC 59 - Miscellaneous Retail

★ 1648 ★
Retailing - Frames (SIC 5900)

Dealer Breakdown of Frame Market

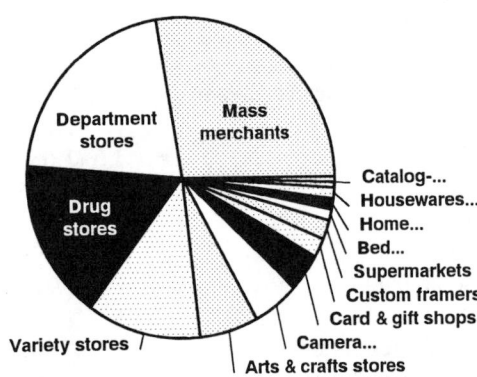

Market shares by distribution channel are shown in percent for 1990.

Mass merchants	.28.0%
Department stores	.21.0
Drug stores	.16.0
Variety stores	.12.0
Arts & crafts stores	.6.0
Camera stores & photo labs	.5.0
Card & gift shops	.4.0
Custom framers	.2.0
Supermarkets	.2.0
Bed, bath & linen stores	.1.0
Home office superstores	.1.0
Housewares chains	.1.0
Catalog-showrooms	.1.0

Source: *HFD*, December 1991, p. 6.

★ 1649 ★
Drugstores (SIC 5912)

Analgesic Sales by Retail Outlet

Shares of 1991 internal analgesic sales, by retail outlet, are shown in percent, based on total of $2.5 billion.

Food stores	.49.0%
Drugstores	.36.1
Mass merchandisers	.14.9

Source: *Drug Topics*, January 6, 1992, p. 74, from Nielsen Marketing Research, Northbrook, Illinois.

★ 1650 ★
Drugstores (SIC 5912)

Analgesics, Digestives, and Miscellaneous Sales by Outlet

Sales of analgesics, digestives, and other miscellaneous products totaled $6.2 billion in 1991. The category includes laxatives, stomach remedies, diarrhea remedies, internal analgesics, arthritis remedies, hemorrhoid preparations, sleeping tablets, diet aids, and vitamins. Shares, by retail outlet, are shown in percent.

Drugstores	.43.5%
Food stores	.38.7
Mass merchandisers	.17.7

Source: *Drug Topics*, April 20, 1992, p. 61.

★1651★

Drugstores (SIC 5912)

Color Cosmetic Sales by Outlet

Sales of color cosmetics totaled $1.9 billion in 1991. The category includes eye makeup, lip makeup, nail color, and face makeup. Shares, by retail outlet, are shown in percent, based on that total.

Drugstores	58.8%
Mass merchandisers	22.5
Food stores	18.7

Source: *Drug Topics*, April 20, 1992, p. 65.

★1652★

Drugstores (SIC 5912)

Cough, Cold, and Flu Remedy Sales by Outlet

Sales of cough, cold, and flu remedies (including nasal sprays, cough syrups, cough drops, cold remedies, sinus remedies, and throat lozenges) totaled $2.9 billion in 1991. Shares, by retail outlet, are shown in percent, based on that total.

Drugstores	45.3%
Food stores	41.8
Mass merchandisers	12.9

Source: *Drug Topics*, April 20, 1992, p. 61.

★1653★

Drugstores (SIC 5912)

Deep-Discount Drugstore Market

Deep-discount drugstores are projected to do $7.589 billion worth of business in 1992. Shares of the group for 1991 and 1992 are shown in precent.

	1991	1992
Phar-Mor	41.5%	42.2%
Drug Emporium (OH)	21.5	21.2
F&M Distributors	10.7	11.1
Marc's	3.9	3.6
Rock Bottom	3.6	3.3
ALP Freddy's	2.9	2.9
Sack N Save	1.5	1.5
Drug Emporium (TX)	1.4	1.4
Drug Palace	1.2	1.2
Rx Place	1.0	1.0
The Pharm	1.0	0.9
Widmann Discount Center	0.9	0.9

	1991	1992
Drugs For Less	0.9%	0.9%
Drug World	0.7	0.7
Drug Barn	0.7	0.7
Cost Cutter's	0.7	0.7
Texas Drug warehouse	0.6	0.6
Colman's	0.6	0.6
Joel & Jenny's	0.6	0.6
Harmon Drug Stores	0.5	0.5
Fazio's	0.4	0.5
Drug Warehouse	0.4	0.4
Price-Less	0.3	0.3
Sid's	0.4	0.3
Ike's	0.3	0.3
Drug Castle	0.3	0.3
Drug Mart	0.4	0.3
Drug Emporium (FL)	0.2	0.3
Lincoln Discount Drugs	0.2	0.2
Great American	0.2	0.2
Mr. Discount	0.2	0.2
Lincoln Drugs	0.1	0.1
RIX Dunnington	0.1	0.1
Harco	0.0	0.0

Source: *DM*, June 1992, p. 73.

★1654★

Drugstores (SIC 5912)

Drug and Cosmetics Sales by Outlet

Shares of 1991 sales by outlet are shown in percent, based on a total of $86.693 million.

Drug and proprietary stores	59.7%
Supermarkets and grocery stores	22.1
Discount stores	9.3
Department stores	6.1
Wholesale clubs	1.0
Variety stores	0.9
Mail order	0.5
Misc. general merchandise stores	0.4

Source: *DM*, June 1992, p. 75.

★1655★

Drugstores (SIC 5912)

Drugstores - U.K.

Market shares are shown in percent.

Boots	8.9%
Lloyds Chemists	5.6

Continued on next page.

★ 1655 ★ *Continued*

Drugstores (SIC 5912)

Drugstores - U.K.

Market shares are shown in percent.

All Co-op's 2.8%
Savory & Moore (McCarthy) 1.5
AAH 1.2
UniChem 1.2
Argyll (Safeway) 0.4
Other 78.4

Source: Investext, Thomson Financial Networks, March 11, 1992, from UBS Phillips & Drew Global Research Group.

★ 1656 ★

Drugstores (SIC 5912)

External Remedies Sales by Outlet

Sales of external and other remedies totaled $1.8 billion in 1991. The category includes foot remedies, acne remedies, eye drops, eye lotions, external analgesics, early pregnancy tests, topical hydrocortisones, contact-lens care, and diaper-rash preventive cream. Shares, by outlet, are shown in percent, based on that total.

Drugstores 48.9%
Food stores 31.1
Mass merchandisers 20.0

Source: *Drug Topics*, April 20, 1992, p. 62.

★ 1657 ★

Drugstores (SIC 5912)

Hair Care Market by Outlet

Sales of hair-care products (including conditioners, shampoos, hair-coloring preparations, hair fixatives, ethnic hair preparations, home permanents, men's hair preparations and hair mousses) totaled $4.3 billion in 1991. Shares, by retail outlet, are shown in percent, based on that total.

Food stores 38.1%
Drugstores 35.7
Mass merchandisers 26.2

Source: *Drug Topics*, April 20, 1992, p. 66.

★ 1658 ★

Drugstores (SIC 5912)

Health and Beauty Care Sales by Outlet

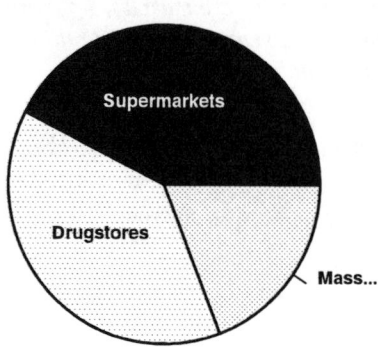

Shares by type of store are shown in percent, based on 1990 total sales.

Supermarkets 42.3%
Drugstores 38.3
Mass merchandisers 19.4

Source: *Grocery Marketing*, November 24, 1991, p. 14, from A.C. Nielsen.

★ 1659 ★

Drugstores (SIC 5912)

Largest Drugstore Sales

Sales of 11 leading drugstore chains totaled $35.769 million in 1991. (Thrifty Drug data include non-drug retail operations). Relative shares are converted to percent.

	Sales ($ mil)	% of Group
Walgreens	$ 6,733,044	18.8%
Eckerd	3,800,000	10.6
Rite Aid	3,784,376	10.6
American Drug Stores . . .	3,730,000	10.4
CVS	3,395,000	9.5
Thrifty Drug	3,300,000	9.2
Phar-Mor	2,875,000	8.0
Longs	2,365,916	6.6
Hooks-SupeRx	1,994,000	5.6
Pay Less Northwest	1,892,000	5.3
Revco	1,900,000	5.3

Source: *Stores*, July 1992, p. 35.

★1660★

Drugstores (SIC 5912)

Leading Drug Stores

Company revenues are shown in thousands of dollars. Percent shares are based on group total.

	Rev. ($ 000)	% of Group
Rite Aid	$ 2,737,900	27.0%
Longs	2,365,916	23.4
Walgreen	1,708,731	16.9
Revco	1,425,651	14.1
Drug Emporium	541,482	5.3
Big B	487,890	4.8
Genovese	447,159	4.4
Arbor Drug	232,238	2.3
Perry	175,454	1.7

Source: *Chain Store Age Executive*, April 1992, p. 72, from company reports.

★1661★

Drugstores (SIC 5912)

Oral Hygiene Market by Outlet

Sales of oral hygiene products, including toothbrushes, mouthwash, dental floss, dental cleaners, denture adhesives, and dentifrices, totaled $2.9 billion in 1991. Shares, by retail outlet, are shown in percent, based on that total.

Food Stores	75.9%
Drugstores	13.7
Mass merchandisers	10.5

Source: *Drug Topics*, April 20, 1992, p. 71.

★1662★

Drugstores (SIC 5912)

OTC Drug Sales by Outlet

Shares of OTC (over-the-counter) drug sales, by outlet, are shown in percent, based on total of $10.9 billion in 1991.

Drugstores	44.4%
Food stores	38.9
Mass merchandisers	16.7

Source: *Drug Topics*, April 20, 1992, p. 56.

★1663★

Drugstores (SIC 5912)

Prescription Drug Providers for Older Americans

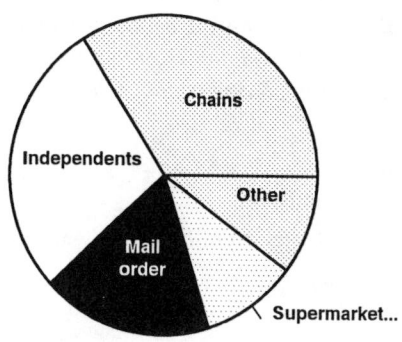

Shares of the prescription drug market for seniors, by outlet, are shown in percent.

Chains	34.0%
Independents	28.0
Mail order	18.0
Supermarket pharmacies	10.0
Other	10.0

Source: *Drug Topics*, May 4, 1992, p. 51.

★1664★

Drugstores (SIC 5912)

Prescription Drug Sales by Outlet

Shares of the total prescription sales market, by type of outlet, are shown in percent for the years 1990 and 1991.

	1990	1991
Chain	25.6%	24.9%
Independent	25.1	23.9
Hospital	23.2	23.0
Food store/pharmacy	6.0	6.2
Mass-merchandiser/pharmacy	5.7	6.0
Mail order	5.1	5.9
Clinic	2.7	3.2
Nursing home	2.6	2.9
Staff/HMO	2.3	2.4
Miscellaneous	1.7	1.6

Source: *Drug Topics*, May 4, 1992, p. 74, from IMS/DDD.

★ 1665 ★

Drugstores (SIC 5912)

Skin-Care Products Sales by Outlet

Sales of skin-care products totaled $2.2 billion in 1991. The category includes suntan lotions, suntan oils, baby lotions, baby oil, depilatories, face creams, and hand-and-body lotions. Shares, by outlet, are shown in percent, based on that total.

Drugstores	46.7%
Food stores	30.4
Mass merchandisers	22.9

Source: *Drug Topics*, April 20, 1992, p. 65.

★ 1666 ★

Drugstores (SIC 5912)

Sundries Market by Outlet

Shares of selected sundries sales, by outlet, are shown in percent, based on a total of $1.6 billion. This category includes batteries, flea collars for pets, and insect repellents.

Food stores	40.1%
Mass merchandisers	32.5
Drugstores	27.4

Source: *Drug Topics*, April 20, 1992, p. 75.

★ 1667 ★

Drugstores (SIC 5912)

Tooth-Whitening Market

Shares by retail outlet are shown in percent, based on total sales of $63 million in 1991.

Drugstores	57.1%
Food stores	42.9

Source: *Drug Topics*, March 23, 1992, p. 96, from Towne-Oller & Associates.

★ 1668 ★

Drugstores (SIC 5912)

Vitamin Sales by Retail Outlet

Shares of 1991 vitamin sales, by retail outlet, are shown in percent, based on a total of $1.1 billion.

Drugstores	54.1%
Food stores	29.7
Mass merchandisers	16.3

Source: *Drug Topics*, April 20, 1992, p. 100, from Nielsen Marketing Research.

★ 1669 ★

Retailing - Books (SIC 5942)

Bookstore Sales - 1992

Shares by type of store are shown in percent, based on 1992 total sales of $8.5 billion.

Multi-unit stores	68.0%
Single-unit stores	32.0

Source: *U.S. Industrial Outlook 1992*, p. 25-9, from U.S. Department of Commerce, Bureau of the Census.

★ 1670 ★

Retailing - Books (SIC 5942)

Children's Book Sales by Distribution Channel

Shares of children's book sales by distribution channel are shown in percent.

Children's only stores	52.7%
General/specialty stores	36.1
National/regional chains	33.2
College/university stores	6.8

Source: *Publishers Weekly*, January 13, 1992, p. 29.

★ 1671 ★

Retailing - Stationery (SIC 5943)

Stationery and Greeting Card Sales by Outlet

Shares of sales by outlet are shown in percent, based on a total of $10.691 million in 1991.

Discount stores	26.6%
Stationery stores	26.3
Drug and proprietary stores	20.1
Supermarkets and grocery stores	9.8
Variety stores	6.3
Department stores	4.0
Bookstores	3.3
Mail order	1.9
Misc. general merchandise stores	1.7

Source: *DM*, June 1992, p. 77.

★ 1672 ★

Retailing - Jewelry (SIC 5944)

Jewelry and Watch Sales by Outlet

Shares of sales by outlet are shown in percent, based on a total of $21.051 million in 1991.

Jewelry stores	61.5%
Department stores	12.9
Discount stores	9.0
Catalog showrooms	8.9
Misc. general merchandise stores	3.6
Gift, novelty and souvenir shops	1.8
Mail order	1.6
Variety stores	0.7

Source: *DM*, June 1992, p. 75.

★ 1673 ★

Retailing - Toys (SIC 5945)

Top Toy Store Chains

Shares are shown in percent based on a total market of $13.3 billion in 1991.

Toys "R" Us	19.0%
Wal-Mart	10.2
KMart	7.1
Target	4.9
Kay-Bee	4.6
Other	54.2

Source: *USA TODAY*, May 28, 1992, p. B1, from Toy Manufacturers of America.

★ 1674 ★

Retailing - Toys and Games (SIC 5945)

Toy, Hobby Goods, Game Sales by Outlet

Shares of sales by outlet are shown in percent, based on a total of $14.004 million in 1991.

Hobby, toy, game stores	38.2%
Discount stores	34.7
Drug and proprietary stores	7.4
Supermarkets and grocery stores	5.0
Variety stores	4.8
Mail order	3.4
Department stores	3.0
Misc. general merchandise stores	2.2
Catalog showrooms	1.3

Source: *DM*, June 1992, p. 76.

★ 1675 ★

Retailing - Photo Supplies (SIC 5946)

Camera and Photo Supply Sales by Outlet

Shares of 1991 sales by outlet are shown in percent, based on a total of $7.996 million.

Camera and photo supply stores	25.8%
Drugstores	26.8
Discount stores	25.4
Supermarket and grocery stores	13.1
Catalog showrooms	3.9
Department stores	2.7
Misc. general merchandise stores	1.6
Variety stores	0.7

Source: *DM*, June 1992, p. 76.

★ 1676 ★

Retailing - Fabrics (SIC 5949)

Linen, Domestics, Fabrics Sales by Outlet

Shares of sales by outlet are shown in percent, based on a total of $20.637 million in 1991.

Discount stores	29.0%
Department stores	19.3
Sewing, piece goods stores	15.2
Wholesale clubs	12.2
Home furnishing stores	6.5
Drapery, fabric stores	6.3
Mail order	3.7
Furniture stores	2.4
Family apparel stores	2.2
Variety stores	2.1
Misc. general merchandise stores	1.1

Source: *DM*, June 1992, p. 74.

★ 1677 ★

Mail Order (SIC 5961)

Mail Order Leaders

Company mail-order sales are shown in millions of dollars. Shares are based on group total.

	Sales ($ mil.)	% of Group
United Services Automobile Assn.	$ 4,867.5	11.6%
Time Warner	3,471.1	8.3
Sears, Roebuck & Co.	3,445.3	8.2
J. C. Penney	3,169.8	7.5
American Assn. of Retired Persons	2,767.5	6.6
Tele-Communications	2,644.9	6.3
Reader's Digest	2,032.1	4.8
GEICO	1,785.0	4.2
Primerica	1,674.6	4.0
AT&T	1,443.5	3.4
Otto Versand	1,383.4	3.3
Comcast Cable	1,102.1	2.6
Marmon Holdings	1,100.0	2.6
Home Shopping Network	1,078.5	2.6
MCI	1,028.5	2.4
H. R. Block	1,000.0	2.4
Digital Equipment Corp.	1,000.0	2.4
United Artists	955.2	2.3
Continental Cablevision	929.8	2.2
QVC Network	921.8	2.2
IBM	900.0	2.1
American Automobile Assn.	886.6	2.1
Leucadia National	873.2	2.1
United Telecommunications	838.8	2.0
21st Century Industries	741.6	1.8

Source: *Direct Marketing*, July 1992, p. 21.

★ 1678 ★

Mail Order (SIC 5961)

Mail Order Leaders - U.K.

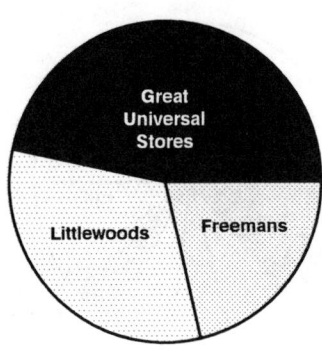

Estimated market shares are shown in percent.

Great Universal Stores 35.0%
Littlewoods 24.0
Freemans 16.3

Source: Investext, Thomson Financial Networks, June 15, 1992, from Barclays de Zoete Wedd Securities.

★ 1679 ★

Mail Order (SIC 5961)

Mail Order Sales

Mail order sales and contributions totaled $200,670 million in 1990 and $211,080 million in 1991. Shares are shown in percent for the same periods.

	1990	1991
Consumer products and services . . .	48.9%	51.2%
Business products and services . . .	26.6	25.6
Charitable contributions	24.4	23.2

Source: *Direct Marketing*, July 1992, p. 30.

★ 1680 ★

Retailing - Flowers (SIC 5992)

Flower Sales

Shares of the total flower retail market, by type of outlet, are shown in percent for the years 1981 and 1991.

	1981	1991
Florists	63.0%	58.0%
Nonflorists	37.0	42.0

Source: *Business Week*, April 27, 1992, p. 44, from Society of American Florists.

★ 1681 ★

Retailing - Tobacco (SIC 5993)

Cigar, Cigarette, Tobacco Sales by Outlet

Shares of sales by outlet are shown in percent, based on a total of $20.89 million in 1991.

Supermarkets and grocery stores 66.7%
Drug and proprietary stores 16.6
Automatic merchandising machines 5.2
Discount stores 5.1
Cigar stores and stands 2.8
Wholesale clubs 1.9
Misc. general merchandise stores 0.8
Department stores 0.7
Variety stores 0.2

Source: *DM*, June 1992, p. 77.

★ 1682 ★

Airport Retailers (SIC 5999)

Airport Retailers

Shares of retail establishments in airports are shown in percent.

Host 45.0-50.0%
Dobbs Houses 23.0
Concession Air 15.0
Other 15.0-17.0

Source: Investext, Thomson Financial Networks, June 30, 1992, from Shearson Lehman Brothers, Inc.

★ 1683 ★

Miscellaneous Retail (SIC 5999)

Foam Pad Retail

Data are based on survey conducted by "Comfort Sleeper" in 1991. Percentages show where consumers expect to purchase pads.

Department stores	55.0%
Specialty stores	21.0
Discount stores	20.0
Not sure	4.0

Source: *HFD*, May 18, 1992, p. 62, from *Comfort Sleeper*.

★ 1684 ★

Retailing - Batteries (SIC 5999)

Rechargeable Battery Sales by Outlet

Market shares by outlet are shown as percent of total sales.

Discount stores	38.0%
Radio Shack	18.0
Hardware stores	11.0
Miscellaneous	8.0
Department stores	7.0
Drugstores	5.0
Catalog-Showroom	5.0
Warehouses	5.0
Food stores	3.0

Source: *HFD*, January 1992, p. 18.

★ 1685 ★

Retailing - Hair Care Appliances (SIC 5999)

Hair Care Appliance Sales by Outlet

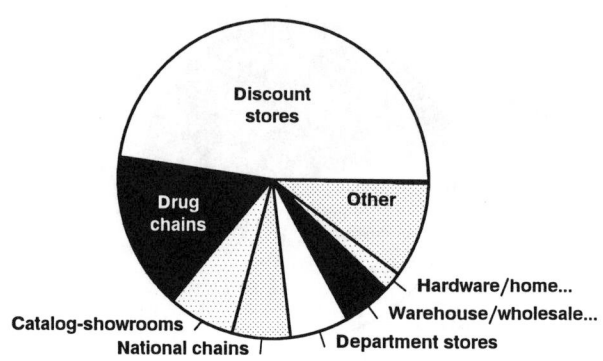

Market shares by channel of distribution are shown in percent for 1989 and 1990.

	1989	1990
Discount stores	48.0%	48.0%
Drug chains	16.0	16.0
Catalog-showrooms	6.0	7.0
National chains	8.0	6.0
Department stores	6.0	6.0
Warehouse/wholesale clubs	2.0	5.0
Hardware/home centers	2.0	2.0
Other	12.0	10.0

Source: *HFD*, January 1992, p. 3.

★ 1686 ★

Retailing - Kitchen Gadgets (SIC 5999)

Kitchen Gadget Sales by Outlet

Shares by retail class are shown as percent of 1990 total sales.

Supermarkets	40.0%
Mass merchants	34.0
Department stores	12.0
Specialty stores	6.9
Hardware	4.0
Other	4.0

Source: *HFD*, February 1992, p. 6.

★ 1687 ★

Retailing - Massagers (SIC 5999)

Massager Sales by Outlet Type

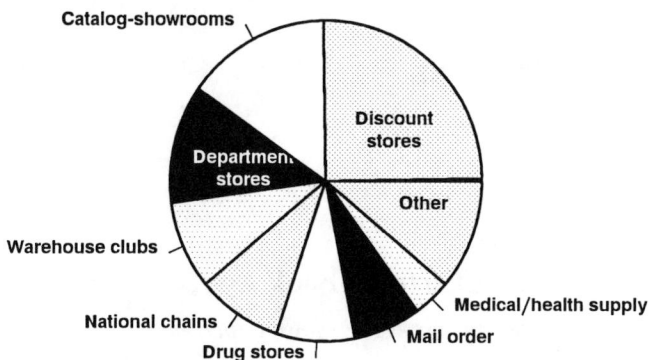

Market shares by channel of distribution are shown in percent.

Discount stores	25.0%
Catalog-showrooms	15.0
Department stores	12.0
Warehouse clubs	9.0
National chains	9.0
Drug stores	8.0
Mail order	7.0
Medical/health supply	4.0
Other	11.0

Source: *HFD*, December 1991, p. 4.

SIC 60 - Depository Institutions

★1688★

Banks (SIC 6000)

Largest Banks in the Asia/Pacific Region

Percentages reflect shares of group total assets under custody. They are defined as cross-border assets held in the Asia/Pacific region.

	Assets ($ bil.)	% of Group
Citicorp	$40	32.8%
Hongkong Bank	38	31.1
Chase Manhattan	30	24.6
Standard Chartered	14	11.5

Source: *Far Eastern Economic Review*, February 27, 1992, p. 55, from Review data.

★1689★

Banks (SIC 6020)

Canada's Leading Banks

Assets of the six leading banks in FY 1991 are shown in billions of Canadian dollars; relative market shares are shown for the same period. Asset figures do not include acceptances.

	Assets ($C bil.)	% of Group
Royal	$125.1	24.3%
CIBC	113.3	22.0
Montreal	95.0	18.4
Scotia	83.3	16.2
Toronto-Dominion	63.2	12.3
National	35.1	6.8

Source: *The Economist*, March 28, 1992, p. 88, from IBCA.

★1690★

Banks (SIC 6020)

Canadian Chartered Bank Assets

Relative market shares are shown in percent for FY1991.

Royal	24.23%
Commerce	22.16
Montreal	18.08
Nova Scotia	16.24
Toronto-Dominion	12.62
National	6.67

Source: Investext, Thomson Financial Networks, January 2, 1992, from Midland Walwyn Capital Inc.

★1691★

Banks (SIC 6020)

Canadian Chartered Bank Deposits

Relative market shares are shown in percent for FY1991.

Royal	24.14%
Commerce	21.95
Montreal	19.03
Nova Scotia	15.41
Toronto-Dominion	12.57
National	6.89

Source: Investext, Thomson Financial Networks, January 2, 1992, from Midland Walwyn Capital Inc.

★1692★

Banks (SIC 6020)

Commercial Banks

Leading banks are shown with assets as of December 31, 1991 in millions of dollars and relative market share in percent.

	Assets ($ mil.)	% of Group
Citicorp	$ 216,922	13.6%
Chemical Banking	138,930	8.7
BankAmerica	115,509	7.3
NationsBank	110,319	6.9
J.P. Morgan	103,468	6.5
Chase Manhattan	98,197	6.2
Security Pacific	76,411	4.8
Bankers Trust New York	63,959	4.0
Wells Fargo	53,547	3.4
First Chicago	48,963	3.1
First Interstate Bancorp	48,922	3.1
Banc One	46,293	2.9
First Union	46,085	2.9
Fleet/Norstar Financial Group	45,445	2.9
PNC Financial	44,892	2.8
Bank of New York	39,426	2.5
Norwest	38,502	2.4
Suntrust Banks	34,554	2.2
Wachovia	33,158	2.1
Barnett Banks	32,721	2.1
Bank of Boston	32,700	2.1
Republic New York	31,221	2.0
First Fidelity Bancorporation	30,215	1.9
NBD Bancorp	29,513	1.9
Mellon Bank	29,355	1.8

Source: *Business Week*, April 27, 1992, p. 98.

★1693★

Banks (SIC 6020)

Five-Star Commercial Banks

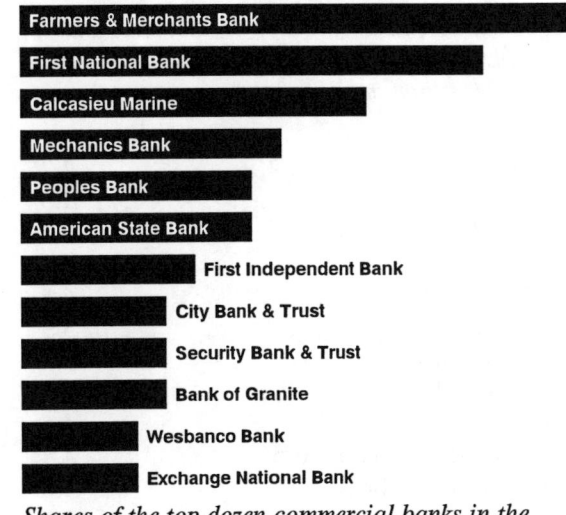

Shares of the top dozen commercial banks in the U.S. in which tangible capital exceeds nine percent, the risk-based capital ratio exceeds nine and a quarter percent, and the bank is soundly invested and profitable. Percentages are based on group total.

	Assets ($ 000)	% of Group
Farmers & Merchants Bank	$ 1,432,963	19.4%
First National Bank	1,210,324	16.3
Calcasieu Marine	884,149	11.9
Mechanics Bank	677,645	9.2
Peoples Bank	560,332	7.6
American State Bank	559,368	7.6
First Independent Bank	431,828	5.8
City Bank & Trust	388,768	5.3
Security Bank & Trust	364,026	4.9
Bank of Granite	334,174	4.5
Wesbanco Bank	302,856	4.1
Exchange National Bank	256,977	3.5

Source: *Bankers Monthly*, May 1992, p. 10, from Bauer Financial Reports.

★1694★

Banks (SIC 6020)

Leading Banks of North America

Relative market shares of the top 16 Canadian and U.S. banks are shown in percent, based on a total of $1,363,734 million in assets for the group.

Citicorp	15.1%
Chemical Banking Corp.	9.4

Continued on next page.

★ 1694 ★ *Continued*

Banks (SIC 6020)

Leading Banks of North America

Relative market shares of the top 16 Canadian and U.S. banks are shown in percent, based on a total of $1,363,734 million in assets for the group.

BankAmerica Corp.	7.7%
Royal Bank of Canada	7.5
Chase Manhattan Corp.	6.8
CIBC	6.8
J.P. Morgan & Co. Inc.	6.5
Security Pacific Corp.	5.9
Bank of Montreal	5.2
Bank of Nova Scotia	5.2
NCNB Corp.	4.5
Bankers Trust New York Corp.	4.4
Toronto-Dominion Bank	4.0
Wells Fargo & Co.	3.9
First Interstate Bancorp.	3.6
C&S/Sovran Corp.	3.6

Source: *The Globe and Mail*, July 16, 1991, p. B2, from InfoGlobe.

★ 1695 ★

Banks (SIC 6020)

Leading Banks Worldwide

Capital of the largest banks worldwide in 1990 is shown in billions of dollars.

Sumitomo	$ 15.7
Dai-ichi Kangyo	14.8
Fuji	13.8
Sanwa	13.4
Union Bank of Switzerland	13.2
Credit Agricole	13.2
Mitsui Taiyo Kobe	12.2
Barclays	11.9
Mitsubishi	11.9
National Westminster	10.7

Source: *The Economist*, May 22, 1992, p. 4, from *The Banker*.

★ 1696 ★

Banks (SIC 6021)

Banks - U.K.

United Kingdom banks are ranked by percent share of capital.

Barclays	10.9%
NatWest	9.7
Abbey National	4.5
Loyds	4.1
Midland	4.1
Royal Bank of Scotland	2.4
TSB	2.0
Bank of Scotland	1.8

Source: Investext, Thomson Financial Networks, April 7, 1992, from Nikko Securities Co., Ltd.

★ 1697 ★

Banks (SIC 6021)

Largest American Banks

Top banks are shown with assets as of 12/31/91 in billions of dollars. Percent shares are based on the group total. BankAmerica merged with Security Pacific.

	Assets ($ bil.)	% of Group
Citicorp	$ 217	28.5%
BankAmerica	192	25.2
Chemical Banking	139	18.2
NationsBank	110	14.4
J.P. Morgan	104	13.6

Source: *USA TODAY*, March 25, 1992, p. 1B, from Keefe, Bruyette & Woods.

★ 1698 ★

Banks (SIC 6021)

Largest Foreign Banks

Banks are ranked by 1990 total assets, shown in millions of dollars. Percent shares are based on group total.

	Assets ($ mil.)	% of Group
Dai-Ichi Kangyo Bank (Japan)	$ 457,024	4.8%
Sumitomo Bank (Japan)	446,321	4.7
Fuji Bank (Japan)	436,822	4.6
Sanwa Bank (Japan)	435,039	4.6
Mitsui Taiyo Kobe Bank (Japan)	434,027	4.6
Mitsubishi Bank (Japan)	381,513	4.0
Industrial Bank of Japan (Japan)	320,394	3.4
Banque Nationale de Paris (France)	291,962	3.1
Credit Lyonnais (France)	287,418	3.0
Tokai Bank (Japan)	268,375	2.8
Deutsche Bank (Germany)	266,504	2.8
Barclays (U.K.)	260,399	2.7
Bank of Tokyo (Japan)	252,181	2.7
National Westminster Bank (U.K.)	233,784	2.5
ABN AMRO Holdings (Netherlands)	233,246	2.5
Long-Term Credit Bank (Japan)	229,639	2.4
Societe Generale (France)	220,050	2.3
Dresdner Bank (Germany)	189,199	2.0
Cie Financiere de Paribas (France)	185,640	2.0
Uninon Bank of Switzerland (Switzerland)	183,515	1.9
Internationale Nederlanden (Netherlands)	163,623	1.7
Cie De Suez (France)	157,819	1.7
HSBC Holdings (Hong Kong)	148,535	1.6
Commerzbank (Germany)	143,808	1.5
Mitsubishi Trust & Banking (Japan)	139,491	1.5
Bayerische Vereinsbank (Germany)	137,081	1.4
Banca Nazionale del Lavoro (Italy)	131,804	1.4
Nippon Crekit Bank (Japan)	130,509	1.4
Swiss Bank Corp. (Switzerland)	130,375	1.4
Daiwa Bank (Japan)	129,769	1.4
Sumitomo Trst & Banking (Japan)	126,417	1.3

	Assets ($ mil.)	% of Group
Kyowa Saitama Bank (Japan)	$ 120,152	1.3%
CS Holding (Switzerland)	117,392	1.2
Gan-Assurances Nationales (France)	116,937	1.2
Bayerische Hypotheken (Germany)	116,174	1.2
Midland Bank (U.K.)	115,127	1.2
Mitsui Trust & Banking (Japan)	108,953	1.2
Royal Bank of Canada (Canada)	107,916	1.1
Lloyds Bank (U.K.)	106,567	1.1
Allianz Holding (Germany)	98,691	1.0
UAP-Union des Assurances (France)	97,876	1.0
Bank of Yokohama (Japan)	97,864	1.0
Canadian Imperial Bank of Commerce (Canada)	97,855	1.0
Yasuda Trst & Banking (Japan)	93,969	1.0
Banca Commerciale Italiana (Italy)	93,161	1.0
Abbey National (U.K.)	89,761	0.9
Westpac Banking (Australia)	88,422	0.9
Banco Bilbao Vizcaya (Spain)	86,673	0.9
Hokkaido Takushoku Bank (Japan)	81,825	0.9
ANZ Group (Australia)	81,605	0.9

Source: *Financial World*, March 1992, p. 64.

★ 1699 ★

Trusts (SIC 6021)

Leading Corporate Trusts

Shares of the market are shown in percent, based on principal outstanding as of December 1990.

Chemical Bank	14.7%
Citibank, N.A.	9.8
Bankers Trust	7.7
Bank of New York	6.5
State Street Bank & Trust	5.6
Security Pacific	5.1
United States Trust Co. of N.Y.	4.8
First Chicago	4.5
Chase Manhattan	4.4
Morgan Guaranty Trust	4.0
Nations Bank	3.3
Fuji Bank & Trust	2.4

Continued on next page.

★ 1699 ★ *Continued*
Trusts (SIC 6021)

Leading Corporate Trusts

Shares of the market are shown in percent, based on principal outstanding as of December 1990.

First Interstate	2.4%
Continental Bank	2.4
Shawmut National	2.4
BankAmerica	2.3
First Fidelity	2.0
Bank of Montreal/Harris Trust	1.9
First Bank System	1.7
IBJ Schroder Bank & Trust Co.	1.5
Mellon Bank	1.5
Bank of Tokyo Trust Co.	1.2
Bank of Boston	1.2
Marine Midland Bank	1.1
Norwest Corp.	1.0
Ameritrust Corporation	1.0
PNC Financial Corp.	1.3
Sun Trust	0.8
First Union Corp.	0.8
Banc One	0.7
Other	20.9

Source: Investext, Thomson Financial Networks, May 15, 1992, from Alex Brown & Sons, Inc.

★ 1700 ★
Trusts (SIC 6021)

New Master Trust/Master Custody Businesses

Company shares are ranked by new tax-exempt business for year ended June 30, 1991. Shares are based on the top 40 companies total of $134.8 million, shown in percent.

Bankers Trust	15.9%
State Street	14.7
Chase Manhattan	12.6
Bank of New York	8.9
Security Pacific	8.9
Mellon Bank	6.4
Northern Trust	6.2
Nations Bank	4.5
U.S. Trust	3.4
Ameritrust	3.1
Boston Safe Deposit	2.4
CoreStates Financial	2.2
First Interstate	1.9

First Nat'l/MD	1.3%
Harris Trust	1.0
NBD Bancorp	0.9

Source: Investext, Thomson Financial Networks, May 15, 1992, from Alex. Brown & Sons, Inc. and Pension & Investments.

★ 1701 ★
Money Orders (SIC 6090)

The Money Order Market

Shares of the total money order market in the U.S. are shown in percent, based on an 1991 industry total of $81.11 billion.

Traveler's Express	29.0%
First Data Corporation	21.0
U.S. Postal Service	20.0
Other	30.0

Source: Investext, Thomson Financial Networks, June 30, 1992, from The First Boston Corporation and The Nilson Report.

★ 1702 ★
Money Orders (SIC 6090)

The Official Check Market

Market shares of the total Official Check (introduced by American Express in 1983) industry, are shown in percent, based on a 1991 industry total of $675 million.

In-house providers	89.0%
First Data Corporation	5.0
Other	6.0

Source: Investext, Thomson Financial Networks, June 30, 1992, from The First Boston Corporation and First Data Corporation.

★1703★

Automated Banking (SIC 6099)

Automated Banking - Canada

Canadian chartered bank shares of ABMs (automated banking machines) are shown in percent based on a total of 10,091 machines at the end of FY1991.

Royal	35.6%
Commerce	23.5
Toronto-Dominion	12.6
Montreal	11.9
Nova Scotia	10.4
National	4.4
Laurentian	1.5

Source: Investext, Thomson Financial Networks, January 2, 1992, from Midland Walwyn Capital Inc.

★1704★

Bank Services (SIC 6099)

Bank Outsourcing Contracts

Biggest bank outsourcing contracts for computer services are shown with estimated revinues in millions of dollars for the 1989-1991 period. Service vendor names appear in parentheses. Relative shares are shown in percent.

	Rev. ($ mil.)	% of Group
First Fidelty (EDS)	$ 450	13.0%
First American Bankshares (Perot)	400	11.6
Continental Bank (IBM, Ernst & Young)	400	11.6
Signet Bank (EDS)	300	8.7
Glendale Federal/Gesco (Flserv)	300	8.7
Great Western Financial (EDS)	300	8.7
Meritor Savings Bank (EDS)	250	7.2
NCNB (Perot)	200	5.8
Riggs National Bank (IBM)	160	4.6
Hibernia National Bank (IBM)	150	4.3
First Tennessee National Bank (IBM)	150	4.3

	Rev. ($ mil.)	% of Group
Bank South (IBM)	$ 120	3.5%
Team Bank (Systematics)	100	2.9
Integra (Union National Bank) (Systematics)	100	2.9
Federal Home Loan Bank S.F. (Systematics)	80	2.3

Source: *Informationweek*, January 6, 1992, p. 13, from Merrill Lynch.

★1705★

Credit Card Management (SIC 6099)

Leading Credit Card Processors

The top ten domestic processors are shown with millions of credit card and EFT (electronic funds transfer) transactions in 1990. Relative market shares are shown in percent for the same period.

	Trans. (mil.)	% of Group
First Data Resources	1,250	21.6%
Total Systems Services	750	12.9
VisaNet Point-of Sale Services	648	11.2
SSBA America	560	9.7
J.C. Penney Business Services	519	9.0
National Processing Company	495	8.5
National Bankcard Corp.	421	7.3
National Data Corp.	410	7.1
BT North America Inc.	400	6.9
BUYPASS Inc.	341	5.9

Source: Investext, Thomson Financial Networks, June 30, 1992, from The First Boston Corporation.

★1706★

Credit Card Management (SIC 6099)

Third Party Processors

Shares of domestic third party bank-card accounts on file are shown in percent for 1991.

First Data Corporation	46.7%
Total Systems Services	27.8
J.C. Penney Business Services	6.2
SSBA America	4.0
Credit Systems Inc.	3.9
Telecredit Card Center	3.4
Electronic Data Systems	2.7
Atlantic States Bankcard Assn.	2.3
First Security Service Co.	1.6

Continued on next page.

★1706★ *Continued*

Credit Card Management (SIC 6099)

Third Party Processors

Shares of domestic third party bank-card accounts on file are shown in percent for 1991.

Rocky Mountain Bankcard 0.5%
Other 0.9

Source: Investext, Thomson Financial Networks, June 30, 1992, from The First Boston Corporation.

SIC 61 - Nondepository Institutions

★1707★
Loans (SIC 6100)

Commercial Lending Institutions for Small Businesses

Commercial lending institutions are ranked according to the amount of credit they provide to small and medium-sized businesses. "Other" includes owners, other individuals or businesses, money-market mutual fund companies, brokerages, mortgage banks, and insurance companies. Shares, by institution type, are shown in percent.

Commercial bank	48.0%
Finance company	14.0
Thrift institution	7.0
Leasing company	5.0
Other	26.0

Source: *INC.*, June 1991, p. 129, from Federal Reserve System.

★1708★
Credit Cards (SIC 6141)

Credit Card Circulation

Circulation in the U.S. is shown in millions with relative market shares in percent.

	No. of Cards	% of Group
Visa	144	47.2%
MasterCard	93	30.5
Sears Discover	42	13.8
American Express	26	8.5

Source: *USA TODAY*, September 30, 1992, p. 10B.

★1709★
Credit Cards (SIC 6141)

Credit Card Market

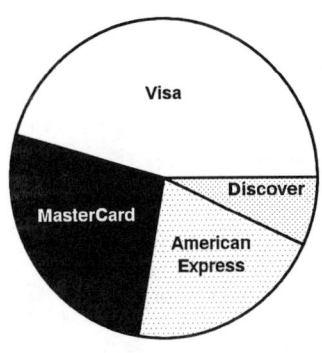

1991 shares of the general-purpose credit card market ($371.1 billion) are shown in percent.

Visa	45.9%
MasterCard	26.6
American Express	20.6
Discover	6.7

Source: *Advertising Age*, August 31, 1992, p. 9, from SMR Research Corp.

★1710★
Credit Cards (SIC 6141)

Credit Cards by Lender

Shares are shown in percent, based on 25 issuers who make up 75% of the domestic market.

	1987	1992
Bank credit cards	80.0%	62.0%
Non-bank credit cards	20.0	38.0

Source: *USA TODAY*, September 9, 1992, p. 1B, from *Credit Card News*.

★ 1711 ★
Credit Cards (SIC 6141)

Revolving Credit Cards - 1991

Companies are ranked by 1991 total accounts, shown in millions of dollars. Percent shares are based on the group total.

	Accts. ($ mil.)	% of Group
Citibank	$ 21.42	29.1%
Chase Manhattan	10.00	13.6
AT&T Universal	7.60	10.3
First Chicago	7.05	9.6
MBNA	5.27	7.2
BankAmerica	4.22	5.7
Household Bank	4.10	5.6
Wells Fargo	3.08	4.2
Bank of New York	3.07	4.2
Manufacturers Hanover	3.30	4.5
Chemical (pre-merger)	2.50	3.4
Security Pacific	2.08	2.8

Source: Investext, Thomson Financial Networks, May 7, 1992, from The First Boston Corporation.

★ 1712 ★
Credit Cards (SIC 6141)

Top Credit-Card Issuers - U.S.

Biggest 1991 card issuers by number of cards outstanding (loans unsettled) and charge volume. 1991 volume shares are shown in percent.

	Cards (mil.)	Volume ($ bil.)	% of Group
Citibank	30.1	$ 42.48	34.7%
First Chicago	10.3	14.08	11.5
AT&T	12.0	13.21	10.8
Chase	13.6	13.11	10.7
MBNA	7.0	12.40	10.1
Bank America	7.5	9.89	8.1
Chemical	6.8	6.54	5.3
Bank of NY	4.5	3.81	3.1
Bank One	4.5	3.71	3.0
Household	5.7	3.12	2.6

Source: *The Wall Street Journal*, April 17, 1992, p. B1, from *The Nilson Report*.

★ 1713 ★
Agricultural Loans (SIC 6159)

Farm Credit Lenders

Shares, by lender, are shown in percent, based on a total farm debt of $139.3 billion in 1991. Commodity Credit Corp. held $4.0 million of debt, the equivalent of 3/10 of one percent of the total.

Commercial banks	35.4%
Farm Credit System	24.7
Farmers Home Administration	12.3
Life insurance companies	7.2
Commodity Credit Corp.	-
Individuals and others	20.4

Source: *Farm Journal*, May 1992, p. 21, from USDA.

★ 1714 ★
Loan Brokers (SIC 6159)

Loan Syndications

Companies are ranked by 1991 sales shown in millions of dollars. Percent shares are based on group totals.

	($ mil.)	% of Group
Citicorp	$ 78,148	10.5%
Chemical	50,992	6.8
J.P. Morgan	45,201	6.1
Barclays	41,955	5.6
First Chicago	32,059	4.3
Credit Suisse/CSFB	30,288	4.1
Natwest	29,224	3.9
Chase Manhattan	28,109	3.8
Bankers Trust	27,481	3.7
NCNB	27,281	3.7
Bank of Nova Scotia	26,467	3.6
Credit Lyonnais	25,956	3.5
Bank of America	25,549	3.4
ABN AMRO	24,586	3.3
Toronto Dominion	24,475	3.3
Manufacturers Hanover	21,560	2.9
Sumitomo Bank	20,406	2.7

Continued on next page.

Loan Brokers (SIC 6159)

Loan Syndications

Companies are ranked by 1991 sales shown in millions of dollars. Percent shares are based on group totals.

	($ mil.)	% of Group
Sanwa	.$ 20,150	2.7%
Bank of New York	17,825	2.4
Union Bank Switzerland	16,490	2.2
Swiss Bank	15,758	2.1
Canadian Imperial	14,570	2.0
Dai-Ichi Kangyo	14,435	1.9
Fuji Bank	13,935	1.9
Royal Bank Canada	13,730	1.8
Continental	13,634	1.8
Long-Term Credit Bank	13,155	1.8
Midland	11,007	1.5
Westpac	10,416	1.4
Industrial Bank of Japan	10,276	1.4

Source: *Investment Dealers' Digest*, January 20, 1992, p. 16, from IDD Loanbase.

★ 1715 ★
Mortgage Loans (SIC 6162)

Canadian Residential Mortgage Shares

Company shares are shown in percent for FY1991.

Royal	26.40%
Commerce	23.24
Montreal	14.87
Nova Scotia	13.24
Toronto-Dominion	14.95
National	7.30

Source: Investext, Thomson Financial Networks, January 2, 1992, from Midland Walwyn Capital Inc.

SIC 62 - Security and Commodity Brokers

★1716★

Investment Banking (SIC 6211)

Biggest 25 Stock Funds

Company assets are shown in billions of dollars and as percent of group total.

	Assets ($ bil.)	% of Group
Fidelity Magellan	$ 19.8	15.3%
Investment Co. of America . . .	11.4	8.8
Washington Mutual Inv.	8.4	6.5
Vanguard Windsor	8.1	6.3
Fidelity Puritan	5.2	4.0
Vanguard Index 500	4.9	3.8
Fidelity Equity-Income	4.5	3.5
20th Century Select	4.4	3.4
American Mutual	4.3	3.3
Pioneer II	4.3	3.3
Templeton World	4.1	3.2
Dean Witter Dividend Gro. . . .	4.1	3.2
Income Fund of America	4.1	3.2
Vanguard Windsor II	4.1	3.2
20th Century Growth	4.0	3.1
AIM Weingarten	3.9	3.0
Janus	3.8	2.9
20th Century Ultra	3.8	2.9
Fidelity Growth & Income . . .	3.7	2.9
Growth Fund of America	3.6	2.8
Affiliated Fund	3.5	2.7
Templeton Growth	3.1	2.4
Putnam Growth & Income A . .	3.0	2.3
Prudential Utility B	2.8	2.2
Dreyfus Fund	2.7	2.1

Source: *USA TODAY*, July 6, 1992, p. 3B, from Lipper Analytical Services.

★1717★

Investment Banking (SIC 6211)

Black Enterprise Underwriters

Largest black-owned investment banks are ranked by amount underwritten in billions of dollars. Relative market shares are shown in percent.

	($ bil.)	% of Group
Pryor, McClendon, Counts & Co., Inc.	$ 19.637	29.1%
Grigsby Brandford & Co., Inc. . .	14.810	21.9
W.R. Lazard & Co.	12.774	18.9
M.R. Beal & Co.	11.958	17.7
Apex Securities, Inc.	2.061	3.1
Ward & Associates, Inc.	1.401	2.1
Weldon, Sullivan, Carmichael & Co.	1.228	1.8
Brooks Securities, Inc.	0.994	1.5
Howard Gary & Co.	0.902	1.3
United Daniels Securities, Inc. . .	0.731	1.1
The Chapman Co.	0.694	1.0
Charles A. Bell Securities Corp. .	0.323	0.5

Source: *Black Enterprise*, October 1991, p. 70, from Securities Data Inc.

★1718★
Investment Banking (SIC 6211)

Brokerage Firms - Leaders

The five leading brokerage firms in the U.S. are ranked according to revenues in millions of dollars. Relative shares are shown in percent. The figure for A. G. Edwards represents a fiscal year ended February 28, 1991; figures for the remaining four brokerage firms represent a fiscal year ended December 31, 1990.

	Rev. ($ mil.)	% of Group
Merrill Lynch	$ 11,200	37.7%
Salomon Inc.	8,900	30.0
Morgan Stanley	5,900	19.9
PaineWebber	3,000	10.1
A.G. Edwards	675	2.3

Source: *St. Louis Business Journal*, January 6, 1992, p. 12, from Value Line and companies listed.

★1719★
Investment Banking (SIC 6211)

Chemical Deal Advisors

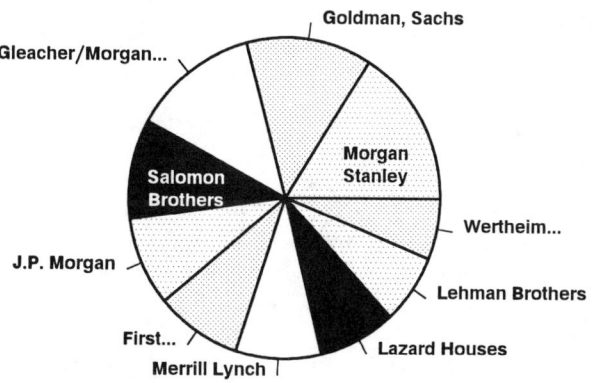

The 10 leading financial advisors in chemical industry deals (closed May 1-October 31, 1991) are ranked by value in millions of dollars. Relative market shares are shown in percent.

	Value ($ mil.)	% of Group
Morgan Stanley	$ 1,428	16.2%
Goldman, Sachs	1,168	13.3
Gleacher/Morgan Grenfell	1,158	13.2
Salomon Brothers	840	9.5
J.P. Morgan	821	9.3
First Boston/Credit Suisse	800	9.1
Merrill Lynch	$ 750	8.5%
Lazard Houses	706	8.0
Lehman Brothers	618	7.0
Wertheim Schroder	510	5.8

Source: *Chemicalweek*, November 27, 1991, p. 27, from Securities Data, investment advisors, and *Chemicalweek* calculations.

★1720★
Investment Banking (SIC 6211)

Chemical Industry Underwriters

The top 10 chemical industry securities (debt and equity) underwriters (full credit to lead manager; May 1 - October 31) are ranked by proceeds in millions of dollars. The relative market share is shown in percent.

	Proceeds ($ mil.)	% of Group
Merrill Lynch	$ 942.2	22.4%
Lehman Brothers	689.7	16.4
Salomon Brothers	498.3	11.9
Lazard Houses	249.4	5.9
Morgan Stanley	248.1	5.9
Goldman, Sachs	229.7	5.5
J.P. Morgan	199.0	4.7
Montgomery Securities	188.9	4.5
Robertson Stephens	162.4	3.9
PaineWebber	119.8	2.9
All others	675.2	16.1

Source: *Chemicalweek*, November 27, 1991, p. 22, from Securities Data and *Chemicalweek* calculations.

★1721★
Investment Banking (SIC 6211)

Common Stock Issuers

Shares, by lead manager, are shown as percent of the total market in the first half of 1990 and 1991. Industry totals were $12,876.0 million in 1990 and $26,009.1 million in 1991.

	1990	1991
Goldman, Sachs	19.1%	20.3%
Alex Brown & Sons	13.2	13.0
Merrill Lynch	10.2	11.8
Morgan Stanley	3.3	8.1

Continued on next page.

Investment Banking (SIC 6211)

Common Stock Issuers

Shares, by lead manager, are shown as percent of the total market in the first half of 1990 and 1991. Industry totals were $12,876.0 million in 1990 and $26,009.1 million in 1991.

	1990	1991
Salomon Brothers	8.9%	7.5%
First Boston	5.5	7.3
Lehman Brothers	8.8	5.9
Donaldson, Lufkin & Jenrette	0.7	4.1
Smith Barney, Harris Upham	4.6	2.8
Prudential Securities	1.8	2.6
PaineWebber	8.7	2.4
Kidder, Peabody	1.1	2.2
Robertson Stephens	0.7	1.5
Hambrecht & Quist	0.7	1.4
Montgomery Securities	0.7	1.3

Source: *Investment Dealers' Digest*, July 8, 1991, p. 21, from IDD Information Services.

★ 1722 ★

Investment Banking (SIC 6211)

CPI Securities Issuers

Leading issuers of new securities (debt and equity in U.S.) in the chemical process industries (May 1-October 31) are ranked by proceeds, excluding overallotments, in millions of dollars. Market shares are shown in percent.

	Proceeds ($ mil.)	Share
Du Pont	$ 323.7	7.7%
M.A. Hanna	250.0	5.9
Pfizer	249.4	5.9
Merck	248.3	5.9
W.R. Grace	231.2	5.5
International Specialty Products	217.0	5.2
Johnson & Johnson	200.0	4.8
Dow Chemical	199.5	4.7
Clorox	199.0	4.7
IMC Fertilizer	154.0	3.7
All others	1,930.6	45.9

Source: *Chemicalweek*, November 27, 1991, p. 20, from Securities Data and *Chemicalweek* calculations.

★ 1723 ★

Investment Banking (SIC 6211)

Domestic Issue Market

Shares, by lead manager, are shown as percent of the total market in the first half in 1990 and in 1991. Industry totals were $163,816.4 million in 1990 and $258,116.3 million in 1991.

	1990	1991
Merrill Lynch	16.3%	18.9%
Goldman, Sachs	13.5	13.3
Salomon Brothers	10.0	10.0
Lehman Brothers	7.1	9.9
First Boston	10.2	9.1
Kidder, Peabody	5.3	8.2
Morgan Stanley	10.7	7.2
Bear, Stearns	6.7	5.8
Prudential Securities	4.4	2.6
Donaldson, Lufkin & Jenrette	2.2	2.1
PaineWebber	2.2	1.8
J.P. Morgan	1.5	1.8
Alex Brown & Sons	1.1	1.3
Smith Barney, Harris Upham	1.4	1.1
Citicorp	0.8	1.1
Other	7.4	5.8

Source: *Investment Dealers' Digest*, July 8, 1991, p. 18, from IDD Information Services.

★ 1724 ★

Investment Banking (SIC 6211)

Eurobonds

Lead manager shares are based on industry totals of $84,143 million for January-June, 1990, and $133,514.6 million for January-June, 1991.

	1990	1991
Nomura Securities	9.1%	8.8%
Deutsche Bank	6.5	6.8
Credit Suisse First Boston/CS	4.3	6.5
Union Bank of Switzerland	3.0	5.9
J.P. Morgan	3.5	5.5
Banque Paribas Capital Markets	6.9	4.8
Daiwa Securities	1.6	4.8
Morgan Stanley	1.0	4.6
Goldman, Sachs	2.8	3.4
Merrill Lynch	2.8	3.1
Nikko Securities	5.1	3.0
Swiss Bank	1.5	2.9
S.G. Warburg	2.5	2.7
Yamaichi International	4.5	2.6

Continued on next page.

★ 1724 ★ *Continued*
Investment Banking (SIC 6211)

Eurobonds

Lead manager shares are based on industry totals of $84,143 million for January-June, 1990, and $133,514.6 million for January-June, 1991.

	1990	1991
Bayerische Vereinsbank	0.2%	2.1%
Other	44.7	32.5

Source: *Investment Dealers' Digest*, July 8, 1991, p. 28.

★ 1725 ★
Investment Banking (SIC 6211)

Euro-Australian Bonds - Top Lead Managers

Shares, by lead manager, are shown as percent of the group total, based on dollar amount of issues from January 1 to March 13, 1992.

Hambros Bank	40.3%
Deutsche Bank	18.7
Merrill Lynch	12.8
National Australia Bank	12.8
Fay Richwhite	5.8
Westpac	5.3
Dresdner Bank	4.3

Source: *Euromoney*, April 1992, p. 62, from *Euromoney Bondware*.

★ 1726 ★
Investment Banking (SIC 6211)

French Franc Issuers - 1991

Top french franc issuers are ranked by percent share of the group total market, based on franc value of issues.

Caisse Nationale de Credit Agricole	12.3%
Credit Foncier de France	11.1
Societe Nationale des Chemins de Fer Francais	10.6
Caisse de Refinancement Hypothecaire	9.6
Societe Generale	8.0
Credit Lyonnais	7.9
Caisse Autonome de Refinancement	6.4
Finansder	5.2
Banque Nationale de Paris	5.0

Credit National	5.0%
France Telecom	4.0
Caisse Nationale des Autoroutes	3.8
Caisse Epargne Ecureuil	3.8
Compagnie Bancaire	3.7
Floral (CDC)	3.4

Source: *Euromoney*, April 1992, p. 46, from Credit Lyonnais.

★ 1727 ★
Investment Banking (SIC 6211)

International Bond Funds

Companies are shown with assets as of 12/31/91, in millions of dollars. Relative market shares are based on the group total, shown in percent.

	Assets ($ mil.)	% of Group
Merrill Lynch Global B	$ 381	37.1%
MFS Worldwide Governments	292	28.5
Fidelity Global Bond	184	17.9
Van Eck World Income	148	14.4
Merrill Lynch Global A	21	2.0

Source: *Fortune*, March 9, 1992, p. 142.

★ 1728 ★
Investment Banking (SIC 6211)

International Debt

Includes Eurobonds, Yankee bonds and foreign bonds not in their home markets. Percent shares are based on industry totals of $91,168.4 million for January-June, 1990, and $259,861.6 million for January-June, 1991.

	1990	1991
Nomura Securities	8.4%	8.4%
Credit Suisse First Boston/CS	7.3	7.7
Deutsche Bank	4.3	6.4
Union Bank of Switzerland	2.8	6.0
Banque Paribas Capital Market	3.0	5.6
J.P. Morgan	3.6	5.2
Daiwa Securities	6.7	4.6
Morgan Stanley	1.1	4.4
Swiss Bank	6.4	3.7
Goldman, Sachs	2.5	3.2
Merrill Lynch	2.6	3.0
Nikko Securities	1.7	2.7
S.G. Warburg	2.3	2.6

Continued on next page.

★ 1728 ★ *Continued*
Investment Banking (SIC 6211)

International Debt

Includes Eurobonds, Yankee bonds and foreign bonds not in their home markets. Percent shares are based on industry totals of $91,168.4 million for January-June, 1990, and $259,861.6 million for January-June, 1991.

	1990	1991
Yamaichi International	4.2%	2.5%
Bayerische Vereinsbank	0.2	2.0
Other	42.9	35.2

Source: *Investment Dealers' Digest*, July 8, 1991, p. 29.

★ 1729 ★
Investment Banking (SIC 6211)

IPO Leading Underwiters

The top 10 firms in IPO (initial public offering) deals in 1991 are shown with total dollar volume in millions and total number of deals.

	Income ($ mil.)	No. of Deals
Alex. Brown & Sons	$ 5,948	38
Merrill Lynch	3,682	21
Goldman, Sachs	2,869	21
First Boston	1,631	20
PaineWebber	961	19
Shearson Lehman Bros.	1,598	17
Montgomery Securities	446	15
Morgan Stanley	1,173	13
Smith Barney, Harris Upham	369	13
Robertson, Stephens	350	13
Other	5,816	205

Source: *Inc.*, May 1992, p. 139, from IDD Information Services.

★ 1730 ★
Investment Banking (SIC 6211)

Junk Bond Funds

Companies are shown with assets in millons of dollars as of 12/31/91. Relative market shares based on group total are shown in percent.

	Assets ($ mil.)	% of Group
Merrill Lynch Corp. High-Inc. A	$ 543	44.3%
Merrill Lynch Corp. High-Inc. B	335	27.3
American High-Income	285	23.2
Plymouth High-Yield	44	3.6
Oppenheimer Champ. High Yield	19	1.5

Source: *Fortune*, March 9, 1992, p. 142.

★ 1731 ★
Investment Banking (SIC 6211)

Leading Offshore Mutual Funds

Relative shares based on group total assets of $3.6185 billion as of December 31, 1991.

Quantum	88.4%
Fleming American Fledgeling	3.1
Pluvalca Fund	2.8
Putnam Emerging Health Sciences	1.6
Putnam Emerging Info. Science	1.1
GAM Tyche	1.1
Falcon Fund International	0.9
EGS Overseas	0.5
Cumber International	0.4
Permal-Drakkar Growth	0.1

Source: *Financial World*, May 12, 1992, p. 10, from *U.S. Offshore Funds Directory, 1992*.

★1732★

Investment Banking (SIC 6211)

Mortgage-Backed Bond Funds

Companies are shown with assets as of 12/31/91, in millions of dollars. Relative market shares are based on group total, shown in percent.

	Assets ($ mil.)	% of Group
Vanguard Fixed Income GNMA	$ 5,298	75.4%
T. Rowe Price GNMA	735	10.5
Benham GNMA Income	703	10.0
Managers Intermediate Mortgage	167	2.4
Lexington GNMA Income . . .	122	1.7

Source: *Fortune*, March 9, 1992, p. 142.

★1733★

Investment Banking (SIC 6211)

Mortgage-Backed Securities Market

Shares, by dealer, are shown as percent of the total market in the first half of 1990 and 1991. Industry totals were $71,639.1 in 1990 and $102,936.5 in 1991.

	1990	1991
Kidder, Peabody	9.8%	17.5%
Bear, Stearns	12.9	12.7
Lehman Brothers	8.4	10.8
Merrill Lynch	7.6	9.8
Goldman, Sachs	10.8	8.2
First Boston	9.1	7.6
Salomon Brothers	8.2	7.5
Prudential Securities	9.2	5.4
Donaldson, Lufkin & Jenrette . . .	4.8	3.3
Morgan Stanley	4.5	3.3
PaineWebber	3.0	2.4
Citicorp	1.4	2.4
Nomura Securities	1.2	2.3
Greenwich Capital Markets	0.6	2.2
Smith Barney, Harris Upham	1.2	1.5
Other	7.3	3.1

Source: *Investment Dealers' Digest*, July 8, 1991, p. 20, from IDD Information Services.

★1734★

Investment Banking (SIC 6211)

Municipal Bond Funds

Companies are shown with assets as of 12/31/91, in millions of dollars. Relative market shares are based on group total, shown in percent.

	Assets ($ mil.)	% of Group
Vanguard Municipal Interm. . .	$ 2,460	52.3%
Vanguard Municipal Long-Term	888	18.9
General Municipal Bond	683	14.5
SAFECO Municipal Long-Term	422	9.0
Financial Tax-Free Inc. Shares .	248	5.3

Source: *Fortune*, March 9, 1992, p. 142.

★1735★

Investment Banking (SIC 6211)

Municipal Bond Issues

Leaders in municipal bond issues are shown with shares, based on a market total of $71,906.5 million from January 1, to June 30, 1991.

Goldman, Sachs	16.7%
Merrill Lynch & Co.	8.3
Lehman Brothers	6.9
First Boston	6.5
Smith Barney, Harris Upham	5.1
Morgan Stanley	4.0
Bear, Stearns	3.9
PaineWebber	3.9
Prudential Securities	3.0
Kidder, Peabody	1.8
Dean Witter Reynolds	1.6
First Chicago Capital Markets	1.5
J.P. Morgan Securities	1.4
Bank of America	1.3
BT Securities	1.3
Other	32.8

Source: *Investment Dealers' Digest*, July 8, 1991, p. 33.

★ 1736 ★

Investment Banking (SIC 6211)

Swiss Franc Foreign Bonds

Shares, by lead manager, are based on total value of Swiss franc foreign bonds.

Credit Suisse	22.08%
Swiss Bank Corp.	21.07
UBS	19.08
Banque Paribas	4.72
Nomura Bank	4.04
Wirtschafts-Und Privatbank	3.94
Yamaichi Bank	3.47
Swiss Volksbank	3.17
Banca Del Gottardo	2.66
Daiwa Securities	2.15
Others	13.62

Source: *Euromoney*, April 1992, p. 14, from *Euromoney Bondware*.

★ 1737 ★

Investment Banking (SIC 6211)

Top IPO Underwriters - 1991

Leading initial public offering (IPO) underwriters are ranked by value of issues underwritten in 1991, shown in millions of dollars. Only those firms with a minimum of three deals are listed. Relative shares are shown in percent, based on the group total of $15.5428 billion.

	Amount ($ mil.)	% of Group
Merrill Lynch	$ 2,796.9	18.8%
Goldman Sachs	2,686.3	18.0
First Boston	1,655.3	11.1
Lehman	1,203.9	8.1
Morgan Stanley	1,113.5	7.5
Alex Brown	677.5	4.5
PaineWebber	560.5	3.8
Salomon	517.3	3.5
Kidder Peabody	491.0	3.3
Montgomery	445.7	3.0
Smith Barney	369.3	2.5
Donaldson Lufkin	310.5	2.1
Robertson Stephens	305.0	2.0
Hambrecht & Quist	283.6	1.9
Prudential	228.6	1.5
Dean Witter	222.6	1.5
Bear Stearns	192.0	1.3
Wm Blair	145.9	1.0

	Amount ($ mil.)	% of Group
Dillon Read	$ 122.3	0.8%
J.C. Bradford	95.0	0.6
Josephthal Lyon	85.3	0.6
Piper Jaffray	84.3	0.6
Robert W. Baird	70.5	0.5
Oppenheimer	62.0	0.4
Dain Bosworth	54.5	0.4
Ladenburg	54.4	0.4
H.J. Meyers	29.1	0.2
Commonwealth	14.4	0.1
J.G. Kinnard	14.2	0.1

Source: *Investment Dealers' Digest*, January 20, 1992, p. 13, from *IDD* Information Services.

★ 1738 ★

Investment Banking (SIC 6211)

Treasury Bond Funds

Companies are shown with assets as of 12/31/91, in millions of dollars. Relative shares are based on group total, shown in percent.

	Assets ($ mil.)	% of Group
Vanguard L-T U.S. Treasury	$ 893	55.0%
Benham Treasury Note	302	18.6
Dreyfus U.S. Treasury L-T	217	13.4
Dreyfus U.S. Treas. Interm.	183	11.3
Stagecoach U.S. Govt. Allocation	30	1.8

Source: *Fortune*, March 9, 1992, p. 142.

★1739★

Investment Banking (SIC 6211)

Underwriters of the East North Central U.S.

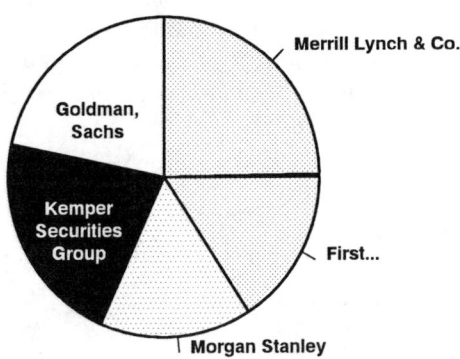

Leading municipal bond underwriters in Ohio, Indiana, Illinois, Michigan, and Wisconsin are ranked by the volume of long-term issues underwritten in 1991. Data are shown in millions of dollars and percent share of the group total.

	($ mil.)	% of Group
Merrill Lynch & Co.	$ 1,850	24.6%
Goldman, Sachs	1,642	21.8
Kemper Securities Group . . .	1,628	21.6
Morgan Stanley	1,213	16.1
First Chicago Capital Markets . .	1,195	15.9

Source: *Governing*, June 1992, p. 79, from IDD Information Services and PSA Municipal Database.

★1740★

Investment Banking (SIC 6211)

Underwriters of the East South Central U.S.

Leading municipal bond underwriters in Kentucky, Tennessee, Alabama, and Mississippi are ranked by the volume of long-term issues underwritten in 1991. Data are shown in millions of dollars and percent share of relative market.

	Vol. ($ mil.)	% of Group
Goldman, Sachs	$ 661	26.0%
Prudential Securities	629	24.7
Merrill Lynch & Co.	562	22.1
First Tennessee Bank, N.A. . . .	393	15.4
Smith Barney, Harris Upham . .	301	11.8

Source: *Governing*, June 1992, p. 79, from IDD Information Services and PSA Municipal Database.

★1741★

Investment Banking (SIC 6211)

Underwriters of the Middle Atlantic U.S.

Leading municipal bond underwriters in New York, New Jersey, and Pennsylvania are ranked by the volume of long-term issues underwritten in 1991. Data are shown in millions of dollars and percent share of group total.

	($ mil.)	% of Group
Goldman, Sachs	$ 5,246	28.6%
Lehman Brothers	4,208	22.9
Merrill Lynch & Co.	3,975	21.7
Bear, Stearns	2,840	15.5
Smith Barney, Harris Upham . .	2,084	11.4

Source: *Governing*, June 1992, p. 79, from IDD Information Services and PSA Municipal Database.

★ 1742 ★

Investment Banking (SIC 6211)

Underwriters of the Mountain Region - U.S.

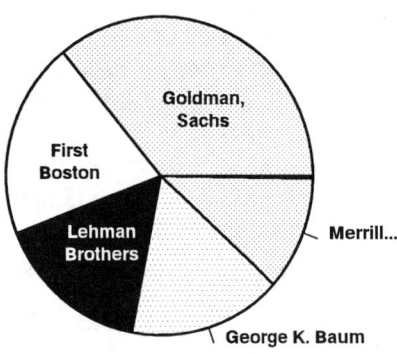

Leading municipal bond underwriters in Montana, Idaho, Wyoming, Colorado, New Mexico, Arizona, Utah, and Nevada are ranked by the volume of long-term issues underwritten in 1991. Data are shown in millions of dollars and percent share of relative market.

	Vol. ($ mil.)	% of Group
Goldman, Sachs	$ 1,856	36.3%
First Boston	1,018	19.9
Lehman Brothers	821	16.0
George K. Baum	801	15.7
Merrill Lynch & Co.	621	12.1

Source: *Governing*, June 1992, p. 79, from IDD Information Service and PSA Municipal Database.

★ 1743 ★

Investment Banking (SIC 6211)

Underwriters of the Northeast U.S.

Leading municipal bond underwriters in Maine, Vermont, New Hampshire, Massachusetts, Connecticut, and Rhode Island are ranked by the volume of long-term issues underwritten in 1991. Data are shown in millions of dollars and percent share of group total.

	($ mil.)	% of Group
Goldman, Sachs	$ 1,740	32.2%
First Boston	1,288	23.8
Bear, Stearns	929	17.2
Merrill Lynch & Co.	856	15.8
Kidder, Peabody	598	11.1

Source: *Governing*, June 1992, p. 79, from IDD Information Services and PSA Municipal Database.

★ 1744 ★

Investment Banking (SIC 6211)

Underwriters of the Pacific U.S.

Goldman, Sachs

Merrill Lynch & Co.

Bank of America

Smith Barney, Harris Upham

Lehman Brothers

Leading municipal bond underwriters in Washington, Oregon, California, Alaska, and Hawaii are ranked by the volume of long-term issues underwritten in 1991. Data are shown in millions of dollars and percent share of relative market.

	Vol. ($ mil.)	% of Group
Goldman, Sachs	$ 5,189	31.0%
Merrill Lynch & Co.	4,373	26.1
Bank of America	3,462	20.7
Smith Barney, Harris Upham . .	1,980	11.8
Lehman Brothers	1,723	10.3

Source: *Governing*, June 1992, p. 79, from IDD Information Services and PSA Municipal Database.

★1745★
Investment Banking (SIC 6211)

Underwriters of the South Atlantic U.S.

Leading municipal bond underwriters in Delaware, Maryland, D.C., Virginia, West Virginia, North Carolina, South Carolina, Georgia, and Florida are ranked by the volume of long-term issues underwritten in 1991. Data are shown in millions of dollars and percent share of group total.

	($ mil.)	% of Group
Merrill Lynch & Co.	$ 2,757	25.8%
Smith Barney, Harris Upham . .	2,447	22.9
Goldman, Sachs	2,034	19.0
First Boston	1,913	17.9
Donaldson, Lufkin & Jenrette . .	1,555	14.5

Source: *Governing*, June 1992, p. 79, from IDD Information Services and PSA Municipal Database.

★1746★
Investment Banking (SIC 6211)

Underwriters of the West North Central U.S.

Leading municipal bond underwriters in Minnesota, Iowa, Missouri, North Dakota, South Dakota, Nebraska, and Kansas are ranked by the volume of long-term issues underwritten in 1991. Data are shown in millions of dollars and percent share of group total.

	($ mil.)	% of Group
Piper, Jaffray & Hopwood . . .	$ 974	32.2%
George K. Baum	554	18.3
Lehman Brothers	552	18.2
Prudential Securities	512	16.9
Smith Barney, Harris Upham . .	433	14.3

Source: *Governing*, June 1992, p. 79, from IDD Information Services and PSA Municipal Database.

★1747★
Investment Banking (SIC 6211)

Underwriters of the West South Central U.S.

Leading municipal bond underwriters in Arkansas, Louisiana, Oklahoma, and Texas are ranked by the volume of long-term issues underwritten in 1991. Data are shown in millions of dollars and percent share of relative market.

	Vol. ($ mil.)	% of Group
Goldman, Sachs	$ 2,554	34.8%
First Boston	1,895	25.8
Merrill Lynch & Co.	1,078	14.7
Rauscher Pierce Refsnes	1,063	14.5
J.P. Morgan Securities	745	10.2

Source: *Governing*, June 1992, p. 79, from IDD Information Services and PSA Municipal Database.

★1748★
Investment Banking (SIC 6211)

Wall Street Underwriters

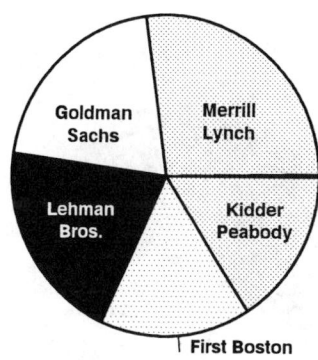

Top Wall Street underwriters collected $3.6 billion in fees in the first half of 1992 for handling stock and bond issues. Company shares are shown in percent.

Merrill Lynch	17.0%
Goldman Sachs	13.0
Lehman Bros.	13.0
First Boston	10.0
Kidder Peabody	10.0

Source: *USA TODAY*, July 15, 1992, p. 1B, from Securities Data and IDD Information Servcies.

★1749★

Investment Banking (SIC 6211)

Yankee Stock Issue Underwriters

Yankee issues are securities sold here to U.S. investors by foreign companies. 1992 proceeds of Yankee Stock issues distributed around major underwriters were $2.503 billion. Shares are shown as percent of that total.

	($ mil.)	% of Group
Goldman Sachs	$ 1,053.4	42.1%
Merrill Lynch	720.8	28.8
Morgan Stanley	466.1	18.6
Salomon Brothers	94.5	3.8
PaineWebber	63.0	2.5
Lehman Brothers	30.3	1.2
Smith Barney	30.2	1.2
Alex. Brown	28.2	1.1
Dean Witter Reynolds	17.0	0.7

Source: *The Wall Street Journal*, June 1, 1992, p. C1, from Securities Data Co.

★1750★

Securities Brokers (SIC 6211)

Brokerage Firms by Type

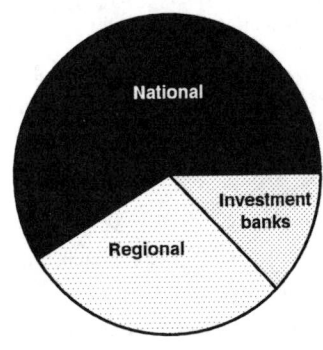

Percent distribution is based on a nationwide total of 75,189 brokers as of September 30, 1991.

National	58.5%
Regional	28.7
Investment banks	12.8

Source: *USA TODAY*, February 17, 1992, p. 1B, from D.A. Davidson & Co.

★1751★

Securities Brokers (SIC 6211)

Brokers on Stock Exchanges: Japan

Company shares are ranked by operating revenue, shown in billions of yen for FY 1991. Shares of the group are shown in percent.

	(Y bil.)	% of Group
Nomura	430	20.2%
Daiwa	320	15.0
Nikko	290	13.6
Yamaichi	250	11.7
Kokusai	115	5.4
New Japan	90	4.2
Kankaku	85	4.0
Sanyo	72	3.4
Wako	68	3.2
Okasan	60	2.8
Cosmo	44	2.1
Tokyo	35	1.6
Universal	31	1.5
Taiheiyo	31	1.5
Dai-ichi	28	1.3
Toyo	24	1.1
Mito	23	1.1
Marusan	21	1.0
National	20	0.9
Yamatane	20	0.9
Meiko	18	0.8
Maruman	17	0.8
Ichiyoshi	16	0.8
Takagi	12	0.6
Kosei	8	0.4

Source: *TOKYO Business Today*, May 1992, p. 46, from *The Financial Business*, Toyo Keizai Inc.

★1752★

Investment Advice (SIC 6282)

Leading Investment Advisers

Companies are ranked by value of portfolio, shown in millions of dollars. Percent shares are based on the group total.

	Value ($ mil.)	% of Group
Wells Fargo Institutional Trust	.$ 55,160	21.4%
Alliance Capital Management . .	26,969	10.4
Wellington Management	19,209	7.4
Fayez Sarofim	19,117	7.4

Continued on next page.

★ 1752 ★ *Continued*

Investment Advice (SIC 6282)

Leading Investment Advisers

Companies are ranked by value of portfolio, shown in millions of dollars. Percent shares are based on the group total.

	Value ($ mil.)	% of Group
Invesco MIM . . . .$	16,949	6.6%
Delaware Management	15,322	5.9
Boston Company	13,808	5.3
Capital Guardian Trust	13,456	5.2
IDS Financial	13,384	5.2
Lazard Freres	11,674	4.5
Oppenheimer LP	11,654	4.5
Investors Research	10,705	4.1
RCM Capital Management . . .	10,636	4.1
Shearson Lehman Brothers . . .	10,423	4.0
Sanford C. Bernstein	9,880	3.8

Source: *Financial World*, March 17, 1992, p. 50, from CDA Investment Technologies.

★ 1753 ★

Money Managers (SIC 6282)

Top Bank Money Managers

Leading bank money managers with top-performing equity funds (September 30, 1990 to September 30, 1991). Relative shares are shown in percent.

	Assets ($ mil.)	% of Group
Norwest Bank of Minnesota . .	$ 131.2	26.2%
UBS Asset Management	117.0	23.4
First Wisconsin/Madison . . .	88.6	17.7
Manufacturers National	42.0	8.4
Fidelity Management Trust . . .	38.0	7.6

	Assets ($ mil.)	% of Group
Security Pacific/ Common Trust	$ 30.7	6.1%
Bank of Boston	25.7	5.1
Princeton Bank & Trust	12.7	2.5
Security Pacific/Aggressive . . .	7.9	1.6
Meridian Trust	7.0	1.4

Source: *Bankers Monthly*, February 1992, p. 15, from CDA Investment Technologies.

SIC 63 - Insurance Carriers

★1754★

Insurance (SIC 6300)

Insurance Companies - Western Germany

Percent shares, by company, are based on total premium income in 1990.

Allianz	27.7%
AMB	7.7
Colonia	6.9
Gerling	5.9
Victoria Versicherungen	4.1
R&V Versicherungen	3.9
SR Beteiligungen	3.8
HDI Group	2.9
Volkfursorge Holding	2.9
Hamburg-Mannheimer	2.8
Other	31.4

Source: *The Economist*, July 25, 1992, p. 76, from AMB.

★1755★

Insurance (SIC 6300)

Largest Life/Health Insurers

The 25 top companies are ranked by total premium written (TPW) in 1991, shown in thousands of dollars. Shares are shown as percent of the group total. The industry total was $285,573.383 million.

	TPW ($ 000)	% of Group
Prudential Ins. Co. of America	$ 24,860,581	16.9%
Metropolitan Life Ins. Co.	19,462,264	13.2
Aetna Life Insurance Co.	8,045,298	5.5
New York Life Insurance Co.	7,646,101	5.2
Travelers Insurance Co.	7,626,039	5.2
Principal Mutual Life	7,333,347	5.0
John Hancock Mutual Life	5,946,984	4.0
Lincoln National Life Ins. Co.	$ 5,325,958	3.6%
Connecticut General Life Ins.	4,723,990	3.2
Northwestern Mutual Life Ins.	4,678,214	3.2
Hartford Life Ins. Co.	4,560,447	3.1
Massachusetts Mutual Life Ins.	4,438,113	3.0
Allstate Life Ins. Co.	3,886,097	2.6
Confederation Life Ins. Co.	3,764,744	2.6
Continental Assurance Co.	3,618,763	2.5
Guardian Life Ins. Co. of America	3,586,151	2.4
Manufacturers Life Ins. Co. CN	3,569,891	2.4
Sunlife Assur. Co. of CN	3,471,468	2.4
Nationwide Life Insurance Co.	3,468,290	2.4
Equitable Life Assurance Society	3,458,268	2.3
Teachers Ins. & Annuity Assn.	3,233,564	2.2
Jackson National Life Ins. Co.	2,869,469	1.9
American Family Life Columbus	2,768,125	1.9
IDS Life Insurance Co.	2,594,396	1.8
Great-West Life Assur. Co.	2,406,509	1.6

Source: *Best's Review*, July 1992, p. 19, from A. M. Best Company.

★1756★

Insurance (SIC 6300)

Largest Life/Health Insurers

The 25 top companies are ranked by net premium written (NPW) in 1991, shown in thousands of dollars. Shares are shown as percent of the group total. The industry total was $209,662.616 million. Companies shown represent only a portion of this total.

	NPW ($ 000)	% of Group
State Farm Group	$ 26,436,759	20.1%
Allstate Insurance Group . .	14,569,772	11.1
American International Group	7,328,810	5.6
Farmers Insurance Group . .	7,240,736	5.5
Aetna Life & Casualty Group	6,675,545	5.1
Liberty Mutual Insurance Cos.	6,434,427	4.9
Nationwide Group	6,285,462	4.8
CNA Insurance Cos.	5,571,500	4.2
ITT Hartford Insurance Group	5,026,486	3.8
Travelers Group	4,327,329	3.3
Continental Insurance Cos. . .	3,665,694	2.8
CIGNA Group	3,634,274	2.8
USAA Group	3,449,365	2.6
Kemper National Ins. Cos. . .	3,164,522	2.4
Zurich Insurance Group - U.S.	3,112,670	2.4
St. Paul Group	3,108,854	2.4
United States Fid. & Guar. Grp.	2,886,415	2.2
Chubb Grp. of Ins. Cos. . . .	2,836,265	2.2
Fireman's Fund Ins. Cos. . .	2,587,183	2.0
Crum & Forster Insurance Cos.	2,422,371	1.8
Prudential of America Grp. .	2,409,941	1.8
Lincoln National Group. . . .	2,303,215	1.8
General Reinsurance Grp. . .	2,122,317	1.6
American Family Insurance Group	2,036,184	1.5
General Accident Insurance Group	1,950,282	1.5

Source: *Best's Review*, July 1992, p. 31.

★1757★

Insurance (SIC 6300)

Leading Life/Health Insurers

Companies are ranked by C&S (capital and surplus), shown in thousands of dollars. Relative market shares are shown in percent.

	C&S ($ 000)	% of Group
Prudential Insurance Co. of America	$ 6,038,137	16.1%
Metropolitan Life Insurance Co.	5,022,544	13.4
Teachers Insurance & Annuity Association	3,261,879	8.7
New York Life Insurance Co. .	2,593,692	6.9
Travelers Insurance Co. . . .	1,974,619	5.3
Aetna Life Insurance Co. . . .	1,742,742	4.6
Northwestern Mutual Life Insurance	1,671,800	4.5
State Farm Life Insurance Co.	1,540,917	4.1
John Hancock Mutual Life . .	1,523,542	4.1
Transamerica Insurance Corp. of CA . . .	1,393,872	3.7
Equitable Life Assurance Society	1,339,362	3.6
Principal Mutual Life	1,302,768	3.5
Connecticut General Life Insurance	1,224,684	3.3
Massachusetts Mutual Life Insurance	1,219,333	3.3
Lincoln National Life Insurance Co.	1,070,878	2.9
American National Insurance Co.	1,012,493	2.7
United Insurance Co. of America	969,963	2.6
Allstate Life Insurance Co. . .	883,191	2.4
AGC Life Insurance Co. . . .	867,793	2.3
Continental Assuance Co. . .	861,307	2.3

Source: *Best's Review*, April 1992, p. 12.

★ 1758 ★

Insurance (SIC 6300)

Long-Term Disability Insurance Carriers

Company shares are shown in percent based on totals of 95,390 in-force cases in 1989 and 102,924 in-force cases in 1990.

	1989	1990
UNUM Corporation	32.0%	33.0%
Mutual Benefit	14.0	16.0
Standard	7.0	7.0
CNA	6.0	7.0
Paul Revere	4.0	6.0
Others	37.0	31.0

Source: Investext, Thomson Financial Networks, May 7, 1992, from The Robinson-Humphrey Company, Inc.

★ 1759 ★

Insurance (SIC 6300)

Mutual Companies - Leaders

The leading 25 mutual companies are ranked by assets, shown in millions of dollars. The 1991 industry total was $649,723,291,000. The companies shown represent 93% of this total.

	Assets ($ 000)	% of Group
Prudential Ins. Co. of Amer.	$ 148,417,569	24.4%
Metropolitan Life Ins. Co.	110,799,477	18.2
Equitable Life Assur. Co.	50,352,793	8.3
New York Life Ins. Co.	42,749,501	7.0
John Hancock Mutual Life	36,220,200	6.0
Northwestern Mutual Life Ins.	35,743,822	5.9
Principal Mutual Life	31,499,392	5.2
Massachusetts Mutual Life Ins.	29,290,591	4.8
Mutual Life Ins. Co. of NY	17,493,473	2.9
New England Mutual Life Ins. Co.	16,947,780	2.8
Connecticut Mutual Life Ins. Co.	11,111,601	1.8
Pacific Mutual Life Ins. Co.	10,650,016	1.8
Guardian Life Ins. Co. of Amer.	6,793,564	1.1
General American Life	6,671,995	1.1

	Assets ($ 000)	% of Group
Phoenix Mutual Life Ins. Co.	$ 6,629,510	1.1%
State Mutual Life Assur. of Amer.	6,584,158	1.1
Minnesota Mutual Life Ins. Co.	6,177,286	1.0
Penn Mutual Life Ins. Co.	6,085,982	1.0
Mutual of Amer. Life Ins. Co.	5,401,502	0.9
American United Life	4,523,083	0.7
National Life Ins. Co.	4,221,471	0.7
Home Life Ins. Co.	3,862,939	0.6
Western & Southern Life Ins. Co.	3,755,262	0.6
Union Central Life Ins. Co.	3,207,833	0.5
Provident Mutual Life Ins. Co.	3,124,393	0.5

Source: *Best's Review*, July 1992, p. 30.

★ 1760 ★

Insurance (SIC 6300)

Stock Companies - Leaders

The 25 leading stock companies are ranked by assets, shown in thousands of dollars. The 1991 industry total was $870,422,567,000. The companies shown represent only a portion of this total.

	Assets ($ 000)	% of Group
Teachers Ins. & Annuity Assoc.	$ 55,575,843	12.4%
Aetna Life Ins. Co.	52,355,001	11.7
Connecticut General Life Ins.	41,692,344	9.3
Travelers Ins. Company	35,662,712	8.0
Lincoln National Life Ins. Co.	23,530,710	5.3
IDS Life Ins. Co.	19,508,675	4.4
Allstate Life Ins. Co.	17,933,916	4.0
Hartford Life Ins. Co.	16,263,228	3.6
Nationwide Life Ins. Co.	15,977,255	3.6
Variable Annuity Life	14,766,530	3.3
State Farm Life Ins. Co.	13,651,713	3.1
Jackson National Life Ins. Co.	13,601,836	3.0
Aetna Life Ins. and Ann. Co.	13,442,123	3.0

Continued on next page.

★ 1760 ★ *Continued*

Insurance (SIC 6300)

Stock Companies - Leaders

The 25 leading stock companies are ranked by assets, shown in thousands of dollars. The 1991 industry total was $870,422,567,000. The companies shown represent only a portion of this total.

	Assets ($ 000)	% of Group
Merrill Lynch Life Ins. Co. . .	$ 11,954,568	2.7%
New York Life Ins. and Ann. Corp.	11,613,393	2.6
Continental Assurance Co. . .	10,943,711	2.5
Equitable Variable Life Ins. Co.	10,103,407	2.3
Great West Life & Ann. Ins.	9,165,030	2.1
Transamerica Life Ins. & Ann.	9,077,417	2.0
Transamerica Occidental Life	8,621,293	1.9
UNUM Life Ins. Co. of Amer.	8,572,502	1.9
Keyport Life Ins. Co.	8,512,724	1.9
American Family Life Columbus	8,475,906	1.9
Provident National Assur. Co.	8,219,623	1.8
American Life Ins. Co.	7,266,363	1.6

Source: *Best's Review*, July 1992, p. 30.

★ 1761 ★

Insurance (SIC 6311)

Net Written Premiums by Insurance Type

Shares by type are shown in percent, based on total net premiums of $217.8 billion written in 1990.

Automobile	43.8%
Workers' compensation	14.2
Liability other than auto	10.1
Homeowners' multiple peril	8.5
Commercial multiple peril	8.1
Fire and allied lines	3.3
Marine, inland and ocean	2.6
Accident and health	2.3
Other lines	7.0

Source: *U.S. Industrial Outlook 1992*, p. 50-6, from *Best's Aggregates and Averages*.

★ 1762 ★

Life Insurance (SIC 6311)

Life Insurance Leaders

Largest 25 life insurance companies are ranked by total premiums, shown in thousands of dollars. Relative market shares are in percent.

	Prem. ($ 000)	% of Group
Prudential Insurance Co. of America	$ 24,108,206	17.3%
Metropolitan Life Insurance Co.	19,530,574	14.0
Aetna Life Insurance Co . . .	9,591,434	6.9
New York Life Insurance Co.	7,709,570	5.5
John Hancock Mutual Life . .	6,822,776	4.9
Principal Mutual Life	6,495,089	4.7
Travelers Insurance Company	4,866,101	3.5
Lincoln National Life Insurance Co.	4,777,397	3.4
Massachusetts Mutual Life Insurance	4,519,196	3.2
Connecticut General Life Insurance	4,418,656	3.2
Northwestern Mutual Life Insurance	4,166,160	3.0
Hartford Life Insurance Co. .	4,118,712	3.0
Equitable Life Assurance Society	4,033,523	2.9
Allstate Life Insurance Co. . .	3,999,585	2.9
Continental Assurance Co. . .	3,650,307	2.6
Mutual Benefit Life Insurance Co.	3,201,171	2.3
Teachers Insurance & Annuity Association	2,978,912	2.1
Guardian Life Insurance Co. of America .	2,928,650	2.1
Jackson National Life Insurance Co.	2,774,260	2.0
Nationwide Life Insurance Co.	2,764,519	2.0
Mutual Life Insurance Co. of New York	2,762,127	2.0
IDS Life Insurance Company	2,296,974	1.7
New England Mutual Life Insurance Co.	2,283,943	1.6

Continued on next page.

★ 1762 ★ *Continued*

Life Insurance (SIC 6311)

Life Insurance Leaders

Largest 25 life insurance companies are ranked by total premiums, shown in thousands of dollars. Relative market shares are in percent.

	Prem. ($ 000)	% of Group
American Family Life Columbus	$ 2,255,048	1.6%
Provident National Assurance Co.	2,061,693	1.5

Source: *Best's Review*, January 1992, p. 14.

★ 1763 ★

Life Insurance (SIC 6311)

Life Insurance Market

Whole life

Universal life

Term

Variable universal life

Variable life

Market share by product is shown in percent for the first three quarters of 1991.

Whole life	57.0%
Universal life	24.0
Term	12.0
Variable universal life	6.0
Variable life	1.0

Source: *Best's Review*, February 1992, p. 93, from LIMRA's monthly survey of life insurance sales in the U.S.

★ 1764 ★

Life Insurance (SIC 6311)

Life Insurance Premium Income

Premium income distribution by product area is shown in percent, based on total premium receipts of $264.0 billion in 1990.

Annuity income	48.9%
Life insurance premiums	29.0
Health insurance premiums	22.1

Source: *U.S. Industrial Outlook*, 1992, p. 50-2, from American Council of Life Insurance.

★ 1765 ★

Life Insurance (SIC 6311)

Life Insurers

Shares of the $1.6 trillion life insurance industry are shown in percent for 1991.

Prudential Insurance of America	7.2%
Metropolitan Life Insurance	6.0
Teachers Insurance & Annuity Assn. of America	3.5
New York Life Insurance	2.6
Aetna Life Insurance	2.4
Equitable Life Assurance Society	2.2
Northwestern Mutual Life Insurance	2.1
John Hancock Mutual Life Insurance	1.9
Travelers Insurance	1.9
Connecticut General Life Insurance	1.8
Principal Mutual Life Insurance	1.2
Massachussetts Mutual Life Insurance . . .	1.2
Lincoln National Life Insurance	1.1
Allstate Life Insurance	1.1
Other	65.7

Source: *USA TODAY*, October 12, 1992, p. 3B, from National Association of Insurance Commissioners.

★ 1766 ★

Disability Insurance (SIC 6321)

Disability Insurance Providers

Shares of the 1990 market for individual disability insurance are shown as percent of sales.

Provident Life and Accident	14.3%
Paul Revere	11.9
Northwestern Mutual	7.4
UNUM	6.5
Other	59.9

Source: Investext, Thomson Financial Networks, March 12, 1992, from The First Boston Corporation.

★ 1767 ★
Disability Insurance (SIC 6321)

Long-Term Disability Insurance Carriers by Premium

| UNUM Corporation |
| CIGNA |
| Mutual Benefit |
| Standard |
| Prudential |
| Others |

Estimated company shares are shown in percent based on a 1989 in-force premium total of $2.5545 billion and a 1990 in-force premium total of $2.7411 billion.

	1989	1990
UNUM Corporation	23.0%	24.0%
CIGNA	14.0	13.0
Mutual Benefit	8.0	7.0
Standard	6.0	6.0
Prudential	6.0	5.0
Others	43.0	45.0

Source: Investext, Thomson Financial Networks, May 7, 1992, from The Robinson-Humphrey Company, Inc.

★ 1768 ★
Auto Insurance (SIC 6331)

Auto Insurers - U.K.

Shares of net premiums written in the United Kingdom are shown in percent for 1990.

Norwich Union	11.0%
General Accident	9.6
Guardian Royal Exchange	8.1
Royal	7.8
Eagle Star	7.3
Sun Alliance	7.0
Commercial Union	4.8
Prudential	4.0
Co-operative	3.3
Cornhill	2.7
National Insurance & Guarantee	2.4
National Farmers Union/Avon	2.3
Zurich	2.1
Provincial	1.8
Minster	1.2
Direct Line	0.9
Legal & General	0.8

Pearl Assurance	0.6%
Iron Trades	0.5
Other	21.7

Source: Investext, Thomson Financial Networks, February 7, 1992, from S.G. Warburg Securities.

★ 1769 ★
Disaster Insurance (SIC 6331)

Largest Insurance Disasters

Total settlements are shown in billions of dollars.

Hurricane Andrew (1992)	$ 10.7
Hurricane Hugo (1989)	4.2
Oakland Fire (1991)	1.2
Loma Prieta earthquake (1989)	1.0

Source: *USA TODAY*, November 13, 1992, p. 1A.

★ 1770 ★
Disaster Insurance (SIC 6331)

Most Costly Insured Catastrophic Events

Data reflect insured loss, by each event, shown in millions of dollars.

Hurricane Andrew (Aug. 1992)	$ 7,300
Hurricane Hugo: Wind, Flooding, Tornadoes (Sept. 1989)	4,195
Oakland Fire (Oct. 1991)	1,200
Loma Prieta, Calif., Earthquake	960
Wind, Snow, Freezing, 41 states (Dec. 1983)	880
Los Angeles Riots (April/May 1992)	775
Hurricane Frederic: Wind, Flooding, Tornadoes (Sept. 1979)	753
Hurricane Alicia (Aug. 1983)	676
Wind, Hail, Tornadoes, Denver, Colo. (July 1990)	625
Hurricane Betsy (Sept. 1965)	515

Source: *The Wall Street Journal*, September 2, 1992, p. A3, from American Services Group, Inc. Property Claim Service division.

★ 1771 ★

Hurricane Insurance (SIC 6331)

Hurricane Damage Estimates

The costliest storms in the history of the U.S. are shown with number of deaths and damage amounts in billions of dollars. Damages for Hurricane Andrew are estimated.

	Deaths (No.)	Damage ($ bil.)
Andrew (1992)	28	$ 20.00
Hugo (1989)	504	7.00
Betsy (1965)	74	6.32
Agnes (1972)	118	6.28
Camille (1969)	256	5.13
Diane (1955)	400	4.12
New England (1938)	600	3.52
Frederic (1979)	31	3.43
Alicia (1983)	17	2.34
Carol (1954)	68	2.32

Source: *The Wall Street Journal*, September 4, 1992, p. A8, from University of Colorado Natural Hazards Center, Federal Emergency Management Agency, *World Almanac*, and National Oceanic and Atmospheric Administration.

★ 1772 ★

Property Insurance (SIC 6331)

Property/Casualty Largest Insurers

Companies are ranked by net premiums written (NPW) in 1991, shown in thousands of dollars. Relative market shares are shown in percent.

	NPW ($ 000)	% of Group
State Farm Group	$ 26,436,759	20.1 %
Allstate Insurance Group .	14,569,772	11.1
Farmers Insurance Group .	7,240,736	5.5
American International Group	7,048,751	5.4
Aetna Life & Casualty Group	6,675,545	5.1
Liberty Mutual Insurance Cos.	6,434,427	4.9
Nationwide Group	6,285,462	4.8
CNA Insurance Companies .	5,571,500	4.2
ITT Hartford Insurance Group	5,026,486	3.8
Travelers Group	4,327,329	3.3
Continental Insurance Companies	3,665,694	2.8

	NPW ($ 000)	% of Group
CIGNA Group	$ 3,634,274	2.8 %
USAA Group	3,449,465	2.6
Kemper National Ins. Companies	3,164,522	2.4
Zurich Insurance Group - U.S.	3,112,670	2.4
St. Paul Group	3,108,854	2.4
United States Fid. & Guar. Group	2,886,415	2.2
Chubb Group of Insurance Cos.	2,836,265	2.2
Fireman's Fund Insurance Cos.	2,587,193	2.0
Crum & Forster Insurance Cos	2,422,371	1.8
Prudential of America Group	2,409,941	1.8
Lincoln National Group . . .	2,303,215	1.8
General Reinsurance Group	2,120,046	1.6
American Family Ins. Group	2,036,184	1.6
General Accident Ins. Group	1,950,282	1.5

Source: *Best's Review*, June 1992, p. 18.

★ 1773 ★

Ransom Insurance (SIC 6331)

Kidnap & Ransom Insurance Providers

Annual premium income for kidnap and ransom insurance totals $70.0 million. "Others" includes Sedgwick.

Lloyd's of London	57.1 %
Others	42.9

Source: *Financial Times*, February 7, 1992, from Control Risks.

★ 1774 ★

Surety Insurance (SIC 6351)

Mortgage Guaranty Insurance Market - U.K.

Shares of the mortgage guaranty business are shown in percent.

Sun Alliance	25.0%
Royal Insurance	17.0
Other	58.0

Source: Investext, Thomson Financial Networks, February 12, 1992, from UBS Phillips & Drew Global Research Group.

★ 1775 ★

Health Funds (SIC 6371)

Health Care Expenditures by Source of Funds

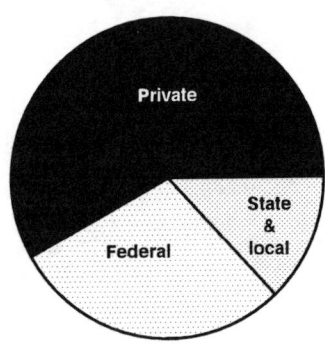

Percent distribution of personal health care expenditures by source of funds is shown for 1990.

Private	57.6%
Federal	29.3
State & local	13.1

Source: *Statistical Bulletin*, January 1992, p. 23.

★ 1776 ★

Pension Funds (SIC 6371)

Pension Fund Leaders

Company assets are shown in billions of dollars. Shares are shown as percent of the $7.283 trillion U.S. equity market.

	($ bil.)	Share
TIAA-CREF (national teachers' retirement system)	$ 95	1.1%
California Public Employees' Retirement System	58	0.6
New York State & Local Retirement Systems	45	0.7
American Telephone & Telegraph	42	0.7
General Motors	41	0.6
New York City Retirement Systems	39	0.6
California State Teachers' Retirement System	32	0.4
General Electric	31	0.4
New Jersey Division of Investment	27	0.5
International Business Machines	27	0.4
Other	6,846	94.0

Source: *Fortune*, July 29, 1991, p. 136, from Money Market Directories Inc. and TIAA.

★ 1777 ★

Pension Funds (SIC 6371)

Self-Directed Pension Managers

Market shares of the $1.0 trillion market for "defined-contribution" plans are shown in percent by type of company.

	1987	1992
Insurance companies	41.0%	39.0%
Banks	37.0	31.0
Mutual fund companies	18.0	9.0
Other	13.0	12.0

Source: *The Wall Street Journal*, September 9, 1992, p. C1, from Access Research, Hartford, CT.

SIC 64 - Insurance Agents, Brokers, and Service

★1778★

Insurance Agents and Brokers (SIC 6411)

Insurance Brokerage Firms

| Marsh & McLennan Cos. |
| Alexander & Alexander |
| ▮ Crawford & Co. |
| ▮ Frank B. Hall |

Sales of the leading insurance brokerage firms are shown in millions of dollars for 1991.

Marsh & McLennan Cos.	$ 2,782
Alexander & Alexander	1,364
Crawford & Co.	516
Frank B. Hall	468

Source: *Forbes*, January 6, 1992, p. 164, from Forbes; Value Line Data Base Service via Lotus CD Investment.

SIC 65 - Real Estate

★ 1779 ★

Commercial Real Estate (SIC 6512)

Leading Banks in Commercial Real Estate

Banks are ranked by commercial real estate assets as of 12/31/91, in millions of dollars. Relative market shares are based on group total, shown in percent.

	Assets ($ mil.)	% of Group
Citicorp	$ 23,000	23.1%
Wells Fargo	14,233	14.3
Security Pacific	12,774	12.8
NationsBank	10,994	11.0
Chemical	10,706	10.7
Chase Manhattan	9,956	10.0
BankAmerica	9,544	9.6
First Chicago	4,131	4.1
Bankers Trust	3,040	3.1
J.P. Morgan	1,259	1.3

Source: *Fortune*, May 18, 1992, p. 76.

★ 1780 ★

Commercial Real Estate (SIC 6512)

Life Insurance Leaders in Commercial Real Estate

Companies are ranked by commercial real estate assets as of 12/31/91, shown in millions of dollars. Relative market shares are based on the group's total, shown in percent.

	Assets ($ mil.)	% of Group
Prudential of America	$ 29,200	18.4%
Metropolitan Life	27,867	17.6
Teachers Insurance & Annuity	21,945	13.8
Aetna Life	19,071	12.0
Travelers	13,404	8.4
Equitable Life Assurance	12,173	7.7
John Hancock Mutual Life	11,135	7.0

	Assets ($ mil.)	% of Group
Connecticut General Life	$ 10,081	6.3%
Northwestern Mutual Life	6,998	4.4
New York Life	6,900	4.3

Source: *Fortune*, May 18, 1992, p. 76.

★ 1781 ★

Military Real Estate (SIC 6519)

Military Base Closings

Acreage due to be sold by the military by the year 1997 is shown by base.

Fort Ord	28,000
Fort Devens	9,311
Williams Air Force Base	5,398
Myrtle Beach Air Force Base	3,793
Fort Benjamin Harrison	2,500
Marine Corps Air Station	1,572
Philadelphia Naval Base	1,425
Naval Construction Battalion Center	900
Hamilton Army Airfield	720
Fort Sheridan	700
Presidio	36

Source: *USA TODAY*, July 28, 1992, p. 9A, from Office of Economic Adjustment, Army Public Affairs, Navy Public Affairs, and Air Force Public Affairs.

★ 1782 ★
Real Estate (SIC 6531)

Commercial Real Estate Values in the U.S. - by Owner

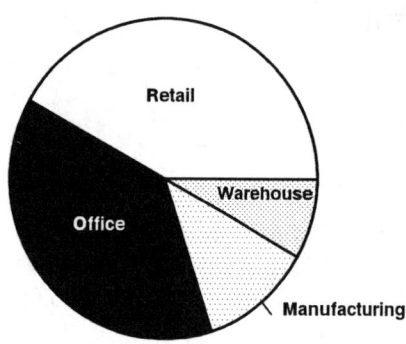

Shares of commercial real estate values in the U.S., by sector, are shown in percent, based on a total of $2,655 billion.

Retail 42.0%
Office 38.0
Manufacturing 11.6
Warehouse 8.4

Source: *Journal of Property Management*, July 1991, p. 41.

★ 1783 ★
Real Estate (SIC 6531)

Hotel Management

The 20 leading hotel management companies are ranked by number of rooms managed. Relative shares are shown in percent.

	No. of Rooms	% of Group
Interstate Hotel Corp.	16,014	9.1%
MHM, Inc.	15,914	9.0
Larken, Inc.	13,000	7.4
The Continental Companies . .	12,300	7.0
Winegardner & Hammons . . .	12,150	6.9
Aircoa Hospitality Services . . .	12,095	6.9
HMS/Economy Lodging Systems	9,400	5.3
Prime Management Co.	8,457	4.8
Westbrooke Hospitality Corp. . .	7,952	4.5
Summit Hotel Management . .	7,555	4.3
Motels of America	7,257	4.1

	No. of Rooms	% of Group
Commonwealth Hospitality Ltd.	6,723	3.8%
American General Hospitality . .	6,546	3.7
Hotel Investors Corp.	6,496	3.7
Vista Host	6,381	3.6
Sage Development Resources . .	6,345	3.6
Ocean Hospitalities	6,170	3.5
Hostmark International	5,862	3.3
Prism Hotel Co.	5,445	3.1
CP Hotel Corp.	4,500	2.5

Source: *Lodging Hospitality*, December 1991, p. 56, from *Lodging Hospitality* research.

★ 1784 ★
Real Estate (SIC 6531)

Real Estate Brokers

The 10 most productive real estate brokers nationwide in 1991 are shown with number of transactions (including both listings and sales). Relative market shares are shown in percent.

	Trans.	% of Group
Coldwell Banker Residential (Mission Viejo, CA)	130,631	37.1%
Weichert Realtors (Morris Plains, NJ)	42,883	12.2
Long & Foster Real Estate (Fairfax, VA)	33,307	9.5
Burnet Realty (Bloomington, MN)	22,932	6.5
Edina Realty (Edina, MN) . . .	22,069	6.3
Realty Executives of Phoenix (Phoenix)	20,890	5.9
The Prudential Preferred Properties (Bethesda, MD) . .	20,058	5.7
The Prudential Florida Realty (Clearwater, FL) . . .	19,988	5.7
Windermere Real Estate (Seattle)	19,712	5.6
Realty One (Cleveland)	19,662	5.6

Source: *USA TODAY*, June 5, 1992, p. 4B, from *Real Trends*.

★1785★
Real Estate (SIC 6531)

Real Estate in the U.S. - by Owner

Individuals	
Corporate	
Partnerships	
Not-for-profits	
Government	
Institutional	
Financial Institutions	
Other	

Shares of real estate ownership in the U.S., by type of owner, are shown in percent, based on a total of $8,777 billion.

Individuals	58.0%
Corporate	19.3
Partnerships	11.5
Not-for-profits	4.7
Government	2.7
Institutional	1.5
Financial Institutions	1.3
Other	1.0

Source: *Journal of Property Management*, July 1991, p. 40.

SIC 67 - Holding and Other Investment Offices

★ 1786 ★
Bank Holding Companies (SIC 6712)

North America's Major Bank Holding Companies

The leading 10 companies are shown with assets (in U.S. dollars) as of December 31, 1991; relative market shares are shown in percent.

	Assets ($ mil.)	% of Group
Citicorp	$ 216.9	18.3%
Chemical Banking	138.9	11.7
Royal Bank of Canada	116.9	9.9
BankAmerica	115.5	9.8
NationsBank	110.3	9.3
J.P. Morgan & Co.	108.7	9.2
Canadian Imperial Bank of Commerce	108.1	9.1
Chase Manhattan	98.2	8.3
Bank of Montreal	88.1	7.4
Bank of Nova Scotia	81.1	6.9

Source: *The New York Times*, April 5, 1992, p. F6, from *American Banker* and Canadian Bankers' Association.

★ 1787 ★
Investment Funds (SIC 6726)

Real Estate Investment Trusts

Federal Realty
Health Care Prop
Weingarten Realty
Kimco Realty
United Dominion
Nationwide Health
Prop. Trust of Amer.

REIT (real estate investment trust) companies are shown with assets in millions of dollars. Percent shares are based on group total.

	Assets ($ mil.)	% of Group
Federal Realty	$ 563	21.4%
Health Care Prop	459	17.4
Weingarten Realty	440	16.7
Kimco Realty	409	15.5
United Dominion	315	12.0
Nationwide Health	306	11.6
Prop. Trust of Amer.	141	5.4

Source: *Forbes*, May 25, 1992, p. 306.

★ 1788 ★
Charitable Organizations (SIC 6732)

Fundraising Charities - U.K.

The top ten fund-raising charities in the United Kingdom are shown with total income in millions of pounds.

National Trust	55.7
Royal National Lifeboat Institution	47.4
Oxfam	45.0
Imperial Cancer Research Fund	42.1
Cancer Research Campaign	40.3
Salvation Army	39.0

Continued on next page.

★ 1788 ★ *Continued*

Charitable Organizations (SIC 6732)

Fundraising Charities - U.K.

The top ten fund-raising charities in the United Kingdom are shown with total income in millions of pounds.

Save the Children Fund	38.6
Barnardos	29.9
Help the Aged	24.5
Guide Dogs for the Blind Association	24.4

Source: *The Economist*, August 29, 1992, p. 54, from Charities Aid Foundation.

★ 1789 ★

Philanthropy (SIC 6732)

Community Foundation Grants

Distribution of community foundation grants by recipient is shown in percent.

Human services	26.6%
Education	25.8
Health	13.8
Public and social benefit	13.5
Arts, culture, and humanities	12.7
Religion	1.9
Other	5.7

Source: *The Chronicle of Philanthropy*, November 5, 1992, p. 16, from Council on Foundations.

★ 1790 ★

Philanthropy (SIC 6732)

Corporate Aid to Education by Purpose

Dollar figures reflect contributions to education made by 326 companies in 1990. Shares by purpose are shown in percent, based on a total of $773,345,000.

	Amt.	Share
Colleges and universities	$ 425,614,000	78.1%
Grants and aids	306,270,000	
Matching gifts	119,344,000	56.2
Pre-college education	58,990,000	21.9
Public and private school support and other	50,609,000	10.8
Matching gifts	8,381,000	9.3

	Amt.	Share
Other educational programs	$ 60,586,000	1.5%
Education-related organizations	32,671,000	11.1
Scholarships and fellowships	27,915,000	6.0

Source: *The Chronicle of Philanthropy*, October 22, 1992, p. 10, from Council for Aid to Education.

★ 1791 ★

Philanthropy (SIC 6732)

Corporate Contributions by Type

Total contributions by type are shown in millions of dollars for 1990. Percent shares are based on a total of $2,069.6 millions.

	($ mil.)	Share
Cash	$ 1,830.7	88.5%
Securities	186.8	186.8
Company products	0.3	0.3
Other property	51.7	2.5

Source: *The Chronicle of Philanthropy*, October 22, 1992, p. 10, from Council for Aid to Education.

★ 1792 ★

Philanthropy (SIC 6732)

Hospital Philanthropy by Source

Shares, by donor type, are shown in percent, based on an estimated total of $1.789 billion in 1991.

Individuals	66.5%
Foundations	13.8
Corporations	13.2
Other	6.5

Source: *Hospitals*, June 20, 1992, p. 16, from Association for Healthcare Philanthropy.

★ 1793 ★

Philanthropy (SIC 6732)

Largest Non-Profit Organizations

America's leading recipients of donations and grants are ranked by amount of private support, shown in dollars. Shares of the group are shown in percent. FJP is the Federaltion of Jewish Philanthropies. JCCA is the Jewish Community Center Association of North America.

	Amt.	% of Group
Salvation Army	$ 658,755,399	11.9%
American Red Cross	520,169,000	9.4
United Jewish Appeal . .	426,399,000	7.7
Second Harvest	394,830,019	7.1
American Cancer Society . .	281,785,285	5.1
American Heart Association	215,860,000	3.9
United Jewish Appeal-FJP of N.Y.C.	213,854,000	3.8
Catholic Charities USA . .	210,887,523	3.8
YMCA of the U.S.A. . . .	207,372,958	3.7
Harvard University . . .	195,941,000	3.5
Boy Scouts of America . . .	194,941,000	3.5
YWCA of the U.S.A. . . .	185,600,000	3.3
Stanford University	180,922,245	3.3
Cornell University	177,100,000	3.2
Shriners Hospital, Tampa, FL	173,308,245	3.1
Boys/Girls Clubs of America	157,319,431	2.8
U of PA	143,384,184	2.6
Catholic Relief Services . .	141,856,000	2.6
World Vision	138,653,464	2.5
Yale University	130,100,000	2.3
JCCA	129,000,000	2.3
Columbia University	128,300,000	2.3
Campus Crusade	123,510,000	2.2
Duke University	113,693,144	2.0
Johns Hopkins	111,814,713	2.0

Source: *The Chronicle of Philanthropy*, November 19, 1992, p. 20.

★ 1794 ★

Philanthropy (SIC 6732)

Leading School Endowments

The top twenty elementary and secondary schools receiving endowments in the 1989-90 school year are shown with endowment in number of dollars. School locations are shown in parentheses.

Phillips Academy (MA)	$ 190,109,654
St. Paul's School (NH)	165,436,204
Phillips Exeter Academy (NH) . . .	151,527,132
Albuquerque Academy (NM)	114,000,000
The Hotchkiss School (CT)	80,859,066
Deerfield Academy (MA)	76,781,000
Choate Rosemary Hall (CT) . . .	66,438,024
Groton School (MA)	64,056,610
The Westminster Schools (GA) . . .	62,818,184
The Culver Academies (IN)	59,909,000
Milton Academy (MA)	57,901,232
Northfield Mount Hermon School (MA)	43,320,000
Woodberry Forest School (VA) . . .	42,856,318
The Taft School (CT)	40,830,130
Punahou School (HI)	40,000,000
The Hill School (PA)	38,547,871
Iolani School (HI)	36,212,653
Rabun-Gap-Nacoochee School (GA)	35,239,053
Western Reserve Academy (OH) . .	32,239,053
The Baylor School (TN)	29,716,000

Source: *Independent School*, "The Reporter", January 1992, p. 5, from Council for Financial Aid to Education.

★ 1795 ★

Philanthropy (SIC 6732)

Philanthropy in 1990 and 1991

Private donations from foundations, organizations, corporations, and individuals are shown in millions of dollars for 1990 and 1991.

	FY '90	FY '91
United Jewish Appeal (National) .	$ 426.4	$ 668.1
Salvation Army	658.8	649.0
Second Harvest	394.8	404.5
American Red Cross	520.2	386.1
Catholic Charities USA	320.2	368.3
American Cancer Society	326.6	346.3
American Heart Association	215.9	235.7
United Jewish Appeal (NYC) . . .	213.9	235.5

Continued on next page.

★1795★ *Continued*

Philanthropy (SIC 6732)

Philanthropy in 1990 and 1991

Private donations from foundations, organizations, corporations, and individuals are shown in millions of dollars for 1990 and 1991.

	FY '90	FY '91
YMCA of the USA	$ 207.4	$ 214.5
Boy Scouts of America	194.9	209.6

Source: *The Wall Street Journal*, November 2, 1992, p. A9, from The Chronicle of Philanthropy.

★1796★

Philanthropy (SIC 6732)

The Largest Foundations

The top 25 foundations are ranked by assets in FY 1990. Shares of the group are shown in percent.

	Assets	% of Group
Ford Foundation . . .	$ 5,460,896,289	12.6%
J. Paul Getty Trust	4,816,152,579	11.1
Lilly Endowment	3,543,648,222	8.2
W.K. Kellogg Foundation	3,509,461,224	8.1
J.D. and C.T. MacArthur Foundation .	3,077,581,000	7.1
Pew Charitable Trusts . .	3,076,891,792	7.1
Robert Wood Johnson Foundation . .	2,914,183,000	6.7
Rockefeller Foundation . .	1,971,970,559	4.5
Andrew W. Mellon Foundation	1,617,441,434	3.7
Kresge Foundation	1,214,208,974	2.8
Annenberg Foundation . .	1,196,093,214	2.8
Duke Endowment	1,054,676,939	2.4
Robert W. Woodruff Foundation	995,893,546	2.3
Charles Stewart Mott Foundation	929,505,650	2.1
McKnight Foundation . .	906,355,455	2.1
Carnegie Corporation of New York	845,268,801	1.9
New York Community Trust . . .	842,116,981	1.9
Richard King Mellon Foundation	836,121,061	1.9

	Assets	% of Group
DeWitt Wallace-Reader's Digest Fund . .	$ 761,826,102	1.8%
W.M. Keck Foundation . .	725,013,250	1.7
Houston Endowment . . .	690,962,560	1.6
Harry and Jeanette Weinberg Foundation . .	639,935,746	1.5
Howard Heinz Endowment	622,403,561	1.4
Starr Foundation	616,002,007	1.4
Alfred P. Sloan Foundation	612,221,359	1.4

Source: *The Chronicle of Philanthropy*, February 24, 1992, p. 12, from Foundation Center.

SIC 70 - Hotels and Other Lodging Places

★ 1797 ★
Lodging Places (SIC 7000)

Lodging Industry Market - North America

Cities are ranked by 1991 room totals. Percent shares are based on group total.

	No. of Rooms	% of Group
Orlando	78,157	11.4%
Los Angeles	74,530	10.9
Las Vegas	70,230	10.2
Chicago	66,371	9.7
Washington	65,343	9.5
New York	64,891	9.5
Atlanta	54,484	7.9
Dallas/Fort Worth	52,664	7.7
San Francisco	43,163	6.3
Anaheim/Santa Ana	41,793	6.1
Toronto	31,472	4.6
Montreal	23,000	3.4
Mexico City	20,266	3.0

Source: *Hotel & Motel Management*, November 4, 1991, p. C1, from Smith Travel Research and Convention and Visitors Bureaus.

★ 1798 ★
Casinos (SIC 7011)

Casino Operator Shares

Shares are shown in percent, based on an Atlantic City gaming win total of $2.9915 billion in 1991.

Trump Taj Mahal	12.8%
Caesar's Boardwalk	10.3
TropWorld	9.6
Harrah's Marina	9.5
Bally's Park Place	8.9
The Sands	8.1
Showboat	8.0
Trump Plaza	7.9

Resorts International	7.4%
Trump Castle	6.6
Bally's Grand	6.4
Claridge	4.5

Source: Investext, Thomson Financial Networks, January 24, 1992, from Donaldson, Lufkin & Jenrette Securities.

★ 1799 ★
Casinos (SIC 7011)

Casino Slot Play

Shares of Atlantic City gaming win in December 1991 are shown in percent, based on an industry total of $121.720 million.

Trump Taj Mahal	13.2%
TropWorld	10.7
Caesar's Boardwalk	10.0
Harrah's Marina	9.1
Trump Plaza	9.1
Bally's Park Place	8.0
The Sands	7.8
Trump Castle	7.4
Showboat	7.3
Resorts International	6.6
Bally's Grand	6.3
Claridge	4.5

Source: Investext, Thomson Financial Networks, January 24, 1992, from Donaldson, Lufkin & Jenrette Securities.

★ 1800 ★
Casinos (SIC 7011)

Casino Table Play

Shares of Atlantic City gaming win in December 1991 are shown in percent, based on an industry total of $203.8 million.

Trump Taj Mahal	13.2%
TropWorld	10.7
Caesar's Boardwalk	10.0

Continued on next page.

★ 1800 ★ *Continued*

Casinos (SIC 7011)

Casino Table Play

Shares of Atlantic City gaming win in December 1991 are shown in percent, based on an industry total of $203.8 million.

Harrah's Marina	9.1%
Trump Plaza	9.1
Bally's Park Place	8.0
The Sands	7.8
Trump Castle	7.4
Showboat	7.3
Resorts International	6.6
Bally's Grand	6.3
Claridge	4.5

Source: Investext, Thomson Financial Networks, January 24, 1992, from Donaldson, Lufkin & Jenrette Securities.

★ 1801 ★

Casinos (SIC 7011)

Riverboat Gambling - Illinois

Riverboat gambling receipts by boat are shown in dollars and as percent of group total in July 1992.

	Receipts	% of Group
Joliet Empress	$ 11,465,712	44.1%
Alton Belle	4,460,410	17.2
E. Peoria Par-A-Dice	4,421,392	17.0
Jo Daviess Silver Eagle	2,838,648	10.9
Casino Rock Island	2,798,504	10.8

Source: *Chicago Tribune*, August 16, 1992, p. C1, from Illinois Gaming Board.

★ 1802 ★

Hotels (SIC 7011)

Asian/African Hotel Chains

Hotel chains are shown with occupancy rates for 1991 and 1992.

	1991	1992
Peninsula (Hong Kong)	75-80%	85-90%
Goodwood Park (Singapore)	83	85
Nikko (Tokyo)	70	78
Regent International (Hong Kong)	68	72
Mandarin Oriental (Hong Kong)	65+	65+
Protea Hotels & Inns (South Africa)	60	65

Source: *Hotels*, January 1992, p. 49.

★ 1803 ★

Hotels (SIC 7011)

European Hotel Chains

Hotel chains are shown with occupancy rates for 1991 and 1992.

	1991	1992
ILA-Chateaux & Hotels (Belgium)	70.0%	80%
Pannonia (Hungary)	65.0	70
Starhotels (Italy)	64.0	70
Treff (Germany)	67.5	70
Relais & Chateau (France)	65.0	67
Queens Moat Houses (UK)	64.0	66

Source: *Hotels*, January 1992, p. 49.

★ 1804 ★

Hotels (SIC 7011)

Hotel Companies

Relative market shares for the world's leading hotel companies are shown as percent of $28.8 billion for the group in 1991.

Accor	34.7%
Marriott	15.3
Best Western	14.9
Hospitality	13.9
Hyatt	11.1

Continued on next page.

★ 1804 ★ *Continued*

Hotels (SIC 7011)

Hotel Companies

Relative market shares for the world's leading hotel companies are shown as percent of $28.8 billion for the group in 1991.

Hilton	3.8%
Holiday Inn	3.5
Sheraton	2.4
Choice	0.3

Source: *USA TODAY*, March 12, 1992, p. 1B, from hotels listed.

★ 1805 ★

Hotels (SIC 7011)

Hotel Management Companies

Sales figures are shown in millions of dollars for 1991. Relative market shares are in percent.

	Sales ($ mil.)	% of Group
Richfield Hotel Management	$ 600	11.2%
Interstate Hotels	514	9.6
TCC	465	8.7
Prime Management	410	7.7
Pratt Hotel Corp.	285	5.3
Hostmark Management Group	281	5.3
Winegarden & Hammons	250	4.7
Columbia Sussex	223	4.2
John Q. Hammons	215	4.0
Larken Inc.	210	3.9
Registry Hotel Corp.	193	3.6
Ocean Hospitalities	177	3.3
Hotel Investors Corp.	171	3.2
American General Hospitality	170	3.2
Summit Hotel Management	135	2.5
Buena Vista Hospitality	125	2.3
Horizon Hotels Ltd.	124	2.3
Universal Hotels	121	2.3
Mariner Hotel Corp.	120	2.2
HI Development Corp.	100	1.9
Boykin Management Group	95	1.8
JP Hotels	90	1.7
Kahler Corp.	90	1.7
Lane Hotels	90	1.7
Victor Management	86	1.6

Source: *Hotel & Motel Management*, June 8, 1992, p. 25.

★ 1806 ★

Hotels (SIC 7011)

Hotel Properties - Top 10

Number of properties owned as of August 1, 1991, except for Choice Hotels International which is shown for May 31, 1991. Percent shares are based on a group total of 11,434 properties.

	No. of Prop.	% of Group
Best Western International	3,400	29.7%
Choice Hotels International	2,190	19.2
Holiday Inn Worldwide	1,432	12.5
Days Inns of America	1,200	10.5
Hospitality Franchise Systems	1,020	8.9
Super 8 Motels, Inc.	843	7.4
Treadway Inns Partners	395	3.5
The Promus Cos.	377	3.3
Hospitality International	302	2.6
Forte Hotels International	275	2.4

Source: *Hotel & Motel Management*, August 19, 1991, p. 47.

★ 1807 ★

Hotels (SIC 7011)

Hotel Rooms - Top 10

Number of rooms owned as of August 1, 1991, except for Choice Hotels International, which is shown for May 31, 1991, and ITT Sheraton which is shown for July 1, 1991. Percent shares are based on a group total of 1,324,382 rooms.

	No. of Rooms	% of Group
Best Western International	274,000	20.7%
Holiday Inn Worldwide	269,110	20.3
Choice Hotels International	207,687	15.7
Hospitality Franchise Systems	154,500	11.7
Days Inns of America	134,000	10.1
ITT Sheraton	64,702	4.9
Radisson Hotels International	61,600	4.7
The Promus Cos.	56,813	4.3
Super 8 Motels, Inc.	52,137	3.9
Hilton Hotels Corp.	49,833	3.8

Source: *Hotel & Motel Management*, August 19, 1991, p. 47.

★ 1808 ★

Hotels (SIC 7011)

Hotel Sales

1990 year-end sales of the top 10 companies. Relative shares are based on a total of 16.5947 billion dollars.

	Sales ($ bil.)	% of Group
Holiday Inn Worldwide	$ 5.1	30.7%
Best Western International . . .	4.0	24.1
Choice Hotels International . . .	1.5	9.0
Hilton Hotels Corp.	1.3	7.8
Hospitality Franchise Systems . .	1.3	7.8
Days Inns of America	1.1	6.6
ITT Sheraton	1.0	6.0
The Promus Cos.	0.8	4.8
Forte Hotels International Inc. . .	0.3	1.8
Hospitality Management Services	0.2	1.2

Source: *Hotel & Motel Management*, August 19, 1991, p. 50.

★ 1809 ★

Hotels (SIC 7011)

Hotels Chains Worldwide

Data show number of hotel and motel rooms worldwide of the top 20 U.S. chains. Relative market shares are shown in percent.

	Rooms	% of Group
Holiday Inn Worldwide		
Holiday Inn Hotels	258,125	15.0%
Holiday Inn Crowne Plaza . .	9,023	0.5
Holiday Inn Express	4,105	0.2
Holiday Inn Garden Court		
Choice Hotels International		
Comfort Inns/Suites	78,543	4.6
Quality Inns/Hotels/Suites . .	56,808	3.3
Clarion Hotels/Suites/ Resorts and Carriage House Inns	11,557	0.7
Sleep Inns	2,573	0.1
Rodeway Inns	15,966	0.9
Econo Lodges	58,706	3.4
Friendship Inns	6,576	0.4
Best Western International		
Best Western	134,861	7.9
Marriott Corp.		
Marriott Hotels/Resorts/ Suites	96,556	5.6
Residence Inn	20,996	1.2

	Rooms	% of Group
Fairfield Inn	10,693	0.6%
Courtyard	26,608	1.6
Hospitality Franchise Systems		
Howard Johnson	57,894	3.4
Ramada	88,322	5.1
Days Inns of America		
Days Inn	128,664	7.5
Daystop	2,939	0.2
Hilton Hotels Corp.		
Hilton Hotels	42,543	2.5
Hilton Inns	49,833	2.9
Hilton Suites	1,095	0.1
ITT Sheraton Corp.		
Sheraton Hotels	51,679	3.0
Sheraton Inns	22,464	1.3
Sheraton Resorts	9,425	0.5
Sheraton Suites	755	0.0
Motel 6		
Motel 6	70,340	4.1
The Promus Companies Inc.		
Embassy Suites	22,949	1.3
Hampton Inn	33,384	1.9
Homewood Suites	2,034	0.1
Harrah's	4,541	0.3
Hyatt Hotels, Inc.		
Hyatt Hotels	57,137	3.3
Hyatt International	444	0.0
Super 8 Enterprises, Inc.		
Super 8 Motels	50,133	2.9
Carlson Hospitality Group, Inc. Radisson Hotels International	39,299	2.3
Colony Hotels & Resorts . . .	7,298	0.4
Country Lodging by Carlson . .	1,906	0.1
Forte Hotels, Inc.		
Travelodge	34,594	2.0
Travelodge Hotels	6,653	0.4
Thriftlodge	237	0.0
Forte Hotels		
La Quinta Motor Inns, Inc.		
La Quinta Inns	26,458	1.5
Hospitality International		
Red Carpet Inn	12,800	0.7
Scottish Inns	10,100	0.6
Master Hosts Inns/Resorts . .	2,600	0.2
R&B Realty Group Oakwood Corporate Apartments	24,761	1.4
Red Roof Inns Red Roof Inns	23,261	1.4

Continued on next page.

★ 1809 ★ *Continued*

Hotels (SIC 7011)

Hotels Chains Worldwide

Data show number of hotel and motel rooms worldwide of the top 20 U.S. chains. Relative market shares are shown in percent.

	Rooms	% of Group
Westin Hotels & Resorts		
Westin Hotels & Resorts . . .	20,439	1.2%
Economy Lodging Systems, Inc.		
Knights Inn	15,120	0.9
Arborgate Inn	1,470	0.1
Knights Court	300	0.0
Knights Stop	200	0.0

Source: *Lodging Hospitality*, December 1991, p. 53.

★ 1810 ★

Hotels (SIC 7011)

Hotels - Federal Travel Vendors

Hotels are shown as federal vendors whose market share in 1990 was greater than 5 percent, as measured in billings through the government's travel card program, administered by Citibank/Diners Club. Data represent fiscal 1990 sales in thousands of dollars which were only one-fifth of the government's travel expenses. Market share is shown in percent.

	Sales ($ 000)	Share
Holiday Inn	$ 68,340	16.6%
Best Western	24,192	5.9
Quality International	21,129	5.1
Other	299,949	72.4

Source: *Government Executive*, August 1991, p. 50, from General Services Administrative.

★ 1811 ★

Hotels (SIC 7011)

Western Hemisphere Hotel Chains

Hotel chains are shown with occupancy rates for 1991 and 1992.

	1991	1992
Aston Hotels (USA)	75.0%	78.0%
Boykin Management Co. (USA) . . .	72.0	73.0
Red Lion Hotels & Inns (USA) . . .	71.0	72.0
Westmark Hotels (USA)	65.0	70.0
Shoney's Inns (USA)	65.0	67.0
Horsa Hotels (Brazil)	56.0	61.0
Hotel des Gouverneurs (Canada) . .	58.0	60.0
Regal Hotels Intl. (USA)	65.0	65.0

Source: *Hotels*, January 1992, p. 49.

★ 1812 ★

Hotels & Motels (SIC 7011)

Hotel & Motel Franchise Companies

Companies are shown with dollar sales for 1990 and relative market shares in percent.

	Sales ($ mil.)	% of Group
Holiday Inn Worldwide . . .	$ 5,100.0	30.0%
Best Western International . . .	3,970.0	23.4
Choice Hotels Corp.	1,540.0	9.1
Hilton Hotels Corp.	1,330.0	7.8
Hospitality Franchise Systems . .	1,330.0	7.8
Days Inns of America	1,100.0	6.5
ITT Sheraton	1,010.0	6.0
The Promus Cos.	834.7	4.9
Forte Hotels International . . .	300.0	1.8
Hospitality Management Services	160.0	0.9
Hospitality International	103.0	0.6
Shoney's Inns	60.0	0.4
Doubletree Club Hotels	55.0	0.3
Nendels Corp.	29.0	0.2
Woodfin Suite Hotels	18.3	0.1
Budgetel	17.4	0.1
ClubHouse Inns of America . .	11.5	0.1
Coachman Inns	4.2	0.0

Source: *Hotel & Motel Management*, August 19, 1991, p. 48.

★ 1813 ★

Campgrounds (SIC 7033)

Campground Bookings - Europe

Shares, by company, are shown in pecent.

Eurocamp	45.0%
Eurosites	25.0
Other	30.0

Source: Investext, Thomson Financial Networks, March 20, 1992, from S. G. Warburg Securities.

SIC 72 - Personal Services

★1814★

Funeral Services (SIC 7261)

Funeral Homes - North American Market

Market shares are shown in percent, based on total of 23,000 funeral homes in operation in North America.

	No. of Homes	Shares
Service Corp.	800	3.5%
Loewen	400	1.7
Other	21,800	94.8

Source: Investext, Thomson Financial Networks, March 6, 1992, from William Blair & Company.

★1815★

Personal Services (SIC 7299)

Gambling Addiction by Game

| Casinos |
| Sports |
| Lottery |
| Horse racing |

Percent of callers to New Jersey's gambling addiction hotline that participated in each type of gambling in 1991.

Casinos	72.0%
Sports	51.0
Lottery	50.0
Horse racing	36.0

Source: *USA TODAY*, June 26, 1992, p. 12A, from The Council on Compulsive Gambling of New Jersey.

★1816★

Personal Services (SIC 7299)

Stop-Smoking Market by Method

Percent distribution is shown for 1989 and projected for 1995 in percent.

	1989	1995
Retail/prescription products	65.8%	79.2%
Clinics	17.5	11.6
Hypnosis	14.3	7.7
Acupuncture	2.4	1.5

Source: *USA TODAY*, November 19, 1992, p. 1A, from Marketdata Enterprises, Inc.

★1817★

Personal Services (SIC 7299)

Weight Control Market by Method

Shares are based on revenue totals of $7.8 billion in 1990 and $8.4 billion in 1991.

	1990	1991
Commercial diet centers	25.6%	26.2%
Low-calorie foods	25.6	26.2
Diet pills and liquids	19.2	20.2
Hospital-based programs	20.5	19.0
Diet books	9.0	8.3

Source: *Business Week*, June 22, 1992, p. 32, from Marketdata Enterprises Inc.

★1818★

Personal Services (SIC 7299)

Weight Control Market by Method

Segment distribution is shown for 1990 and projected for 1996, based on respective totals of $6.17 billion and $10.3 billion in sales.

	1990	1996
Commercial weight-loss programs	32.4%	31.1%
Diet foods	32.4	31.1
Appetite suppressants	24.3	27.2
Diet books/cassettes	10.9	10.7

Source: *USA TODAY*, June 16, 1992, p. 1D, from Marketdata Enterprises Inc.

SIC 73 - Business Services

★1819★

Advertising (SIC 7310)

Advertising Agencies

Sales of the leading advertisers are shown in millions of dollars for 1991.

WPP Group	$ 2,176
Interpublic Group	1,541
Omnicon Group	1,184
ADVO-System	697
Grey Advertising	514

Source: *Forbes*, January 6, 1992, p. 142, from Forbes; Value Line Data Base Service via Lotus CD Investment.

★1820★

Advertising (SIC 7310)

Advertising Expenditures by Medium

Shares are shown as percent of the total market, based on advertising expenditures in 1990. Production costs are included in the total.

	Expend. ($ mil.)	Market Share
Newspapers	$ 32,281	25.1%
Television	28,405	22.1
Radio	8,726	6.8
Magazines	6,803	5.3
Others	52,425	40.8

Source: *Newspaper and Newsprint Facts at a Glance 1991-92*, from McCann-Erickson Inc.

★1821★

Advertising (SIC 7310)

Advertising Expenditures by Medium

Media are ranked according to millions of advertising dollars spent in 1992. Market shares are shown as percent of total expenditures.

	($ mil.)	Shares
Local newspapers	$ 27,925	34.9%
Direct mail	25,560	31.9
Network TV	9,335	11.7
Magazines	6,880	8.6
Local radio	6,730	8.4
Syndicated TV	2,020	2.5
Cable TV	1,610	2.0

Source: *The Wall Street Journal*, June 3, 1992, p. B5, from Robert J. Coen, McCann-Erickson.

★1822★

Advertising (SIC 7310)

Media Billing by Category - 1990

Shares by category are shown in percent, based on total billings of $33,822.2 million in 1990.

Network TV	30.2%
Spot TV	25.1
Magazine	14.3
Newspaper	8.3
Spot radio	6.6
Cable TV	3.0
Business publications	2.6
Yellow Pages	2.6
Outdoor	2.2
Syndicated TV	1.8
Network radio	1.4
Medical journals	1.4
Sunday newspaper magazines	0.3
Farm publications	0.1
Transit	0.1

Source: *U.S. Industrial Outlook 1992*, p. 53-3, from *Advertising Age*.

★ 1823 ★

Advertising (SIC 7310)

Top Advertising Agencies in Europe

Figures for 1991 are in thousands. Percentages reflect shares of group total.

	Gross Income	% of Group
Euro RSCG	$ 837,679	15.2%
Publicis FCB	503,416	9.1
Saatchi & Saatchi Advertising . .	382,579	6.9
Young & Rubicam	380,855	6.9
McCann-Erickson Worldwide . .	362,104	6.6
Ogilvy & Mather Worldwide . .	325,388	5.9
Lintas: Worldwide	309,761	5.6
Backer Spielvogel Bates . . .	309,651	5.6
J. Walter Thompson Co. . . .	306,939	5.6
DDB Needham Worldwide . .	282,599	5.1
Grey Advertising	276,937	5.0
D'Arcy Masius Benton & Bowles	234,653	4.3
BBDO Worldwide	206,278	3.7
BDDP Worldwide	205,155	3.7
Leo Burnett Co.	149,735	2.7
Lowe Group	139,203	2.5
TBWA Advertising	99,249	1.8
N W Ayer	71,945	1.3
FCA Group	69,034	1.3
Armando Testa Group	66,449	1.2

Source: *Advertising Age International*, April 27, 1992, p. I-4, from *Advertising Age*.

★ 1824 ★

Advertising (SIC 7310)

Top Advertising Agencies in Latin America

Income figures for 1991 are shown in thousands. Percentages reflect shares of the group total.

	Gross Income	% of Group
McCann-Erickson Worldwide . .	$ 84,857	20.7%
Lintas: Worldwide	81,929	20.0
J. Walter Thompson Co. . . .	41,249	10.1
Dualibi, Petit, Zaragoza . . .	39,450	9.6
Leo Burnett Co.	36,502	8.9
Ogilvy & Mather Worldwide . .	34,189	8.3
Young & Rubicam	32,216	7.9
Foote, Cone & Belding	20,240	4.9

	Gross Income	% of Group
BBDO Worldwide	$ 20,135	4.9%
Grey Advertising	19,003	4.6

Source: *Advertising Age International*, April 27, 1992, p. I-4, from *Advertising Age*.

★ 1825 ★

Advertising (SIC 7310)

Top Advertising Agencies in the Asia/ Pacific Region

Income figures for 1991 are shown in thousands. Percentages reflect shares of the group total.

	Gross Income	% of Group
Dentsu	$ 1,326,045	41.1%
Hakuhodo	574,053	17.8
Daiko	174,329	5.4
Asatsu	149,261	4.6
Dai-Ichi Kikaku	129,690	4.0
I&S Corp.	106,125	3.3
McCann-Erickson Worldwide	103,156	3.2
Cheil Communications	101,600	3.1
Backer Spielvogel Bates . . .	100,667	3.1
Dentsu, Young & Rubicam . .	98,997	3.1
J. Walter Thompson Co. . . .	81,628	2.5
Ogilvy & Mather Worldwide .	81,266	2.5
Leo Burnett Co.	79,023	2.4
Clemenger/BBDO	67,063	2.1
Chuo Senko Advertising Co. . .	52,836	1.6

Source: *Advertising Age International*, April 27, 1992, p. I-4, from *Advertising Age*.

★ 1826 ★

Advertising (SIC 7311)

Ad Leaders - Japan

Top ten Japanese advertising agencies are shown with percent share, based on group total revenues in 1991.

Dentsu	45.0%
Hakuhodo	19.6
Tokyu	6.6
Daiko	6.0
Asatsu	5.0
Yomiko	4.2
I&S	4.0
Dai-Ichi Kikaku	3.9
McCann-Erickson	3.1
Hakuhodo Asahi	2.6

Source: *Business TOKYO*, June 1992, p. 54, from Nikkei Songyo Shimbun.

★ 1827 ★

Advertising (SIC 7311)

Advertising Leaders - Japan

1991 billings are shown in billions of U.S. dollars; relative market share for the same period is shown in percent.

	($ bil.)	% of Group
Dentsu Inc.	$ 9.61	44.7%
Hakuhodo Inc.	4.19	19.5
Tokyu Agency	1.48	6.9
Daiko Advertising	1.28	6.0
Asatsu	1.07	5.0
Yomiko Advertising	0.89	4.1
I&S	0.85	4.0
Dai-Ichi Kikaku	0.83	3.9
McCann-Erickson Hakuhodo . .	0.70	3.3
Asahi Advertising	0.58	2.7

Source: *The Wall Street Journal*, August 11, 1992, p. B4, from *Advertising Age*.

★ 1828 ★

Advertising (SIC 7311)

Largest Advertising Firms - 1990

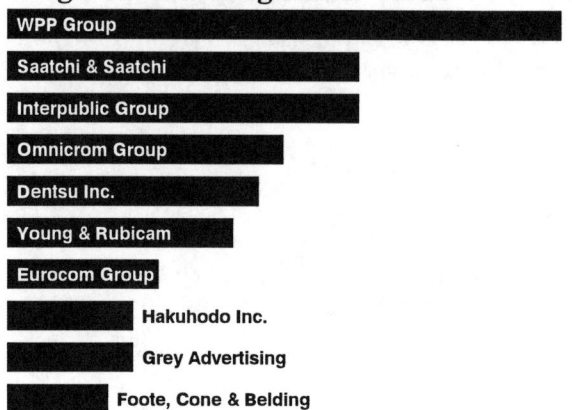

Gross income of the top 10 ad agencies worldwide totaled $12.2093 billion in 1990. Relative shares are shown in percent.

	Income ($ mil.)	% of Group
WPP Group	$ 2,712.0	22.2%
Saatchi & Saatchi	1,729.3	14.2
Interpublic Group	1,649.8	13.5
Omnicrom Group	1,335.5	10.9
Dentsu Inc.	1,254.8	10.3
Young & Rubicam	1,073.6	8.8
Eurocom Group	748.5	6.1
Hakuhodo Inc.	586.3	4.8
Grey Advertising	583.3	4.8
Foote, Cone & Belding	536.2	4.4

Source: *U.S. Industrial Outlook 1992*, p. 53-2, from *Advertising Age*.

★ 1829 ★

Advertising (SIC 7311)

South Africa's Top Advertisers

Agencies are ranked by value of billings in 1990, shown in millions of dollars. Percent shares are based on the group total.

	($ mil.)	% of Group
Ogilvy & Mather Rightford . . .	$ 94.1	27.1%
Lindsay Smithers-FCB	71.8	20.7
Grey Holdings	66.9	19.3
Young & Rubicam	66.6	19.2
BSB/Bates	48.0	13.8

Source: *Adweek*, September 9, 1991, p. 23, from *Advertising Focus*.

★ 1830 ★

Advertising (SIC 7313)

Broadcast Advertising Market

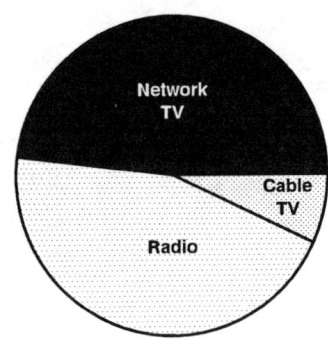

Segment distribution is shown in percent, based on a total of $14.8 billion (dollar figure adjusted for inflation) in 1991.

Network TV	48.0%
Radio	44.6
Cable TV	7.4

Source: *Fortune*, August 12, 1991, p. 68.

★ 1831 ★

Advertising (SIC 7313)

Magazine Ads by Category

Percent shares are based on a total of $3.35 billion in revenues for the first half of 1992. The automotive category includes accessories and equipment; the apparel category includes footwear and accessories.

Automotive	21.7%
Toiletries	13.7
Direct response companies	12.4
Business and consumer services	9.6
Food	9.2
Apparel	8.7
Travel, hotels, and resorts	8.3
Computers and office equipment	6.7
Drugs	5.1
Cigarettes and tobacco	4.6

Source: *Advertising Age*, July 20, 1992, p. 26, from Publishers Information Bureau.

★ 1832 ★

Magazine Advertising (SIC 7313)

Magazine Ad Revenues

Five top high-tech magazine ad revenues totaled $70.6 million in 1989 and $98.2 million in 1990. Relative shares are shown in percent, based on 1990 total. (Publishers are shown in parentheses). Source for Tour & Travel News *data is publisher's figures and MMS/Rome Reports.*

	1989 ($ mil.)	1990 ($ mil.)	% of Group
PC Computing (Ziff-Davis)	$ 17.7	$ 27.8	28.3%
Tour & Travel News (CMP Publications)	20.4	23.6	24.0
MacWeek (Ziff-Davis)	15.2	20.7	21.1
VAR Business (CMP Publications)	9.6	14.1	14.4
LAN Times (McGraw-Hill)	7.7	12.0	12.2

Source: *Business Marketing*, September 1991, p. 40, from Adscope Inc.

★1833★

Media Companies (SIC 7313)

Advertising Media by Type

Media categories are shown with number of companies and revenues in billions of dollars. Shares are shown in percent based on total revenues of $108.5 billion in 1990.

	No. of Cos.	Rev. ($ bil.)	Share
Newspaper publishing . .	38	$ 19.0	17.50%
Television & radio broadcasting	64	17.9	16.50
Business information services . .	52	16.6	15.30
Cable TV	44	14.9	13.70
Filmed entertainment . .	38	12.3	11.40
Magazine publishing . .	24	8.5	7.80
Advertising agencies . .	9	6.8	6.30
Book publishing	25	6.4	5.90
Recorded music	6	6.1	5.60

Source: *Sales & Marketing Management*, January 1992, p. 64, from Vernonis, Suhler & Assoc.

★1834★

Media Companies (SIC 7313)

Media Sales - 1990

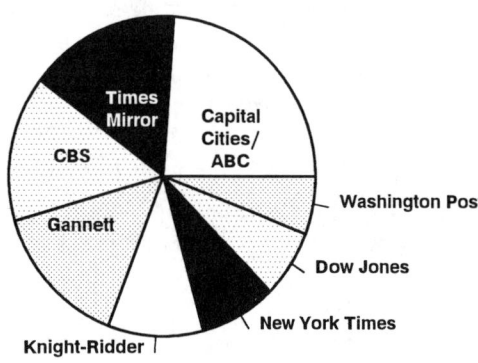

Sales of leading media companies totaled $23.324 billion dollars in 1990. Relative shares are shown in percent.

	Sales ($ mil.)	% of Group
Capital Cities/ABC	$ 5,480	23.5%
Times Mirror	3,633	15.6
CBS	3,516	15.1
Gannett	3,446	14.8

	Sales ($ mil.)	% of Group
Knight-Ridder	$ 2,305	9.9%
New York Times	1,777	7.6
Dow Jones	1,728	7.4
Washington Post	1,439	6.2

Source: *Sales & Marketing Management*, January 1992, p. 64, from *Fortune*.

★1835★

Television and Radio Advertising (SIC 7313)

Advertising ECI Revenues

Electronic Communications Index revenues, which advertising agencies derive from TV and radio advertising, are shown in millions of dollars. Company shares are shown in percent. (Data for Saatchi & Saatchi, WPP, Interpublic, Omnicom, and Grey reflect U.S. operations only).

	Rev.	Share
Saatchi & Saatchi	$ 440.0	16.9%
WPP	339.9	13.1
Interpublic	283.4	10.9
Dun & Bradstreet	280.0	10.8
Omnicom	281.4	10.8
GM Hughes	215.3	8.3
Control Data	201.7	7.8
Grey	166.2	6.4
FCB	125.2	4.8
Comsat	77.4	3.0
Reuters	54.8	2.1
IDB	53.5	2.1
Unitel Video	45.9	1.8
Burnup & Sims	32.4	1.2

Source: *Broadcasting*, June 22, 1992, p. 49, from company estimates, securities analysts, and industry associations.

★1836★
Yellow Pages Advertising (SIC 7313)

Yellow Pages Revenues

Top directory publishers are ranked by 1991 Yellow Pages ad revenues. Relative shares are based on a total of $8.599 billion.

	Rev. ($ mil.)	% of Group
BellSouth Corp.	$ 1,426.3	16.6%
GTE Corp.	1,200.0	14.0
Bell Atlantic	994.6	11.6
Pacific Telesis Group	990.0	11.5
U.S. West	853.7	9.9
NYNEX Corp.	849.2	9.9
Southwestern Bell Corp. . . .	847.7	9.9
Ameritech Corp.	515.4	6.0
Dun & Bradstreet Corp. . . .	463.1	5.4
DonTech	459.6	5.3

Source: *Advertising Age*, August 10, 1992, p. S-10, from company reports.

★1837★
Sales Promotion (SIC 7319)

Promotional Services Agencies

U.S. gross income of the top 10 firms is shown in thousands of dollars for 1991; relative market shares are shown in percent for the same period.

	Gross Income ($ 000)	% of Group
DCI Marketing	.$ 61,548	33.5%
Lintas: Marketing Communications	34,459	18.7
MarketSource	27,500	15.0
Stratmar Systems	14,000	7.6

	Gross Income ($ 000)	% of Group
Merchandising Workshop . . .	$ 9,500	5.2%
BDS Marketing	9,377	5.1
Communications Diversified . .	8,900	4.8
Einson Freeman	7,032	3.8
Diamond Promotion Group . .	6,280	3.4
Strottman Group	5,259	2.9

Source: *Advertising Age*, May 4, 1992, p. 32, from *Ad Age* survey.

★1838★
Sales Promotion (SIC 7319)

Sales Promotion Agencies

U.S. gross income of the top 10 firms is shown in thousands of dollars for 1991; relative market shares are shown in percent for the same period.

	Gross Income ($ 000)	% of Group
Alcone Sims O'Brien	.$ 41,709	16.9%
D.L. Blair	33,323	13.5
Marketing Corp. of America . .	27,134	11.0
Clarion Marketing & Communications	26,809	10.9
Ross Roy Group	25,384	10.3
Cato Johnson Worldwide . . .	23,891	9.7
Frankel & Co.	22,376	9.1
Comart	16,064	6.5
Flair Communications	15,185	6.2
Ryan Partnership	14,699	6.0

Source: *Advertising Age*, May 4, 1992, p. 29, from *Ad Age* survey.

★1839★
Equipment Leasing (SIC 7350)

Leasing of Company Equipment

Shares of the total leasing market, by type of equipment leased, are shown in percent for 1990.

Computer systems	23.2%
Aircraft	14.7
Office machines	11.5
Construction equipment	8.1
Trucks/trailers	6.1
Manufacturing equipment	5.1

Continued on next page.

★ 1839 ★ *Continued*

Equipment Leasing (SIC 7350)

Leasing of Company Equipment

Shares of the total leasing market, by type of equipment leased, are shown in percent for 1990.

Medical equipment	4.8%
Furniture/fixtures	4.6
Industrial equipment	4.4
Telecommunications equipment	3.8
Railroad equipment	3.1
Other	10.6

Source: *INC.*, November 1991, p. 190, from American Association of Equipment Lessors, *Survey of Industry Activity and 1990.*

★ 1840 ★

Employment Agencies (SIC 7361)

Executive Recruiting Firms

Relative market shares of the leading firms are shown in percent, based on a total of $271.7 million in U.S. revenue for the group. The figures for SpencerStuart, Lamalie Associates, and Egon Zehnder Intl. are based on fiscal year revenues.

Korn/Ferry Intl.	23.9%
Russell Reynolds	20.1
Heidrick & Struggles	16.5
SpencerStuart	13.3
Paul Ray & Carre Orban	5.4
Lamalie Associates	5.0
Ward Howell Intl.	4.8
A.T. Kearney	4.4
Egon Zehnder Intl.	3.4
Boyden Intl.	3.2

Source: *The Wall Street Journal*, August 2, 1991, p. B1, from *Executive Search Review.*

★ 1841 ★

Employment Agencies (SIC 7361)

Top Executive Search Firms

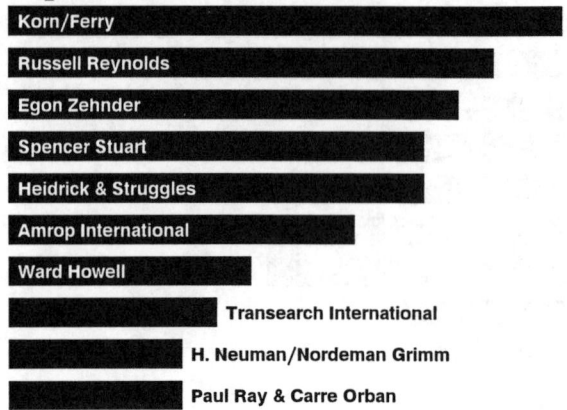

Top 10 executive search firms are ranked by worldwide revenues of $667.6 million in 1990. Relative shares are shown in percent.

	Rev. ($ mil.)	% of Group
Korn/Ferry	$ 107.3	16.1%
Russell Reynolds	92.5	13.9
Egon Zehnder	89.4	13.4
Spencer Stuart	79.0	11.8
Heidrick & Struggles	77.3	11.6
Amrop International	69.2	10.4
Ward Howell	47.5	7.1
Transearch International	38.0	5.7
H. Neuman/Nordeman Grimm	35.0	5.2
Paul Ray & Carre Orban	32.4	4.9

Source: *U.S. Industrial Outlook 1992*, p. 53-4, from *Executive Recruiter News.*

★ 1842 ★

Staffing Services (SIC 7363)

Leading Staffing Companies

Revenues of nine publicly held staffing companies are shown in millions of dollars in 1991.

MANPOWER	$ 2,799.9
Kelly	1,437.9
Olsten	843.5
Lifetime	778.7
CDI Corp.	768.1
Adia	643.7
Robert Half	209.5

Continued on next page.

★1842★ *Continued*

Staffing Services (SIC 7363)

Leading Staffing Companies

Revenues of nine publicly held staffing companies are shown in millions of dollars in 1991.

Staff Builders	$ 168.5
Uniforce	91.6

Source: *The Wall Street Journal*, July 28, 1992, p. B4, from Robert W. Baird & Co., Inc.

★1843★

Computer Services (SIC 7370)

Computer Outsourcing Vendors

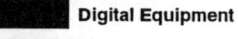

1990 estimated outsourcing revenues are shown for the seven largest vendors in the industry worldwide. The seven American companies account for $16.730 billion or 56.7% of the world market. Revenues are shown in millions of dollars. Global market shares are shown in percent.

	Rev. ($ mil.)	Share
EDS	$ 6,110	20.7%
IBM	3,900	13.2
Andersen Counsulting	1,880	6.4
Digital Equipment	1,800	6.1
Computer Sciences	1,500	5.1
KMPG Peat Marwick	780	2.6
AT&T	760	2.6
Other	12,870	43.3

Source: *Fortune*, September 23, 1991, p. 104, from Yankee Group.

★1844★

Computer Services (SIC 7370)

Computer Outsourcing Vendors

Estimated company computer system outsourcing revenue totaled $3.535 billion in 1991 and $8.750 billion in 1995. Market shares are shown in percent.

	1991	1995
EDS	33.9%	37.7%
IBM	9.9	13.7
Computer Sciences	11.3	11.4
Perot Systems	4.5	5.7
Affiliated Comp. Systems	4.4	4.9
Fiserve	6.4	4.3
Systematics	6.4	4.0
Shared Medical Systems	4.0	0.0
First Financial Mgmt.	2.3	0.0
Others	17.0	18.3

Source: *Stores*, July 1992, p. 61, from Merrill Lynch.

★1845★

Software (SIC 7372)

CAD Packages

Estimated shares of the 1991 CAD (computer-aided design) market for personal computers are shown in percent, by brand.

Autodesk	71.8%
Intergraph	6.9
ComputerVision	4.0
Cadkey	4.0
Cadam	3.9
Other	9.4

Source: *The Wall Street Journal*, May 28, 1992, p. A14, from Daratech Inc.

★1846★

Software (SIC 7372)

CD-ROM Manufacturers - Library Materials

Library preferences for vendors are shown in percent based on a survey of 125 purchasers. Total exceeds 100% due to multiple responses.

SilverPlatter	19.2%
Information Access Co.	15.2
EBSCO	12.8
UMI	9.6

Continued on next page.

★ 1846★ *Continued*

Software (SIC 7372)

CD-ROM Manufacturers - Library Materials

Library preferences for vendors are shown in percent based on a survey of 125 purchasers. Total exceeds 100% due to multiple responses.

The H.W. Wilson Co.	9.6%
R.R. Bowker	5.6
CD Plus	4.8
Michigan Library Consortium	4.0
Library Corp. (BiblioFile)	4.0
DIALOG	3.2
Faxon Co.	3.2
PALINET	3.2
SOLINET	3.2
OCLC	3.2
WLN	2.4
Ingram	2.4
NELINET	2.4
Baker & Taylor	2.4
AMIGOS	2.4
CMC ReSearch	1.6
Gale Research	1.6
NewsBank	1.6
BCR	1.6
UpData	1.6
General Research	1.6
MLNC	0.8
Auto-Graphics	0.8
Compact Cambridge	0.8
Gaylord	0.8
Oxford University Press	0.8
GPO	0.8
Other	17.6

Source: *Library Journal*, February 1, 1992, p. 47.

★ 1847★

Software (SIC 7372)

Computerized Reservation Systems

Shares are shown in percent.

Sabre (American Airlines)	40.2%
Apollo (United Airlines)	22.7
Worldspan (Delta, Northwest, TWA)	21.2
System One (Continental)	15.9

Source: *Advertising Age*, June 15, 1992, p. 42.

★ 1848★

Software (SIC 7372)

Database Packages Worldwide

Estimated shares of the $450 million market are shown in percent. Manufacturers' names are shown in parentheses.

Paradox (Borland)	38.0%
dBase (Borland)	25.0
FoxPro (Microsoft)	10.0
Other	27.0

Source: *The Wall Street Journal*, November 16, 1992, p. B10, from Shearson Lehman Brothers Inc.

★ 1849★

Software (SIC 7372)

DBMS Software Developers

Company shares are based on 1991/1992 planned usage of DBMS (database management system) software, developed for PC LAN (personal computer local area network) platforms.

Oracle	73.0%
Sybase	14.0
Computer Associates	7.0
ASK/Ingres	3.0
Informix	3.0

Source: *Datamation*, November 15, 1991, p. 70, from *Datamation*/ Cowen & Co.

★1850★

Software (SIC 7372)

DBMS Software Developers - UNIX

Company shares are based on 1991/1992 planned usage of DBMS (database management system) software developed for UNIX multiuser operating systems.

Informix	38.0%
Oracle	32.0
Sybase	14.0
Progress	11.0
ASK/Ingres	5.0

Source: *Datamation*, November 15, 1991, p. 70, from *Datamation/* Cowen & Co.

★1851★

Software (SIC 7372)

Desktop-to-High-End Link Market

Market penetration, by brand, of links that join desktop-designed pages to scanning and output systems is shown in percent. Numbers exceed 100% due to multiple responses.

Visionary	51.2%
StudioLink	17.1
Scriptmaster	14.6
VIP	9.8
Lightspeed	2.4
Don't know/no answer	19.5

Source: *Folio*, August 1991, p. 58, from survey.

★1852★

Software (SIC 7372)

DOS Software Sales Worldwide

MS DOS

DR DOS

Data are shown in millions of dollars.

MS DOS	$ 20.3
DR DOS	2.2

Source: *PC Week*, March 23, 1992, p. 129, from International Data Corp.

★1853★

Software (SIC 7372)

Editorial Software

Microsoft Word

XyWrite

WordPerfect

Atex

Bestinfo

Other

Market penetration, by brand, is shown in percent. Figures, based on a survey of production executives, exceed 100% due to multiple responses.

Microsoft Word	30.9%
XyWrite	30.3
WordPerfect	17.6
Atex	10.3
Bestinfo (WordWright)	1.8
Other	13.3

Source: *Folio*, August 1991, p. 59, from survey.

★1854★

Software (SIC 7372)

Financial Software Market

Data reflect company shares of financial software in use vs. planned for purchase in '91-'92.

	In Use	Planned '91-'92
Oracle Financials	4.0%	27.0%
DBS	30.0	23.0
CA	22.0	23.0
Ross	13.0	11.0
ASK	13.0	8.0
J.D. Edwards	8.0	4.0
SSA	5.0	4.0
Pansophic	5.0	-

Source: *Datamation*, May 1992, p. 4, from Cowen & Co.

★1855★
Software (SIC 7372)

Intel Operating Systems

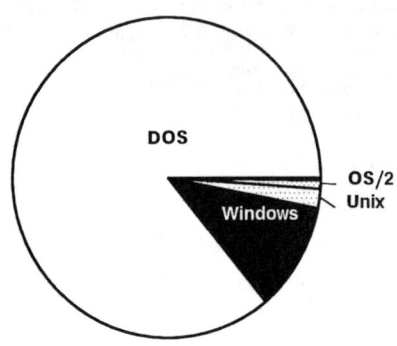

Brand shares of market for desktop operating systems which are compatible with the Intel X86 platform are shown in percent.

DOS	86.0%
Windows	11.0
Unix	2.0
OS/2	1.0

Source: *Informationweek*, January 6, 1992, p. 42, from Meta Group.

★1856★
Software (SIC 7372)

LAN E-Mail Software Worldwide

Brand shares of the global market in 1990 are shown in percent, with manufacturers' names in parentheses. Ashton-Tate and Banyan were acquired by Borland in 1991. cc:Mail was acquired by Lotus in 1991.

cc:Mail (cc:Mail)	23.0%
Microsoft Mail (Microsoft)	17.0
e-Mail (DaVinci Systems)	8.0
WordPerfect Office (WordPerfect)	8.0
Coordinator (Action Technologies)	7.0
3 + Mail (3Com)	6.0
Higgins (Enable OA)	6.0
QuickMail (CE Software)	6.0
Right Hand Man (Futurus)	6.0
Banyan Mail (Banyan)	5.0
InBox (Sitka)	3.0
Office Works (Data Access)	3.0
Framework III LAN (Ashton-Tate)	2.0
Notes (Lotus)	1.0

OfficeVision/2 LAN (IBM)	0.0%
Wang Office (Wang)	0.0
Other	2.0

Source: *Software Magazine*, January 1992, p. 95, from International Data Corporation.

★1857★
Software (SIC 7372)

Laser Disc Software Production Market - Japan

Production shares, by company, are shown in percent for 1991.

Pioneer	70.0%
Sony	20.0
Other	10.0

Source: Investext, Thomson Financial Networks, May 14, 1992, from Sanyo Securities America.

★1858★
Software (SIC 7372)

Macintosh Compatible Graphics Software

1989 brand shares of Macintosh compatible graphics software are shown in percent. (Manufacturers are shown in parentheses).

Powerpoint (Microsoft)	28.4%
Cricket Graph and Presents (Computer Associates)	27.6
More II (Symantec)	19.9
Persuasion (Aldus)	14.2
Others	9.9

Source: *UnixWorld*, April 1991, p. 58, from International Data Corp.

★1859★
Software (SIC 7372)

MCAE Software Producers

Shares of the 1991 market for mechanical computer-aided engineering market are shown in percent, based on a total of $1.550 billion in software revenues.

Prime/Computervision	20.0%
IBM	18.0

Continued on next page.

★ **1859** ★ *Continued*

Software (SIC 7372)

MCAE Software Producers

Shares of the 1991 market for mechanical computer-aided engineering market are shown in percent, based on a total of $1.550 billion in software revenues.

Structural Dynamics	9.0%
EDS	7.0
Autodesk	7.0
Hewlett-Packard	5.0
Schlumberger	5.0
Parametric	3.0
MacNeal-Schwendler	3.0
Intergraph	2.0
Other	19.0

Source: Investext, Thomson Financial Networks, March 31, 1992, from Morgan Stanley & Co. Inc.

★ **1860** ★

Software (SIC 7372)

Microcomputer Software - North America

Software sales, by application, are shown in millions of dollars for 1991. Percentages are based on 1991 total.

	Sales	Share
Word processors	$ 1,136.0	19.9%
Spreadsheets	946.7	16.6
Graphics	724.4	12.7
Databases	396.8	7.0
Entertainment	376.0	6.6
Education	215.9	3.8
Languages/tools	173.6	3.0
Integrated	163.6	2.9
Desktop publishing	152.6	2.7
Other	1,418.1	24.9

Source: *Datamation*, July 15, 1992, p. 106.

★ **1861** ★

Software (SIC 7372)

Network Operating Software Providers

Shares, by company, are based on organizational installations, planned over 12 months in 1991/1992.

All NetWare	53.0%
UNIX	17.0
All LAN MAN	13.0
VINES & Wang	5.0
IBM	2.0
Other	10.0

Source: *Datamation*, November 15, 1991, p. 68, from *Datamation* / Cowen & Co.

★ **1862** ★

Software (SIC 7372)

Network Software Manufacturers

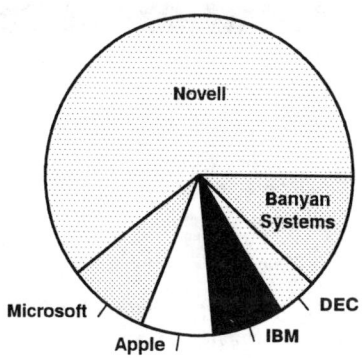

Shares of the U.S. market as of January 1992 are shown in percent.

Novell	57.0%
Microsoft	8.0
Apple	7.0
IBM	7.0
DEC	4.0
Banyan Systems	11.0
Other	

Source: *Financial World*, April 12, 1992, p. 22, from Shearson Lehman Brothers and Computer Intelligence.

★ 1863 ★

Software (SIC 7372)

Office Automation Software

Company shares of $512 million in worldwide revenue for office automation software (PC and non-PC) are shown in percent. This groupware integrates E-mail, word processing, forms routing, group conferencing, data manipulation, and other office-related processes in one package.

DEC (All-in-1)	.27.0%
IBM (Office Vision, Profs)	.26.0
HP (NewWave Office)	7.0
Uniplex (Uniplex)	6.0
Other	.34.0

Source: *Informationweek*, November 25, 1991, p. 67, from IDC.

★ 1864 ★

Software (SIC 7372)

Operating Systems

DOS	
DOS	
Macintosh	
UNIX	
OS/2	
Proprietary	
All other	

Distribution of PC operating systems is shown in percent based on an estimated 84 million PCs worldwide in 1991.

DOS (alone)	.71.0%
DOS (with Windows)	9.0
Macintosh	7.0
UNIX	2.0
OS/2	1.0
Proprietary	9.0
All other	1.0

Source: *The New York Times*, April 5, 1992, p. E5, from InfoCorp.

★ 1865 ★

Software (SIC 7372)

Operating Systems for PCs Worldwide

Percent shares, by brand, are based on a total of 90.0 million systems installed as of 1991.

MS-DOS	.78.0%
Windows	.11.0
Macintosh	9.0
Other	2.0

Source: *The Economist*, April 4, 1992, p. 88, from Datastream Text 100 and company reports.

★ 1866 ★

Software (SIC 7372)

Page Composition Software

Market penetration, by brand, is shown in percent. Figures, based on a survey of production executives, exceed 100% due to multiple responses.

Quark XPress	.50.3%
Aldus PageMaker (Mac)	.29.7
Aldus PageMaker (PC)	6.7
Bestinfo	4.8
Ventura Publisher	3.6
Other	.10.3

Source: *Folio*, August 1991, p. 59, from survey.

★ 1867 ★

Software (SIC 7372)

PC LAN Protocols

1991 shipments of PC LAN (local area network) protocol software totaled 2,911,510 units. Shares are shown in percent.

Novell IPX	.53.0%
Netbeui	.12.0
TCP/IP	.10.0
Other	.25.0

Source: *UnixWorld*, June 1991, p. 69, from Forrester Research Inc.

★1868★

Software (SIC 7372)

PC Software Producers Worldwide

Shares are shown as percent of the 1991 global market for all types of PC software.

Microsoft	39.8%
Lotus	5.7
Word Perfect	4.7
Borland	3.1
Other	46.7

Source: *USA TODAY*, March 31, 1992, p. 2B, from Dataquest.

★1869★

Software (SIC 7372)

PC/MS-DOS Compatible Graphics Software

1989 brand shares of PC/MS-DOS compatible graphics software are shown in percent. (Manufacturers are shown in parentheses).

Harvard Graphics (Software Publishing)	36.9%
Freelance (Lotus Development)	21.1
Graph-in-the-Box (New England Software)	6.3
GrafTalk (Software Solutions)	6.3
GraphWriter (Lotus Development)	6.2
Others	23.2

Source: *UnixWorld*, April 1991, p. 58, from International Data Corp.

★1870★

Software (SIC 7372)

Peer-to-Peer LAN OS Developers

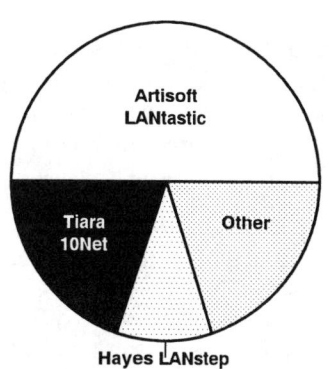

Company shares in 1991 are shown in percent. LAN OS stands for Local Area Network Operating System.

Artisoft LANtastic	50%
Tiara 10Net	20
Hayes LANstep	10
Other	20

Source: *PC Week*, February 24, 1992, p. 15, from Montgomery Securities.

★1871★

Software (SIC 7372)

Sales/Marketing Automation Software

Nine best-selling SMA (sales and marketing automation) software titles are shown with number of installed bases. (Vendor names are shown in parentheses). Relative shares are shown in percent.

	No. of Bases	% of Group
Market Force Plus (Software of the Future)	20,000	46.1%
Brock Activity Manager (Brock Control Systems)	8,000	18.4
Goldmine (ELAN Software)	5,000	11.5
Sales CTRL2 (Sales & Marketing Systems)	4,500	10.4
Action Plus (Action Plus Software)	2,000	4.6
Contact Plus (Contact Plus)	2,000	4.6
EMIS II (EMIS Software)	1,500	3.5

Continued on next page.

★ 1871 ★ *Continued*

Software (SIC 7372)

Sales/Marketing Automation Software

Nine best-selling SMA (sales and marketing automation) software titles are shown with number of installed bases. (Vendor names are shown in parentheses). Relative shares are shown in percent.

	No. of Bases	% of Group
MSM (Marketing Information System)	350	0.8%
Matrix Information Technology (Market Power) . .	50	0.1

Source: *Sales & Marketing Management*, June 1992, p. 158, from Information Systems Marketing, *Guide to Sales, Customer Service, and Marketing Automation*, and *Sales & Marketing Management*.

★ 1872 ★

Software (SIC 7372)

Sales/Marketing Software

Most popular sales/marketing-oriented computer programs are shown with number of installations, based on information provided by software vendors. Shares of the group are shown in percent.

	Instal- lations	% of Group
Storyboarder	2,500,000	44.8%
PC-File 6.0	850,000	15.2
Aldus Persuasion	500,000	9.0
Applause II 1.5	500,000	9.0
Harvard Graphics 3.0	300,000	5.4
Sales Management Solutions 6.0	300,000	5.4
Act! 2.0.	250,000	4.5
DrawPerfect 1.1	150,000	2.7
GoldSpread	125,000	2.2
Your Way	100,000	1.8

Source: *Sales & Marketing Management*, May 1992, p. 82, from *Sales & Marketing Management* and "1991 Directory of PC-Based Sales & Marketing Applications Software".

★ 1873 ★

Software (SIC 7372)

Software Application Compatibility

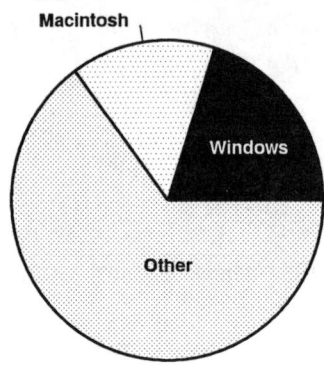

Brand shares are shown in percent for 1990 and 1991, based on total sales.

	1990	1991
Windows	8.5%	20.2%
Macintosh	12.9	14.5
Other	78.6	65.3

Source: *PC Week*, May 11, 1992, p. 121, from Software Publishers Association.

★ 1874 ★

Software (SIC 7372)

Software OS Compatibility

Shares, by brand, are shown in percent based on total sales for the last quarters of 1990 and 1991. OS stands for operating system.

	4Q '90	4Q '91
DOS	72.0%	58.0%
Macintosh	13.0	13.0
Windows	10.0	26.0
OS/2	1.0	1.0
Other	4.0	2.0

Source: *PC Week*, March 30, 1992, p. 131, from Software Publishers Association.

★1875★
Software (SIC 7372)

Software Tools Usage

Shares of software tools usage, by tool type, are shown in percent for current and future usage.

	Curr.	Fut.
SQL Databases	50.0%	37.0%
4GL/PICK	30.0	8.0
Object-Oriented Languages	23.0	20.0
Groupware	23.0	14.0
RPC/DCE Tools	13.0	16.0
Reverse Engineering	11.0	6.0
Upper CASE	11.0	25.0
Lower CASE	5.0	10.0

Source: *Datamation*, May 15, 1991, p. 57.

★1876★
Software (SIC 7372)

Software Vendors - Europe

Shares of independent software and service in Western Europe are shown in percent, based on a total market of $48.0 billion in 1991.

Cap Gemini Sogeti	3.1%
EDS	2.1
Finsiel	1.9
Andersen Consulting	1.9
Microsoft	1.5
Sema Group	1.4
Oracle	1.1
OIS	1.1
Computer Associates	1.0
Datev	1.0
Other	84.0

Source: *The Economist*, October 10, 1992, p. 82, from International Data Corporation.

★1877★
Software (SIC 7372)

Software - Leading Producers

Company sales are shown in millions of dollars for fiscal year 1991. Relative market shares are shown in percent.

	Sales ($ mil.)	% of Group
Microsoft	$ 1,843.4	20.7%
Computer Associates Int'l	1,348.2	15.2
Oracle Systems	1,027.9	11.6
Lotus Development	828.9	9.3
Novell	640.1	7.2
Cadence Design Systems	392.3	4.4
ASK Computer Systems	343.9	3.9
Autodesk	274.0	3.1
Adobe Systems	229.7	2.6
Borland International	226.8	2.6
Legent	203.3	2.3
Informix	179.8	2.0
Sybase	159.4	1.8
System Software Associates	149.1	1.7
Structural Dynamics Research	146.3	1.6
BMC Software	139.5	1.6
Goal Systems International	127.8	1.4
Knowledgeware	124.3	1.4
Symantec	116.3	1.3
Electronic Arts	101.9	1.1
American Software	101.8	1.1
Boole and Babbage	98.6	1.1
Interleaf	84.3	0.9

Source: *Electronic Business*, May 18, 1992, p. 91.

★1878★
Software (SIC 7372)

Spreadsheet Developers

Manufacturer shares of the IBM-compatible spreadsheet software market are shown as percent of 2.644 million units shipped in the first half of 1991.

Lotus	39.7%
Microsoft	28.6
Borland	25.0
Computer Associates	2.8

Continued on next page.

★ 1878★ *Continued*

Software (SIC 7372)

Spreadsheet Developers

Manufacturer shares of the IBM-compatible spreadsheet software market are shown as percent of 2.644 million units shipped in the first half of 1991.

Microsoft Multiplan 2.8%
Wordperfect 0.6
Informix 0.4
Other 0.1

Source: *The New York Times*, November 22, 1991, p. C1, from Datastream and International Data Corporation.

★ 1879★

Software (SIC 7372)

Spreadsheet Developers

Shares of the 1991 market are shown in percent.

Lotus 46.0%
Borland 27.0
Microsoft 12.0
Other 15.0

Source: *Advertising Age*, September 28, 1992, p. 14, from InfoCorp.

★ 1880★

Software (SIC 7372)

Super Client Operating Systems

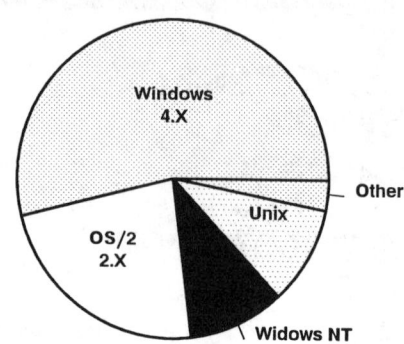

1995 forecast market shares by brand are shown in percent. A "super client" operating system is defined as business applications migrating from minicomputers and mainframes onto PC LANs.

Windows 4.X 54.0%
OS/2 2.X 23.0
Widows NT 10.0
Unix 10.0
Other 3.0

Source: *PC Week*, June 22, 1992, p. 8, from Forester Research Inc.

★ 1881★

Software (SIC 7372)

Top Software Vendors

Shares shown in percent are based on revenue per employee. Revenue totaled $1.844 million in 1990 and $1.989 in 1991.

	1990	1991
BMC Software	12.4%	14.6%
Software Eng. of America	13.8	13.7
Ask Computer	12.6	12.0
Computer Associates	10.8	10.1
Oracle	7.6	8.9
BSG Systems	8.3	8.5
Legent	9.6	8.2
Candle	8.2	8.2
Systems Center	7.4	7.9
Landmark Systems	9.2	7.9

Source: *Software Magazine*, January 1992, p. 24, from Sentry Market Research.

★ 1882 ★

Software (SIC 7372)

UNIX Software Vendors

The leading five UNIX software vendors are shown with 1991 total revenues in millions of dollars and relative shares in percent.

	Rev. ($ mil.)	% of Group
Oracle Corp.	$ 563	53.7%
Informix Software Inc.	162	15.4
The Santa Cruz Operation . . .	140	13.3
Ask Computer Systems Inc. . .	100	9.5
Sybase Inc.	84	8.0

Source: *UnixWorld*, December 1991, p. 53.

★ 1883 ★

Software (SIC 7372)

Windows Spreadsheets

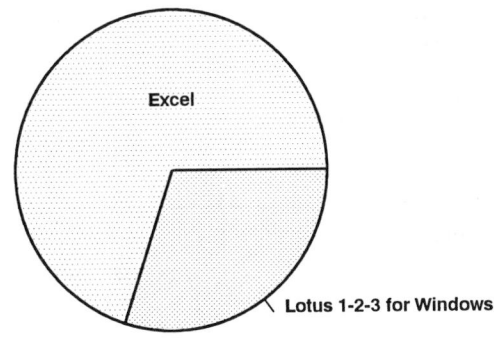

Shares are shown in percent for 1991.

Excel (Microsoft) 70.0%
Lotus 1-2-3 for Windows (Lotus) 30.0

Source: *Advertising Age*, September 28, 1992, p. 14, from InfoCorp.

★ 1884 ★

Data Communications (SIC 7373)

Datacom Networks - Europe

Data are based on a survey of 512 users in the largest companies of nine Western European countries. Shares are shown in percent.

Ethernet 52.0%
Token Ring 27.0
StarLAN 9.0
Arcnet 4.0
Localtalk 3.0
FDDI 0.0
Other 5.0

Source: *Data Communications*, January 21, 1992, p. 8, from Business Research Group.

★ 1885 ★

Image Processing (SIC 7373)

Commercial Image Processing Systems Market

Market segment sales are shown in millions of dollars for 1990. Percent shares are based on group total.

	Sales ($ mil.)	% of Group
Equipment	$ 1,452	62.4%
Input devices	373	16.0
Service	332	14.3
Output devices	89	3.8
Software	82	3.5

Source: *Tooling & Production*, February 1992, p. 51, from Frost & Sullivan, Inc.

★ 1886 ★

Image Processing (SIC 7373)

Image Processing Industry by Segment

Shares of the total image processing market, by segment, are shown in percent.

Banking 23.0%
Government 19.9
Manufacturing 17.9
Insurance 16.0
Transportation 5.8
Communications/Utilities 5.0
Continued on next page.

★ 1886★ *Continued*

Image Processing (SIC 7373)

Image Processing Industry by Segment

Shares of the total image processing market, by segment, are shown in percent.

Business services	4.7%
Other	7.7

Source: *Datamation*, November 15, 1991, p. 81, from IDC/Avante.

★ 1887★

Integrated Systems (SIC 7373)

CAD/CAM Forecast

1991 computer-aided design, computer-aided manufacture and computer-aided engineering industry revenues projection by company. Shares are shown in percent, based on total revenue of $7.3 billion.

IBM	29.9%
Intergraph	15.8
Computervision	13.3
Hewlett-Packard	6.1
Mentor Graphics	5.4
McDonnell Douglas	4.8
Autodesk	3.9
Cadence	3.2
Schlumberger CAD/CAM	2.0
Valid	1.7
Other	13.9

Source: *American Machinist*, January 1992, p. 23, from Daratech Inc.

★ 1888★

Integrated Systems (SIC 7373)

CAD/CAM/CAE Industry - Forecast

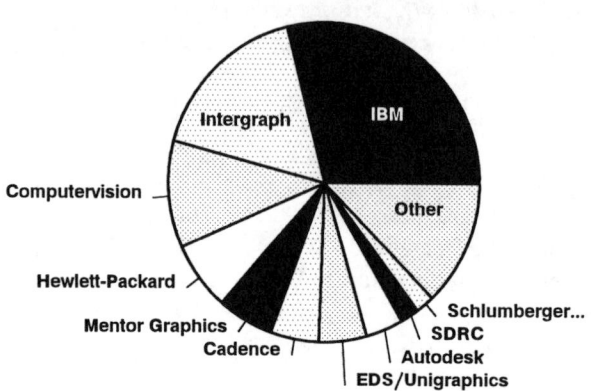

Company shares are based on 1992 total revenues of $8.1 billion, shown in percent.

IBM	29.0%
Intergraph	17.0
Computervision	11.1
Hewlett-Packard	6.7
Mentor Graphics	5.7
Cadence	5.3
EDS/Unigraphics	4.7
Autodesk	4.1
SDRC	1.9
Schlumberger CAD/CAM	1.6
Other	12.9

Source: *Electronic News*, May 18, 1992, p. 19, from Daratech, Inc.

★ 1889★

Integrated Systems (SIC 7373)

Data Processing Market

Market shares, by company, are shown in percent. The figures for 1992 are estimates. SSL is a division of Raytheon.

	1991	1992
Western Atlas	29.1%	28.3%
Halliburton Co.	16.4	16.9
CGG	10.9	10.8
Schlumberger Ltd.	9.1	9.2

Continued on next page.

★**1889**★ *Continued*

Integrated Systems (SIC 7373)

Data Processing Market

Market shares, by company, are shown in percent.
The figures for 1992 are estimates. SSL is a division
of Raytheon.

	1991	1992
Digicon	6.4%	6.9%
SSL	5.5	5.4
Grant Tensor	2.7	3.5
Other	20.0	18.9

Source: Investext, Thomson Financial Networks, June 2, 1992, from Paine Webber, Inc.

★**1890**★

Integrated Systems (SIC 7373)

EMS/SCADA System Developers

Shares of the 1990 market for EMS (energy
management systems) and SCADA (supervisory
control and data acquisition) systems are shown in
percent, based on a total of $157 million.

Harris Corp.	36.4%
Landis & Gyr Inc.	17.5
Empros System International	11.9
ESCA Corp	7.6
Advanced Control Systems	4.5
CAE Electronics	4.1
Stagg Systems	4.4
Other	13.6

Source: *Electrical World*, December 1991, p. 62, from CSR Inc.

★**1891**★

Integrated Systems (SIC 7373)

IS Companies

1991 IS (integrated system) revenues are shown in
millions of dollars; relative market shares are shown
in percent for the same period. Data refer only to
projects valued at more than $1.0
million.

	Rev. ($ mil.)	% of Group
IBM	$ 3,400	40.3%
Electronic Data Systems	1,200	14.2
Andersen Consulting	1,000	11.9
Digital Equipment	700	8.3
Computer Sciences	527	6.3

	Rev. ($ mil.)	% of Group
Cap Gemini	$ 420	5.0%
Groupe Bull	300	3.6
Unisys	230	2.7
TRW	220	2.6
Boeing Computer Services	220	2.6
Planning Research	215	2.5

Source: *The New York Times*, April 22, 1992, p. C7, from The Gartner Group.

★**1892**★

Integrated Systems (SIC 7373)

POS System Manufacturers

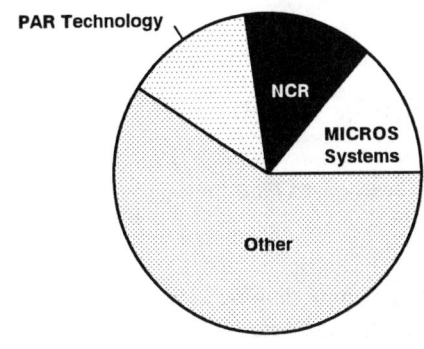

Leaders' shares in the development and application
of POS (point-of-sale) systems technology are shown
in percent.

MICROS Systems	15.0%
NCR	15.0
PAR Technology	15.0
Other	65.0

Source: Investext, Thomson Financial Networks, June 25, 1992, from Anderson & Strudwick, Inc.

★ 1893 ★

Integrated Systems (SIC 7373)

UNIX Systems Vendors - Leaders

The leading five UNIX systems vendors are shown with 1991 total revenues in millions of dollars and relative shares in percent.

	Rev. ($ mil.)	% of Group
Sun Microsystems	$ 3.6300	30.8 %
Hewlett-Packard Co.	3.6000	30.5
IBM Corp.	2.0000	17.0
Digital Equipment Corp.	1.6400	13.9
AT&T Computer Systems Inc.	0.9155	7.8

Source: *UnixWorld*, December 1991, p. 53.

★ 1894 ★

Integrated Systems (SIC 7373)

Who Uses SI?

SI (systems integration) distribution, by application, is shown in percent, based on a total of $3.2 billion in revenue in 1990.

Manufacturing	28.0 %
Transportation, communications, utilities	17.0
Finance, insurance, real estate	13.0
Services	12.0
State & local government	11.0
Retail	10.0
Wholesale	5.0
Construction	3.0
Agriculture, fishing, forestry	1.0

Source: *Networking Management*, August 1991, p. 15, from Frost & Sullivan Inc.

★ 1895 ★

Networks (SIC 7373)

Client/Server Computing Market Worldwide

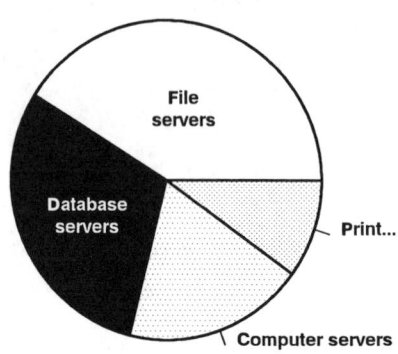

Segment distribution of the worldwide server market is shown in percent, based on vendor revenues in 1991.

File servers	41.0 %
Database servers	30.0
Computer servers	19.0
Print and other servers	10.0

Source: *Networking Management*, July 1992, p. 45, from Dataquest.

★ 1896 ★

Networks (SIC 7373)

Data Network Consumption by Industry

Figures represent percentage of each industry that uses data network devices.

Federal government	66.0 %
Wholesale	64.0
State/local government	62.0
Manufacturing	60.0
Health care	59.0
Transportation	59.0
Education	58.0
Ag/mining/construction	56.0
Utilities	55.0
Banking/financial	52.0
Business services	52.0
Insurance	41.0
Retail	40.0

Source: *Network Management*, March 1992, p. 27.

★ 1897 ★
Networks (SIC 7373)

LAN Leaders

LAN (local area network) market preferences are shown in percent, based on a survey.

IBM LAN Network Manager/Netview . . .	16.9%
Novell NetWare	15.4
Banyan Vines	3.8
SynOptics	3.8
DEC	3.1
3Com	2.3
SunNet LAN Manager	1.5
In-house/proprietary	1.5
Cabletron	1.5
Microsoft LAN Manager	0.8
Other	13.1
Don't know/not available	36.3

Source: *Data Communications*, September 21, 1991, p. 10, from Business Research Group.

★ 1898 ★
Networks (SIC 7373)

Network Devices Market

A survey of 600 readers shows percent of respondents using the devices indicated.

T1	55.0%
Bridges/routers	54.0
Leased analog	53.0
Other leased digital	50.0
Voice/data on backbone	32.0
Fiber optics	29.0
Microwave	26.0
Fractional T1	24.0
Virtual voice	22.0
ISDN	19.0
Satellite circuits	19.0
Virtual data	18.0
T3	14.0
FDDI	13.0
ANI	11.0
VSAT	8.0
Frame relay	6.0
Fractional T3	4.0

Source: *Network Management*, March 1992, p. 24, from *Network Management* survey.

★ 1899 ★
Networks (SIC 7373)

Network Server Market - U.S.

Shares of the U.S. server market, by server type, are shown in percent for 1990 and 1996.

	1990	1996
Super servers	55.0%	57.0%
Enhanced PC servers	31.0	36.0
Terminal servers	14.0	7.0

Source: *Network Management*, September 1991, p. 73.

★ 1900 ★
Networks (SIC 7373)

Protocol Analyzer Manufacturers

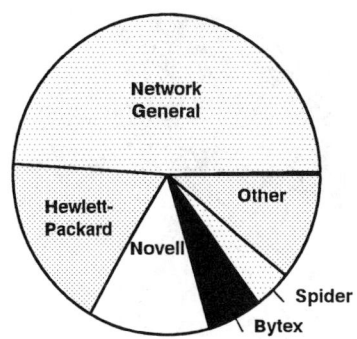

Shares, by manufacturer, are shown in percent, based on 1990 shipments.

Network General	49.2%
Hewlett-Packard	18.1
Novell	12.6
Bytex	6.1
Spider	3.5
Other	10.5

Source: *PC Week*, May 11, 1992, p. 14.

★ 1901 ★

Networks (SIC 7373)

Remote Procedure Calls

Percent distribution of currently used RPCs (remote procedure calls) are shown in percent by company and brand.

IBM (LU6.2/APPC)	.76.0%
Sun (Netwise RPC)	.15.0
Hewlett-Packard (Apollo NCS)	9.0

Source: *Datamation*, May 15, 1991, p. 56.

★ 1902 ★

Networks (SIC 7373)

Token-Ring Port Global Market

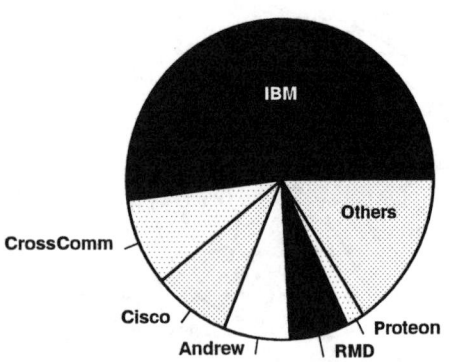

Company shares, based on 1991 total shipments of 42,480 units, are shown in percent.

IBM	.51.8%
CrossComm	9.4
Cisco	7.8
Andrew	6.8
RMD	5.9
Proteon	2.3
Others	.16.0

Source: *PC Week*, April 27, 1992, p. 45, from International Data Corp. and Cross Comm.

★ 1903 ★

Networks (SIC 7373)

Voice Network Market Penetration

Average spending on voice networks, by industry, is shown in percent for 1991.

Retail	.60.0%
Insurance	.59.0

Banking/financial	.48.0%
Business services	.48.0
Utilities	.45.0
AG/mining/construction	.44.0
Education	.42.0
Transportation	.41.0
Health care	.41.0
Manufacturing	.40.0
State/local government	.38.0
Wholesale	.36.0
Federal government	.34.0

Source: *Network Management*, March 1992, p. 27.

★ 1904 ★

Networks (SIC 7373)

WAN Analyzer Vendors

Percent shares are based on total end-user revenues of $106.0 million in sales of wide-area network protocol analyzers. Shares, by vendor, are shown for the 1990 domestic market.

Hewlett-Packard CTD	.30.7%
Tekelec	.19.2
Telenex	.10.0
Hewlett-Packard Idacom	7.7
Network Communications	6.7
CRX/Dialog	6.6
Others	.19.1

Source: *Data Communications*, April 1992, p. 67, from Dataquest.

★ 1905 ★

Networks (SIC 7373)

Wireless LAN Worldwide Market

Shares by storage capacity are shown as percent of the $3.5 million market in 1991 and for the year 1995 (projected $49.5 million). LAN stands for local area network.

	1991	1995
< 10 Mbit/s	86.0%	84.0%
10-50 Mbit/s	14.0	13.0
50 Mbit/s - 1Gbit/s	0.0	3.0
>1 Gbit/s	0.0	0.0

Source: *Data Communications*, November 21, 1991, p. 10, from ElectroniCast Corp.

★ 1906 ★
Information Technology (SIC 7375)

Electronic Information Services

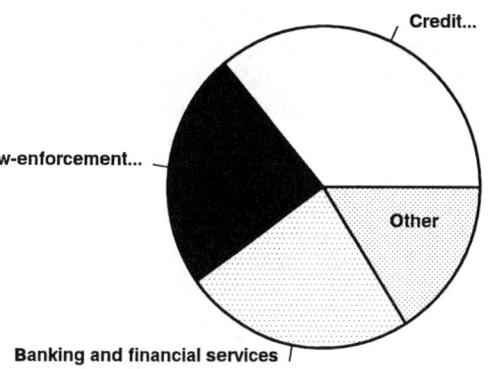

Shares, by use, are shown in percent for 1991.

Credit and collections industry	36.0%
Law-enforcement and investigative services	24.0
Banking and financial services	24.0
Other (including corporate and consumer uses)	16.0

Source: *Wall Street Journal*, April 6, 1992, p. B1, from Jupiter Communications Co.

★ 1907 ★
Information Technology (SIC 7375)

Information Technology Spending

Spending on information technology services is shown in billions of dollars for 1990. Market segments are shown in percent.

	($ bil.)	Share
Database services	$ 9.675	50.3%
On-line transaction processing . .	2.753	14.3
Alarm monitoring/telemetry . . .	2.502	13.0
Telemessaging services	1.096	5.7
Voice information services . . .	1.048	5.5
Value-added network services . .	0.790	4.1
Electronic messaging	0.580	3.0
Residential data services	0.272	1.4
Voice messaging	0.220	1.1
Electronic data interchange . . .	0.160	0.8
Business video services	0.078	0.4
Enhanced facsimile	0.045	0.2

Source: *Data Communications*, September 1991, p. 22, from Link Resources Corp.

★ 1908 ★
Information Technology (SIC 7375)

Online Newspaper Services

Shares of 1990 online newspaper coverage by provider to the 100 most populous U.S. cities and their newspapers. (Newspaper may be provided by more than one online service. City may have more than one paper online).

	Cities	Papers
DataTimes	45	56
VU/Text	42	52
Dialog	26	29
Nexis	15	18

Source: *Database*, August 1992, p. 41, from *Database* survey, *World Almanac*, U.S. Census Bureau, and *Editor and Publisher*.

★ 1909 ★
Computer Consultants (SIC 7379)

Computer Services Leaders

Company shares in the $41.5 billion worldwide market (1992) for consulting, software development, education and training are shown in percent.

IBM	13.5%
EDS	8.1
Andersen Consulting	6.6
Cap Gemini	6.3
Digital Equipment	4.3
Other	61.2

Source: *The New York Times*, September 6, 1992, p. 6F, from Gartner Group.

★ 1910 ★
Security Guard Service (SIC 7381)

Security Guard Companies - Leaders

The ten leading security guard companies in 1991 are shown ordered by number of guards employed.

	(000)
Pinkerton Security	650
Whelan Security Co.	600
Stoehner Security Service Inc.	412
Burns International Security Services . . .	400
Sentry Security Inc.	400
Wells Fargo Guard Service	300
Allied Security Inc.	300
National Industrial Security Corp.	270

Continued on next page.

★ 1910 ★ *Continued*

Security Guard Service (SIC 7381)

Security Guard Companies - Leaders

The ten leading security guard companies in 1991 are shown ordered by number of guards employed.

	(000)
McCormick Professional Service	138
Yale Enforcement	129

Source: *St. Louis Business Journal*, September 32, 1991, p. B1, from security firms listed.

★ 1911 ★

Security Services (SIC 7382)

Alarm Monitoring Leaders - U.K.

Company shares are shown as a percent of the total U.K. market in 1990.

Automated Security Holdings	23.0%
ADT Security (ADT Ltd.)	11.0
Chubb (Racal Elec.)	8.0
Shorrock (BET)	6.0
Securicor	5.0
Thorn	5.0
Others	42.0

Source: Investext, Thomson Financial Networks, March 5, 1992, from Shearson Lehman Brothers, Inc.

★ 1912 ★

Security Services (SIC 7382)

Alarm Monitoring Market Leaders - U.S.

Company shares are shown as a percent of the domestic market in 1990.

ADT Security (ADT Ltd.)	7.4%
Honeywell	2.4
Wells Fargo	2.2
National Guardian (LEP Group)	2.0
Alert Center	1.0
Holmes Protection	0.9
Security Link	0.8
Westec/Secom	0.8

API Alarms (Automated Security Holdings)	0.7%
Rollins Protective	0.6
Brinks	0.6
Others	80.6

Source: Investext, Thomson Financial Networks, March 5, 1992, from Shearson Lehman Brothers, Inc., Support Services Group, and Security Distribution & Marketing.

★ 1913 ★

Security Services (SIC 7382)

Security Service Market

Percent distribution of service revenue is shown for 1990 and 1995 (projected), based on respective totals of $11.835 billion and $17.575 billion.

	1990	1995
Officer and investigative	71.0%	69.4%
Central station monitoring	25.3	26.2
Consulting	3.7	4.4

Source: *Security*, December 1991, p. 58, from The Freedonia Group.

★ 1914 ★

Security Services (SIC 7382)

Security System Market

Security systems by type are shown based on a total of 17 million installed to-date.

Residential	52.0%
Commercial	42.0
Government	6.0

Source: *The Wall Street Journal*, July 1, 1992, p. B3, from STAT Resources Inc.

★1915★
Photo Industry (SIC 7384)

Photofinishing by Outlet

Estimated shares of the photofinishing market are shown in percent. Category includes wholesale, captive and mail order as well as processing by minilab equipment.

	1988	1989	1990
Standalone minilabs	28.4%	26.0%	27.0%
Drugstores	21.5	22.0	22.9
Camera stores	13.9	15.5	15.7
Mass merchandisers	14.2	14.4	14.2
Supermarkets	9.9	10.3	10.0
Mail order	6.7	5.9	5.6
Other	5.4	6.0	4.6

Source: Investext, Thomson Financial Networks, January 10, 1992, from Smith Barney, Harris Upham & Co.

★1916★
Appraisal Services (SIC 7389)

Jewelry Appraisals by Type

Insurance	81.8%
Estates	12.2
Divorce	2.0
Comparison	4.0

Source: *Jewelers' Circular - Keystone*, April 1992, p. 67, from JCK Retail Jewelers panel.

★1917★
Interior Design (SIC 7389)

Interior Design Leaders

The top twenty interior design firms are shown with annual fee volume in millions of dollars and relative market shares in percent. Data refer to 1992.

	($ mil.)	% of Group
Gensler and Associates/ Architects	$ 48.96	16.3%
ISD + AI	25.00	8.3
Howard Needles Tamman & Bergendoff	20.32	6.8
Swanke Hayden Connell Architects	17.25	5.8
R.J. Pavlik, Inc., D/B/A The Pavlik Design Team	16.69	5.6

	($ mil.)	% of Group
Hellmuth, Obata & Kassbaum, Inc.	$ 16.47	5.5%
Sverdup Corporation	16.14	5.4
Leo A Daly	16.11	5.4
Space Design International	12.20	4.1
RTKL Associates, Inc.	11.29	3.8
CRSS Architects, Inc.	11.28	3.8
Smith, Hinchman & Grylls Associates, Inc.	10.92	3.6
The Callison Partnership, Ltd.	10.72	3.6
Walker Group/CNI, Inc.	10.33	3.4
Gwathmey Siegel & Associates Architects	10.00	3.3
Kohn Pederson Fox Conway Associates, Inc.	9.80	3.3
NBBJ Interiors	9.78	3.3
Perkins & Will	9.00	3.0
Mancini-Duffy Associates	8.84	3.0
STUDIOS Architecture	8.56	2.9

Source: *Interior Design*, January 1992, p. 67.

★1918★
Mergers and Acquisitions (SIC 7389)

Cross-Border M&A Deals - Worldwide

The top 5 cross-border merger and acquisition (M&A) deals, announced January 1 to September 30, 1991, are shown in billions of U.S. dollars. Percent shares are based on group total.

	($ bil.)	% of Group
Royal Dutch Shell (Guangdong Petrochemical)	$ 2.50	31.4%
Schneider (Square D)	2.23	28.1
Aberdeen Trust (Ivory & Sime Luxembourg)	1.14	14.3
Ahold (Tops Markets)	1.10	13.8
AXA (Equitable Life)	.98	12.3

Source: *Hispanic Business*, February 1992, p. 70, from KPMG Peat Marwick.

★ 1919 ★

Mergers and Acquisitions (SIC 7389)

Japanese Investments in U.S. Companies

Japanese investment and acquisition deals are ranked by price, shown in millions of dollars. U.S. companies are shown in parentheses.

Nippon Mining (Gould)	$ 1,100
Kyocera (AVX)	575
Hitachi (Natl. Advanced Systems)	398
Yamanouchi Pharmaceuticals (Shaklee) . .	395
Mitsubishi Kasei (Verbatim)	250
Kobe Steel (Electronic Metallurgy)	250
Kyocera (Elco (div. of Wickes))	250
Mitsubishi (UCAR Carbon)	233
Nippon Steel (Oracle Systems)	200
Pioneer Electronics (Discovision)	200
TDK (Silicon Systems)	200
Asahi (Wiltron)	180
Mitsui (Unisys)	150
CIT Group (Chase Aircraft)	130
Chugai Pharmaceuticals (Gen-Probe) . . .	110
Kawasaki Steel (ICI)	100
Canon (Next)	100
Yamanouchi Pharmaceuticals (Roberts Pharmaceuticals)	95
Nippon Sanso (Tri Gas)	88
Dainippon Ink & Chemical (NL Spencer Kellogg)	86

Source: Fortune, June 15, 1992, p. 116, from Economic Strategy Institute.

★ 1920 ★

Mergers and Acquisitions (SIC 7389)

Largest Deals in Mergers and Acquisitions

Target companies are ranked by price of deal, shown in millions of dollars.

NCR Corp.	$ 7,893.4
MCA	7,406.0
Contel Corp	6,243.3
C&S/Sovran Corp.	4,259.0
Fireman's Fund Insurance Co.	3,100.0
Cellular Communications	2,980.0
E.I. du Pont de Nemours & Co.	2,500.0
Societe National Elf Aquitaine's Sanofi unit	2,400.0
Manufacturers Hanover Corp.	2,044.2
R.H. Macy & Co.'s Macy Credit Corp. . .	$ 1,600.0
Harcourt Brace Jovanovich	1,500.0
IBM Corp.	1,500.0

Source: Institutional Investor, March 1992, p. 90, from Securities Data Co.

★ 1921 ★

Mergers and Acquisitions (SIC 7389)

M&A Advisors in Banking

Companies are ranked by 1991 announced volume of transactions, shown in millions of dollars. Relative market shares are shown in percent.

	($ mil.)	% of Group
First Boston Corporation . .	$ 13,200.6	21.8%
Morgan Stanley & Company . .	12,905.4	21.3
Merrill Lynch & Company . . .	7,367.6	12.2
Salomon Brothers	6,842.8	11.3
Goldman Sachs & Company . .	6,060.0	10.0
Lehman Brothers	4,942.1	8.2
Dillon, Read & Company . . .	4,901.9	8.1
Montgomery Securities	1,235.0	2.0
Wasserstein Perella	1,000.0	1.7
Chicago Corporation	658.4	1.1
Keefe, Bruyette & Woods . . .	319.5	0.5
Donaldson, Lufkin & Jenrette .	283.0	0.5
Austin Associates	134.9	0.2
Alex Sheshunoff & Company . .	149.1	0.2
Scott & Stringfellow Investment	124.0	0.2
McDonald & Company	110.8	0.2
Kemper Securities	102.0	0.2
Prudential Securities	88.0	0.1
Sandler O'Neill & Partners . . .	73.0	0.1
J.C. Bradford & Company . . .	72.0	0.1

Source: Banker, May 1992, p. 14.

★ 1922 ★

Mergers and Acquisitions (SIC 7389)

M&A Advisors - 1991

The top 10 M & A (mergers and acquisitions) advisors are shown with value of transactions in millions of dollars and relative market shares in percent. Data are shown for 1991.

	($ mil.)	% of Group
Lehman Brothers	$ 4,509	25.1 %
Blackstone Group	3,450	19.2
First Boston/Credit Suisse . . .	2,391	13.3
Morgan Stanley	2,286	12.7
Wasserstein, Perella	1,044	5.8
J.P. Morgan	1,001	5.6
Robertson Stephens	897	5.0
Lazard Houses	894	5.0
Goldman, Sachs	891	5.0
Salomon Brothers	621	3.5

Source: *Chemicalweek*, March 18, 1992, p. 22, from Securities Data Corp.

★ 1923 ★

Mergers and Acquisitions (SIC 7389)

Top Players in Mergers and Acquisitions

Leaders in mergers and acquisitions in 1991 are ranked by their transaction volumes, shown in millions of dollars. Percent shares are based on group total.

	Vol. ($ mil.)	% of Group
Goldman Sachs	$ 27,846.0	13.6 %
Morgan Stanley	21,364.3	10.5
Salomon Brothers	18,529.6	9.1
Lehman Brothers	17,212.7	8.4
Lazard Freres	16,664.1	8.2
Merrill Lynch	16,632.9	8.1
First Boston	16,052.1	7.9
Dillon Read	14,982.0	7.3
Wasserstein Perella	10,308.2	5.0
PaineWebber	8,517.2	4.2
Allen & Co.	7,471.2	3.7
James D. Wolfensohn	5,066.0	2.5
Donaldson, Lufkin & Jenrette .	4,271.2	2.1
J.P. Morgan	4,215.5	2.1

	Vol. ($ mil.)	% of Group
Smith Barney, Harris Upham .	.$ 4,072.3	2.0 %
Prudential Securities	1,483.3	0.7
Blackstone Group	1,325.0	0.6
Chase Manhattan	1,306.0	0.6
Kidder Peabody	1,243.2	0.6
Montgomery Securities	1,122.2	0.5
Gleacher	1,046.5	0.5
Bear Stearns	1,005.1	0.5
Robertson Stephens	997.1	0.5
Dean Witter	819.6	0.4
Petrie Parkman	763.4	0.4

Source: *Institutional Investor*, March 1992, p. 87, from Securities Data Co.

★ 1924 ★

Mergers and Acquisitions (SIC 7389)

Top Takeovers of 1992

The leading acquirers as of June 1992, are shown with target companies in parentheses and value of deals in billions of dollars.

Sprint (Centel)	$ 2.85
Entergy (Gulf States)	2.28
KKR (American Re)	1.40
BancOne (Valley National)	1.19
Fifth Third Bancorp (Star Banc)	1.16

Source: *The Wall Street Journal*, June 10, 1992, p. C1, from Securities Data Corp.

SIC 75 - Auto Repair, Services, and Parking

★1925★

Trailer Rental (SIC 7513)

Trailer Rental Firms - U.K.

Shares of vehicles rented are shown in percent.

Tiphook	32.0%
TIP Europe	13.0
BRS (NFC)	2.0
Other	53.0

Source: Investext, Thomson Financial Networks, January 15, 1992, from UBS Phillips & Drew Global Research Group.

★1926★

Car Rental (SIC 7514)

Car Rental Firms Worldwide

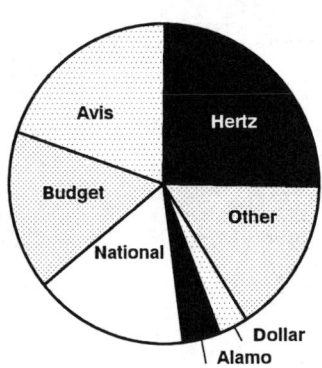

Company shares of the 1990 market are shown in percent, based on an estimated total of $15.8 billion. The figure for National includes operations of Europcar and Tilden Rent-A-Car. The figure for Dollar includes operations of Euro-Dollar. The figure for Avis is based on estimated revenue.

Hertz	25.3%
Avis	20.3
Budget	15.8
National	15.8
Alamo	3.8
Dollar	3.2
Other	15.8

Source: *The New York Times*, January 19, 1992, p. 10F, from *Business Travel News*.

★ 1927 ★

Car Rental (SIC 7514)

Car Rentals - Federal Travel Vendors

Car rental companies are shown as federal vendors whose market share in 1990 was greater than 5 percent, as measured in billings through the government's travel card program, administered by Citibank/Diners Club. Data represent fiscal 1990 sales in thousands of dollars which were only one-fifth of the government's travel expenses. Market share is shown in percent.

	($000)	Share
Budget	$ 25,528	27.5 %
National	17,245	18.5
Hertz	14,662	15.8
Avis	12,149	13.1
Dollar	5,369	5.8

Source: *Government Executive*, August 1991, p. 50, from General Services Administration.

★ 1928 ★

Car Rental (SIC 7514)

Leading Car Rental Companies

Relative market shares of the top companies are shown as percent of 22,364 locations worldwide and 1,817,568 vehicles.

	Locations	Vehicles
Hertz	24.6 %	22.0 %
Avis	21.5	22.0
National	20.6	15.2
Budget	15.5	13.8
Alamo	0.5	7.0
Enterprise	4.9	6.1
Dollar	3.8	5.4
American International	4.3	4.5
Thrifty	2.9	2.5
General	0.3	1.0
Payless	0.8	0.4
Advantage	0.3	0.3

Source: *The New York Times*, January 15, 1992, p. C1, from *Corporate Travel*.

★ 1929 ★

Automotive Services (SIC 7549)

Tuneups by Type of Service Outlet

Tuneup market shares by type of service outlet are shown in percent for 1991.

New car dealers	25.3 %
Repair shops	15.5
Auto parts retail	15.1
Service stations	12.2
KMart/Wal-Mart	6.0
Tuneup specialists	5.9
Auto parts wholesale	5.5
All other	14.5

Source: *National Petroleum News*, June 1992, p. 171, from Champion Spark Plug Co. survey.

SIC 78 - Motion Pictures

★1930★

Entertainment (SIC 7800)

Showbiz Production - Australia

Shares are shown in percent, based on revenues in Australian dollars.

In-house television	47.8%
Commercials	27.6
Independent television dramas	12.9
Feature films	10.5
Corporate	5.0
Documentaries	1.8
Music videos	0.4

Source: *Variety*, April 27, 1992, p. 66.

★1931★

Motion Pictures (SIC 7812)

Box Office Market Shares

Domestic motion picture box office market share by studio for 1989, 1990, and 1991.

	1989	1990	1991
Warner Bros.	17.4%	13.1%	13.9%
Buena Vista	13.9	15.5	13.7
Paramount	13.8	14.9	12.0
20th Fox	6.5	13.1	11.6
Universal	16.6	13.1	11.0
Tri-Star	7.9	9.0	10.9
Columbia	8.1	4.9	9.1
Orion	4.2	5.6	8.5
New Line	1.3	4.4	4.0

	1989	1990	1991
MGM	6.3%	2.8%	2.3%
Other	4.0	3.6	3.0

Source: *Variety*, January 13, 1992, p. 7.

★1932★

Motion Pictures (SIC 7812)

Box Office Shares

Shares are shown in percent, based on revenue totals of $5.02 billion in 1990 and $4.53 billion in 1991. Figures for 1991 are estimated.

	1990	1991
Columbia/Tri-Star	12.4%	18.7%
Warner	11.1	13.2
Disney	13.3	13.0
Paramount	12.7	11.3
Universal	11.5	11.3
20th Century Fox	10.9	10.9
Orion	5.0	8.5
MGM/United Artists	2.2	2.3
Other	20.8	10.8

Source: Investext, Thomson Financial Networks, January 7, 1992, from Paine Webber Inc.

★1933★

Motion Pictures (SIC 7812)

Box Office Shares - 1992

Studio market shares are shown for the period from January 1st through March 8, 1992.

Disney	27.7%
Universal	14.7
Warner Bros.	14.6
Paramount	14.5

Continued on next page.

★ **1933** ★ *Continued*

Motion Pictures (SIC 7812)

Box Office Shares - 1992

Studio market shares are shown for the period from January 1st through March 8, 1992.

20th Century Fox	8.1%
Tri-Star	7.8
Columbia	7.6
MGM	1.3

Source: Investext, Thomson Financial Networks, March 30, 1992, from Oppenheimer & Co., Inc.

★ **1934** ★

Motion Pictures (SIC 7812)

Studio Shares - 1991

Company shares are shown in percent based on total box office gross revenue in 1991. Sony Pictures includes Columbia and Tri-Star.

Sony Pictures	20.0%
Warner Bros.	13.9
Walt Disney	13.7
Paramount Pictures	12.0
20th Century Fox	11.6
Universal	11.0
Orion	8.5
Other	9.3

Source: *The Wall Street Journal*, January 15, 1992, p. B1, from *Variety*.

★ **1935** ★

Motion Pictures (SIC 7812)

Theatrical Box Office Shares

Domestic box office shares, by producer/distributor, are shown in percent.

	1990	1991
Warner	13.1%	14.2%
Columbia/Tri-Star	10.1	14.0
Disney	15.5	13.8
Paramount	14.9	12.2
Fox	13.1	11.6
Orion	5.6	8.5
MCA	11.6	6.6
Carolco	3.8	6.3
Imagine	1.5	4.7
New Line	4.4	4.2

	1990	1991
MGM/UA/Pathe	2.8%	2.4%
Other	3.6	1.5

Source: Investext, Thomson Financial Networks, February 26, 1992, from Seidler Amdec Securities Inc.

★ **1936** ★

Motion Pictures (SIC 7812)

Top Films in Summer Season

Top films are ranked by cumulative box-office gross in summer season through July 12.

	($ mil.)	% of Group
Batman Returns (Warner)	$ 137.5	22.3%
Lethal Weapon 3 (Warner)	134.2	21.7
Sister Act (Disney)	89.2	14.5
Patriot Games (Paramount)	70.0	11.3
Alien 3 (Fox)	53.1	8.6
Far and Away (Universal)	51.4	8.3
Housesitter (Universal)	42.8	6.9
A League of Their Own	38.9	6.3

Source: *The Wall Street Journal*, July 14, 1992, p. B1, from *Exhibitor-Relations*.

★ **1937** ★

Film Distribution (SIC 7822)

Film Distributors - Italy

Film distributors grossed $186.183 million for the period of September 1, 1990 to January 12, 1991 and $191.699 million for the period of September 1, 1991 to January 12, 1992. (All companies listed are Italian except UIP, Fox, Warner Bros., and Columbia Tri-Star. $1.00 = 1,180 lire). Shares are shown in percent.

	1991	1992
Penta	29.8%	38.3%
Filmauro	8.6	12.6
UIP	22.2	9.3
Artosti Associati	1.9	8.9
Fox	1.5	7.3
Warner Bros.	26.6	5.9
Columbia Tri-Star	2.7	5.6
Italian Int. Film	0.2	3.9
Titanus Distrib.	0.6	3.2
Life	1.1	1.4

Continued on next page.

★ 1937 ★ *Continued*
Film Distribution (SIC 7822)

Film Distributors - Italy

Film distributors grossed $186.183 million for the period of September 1, 1990 to January 12, 1991 and $191.699 million for the period of September 1, 1991 to January 12, 1992. (All companies listed are Italian except UIP, Fox, Warner Bros., and Columbia Tri-Star. $1.00 = 1,180 lire). Shares are shown in percent.

	1991	1992
Mikado	0.9%	1.2%
Other	3.9	2.4

Source: *Variety*, January 20, 1992, p. 39.

★ 1938 ★
Film Distribution (SIC 7822)

Film Rentals - Australia

Crocodile Dundee
Crocodile Dundee 2
E.T.
Pretty Woman
The Man From Snowy River
Indiana Jones and the Last Crusade
Ghost
Three Men and a Baby
Star Wars
Fatal Attraction

1991 shares of top 10 film rentals by movie title in Australia, distributed in millions of Australian dollars. Relative shares are converted to percent.

	(Aus. $ mil.)	% of Group
Crocodile Dundee	$ 19.77	20.7%
Crocodile Dundee 2	12.31	12.9
E.T.	11.42	11.9
Pretty Woman	8.67	9.1
The Man From Snowy River	7.82	8.2
Indiana Jones and the Last Crusade	7.71	8.1
Ghost	7.61	8.0
Three Men and a Baby	7.45	7.8
Star Wars	6.41	6.7
Fatal Attraction	6.40	6.7

Source: *Variety*, April 27, 1992, p. 64, from MPDAA.

★ 1939 ★
Film Distribution (SIC 7822)

Film Rentals - Foreign

Top film distributors are ranked by film rental revenues overseas ($1.223 billion, 1991). Company shares are shown in percent.

	($ mil.)	% of Group
20th Century Fox	$ 265	21.7%
Columbia Tri-Star	210	17.2
Buena Vista Intl.	190	15.5
Paramount	155	12.7
Warner Bros	141	11.5
Universal	139	11.4
Orion	70	5.7
MGM	53	4.3

Source: *Variety*, January 27, 1992, p. 71, from studios and *Variety* estimates.

★ 1940 ★
Movie Theaters (SIC 7832)

Top Movie Theaters - North America

Top 10 film exhibitors in the U.S. and Canada are ranked by number of screens. Shares of group are shown in percent.

	Screens	% of Group
United Artist Theater Circuit	2,451	20.5%
Cineplex Odeon	1,716	14.3
American Multi Cinema	1,626	13.6
General Cinema	1,466	12.2
Carmike Cinemas	1,400	11.7
Loews	866	7.2
Cinemark USA	865	7.2
National Amusements	628	5.2
Mann	486	4.1
Famous Players	479	4.0

Source: *Variety*, March 30, 1992, p. 58.

SIC 79 - Amusement and Recreation Services

★ 1941 ★

Entertainment (SIC 7900)

Event Sponsorship by U.S. Firms

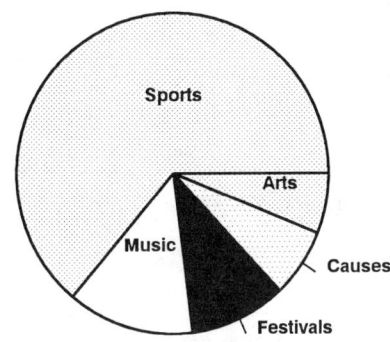

Segment distribution is shown in percent, based on 1991 total spending of $2,940 million.

Sports	64.3%
Music	12.9
Festivals	9.9
Causes	7.0
Arts	6.0

Source: *Jewelers' Circular-Keystone*, February 1992, p. 206, from *Special Events Report*.

★ 1942 ★

Television Programs (SIC 7922)

Late-Night TV Market Penetration

Favorite late-night network TV shows for 1990-92 are represented by percent of household penetration. "Late Night I" and "Late Night II" aired one-half hour later (12:00 a.m. ET) last season.

	'90-'91	'91-'92
Saturday Night Live (NBC)	22.0%	24.0%
Tonight Show (NBC)	16.0	16.0
David Letterman II (NBC)	15.0	15.0
David Letterman I (NBC)	15.0	14.0

	'90-'91	'91-'92
Nightline (ABC)	16.0%	13.0%
Arsenio Hall (Syndicated)	12.0	12.0
Friday Night Videos (NBC)	12.0	11.0
Later With Bob Costa (NBC) . . .	12.0	11.0
Late Night I (CBS)	8.0	10.0
Comic Strip Live (Fox)	7.0	7.0
ABC's in Concert (ABC)	-	6.0
Late Night II (CBS)	7.0	6.0

Source: *Advertising Age*, April 20, 1992, p. 44, from N.W. Ayer analysis and Nielsen Media Research.

★ 1943 ★

Television Programs (SIC 7922)

Programming ECI Revenues

1991 Electronic Communications Index revenues which companies derive from television programming, shown in millions of dollars. Company shares are shown in percent.

	Rev.	Share
Viacom	$ 1,711.6	21.2%
Turner Broadcasting	1,383.0	17.1
Home Shopping Network	1,035.5	12.8
QVC Network	921.8	11.4
Paramount	810.4	10.0
Walt Disney Co.	752.3	9.3
King World Productions	475.9	5.9
Gaylord Entertainment	361.0	4.5
Westwood One	144.4	1.8
Charter Co. (8 months)	122.7	1.5
International Family Ent.	113.7	1.4
Liberty Media	106.8	1.3

Continued on next page.

★ 1943 ★ *Continued*

Television Programs (SIC 7922)

Programming ECI Revenues

1991 Electronic Communications Index revenues which companies derive from television programming, shown in millions of dollars. Company shares are shown in percent.

	Rev.	Share
Republic Pictures	$ 47.4	0.6%
Dick Clark Productions	41.8	0.5
All American Communications	27.5	0.3
Playboy Enterprises	26.7	0.3

Source: *Broadcasting*, June 22, 1992, p. 48, from company estimates, securities analysts, industry associations.

★ 1944 ★

Theatrical Production (SIC 7922)

Broadway Production Profile

Shares are shown in percent, based on a total of 36 productions in FY 1991-92.

Plays

New	41.7%
Revivals	27.8

Musicals

New	19.4
Revivals	8.3
Return shows	2.8

Source: *Variety*, June 8, 1992, p. 58.

★ 1945 ★

Theatrical Productions (SIC 7922)

Broadway Hits

The 20 longest-running Broadway shows that have played at least 1,000 performances, as of June 3, 1992, not including previews. The table ranks plays and musicals by total number in attendance. ("O, Calcutta!" is the only revival included in the table because it played more than 1,000 performances in both original and revival productions). Relative shares are shown in percent.

	Atten-dance	% of Group
A Chorus Line	6,137	10.4%
O, Calcutta!	5,852	9.9
Cats	4,033	6.9

	Atten-dance	% of Group
42nd Street	3,486	5.9%
Grease	3,388	5.8
Fiddler on the Roof	3,242	5.5
Life With Father	3,224	5.5
Tobacco Road	3,182	5.4
Hello, Dolly!	2,844	4.8
My Fair Lady	2,717	4.6
Annie	2,377	4.0
Man of La Mancha	2,328	4.0
Abie's Irish Rose	2,327	4.0
Oklahoma!	2,212	3.8
Les Miserables	2,119	3.6
Pippin	1,944	3.3
South Pacific	1,925	3.3
Magic Show	1,920	3.3
Phantom of the Opera	1,819	3.1
Deathtrap	1,792	3.0

Source: *Variety*, June 8, 1992, p. 58.

★ 1946 ★

Concert Artists (SIC 7929)

Top Concert Tours - 1991

Performer shares are shown in percent based on concert tour revenue totaling approximately $825.0 million.

The Grateful Dead	4.2%
ZZ Top	3.0
The Judds	2.8
Rod Stewart	2.7
Paul Simon	2.6
Guns N' Roses	2.5
Bell Biv De Voe/Johnny Gill/Keith Swaet	2.1
Michael Bolton	2.1
Garth Brooks	2.1
Clint Black	1.8
Other	74.2

Source: *The Wall Street Journal*, May 20, 1992, p. B1, from *Pollstar*.

★ 1947 ★

Sport Events (SIC 7941)

Barcelona Olympic Games - Forecast Receipts

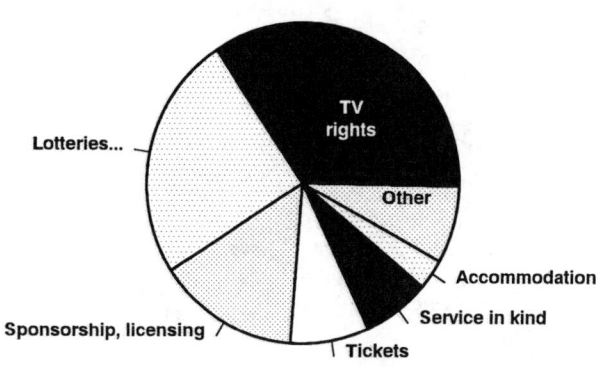

Forecast receipts of Barcelona Olympics organizing committee are $1.52 billon. Percent shares are shown by source. "Accommodation" includes media, VIPs etc.

TV rights	35.0%
Lotteries, coins, medals, stamps	25.0
Sponsorship, licensing	15.0
Tickets	8.0
Service in kind	7.0
Accommodation	3.0
Other	8.0

Source: *The Economist*, July 25, 1992, p. 18, from COOB.

★ 1948 ★

Sport Events (SIC 7941)

Television-Rights for Sport Events

Television-rights contracts, by type of sport event, are shown in millions of dollars and as percent of group total.

	($ mil.)	% of Group
1992 Summer Olympics	$ 635	62.3%
1992 Winter Olympics	295	28.9
1994 FIFA World Cup	90	8.8

Source: *The Economist*, July 25, 1992, p. 4.

★ 1949 ★

Amusement Parks (SIC 7996)

Leading Theme Parks

Companies are ranked by estimated 1991 attendance, shown in millions of visits. Percent shares are based on total for the group.

	Visits	%
Disney Magic K./Epcot/MGM	28.0	40.0%
Disneyland	11.6	16.6
Universal Studios Florida	5.9	8.4
Universal Studios Hollywood	4.6	6.6
Knott's Berry Farm	4.0	5.7
Sea World of Florida	3.4	4.9
Sea World of California	3.3	4.7
Six Flags Magic Mountain	3.2	4.6
Cedar Point	3.0	4.3
Santa Cruz Beach Boardwalk	3.0	4.3

Source: *The Wall Street Journal*, May 27, 1992, p. B1, from Amusement Business.

★ 1950 ★

Bowling (SIC 7997)

ABC Bowling Memberships

1990-91 memberships for the 25 largest local American Bowling Congress associations amounted to 652,716, which represents 22.33% of ABC's 2,922,829 total membership. Relative shares are shown in percent.

	No. Memb.	% of Group
Greater Detroit	98,230	15.0%
Chicago Metropolitan	52,008	8.0
Nation's Capital Area	35,749	5.5
Eastern Long Island	31,019	4.8
Minneapolis District	28,120	4.3
Denver	26,216	4.0
Citrus Belt	25,138	3.9
Greater St. Louis	23,965	3.7
Buffalo	23,823	3.6
Rochester	23,312	3.6
Greater Cleveland	23,177	3.6
Greater Milwaukee	22,750	3.5
New York	22,085	3.4
Greater Cincinnati	19,822	3.0
Houston	19,273	3.0
Greater Philadelphia	19,032	2.9
Greater Phoenix	18,619	2.9
Greater Baltimore	18,514	2.8

Continued on next page.

★ 1950 ★ *Continued*

Bowling (SIC 7997)

ABC Bowling Memberships

1990-91 memberships for the 25 largest local American Bowling Congress associations amounted to 652,716, which represents 22.33% of ABC's 2,922,829 total membership. Relative shares are shown in percent.

	No. Memb.	% of Group
Orange County	18,411	2.8%
Greater Columbus	17,911	2.7
Toledo	17,637	2.7
Los Angeles	17,546	2.7
Greater Indianapolis	17,418	2.7
Greater Louisville	16,885	2.6
Greater Grand Rapids	16,056	2.5

Source: *American Bowling Congress Annual Report 1990-91*, 1991, p. 14.

★ 1951 ★

Bowling (SIC 7997)

Bowling League Majors

Top 10 local Women's Bowling Associations measured by number of leagues. Share of group shown in percent.

	Leagues	%
Detroit WBA	2,425	19.2%
Chicago WBA	1,491	11.8
Citrus Belt WBA	1,353	10.7
Washington D.C. Area WBA . .	1,281	10.1
Denver WBA	1,242	9.8
Minneapolis WBA	1,012	8.0
Orange County WBA	999	7.9
Milwaukee WBA	978	7.7
Phoenix WBA	936	7.4
Houston WBA	917	7.3

Source: *1990-91 WIBC Annual Report*, 1991, p. 48.

★ 1952 ★

Bowling (SIC 7997)

Bowling Member Majors

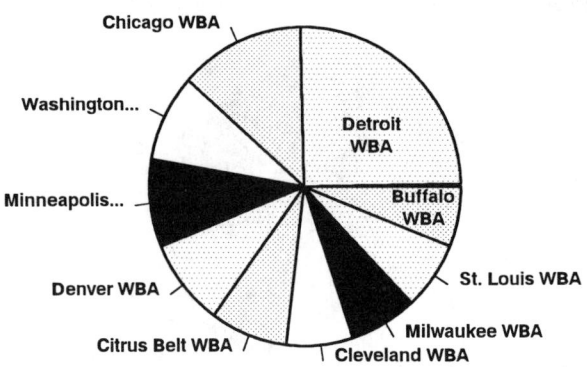

Top 10 local Women's Bowling Associations measured by number of members. Share of group shown in percent.

	Members	%
Detroit WBA	76,055	24.5%
Chicago WBA	41,491	13.4
Washington D.C. Area WBA . .	28,109	9.1
Minneapolis WBA	27,831	9.0
Denver WBA	26,429	8.5
Citrus Belt WBA	24,403	7.9
Cleveland WBA	22,300	7.2
Milwaukee WBA	22,272	7.2
St. Louis WBA	21,570	6.9
Buffalo WBA	19,981	6.4

Source: *1990-91 WIBC Annual Report*, 1991, p. 48.

★ 1953 ★

Golf Clubs (SIC 7997)

Most Expensive Golf Clubs in Tokyo

Golf clubs are shown with number of members. Shares shares, based on the group's membership total, are shown in percent.

	Members	%
Totsuka Country Club	2,328	22.4%
Sagamihara Golf Club	2,091	20.1
Hakone Country Club	1,804	17.4
Takanodai Country Club	1,487	14.3
Atsugi Country Club	1,180	11.4
Yomiuri Golf Club	1,038	10.0
Koganei Country Club	467	4.5

Source: *International Real Estate Journal*, July 1991, p. 32, from *Asahi Golf 1991* and *National Course Guide*.

★ 1954 ★

Gambling (SIC 7999)

Legal Betting in Sport

Pari-mutuel wagering for the sports on which betting is legal is shown in billions of dollars for 1990. Relative market shares are in percent.

	($ bil.)	% of Group
Horse racing	$ 14.3	88.3%
Greyhound racing	1.4	8.6
Jai alai	0.5	3.1

Source: *USA TODAY*, June 29, 1992, p. C1.

★ 1955 ★

Leisure Activities (SIC 7999)

Favorite Outdoor Leisure Activities in U.S.

Favorite outdoor leisure activities are shown with percentage of respondents participating in each activity.

Walking/jogging	88.0%
Driving	82.0
Swimming	55.0
Bicycling	44.0
Fishing	37.0
Boating	36.0
Camping	29.0
Backpacking/hiking	18.0
Skiing	15.0

Source: *Sporting Goods Business*, June 1991, p. 16, from Peter Market Research Associates.

★ 1956 ★

Professional Baseball (SIC 7999)

Baseball Revenues

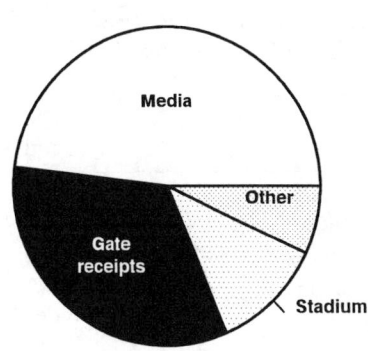

Shares of revenues, by source, are shown in percent, based on a total of $1.35 billion.

Media	48.5%
Gate receipts	33.5
Stadium	11.6
Other	6.5

Source: *Financial World*, July 1991, p. 36.

★ 1957 ★

Professional Baseball (SIC 7999)

Baseball Teams - Major League

Revenues for 1991 are shown in millions of dollars; shares are shown in percent for the same period.

	Rev. ($ mil.)	Share
N.Y. Mets	$ 91.1	6.5%
N.Y. Yankees	90.0	6.4
Toronto Blue Jays	88.7	6.3
Boston Red Sox	81.5	5.8
L.A. Dodgers	79.3	5.6
Chicago White Sox	78.0	5.6
Oakland Athletics	64.9	4.6
Chicago Cubs	64.5	4.6
Texas Rangers	61.5	4.4
St. Louis Cardinals	59.1	4.2
California Angels	54.1	3.8
Kansas City Royals	53.6	3.8
Detroit Tigers	51.6	3.7
Cincinnati Reds	49.0	3.5
S.F. Giants	48.9	3.5
San Diego Padres	48.4	3.4
Houston Astros	46.0	3.3

Continued on next page.

★ 1957 ★ *Continued*
Professional Baseball (SIC 7999)

Baseball Teams - Major League

Revenues for 1991 are shown in millions of dollars; shares are shown in percent for the same period.

	Rev. ($ mil.)	Share
Pittsburgh Pirates	$ 45.8	3.3%
Seattle Mariners	44.7	3.2
Minnesota Twins	44.1	3.1
Cleveland Indians	42.0	3.0
Atlanta Braves	40.3	2.9
Montreal Expos	39.4	2.8
Milwaukee Brewers	38.8	2.8

Source: *USA TODAY*, June 16, 1992, p. 2C, from *Financial World*.

★ 1958 ★

Professional Baseball (SIC 7999)

Baseball - Professional Franchises

Baseball franchises are ranked by 1990 revenues in millions of dollars. Shares are shown in percent.

	Rev. ($ mil.)	Share
New York Yankees	$ 98.0	7.5%
New York Mets	81.1	6.2
Toronto Blue Jays	77.5	5.9
Boston Red Sox	68.5	5.2
Los Angeles Dodgers	64.4	4.9
Philadelphia Phillies	61.9	4.7
Oakland Athletics	57.9	4.4
St. Louis Cardinals	55.8	4.3
Kansas City Royals	53.2	4.1
Chicago Cubs	50.3	3.8
Texas Rangers	50.3	3.8
San Francisco Giants	50.0	3.8
Chicago White Sox	49.0	3.7
Cincinnati Reds	48.7	3.7
California Angels	48.6	3.7
Baltimore Orioles	47.9	3.7
San Diego Padres	47.2	3.6
Pittsburgh Pirates	41.1	3.1
Houston Astros	40.0	3.1
Minnesota Twins	38.6	2.9
Milwaukee Brewers	38.4	2.9
Detroit Tigers	38.0	2.9
Atlanta Braves	35.4	2.7

	Rev. ($ mil.)	Share
Montreal Expos	$ 35.3	2.7%
Seattle Mariners	34.0	2.6

Source: *Financial World*, July 9, 1991, p. 41.

★ 1959 ★

Professional Basketball (SIC 7999)

Basketball Revenues

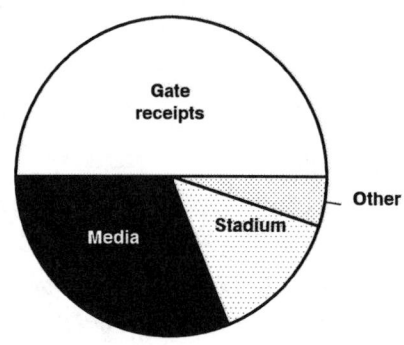

Shares of revenue, by source, are shown in percent, based on a total of $606 million.

Gate receipts	50.2%
Media	31.2
Stadium	14.2
Other	4.5

Source: *Financial World*, July 1991, p. 37.

★ 1960 ★

Professional Basketball (SIC 7999)

Basketball Teams - NBA

Revenues for 1991 are shown in millions of dollars; shares are shown in percent for the same period.

	Rev. ($ mil.)	Share
L.A. Lakers	$ 62.6	7.4%
Detroit Pistons	45.0	5.3
Boston Celtics	41.8	5.0
Chicago Bulls	41.2	4.9
Portland Trail Blazers	36.2	4.3
Clevland Cavaliers	35.3	4.2
Charlotte Hornets	34.4	4.1
N.Y. Knicks	33.8	4.0
San Antonio Spurs	33.0	3.9

Continued on next page.

★**1960**★ *Continued*

Professional Basketball (SIC 7999)

Basketball Teams - NBA

Revenues for 1991 are shown in millions of dollars; shares are shown in percent for the same period.

	Rev. ($ mil.)	Share
Minneapolis Timberwolves . . .	$ 32.7	3.9%
Golden State Warriors	30.8	3.7
Philadelphia 76ers	30.1	3.6
Phoenix Suns	29.9	3.5
Dallas Mavericks	29.3	3.5
Houston Rockets	28.4	3.4
L.A. Clippers	28.3	3.4
Utah Jazz	27.5	3.3
Orlando Magic	27.3	3.2
New Jersey Nets	26.8	3.2
Miami Heat	26.3	3.1
Sacramento Kings	26.3	3.1
Atlanta Hawks	24.7	2.9
Milwaukee Bucks	24.2	2.9
Seattle SuperSonics	22.4	2.7
Indiana Pacers	21.7	2.6
Washington Bullets	21.6	2.6
Denver Nuggets	21.5	2.6

Source: *USA TODAY*, June 16, 1992, p. 2C, from *Financial World*.

★**1961**★

Professional Basketball (SIC 7999)

Basketball - Professional Franchises

Professional basketball franchises are ranked by 1990 revenues in millions of dollars. Shares are shown in percent.

	Rev. ($ mil.)	Share
Los Angeles Lakers	$ 62.2	10.3%
Detroit Pistons	47.3	7.8
Boston Celtics	30.7	5.1
Chicago Bulls	27.4	4.5
New York Knicks	25.6	4.2
Charlotte Hornets	22.8	3.8
Cleveland Cavaliers	22.6	3.7
Orlando Magic	22.5	3.7
Houston Rockets	22.3	3.7
Miami Heat	21.7	3.6
Portland Trailblazers	21.4	3.5
Dallas Mavericks	20.9	3.4

	Rev. ($ mil.)	Share
Phoenix Suns	$ 20.7	3.4%
Philadelphia 76ers	20.4	3.4
Golden State Warriors	19.5	3.2
Atlanta Hawks	19.1	3.2
Milwaukee Bucks	19.1	3.2
Minnesota Timberwolves	19.0	3.1
Sacramento Kings	18.9	3.1
San Antonio Spurs	17.2	2.8
Los Angeles Clippers	16.5	2.7
New Jersey Nets	16.4	2.7
Utah Jazz	16.0	2.6
Denver Nuggets	15.6	2.6
Washington Bullets	13.9	2.3
Seattle Supersonics	13.8	2.3
Indiana Pacers	12.8	2.1

Source: *Financial World*, July 9, 1991, p. 41.

★**1962**★

Professional Football (SIC 7999)

Football Revenues

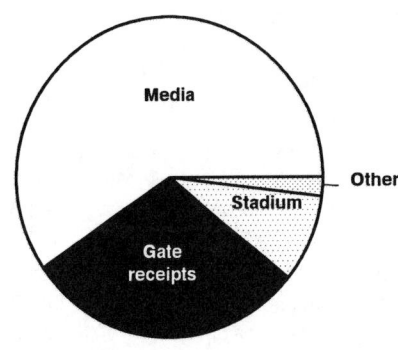

Shares of revenue, by source, are shown in percent, based on a total of $1.31 billion.

Media	59.5%
Gate receipts	29.6
Stadium	9.1
Other	1.8

Source: *Financial World*, July 1991, p. 37.

★ 1963 ★
Professional Football (SIC 7999)

Football Teams - NFL

Revenues for 1991 are shown in millions of dollars; shares are shown in percent for the same period.

	Rev. ($ mil.)	Share
Miami Dolphins	$ 66.0	4.5%
Buffalo Bills	61.0	4.2
Cleveland Browns	59.8	4.1
Philadelphia Eagles	57.4	3.9
Houston Oilers	56.8	3.9
Chicago Bears	56.6	3.9
N.Y. Giants	56.6	3.9
Dallas Cowboys	55.8	3.8
S.F. 49ers	55.5	3.8
Cincinnati Bengals	53.9	3.7
Seattle Seahawks	52.6	3.6
Washington Redskins	52.2	3.6
L.A. Raiders	51.9	3.5
L.A. Rams	51.6	3.5
Kansas City Chiefs	50.6	3.4
Minnesota Vikings	50.5	3.4
New Orleans Saints	50.5	3.4
Pittsburgh Steelers	50.2	3.4
Phoenix Cardinals	49.8	3.4
Denver Broncos	49.6	3.4
N.Y. Jets	49.0	3.3
Atlanta Falcons	48.9	3.3
Detroit Lions	48.3	3.3
San Diego Chargers	48.3	3.3
Indianapolis Colts	48.2	3.3
Tampa Bay Buccaneers	46.7	3.2
New England Patriots	45.6	3.1
Green Bay Packers	45.0	3.1

Source: *USA TODAY*, June 16, 1992, p. 2C, from *Financial World*.

★ 1964 ★
Professional Football (SIC 7999)

Football - Professional Franchises

Professional football franchises are ranked by 1990 revenues in millions of dollars. Shares are shown in percent.

	Rev. ($ mil.)	Share
Miami Dolphins	$ 62.4	4.8%
Dallas Cowboys	52.5	4.0
Cleveland Browns	51.8	3.9
San Francisco 49ers	51.7	3.9
New York Giants	50.5	3.8
Chicago Bears	50.4	3.8
Philadelphia Eagles	50.4	3.8
Los Angeles Rams	49.4	3.8
Buffalo Bills	48.3	3.7
New Orleans Saints	47.7	3.6
Seattle Seahawks	46.4	3.5
Los Angeles Raiders	46.2	3.5
Phoenix Cardinals	46.1	3.5
Houston Oilers	45.9	3.5
Minnesota Vikings	45.8	3.5
Washington Redskins	45.5	3.5
Denver Broncos	45.3	3.4
Indianapolis Colts	44.6	3.4
Detroit Lions	44.5	3.4
New York Jets	44.3	3.4
Cincinnati Bengals	44.0	3.3
Tampa Bay Buccaneers . . .	43.9	3.3
Kansas City Chiefs	43.7	3.3
San Diego Chargers	43.6	3.3
Atlanta Falcons	43.4	3.3
Pittsburgh Steelers	43.2	3.3
Green Bay Packers	42.2	3.2
New England Patriots	39.9	3.0

Source: *Financial World*, July 9, 1991, p. 41.

★ 1965 ★

Professional Hockey (SIC 7999)

Hockey Revenues

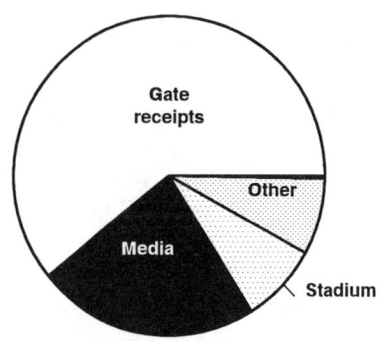

Shares of revenue, by source, are shown in percent, based on a total of $465 million.

Gate receipts	60.9%
Media	22.6
Stadium	8.2
Other	8.4

Source: *Financial World*, July 1991, p. 37.

★ 1966 ★

Professional Hockey (SIC 7999)

Hockey Teams - NHL

Revenues for 1991 are shown in millions of dollars; shares are shown in percent for the same period.

	Rev. ($ mil.)	Share
Detroit Red Wings	$ 42.6	8.2%
L.A. Kings	35.7	6.9
Boston Bruins	32.0	6.2
Montreal Canadiens	29.0	5.6
N.Y. Rangers	29.0	5.6
Chicago Black Hawks	25.3	4.9
N.Y. Islanders	24.2	4.7
Calgary Flames	24.1	4.6
Toronto Maple Leafs	23.8	4.6
Hartford Whalers	23.6	4.5
Philadelphia Flyers	23.1	4.4
St. Louis Blues	22.7	4.4
New Jersey Devils	22.5	4.3
Pittsburgh Penguins	22.2	4.3
Vancouver Canucks	22.1	4.3
Edmonton Oilers	21.6	4.2
Minnesota North Stars	21.2	4.1

	Rev. ($ mil.)	Share
Buffalo Sabres	$ 20.5	3.9%
Washington Capitals	19.9	3.8
Quebec Nordiques	18.0	3.5
Winnepeg Jets	16.6	3.2

Source: *USA TODAY*, June 16, 1992, p. 2C, from *Financial World*.

★ 1967 ★

Professional Hockey (SIC 7999)

Hockey - Professional Franchises

Professional hockey franchises are ranked by 1990 revenues in millions of dollars. Shares are shown in percent.

	Rev. ($ mil.)	Share
New York Islanders	$ 28.8	6.5%
Boston Bruins	28.7	6.5
New York Rangers	27.2	6.2
Hartford Whalers	25.2	5.7
Los Angeles Kings	24.3	5.5
Montreal Canadiens	24.1	5.5
Chicago Black Hawks	23.3	5.3
Calgary Flames	22.1	5.0
Edmonton Oilers	21.9	5.0
Philadelphia Flyers	21.4	4.9
Quebec Nordiques	21.3	4.8
Detroit Red Wings	20.8	4.7
Toronto Maple Leafs	20.2	4.6
Washington Capitals	20.0	4.5
Vancouver Canucks	19.6	4.5
Buffalo Sabres	18.5	4.2
New Jersey Devils	16.8	3.8
Pittsburgh Penguins	16.6	3.8
St. Louis Blues	15.8	3.6
Winnipeg Jets	12.2	2.8
Minnesota North Stars	11.1	2.5

Source: *Financial World*, July 9, 1991, p. 41.

SIC 80 - Health Services

★ 1968 ★

Health Care (SIC 8000)

Cancer Treatment Projections

Estimated market shares, by company, are shown in percent for 1992, 1993, and 1994.

	1992	1993	1994
Amgen/Neupogen	83.0%	80.0%	77.0%
Immunex	11.0	11.0	12.0
Schering-Plough/Sandoz . . .	3.0	6.0	8.0
HRPI	3.0	3.0	3.0

Source: Investext, Thomson Financial Networks, February 14, 1992, from Alex Brown & Sons.

★ 1969 ★

Health Care (SIC 8000)

Health Care Expenditures by Source

Distribution of health care expenditures by source is shown in percent, based on a total of $768.0 billion in FY1992.

Private out-of-pocket	20.0%
Private health insurance employer share . . .	19.0
Medicare	17.0
Medicaid	14.0
Federal tax subsidies	8.0
Private health insurance employee share . .	7.0
State tax subsidies	2.0
Other private	3.0
Other public	10.0

Source: *Hospitals*, January 5, 1992, p. 41, from American Enterprise Institute.

★ 1970 ★

Health Care (SIC 8000)

Health Care Industry

Segment distribution of the $809 billion industry is shown in percent.

Hospital care	38.8%
Physician services	20.5
Dental and other professional services . . .	9.6
Nursing home care	8.0
Drugs	6.9
Private insurance	5.7
Public health programs	2.6
Vision products	2.0
Personal health care	1.8
Research	1.6
Construction	1.5
Home health care	1.1

Source: *USA TODAY*, October 15, 1992, p. 5A, from Health Care Financing Administration, Public Opinion Strategies, Mellman & Lazarus, Public Citizen Research Group, Office of Management and Budget, and Families USA.

★ 1971★

Health Care (SIC 8000)

Health Care Institutions

Distribution of institutions in the U.S., by type, is shown in percent, based on a total of 59,880 establishments.

Nursing and personal care facilities	. . . . 30.1%
Medical and dental labs	23.9
Home health care services	12.5
Hospitals	8.7
Other	24.9

Source: *Graphic Arts Monthly*, January 1992, from Department of Commerce.

★ 1972★

Health Care (SIC 8000)

Health Care Plans

Health care plans are shown with percentage of employees enrolled in each type of plan in 1991.

Traditional indemnnity	55.0%
Health maintenance organization	23.0
Preferred provider	17.0
Point-of-service plan	5.0

Source: *The Wall Street Journal*, July 29, 1992, p. B1, from A. Foster Higgins & Co.

★ 1973★

Health Care (SIC 8000)

Health Care Service Companies

Company sales are shown in millions of dollars for 1991. Percent shares are based on group total of $27,327 million.

	($ mil.)	% of Group
Humana	$ 6,099	26.3%
National Medical Enterprises . .	3,973	17.2
American Medical Holdings . .	2,452	10.6
Beverly Enterprises	2,301	9.9
Healthtrust	2,104	9.1

	($ mil.)	% of Group
U.S. Healthcare	$ 1,709	7.4%
Manor Care	868	3.7
United Healthcare	847	3.7
National Health Laboratories . .	604	2.6
Continental Medical Systems . .	491	2.1
Community Psychiatric Centers . .	393	1.7
Medical Care International	282	1.2
Critical Care America	233	1.0
Novacare	230	1.0
HealthSouth Rehabilitation . . .	225	1.0
Surgical Care Affiliates	170	0.7
T2 Medical	166	0.7

Source: *The 1992 Business Week 1000*, p. 182.

★ 1974★

Health Care (SIC 8000)

Health Maintenance Organizations by Type

Distribution of HMOs (health maintenance organization) and HMO enrollees, by model type, is shown in percent.

	% of HMO	% of Enrls
IPA	61.7%	45.8%
Group	12.	27.1
Network	15.6	15.3
Staff	10.5	11.8

Source: *American Medical News*, July 16, 1992, p. 21, from Group Health Assn. of America.

★ 1975 ★

Health Care (SIC 8000)

Health Practitioners

Distribution of offices and clinics, by type, is shown in percent, based on a total of 411,031 establishments.

Medical doctors	46.7%
Dentists	24.9
Chiropractors	4.9
Optometrists	3.7
Podiatrists	1.8
Osteopaths	1.7
Other	16.3

Source: *Graphic Arts Monthly*, January 1992, from Department of Commerce.

★ 1976 ★

Health Care (SIC 8000)

Personal Health Care Expenditures

Personal health care expenditures by type are shown in billions of dollars for 1990. Percent distribution is based on total of $585.3 billion

	($ bil.)	Share
Hospital care	$ 256.0	43.7%
Physicians' services	125.7	21.5
Dentists' services	34.0	5.8
Other professional services . . .	31.6	5.4
Home health care	6.9	1.2
Drugs and other medical nondurables	54.6	9.3
Vision products and other medical nondurables	12.1	2.1
Nursing home care	53.1	9.1
Other personal health care . . .	11.3	1.9

Source: *Statistical Bulletin*, January 1992, p. 23.

★ 1977 ★

Surgery (SIC 8011)

Replacement Surgery in the U.S.

Average annual replacement surgeries in the United States are shown in thousands of procedures.

Hip replacement	123,000
Knee replacement	95,000
Foot/Toe replacement	11,000
Hand/Finger	7,000
Shoulder	3,000
Wrist	2,000

Source: *USA TODAY*, March 24, 1992, p. 1C, from American Academy of Orthopedic Surgeons.

★ 1978 ★

Hospitals (SIC 8060)

Overnight Medical Care

Hospitals, by type of facility, are shown with estimated 1992 revenues in billions of dollars. Shares are shown in percent.

	Rev. ($ bil.)	Share
Acute-care hospital	$ 321	81.3%
Subacute-care facility	1	0.3
Rehabilitation hospital	3	0.8
Skilled nursing facility	70	17.7

Source: *The Wall Street Journal*, July 23, 1992, p. B1, from Health Care Investment Analysts.

★ 1979 ★

Hospitals (SIC 8060)

Rehab Operators

Revenue of the leading rehabilitation hospital operators is shown in millions of dollars for the latest fiscal year; relative market shares are shown in percent for the same period. Figures for Natl. Med. Enterprises are estimated. NovaCare acquired Rehab Systems in August 1991.

	Rev. ($ mil.)	% of Group
Natl. Med. Enterprises Rehab.	$ 525.0	41.9%
Continental Medical Systems	340.0	27.2
HealthSouth Rehab.	226.0	18.1
NovaCare/Rehab Systems	66.0	5.3
AdvantageHealth Corp.	53.0	4.2
ReLife Inc.	41.5	3.3

Source: *The Wall Street Journal*, from *Modern Healthcare* and company reports.

★ 1980 ★

Home Health Care (SIC 8082)

Home Infusion Market

Manufacturers' market shares are shown in percent for 1991.

Caremark (Baxter)	28.8%
Critical Care America	7.9
T2	5.0
HMSS	4.6
National Medical Care (W. R. Grace)	4.1
Home Nutritional Services, Inc.	3.5
Homedco	1.7
Other	44.4

Source: Investext, Thomson Financial Networks, February 19, 1992, from Donaldson, Lufkin & Jenrette Securities.

★ 1981 ★

Home Health Care (SIC 8082)

Home Infusion Providers

Shares of the 1991 home infusion market are shown in percent, based on a total of $2.933 billion in revenues.

Caremark	26.3%
Critical Care America	7.7
HMSS	4.7

National Home Care	4.7%
Home Nutritional Services	4.2
Tokos Medical	3.9
T2 Medical	3.6
Quantum Health Resources	2.6
Homedco Group	1.8
Home Intensive Care	1.7
Curaflex Health Services	1.3
Health Infusion	1.1
Total Pharm. Care of America	1.1
US Homecare	0.2
Other	35.3

Source: Investext, Thomson Financial Networks, June 10, 1992, from Morgan Stanley & Co. Inc.

★ 1982 ★

Home Health Care (SIC 8082)

Home Infusion Therapy Industry

Market segmentation is shown in percent, by type of therapy, based on a total market of nearly $3.0 billion. "Other" includes aerosolized pentamidine. The categories antibiotics, total parenteral nutrition, pain management, and aerosolized pentamidine all serve AIDS patients.

Antibiotics	32.0%
Total parenteral nutrition	31.0
Enteral nutrition	21.0
Chemotherapy	4.0
Pain management	4.0
Other therapies	8.0

Source: Investext, Thomson Financial Networks, June 10, 1992, from Morgan Stanley & Co. Inc.

★ 1983 ★

Health Services (SIC 8099)

Organ Transplants by Type

Numbers of people waiting for organ transplants are shown by type of transplant.

Kidney	20,922
Heart	2,563
Liver	2,136
Lung	852
Pancreas	756
Heart/lung	162

Source: *USA TODAY*, July 6, 1992, p. 11A, from United Network for Organ Sharing.

★1984★

Health Services (SIC 8099)

Transplants in the U.S.

Percent distribution of the most common organ transplants is based on a total of 16,012 transplants. 22.4% of the kidney transplants were from living donors.

Kidney	62.1%
Liver	18.4
Heart	13.3
Pancreas	3.3
Lung	2.5
Heart/lung	0.3

Source: *USA TODAY*, November 12, 1992, p. 15A, from United Network for Organ Sharing, and U.S. Dept. of Health and Human Services.

SIC 81 - Legal Services

★1985★

Legal Services (SIC 8111)

Biggest Law Firms by Revenue

Companies are ranked by revenue, shown in millions of dollars. Percent shares are based on group total.

	Rev. ($ mil.)	% of Group
Skadden, Arps/New York . . .	$ 490.0	16.6%
Baker, McKenzie/Chicago . . .	477.5	16.2
Jones, Day/Cleveland	406.0	13.7
Gibson, Dunn/Los Angeles . . .	277.0	9.4
Shearman, Sterling/New York .	273.5	9.3
Sullivan, Cromwell/New York .	255.0	8.6
Davis, Polk/New York	252.0	8.5
Weil, Gotshal/New York . . .	252.0	8.5
Latham, Watkins/Los Angeles .	138.5	4.7
Cleary, Gottlieb/New York . . .	135.0	4.6

Source: *USA TODAY*, June 30, 1992, p. 6B, from *American Lawyer*.

★1986★

Legal Services (SIC 8111)

Civil Cases by Type

Distribution of civil suits filed in 24 state courts in 1990 is shown in percent.

Domestic relations	33.0%
Contract	14.0
Small claims	12.0
Tort	10.0
Property	9.0
Estate	7.0
Other	15.0

Source: *The Economist*, July 18, 1992, p. 12.

★1987★

Legal Services (SIC 8111)

Largest Law Firms

Skadden, Arps
Baker & McKenzie
Jones, Day
Shearman & Sterling
Gibson, Dunn & Crutcher
Vinson & Elkins
Davis Polk & Wardwell
Sullivan & Cromwell
Latham & Watkins
O'Melveny & Myers

Top 10 U.S. legal services firms ranked by worldwide gross revenues of $3.115 billion in 1990. Shares of the group are shown as percent.

	Rev. ($ mil)	% of Group
Skadden, Arps	$ 503.0	16.1%
Baker & McKenzie	404.0	13.0
Jones, Day	390.0	12.5
Shearman & Sterling	299.0	9.6
Gibson, Dunn & Crutcher . . .	290.0	9.3
Vinson & Elkins	275.5	8.8
Davis Polk & Wardwell	250.0	8.0
Sullivan & Cromwell	240.0	7.7
Latham & Watkins	234.0	7.5
O'Melveny & Myers	230.0	7.4

Source: *U.S. Industrial Outlook*, 1992, p. 53-4, from *The American Lawyer*.

★ 1988 ★

Legal Services (SIC 8111)

Leading Law Firms - U.S.

10 leading U.S. law firms ranked by 1990 revenues in millions of dollars. Headquarters locations are shown in parentheses. Shares of group are shown as percent.

	Sales ($ mil.)	% of Group
Skadden, Arps, Slate, Meagher & Flom (New York)	$ 503.0	16.1%
Baker & McKenzie (Chicago) . .	404.0	13.0
Jones, Day, Reavis & Pogue (Cleveland)	390.0	12.5
Shearman & Sterling (New York)	299.0	9.6
Gibson, Dunn & Crutcher (Los Angeles) . . .	290.0	9.3
Vinson & Elkins (Houston) . .	275.0	8.8
Davis Polk & Wardwell (New York)	250.0	8.0
Sullivan & Cromwell (New York)	240.0	7.7
Latham & Watkins (Los Angeles)	234.0	7.5
O'Melveny & Myers (Los Angeles)	230.0	7.4

Source: *American Lawyer* and *The New York Times*, 1992.

★ 1989 ★

Legal Services (SIC 8111)

Leading Prepaid Legal Services

Shares of the eight largest firms are shown as percent of approximately 58.0 million subscribers to prepaid legal services across the U.S. in 1990.

Lawphone	30.3%
Caldwell Legal USA	8.6
Signature Group	2.2
Hyatt Legal Plans	1.6
Midwest Legal Services	0.9
Pre-Paid Legal Services	0.6
Prudential Group Legal Services	0.4
National Legal Shield	0.4
Other	55.0

Source: *The Wall Street Journal*, August 6, 1991, p. B1.

★ 1990 ★

Legal Services (SIC 8111)

M&A Legal Advisors

Total transaction amounts of merger and acquisition deals in 1991 are shown in millions of dollars for the leading 10 advisors. Relative market shares are shown in percent for the same period.

	Rev. ($ mil.)	% of Group
Richards Layton	$ 29,960.0	18.3%
Wachtell Lipton Rosen & Katz	26,493.3	16.1
Simpson Thacher	23,291.1	14.2
Lierderkerke, Worters, Waelbroeck	15,475.1	9.4
Morris Nichols	15,098.7	9.2
Cahill Gordon	13,731.9	8.4
Sullivan & Cromwell	12,749.7	7.8
Cravath, Swaine & Moore . . .	10,022.6	6.1

Continued on next page.

Legal Services (SIC 8111)

M&A Legal Advisors

Total transaction amounts of merger and acquisition deals in 1991 are shown in millions of dollars for the leading 10 advisors. Relative market shares are shown in percent for the same period.

	Rev. ($ mil.)	% of Group
Weil Gotshal	$ 8,784.6	5.4%
Sidley Austin	8,447.2	5.1

Source: *Investment Dealers Digest*, May 25, 1992, p. 15, from IDD Information Services.

SIC 82 - Educational Services

★1991★

Education (SIC 8200)

Educational Establishments

Distribution of establishments in the U.S. is shown in percent.

Elementary and secondary schools 42.8%
Vocational schools 14.0
Colleges and universities 9.6
Libraries 5.2
Other 28.4

Source: *Graphic Arts Monthly*, May 1992, from Department of Commerce, and Department of Education.

★1992★

Minority Education (SIC 8220)

Hispanic Enrollment in Undergraduate Institutions

Academic institutions are ranked by Hispanic enrollment. These colleges and universities listed have 25 percent or higher Hispanic enrollment. Percent shares are based on total for the group.

	No. of Students	% of Group
University of Texas-Pan America	10,344	15.1%
University of Texas at El Paso .	9,508	13.9
Florida International University	9,455	13.8
Cal State University, Los Angeles	5,856	8.6
University of Texas at San Antonio	4,687	6.8
New Mexico State University .	4,039	5.9
Herbert H. Lehman College (NY)	3,712	5.4
City College (NY)	3,642	5.3
Texas A&I University	3,540	5.2
Barry University (FL)	1,722	2.5

	No. of Students	% of Group
New Mexico Highlands University	1,690	2.5%
St. Mary's University (TX) . .	1,469	2.1
Our Lady of the Lake University (TX)	1,299	1.9
Mercy College (NY)	1,292	1.9
Corpus Christi State University (TX)	1,234	1.8
Incarnate Word College (TX) .	1,099	1.6
Boricua College (NY)	1,027	1.5
St. Thomas University (FL) . .	867	1.3
Western New Mexico University	728	1.1
Sul Ross State University (TX)	599	0.9
Mt. St. Mary's College (CA) . .	370	0.5
College of Santa Fe	306	0.4

Source: *Hispanic Business*, April 1992, p. 16, from Hispanic Association of Colleges and Universities and September 1991 annual report.

★1993★

Minority Education (SIC 8220)

Institutions with the Top Master's Programs in Hispanic Enrollment

Colleges and universities are ranked by Hispanic enrollment in master's programs. Percent shares are based on group total.

	No. of Students	% of Group
Florida International University (FL)	231	23.7%
Baruch College-CUNY (NY) .	94	9.7
Pace University (NY)	94	9.7
University of Texas-Austin (TX)	72	7.4
Pepperdine University (CA) . .	70	7.2

Continued on next page.

538

★1993★ *Continued*

Minority Education (SIC 8220)

Institutions with the Top Master's Programs in Hispanic Enrollment

Colleges and universities are ranked by Hispanic enrollment in master's programs. Percent shares are based on group total.

	No. of Students	% of Group
Laredo State University (TX) .	58	6.0%
St. Mary's University (TX) . .	55	5.6
University of Michigan- Ann Arbor (MI)	51	5.2
Harvard University (MA) . . .	47	4.8
New York University (NY) . .	39	4.0
University of Texas-El Paso (TX)	37	3.8
Fairleigh Dickinson University (NJ)	35	3.6
De Paul University (IL)	34	3.5
University of Dallas (TX) . . .	29	3.0
Rutgers-State U. of NJ/ Newark (NJ)	28	2.9

Source: *Hispanic Business*, April 1992, p. 20, from American Assembly of Collegiate Schools of Business.

★1994★

Libraries (SIC 8231)

Public Library Funding

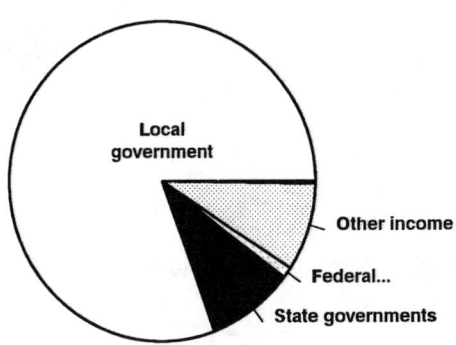

Shares of funding of public libraries, shown in percent.

Local government 80.2%
State governments 9.0
Federal governments 1.4
Other income (private donations,
    fines, fees, etc.) 9.4

Source: *CQ Researcher*, June 26, 1992, p. 553, from American Library Association.

SIC 83 - Social Services

★ **1995** ★

Child Care (SIC 8351)

Child Care Alternatives

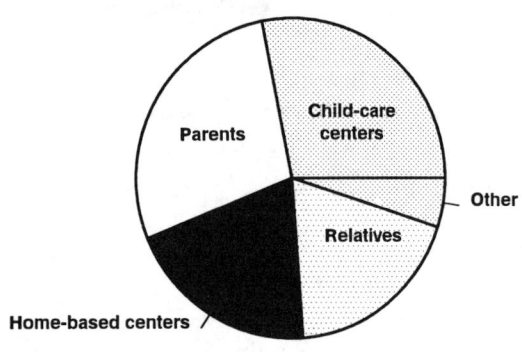

Distribution of child care providers is shown for 1990 in percent.

Child-care centers	28.0%
Parents	28.0
Home-based centers	20.0
Relatives	19.0
Other	5.0

Source: *USA TODAY*, November 25, 1992, p. 6B, from *Child Care Information Exchange*.

★ **1996** ★

Child Care (SIC 8351)

For-Profit Child Care Leaders

The four top for-profit child care providers are shown with number of children in full-day care.

KinderCare Learning Centers	144,545
La Petite Academy	90,000
Children's World Learning Centers . . .	63,000
Childtime Childcare Inc.	13,256

Source: *USA TODAY*, November 12, 1992, p. 2A, from *Child Care Information Exchange*.

SIC 84 - Museums, Botanical, Zoological Gardens

★ 1997 ★

Museums and Parks (SIC 8400)

Top 20 Attractions in U.K.

Top British attractions charging admission are shown with number of visits in 1990. Shares for the group are shown in percent.

	No. of Visits	% of Group
Madame Tussaud's	2,547,000	9.7%
Tower of London	2,298,000	8.8
Alton Towers	2,070,000	7.9
Natural History Museum	1,534,000	5.9
Chessington	1,515,000	5.8
Blackpool Tower	1,426,000	5.5
Royal Academy	1,309,000	5.0
Science Museum	1,303,000	5.0
London Zoo	1,250,000	4.8
Kew Gardens	1,196,000	4.6
Flamingo Land, N. Yorkshire	1,138,000	4.4
Edinburgh Castle	1,078,000	4.1
Windsor Safari Park	1,050,000	4.0
Chester Zoo	1,000,000	3.8
Drayton Manor Park	990,000	3.8
Thorpe Park, Surrey	974,000	3.7
Roman Baths, Bath	950,000	3.6
Windsor Castle	855,000	3.3
Jorvik Centre, York	846,000	3.2
Swansea Leisure Centre	812,000	3.1

Source: *Focus*, June 1991, p. 12.

SIC 86 - Membership Organizations

★ 1998 ★
★ 1998 ★

Membership Organizations (SIC 8631)

Union Membership - Federal Government

Distribution of federal labor union memberships by organization is shown in number of members and as percent of group total for 1991.

	(000)	% of Group
American Federation of Government Employees	177	64.6%
National Treasury Employees Union	65	23.7
National Federation of Federal Employees	32	11.7

Source: *Government Executive*, September 1991, p. 24, from *Working for the Sovereign*, *Directory of U.S. Labor Organizations*, and individual unions.

★ 1999 ★

Political Organizations (SIC 8651)

Political Fund-Raising for Women

Top 1988 political fund-raisers for women by organization are shown in millions of dollars raised. Shares of group are in percent.

	($ mil.)	% of Group
National Association of Realtors . .	$ 3.0	23.8%
Teamsters Union	2.9	23.0
American Medical Association . .	2.6	20.6
National Education Association . .	2.2	17.5
National Association of Retired Federal Employees . . .	1.9	15.1

Source: *USA TODAY*, August 18, 1992, p. 1A, from *USA TODAY* research.

★ 2000 ★

Religion (SIC 8661)

Shrines and Temples - Japanese New Year

Top Japanese shrine and temple visitations for Shinto and Buddhist New Year's festivals were 77,420,000 in 1991, down 2.8% from 1990. Religious destinations are shown in percent.

	Visitors (mil.)	% of Group
Meiji Jingu Shrine	3.55	14.7%
Kawasaki Daishi Temple . . .	3.17	13.1
Naritasan Shinshoji Temple . .	3.02	12.5
Sumiyoshi Taisha Shrine	2.83	11.7
Fushimi Inari Taisha Shrine . .	2.23	9.2
Atsuta Jingu Shrine	2.11	8.7
Hachimangu Shrine	1.98	8.2
Dazaifu Tenmangu Shrine . . .	1.95	8.1
Omiya Hikawa Jinja Shrine . .	1.67	6.9
Sensoji Temple	1.64	6.8

Source: *Intersect*, January 1992, p. 46, from Agency for Cultural Affairs, "Coping with Japan," by John Randle and Mariko Watanabe, Japan Travel Bureau, and Yomiuri Shimbun.

SIC 87 - Engineering and Management Services

Engineering (SIC 8710)

Engineering and Architectural Services Firms

Companies are ranked by 1991 sales, shown in millions of dollars. Shares of the group are shown in percent.

	Sales ($ mil.)	% of Group
Fluor	$ 6,580	36.9%
McDermott International	3,544	19.9
EG&G	2,689	15.1
Foster Wheeler	1,992	11.2
Morrison Knudsen	1,980	11.1
Jacobs Engineering Group	1,026	5.8

Source: *The 1992 Business Week 1000*, p. 190.

★2002★

Engineering (SIC 8711)

Environmental Engineering Market

Segment distribution of the 1991 market, based on total projected revenue of $134.2 billion, is shown in percent.

Solid waste management	23.0%
Resource recovery	14.7
Water infrastructure	11.5
Hazardous waste management	11.5
Environmental consulting/engineering	10.6
Water utilities	8.9
Waste management equipment	7.7
Air pollution control	4.7
Asbestos abatement	3.1
Analytical services	1.7
Environmental energy sources	1.4
Instrument manufacturing	1.4

Source: *The Wall Street Journal*, October 21, 1991, p. B1, from *Environmental Business Journal*.

★2003★

Accounting Services (SIC 8721)

Accountancy Firm Revenues

Companies are ranked by revenue, shown in millions of dollars. Shares of the group are shown in percent.

	Rev. ($ mil.)	% of Group
Arthur Andersen	$ 2,463	20.6%
Ernst & Young	2,240	18.7
Deloitte & Touche	1,952	16.3
KPMG Peat Marwick	1,813	15.1
Coopers & Lybrand	1,470	12.3
Price Waterhouse	1,282	10.7
Grant Thornton	206.0	1.7
McGladrey & Pullen	188.0	1.6
Kenneth Leventhal & Co.	182.0	1.5
BDO Seidman	181.0	1.5

Source: *Accountancy*, September 1992, p. 16, from *Public Accounting Report*.

★2004★

Accounting Services (SIC 8721)

Accounting Firms Worldwide

The top six firms in 1991 are shown with worldwide fee income in billions of dollars; relative market shares are shown in percent for the same period.

	Fees ($ bil.)	% of Group
KPMG	$ 6.01	20.4%
Ernst & Young	5.41	18.4
Coopers & Lybrand	5.00	17.0
Arthur Andersen	4.95	16.8
Deloitte Touche Tohmatsu	4.50	15.3
Price Waterhouse	3.60	12.2

Source: *The Economist*, October 17, 1992, p. 19, from Lafferty Business Research.

★ 2005 ★

Accounting Services (SIC 8721)

Accounting Services - U.K.

Companies are ranked by 1992 income fees, shown in millions of pounds. Income fees in 1992 totaled 3,330 million pounds for the group. Relative shares are shown in percent. (Figures for Price Waterhouse reflect year-end June media figures. Income fees for Moores Rowland do not include those of MRI Associates. Figures for Finnies have been estimated and adjusted for its office demerger of 1990-91. The figure for Casson Beckman is an estimate. "FT" provided the figure for Fraser & Russel; it includes 1.8 million pounds from Fraser Smith Financial Services.)

	(L mil.)	% of Group
Coopers & Lybrand	577	17.3%
KPMG Peat Marwick	494.7	14.9
Price Waterhouse	400.5	12.0
Ernst & Young	398.9	12.0
Touche Ross	349.7	10.5
Arthur Andersen	330.8	9.9
Grant Thornton	118.4	3.6
BDO Binder Hamlyn	114.4	3.4
Pannell Kerr Forster	85.7	2.6
Stoy Hayward	68.3	2.1
Kidsons Impey	60.1	1.8
Clark Whitehill	53.6	1.6
Robson Rhodes	36.7	1.1
Moore Stephens	35.5	1.1
Neville Russell	33.4	1.0
Moores Rowland	30.6	0.9
Baker Tilly	25.8	0.8
Haines Watts	20.6	0.6
Saffery Champness	16.6	0.5
Finnies	14.2	0.4
Hacker Young	14	0.4
Chantrey Vellacott	12.6	0.4
Levy Gee	12.4	0.4
Casson Beckman	11.7	0.4
Fraser & Russell	11.1	0.3

Source: *Accountancy*, July 1992, p. 16.

★ 2006 ★

Accounting Services (SIC 8721)

CPA Revenues - "Big Six"

KPMG Peat Marwick
Ernst & Young
Deloitte & Touche
Arthur Andersen
Coopers & Lybrand
Price Waterhouse

Revenues of the six leading U.S. certified public accounting (CPA) firms worldwide were $25.766 billion in 1990. Relative shares are shown as percent. (Data for Arthur Andersen include Andersen Consulting).

	Rev. ($ mil.)	% of Group
KPMG Peat Marwick	$ 5,400	21.0%
Ernst & Young	5,006	19.4
Deloitte & Touche	4,200	16.3
Arthur Andersen	4,160	16.1
Coopers & Lybrand	4,100	15.9
Price Waterhouse	2,900	11.3

Source: *U.S. Industrial Outlook 1992*, 1992, p. 53-2, from *Public Accounting Report*.

★ 2007 ★

Biological Research (SIC 8731)

Biotech Sales - 1991

1991 sales of bioengineered products by company shown in millions of dollars and percent share of market.

	($ mil.)	Share
Amgen	$ 682.0	31.8%
Genentech	459.6	21.4
Life Technologies	171.3	8.0
Applied Biosystems	163.9	7.6
Alza	162.4	7.6
Genzyme	109.5	5.1
Genetics Institute	82.6	3.9
Biogen	61.4	2.9
Centocor	53.2	2.5
Immunex	52.7	2.5
Cambridge Biotech	29.0	1.4
Calgene	26.1	1.2
Mycogen	18.3	0.9
Xoma Corp.	17.1	0.8

Continued on next page.

★ 2007 ★ *Continued*

Biological Research (SIC 8731)

Biotech Sales - 1991

1991 sales of bioengineered products by company shown in millions of dollars and percent share of market.

	($ mil.)	Share
Carrington Labs	$ 15.4	0.7%
Synergen	14.2	0.7
DNA Plant Technology	9.1	0.4
Repligen	7.6	0.4
Scios	7.4	0.3

Source: *Chemicalweek*, May 6, 1992, p. 30, from Standard & Poor's Compustat Services.

★ 2008 ★

Biological Research (SIC 8731)

Top Biotech Firms

Latest fiscal year revenues of the 12 largest biotech firms are shown in millions of dollars. Shares are shown in percent.

	Rev. ($ mil.)	% of Group
Genentech	$ 476.1	39.4%
Amgen	361.4	29.9
Chiron	78.5	6.5
Biogen	59.4	4.9
Genzyme	54.8	4.5
Genetics Institute	40.4	3.3
Cetus	38.9	3.2
Immunex	34.9	2.9
Centocor	32.9	2.7
Synergen	12.7	1.1
California Biotechnology	12.4	1.0
Xoma	4.7	0.4

Source: *Fortune*, August 12, 1991, p. 81, from Ernst & Young.

★ 2009 ★

Commercial Research (SIC 8732)

Market Research Shares

Shares of market research done at the retail level are shown in percent. "Other" includes Information Resources.

Nielsen Market Research	60.0%
Other	40.0

Source: Investext, Thomson Financial Networks, March 13, 1992, from Brown Brothers Harriman & Co.

★ 2010 ★

Management Consulting Services (SIC 8742)

Management Consulting Leaders

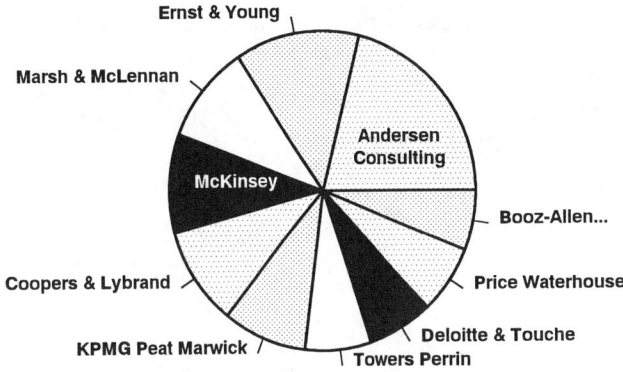

Worldwide revenues of the 10 largest U.S. management consulting firms were $8.971 billion in 1990. Relative shares are shown as percent.

	Rev. ($ mil.)	% of Group
Andersen Consulting	$ 1,875	20.9%
Ernst & Young	1,169	13.0
Marsh & McLennan	910	10.1
McKinsey	900	10.0
Coopers & Lybrand	898	10.0
KPMG Peat Marwick	785	8.8
Towers Perrin	640	7.1
Deloitte & Touche	639	7.1
Price Waterhouse	634	7.1
Booz-Allen Hamilton	521	5.8

Source: *U.S. Industrial Outlook*, 1992, p. 53-5, from *Consultants News*.

Systems Management (SIC 8742)

Systems Management Companies

The top 10 system management firms are ranked by 1991 system management revenue (defined as all post-implementation services bundled under one pact). Company shares are based on a group total of $8.4 billion, shown in percent.

	Rev. ($ mil.)	% of Group
EDS Corp.	$ 2000	51.0%
IBM	600	15.3
Digital Equipment Corp.	400	10.2
Andersen Consulting	200	5.1
Systematics Inc.	170	4.3
Boeing Computer Services . . .	155	4.0
Computer Sciences Corp. . . .	120	3.1
Unisys Corp.	115	2.9
Policy Management Systems Corp.	100	2.6
SHL Systemhouse Inc.	60	1.5

Source: *InformationWeek*, July 13, 1992, p. 42, from G2 Research.

Business Consulting Services (SIC 8748)

Employee Benefits Consultants

Company shares are based on revenue totals of $2,489 million for 1990 and $2,672 million for 1991, shown in percent.

	1990	1991
William M. Mercer Co.	25.6%	24.3%
Towers Perrin	16.8	16.2
Wyatt Co.	14.4	15.0
Hewitt Associates	10.1	10.4
Noble Lowndes	6.7	7.2
Alexander Consulting Group Inc. . . .	6.8	7.1
Buck Consultants Inc.	6.2	6.1
A. Foster Higgins & Co.	5.9	5.9
Coopers & Lybrand Benefits Group .	4.7	4.9
Godwins International Holdings Inc.	2.8	2.9

Source: *The Wall Street Journal*, July 29, 1992, p. B4.

SIC 89 - Services, NEC

★ 2013 ★
Geophysical Data (SIC 8999)

Geophysical Companies Worldwide

Shares of the global market are shown in percent.

GECO Prakla	22.0%
Western Atlas	22.0
Halliburton	20.0
CGG	18.0
Other	18.0

Source: Investext, Thomson Financial Networks, June 25, 1992, from The Robinson-Humphrey Company, Inc.

SIC 91 - Executive, Legislative, and General

★ 2014 ★

Contractors (SIC 9100)

Leading Government Contractors

Prime contracts awarded in fiscal year 1990 are shown in thousands of dollars; percent shares are based on total purchases of $177.64577 billion.

	($000)	Share
McDonnell Douglas	$ 9,791,433	5.5%
General Electric	6,692,079	3.7
General Dynamics	6,613,547	3.7
Martin Marietta	6,451,475	3.6
Westinghouse Electric	5,762,783	3.2
Lockheed	5,036,152	2.8
General Motors	4,532,880	2.5
Rockwell International	4,387,972	2.5
Raytheon	4,369,484	2.4
United Technologies	3,336,201	1.9
Boeing	3,130,836	1.8
Grumman	2,840,651	1.6
AT&T	2,409,497	1.3
Tenneco	2,371,865	1.3
University of Calif. System	2,364,417	1.3
Dynacorp	509,090	0.3
Mitre	500,924	0.3
Hercules	483,203	0.3
E-Systems	468,847	0.3
Morrison-Knudsen	467,434	0.3
Texas Instruments	749,837	0.4
Computer Sciences Corp.	719,754	0.4
McDermott	673,662	0.4
Science Applications Intl.	655,036	0.4
FMC	650,071	0.4
Royal Dutch Petroleum	625,205	0.4
Honeywell	580,775	0.3
Loral	557,921	0.3
Avondale Industries	546,162	0.3
Olin	539,025	0.3

Source: *Government Executive*, August 1991, p. 14.

★ 2015 ★

Government Contractors (SIC 9100)

Leading Civilian Government Contractors

Civilian contracts awarded in fiscal year 1990 are shown in thousands of dollars; percent shares are based on total purchases of $43.471 billion. Ford's Aerospace Division was sold to Loral in December, 1990.

	($000)	Share
Westinghouse Electric	$ 3,488,406	7.9%
University of Calif. System	2,324,272	5.2
Martin Marietta	2,205,443	5.0
Rockwell International	2,157,583	4.9
AT&T	1,464,741	3.3
EG&G	1,357,929	3.1
Lockheed	1,181,530	2.7
California Inst. of Technology	1,114,804	2.5
General Electric	868,582	2.0
McDonnell Douglas	867,976	2.0
Allied-Signal	718,467	1.6
Boeing	707,289	1.6
McDermott	654,568	1.5
Thiokol	498,936	1.1
University of Chicago	415,498	0.9
IBM	400,890	0.9
Universities Space Res. Assn.	391,962	0.9
United Technologies	385,269	0.9
Computer Sciences Corp.	342,104	0.8
Battelle Memorial Institute	322,051	0.7
Diversified Energy Inc.	316,819	0.7
Associated Universities	286,537	0.6
TRW	280,723	0.6
Ford Motor Co.	271,995	0.6
General Motors	242,431	0.5

Source: *Government Executive*, August 1991, p. 33.

SIC 92 - Justice, Public Order, and Safety

★2016★
Crime (SIC 9220)

Crime in the U.S.

Percent distribution of crimes reported is shown, in percent, based on a total of 14.87 million reports filed with law enforcement authorities in 1991.

Larceny theft	55.0%
Burglary	21.0
Motor vehicle theft	11.0
Aggravated assault	7.0
Robbery	5.0
Forcible rape	1.0
Murder	0.2

Source: *USA TODAY*, September 18, 1992, p. 12A, from FBI, *Crime in the United States, 1991*.

★2017★
Crime (SIC 9220)

Crime in the U.S. - 1981 and 1991

Crimes committed in the U.S., by type, are shown in occurrences (rounded to the nearest thousand) for the years 1981 and 1991.

	'81	'91
Assaults	700	1,900
Car thefts	1,100	1,700
Drug arrests	560	1,010
Rapes	83	107
Homicides	23	25

Source: *USA TODAY*, October 26, 1992, p. 10A, from *FBI Uniform Crime Report* and Bureau of Justice Statistics.

★2018★
Crime (SIC 9220)

Criminal Justice Expenditures

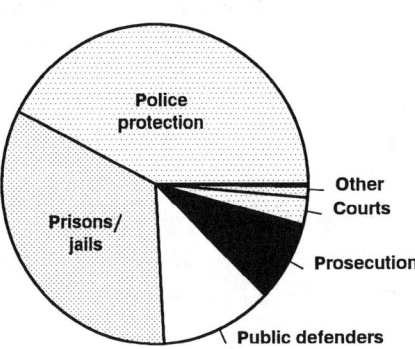

Expenditures for criminal justice in 1990, by category, are shown in billions of dollars, based on total expenditures of more than $74 billion.

Police protection	31.8
Prisons/jails	25.0
Public defenders	9.3
Prosecution	5.5
Courts	1.7
Other	0.9

Source: *USA TODAY*, October 26, 1992, p. 10A, from *FBI Uniform Crime Report* and Bureau of Justice Statistics.

★ 2019 ★

Crime (SIC 9220)

Homicide Weapons

Weapons most used in the commission of homicides in 1991 are shown, by type, in thousands of units.

Handguns 7,847
Knives 3,643
Shotguns/rifles 1,877
Hands/fists/feet 1,165
Blunt objects 1,045

Source: *USA TODAY*, October 26, 1992, p. 10A, from *FBI Uniform Crime Report* and Bureau of Justice Statistics.

★ 2020 ★

Crime (SIC 9220)

Telephone Fraud

Most costly categories of telephone fraud are shown as percent of $2,233 million total for 1991.

Long distance 80.6%
"800" charges. 15.7
Victim management and staff time 1.8
Victim consultant and staff fees 0.5
Carrier and vendor consultant and
   attorney fees 0.8
Carrier and vendor management and staff . . 0.7

Source: *The New York Times*, August 22, 1992, p. 19, from *Telecommunication Advisors*.

★ 2021 ★

Law Enforcement (SIC 9221)

Federal Drug Control Budget

Distribution of the current $12.7 billion budget is shown in percent.

Domestic law enforcement 44.1%
Demand reduction 32.3
International aid and interdiction 23.6

Source: *USA TODAY*, September 8, 1992, p. 13A, from "National Household Survey on Drug Abuse '91", Office of National Drug Control Policy, and National Institute of Drug Abuse.

★ 2022 ★

Correctional Institutions (SIC 9223)

Adult Correctional Institutions

Distribution of total inmates by type of correctional institution is shown in percent based on total of 802,428 prisoners as of January 1, 1991.

State & D.C. prisons 83.7%
Federal prisons 7.6
Other facilities 5.2
Jails 3.6

Source: *The Corrections Yearbook*, Adult Corrections, 1991, p. 1.

SIC 93 - Finance, Taxation, and Monetary Policy

Federal Budget (SIC 9311)

Mandatory Dollars of Federal Budget

Federal budget mandatory dollar distribution is shown in percent.

	($ bil.)	Share
Social Security	$ 300	38.9 %
Medicare	127	16.5
Medicaid	85	11.0
Federal retirement	81	10.5
Means-tested entitlements	77	10.0
Deposit insurance	76	9.8
Unemployment insurance	26	3.4

Source: *USA TODAY*, July 1992, p. 13A, from 1993 Federal Budget.

★ 2024 ★

Federal Traveling (SIC 9311)

Per Diem Rates for 10 Popular Destinations

Per diem rates for 10 popular destinations for federal travelers are shown in dollars. New per diem rates are effective January 1, 1991. The allowance for meals and incidental expenses in each of these cities is $34, with the balance allocated to lodging expenses.

	Old	New
New York	$ 147	$ 151
Washington	127	131
Chicago	123	127
Boston	121	125
Los Angeles	120	124
San Francisco	112	122

	Old	New
Atlanta	$ 108	$ 112
Baltimore	99	105
Denver	99	103
Miami	94	96

Source: *Government Executive*, February 1991, p. 6, from Federal Register.

★ 2025 ★

Federal Traveling (SIC 9311)

Per Diem Rates Worldwide

Figures reflect lodging and total per diem rates all over the world for federal travelers, effective December 1, 1990.

	Lodg.	Total
Tehran	$ 139	$ 285
Tokyo	133	242
London	144	241
Moscow	170	212
Rome	128	207
Paris	123	201
Hong Kong	126	196
Geneva	111	193
Brussels	105	191
Baghdad	83	186
Berlin	94	184
Prague	128	178
Managua	98	165
Kuwait	92	159
Addis Ababa	100	149
Riyadh	80	149
Istanbul	102	148
New York	113	147
Ottowa	80	144
Seoul	79	140
Beijing	91	138
Bucharest	87	138
Jerusalem	62	136
Warsaw	95	135

Continued on next page.

★ 2025 ★ *Continued*

Federal Traveling (SIC 9311)

Per Diem Rates Worldwide

Figures reflect lodging and total per diem rates all over the world for federal travelers, effective December 1, 1990.

	Lodg.	Total
Lagos	$ 94	$ 135
Panama city	75	132
Washington	93	127
Bangkok	76	126
Budapest	80	124
Chicago	89	123
Manila	75	122
Los Angeles	86	120
Cairo	72	110
Bogota	66	107
Nairobi	65	104
Cape Town	69	99
San Salvador	49	77
Katmandu	49	72
Cambodia	35	58
Lebanon	25	50

Source: *Government Executive*, January 1992, p. 44, from Federal Register.

★ 2026 ★

Government Spending (SIC 9311)

Certificate of Participation (COP) Financing

Shares of the total COP market, by mortgage issuer, are shown in percent for the period from January 1985 to May 1990, based on an industry total of $21,908.3 million. The Certificate of Deposit is a tax-exempt financing vehicle used by local and state governments and their related authorities to build public facilities.

City, town, or village	24.0%
District (school, utility, etc.)	21.3
Local authority	17.3
County/parish	17.0
State	10.7
State authority	8.4
College or university	1.4

Source: *Journal of Housing*, May 1992, p. 110, from Securities Data Company, Basile Baumann Prost & Associates, Inc.

★ 2027 ★

Government Spending (SIC 9311)

Certificate of Participation (COP) Financing by End Use

Shares of the total COP financing market, by end use, are shown in percent for the period from January 1985 to May 1990, based on an industry total of $21,848 million. Numbers may not add due to rounding.

General purpose/public improvements	34.4%
Primary/secondary education	17.9
Waste/sewer facilities	8.3
Civic and convention centers	5.9
Correctional facilities	5.2
Higher education	4.3
Hospitals	3.6
Electric and public power	3.3
Government buildings	2.7
Parking facilities	2.6
Other	11.6

Source: *Journal of Housing*, May 1992, p. 112, from Securities Data Company, Basile Baumann Prost & Associates, Inc.

★ 2028 ★

Government Spending (SIC 9311)

Domestic Spending in 1993

Projected domestic spending for 1993 is shown, by segment, in billions of dollars.

Entitlement programs	$ 694.8
Defense	291.6
Discretionary domestic spending	224.7
Federal debt interest	213.8
Other	91.8

Source: *USA TODAY*, May 19, 1992, p. 4A, from Office of Management and Budget, and Congressional Budget Office.

★ 2029 ★

Government Spending (SIC 9311)

State and Local Purchasing

| Education |
| Health and hospitals |
| Civilian safety |
| Transportation |
| Administrative/judicial |
| Other |

The estimated distribution of goods and services, by category, is shown in percent for 1991. Shares are based on an estimated total expenditure of $702 billion.

Education	43.0%
Health and hospitals	11.2
Civilian safety	10.3
Transportation	10.0
Administrative/judicial	6.5
Other	19.0

Source: *Industrial Distribution*, January 15, 1992, p. 39.

★ 2030 ★

Taxation (SIC 9311)

Distribution of Federal Income Taxes - 1990

Share of federal income tax revenues paid by each income group. Data are in percent.

Upper

Top 1% (income over $220,000)	25.4%
Top 5% (income over $102,400)	44.1
Top 20% (income over $61,490)	71.8
Next-to-top ($42-$61,000)	17.0

Mid and lower

Bottom 60% (income below $42,040) . . .	11.0
Bottom 40% (income below $29,044) . . .	2.4

Source: *Forbes*, May 11, 1992, p. 93, from Congressional Budget Office.

SIC 94 - Administration of Human Resources

★ 2031 ★

Health and Human Services (SIC 9400)

Health and Human Services Budget

The budgets for health and human services totaled $486.3 billion in 1991 and $505 billion in 1992 (projected). Distribution, by fund or program, are shown in percent based on the 1991 total.

Social Security Administration	58.3%
Medicare	21.0
Medicaid	10.6
Discretionary funds	5.8
Entitlement programs	4.4

Source: *Black Enterprise*, September 1991, p. 94, from Department of Health and Human Services.

★ 2032 ★

Health Services (SIC 9431)

National Spending on Health Care

National spending on health care by segment is shown in billions of dollars for 1992 and 2000.

	1992 ($ bil.)	2000 ($ bil.)
Hospital care	$ 313.9	$ 65.2
Physician services	165.5	360.5
Nursing home care	64.9	130.8
Drugs	55.5	91

Source: *USA TODAY*, June 29, 1992, p. 5A, from Health Care Financing Administration.

★ 2033 ★

Public Health (SIC 9431)

Health Initiatives for Minorities

Minority health initiatives launched by the National Institutes of Health are shown with budgets in millions of dollars for 1992 (estimate) and 1993 (proposed).

	1992	1993
Infant Mortality	$ 0.5	$ 5.0
Adolescent Health	2.0	5.0
Young Adults	0.5	5.0
Older Adults	0.6	2.0
Minority Male at Risk	-	8.0
Regional Training and Research Centers	-	5.0
M.S./Ph.D. Program in Biological Sciences	1.2	5.0
2-Year/4-Year Bridge Program	0.8	5.0
Pre-College Intervention Program	2.5	5.0
Evaluation of NIH Minority Training	-	-

Source: *Science*, April 3, 1992, p. 24.

★ 2034 ★

Public Health (SIC 9431)

National Institutes of Health

Shares of NIH (National Institutes of Health) final budget are shown in percent, based on totals of $8276.7 thousand in 1991 and $9010.4 thousand in 1992 (appropriation). NI stands for "National Institute". Names of some agencies have been further abbreviated.

	1991	1992
National Cancer Institute	20.7%	22.1%
National Heart, Lung, & Blood Institute	13.6	13.3
NI of Allergy & Infectious Diseases	11.0	10.8

Continued on next page.

★ 2034 ★ *Continued*

Public Health (SIC 9431)

National Institutes of Health

Shares of NIH (National Institutes of Health) final budget are shown in percent, based on totals of $8276.7 thousand in 1991 and $9010.4 thousand in 1992 (appropriation). NI stands for "National Institute". Names of some agencies have been further abbreviated.

	1991	1992
NI of General Medical Sciences . . .	9.2%	9.1%
NI of Diabetes, Digestive, Kidney Diseases	7.4	7.4
NI of Neurological Disorders & Stroke	6.5	6.5
NI of Child Health & Human Development	5.8	5.8
NI on Aging	3.9	4.3
National Eye Institute	3.1	3.0
NI of Environmental Health Sciences	2.9	2.8
NI of Arthritis, Musculoskeletal, & Skin Diseases .	2.3	2.3
NI of Dental Research	1.8	1.8
NI on Deafness & Communication Disorders	1.6	1.7
Other	10.1	9.2

Source: *News & Comment, Science*, November 1992, p. 791.

★ 2035 ★

Public Health (SIC 9431)

National Institutes of Health - Budget Segments

Segment distribution is shown in percent, based on totals of $8,953 million in 1992 and $9,396 million in 1993 (forecast).

	1992	1993
Research project (grants)	55.0%	56.2%
Centers	8.8	8.4
Research training	3.5	3.3
R&D contracts	7.2	6.9
Intramural research	11.1	11.1
Research support	4.6	4.6
Extramural construction	0.1	0.1
Women's health	0.3	0.5
Minority health	0.0	0.5

	1992	1993
Other research	8.3%	7.8%
NIH facilities repairs	1.2	0.8

Source: *News & Comment, Science*, February 7, 1992, p. 674, from HHS.

★ 2036 ★

Food Assistance (SIC 9441)

Food Assistance in Schools

1990 expenditures for food assistance in schools totaled $4.482 billion. Shares, by type service, are shown in percent.

School lunch	71.6%
Commoditites	14.7
School breakfast	13.3
Special milk	0.4

Source: *FoodReview*, July 1991, p. 45.

★ 2037 ★

Food Assistance (SIC 9441)

Food Assistance Spending

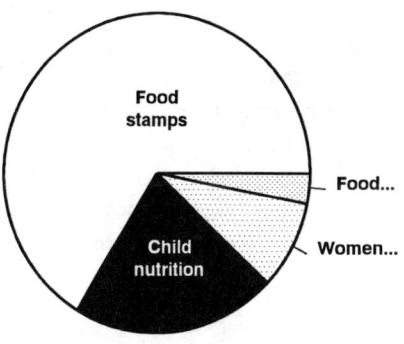

Food assistance spending in 1990 totaled $24.869 billion. Distribution by food assistance program is shown in percent.

Food stamps	66.5%
Child nutrition	22.3
Women, infants, and children	8.6
Food distribution	2.6

Source: *FoodReview*, July 1991, p. 44.

SIC 95 - Environmental Quality and Housing

★ 2038 ★

Environmental Services (SIC 9511)

Environmental Services

1991 sales of environmental services by company and percent share of $6,704.5 market.

	Sales ($ mil.)	Share
Browning-Ferris Inds.	$ 3,183.3	47.5%
Safety-Kleen	695.0	10.4
Pall Corp.	657.0	9.8
ICF International	625.0	9.3
International Technology . . .	407.2	6.1
Rollins Environmental Svcs. . . .	220.8	3.3
OHM Corp.	175.5	2.6
Clean Harbors	142.9	2.1
Environmental Systems	138.6	2.1
Oil Dri Corp. of America	102.3	1.5
Tetra Technologies	85.3	1.3
Harding Associates	72.4	1.1
Horsehead Resource Devel. . . .	71.1	1.1
C.H. Heist Corp.	70.1	1.0
Versar	58.2	0.9

Source: *Chemicalweek*, May 6, 1992, p. 33, from Standard & Poor's Compustat Services.

★ 2039 ★

Recycled Materials (SIC 9511)

Recycled Materials

Newspapers

Clear glass

Green glass

HDPE/PET

Steel cans

Brown glass

Aluminum

Shares are shown in percent, based on a collection total of 6,000 lbs. per day.

Newspapers	66.0%
Clear glass	14.0
Green glass	6.0
HDPE/PET	5.0
Steel cans	5.0
Brown glass	3.0
Aluminum	1.0

Source: *Food Engineering*, March 1992, p. 127, from The Council for Solid Waste Solutions.

★ 2040 ★

Waste Management (SIC 9511)

Environmental and Waste-Management Companies

Sales of the leading environmental and waste-management companies are shown in millions of dollars for 1991.

Waste Management	$ 7,397
Thermo Electron	801
ICF International	683
Zurn Industries	620

Source: *Forbes*, January 6, 1992, p. 100, from *Forbes*; Value Line Data Base Service via Lotus CD Investment.

★2041★
Waste Management (SIC 9511)

Municipal Solid Waste Components

Components of the solid waste stream, shown in percent.

Containers/packaging	31.6%
Nondurable goods	28.1
Yard wastes	17.6
Durable goods	13.9
Food wastes	7.3
Other	1.5

Source: *Food Review*, April 1991, p. 32.

★2042★
Waste Management (SIC 9511)

Plastics Recovery - Western Europe

West European waste plastics weighed 11,428 metric tons in 1989. Destination of the wastes is shown in percent.

Municipal solid waste	73.0%
Distribution	11.6
Auto	5.4
Construction	5.3
Agricultural	4.7

Source: *Chemicalweek*, December 25, 1991, p. 38.

★2043★
Waste Management (SIC 9511)

Pollution Control - Leading Firms

Companies are ranked by 1991 sales, shown in millions of dollars. Shares of the group are shown in percent.

	Sales ($ mil.)	% of Group
Waste Management	$7,551	57.8%
Browning-Ferris Industries	3,183	24.4
Chemical Waste Management	1,358	10.4
Chambers Development	322	2.5
Calgon Carbon	308	2.4
Rollins Environmental Services	223	1.7
Mid-American Waste Systems	120	0.9

Source: *The 1992 Business Week 1000*, p. 190.

★2044★
Waste Management (SIC 9511)

Solid Waste Management Methods

	1988	1995
Landfilling	72.7%	53.1%
Recycling	12.9	19.4
Incineration	14.2	22.8
Composting	0.3	4.8

Source: *Independent Energy*, February 1992, p. 36, from U.S. Environmental Protection Agency.

★2045★
Waste Management (SIC 9511)

Waste Managers - Europe

Estimated 1991 turnover by Europe's 10 largest waste management companies reached 3.175 billion ECUs (European currency units). Relative distribution is in percent.

	(ECU mil.)	% of Group
Waste Management International	650	20.5%
Generale des Eaux	615	19.4
SITA	400	12.6
Edlehoff	310	9.8
Browning-Ferris International	270	8.5
RWE	255	8.0
Otto	215	6.8
FOCSA	200	6.3
Shanks & McE	130	4.1
SVT/Biffa	130	4.1

Source: *The European*, August 6, 1992, p. 41, from ECOFIN.

★2046★
Waste Management (SIC 9511)

Waste-to-Energy Companies

Capacity shares of the 1991 market are shown in percent.

Ogden Projects	21.0%
Wheelabrator	20.0
Other	59.0

Source: Investext, Thomson Financial Networks, May 12, 1992, from Donaldson, Lufkin & Jenrette Securities.

★ 2047 ★
Waste Management (SIC 9511)

Waste-to-Energy Forecast

Company shares are shown as percent of anticipated industry capacity in 1994.

Ogden	.27.0%
Wheelabrator	.22.3
Westinghouse Electric	8.1
American Ref-Fuel	7.0
ABB Resource Recovery	4.2
Foster Wheeler	4.2
Other	.22.6

Source: Investext, Thomson Financial Networks, January 22, 1992, from Prudential Securities Inc.

★ 2048 ★
Waste Management (SIC 9511)

Waste-to-Energy Plants

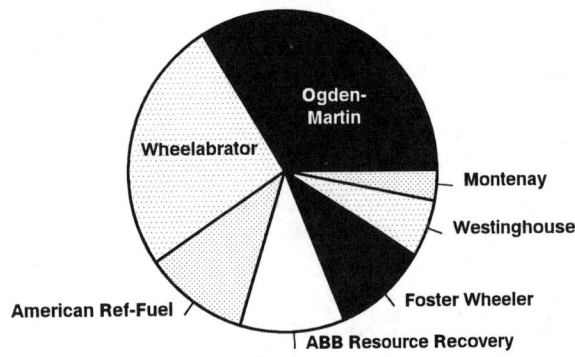

Leading waste-to-energy company shares of tons per day (TD) of capacity for 1992. Shares of group are in percent.

	TD	%
Ogden-Martin	.28,000	33.5%
Wheelabrator	.21,900	26.2
American Ref-Fuel	9,100	10.9
ABB Resource Recovery	9,000	10.8
Foster Wheeler	8,200	9.8
Westinghouse	5,000	6.0
Montenay	2,350	2.8

Source: *Independent Energy*, July 1992, p. 53, from Kidder, Peabody & Co.

★ 2049 ★
Water Management (SIC 9511)

Home Water Filtration Market

The water filtration market is shown in percent for 1990.

Ecolochem	.47.0%
Arrowhead Industrial	.25.0
Polymetrics	.13.0
Ionics	8.0
MPW and Mobile Water	7.0

Source: Investext, Thomson Financial Networks, March 27, 1992, from Rauscher Pierce Refsnes, Inc.

SIC 96 - Administration of Economic Programs

★ 2050 ★
Urban Aid (SIC 9611)

Federal Aid to Cities

Distribution, by program, is shown in percent, based on totals of $23.4 billion in 1981 and $14.0 billion in 1992.

	1981	1992
Employment/training	25.2%	28.6%
Mass transit aid	16.2	27.9
Community development	17.1	24.3
Water/sewer plants	16.2	17.1
Economic development	1.7	2.1
Revenue sharing	21.8	0.0
Urban development	1.7	0.0

Source: *USA TODAY*, November 19, 1992, p. 4A, from U.S. Conference of Mayors.

★ 2051 ★
Highway Administration (SIC 9621)

Highway Funding

Distribution of $119.5 billion in highway spending is shown in percent.

Surface Transportation Program	20.3%
National Highway System	17.9
Interstate maintenance	14.5
Bridge Program	13.7
Minimum allocation and guarantees	8.8
Interstate construction and transfer	7.0
Demonstration projects	5.5
Congestion mitigation/air quality	5.1
Toll Reimbursement Program	3.4
Miscellaneous	3.9

Source: *Constructor*, December 1991, p. 9.

★ 2052 ★
Transportation Regulation (SIC 9621)

Federal Transit Bus Commitments

Percent distribution by type of bus is based on 1990 total of 77,355 vehicles.

35' & 40' standard	78.1%
Less than 35'	12.4
Vans	6.3
Articulated	2.8
Electric trolley	0.4

Source: *METRO Magazine*, 1991-92 Annual Fact Book, 1992, p. 16.

★ 2053 ★
Agricultural Programs (SIC 9641)

Shares of EPP Sales

Shares of EEP (Export Enhancement Program) sales value are shown for 1985 through April 1991.

Wheat	72.0%
Feed grains	9.1
Flour	7.1
Frozen poultry	3.7
Dairy cattle	2.8
Vegetable oils	2.1
Others	2.6

Source: *FoodReview*, July 1991, p. 54, from USDA and FAS.

★ 2054★

Agricultural Programs (SIC 9641)

Shares of TEA Program Funds

Distribution of TEA (Targeted Export Assistance) program funds, by commodity, is shown in percent for 1986-89. High-value product promotion organizations include national and regional associations of state departments of agriculture and trade organizations representing candy and bourbon manufacturers.

Horticultural products	52.6%
Animals and animal products	14.0
Oilseeds and products	11.1
Grains and products	8.5
Cotton, seeds, and tobacco	6.8
High-value products	5.4
Wood products	1.6

Source: *FoodReview*, July 1991, p. 55, from USDA and FAS.

SIC 97 - National Security and International Affairs

★ 2055 ★

Defense (SIC 9711)

DIB Output by Sector - Canada

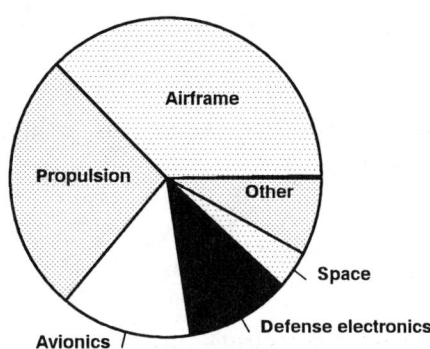

Shares of Defense Industrial Base (DIB) by sector are shown in percent for 1990. Total may not equal 100 percent due to rounding.

Airframe	37.7%
Propulsion	26.6
Avionics	13.8
Defense electronics	11.3
Space	4.3
Other	7.8

Source: *National Defense*, July 1992, from Canadian Ministry of Industry, Science, and Technology.

★ 2056 ★

Defense (SIC 9711)

Leading Defense Contractors

Prime contracts awarded in fiscal year 1990 are shown in thousands of dollars; percent shares are based on total purchases of $134.174 billion.

	Awards	Share
McDonnell Douglas	$ 8,923,457	6.7%
General Dynamics	6,569,018	4.9
General Electric	5,823,497	4.3
General Motors	4,305,974	3.2

	Awards	Share
Martin Marietta	$ 4,246,032	3.2%
Raytheon	4,166,633	3.1
Lockheed	3,854,622	2.9
United Technologies	2,950,932	2.2
Grumman	2,725,294	2.0
Boeing	2,423,547	1.8
Tenneco	2,370,675	1.8
Westinghouse Electric . . .	2,274,377	1.7
Rockwell International	2,230,389	1.7
Litton Industries	1,562,349	1.2
Unisys	1,457,445	1.1
GTE	1,304,641	1.0
Textron	1,245,562	0.9
IBM	1,235,234	0.9
TRW	1,097,223	0.8
Gencorp	1,094,966	0.8
LTV	1,054,864	0.8
ITT	947,110	0.7
AT&T	944,756	0.7
Foundation Health Corp. . . .	865,272	0.6
Alliant Techsystems	855,841	0.6
Ford Motor Co.	799,874	0.6
MIT	787,850	0.6
Allied-Signal	783,379	0.6
Northrop	748,478	0.6
Texas Instruments	745,631	0.6
Other	63,598,484	47.4

Source: *Government Executive*, August 1991, p. 24.

★ 2057 ★

Defense (SIC 9711)

Leading DoD Weapon Systems

The top 10 Defense Department acquisitions approved in 1991 are shown with service branch in parentheses and cost in millions of dollars.

B-2 (USAF)	$ 4,185
DDG-51 (USN)	3,246
SDI (DoD)	2,874

Continued on next page.

★ 2057 ★ *Continued*

Defense (SIC 9711)

Leading DoD Weapon Systems

The top 10 Defense Department acquisitions approved in 1991 are shown with service branch in parentheses and cost in millions of dollars.

SSN-21 (USN)	$ 2,340
F-16 (USAF)	2,154
F/A-18 (USN)	1,683
Trident II Missile (USN)	1,671
C-17 (USAF)	1,026
ATF (USAF)	955
Tomahawk (USN)	710
KC-135 Reengine (USAF)	583
AMRAAM (USAF)	561
Adv Cruise Missile (USAF)	506
E-2C (USN)	466
Space Boosters (USAF)	345
LHX (USA)	340
CH/MH-53 (USN)	336
Tac Missile Def Initiative (DoD)	218
UH-60 (USA)	105
AOE Ship (USN)	4

Source: *Armed Forces Journal International*, March 1991, p. 22, from Dept. of Defense, *Program Acquisition Cost by Weapon System, FY92-93.*

★ 2058 ★

Defense (SIC 9711)

Military Manpower

Personnel counts are shown in thousands for fiscal years 1991 through 1992.

	1991	1992
Active military		
Army	702	660
Navy	570	551
Marine Corps	194	188
Air Force	509	487
Selected Reserves	1,176	1,068
Civilians	1,052	1,003

Source: *Government Executive*, April 1991, p. 36, from Department of Defense.

★ 2059 ★

Defense (SIC 9711)

Military Spending in Asian Countries

Asian country military spendings are shown as percent of gross national product (GNP) in 1989.

North Korea	20.0%
Pakistan	6.8
Taiwan	5.4
Singapore	5.1
South Korea	4.3
China	3.7
India	3.1
Malaysia	2.9
Thailand	2.7
Indonesia	1.7

Source: *The Economist*, June 20, 1992, p. 34, from *The Washington Quarterly*.

★ 2060 ★

Defense (SIC 9711)

Military Spending - Japan

Shares of military spending in Japan, by major segments, are shown in percent, based on total of $32.9 billion in 1991.

Personnel	40.0%
Arms, equipment and supplies	28.0
Operations and maintenance	16.0
Support for U.S. forces in Japan	10.0
Construction	3.0
Research and development	2.0

Source: *Detroit Free Press*, June 21, 1992.

★ 2061 ★

Defense (SIC 9711)

Military Spending - U.S.

Shares of U.S. military spending, by major segments, are shown in percent based on a total of $273 billion in 1991.

Operations and maintenance	30.0%
Arms, equipment and supplies	27.0
Personnel	27.0
Research and development	13.0
Construction	3.0

Source: *Detroit Free Press*, June 21, 1992, p. 4F.

★2062★

Defense (SIC 9711)

Pentagon Prime Contract Awards by Company

The top 50 companies are ranked by Pentagon prime contract awards, shown in millions of dollars. Percent shares are based on group total. Data refer to fiscal year 1991.

	(000)	% of Group
McDonnell Douglas Corp.	$ 8,057,307	14.0%
General Dynamics Corp.	7,848,241	13.7
General Electric Co.	4,866,488	8.5
General Motors Corp.	4,427,169	7.7
Raytheon Co.	4,089,761	7.1
Northrop Corp.	3,319,215	5.8
United Technologies Corp.	2,825,134	4.9
Martin Marietta Corp.	2,689,206	4.7
Lockheed Corp.	2,666,573	4.6
Grumman Corp.	2,363,479	4.1
Westinghouse Electric Corp.	1,811,664	3.2
Rockwell International Corp.	1,707,779	3.0
Litton Industries Inc.	1,600,954	2.8
FMC Corp.	1,466,587	2.6
Unisys Corp.	1,378,865	2.4
Aerospace Corp.	395,136	0.7
World, Rosenbalm, Key, et al. JV	388,552	0.7
Coastal Corp.	384,767	0.7
Royal Dutch Shell Group	376,754	0.7
Hercules Inc.	365,393	0.6
Science Applications Int'l Corp.	513,426	0.9
Teledyne Inc.	476,718	0.8
Dyncorp	460,245	0.8
Oshkosh Truck Corp.	455,144	0.8
Arco Products Co.	440,107	0.8
Mitre Corp.	436,052	0.8
Foundation Health Corp.	433,279	0.8
Computer Sciences Corp.	405,875	0.7
Johns Hopkins Univ.	404,203	0.7
Massachusetts Inst. of Technology	401,525	0.7

Source: Aviation Week & Space Technology, May 25, 1992, p. 59.

★2063★

Defense (SIC 9711)

Top Defense Contractors in Japan

Top 10 companies are ranked by military spending in millions of dollars. Percent shares are based on 1991 total military budget of $10,733 million.

	($ mil.)	Share
Mitsubishi Heavy Industries	$ 2,686	25.0%
Kawasaki Heavy Industries	1,071	9.9
Ishikawajima-Harima Heavy Ind.	798	7.4
Mitsubishi Electric Corp.	729	6.8
Nippon Electric Co.	428	4.0
Toshiba Corp.	364	3.4
Fuji Heavy Industries	243	2.3
Japan Steel Corp.	208	1.9
Komatsu Corp.	173	1.6
Hitachi Corp.	134	1.2

Source: Aviation Week & Space Technology, April 20, 1992, p. 24.

★2064★

Defense (SIC 9711)

U.S. Intelligence Agency Budgets

Estimated agency budgets for fiscal year 1992 are shown in millions of dollars; shares of intelligence spending are shown in percent for the same period. "Tactical intelligence" refers to all military tactical intelligence collection activities.

	Budget ($ mil.)	% of Group
National Reconnaissance Office	$ 6,200	21.1%
National Security Agency	3,900	13.3
Central Intelligence Agency	3,200	10.9
Army Intelligence	1,500	5.1
Air Force Intelligence Agency and Electronic Security Command	1,500	5.1
Defense Intelligence Agency	582	2.0
Defense Reconnaissance Support Program	536	1.8
Office of Naval Intelligence	500	1.7
Department of Energy	150	0.5
Intelligence Community Staff	100	0.3
Federal Bureau of Investigation	100	0.3

Continued on next page.

★ 2064 ★ *Continued*

Defense (SIC 9711)

U.S. Intelligence Agency Budgets

Estimated agency budgets for fiscal year 1992 are shown in millions of dollars; shares of intelligence spending are shown in percent for the same period. "Tactical intelligence" refers to all military tactical intelligence collection activities.

	Budget ($ mil.)	% of Group
State Department intelligence and research . . .	$ 50	0.2%
Tactical intelligence	11,000	37.5

Source: *Government Executive*, March 1992, p. 12, from Federation of American Scientists.

★ 2065 ★

National Security (SIC 9711)

Department of Defense Budget

The fiscal year 1992 budget for the Department of Defense is shown in billions of current-year dollars. The costs of Operation Desert Shield and Operation Desert Storm are not included in the total. Shares by program are shown in percent.

	($ bil.)	Share
Navy	$ 84.8	30.3%
Air Force	80.2	28.6
Army	67.0	23.9
Defense Agencies	21.2	7.6
Defense-Wide	17.7	6.3
Defense Medical Program	9.1	3.3

Source: *Armed Forces Journal International*, March 1992, p. 8.

★ 2066 ★

National Security (SIC 9711)

Department of Defense Manpower

Percent shares by branch are based on a total of 1.865 million active personnel in fiscal year 1992.

Army	34.4%
Navy	29.5
Air Force	26.0
Marine Corps	10.1

Source: *Armed Forces Journal International*, March 1992, p. 11.

SOURCE INDEX

This index is divided into *primary sources* and *original sources*. Primary sources are the publications where the market shares were found. Original sources are sources cited in the primary sources. Numbers following the sources are entry numbers, arranged sequentially; the first number refers to the first appearance of the source in *Market Share Reporter*. The index lists more than 1,600 organizations.

Primary Sources

Original Sources

Source Index: Original

Source Index: Original

PLACE NAMES INDEX

This index shows global regions, political entities, states and provinces, regions within countries, and cities. The numbers that follow listings are entry numbers; they are arranged sequentially so that the first mention of a place is listed first.

PRODUCTS, SERVICES, AND ISSUES INDEX

This index shows, in alphabetical order, references to products, services, and issues covered in *Market Share Reporter*, 3rd Edition. Nearly 3,000 terms are included. Terms include subjects not readily categorized as products and services, including such subjects as *crime* and *welfare*. The numbers that follow each term refer to entry numbers and are arranged sequentially so that the first mention is listed first.

3D graphics workstations, 986
900 & 976-line services, 1457
ABMs, 1703
Abrasive cleansers, 730, 731
Abrasive products, 878
ABS resins, 593, 599, 607
Accessories, automotive, 1248
Accessories, boys', 441
Accessories, decorative, 1583, 1588
Accessories, fashion, 51, 440, 1339
Accessories, laundry, 934
Accessories, men's, 443
Accident insurance, 1761
Accounting services, 2003, 2004, 2005, 2006
ACE inhibitors, 627, 628
Acetaminophen, 694
Acetic acid, 772
Acne remedies, 630, 631, 1656
Acquisitions, 1919, 1922, 1924, 1990
Acrylic fibers, 618
Acrylonitrile, 772
Acrylonitrile-butadiene-styrene, 593, 599
Action figures, 1325
Activated carbon, 806, 807
Activewear, 425, 436, 441, 442, 443
Acupuncture, 1816
Acute-care hospitals, 1978
Acute-care monitoring equipment, 1310
Add-on displays, 1069
Addiction programs, gambling, 1815
Addiction programs, smoking, 1816
Additives, automotive, 1248
Adhesives, 787, 788, 789, 790, 791, 792
Administration, public, 2031, 2033
Advanced armor, 1, 2
Advanced ceramics, 3, 865, 866, 867, 868, 869
Advanced materials, 3, 4
Advertising, 1819, 1820, 1821, 1822, 1823, 1824, 1825, 1826, 1827, 1828, 1829, 1833, 1835
—broadcast, 1830
—magazine, 1831, 1832

Advertising - continued
—yellow pages, 1836
AEM, 981
Aerobics, 430
Aerobics shoes, 842
Aerosols, 663, 667
Aerospace, 790, 1257, 1285, 1286
After-shave preparations, 754
Aggregate mining, 154
Agrichemicals, 553, 554, 555, 780, 781, 782, 783, 784
Agricultural loans, 1713
Agricultural production, 45, 46, 97, 99, 101, 103, 105, 106, 107, 108, 111, 116, 2053
AGV systems, 966, 981
AIDS, 5, 1982
Air, 94
Air bag initiators, 1250
Air cargo, 93, 1260, 1262, 1368, 1380, 1384, 1419, 1420, 1421, 1422, 1424
Air carriers, 1262, 1372, 1373, 1374, 1386
Air cleaners, electronic, 1072
Air conditioners, 1047, 1072, 1073
Air filtration, 980
Air freight, 1260, 1262, 1368, 1422
Air fresheners, 90, 719, 728
Air pollution control, 2002, 2051
Air purifiers, 1080
Air tickets, 1434
Air transportation, 1262, 1268, 1372, 1373, 1374, 1375, 1401, 1406, 1407, 1413, 1420, 1422
Air travel, 1368, 1372, 1373, 1374, 1375, 1403, 1406, 1413
Airbags, 1245, 1251
Aircraft, 1, 1255, 1256, 1258, 1259, 1261, 1263, 1264, 1265, 1266, 1267, 1268, 1369
—business, 1260, 1262
—civil, 1266
—jet, 1265
—military, 1257, 1266, 1269
—small craft, 1270
—U.S. Navy, 1269
Aircraft accessories, 418

Products, Services, and Issues Index

Products, Services, and Issues Index

COMPANY INDEX

The more than 5,600 companies and institutions in this book are indexed here in alphabetical order. Numbers following the terms are entry numbers. They are arranged sequentially; the first entry number refers to the first mention of the company in *Market Share Reporter*. Although most organizations appear only once, some entities are referred to under abbreviations in the sources and these have not always been expanded. Thus a few companies may appear more than once.

1928 Jewelry Co., 1339
20th Century Fox, 1932, 1933, 1934, 1939
20th Century Growth, 1716
20th Century Select, 1716
20th Century Ultra, 1716
20th Fox, 1931
21st Century Industries, 1677
3-Glocken, 367
3 Rivers Terminal, 1360
3Com/BICC, 1147
3Com Corp., 987, 1045, 1137, 1144, 1160, 1856
3M Co., 483, 570, 1126, 1197
A&E, 1480, 1483
A&G Coal, 130
A&P Supermarkets, 74, 1548, 1556, 1557, 1561
A&S, 921
A&W Brands, Inc., 289, 320, 328, 331, 336, 337, 586
A&W Restaurants, 1647
A. Duda & Sons, Inc., 106
A. Foster Higgins & Co., 2012
A. L. Laboratories, 668
A League of Their Own, 1936
A-P-A Transport Inc., 1356
AAA Cooper Transportation, 1356
AAFES, 1536
AAH, 1655
AAR Corp., 1380
ABB, 1063, 1280, 1491
ABB Resource Recovery, 2047, 2048
Abbey National, 1696, 1698
Abbott, 637, 655, 664, 678, 699, 711
ABC, 1467, 1470, 1472, 1942
ABC Appliance Center, 1620
Aberdeen Trust, 1918
ABF Freight System, 1356
Abitibi-Price Inc., 479, 480, 484
ABN AMRO Holdings, 1698, 1714
Abt Associates, 68
Abuelita (Mexican candies), 260
A.C. Nielsen Co., 68, 69

Academy Lines Inc., 1352
ACBL, 1363
Accessories Associates Inc., 1339
Accor, 1804
Ace Novelty Co., 1339
Aceto, 568
Ackerley Communications, 1464, 1468
Acklands Limited, 1495
Acme, 890
ACS, 1293, 1294, 1295, 1296
Action, 464, 466
Action Plus Software, 1871
Action Technologies, 1856
Action Transit, 1353
A.D. Makepeace Co., 101
Adaptec, 1034
Addison-Wesley, 543
Adelphia, 1476
Adelphia Communications Corp., 1475, 1482
Adia, 1842
Adidas, 837, 838, 840, 841, 844, 1333
Adkin Blue Ribbon Pkg. Co. Inc., 101
ADM Milling Co., 230, 231, 240, 286
Adobe Systems, 1877
Adolph Coors, 292, 296, 303, 304
Adray's, 1620
Adria, 699, 1368
Adriasebina, 863
Adrienne Vitadinni, 53
ADT Ltd., 1911, 1912
ADT Security, 1911, 1912
Advance Chemical Distribution Inc., 1360
Advance Circuits, 1161
Advance Publications, 516, 520, 531, 1475
Advance Quick Circuits, 1161
Advanced Control Systems, 1492, 1890
Advanced Logic Research Inc., 994, 999, 1006
Advanced Micro Devices, 89, 1056, 1157, 1166, 1179
Advantage, 1928
AdvantageHealth Corp., 1979

American Trans Air, 1418
American United Life, 1759
American Urban, 1462
American Woodmark, 452
Americo, 229
Amerijet, 1420
Ameritech, 1116, 1117, 1118, 1436, 1443, 1445, 1836
Ameritech Audiotex Services Inc., 1460
Ameritrust Corporation, 1699, 1700
Ames, 1545, 1546
Ames/Zayre, 1620
Ametek, 1288
Amgen, 648, 661, 2007, 2008
Amgen/Neupogen, 1968
AMIGOS, 1846
Amoco, 134, 137, 138, 140, 141, 142, 143, 514, 555, 810
Amoco Ankina Production Co, 139
Amoco Chemical, 561, 564
AMP, 1056, 1088, 1158, 1179, 1249
AMP-AKZO Corp., 1161
Ampex, 1126
AMR Corp., 1380
Amrop International, 1841
AMSCO, 1304
Amsted Industries, 882
Amstrad, 1014
Amtico, 852
Amurol Products, 271
Anadarko Petroleum, 134, 140, 142, 143
Analog Devices, 89, 1056
Anaren Microwave Inc., 24
Anchor Glass, 7, 860, 861
Anchorage Int'l, 1424
Anchorage News, 524
Anchorage Times, 524
Ancient Age, 297
Andersen Consulting, 1843, 1876, 1891, 1909, 2010, 2011
Andrew, 1902
Andrew W. Mellon Foundation, 1796
Anglesey Aluminum, 906
Anglia, 1473
Anheuser-Busch Cos. Inc., 176, 251, 289, 292, 296, 303, 304, 514
Anjou International, 322
Annenberg Foundation, 1796
ANR Freight Systems, 1356
Ansaldo, 1280
Ansell-Americas, 854
Ansett, 1401
Ansett Express, 1401
Ansett NT, 1401
Ansett WA, 1401
Antarctica, 303, 304

Antelope Valley Bus Inc., 1352
ANZ Group, 1698
Aoki, 43
Apache Corp., 134, 140, 142, 143
Apertus Technologies, Inc, 1289
Apex Securities, Inc., 1717
API Alarms, 1912
Apothecon, 632, 633, 652, 697
Apple Computer Co., Inc., 24, 988, 989, 990, 994, 999, 1004, 1005, 1006, 1007, 1008, 1009, 1010, 1012, 1013, 1037, 1038, 1042, 1043, 1157, 1158, 1862
Apple Japan, 1015
Applebee's, 1639
Appleton, 485
Appleton Papers, Inc., 483
Appliance Store, 1620
Applied Biosystems, 2007
Applied Magnetics, 1154
Applied Materials, 89, 940, 1176
Aquafil, 619
A.R. Demarco Enterprises Inc., 101
Arbitron Co, 68
Arbor Drug, 1660
Arby's Inc., 1629, 1635, 1647
Arcadian, 563
Arcata Graphics Company, 515, 546
Archer Daniels Midland, 174, 175, 176, 779
Archive, 1034
ARCO, 140, 142, 143, 553, 559, 561, 617, 810, 907, 1249, 2062
Arctic Region Supercomputing Center, 81
Argo Industries Ltd., 164
Argos, 1586
Argyll, 1553
Argyll (Safeway), 1655
Ariana Afghan 2, 1368
Aries, 1341
Aritmos, 838
Arizona Star, 523
Arkansas Steel, 889
Arm & Hammer, 729
Armando Testa Group, 1823
Armbro Inc., 164
Armco, 882, 888, 890, 892, 893, 922
Armour, 705
Arms Technology, 927
Armstrong World Industries, 7, 408, 456, 833, 846, 852, 881, 1074
Army & Air Force Exchange Service, 1536
Aron J & Co., 820
Arrow, 437, 1420
Arrowhead Industrial, 2049
Art Van, 1585

Company Index

Company Index

Company Index

Company Index

Company Index

M&N Standard Cogar, 399
M. Grossman and Sons Inc., 440
M.A. Hanna, 1722
Macaroni Grill, 1639
MacDermid, 568
MacFarms of Hawaii, Inc., 105
Mack, 1238, 1239, 1240, 1241
MacMillan Bloedel Ltd., 449, 453, 479, 480, 484, 543
Macmillan/McGraw Hill, 513
MacNeal-Schwendler, 1859
MACSTEEL, 888
Macy's, 1535, 1620
Madame Tussaud's, 1997
Madison Paper Co., 485
Maersk Line, 1365
MAG, 471
Maggioni Winthrop/Sterling, 686
Magil Construction Ltd., 163, 165
Magma Copper, 882, 884, 923
Magna, 376, 1249
Magnesium Products Ltd., 911
Magnet, 1586
Magnetek, 1056, 1067, 1068
Maines Paper & Food, 1503
Mainichi Shimbun,Japan, 512
Majestic Contractors Ltd., 163
Major Pharmaceutical, 668, 669
Malaysia Airlines, 1386
Malibu, 376
Mallard Coach Co. Inc., 1287
MAN, 939, 1242
Managers Intermediate Mortgage, 1732
Mancini-Duffy Associates, 1917
Mandarin Oriental, 1802
Manistique Papers Inc., 481, 485
Manitoba Rolling Mills Ltd., 887
Mann, 1940
Mannesmann, 939
Mannington, 846
Manor Care, 1973
Manpower, 1842
Manufacturers Hanover Corp., 1711, 1714, 1920
Manufacturers Life Insurance Co., 1755
Manufacturers National, 1753
Manville, 47
Mapco, 134
Maple-Vail Book Mfg. Corp., 546
Marathon, 227, 810
Marathon-LeTourneau, 889
Marchese Farms, 108
Marc's, 1653
Marcus Restaurants, 1637
Marian Merrell Dow, 665

Marine Midland Bank, 1699
Mariner Hotel Corp., 1805
Marion, 641, 681
Marion Labs, 708
Marion Merrell Dow, 644, 661, 662, 688, 689
Mark IV Industries, 1056, 1353
MarkAir, 1410
Market Facts, 68
Market Measures, 68
Market Power, 1871
Marketeam/Doane Marketing Research, 68
Marketing Analysts, 68, 69
Marketing Corp. of America, 1838
Marketing Information System, 1871
Marketing Metrics, 69
MarketSource, 1837
Marks & Spencer, 1567, 1571, 1573, 1578
Marley, 847
Marlin Firearms, 928
Marlitz Marketing Research, 68
Marmon Holdings, 1677
Marquette, 1311
Marriott Corp., 1804, 1809
Marriott Resorts, 1809
Marriott Suites, 1809
Mars Inc., 244, 247, 257, 276
Marsh & McLennan Cos., 1778, 2010
Marshall Durbin Companies, 116, 191
Marshall Field, 1535
Marshalls, 1545
Martin County, 133
Martin Marietta, 153, 154, 1255, 1256, 1259, 2014, 2015, 2056, 2062
Marubeni Co., 14, 92
Marui, 1538
Maruman, 1751
Marusan, 1751
Maruzen Co. Ltd., 1358
Marwood College, PA, 81
Marysville Underground Storage Terminal, 1360
Masco Industries, 452, 456, 459, 460, 465, 913, 918, 1074, 1249
Massachusetts Institute of Technology, 2062
Massachusetts Mutual Life Insurance, 1755, 1757, 1759, 1762, 1765
Massalin Particulares, 377
Massey Ferguson, 941, 942, 943, 944, 945, 951, 953, 955, 956, 957
Match, 1549
Material Service, 154
Matra S.A., 1135, 1201, 1286
MATRIXX Marketing Inc., 1460
Matsushita Electric Industrial Co. Ltd., 25, 43, 471, 873,

Company Index

Northwestern Steel & Wire Co., 888, 890
Northwood Pulp & Timber Ltd., 449, 453
Norwalk Galleries, 1581
Norwegian Telecom, 1123, 1440
Norwest Bank of Minnesota, 1692, 1699, 1753
Norwich Park, 132
Norwich Union, 1768
Nova Scotia, 1690, 1691, 1703, 1715
Novacare, 1973, 1979
Novaky, 601
Novatel, 1439
Novell, 1862, 1877, 1900
Now, 376
NRTA/AARP News Bulletin, 529
NS Group Inc., 133, 888, 890
N.T. Gaurgiulo, Inc., 101
NTT, 25
Nu West Industries, 780
Nuclear Electric, 1066
Nucor Corp., 882, 888, 889, 890
Nuevo, 140, 142, 143
Nuts Unlimited, Inc., 105
NVF Company, 483
NYNEX Corp., 1116, 1117, 1118, 1436, 1443, 1445, 1474, 1836
O-B, 507
Oak Ridge Vyds./Royal Host Brandy, 313
Oakland Athletics, 1957, 1958
Oakland Int'l, 1424
Oakwood Homes, 454
Occidental, 134, 139, 140, 142, 143, 553, 555, 561, 564, 586, 587
Ocean Hospitalities, 1783, 1805
Ocean Spray, 174, 340
OCLC, 1846
OCLI, 1035
Octel, 1461
Octel Communications, 987
ODI, 1035
ODS, 1147
Odzaci 'Hipol' Works, 560
OEA Inc., 1250, 1251, 1255, 1256
O.F. Mossberg, 928
Office Depot, 1532, 1620
Ogden, 1624, 2047
Ogden-Martin, 2048
Ogden Projects, 2046
Ogilvy & Mather Worldwide, 1823, 1824, 1825, 1829
Ohbayashi Corp., 18
Ohis, 601
OHM Corp., 2038
Oil Dri Corp. of America, 2038
Oil Rail Terminals Ltd., 1359

Oiltanking Inc., 1360
OIS, 1876
Okasan, 1751
Oki, 1172, 1173
Okidata, 1042, 1043
Okuma Machinery Works, 968
Olde English, 315
Olin Corp., 555, 563, 586, 2014
Olivetti & Co., 78, 985, 989, 990, 996, 997, 1006
Olsten, 1842
Olympia Brewery, 302
Omar, 133
O'Melveny & Myers, 1987, 1988
Omnicon Group, 1819, 1828, 1835
Omron Corp., 1006
One Price Clothing Stores Inc., 1543
Oneita, 439
Ontario Express, 1387
Ontario Int'l, 1424
Ontario Paper Co., 484
Ontario Power, 1490
Onyx, 1623
Opel, 1211, 1217
Oppenheimer, 1730, 1737, 1752
Optical Data Systems Inc., 1144
Oracle Corp., 1849, 1850, 1854, 1876, 1881, 1882
Oracle Systems, 1877, 1919
Orange-Co. of Florida, 106
Orange County Register, 521
Orange County WBA, 1951
Orange Julius, 1635, 1647
Orchard Management Co./Senseny South Corp., 107
Oregon Metallurgical Corp., 126, 1255, 1256
Oremet, 908
Organon Teknika, 711
Orion, 1931, 1932, 1934, 1935, 1939
Orlando Magic, 1960, 1961
Ortho, 711
Oryx Energy, 134, 140, 142, 143
Osaka Titanium, 908
Oscar Mayer Foods Corp., 188
Oshkosh Truck Corp., 2062
Oshman's Sporting Goods, 70, 1540
Osma, 847
O'Sullivan, 460, 465
Oswiecim, 601
OTE, 1440
Otto, 427, 2045
Otto Versand, 1677
Our Lady of the Lake University (TX), 1992
Outback Steakhouse, 1639
Outer Banks, 433
Outlet Communications, 1468

Company Index

Wickes Lumber, 1512
Widmann Discount Center, 1653
Wigley, 279
Willamette Industries, Inc., 47, 474, 483, 486
Willett, 1040
William M. Mercer Co., 2012
Williams, 1447
Williams Air Force Base, 1781
Wills, 382
Wiltel/Telesphere, 1447
Wiltron, 1919
Wimpy, 1631
Windermere Real Estate, 1784
Windsor Castle, 1997
Windsor Safari Park, 1997
Windward Islands, 1368
Wine Alliance, 313
Wine Group, 313
Wine World, 313
Wine World Estates, 103
Winegarden & Hammons, 1783, 1805
Winn-Dixie Stores, 74, 1548, 1556, 1557, 1561
Winnipeg Jets, 1966, 1967
Winterpark Investment Group, 346
Wirthlin Group, 68, 69
Wirtschafts- und Privatbank, 1736
Wisconsin Dairies Coop., 174
Witco Chemical, 797, 799, 800
Wiz, The, 1620
W.K. Kellogg Foundation, 1796
WLN, 1846
Wloclawek, 601
Wm Blair, 1737
Wm Grant, 319
W.M. Keck Foundation, 1796
Wm. Wrigley Jr. Co., 174, 175, 257, 267, 277, 278, 279, 281
Wolohan Lumber, 1507
Wolverine, 843
Woman's Day, 529
Woodberry Forest School (VA), 1794
Woodfin Suite Hotels, 1812
Woodhaven Foods, 1503
Woodpecker, 315
Woodward & Lathrop, 1535
Woolworth, 74, 223, 1522, 1532, 1534, 1540, 1568
WordPerfect, 1856, 1868, 1878
World, 1410
World Color Press, Inc., 515
World Vision, 1793
Worldcorp Inc., 1380
World, Rosenbalm, Key, et al. JV, 2062
Worthington Ind., 882

WPP Group, 1819, 1828, 1835
W.R. Grace, 553, 555, 559, 561, 563, 568, 1722
W.R. Lazard & Co., 1717
Wrangler, 426, 1420
Wrigley (see Wm. Wrigley)
W.S. Babcock, 1585, 1596
WTBS, 1478, 1480, 1483
WTD Industries Inc., 449, 453
W.W. Grainger, Inc, 1495
Wyatt Co., 2012
Wyco Pipeline Co., 1360
Wyeth-Ayerst, 633, 677, 680, 697, 709
Wyman-Gordon Co., 1255, 1256
Wymondham Oil Storage Co. Ltd., 1359
Wyse Technology, 999, 1006
Xerox, 26, 1046, 1157, 1158
Xianyang, 1159
Xilinx, 1179
Xoma Corp., 661, 2007, 2008
Xomox, 932
Yale Enforcement, 1910
Yale University, 1793
Yamaha, 1283
Yamaichi International, 1724, 1728, 1736, 1751
Yamanouchi, 665
Yamanouchi Pharmaceuticals, 1919
Yamatane, 1751
Yamazaki Mazak, 968
Yanmar, 941, 953, 956, 957
Yasuda Trst & Banking, 1698
Yellow Freight System, 1356
YMCA of the USA, 1793, 1795
Yodogawa Steel Works, 900
Yokahama Rubber, 834
Yokohama, 835
Yokohama Takashimaya, 1538
Yomiko Advertising, 1826, 1827
Yomiuri Golf Club, 1953
Yomiuri Shimbun, 512
Yomo, 206
Yoplait, 204, 207
York International, 940
Yorkshire, 1473
Young An, 427
Young & Rubicam, 1823, 1824, 1828, 1829
Yukong, 815
YWCA of the USA, 1793
Zale Jewelry, 1532
Zantop, 1420
Zehnder's, 1636
Zenith, 652, 660, 995, 1122, 1126
Zenith Data Systems Inc., 999, 1012
Zenith Electronics Corp., 24, 1056

BRANDS INDEX

This index shows more than 1,500 brands—including names of periodicals, television programs, popular movies, and other "brand-equivalent" names. Each brand name is followed by one or more numerals; these are entry numbers; they are arranged sequentially, with the first mention of the brand shown first.

Brands Index

Brands Index

Brands Index

APPENDIX

SIC COVERAGE

This appendix lists the Standard Industrial Classification codes (SICs) included in *Market Share Reporter*. Page numbers are shown following each SIC category; the page shown indicates the first occurrence of an SIC. *NEC* stands for not elsewhere classified.

Appendix: SIC Nomenclature

Appendix: SIC Nomenclature

Engineering and Management Services

8710 Engineering & architectural services, p. 543
8711 Engineering services, p. 543
8721 Accounting, auditing, & bookkeeping, p. 543
8731 Commercial physical research, p. 544
8732 Commercial nonphysical research, p. 545
8742 Management consulting services, p. 545
8748 Business consulting, nec, p. 546

Services, NEC

8999 Services, nec, p. 547

Executive, Legislative, and General

9100 Executive, legislative, & general, p. 548

Justice, Public Order, and Safety

9220 Public order & safety, p. 549
9221 Police protection, p. 550
9223 Correctional institutions, p. 550

Finance, Taxation, and Monetary Policy

9311 Finance, taxation, & monetary policy, p. 551

Administration of Human Resources

9400 Administration of human resources, p. 554
9431 Admin. of public health programs, p. 554
9441 Admin. of social & manpower programs, p. 555

Environmental Quality and Housing

9511 Air, water, & solid waste management, p. 556

Administration of Economic Programs

9611 Admin. of general economic programs, p. 559
9621 Regulation, admin. of transportation, p. 559
9641 Regulation of agricultural marketing, p. 559

National Security and International Affairs

9711 National security, p. 561

Appendix: SIC Nomenclature